MOTOR LEARNING AND DEVELOPMENT

Third Edition

Pamela S. Beach, PhD

SUNY Brockport

Melanie E. Perreault, PhD

SUNY Brockport

Ali S. Brian, PhD, CAPE

University of South Carolina

Douglas H. Collier, PhD

SUNY Brockport

HUMAN KINETICS

Library of Congress Cataloging-in-Publication Data

Names: Haibach-Beach, Pamela S., 1977- author. | Perreault, Melanie
  Elizabeth, 1983- author. | Brian, Ali Sara, 1978- author. | Collier,
  Douglas Holden, 1953- author.
Title: Motor learning and development / Pamela S. Beach, Melanie E.
  Perreault, Ali S. Brian, and Douglas H. Collier.
Description: Third edition. | Champaign, IL : Human Kinetics, [2024] |
  Includes bibliographical references and index.
Identifiers: LCCN 2022031109 (print) | LCCN 2022031110 (ebook) | ISBN
  9781718211711 (paperback) | ISBN 9781718211728 (epub) | ISBN
  9781718211735 (pdf)
Subjects: LCSH: Motor learning. | Motor ability in children. | Movement
  education.
Classification: LCC BF295 .H25 2024 (print) | LCC BF295 (ebook) | DDC
  152.3/34--dc23/eng/20220817
LC record available at https://lccn.loc.gov/2022031109
LC ebook record available at https://lccn.loc.gov/2022031110

ISBN: 978-1-7182-1171-1 (print)

Copyright © 2024 by Pamela S. Beach, Melanie E. Perreault, Ali S. Brian, and Douglas H. Collier

Copyright © 2018, 2011 by Pamela S. Haibach-Beach, Gregory D. Reid, and Douglas H. Collier

Human Kinetics supports copyright. Copyright fuels scientific and artistic endeavor, encourages authors to create new works, and promotes free speech. Thank you for buying an authorized edition of this work and for complying with copyright laws by not reproducing, scanning, or distributing any part of it in any form without written permission from the publisher. You are supporting authors and allowing Human Kinetics to continue to publish works that increase the knowledge, enhance the performance, and improve the lives of people all over the world.

Notwithstanding the above notice, permission to reproduce the following material is granted to persons and agencies who have purchased this work: pp. 124, 180, 198, 281, 347, 367.

The online video and learning content that accompanies this product is delivered on HK*Propel*, **HKPropel.HumanKinetics.com**. You agree that you will not use HK*Propel* if you do not accept the site's Privacy Policy and Terms and Conditions, which detail approved uses of the online content.

To report suspected copyright infringement of content published by Human Kinetics, contact us at **permissions@hkusa.com**. To request permission to legally reuse content published by Human Kinetics, please refer to the information at **https://US.Human Kinetics.com/pages/permissions-information**.

The web addresses cited in this text were current as of September 2022, unless otherwise noted.

Acquisitions Editor: Diana Vincer; **Managing Editor:** Anna Lan Seaman; **Copyeditor:** Janet Kiefer; **Proofreader:** Erin Cler; **Indexer:** Dan Connolly; **Permissions Manager:** Laurel Mitchell; **Senior Graphic Designer:** Joe Buck; **Cover Designer:** Keri Evans; **Cover Design Specialist:** Susan Rothermel Allen; **Photograph (cover):** MoMo Productions/DigitalVision/Getty Images; **Photographs (interior):** Filmwell Studios/© Human Kinetics; © Human Kinetics, unless otherwise noted; **Photo Asset Manager:** Laura Fitch; **Photo Production Manager:** Jason Allen; **Senior Art Manager:** Kelly Hendren; **Illustrations:** © Human Kinetics, unless otherwise noted; **Printer:** Versa Press

We thank SUNY Brockport in Brockport, New York, for assistance in providing the location for the video and photo shoot for this book.

Printed in the United States of America

10 9 8 7 6 5 4 3 2 1

The paper in this book is certified under a sustainable forestry program.

Human Kinetics
1607 N. Market Street
Champaign, IL 61820
USA

United States and International
Website: **US.HumanKinetics.com**
Email: info@hkusa.com
Phone: 1-800-747-4457

Canada
Website: **Canada.HumanKinetics.com**
Email: info@hkcanada.com

To my children who humble and inspire me every day. I am blessed to watch your growth and development. And to my husband for his endless support of my adventures and academic pursuits.

—Pamela Beach

To my husband for his unconditional love and support, and our children, Sylvie and Leo, for inspiring me every day and providing an endless supply of motor development examples.

—Melanie Perreault

To my parents, Gary and Vicki Brian, and to my sister, Lauren.

—Ali Brian

To *Sneaky Pete,* who, more than 45 years in, remains my very best friend.

—Doug Collier

CONTENTS

PREFACE

From the day we are born until the end of our lives, we never stop moving, changing, and adapting. Motor learning and development are at the core of our existence. We are movers who must learn to adapt to our changing bodies, environment, and task. Whether it be outsmarting the opponent on the field of play or simply walking down the street, we are consistently faced with the challenge of solving movement problems. When we walk down the street, we often must avoid obstacles or other pedestrians while keeping in mind the wet, slippery pavement. In a competitive sporting environment, we may have to consciously think about faking out an opponent. No matter the setting, our skill level, or our age, we cannot avoid the fact that movement is a vital part of our lives and affects us in terms of our overall physical well-being, our intellectual functioning, and the development of our social skills. These effects are ever present—and ever changing—and take place over the course of our lives.

Clearly, then, how we develop, in addition to our previous movement experiences, affects how we acquire new motor skills and how we refine old skills. The learning of new motor skills and the refinement and adjustment of existing motor skills are critical aspects of our lives—aspects that we don't always appreciate. When performing everyday movements, we often do not appreciate how difficult it is to coordinate our limbs so that we can execute activities. As an example, we use a knife and fork to eat without giving these actions a second thought; however, this was a very difficult task when we were small children. We had to learn how to control both limbs in a coordinated

fashion to cut meat and feed ourselves. Over time, though, this initially challenging feat became second nature, and the frustration caused by the complexity of these actions was soon forgotten. However, that feeling of frustration in learning those early everyday tasks returns if, as adults, we must relearn these basic movements following a serious accident or medical event such as a stroke. The intense physical and occupational therapy required to relearn even the simplest of tasks reminds us of the intricacy of motor skills. No matter the time of life—infancy through old age—the ongoing interactions between our ever-changing abilities, the environment, and the task determine how we proceed.

Motor Learning and Development, Third Edition, provides a framework for understanding both fields and for exploring how motor learning and motor development interact with and affect each other. Having a thorough understanding of the factors that "push" the development of motor skill across the life span will better prepare you to teach movement skills effectively to learners at any chronological age and at any skill level. *Motor Learning and Development, Third Edition,* examines the development of movement skill in humans from infancy to older adulthood (referred to as life span motor development) and examines how having different motor, cognitive, and social abilities affects how, when, and why we learn motor skills. As movement educators, we must understand the complexities of teaching movement skills to people of various backgrounds, interests, experiences, and abilities. As we have noted, learning a motor skill (or a combination of motor skills) can be quite challenging, and many elements must be taken into consideration. *Motor Learning and Development, Third Edition*, guides you in an accessible and interesting manner into the fields of motor development and motor learning. The book includes a variety of methods to facilitate learning and keep you engaged with the material.

Motor Learning and Development, Third Edition, is an undergraduate text written for students and professionals pursuing careers in physical education, athletic training, early childhood education, gerontology, kinesiology, special education, adapted physical education, primary and secondary education, physical therapy, occupational therapy, and related fields. The text presents a strong theoretical foundation in an engaging and accessible way. You will learn how to develop, implement, and critically assess motor skill programs for learners at all developmental levels.

Although the fields of motor learning and motor development have been addressed in a variety of undergraduate texts, none have merged these two fields into one textbook. *Motor Learning and Development, Third Edition*, fills this void. The content is based on the latest research in the fields of motor development and motor learning. This text also provides a framework for developing movement programs that facilitate skill acquisition for all types of learners—from those with significant disabilities to elite athletes. This book also prepares you for meeting national standards and Praxis exams.

LIFE SPAN PERSPECTIVE

This book adopts a life span perspective that goes beyond the developmental and neuromotor changes associated with childhood and younger adulthood. This perspective provides an in-depth look at all ages throughout the human life span, including the many large life changes associated with younger and older adults. These changes can

include leaving home, entering the workforce, getting married, and having children. We also examine the social and psychological changes associated with life transitions. Societal mores and expectations can have a huge impact on the motor development of various cohorts. For instance, in today's highly technological age, adolescents are much more likely to spend a larger portion of their free time playing with smartphones, tablets, and video games than participating in physical activity. On the other hand, many adults have changed their focus to health and wellness, which has resulted in a surge of people who are eating healthier meals, giving up unhealthy habits such as cigarette smoking, and participating in more physical activity. These healthy decisions are certainly having a large impact on older adults' motor development and on slowing their rate of functional decline. However, what motivates an adolescent to participate in sport or physical activity may be of little interest to a middle-aged adult or, indeed, a child.

It is important to take a broad view and consider many variables when examining individual motor development and performance. This book details these variables to prepare movement educators to teach motor skills to a broad array of people representing many ages, developmental levels, and degrees of physical proficiency in a variety of settings, including educational, athletic, clinical, and fitness settings.

CHANGES TO THE THIRD EDITION

Motor Learning and Development has undergone a thorough revision since the second edition, including the addition of four chapters. The HK*Propel* content also includes many new videos illustrating fundamental motor skills, motor milestones, and reflexes; several new ancillaries; more PowerPoint slides and test bank questions; updated material based on the latest research throughout the textbook; and revised examples throughout the book. A focus of these changes has been to cover both motor learning and motor development more thoroughly as well as to unite these fields to best prepare practitioners to devise developmentally appropriate programs for people of any age or skill level. New chapters added to the text include chapter 11, Assessment of Gross Motor Development, chapter 16, Sociocultural Constraints, chapter 17, Developmental Models for Instruction, and chapter 21, Program Design. The skill classification content formerly located in chapter 1 has been expanded and extracted into a new chapter. Similarly, fundamental motor skills have been expanded and divided into two chapters, chapter 8, Locomotor and Stability Skills in Childhood, and chapter 9, Object Control Skills in Childhood.

Ancillaries in the third edition have been expanded to include more PowerPoint slides and more than double the number of exam questions in the test bank. In addition, new videos on infant motor development, fundamental motor skills, older adult movement, and skill transfer have been added to the web resources. This edition has also been updated with the latest research. Many chapters have new opening vignettes.

ORGANIZATION

Part I, Theory and Foundational Concepts, provides a basic outline of the fundamental concepts in motor learning and motor development. Chapter 1 introduces the subfields of motor behavior, motor control, motor learning, and motor development, as well as important concepts and terminology. Chapters 2 and 3 have been updated, and their order has been reversed for better flow of the historical content on motor development to flow into the behavioral theories and set the stage for the theoretical underpinnings used throughout the text. First, the major tenets and theoretical per-

spectives from the fields of motor behavior are explained in chapter 2. Then, chapter 3 emphasizes movement control, including reaction time, attention, arousal, sensory contributions, and memory. Chapter 4 is a new chapter that includes the skill classification content formerly housed in chapter 1. Chapter 5 discusses motor skill progression as well as three models of motor learning stages. Instructors who have a thorough understanding of the strengths and shortcomings of each model will have more and better developed tools to engender positive behavioral, cognitive, and physical changes in performers. It is at this point (chapter 6) that we discuss important methodological considerations, including how to measure and assess motor learning and organize the learning experience to facilitate positive transfer and long-term retention.

Part II, Life Span Physical Activity and Movement, provides a solid background on movement patterns across the life span, from infancy to older adulthood. Chapter 7 examines infant motor development, including prenatal growth and development, spontaneous and reflexive movements in early infancy, and the development of motor milestones. Chapter 8 picks up where chapter 7 ends by defining fundamental motor skills and examining locomotor and stability skills developed during childhood. The development of fundamental movement skills is essential to healthy development in childhood. Children who are given a strong movement foundation will have the skill sets and the confidence to be physically active with their families, with peers, and on their own. Chapter 9 continues the topic of fundamental motor skills by discussing the object control skills typically developed during childhood. Chapter 10 explores physical activity and movement in young, middle, and older adulthood. The discussion focuses first on physical activity in adulthood and peak athletic performance and then explores the changing movement patterns observed in older adults. The final chapter (chapter 11) in part II is a new chapter on gross motor assessment in which the importance of assessment and assessment considerations for individuals across the life span are discussed.

Part III, Individual and Environmental Constraints, examines the changing individual and environmental constraints throughout the life span. Chapter 12 discusses some of the structural factors that constrain the acquisition and development of movements throughout childhood and adolescence. Chapter 13 discusses the physiological changes that affect physical function and movement, including age-related changes in the skeletal, muscular, cardiovascular, nervous, endocrine, and sensory systems. Movement educators who work with older adults must understand the effects of aging on the physiological systems and the impact these changes have on movement. Chapter 14 addresses how structural and functional constraints may interact with tasks that affect the learning of movement skills over the life span. Part III concludes with chapter 15 and chapter 16, a new chapter, examining the interaction between individual and environmental constraints that influence opportunities and engagement in movement experiences and physical activity.

Part IV, Designing Developmentally Appropriate Programs, gets you ready to prepare, design, and implement developmentally appropriate movement programs. Chapter 17 is a new chapter that examines how practitioners can use motor development and sport development models to guide developmentally appropriate instruction in multiple contexts. Chapter 18 discusses prepractice considerations, including how to set goals and introduce motor skills using demonstrations, verbalizations, attention directing, and physical guidance. The discussion continues in chapter 19, which addresses the design and structure of effective practice sessions. Topics include variable practice, practice specificity, part and whole practice, and practice distribution. Just like practice, feedback should be designed around the person and the task. Chapter 20 discusses the functions and types of feedback as well as effective feedback scheduling. The book closes with a new chapter (chapter 21), Program Design, which prepares the practitioner for designing developmentally appropriate programs. The chapter includes a discussion of the teaching style continuum, task analyses, differentiation, and universal design. Students can apply their knowledge gained with a variety of case studies located in the labs.

PEDAGOGICAL FEATURES

Many features throughout the book will help you understand the concepts introduced in each chapter.

- *Opening vignette:* Each chapter opens with a vignette, a practical example that introduces one or more of the main concepts explored in the chapter.

- *Research Notes:* Each chapter includes sections that present important research experiments. Many of these research notes have been updated for the third edition.

- *Try This:* This feature supplements the text with a variety of short applications that you can perform at home or at your desk. Answering questions will help you think critically about the concepts.

- *What Do You Think?:* Each chapter includes opportunities to stop and think about the material. This feature provokes critical thinking and stimulates further thought about the material. You can answer these questions on your own or discuss them in class.

- *Summary:* A brief summary of the key elements and concepts is provided at the conclusion of each chapter.

- *Supplementary Activities:* Two additional activities are presented at the conclusion of every chapter. These are intended either as outside activities or as classroom laboratory activities.

- *Glossary:* Key terms and concepts are printed throughout the text in bold type for emphasis and are defined at the end of each chapter.

Note: In this text we use English measurements followed by metric conversions in parentheses. The exception is with yards, which convert to approximately the same number of meters.

HK*PROPEL*

The online student resource in HK*Propel* includes laboratories for each chapter, the What Do You Think? and Try This activities, and videos for chapters 6, 7, 8, 9, 10, 11, and 20 with accompanying study questions. The labs provide experiential learning for difficult concepts or topics and typically require some equipment and additional space, such as a gymnasium or outside area. The videos accompany the laboratory activities for chapters 6 (assessing motor learning), 7 (infant motor development), 8 (locomotor and stability skills in childhood), 9 (object control skills in childhood), 10 (movement in adulthood), 11 (assessment of gross motor development), and 20 (feedback) and can be used as part of a lecture.

The student resource can be accessed online at HK*Propel*. If you purchased a new print book, follow the directions included on the orange-framed page at the front of your book. That page includes access steps and the unique key code that you'll need the first time you visit the *Motor Learning and Development* website. If you purchased an ebook from HumanKinetics.com, follow the access instructions that were emailed to you following your purchase.

Although there are many excellent books that examine motor development from a life span perspective and books that explore the field of motor learning, there is not, to our knowledge, a book that combines the two. You will find that *Motor Learning and Development, Third Edition,* achieves the goal of combining the two fields in an accessible and interesting way, and it explains how motor development and motor learning inform each other and intersect.

Those with a thorough understanding of the multiple factors that inspire into motion the development of motor skills from infancy to older adulthood are in a good position to teach movement skills efficiently and to individualize their instruction. This individualization is a point of emphasis throughout the text, given the complexity of teaching learners of various backgrounds, interests, abilities, and ages. Furthermore, learners' abilities and interests are hardly static; rather, they are very dynamic. Thus, to work with learners at all life stages, we must be continually aware of the ongoing interactions between ever-changing abilities, an ever-changing environment, and the tasks at hand. The intersection of these three factors determines how to proceed.

And so, this textbook—based on the latest research in the fields of motor learning and motor development—provides both the theoretical foundation and applied information for developing movement programs for all types of learners—from those with identifiable disabilities to those at both ends of the ability spectrum.

Motor Learning and Development, Third Edition, is divided into four parts. Part I, Theory and Foundational Concepts, lays the groundwork by outlining the fundamental concepts of motor control, motor learning, and motor development. Part II, Life Span Physical Activity and Movement, provides a solid background in physical activity and movement patterns from infancy through older adulthood, examining not only *what* skills are developed but also *how* they are developed and change with age. Part III, Individual and Environmental Constraints, delineates the constraints that may, in combination, hinder or promote optimal development. The fourth and final part, Designing Developmentally Appropriate Programs, gives detailed information that prepares students to organize, develop, implement, and evaluate movement programs for a variety of learners. Although the material that precedes part IV has a direct bearing on the development of appropriate programs, the students need not have read every chapter of the text to benefit from part IV.

Although this textbook is written from a life span perspective and details how skill is acquired over the course of one's life, a particular course may emphasize a certain time frame. If, as an example, motor learning and motor development in school-age children and adolescents is the focus of the course, you may decide to bypass chapters 7 (Infant Motor Development), 10 (Movement in Adulthood), and 13 (Physical Aging). The same applies to a course focusing more on adult development and aging. In this case, the emphasis may be on chapters 10 and 13 in addition to parts I and IV.

Each chapter in *Motor Learning and Development, Third Edition,* has the following features that engage students in their reading and help them to understand the concepts.

• *Chapter Objectives:* Each chapter begins with approximately six learning objectives related to the most important concepts. These objectives guide the students' reading and allow you to spend less class time lecturing and more time on interactive, student-focused learning activities and skill development. If you believe that the best approach to teaching the material is to use the lecture as your primary methodology, the chapter objectives provide a road map for both you and the students.

• *Research Notes:* Research experiments pertinent to the chapter material are presented throughout the text. Beyond their importance to the fields of motor learning and motor development, these research notes allow you to engage the students in debates and discussions about topics such as research design, the appropriateness of the question (i.e., why is this a good question to ask—or is it?), what the next question might be, and how to design the next question. Students can work on these questions and others during or outside of class, either individually or in small groups. Much of the research presented can lead to robust debate.

• *What Do You Think?:* This feature gives students the opportunity to think about the course content both critically and creatively. Examples include thinking back to how the students acquired a challenging skill, considering how to teach a diverse group of learners, and explaining how plasticity is demonstrated when a stroke patient regains the ability to hit a slice backhand. The key point is to stimulate critical thinking. Students can use this feature individually, in pairs, as a group, or in a class discussion either inside or outside of the classroom.

• *Try This:* This feature engages students in a practical application that clarifies a given concept. Students actively engage in a physical activity to attain a more thorough understanding of the concept at hand. This feature stimulates critical thinking and can be incorporated into the course either in or outside of the classroom.

• *Supplemental Activities:* At the end of each chapter, two activities are provided that can be completed as either classroom laboratory activities or at-home activities. These activities give students a chance to deepen their understanding of the topics presented in the chapter.

• *Key terms:* Key terms are the most important concepts in the chapter and appear in bold text. They are defined at the end of each chapter.

Five ancillaries facilitate the teaching of this material:

• *Instructor's guide:* This ancillary includes sample answers to the What Do You Think? sections and, as appropriate, the Try This activities. It also includes troubleshooting and instructor tips for each chapter and its labs.

• *Test package:* This ancillary includes more than 450 multiple-choice, true-or-false, and short-answer questions, as well as their answers. These test questions can be used for building quizzes or as a supplement to your own exam questions.

• *Laboratories:* Labs for chapters 1 through 21 are available to students through the web resource. The labs engage students in practical applications of important concepts from the chapters; they also require more time and preparation than the Try This activities. Most labs require students to complete an activity, record their data, and for some, calculate and compare their data to class data. Instructor tips for the labs are available in the instructor's guide.

• *Presentation package:* PowerPoint presentations are available for each chapter with approximately 30 slides per chapter. Each chapter's PowerPoint slide deck includes objectives, important figures and tables, key concepts, and summary points.

• *Video clips:* Video clips are available in the web resource for chapter 6, Assessing Motor Learning; chapter 7, Infant Motor Development; chapter 8, Locomotor and Stability Skills in Childhood, chapter 9,

Object Control Skills in Childhood; chapter 10, Movement in Adulthood; chapter 11, Assessment of Gross Motor Development; and chapter 20, Feedback. The study question links in the web resources contain questions focused on these videos, but you can use these videos to demonstrate these reflexes, motor milestones, and motor skills as you see fit.

The ancillaries are available online.

We hope we have laid some groundwork for using *Motor Learning and Development, Third Edition,* in your course, allowing you to teach and, more important, engage students in these essential subjects. Be sure to familiarize yourself with the text so that you can manage your time to ensure that you cover the appropriate material for your course. Clearly, you will need to determine the amount of time required for covering each chapter and concept. Keeping track of material that required more time or less time to cover than you anticipated will help you make informed changes to future courses.

How much time you take to cover material from the text is, of course, an individual decision that has much to do with your pedagogical philosophy and course content goals.

We wish you the best as you use the first textbook to combine the fields of motor learning and motor development.

ACKNOWLEDGMENTS

Motor Learning and Development, Third Edition, is a comprehensive book, combining two fields of study into one textbook. We have presented the material that we felt was most relevant and current, while also unifying these two fields. There are many topics covered throughout this book, so for some areas we have called on the expertise of others. Therefore, we are grateful to colleagues who have provided input. We would first like to recognize Greg Reid for his invaluable authorship and collegial support as the second author in the first and second editions of *Motor Learning and Development*. Much of his work continues in this third edition. We are truly grateful for all of his contributions as well as his important role in shaping this textbook.

We would also like to extend our deep appreciation to Dr. Jason Rich for his contributions toward opening vignettes and applicable photographs and to Layne Case for her contributions to chapter 9 on object control skills. We are also deeply grateful to our colleagues who read drafts of the content and provided editorial suggestions throughout the process.

In addition, we would like to acknowledge the many individuals who made possible the photos used in chapters 8 and 9 and the videos for chapters 6, 8, 9, and 11 featured in HK*Propel*—the children, who demonstrated the fundamental motor skills during the photo shoot; the parents, who facilitated their children's involvement; Jim Dusen, whose photography was exceptional; Gregory Payne for acquiring permission to use the infant videos; and Filmwell Studios for their fine videography of motor skill performance.

PART I

Theory and Foundational Concepts

In the first chapter of this part of the text, we define the three fields of motor behavior: motor control, motor learning, and motor development. The key terms of each field are explained, and some core areas of research in each field are introduced. We then turn to the evolution of the field of motor development from its inception in the late 18th century to the present day. We then turn to the theoretical constructs of motor behavior in chapter 2. The three main theoretical constructs that drive research in motor behavior (the information-processing theory, the ecological approach, and the dynamic systems approach) differ not only in the way they define development and learning, but also in how they examine behavior. Chapter 3 examines the many factors involved in understanding movement control, including reaction time, attention, arousal, sensory contributions, and memory. Because these factors have a profound impact on movement throughout the life span, they are discussed throughout the book.

In chapter 4, we detail motor skill classification, including sport skills, developmental classifications, single-dimensional classifications, and multi-dimensional classifications. The classification of motor skills is important for any movement educator with an interest in rehabilitation, education, or athletics, because the appropriate practice and feedback schedules often depend on the type of motor skills. In chapter 5, we examine the developmental and motor learning stages. This includes a discussion of the stages of learning, including Fitts and Posner's, Bernstein's, and Gentile's learning stages, providing a framework for categorizing the skill level of learners from novices to experts. These models enable practitioners to assess the level of the learner and, more appropriately, to prepare practice sessions. Part I concludes with methodological considerations (chapter 6), including how to measure and assess motor learning. Indicators of motor learning beyond basic performance measures are described (the best indicator of motor learning is performance following a retention interval). Also examined is transfer of learning, which is a critical component of learning a motor skill. Practitioners need to know how to promote positive transfer in any setting.

1

PERSPECTIVES IN MOTOR BEHAVIOR

CHAPTER OBJECTIVES

After reading this chapter, you should be able to do the following:

- Define motor behavior and the subfields of motor learning, motor control, and motor development.
- Explain several lines of motor control research.
- Compare motor performance and motor learning.
- Summarize the four characteristics of motor learning.
- Discuss the importance of motor competence.
- Understand the evolution of motor development.
- Explain why the fields of motor behavior are important for teaching and assessing motor skills in sport, physical activity, and health professions.

Choke Up on the Bat!

Harper, an active six-year-old child, enthusiastically attended her first baseball practice. She had not been involved in any team-affiliated activity before and was anxious to begin. The first day of practice began with skill assessment on batting, catching, and throwing. Harper regularly played ball with her dad and older brother after school and was confident with her ability to perform these skills. After performing well on both the catching and throwing tasks, Harper was poised going into the final task of batting. As Harper was about to bat, the coach instructed her to "choke up on the bat." Not knowing what that phrase meant, Harper proceeded to lift her arms higher, rather than moving her hands higher on the bat. With this awkward position, it is not surprising that Harper performed very poorly in the batting exercise even though she was well practiced with batting.

As a practitioner, it is important to understand not only motor learning and motor development but also motor control and how these fields of study influence one another. These fields are strongly related but often separated in textbooks. This chapter provides a background for each of these fields, discussing the main concepts, tenets, and theoretical frameworks of each field. Subsequent chapters use a life span perspective to explain how to prepare, implement, and assess motor skill programs for any group of individuals regardless of age, developmental level, or motor skill. In the batting example, the coach did not realize that he was not using developmentally appropriate terminology when providing feedback to Harper, which caused confusion rather than effective instruction.

DEFINING THE FIELDS OF MOTOR BEHAVIOR

A full understanding of the fields of motor behavior is necessary before designing, implementing, or assessing a motor skill program. **Motor behavior** is an umbrella term for the fields of motor control, motor learning, and motor development. **Motor control** researchers investigate the neural, physical, and behavioral aspects of human movement. An understanding of all three fields optimizes skill acquisition. **Motor learning** is the study of the processes involved in the acquisition of a motor skill and the factors that enhance or inhibit the ability to perform a motor skill. Researchers in the field of **motor development** examine the products and underlying processes of motor behavior changes across the life span. (See table 1.1 for a summary of each field.)

A practitioner with a strong background in motor behavior has a solid foundation in how humans develop across the life span, can explain why particular behaviors have manifested, and can design programs that assess, diagnose, or teach motor skills for the purposes of instruction or rehabilitation. In this book, the term *practitioner* refers to any type of movement educator, including physical education teachers, clinicians, trainers, instructors, and coaches. **Motor skills** are the learned ability to bring about predetermined results with maximal certainty, often with a minimum outlay of time or energy (Knapp, 1963). Athletes or performers are considered **skillful** if they have achieved a criterion of excellence and are capable of performing at a high level most of the time. Motor skills have also been defined as activities that require a chain of sensory (vision, hearing, touch, smell), central (brain and nervous systems), and motor mechanisms whereby the performer is able to maintain constant control of the sensory input and in accordance with the goal of the movement (Argyle & Kendon, 1967). Physical activities

Table 1.1   Summary of the Fields of Motor Behavior

Field	Key points
Motor control	• Addresses the underlying processes of movement. • Investigates the degrees of freedom problem (how the system can constrain the number of degrees of freedom to produce a coordinated movement pattern). • Examines the serial order problem (sequencing and timing of movement behaviors). • Investigates the perceptual–motor integration problem (how perception and action are incorporated).
Motor learning	• Addresses the process of acquiring a capability for producing skilled actions. • Is a direct result of practice and not due to maturation or physiological changes.
Motor development	• Addresses the performance product (outcome) and process (underlying mechanisms). • Addresses successive development (following in uninterrupted order) and systematic development (step-by-step procedures). • Is related to but not dependent on age.

can be categorized. Each activity is unique with respect to the structure of the task, task goals, and obstacles. Although physical activities have many unique qualities, there are also commonalities across activities, such that proficiency in one skill can lead to increased competence in another (i.e., positive transfer of learning).

Let's take a closer look at the fields of motor behavior, beginning with motor control.

MOTOR CONTROL

Motor control is a subdiscipline of motor behavior that focuses on the neural, physical, and behavioral aspects of human movement. One area of study for motor control researchers is the role of the neurological system in the function of the body. Some researchers examine reaction time as an indicator of processing speed and nerve conduction velocities under various conditions. Researchers in the field of motor control also investigate how the system moves in a controlled and coordinated fashion. Even fundamental motor skills and movements are quite complex. The number of possible movements is nearly infinite because of the degrees of freedom available. The field of motor control is often concerned with three core issues: (a) the degrees of freedom problem, (b) the serial order problem, and (c) the perceptual–motor integration problem. This section provides a brief overview of these motor control problems.

Degrees of Freedom Problem

Degrees of freedom are the number of independent elements that must be constrained to produce coordinated motion (Bernstein, 1967). At the joint level, there are dozens of movement possibilities even for simple actions such as reaching for a glass. Minimally, the reach involves the wrist, elbow, and shoulder, each of which has multiple axes of rotation. If the person

is standing during the reach, the hips, knees, and ankles are also involved in coordinating the movement. At the muscular level, the number of movement possibilities—or degrees of freedom—increases to the hundreds. If extended to the neuronal level, there could be millions, if not billions, of movement possibilities.

Coordination involves constraining the number of degrees of freedom to decrease the complexity of the movement task to produce a movement pattern and achieve a task goal (Sparrow, 1992). Coordination involves bringing parts into proper relationship with one another (Turvey, 1990). Increased coordination leads to a more positive task outcome. But in addition to coordinating the body parts, the person must also complete the task with **control**. The person must be able to manipulate the movements to meet the demands of the task. For example, a dancer can coordinate her body parts to execute all the correct steps. However, what distinguishes her as a dancer is her ability to accentuate certain movements while also moving with style and grace, making each movement appear seamless and effortless. A softball pitcher must constrain his degrees of freedom by deciding when to initiate the pitch and the speed of the pitch. The timing, the initiation and release, and the speed of the pitch are all variables of control. To maximize speed and preserve energy, a competitive swimmer must have good form, and a cross country skier must maintain appropriate knee bend to increase glide and maintain forward momentum while avoiding any lateral movements that may result in a loss of balance or movement efficiency. Movement demands and coordination requirements are unique to every skill, and this uniqueness becomes even more apparent with increasing skill level.

Movement is quite complex, and skillful movement is even more complex. Understanding how the body parts can coordinate—particularly while acquiring a new movement pattern—has long been a popular area of research. It is hard to conceptualize how the many degrees of freedom are coordinated. For example, it is not as simple as determining how a baseball player's lower body should move with respect to the upper body when batting. The bat could be moved by a rotation of the wrist, a lower arm rotation around the elbow, a shoulder joint rotation with the arm, an upper body rotation around the hip joint, or any combination of these rotations. This is a simplistic description because it only explains the joint level. At the muscular level there are six muscles in the elbow joint, enabling more variations of the movement. Each option of movement is considered one degree of freedom. With so many options for movement, how are we able to condense these options and move in a fluid and controlled manner? This problem will be further discussed in chapter 5 when we explore learning stages; however, if you're curious about the baseball example, baseball players solve the degrees of freedom problem by coupling their swing coordination (Gray, 2020). This coupling can be acquired through much variability in practice, which is discussed in chapter 19.

Serial Order Problem

The **serial order problem** refers to the sequencing and order of movement behaviors. The timing and order of an activity are critical for nearly every movement we produce. Think about the importance of the sequence of sounds in speech or the movements in walking, running, or throwing. In speech, if the order is changed, the sounds and meanings of the words and sentences change. In speech there are at least two serial order problems. The sequence of words must be maintained in short-term memory, and there must be a sequential order of coordinating the jaw, lips, tongue, and larynx to produce the appropriate sounds (Snyder & Logan, 2014). For example, a speech error would occur if you misspoke by saying *dirthbay* instead of *birthday*. Errors in speech

that result from exchanging letters in adjacent words have been termed **spoonerisms** after an Oxford professor, William Spooner, who was known to often make such errors (Rosenbaum, 2010). He has been quoted as having made the slip, "You hissed all my mystery lectures" instead of "You missed all my history lectures." In general, these sequencing errors occur in a specific way. Consonants switch with other consonants, vowels with other vowels, nouns with nouns, and verbs with verbs.

Serial order errors are not limited to speech. People make performance-related action errors all the time. Have you ever put something away in an obviously wrong place (e.g., silverware in the trash instead of the dishwasher), missed your exit when driving, or sent a text to the wrong person? These errors occur when we are not paying attention to what we are doing. With these errors, you clearly knew what you intended to do; however, the problem arose because you were thinking about the action rather than the specifics of the task. For example, you could visually identify the dishwasher and the trash but perhaps were more focused on the goal of clearing the plate and not on what you were throwing away. This type of error is referred to as an **action slip**. Everyone makes these errors from time to time. So, why are they particularly interesting? These examples indicate that people prepare an action plan rather than planning and then executing one thought at a time (Lashley, 1951); this allows us to be much more efficient with our actions.

The serial order problem has also been found in the production of correct, or accurate, movements through coarticulation. **Coarticulation** refers to the simultaneous motions that occur in sequential tasks (Rosenbaum, 2010). This means that we are preparing for subsequent movements rather than completing one movement before preparing for the next. Coarticulation suggests that we preplan activities to move efficiently.

TRY THIS

Coordination

Exercise 1.1

Generally, coordination is thought of as performing an activity more fluidly through practice, but our limbs are already coordinated to perform actions together, such as the right arm and the left arm or even the upper body with the lower body. To see for yourself, try each of these activities and notice how the limbs influence each other.

1. Writing activity

   a. Regardless of your hand dominance, write your name backward with your left hand. How difficult was this task? Did you have to concentrate on what you were doing? Did you think about which direction the letters should be facing? Perhaps you even made an error and one of your letters was correct rather than backward.

   b. Take a second writing utensil in your right hand (you should have one writing utensil in each hand). While writing backward with your left hand, write forward with your right hand. Were you able to accomplish this task? Was it harder or easier than only writing backward with your left hand?

   c. Try writing with both hands again a second time to see if you can complete the activity faster while thinking only about writing with your right hand. Were you able to increase the speed and complete both tasks while not even thinking about writing backward with your left hand? How do you think your hand dominance affects this task?

2. Hand and foot activity

   a. Make circular motions clockwise in the air with one foot. After you've done that for a little while, add drawing 6s in the air with your finger while continuing to make circular clockwise motions with your foot. What happened when you added the second task?

   b. In both activities, what did you notice about your limb coordination?

Preparing simultaneous movements enables us to type fast, speak clearly, and transport objects efficiently. Learning how to write involves the ability to write one letter while also preplanning how to produce the subsequent letters. The way the letter is formed changes based on the following letters. Research suggests that this coarticulation of writing reaches an adult level at around the age of nine years (Kandel & Perret, 2015). Coarticulation also occurs in grasping. The position we use to grasp an object depends on where we are going to move the object. In a study by Cohen and Rosenbaum (2004), participants were asked to grasp a plunger and place it in either a high or a low final position. The position of the grasp on the plunger changed based on the final position. Participants grasped the plunger high when they were going to place the plunger in a low position; conversely, they grasped it low when placing it in a high position. Refer to exercise 1.2 for a speech example of coarticulation.

TRY THIS

Action Planning

Exercise 1.2

Look in the mirror and say the word *twilight*. Did you notice that your lips rounded prior to producing the *t* sound? Look at your lips as you say the words *gold* and *cupid*. Did you notice the same thing? These examples indicate that there is an action plan for the entire word prior to the utterance of the first sound. If each sound were planned separately, your mouth would not have changed shape until after the *t, g,* or *c* sounds.

1. What are some other words in which you can notice a preparatory action plan?
2. Provide examples of performances other than typing and grasping in which movements are prepared in advance. What is the motor control term that explains preparing movements in advance?
3. What are some examples of action slips that you have experienced?

Perceptual–Motor Integration Problem

As the name implies, the **perceptual–motor integration problem** addresses how perception and motor control are integrated. For example, how is movement affected by perception, and conversely, how is what we perceive affected by our actions? This is not a problem like deciding whether the chicken or the egg came first. Rather, perception and movement work together, continuously influencing one another. You might move closer to an object to see it better or closer to a sound to hear it better. In those cases, movement improves perception.

Movement can also inform perception. Our perception is affected by our actual or intended actions. Hirsiger and colleagues (2012) examined the influence of size and weight cues on perception and action. Every day, we make inferences on the sizes and weights of objects. This information affects how we grasp things; whether we need two fingers, a full hand, or two hands; and how much force we need to exert. Perceptions of object weight are biased by expectations of size, and perceptions of object size are biased by expectations of the weight. Lighter objects are often perceived as being smaller

than they are, whereas heavier objects are often perceived as being larger. Therefore, the perception of the size or the weight influences the action response to grasp and lift the object. This topic is discussed further in chapter 7.

Neurophysiological research has provided further insights into the perceptual–motor integration problem. It was discovered that the same motor neurons fired when macaque monkeys watched an activity being performed as when they were producing the movement themselves (di Pellegrino et al., 1992). This observation occurred by chance when one of the researchers picked up some food and ate it. The researcher noticed that the same neurons in the monkey's brain were firing as they would be firing if the monkey were picking up food and eating it himself. Mirror neurons were also found in humans (Mukamel et al., 2010). These neurons are referred to as mirror neurons because they fire when people witness an action that they could perform themselves. Research on mirror neurons was conducted with ballet and capoeira dancers (Calvo-Merino et al., 2005). The brain activity of the dancers was higher when they watched

RESEARCH NOTES

Infant Walkers

One of the biggest motor challenges infants overcome is independent walking. Walking requires adequate strength, balance, and coordination to be able to hold the body upright and progress forward while exchanging balance from one foot to the next. Not surprisingly, an infant's first steps are very awkward with legs out, arms up and to the side, and very small steps. With time, infants narrow their base of support, lower their arms, and take larger steps. The incredible motor act of independent walking does not occur without important sensory cues that provide relevant information about the toddler's body in relation to the environment. While we see the toddler gaining more control over his movements, the toddler is mastering how to use this sensory information to navigate his body through different surfaces and over or around obstacles. To examine perceptual–motor integration in young walkers, Viera and colleagues (2019) examined the effects of age and walking experience on infants encountering obstacles. Three groups of infants with varying amounts of walking experience (one, three, or six months) were assessed walking with and without an obstacle. Infants with less experience walked slower and with a shorter stride than the infants with more experience. These infants also did not modulate their responses to the obstacle, indicating poor sensory motor coupling. The more experienced walkers made several changes to their steps when approaching the obstacle. The results indicate that sensory motor coupling increases with age and experience in infant walkers.

others performing the dances that they were skilled in (e.g., ballet dancers had more brain activity when watching ballet, and capoeira dancers had more brain activity when watching capoeira). The results further indicate that learning new motor skills can change the amount of neuronal firing during observations of those motor skills.

MOTOR LEARNING

Motor learning is a subdiscipline of motor behavior that examines how people acquire motor skills and the factors that affect them. Motor learning is a relatively permanent change in the ability to execute a motor skill because of practice or experience rather than maturation or physiological training.

Before proceeding, it is important to clarify the difference between motor learning and motor performance since the two

terms are often confused. Motor learning contrasts with **performance**, the observable act of executing a motor skill that results in a temporary, nonpermanent change. One way to conceptualize this difference is to consider the change of state of an egg and water (Schmidt & Lee, 2014). When an egg is boiled, there is a permanent change in the state of that egg. The inside of the egg has irreversibly transformed into a solid. However, when water temperature drops below 32 degrees Fahrenheit (0 degrees Celsius), it solidifies to ice. This is not a permanent change because water will convert back to its original form if temperatures increase again to above 32 degrees Fahrenheit. The permanent change that results from boiling an egg is analogous to the permanent change in the ability to perform a motor skill, or motor learning. On the other hand, the change in water resulting from temperature increases or decreases is analogous to performance changes because of its lack of permanency.

Now let's return to the definition of motor learning. Recall that motor learning is the process of acquiring the ability to produce skilled actions. The first characteristic of motor learning is that a process is required to induce a change in the ability to perform skillfully. A process, regarding acquiring a skill, is a set of events or occurrences resulting in a change in the state or end product. Dropping temperatures would be the process that causes water to change form. Drills in sport are processes with the goal of improving the capability to perform skillfully. For instance, soccer juggling is a common method (process) to improve ball control by soccer players. A player who tears her anterior cruciate ligament must undergo months of physical therapy (process) to rehabilitate her knee and regain her strength and flexibility. The goal of conducting a process is to increase the strength of this state, be it altering the temperature to change the state of water or promoting motor learning through practice drills or physical therapy sessions.

Capability implies that skilled behavior *may* occur if the conditions are favorable. Love him or hate him, there is certainly no question that Tom Brady acquired the capability to play the game of American football. However, even Brady has his off days, although his off-day passing skills most likely still far exceed many, if not all, of our passing skills. Certain variables can prevent optimal performance even when the capability is attained, such as external conditions (e.g., rain, snow, sleet, cold, wind), motivation, wellness, or fatigue. Regardless of our skill levels, our performances go down when we are ill or tired. Motivation fluctuates throughout the day, and, depending upon your current motivation level, your performance may be temporarily impaired. Motivation is an important component in performance and will be discussed in multiple chapters throughout this book. While

these variables may reduce your performance, it is important to note that if the skill is learned, these reductions in performance are only temporary.

The second characteristic of motor learning is that it must occur as a direct result of practice. Motor learning is not due to maturation or physiological training. A change that occurs because of maturation is a motor development change. For instance, learning to walk is motor development, not motor learning, because it is a motor skill that almost all humans acquire; in contrast, learning to shoot a basketball requires practice and is due to motor learning.

The third characteristic of motor learning is that it cannot be observed directly. It can only be assumed based on long-term performance changes. Motor learning, like love or success, is a construct. It cannot be seen but is assumed to have occurred when relatively permanent changes in the capability of skilled behavior are observed through performance changes. The fourth characteristic of motor learning is that it is assumed to produce positive, irreversible effects in the capability for skilled behavior, meaning that these changes are not temporary, as reflected in the saying, "It's like learning to ride a bicycle."

Stages of Learning

A big focus in the field of motor learning is examining the progression in skill from a novice who is first attempting a motor skill to a skillful performer. Regardless of the skill, all learners progress through the same distinct stages of learning. Understanding these distinct stages and how to most efficiently teach learners how to progress from one stage to the next stage is an important component to an effective movement educator, coach, or therapist. Although the stages of learning are distinct, there are several different models that define these stages. Practitioners who understand each of these models are better equipped to tailor their instruction and feedback to their learners.

RESEARCH NOTES

Power Law of Practice

For most learners, performance improves the most during the beginning stages of learning with improvements subsequently continuing at a much lower rate of improvement. Such performance occurs because of extensive practice resulting in large skill improvements. This learning improvement as a function of practice occurs so often across so many motor skills that it has been referred to as the **power law of practice** (Logan, 1988; Newell & Rosenbloom, 1981). This law is of particular importance because in the fields of motor behavior, there are very few laws due to the many variables that influence movements. For a hypothesis or theory to become a law, it must be very well supported across different motor skills, conditions, and groups of learners. Although a law such as the power law of practice describes the patterns we see such as the effect of extensive practice upon the rate of learning, it does not explain this relationship. The power law of practice is of particular concern for coaches, physical educators, trainers, and rehabilitation specialists to help them to understand the rates at which performance will likely improve. They should also understand how individual differences affect motor skill improvement and learning (Howard, 2014).

Because learning cannot be observed, practitioners must be aware of a variety of indicators of motor skill learning. The most common indicator of learning is through observing performance improvement. However, it is important to understand that performance is a nonpermanent change. To test whether an individual has learned a motor skill, practitioners must administer retention tests, which are performance assessments after a longer break in practice. Learners who are still able to perform at a higher level after this break demonstrate the retention of the motor skill. Practitioners should also be aware of other indicators of motor learning such as performance consistency, decreased physical and mental effort, reduced attentional demands, and increased adaptability.

Practice and Feedback

While it is likely not surprising that the most important variable in improving performance and retention is practice itself, it may be surprising how many types of practice there are as well as how many variables affect practice. Practice can be variable or constant, physical or mental, part or whole, and massed or distributed. This is only the beginning of the many types of practice. In addition, there are many considerations for effective practice. Variables such as age, experience, and type of skill affect whether a particular form of practice actually accelerates learning compared to another.

While practice is the most important variable in motor learning, the second most important variable is feedback. While it is likely that all practitioners—whether coaches, educators, trainers, or therapists—provide feedback when instructing motor skills, many are not providing feedback most effectively. Just like there are many variables that affect designing effective practice schedules, there are many important implications for providing effective feedback. It is also of critical importance that the learner be open to accepting the feedback. You have probably experienced times in which you were frustrated when attempting to learn a new motor skill or refining a motor skill that you already

WHAT DO YOU THINK?

Exercise 1.3

1. Think about a time you learned a new motor skill or when you taught someone a motor skill. List several indicators that helped you to determine that learning had occurred.

2. Think about how you can determine an individual's skill level based on these indicators. Choose a motor skill and describe how these indicators would help you to determine someone's skill level.

had. Frustrated learners are likely not very receptive to feedback. As such, you are likely not surprised that the learner's openness to receiving feedback is a critical component for that feedback to be effective.

In addition, other critical aspects of effective feedback include the type, accuracy, and frequency of delivering feedback. These aspects vary depending on the age and skill level of the learner as well as the difficulty of the motor skill. Siedentop and Tannehill (2000) reported that most coaches and therapists are not effectively delivering feedback. Many practitioners do not understand how the benefits of the type, frequency, and timing of their feedback can be very impactful upon the learning process. As such, it is important for practitioners to consider these factors when providing feedback regardless of the situation (e.g., an unskilled person learning a new motor skill or someone recovering from injury or illness). Feedback is critical not only when learning new motor skills but also for highly skilled athletes and injured people trying to reacquire motor skills. This includes both sport-specific skills (e.g., controlling the ball on the soccer field following an anterior cruciate ligament tear) and functional skills (e.g., relearning to walk, write, or even brush one's teeth). Injured people often have to either relearn a motor skill, modify a motor skill, or learn a new motor skill. Occupational and physical therapists must understand how to provide feedback in a way that maximizes patients' learning. In this book, you will learn how to effectively design practice (chapter 19) and feedback schedules (chapter 20) to maximize learning.

MOTOR DEVELOPMENT

Motor development is a subdiscipline of motor behavior that examines the age-related, successive changes that occur over the life span and the processes and factors that affect these changes. Changes that occur during a short period that are not associated with practice or experience, such as a child throwing farther or running faster between the ages of two and three, would likely be due to motor development. Motor development maps chronological age (i.e., age from birth) to the emergence of a new motor milestone (e.g., sitting, crawling, standing) or a new motor skill (e.g., throwing, kicking, or galloping; Shirley, 1931). The field of motor development combines biology, the study of the growth and maturation of living organisms, and psychology, the study of human behavior (Clark & Whitall, 1989). Motor development is an expression of the integration of many body systems, each of which has an important role in movement, including musculoskeletal, sensory, cardiorespiratory, and neurological systems (Dwyer et al., 2009). The interaction with the environment is particularly important in motor development (Malina, 2014); as such, the research tends to focus more on the behavioral aspects, which makes it more aligned with psychology than biology.

WHAT DO YOU THINK?

Exercise 1.4

1. Provide an example of a product and a process outcome for each of the following:
   a. Kicking a ball
   b. Running
   c. Dancing
   d. Rehabilitation
2. What are some advantages to using product-oriented assessments?
3. What are some advantages to using process-oriented assessments?
4. Which (product or process) do you recommend practitioners use when assessing motor competence? Explain your answer.

The measurement aspect of a movement is termed **motor competence** (Barnett et al., 2020). It is critical that young children develop a wide variety of movement patterns during their earlier years to provide a foundation for more complex movements (Clark & Metcalfe, 2002; Hulteen et al., 2018). A child's growth and development require the development of locomotor skills, ball skills, and balance competence. The development of motor competence should be a critical focus for parents, physical educators, youth specialists, and other practitioners of young children. A minimal threshold of motor competence was deemed necessary to develop more complex skills (Seefeldt, 1980). This threshold was termed a proficiency barrier and will be further discussed in chapter 17. Developing adequate levels of motor competence is associated with higher levels of physical activity participation, improved health and weight status, and a continued development of motor competence throughout an individual's life span (Stodden et al., 2008). In this book, we will discuss an individual's proficiency using the term *competence*. A child who is competent has reached a higher level of proficiency. A competent performer is one who can not only efficiently perform various locomotor, ball, and balance skills but also adapt their movements to changing task demands in an efficient and coordinated manner.

Motor competence is assessed according to the **product** (the outcome of performance) or the **process** (the underlying mechanisms of change). The amount of weight lifted, the distance a javelin is thrown, running speed, or number of successful attempts are examples of movement products, whereas the action that was performed to produce the throw is a movement process. Motor development, however, is not simply change. Motor development must be organized and systematic, such as an infant progressing through the motor milestones of raising their head, to rolling over, to crawling, and then to walking. The changes also need to be successive—that is, they must occur in an uninterrupted order. Motor development, therefore, is systematic and marked by successive changes over time. Changes that occur because of practice or experience, however, are due to motor learning, not motor development. For example, if a physical education teacher instructs a student to snap his wrist in a squash swing as opposed to using a solid-arm swing in the tennis stroke, the resultant change would be considered motor learning. A therapist teaching someone alternative ways to lift objects overhead following a shoulder injury would also be dealing with motor learning rather than motor development.

Development can occur over various time periods, from a very long time (phylogeny) to very brief in response to immediate task demands. **Phylogeny** refers to the evolutionary development of a species, which may take many hundreds, even thousands, of years. **Ontogeny** refers to development that occurs over the life span of one individual. The developmental sequence for running is likely phylogenetic in that most individuals can run proficiently; however, other skills such as high jumping, throwing a football, or juggling a soccer ball would require much practice to acquire, making these skills ontogenetic. The focus throughout this book is on ontogenetic development, that which is affected by experience. In addition to phylogenetic and ontogenetic timescales, there are also local dynamics, such as biological and psychological changes that occur in short timescales including changes in the surface of support, motivation, or instructions (Newell, 1986, 2020).

Although laypeople often use the terms *growth* and *development* interchangeably, these terms refer to different changes. **Physical growth** refers to an increase in body size or in individual parts that occurs through maturation. However, the term *growth* is more inclusive of overall body changes, as defined by development. The process of development is not limited to the changes occurring during infancy and childhood. Development occurs throughout the life span as people continually undergo cognitive, physical, and psychosocial changes regardless of their age. The term **maturation** refers to the fixed transitions or order of progressions that enables a person to progress to higher levels of function. Maturation includes internal processes that are unaffected by external factors such as the environment. Of course, aspects of the environment such as learning experiences, parental influence, and physical surroundings certainly can alter the timing of developmental transitions. For example, a child who is given a ball during infancy is much more likely to be able to catch and throw at an early age than a child who is only given a doll. Not receiving a ball does not prevent the child from learning how to catch and throw but will delay the development of these skills.

Aging refers to a process or group of processes occurring in living organisms that with the passage of time leads to a loss of adaptability, functional impairment, and eventually death (Spirduso et al., 2005). Aging is the progression of life from birth whereby a person matures, and this process continues through physical decline, ending with death. People are often classified by chronological age (see table 1.2) to avoid confusion in defining age groups. For instance, one professional may define a four-year-old as a child, whereas another professional may refer to a four-year-old as a preschooler. The importance of age classifications becomes even more prominent in the upper continuum of life, where age classification discrepancies can be as much as 20 years (i.e., determining whether old adulthood begins at age 55, 65, or 75). It is

Table 1.2 Age Classifications

Description	Age or transition marker
Newborn	Birth to 6 weeks
Infant	Age 6 weeks to age at walking
Toddler	Age at walking to 2 years
Preschooler	Age 3 to age at start of school
Young child	Age at start of school to 7 years
Child	Age 8 to 10
Preadolescent	Age 11 to onset of puberty
Adolescent	Onset of puberty to 20 years
Young adult	Age 21 to 40
Middle-aged adult	Age 41 to 60
Young-old adult	Age 61 to 74
Old adult	Age 75 to 99
Centenarian	Age 100+

WHAT DO YOU THINK?

Exercise 1.5

In this chapter you are learning about each of the subfields of motor behavior. While each subfield has a variety of similar features, each subfield also has distinct differences. In this exercise, determine which subfield each scenario hinges upon most: motor control, motor learning, or motor development. Fully explain how you came to your conclusion for each. Hint: Think about the age of the individuals and timeline.

1. A 20-year-old collegiate soccer player tears his anterior cruciate ligament and undergoes physical therapy to rehabilitate his knee. After six months, including three months of intensive therapy, the soccer player is back on the field.

2. A toddler begins to run six months after learning to walk.

3. A 12-year-old joins the track team and is not able to jump over the high jump bar. Following a month of practice, he can successfully high jump 1.75 yd (1.60 m).

4. A 62-year-old continues to play racquetball competitively and regularly beats many athletes a third of her age with her capability of controlling her shots.

also important to denote that most transitions are at a designated age while the transition from infancy to toddlerhood is the onset of independent walking and the transition from preadolescence to adolescence is puberty.

HISTORY OF MOTOR COMPETENCE RESEARCH

The history of the fields of motor behavior began several hundred years ago and has evolved to the multidisciplinary approach of today. The interest in assessing motor competence can be traced back even further to 800 BCE with assessments of Spartans' fitness for citizenship (Van Dalen & Bennett, 1971). Examining motor competence highlights a variety of mechanisms, including biological (i.e., growth, maturation, reflexes), social (e.g., parents, culture, practitioners), and environmental (e.g., home, community, schools) factors that influence functional and healthy lifestyles. To best understand the origins of motor competence assessments, we must follow the four periods: the precursor period, the maturational period, the normative period, and the process-oriented period (Clark & Whitall, 1989) (see table 1.3).

Table 1.3 Periods in the Evolution of the Field of Motor Development

Period	Characteristics
Precursor (1787-1928)	• Focus on product development • Nature versus nurture argument
Maturational (1928-1946)	Focus on maturation
Normative (1946-1970)	Focus on movement skills in school-age children
Process oriented (1970-present)	• Hypothesis-driven research • Emergence of the information-processing theory, ecological approach, and dynamic systems approach

Precursor Period

Motor competence research has its roots in the precursor period, beginning in the late 18th century. During this time, the main method for studying motor development was through descriptive observations, with the focus on the product, or outcome of development. It was also during the precursor period that Charles Darwin developed one of the main arguments for understanding the processes of motor development—the nature-versus-nurture debate. The perspective that development occurs as a function of nature assumes that maturation occurs because of genetic or internal factors (Gesell, 1928, 1954). This view, known as the **maturational perspective**, became quite popular in the 1930s during the maturational period. The **environmentalism perspective** assumes the converse: It is not heredity that molds the maturational process; rather, humans are nurtured by their environment. This argument ensued for many decades and continues to some degree even today. Charles Darwin did not believe that nature or nurture favors one developmental process over another. Instead, the environment (nurture) and genetic factors (nature) interact. Maturationists assume that a child born with the underlying abilities to excel at certain sports will eventually exhibit excellence in those sports. However, environmentalists propose that even basic skills must be developed through interaction with the environment. According to environmentalists, either individuals who are not given the appropriate equipment or environment to learn such skills will be delayed in developing them, or the skills will never materialize. Research has found high genetic contributions to development in twins who were either raised with (Williams & Gross, 1980) or apart from their family (Fox et al., 1996). Although there is research to support the high genetic component, there are also many environmental influences that affect motor development as well (Sasaki & Kim, 2017).

Charles Darwin's work was seminal in the study of motor behavior. It provided insights into the effect of the environment on the animal. Darwin theorized about how animals adapt to changing environments and discussed developmental sequences found across species (Darwin, 1859, 1871, 1872). He also wrote about the importance of studying both the product of the behavior and the process.

Maturational Period

A boom in motor development studies occurred in the 1930s following the emergence of the field of developmental psychology. As the name of this period implies, the focus was on maturation. Arnold Gesell led the maturationist movement, asserting that infant maturity is genetically predetermined, meaning that the infant moves from one developmental cycle to the next under the control of the central nervous system (composed of the brain and the spinal cord). Each cycle occurs in a very orderly and predetermined fashion; for example, infants roll over at around five months, sit up at six

---

WHAT DO YOU THINK?

Exercise 1.6

Think about your own family. Perhaps you have a large family with many siblings; maybe you are an only child; or maybe you were adopted. From a personal perspective, discuss how you believe your genetics and environment (parents and family) affected your motor development. From these personal experiences, do you lean more toward nature or nurture? Explain your response.

months, and stand at eight months. Maturationists assume that these transitions are set and controlled by nature. Children progress to the next step when they are ready. External influences are not included in these transitions; an internal clock, so to speak, simply determines precisely when the infant will progress. More recent research has shown that the environment can certainly influence the onset of these transitions. For instance, a child who never lies on his belly will crawl much later than a child who receives regular belly time (Mendres-Smith et al., 2020). The no-belly-time child's environment has delayed this transition because the infant was not given the opportunity to strengthen the arm, leg, and core muscles necessary for crawling. Children who are blind have been found to be significantly delayed in reaching many milestones (Elisa et al., 2002), such as manipulative and locomotor skills (Wagner et al., 2013) as well as **stability** skills (Haibach et al., 2011). It is doubtful that the delay is genetically predetermined. Rather, it is more likely that the delay results from the lack of visual stimuli that would motivate them to reach objects of interest as well as help them to replicate actions that their peers are doing.

Esther Thelen and colleagues' research on the infant stepping reflex and walking was seminal in this area. According to the maturation perspective, infants do not walk following the disappearance of the stepping reflex because neuronal paths need to first mature. The persistence of the stepping reflex in some infants had been viewed as an indication of a developmental delay. Thelen examined the effects of body build and arousal on infant stepping and found that the disappearance of the stepping reflex was due to increased body mass in proportion to strength (Thelen et al., 1982). Infants decrease their number of steps simply because they do not have the muscle strength to lift their heavy legs.

Growth occurs in a **cephalocaudal** direction, meaning that the head develops first and distal structures grow more slowly. Essentially, growth occurs from the head to the foot. An infant can control movements of the head much earlier than movements of the trunk or limbs. For instance, the eyes and mouth develop earlier than the hands and feet. Controlled eye movements can be seen postnatally at very early ages. On a personal note, one of the authors of this book was surprised to see that immediately following birth, her firstborn child was able to track his mother's eye movements. He would lie peacefully when eye contact was maintained but would scream when eye contact was removed, even for just a moment. With respect to his vision, he was not only alert but also very aware of his surroundings. It was also quite clear that although he was able to control his eye movements, it would be quite some time before he could control his head, neck, trunk, and limb movements.

While growth is occurring in a cephalocaudal direction, it is concurrently developing in a **proximodistal** direction; as the body is growing from head to foot, the trunk is advancing at a faster rate than the limbs. This can be examined in the prehension, or grasping, stages in infants. Initially, infants attempt to grasp an object with the whole palm. As they mature, they begin to use three fingers and then finally add the thumb and forefinger.

A secondary focus during the maturational period was on motor learning (McGraw, 1935). McGraw explained that "maturation and learning are not different processes, merely different facets of the fundamental process of growth" (McGraw, 1945/1969, pp. 130-131). Comparing the development of twins in a study in which one twin was taught motor skills and the other merely matured, McGraw found not only that the environment has a strong influence on motor development but also that there appear to be critical periods in which improvement can be optimized through advanced opportunities and instruction (McGraw, 1935, 1940).

Normative Period

Following World War II, the study of motor behavior was largely influenced by several physical educators, with a focus on movement skills in school-age children. The focus was less on cognitive development and more on the physical aspects of development, which caused a shift from process- to product-oriented research. Physical educators and researchers were also interested in anthropometric measures (growth measures) through childhood and the role of maturation and strength changes in children (Clark & Whitall, 1989, p. 189). Part of this shift was due to physical educators' interests at the time. They wanted to improve motor skill instruction through understanding changes in motor performance (Halverson, 1970). Motor learning researchers focused on the processes underlying performance changes when new simple motor skills are learned and on the evaluation of such performances. Unfortunately, it was not until the 1980s that motor developmentalists and motor learning and control researchers began appreciating the value of each other's work (Clark & Whitall, 1989).

Process-Oriented Period

A reemergence of motor behavior research occurred in the early 1970s as psychologists developed a renewed interest in the field and much study focused on hypothesis-driven research. During this period, three theoretical constructs emerged, each of which is still prominent today: the information-processing theory, the ecological approach, and the dynamic systems approach. It is important to have a basic understanding of the theories that drive research in motor development and motor learning to understand and interpret experimental findings in these fields. These theories are discussed in chapter 2 and are the theoretical basis for this book.

SUMMARY

This chapter provided a background for the fields of motor control, motor learning, and motor development. It is important to understand the similarities and differences between these fields of knowledge and to appreciate the importance of bringing them together when planning a motor skill program for learners of any age, developmental level, or background. It is also critical to understand the differences between growth and development and between learning and performance because they are very often overlooked.

We all stop growing at some point, but we never stop developing. Many people falsely assume that development is confined to infancy and childhood; however, development occurs throughout the life span. Another common misconception is that performance changes equate to learning changes, but this is not always the case. Learning results in a permanent change in the ability to perform skilled movement, whereas performance changes are the observable products of movement. Shooting a one-time half-court shot for a million dollars and shooting a free throw shot the next day are examples of performance. In a moment of extreme luck, someone could make the million-dollar shot but not be able to make a foul shot the following day. This person's performance would not reflect learning because a permanent change in the capability to shoot a basketball has not occurred. Finally, this chapter also presented the historical progression of the field of motor development leading into the current theoretical perspectives that are explained in chapter 2.

> **› ONLINE ACTIVITIES**

The student material found in HK*Propel* includes exercises, labs, and videos to enhance learning and encourage practical application of important concepts.

LEARNING AIDS

Supplemental Activities

1. Search the Internet for products related to motor development and make a list. Who are these products targeted toward? What age range are they designed for? Describe how the products are expected to help infants or children develop. Do you think these products will help infants or children develop the abilities or skills they are intended to develop? Why or why not?

2. Search the Internet for mainstream articles on motor behavior. This search should not be directed toward research articles, but rather magazines or news articles. Summarize the article. What are the main points the author is discussing? Who is the intended audience for this article? Then, in the same manner as in exercise 1.6, discuss which subfield this article most hinges upon—motor learning, motor development, or motor control—and explain how you came to this conclusion.

Glossary

action slips—Performance-related errors that typically occur when the person is not consciously attending to the movement.

aging—A process or group of processes occurring in living organisms that, with the passage of time, lead to a loss of adaptability, functional impairment, and eventually death.

cephalocaudal—Proceeding from the head to distal structures; development begins with the head, and distal structures grow more slowly.

coarticulation—Simultaneous motions that occur in sequential tasks.

control—Manipulation of movements in such a way as to meet the demands of the task.

coordination—The constraint of the number of degrees of freedom to decrease the complexity of the movement task to produce a movement pattern and achieve a task goal.

degrees of freedom—The number of independent elements that must be constrained to produce coordinated motion.

environmentalism perspective—A perspective that assumes that heredity does not mold the maturational process; rather, maturation occurs as humans are nurtured by their environment.

maturation—The fixed transition or order of progression that enables a person to progress to higher levels of function.

maturational perspective—A perspective that development occurs as a function of nature (i.e., because of genetic or internal factors).

motor behavior—An umbrella term for the fields of motor control, motor learning, and motor development.

motor competence—The measurement aspect of a movement, either product or process.

motor control—The underlying neural, physical, and behavioral processes of movement.

motor development—The products and underlying processes of motor behavior changes across the life span.

motor learning—The processes involved in the acquisition of a motor skill and the factors that enhance or inhibit the capability to perform a motor skill.

motor skills—Voluntary, goal-oriented physical elements that enable movement.

ontogeny—The level of development occurring over the life span of one individual.

perceptual–motor integration problem—Line of research in motor control that examines how perception and motor control are integrated.

performance—The act of executing a motor skill.

phylogeny—The evolutionary development of the history of a species, which can occur over many hundreds or thousands of years.

physical growth—An increase in body size or in individual parts that occurs through maturation.

power law of practice—The learning improvement as a function of practice such that performance from extensive practice improves the most during the beginning stages of learning with improvements subsequently continuing at a much lower rate of improvement.

process—A set of events or occurrences resulting in a change in the state or end product.

product—The outcome of performance.

proximodistal—In relation to development, the earlier advancement of the trunk than of the limbs.

serial order problem—The study of the importance of the sequencing, order, and timing of movement behaviors.

skillful—A criterion of excellence for performing a motor skill.

spoonerisms—Speech errors that occur because of exchanging letters in adjacent words.

stability—The ability to maintain body position against forces of gravity, which may include other circumstances that increase the difficulty of the task.

THEORETICAL CONSTRUCTS IN MOTOR BEHAVIOR

CHAPTER OBJECTIVES

After reading this chapter, you should be able to do the following:

- Defend the theoretical constructs in motor behavior.
- Develop invariant features and parameters in generalized motor programs.
- Explain open-loop and closed-loop control.
- Differentiate information-processing theory and the ecological approach to perception.
- Construct the constraints model, such as how movement patterns are constrained by boundaries that limit movement possibilities.

Transitions

Chante and Darius were proud parents of their first child, Keenan. Keenan was born a healthy baby boy three days after his due date. He progressed in his milestones at typical developmental periods, and with each milestone, his parents beamed with joy. He began crawling at a developmentally young age at seven months, which made his parents begin to think he may be physically advanced. They expected him to be independently walking well before his first birthday at this rate. However, to their surprise, Keenan's first birthday passed, and Keenan showed little interest in walking. Keenan had found that he could get around much quicker on four limbs than on his unstable two legs, and therefore was not interested. Perhaps this lengthy period of crawling made the moment of first steps even that much more exciting for his parents.

It is nothing short of remarkable witnessing a child's firsts—first smile, first time sitting up alone, first step, to mention only a few. They can certainly make us wonder what underlies these changes. In one moment, an infant cannot take any independent steps; then in another moment they are able to walk from one parent to the other. What has enabled this transition? Transitions are not limited to infancy and childhood but continue across the life span. Maybe you recently learned how to juggle and struggled through many failed attempts before you could make several catches, then a few more; finally, you were able to juggle. What changed? How were you able to suddenly accomplish this seemingly impossible task?

Transitions also occur following an injury such as a ligament tear. More and more baseball pitchers are undergoing surgery to repair the ulnar collateral ligament. This surgery is commonly referred to as Tommy John surgery. Although this surgery is popular, the recovery is long, and there are certainly no guarantees of returning to a preinjury level of play. Also, many variables can affect the recovery outcome. In the case of injury, rehabilitation drives movement pattern changes, whereas in the case of learning new movements, development, practice, or training induces change.

To explain what drives the many remarkable changes that occur throughout our life spans, three theoretical constructs were developed during the early part of the process-oriented period in the history of motor development theory, as discussed in chapter 1. These theoretical constructs—the information-processing theory, ecological approach, and dynamic systems approach—still drive research today. These theories differ in the way they define development and learning as well as in how they examine behavior. According to the **information-processing theory**, the brain receives, processes, and interprets information to send signals to produce skilled coordinated movements, similar to how a computer functions. Proponents of the **ecological approach**, however, state that movement is much more complex than a simple input–output relay of information from the brain to the other systems. Instead, actions are determined by many internal factors (e.g., goals and capabilities) and external factors (e.g., what is available in the environment). The third theoretical perspective, the **dynamic systems approach**, has been viewed as an offshoot of ecological psychology. In this perspective, movement does not occur because of a set of instructions but rather as the result of the interplay of the task, the environment, and the individual. Movement is "softly" assembled, meaning that it emerges because of these three factors.

INFORMATION-PROCESSING THEORY

The basis of the information-processing theory is the idea that the brain acts like a computer, working as a receiver and processor of information (Fitts & Posner, 1967; Keele, 1973; Marteniuk, 1976; Schmidt, 1975). A key area of this research addressed the processes involved in movement behavior. Although the process of development was a key area of interest in earlier research, there was a shift from investigating ontogenetic (life span) changes to processes of change within a life span, such as memory, feedback, attention, and perception (Clark & Whitall, 1989).

A **generalized motor program (GMP)** is a representation of a pattern of movements that is modifiable to produce a movement outcome. A GMP can be thought of as a set of instructions stored in the brain. When we perform a particular skill, we retrieve this set of instructions, sending the message to the appropriate muscles. The time needed to organize a motor program depends on the complexity of the task; more complex tasks require more time to organize than less complex tasks do. Henry and Rogers (1960) illustrated this by measuring reaction time for three tasks varying in complexity. They found that reaction time (the time from the onset of a stimulus to the initiation of the response) increased with increasing complexity. When participants had to simply lift a finger from a switch, reaction time was only 165 milliseconds, but it went up to 199 milliseconds, when the task increased in complexity to lifting the finger from the switch and then grasping a hanging tennis ball. It increased to 212 milliseconds for lifting the finger, striking the ball, pushing a button, and grasping another ball. These results indicate that movements are planned prior to initiating a response, because more time is required to prepare motor programs for more complex tasks.

To be classified into a particular GMP, an action must include **invariant features**—that is, features that cannot be modified between attempts. Invariant features are unique to their GMP much as the features of a person's signature are unique. If you were asked to write your name under varying conditions (e.g., with your dominant hand, with your nondominant hand, in large letters or small letters, or even with your feet), the general stroke and structure of your signature would be the same. Of course, the writing may be a bit sloppier with your feet, but it will still have the same general features as your signature with your dominant hand. The difference in the signatures is the effect of experience and reduced coordination and control in the nondominant limb, not the structure of the letters. A classic example that illustrates the effects of invariant features is shown in figure 2.1.

The three invariant features of a GMP are the *sequence of actions, relative timing,* and *relative force.* Sequence of actions include the coordination or movement sequences for a motor skill. For example, a basketball layup includes dribbling, two steps, and then a shot, or a punt would include a catch, approach, dropping the ball, and then kicking the ball. If the sequence of actions were changed, the motor skill likely couldn't even be performed. Relative timing and relative force enable the rhythm of the movement pattern. Movements can be performed with more force or less force, or faster or slower (timing), but *all* components of the skill must increase or decrease in force or speed, not just one component. By changing only one component, the rhythm of the motor skill will change. For example, if proportionally more time were spent on any one action of a volleyball serve, such as slowing down the

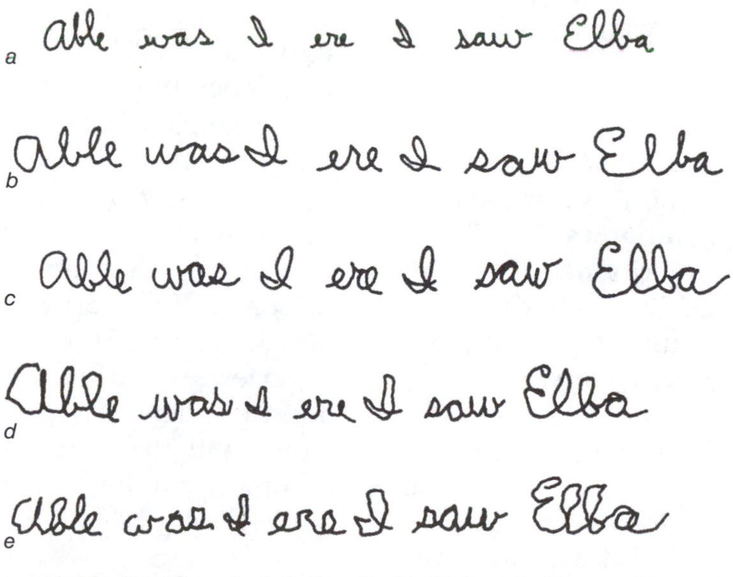

Figure 2.1   Invariant features affected this person's ability to write *(a)* with the right (dominant) hand, *(b)* with the wrist immobilized, *(c)* with the left hand, *(d)* with the pen gripped in the teeth, and *(e)* with the pen taped to the foot.

Reprinted by permission from M.H. Raibert, *Motor Control and Learning by the State Space Model,* Technical Report AI-TR-439 (Cambridge, MA: MIT Artificial Intelligence Laboratory, 1977), 50.

toss of the ball but not slowing down the swing, the overall movement pattern would be compromised. This would be an example of a relative timing change. A person can walk at many speeds; however, the relative timing will remain the same unless the person transitions to running. The same is true for relative force. To kick a ball harder, an athlete must proportionately increase the amount of force produced when planting the nondominant foot, swinging the dominant foot back, swinging the dominant foot forward, and contacting the ball. Altering the relative timing or relative force of only one or two components and not all the components will compromise the rhythm of the movement pattern.

Examples of each type of invariant features of a generalized motor program

- *Sequence of actions:* An American football punt sequence is catch, approach, drop, kick.
- *Relative timing:* A swing to hit a volleyball during a serve must be relative to the timing of the toss.
- *Relative force:* The force of your foot contacting a ball during a kick should be relative to the force with which you approached the ball and the movement of your leg.

The features of a GMP that *can* be modified during the execution of a movement pattern are called **parameters**. Modifying parameters allows practitioners to adapt their responses (e.g., walk at different speeds, shoot a basketball from different positions on the court, kick with more force or less force). The three types of parameters are *muscle selection*, *overall duration*, and *overall force*. In the signature example in figure 2.1, similar features were found for writing with the dominant and with the nondominant hand. Writing with a different hand is a parameter change, not an invariant feature change, because of the use of different muscle groups (muscle selection).

A quarterback in American football can throw a short pass to a running back or throw much farther for a Hail Mary pass to a wide receiver. The GMP used is the same whether you are unscrewing a very tight lid or a loose one or whether you are kicking a penalty kick from the right or the left side of the goal.

As a reminder, GMPs are defined by their invariant features (inflexible features) and parameters (flexible features). It is important to recognize the differences between invariant features and parameters; here is a quick recap of each.

Examples of each type of parameter of a generalized motor program

- *Muscle selection:* The GMP is the same for throwing with your left hand as it is for throwing with your right hand.
- *Overall duration:* The GMP is the same for running slowly as it is for running fast.
- *Overall force:* The GMP is the same for batting with more overall force as it is for batting with less overall force.

Varying parameters appropriate to the situation is particularly essential for open skills. Basketball players must vary each shot depending on their position relative to the basket, and shortstops in baseball must vary their throws to reach different bases. By practicing under varying conditions, learners develop rules or relationships that help them make appropriate movement responses. These are called **schemas**. Schemas develop over time through accumulated experiences within a generalized motor program. The more someone practices a motor skill, the more developed the schema becomes, enabling the person to react more quickly and perform more accurately.

Modes of Control

Prior to executing a movement, the mover must retrieve the appropriate GMP and

RESEARCH NOTES

Monkey Business

A seminal paper by Polit and Bizzi (1978) investigated the notion of the GMP by deafferenting monkeys. Deafferentation is a technique whereby the sensory receptors are severed so that no proprioceptive feedback can be received. In other words, there is no longer any feeling in the deafferented limb. Polit and Bizzi trained several monkeys to perform pointing tasks. After the movement pattern was acquired, the monkeys were deafferented. In addition, to remove other sensory information, the monkey's vision was blocked so that they could neither see nor feel where their deafferented limb was located. Even without the sensory feedback, the monkeys were still able to accurately point to the target just as they had with vision and kinesthesis (feeling movement). These findings provide support for the notion of motor programs and the information-processing theory because the monkeys were able to plan for movement, initiate that plan, and continue the movement without feedback.

TRY THIS

When Is a Throw Not a Throw?

Exercise 2.1

Early motor program theories postulated that every task required a separate motor program. A new program was required to catch a tennis ball versus a softball, or to throw a ball 10 feet (3 m) rather than 15 feet (4.5 m). If a new program was required for every variation of a movement, an immense amount of space in memory would be needed for all the information. A theory of generalized motor programs was developed to address this issue. If a new coordination pattern was not required to perform a motor skill, it could be controlled by the same generalized motor program. To test this, try the following variations of throwing a small ball at a target. For *a* through *d*, the goal is to throw for accuracy; for *e*, the goal is to throw as hard as you can.

a. Find a target that is only 5 feet (1.5 m) away and throw at it a few times.

b. Take several big steps back so that you are 15 feet (4.5 m) from the target; then aim and throw at the target.

c. From the same spot, aim and throw the ball more slowly.

d. Using the same target and position, throw with your nondominant hand.

e. Now take several big steps back until you are 30 feet (9 m) or more from the target and throw as hard as you can at the target.

Answer the following questions based on your experience:

1. Which of the throws were controlled by the same generalized motor program? If one or more was not, describe how you know that it was controlled by a different GMP.

2. Which of the variations of throwing a small ball was a variation of a parameter? Describe what type of parameter was varied.

(continued)

Answer these questions on a motor skill of your choice:

1. Provide two examples of invariant features for a movement skill of your choice. Discuss why these features would place this movement into a different GMP rather than being a parameter change.
2. Now provide two examples of how you could vary this skill without compromising the movement pattern (parameter change).
3. If an adaptation in a motor skill has caused a change in the invariant features, should the learner practice under these conditions? Explain why they should or should not.

choose the appropriate parameters for that situation. These decisions occur at a subconscious level and do not explain how the movement is controlled. There are many options for adapting any movement pattern, and as such, there is a wide variety of ways to control skill production. In a broad sense, two control systems underlie movements: closed-loop control and open-loop control.

Closed-Loop Control

Closed-loop control is used for relatively long-duration, continuous activities during which the person can make corrections based on feedback received while moving. In closed-loop control, the information used to make corrections travels through the stages of information processing. First, the information is processed, and a motor program is initiated. Sensory information regarding the movement (i.e., response-produced feedback) is compared to the desired movement, and corrections to the movement pattern can be made if necessary. For example, when you are walking to class, you have a plan for the route you are going to take, but you cannot plan exactly for the disturbances you may encounter, such as potholes, people walking toward you, and cars coming when you approach a crosswalk. When you encounter these things, you adjust, such as changing direction, slowing down, or even stopping. These changes occur throughout the execution of the movement of walking to class.

A thermostat is a good example of a closed-loop system. A thermostat regulates the room temperature based on the set temperature. It continuously monitors the temperature and makes a change only when the actual temperature doesn't match the set temperature. If the temperature is set to 68 degrees Fahrenheit (20 degrees Celsius), and the room temperature is detected to be 67 degrees, the heater will turn on. Once the heat reaches the desired temperature of 68 degrees, the heater turns off.

Open-Loop Control

Closed-loop control can only be used for slower actions that last long enough for feedback to be used during the movement. For movements that are more rapid and discrete, the control made is called **open-loop control**. To use open-loop control, the performer needs to preplan the movement by choosing a generalized motor program and then execute the action. A good example is composing a text message. You choose the person you are going to text, type your message, and then tap Send. Once you tap Send, there is no return; you cannot go back and change the text. Most of us have sent a text to the wrong person, and there's simply no way to unsend that text. Perhaps there was an error in the text because you typed incorrectly or autocorrect changed what you wrote. If you want to make a change to your text, your only option is to send a follow-up text with the correct information. This action is not considered closed loop because sending the subsequent text cannot eliminate and correct the original text. Open-loop control of movements is very common and is often part of the end of a movement. Examples include pressing an elevator button, heading a ball in soccer, flipping a light switch, and catching a line drive in baseball. Refer to figure 2.2a and 2.2b, for a comparison of closed- and open-loop control.

In some cases, a rapid action can be quickly adjusted following the initial movement. You may have started to shut a door and midway through realized that you didn't have your keys. If you made the adjustment quickly enough, you may have been able to prevent the door from shutting and locking you out. A good sporting example is the checked swing in baseball. The swing can be prevented if a second decision to not swing is made early enough. However, if the decision is made too late, the batter may not have enough time to check the swing. Nonetheless, the batter is aware that he should not have swung even as he is swinging, thus receiving response-produced feedback during the movement. This awareness, or feeling of incorrectness, is possible in many movements controlled by open-loop processes, such as knowing you

made a poor basketball shot well before the ball reaches the basket.

Most activities incorporate a combination of both modes of control, such as the earlier texting example. Composing the text is controlled by closed-loop processes because you can make changes; however, tapping Send is controlled by open-loop processes. When assessing how a movement is controlled, think about how long it takes to produce the movement. If there is time to adjust, then the movement is controlled by closed-loop processing. If the movement is very rapid and has a point of no return (i.e., there is no option to alter the movement while it is happening), then it is controlled by an open-loop process. For a comparison of open- and closed-loop control, see table 2.1.

Speed–Accuracy Trade-Off

Speed and accuracy are important in many motor skills, particularly those that have a temporal and spatial component such as in racket sports and fielding games. Although both accuracy and speed may be important in these motor skills, when a person focuses on one, the other is compromised—hence, the term **speed–accuracy trade-off**. For example, batters must be able to produce a quick and forceful swing that is also accu-

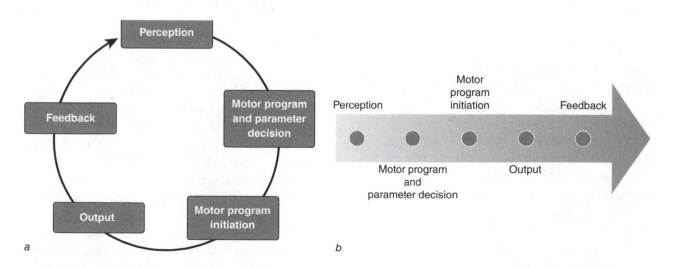

Figure 2.2 Systems of control can be (a) closed or (b) open.

Table 2.1 Comparison of Open- and Closed-Loop Systems of Control

Characteristics	Open-loop control	Closed-loop control
Speed of movement	Rapid	Slow
Accuracy of response	Low accuracy	Very accurate
Feedback	Adjustments can't be made	Adjustments can be made

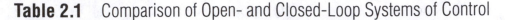

Figure 2.3 Fitts' tapping task in which participants tapped between the two target plates of varying widths separated by varying amplitudes using a stylus.

rate. Given that pitchers can throw balls over 90 miles per hour (145 km/h) and batters are only 18 yards away, batters not only have minimal time to react but also must accurately position their bats to contact the ball.

Woodworth (1899) conducted some of the first research in motor behavior that focused on the relationship between speed and accuracy when drawing lines from one target to another. He found that accuracy diminished when speed or distance between targets increased. Fitts (1954) extended this research and discovered that speed decreased when either the distance between the targets was increased or the size of the targets was decreased when focusing on accuracy (see figure 2.3). Interestingly, this relationship exists only for spatial accuracy. Regarding temporal accuracy, such as the speed of a swing, accuracy improves with increased speed. Estimates of time are more accurate with less time than with more time. You could try this by estimating time with a stopwatch. Compare your estimates of shorter periods of time (e.g., one or five seconds) to longer periods of time (e.g., one minute). Were you more accurate estimating shorter periods of time or longer periods of time?

The effect of spatial and temporal accuracy instructions was examined in a speed–accuracy trade-off study in children (Rival et al., 2003). Children aged 6 to 10 years and adults completed three experimental conditions with different verbal instructions. The task was to point to a lit target and (a) move as quickly as possible, (b) move as accurately as possible, or (c) move as accurately *and* quickly as possible. Reaction time was slower when participants were instructed to focus on accuracy or instructed to focus on both speed and accuracy. These results revealed that not only was the speed–accuracy trade-off present for all age groups, but all age groups were able to comply with the instructions and adapt their movements accordingly.

ECOLOGICAL APPROACH

Perception, the act of attaching meaning to something, is essential and intricately linked to movement. Essentially, perception enables us to interact with the environment in a meaningful way. For instance, we perceive the sizes of objects and determine how to adjust our grip to manipulate them. We perceive through our senses (vision, hearing, and kinesthesis), but perception is also affected by our personal experiences and understanding.

The relationship of perception and action is viewed very differently between the ecological approach and the information-processing theory. The ecological approach to perception is known as a direct process

---

TRY THIS

Haste Makes Waste

Exercise 2.2

1. On a piece of paper, draw five sets of two circles separated by approximately 5 inches (13 cm) for the first four sets and approximately 10 inches (25 cm) for the last set. The circles for the fourth set should be smaller in diameter. The circles are your targets. The task is to draw lines from one target to the other and continue moving back and forth under varying conditions, changing either the goal or the targets.

Condition 1: Start with your pen in one circle in the first set of circles. Your goal is to move your pen back and forth from one circle to the other circle in the same set as *quickly* as possible. Do this at least 10 times.

◯   ◯

Condition 2: Starting with your pen in one circle in the second set of circles, move your pen back and forth from one circle to the other circle in the same set and back as *accurately* as possible 10 times. Your goal is to never go beyond either the circle.

◯   ◯

Condition 3: Starting with your pen in one circle in the third set of circles, move your pen from one circle to the next circle and back as *quickly and accurately* as possible 10 times.

◯   ◯

Condition 4: Starting with your pen in one circle in the fourth set of circles, move your pen as *quickly and accurately* as possible back and forth from one to the other a total of 10 times.

◯   ◯

Condition 5: Starting with your pen in one circle in the fifth set of circles, move your pen back and forth as *quickly* and *accurately* as possible 10 times.

◯   ◯

2. Discuss how your speed and accuracy changed in the varying conditions.

---

because it holds that using memory stores is not necessary to provide meaning to objects or events in the environment (Gibson, 1966). In contrast, the information-processing theory holds that action occurs as an *indirect process* of perception; that is, to act on the environment, a person must go through a series of steps. For instance, if a person comes across a steaming hot cup of coffee, he must first perceive the cup of coffee by locating memory stores of a cup of coffee. He then decides whether he wants to drink the coffee. If he is interested in drinking it, a message is sent from the brain to the limbs to reach for the cup of coffee. An example of this can be seen in figure 2.4.

Ecological psychologists explain that we do not go through a long series of processes to complete a task such as drinking a cup of coffee (see figure 2.4). Rather, as movers, we act upon the environment in the manner *afforded* by the object. We cannot move without perceiving, just as we cannot perceive without acting. For example, a hiker walking through the woods who sees a fallen log does not see the log, perceive what it is, decide how to act on it, and then act on it. Instead, the log affords the hiker a place to sit. The perception and action are the same. **Affordances** are the action possibilities of the environment and task in relation to the perceiver's capabilities (Gibson, 1977, 1979). Perceiving and acting is guided by body-scaled ratios. For example, a person's leg length affects how that person climbs a set of stairs. Toddlers have much shorter legs and must compensate for a reduced ratio between leg length and the action space of the step height (Warren, 1984). Because children are tuned in to this body-scaled ratio, they do not have to learn new movement patterns as they grow and mature. Depending on individual differences and goals, action possibilities for a particular object can vary quite widely. A chair will most often afford a place to sit; however, a person who needs to reach for a high object may use a chair as a stool. A stool may afford small children a seat because of their shorter height and leg length; however, an adult might not be able to sit comfortably on a stool.

Ecological psychology rejects the idea that there is a need to search for memory stores for object representations. Instead, the acts of perceiving and moving occur simultaneously (Michaels & Carello, 1981). Objects are used to suit goals or needs (direct perception), not because there is a prior memory of using that object (indirect perception). This effect was illustrated in a locomotor task with toddlers and crawling infants ascending and descending a sloping walkway (Adolph et al., 1993). Both groups overestimated their ability to ascend the slopes, but only the toddlers altered their movement patterns during the steeper descents. The toddlers often switched to a sliding movement, whereas the infants continued to crawl headfirst down the steep descents, often resulting in a fall. The infants hesitated only prior to the steeper descents, but they did not attempt an alternate means of negotiating the slope. The toddlers, on the other hand, hesitated on the lower slopes and then switched to the more stable sliding method for the steeper slopes. These findings indicate that the perception of affordances (the degree to which a surface is walkable) is influenced by locomotor skills. Children learn how to perceive locomotion affordances through movement exploration.

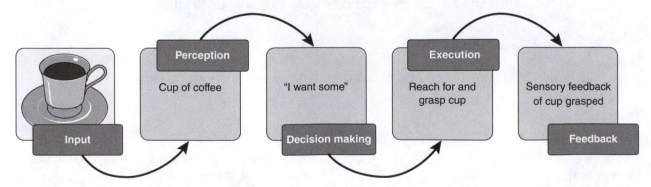

Figure 2.4 Example of an indirect process of action and perception as viewed by the information-processing theory. The person must perceive first and then act on the environment.

WHAT DO YOU THINK?

Exercise 2.3

Affordances relate to action possibilities for a person and a particular environment. Movement patterns are specified by body-scaled ratios between the piece of equipment or elements in the environment and the size of the person. The following examples address how a person's size affects the person's movement pattern.

1. If an adult were teaching a six-year-old the basics of tennis, how do you expect their grips (both the adult's and the child's) to be affected if both use the same size racket? Discuss in terms of affordances.

2. How would you expect two-, four-, and eight-year-olds to catch a beach ball? A soccer ball? A softball?

3. Why is body scaling particularly important in physical therapy? Provide a couple of examples.

DYNAMIC SYSTEMS APPROACH

During the early 1980s, Kugler, Kelso, and Turvey (1982) introduced the dynamic systems approach. They emphasized that movements are controlled by more than just the central nervous system; they are also controlled by interactions within various body systems as well as with the environment. Many factors are involved in how we move, which can cause us to move differently from one day to the next because of changes in the environment (physical or sociocultural), the task (goal, equipment, rules), or personal factors (height or intellect). For example, children's ability to jump high is affected by the muscular system (they need the strength to propel themselves into the air), the skeletal system (taller children have a height advantage in jumping), the adipose system (children with more body fat have more difficulty jumping high), and the neurological system (to coordinate the body to jump). In addition, the experience children have with jumping certainly influences their capability to jump. Psychological factors such as how motivated children are to jump also affect how high they will jump. The task goal can also significantly affect height of a jump, such as when jumping for a basketball rebound.

The information-processing theory asserts that functioning occurs in a hierarchical manner; that is, all signals go to the brain and the brain issues commands to be sent to the muscles. However, the information-processing theory does not account for the continuous interaction of the person with the environment. Proponents of the dynamic systems approach contend that coordinated behavior occurs because of many variables that are continuously interacting to constrain movement. Researchers who favor the maturational perspective suggest that a predetermined plan specifies the sequence of movement behaviors. They suggest that movement is hardwired and preset, whereas the dynamic systems theorists suggest that movement emerges as a function of the person, the task, and the environment.

The dynamic systems approach characterizes movement as a self-organizing process. **Self-organization** is the system's ability to change states or acquire a new structure or pattern by itself. This perspective defines movement and coordination as a complex and evolving process. The system is constantly looking for stable states, or **attrac-**

tors. When the system is perturbed enough (e.g., if movement speed has increased or the person has been injured), the system will be disrupted and pushed into a new attractor, or stable, state (Thelen & Ulrich, 1991). An example of disruption because of injury is a racquetball player who suddenly cannot grip the racket tightly because of a strained ring finger. Interestingly, this looser grip results in a more mechanically efficient swing that can lead to the player swinging with more accuracy and velocity. Once the injured finger heals, the player, realizing the benefits, may stay with the new and improved grip. The finger injury perturbed her physical status (the system), pushing the athlete to a new way of hitting the ball (a new attractor state).

Basic developmental phases such as sitting, crawling (belly on the ground), and creeping (belly off the ground) can also be viewed as attractor states. During development, new attractors emerge as infants mature and increase strength and coordination, causing former attractor states to disappear. When infants are first learning to walk, they often switch back to their more comfortable state of creeping. However, after they have been walking for several months, they leave the attractor state of crawling and usually do not crawl except on rare occasions to negotiate the environment.

The stability of attractors has been compared to the depth of a basin or well; the deeper the well is, the more stable the behavior is (Ennis, 1992). Very stable patterns (deep wells) are quite difficult to change, such as a movement skill or pattern that is well learned, whereas shallow wells are volatile and very susceptible to switching into a new attractor state. A swimmer who has learned an unorthodox way of performing the butterfly stroke may have a difficult time using the correct technique introduced by a new instructor. The swimmer most likely will go through a period of slower sprint times and uncomfortable movement patterns before a phase shift pushes her movement pattern into a new attractor state. Likewise, physical therapists strongly encourage patients to walk without a limp so that they do not develop a stable pattern of limping once they have recovered from injury, which would require them to progress through phase shifts to return to their previous walking pattern without a limp.

A **phase shift** is the change in a state that causes a reorganization to a new attractor state, whereas **control parameters** are the variables that induce the shift to a new attractor state. Movement speed, injury, weight, force, and sensory information can all act as control parameters. In the example of the racquetball player, the finger injury was the control parameter that caused a phase shift to a new grip. Increasing the speed on a treadmill can be a control parameter that causes a phase shift from walking to running. Control parameters can also limit or hinder performance. When this

---

WHAT DO YOU THINK?

Exercise 2.4

What would cause a change in self-organization in each of the following comparisons?

1. Compare hiking in the woods—encountering branches, fallen logs, and so on—to hiking in deep snow.
2. Compare dancing in a crowded club to dancing on an open floor.
3. Compare bench pressing at 60 percent of your maximum to bench pressing at 95 percent of your maximum.

occurs, the control parameter is referred to as a **rate limiter**. Fear is a common rate limiter because it often causes people to alter their movement patterns. A toddler who is afraid of being hurt by a thrown ball will likely close his eyes and protect his face rather than place his hands out in preparation to catch the ball. A bowling ball or a bat that is too heavy could also act as a rate limiter. Physical and occupational therapists work with patients to resolve some of the changes resulting from rate limiters. For example, a physical therapist may work with a stroke patient who must relearn to walk or even pick up objects with the affected limb. Injuries and arthritis are other examples of rate limiters that physical or occupational therapists often encounter. Bench pressing with a comfortable weight is an example of a strong attractor. As the amount of weight is increased (control parameter), the person's form will become progressively less stable until at some point the person will change form to be able to continue to lift. The amount of increased weight that causes this change to poor form is an example of a rate limiter. The change from good form to bad form is an example of a phase shift. Following are brief descriptions and practical examples of these terms:

Attractor: A stable state, such as bench pressing with good form

Control parameter: The cause of a change, such as increasing the amount of weight used in a bench press

Rate limiter: The cause of a negative change, such as increasing the weight used in a bench press beyond the capability of the lifter

Phase shift: A change that causes a shift to a new attractor, such as too much weight used in a bench press, which leads to a change in the lifter's form

Kugler, Kelso, and Turvey (1982) proposed that coordination is developed by changing constraints imposed by the interaction of the person with the environment, which they called the **constraints model**. Newell (1986) asserted that movement is constrained by boundaries that limit movement possibilities. These boundaries are termed **constraints**. People choose movement patterns based on the interaction of themselves, the task, and the environmental constraints (see figure 2.5).

Individual Constraints

Individual constraints are divided into two categories, structural and functional. **Structural constraints** include physical characteristics such as gender, height, weight, and body makeup. We would expect a 6-foot, 5-inch (196 cm) man to perform very differently on a basketball court than a 4-foot, 7-inch (140 cm) female. We would also expect the tall male and the petite female to move differently on the dance floor or even when walking down the street. **Functional constraints** include psychological and cognitive variables, such as motivation, arousal, and intellect. A dancer may perform a dance routine with more small errors when she is under much stress, ill, or fatigued, even though the structural constraints have not changed.

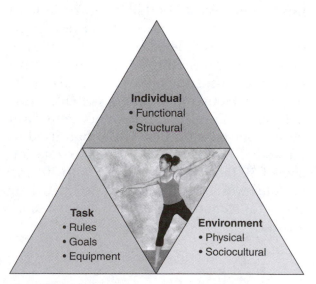

Figure 2.5 Model of the three constraints: individual, task, and environment.

WHAT DO YOU THINK?

Exercise 2.5

Because the goal of any motor skill program is to promote increased proficiency in motor skill performance, practitioners must understand what may limit the progression of a skill. For the following examples, list the potential rate limiters that are preventing or delaying progression in the motor skill.

1. An older adult can walk and climb stairs normally, but when descending he must go down backward. What rate limiter is preventing him from moving forward when stepping downstairs?

2. An infant cannot hold her body upright to stand without supporting herself with a solid stationary object. What is preventing her from standing without support?

3. A four-year-old can hit a ball from a tee but cannot contact the ball when it is pitched to him. What rate limiters are preventing him from hitting the ball?

Task Constraints

Task constraints include the goals of the movement, rules, and equipment (Newell, 1986). All movement tasks are constrained by the goal of the movement. The goal of basketball is to outscore the opponent by shooting basketballs through a regulation-sized hoop while the other team is attempting to steal the ball. Because of this goal, athletes practice the motor skill of jump shooting. The rules of basketball also govern the body movements. Basketball players are allowed to take only one step after they have stopped dribbling. This rule adds to the complexity of the sport, preventing athletes from simply running up and down the court and requiring them to outsmart their opponents while dribbling. Finally, implements constrain movement possibilities. If the ball used in basketball were changed from a regulation size of 30 inches to 12 inches (76 to 30 cm), athletes would certainly have to alter their shots to accommodate this new task constraint.

Environmental Constraints

Environmental constraints are constraints that are external to the mover. These can be either physical or sociocultural. **Physical environmental constraints** include external conditions such as weather, temperature, lighting, floor surface, and step height. Tennis players play differently on grass courts than they do on clay or concrete courts. American football players change to shorter passes during rainy games because of the increased difficulty of grasping the wet ball. Physical environmental constraints do not affect only athletes; they affect us all every day. We walk differently on icy ground than we do on the beach. A high curb may be very difficult for someone in a wheelchair or on crutches to overcome. Even a young, able-bodied person may misjudge the curb and trip. **Sociocultural environmental constraints** are imposed by social and cultural norms and pressures. For instance, young women in some Eastern cultures may be less likely to participate regularly

TRY THIS

Constraints

Exercise 2.6

Individual Constraints

Place one hand over and behind your head and the other hand behind your back. Now attempt to grasp your fingers with the opposite hands.

1. Were you able to accomplish this task? If not, what prevented you from grasping your fingers?
2. Would this be considered a structural or a functional constraint?
3. Sit on the floor with your legs crossed. Stand without the use of your hands.
   a. Were you able to accomplish this task?
   b. If so, did you or other students find it challenging?
   c. What constraints made this task more challenging or less challenging for some students than others?
   d. How might this task be particularly challenging for older adults?

Task Constraints

Crumple up a piece of paper into a ball and throw it into a basket (a wastebasket if necessary). Now throw a racquetball into the same basket from the same distance. Place the basket on top of a table or a shelf. Throw each ball into the basket again.

1. Did you use the same movement pattern for each ball? Describe your movement pattern(s).
2. Did you use the same movement pattern for each basket height? Describe your movement pattern(s).

Label the three types of task constraints. Provide an example of how you could vary one of these types of task constraints for a therapy-related exercise or a physical education class activity.

Environmental Constraints

Shoot your paper ball and the racquetball into the basket again, this time with a fan blowing across the basket.

1. Did the added influence of wind influence the accuracy of your shot?
2. Did it affect both the paper ball and the racquetball?
3. Did you alter your movement pattern to overcome the increased airflow produced by the fan?

(continued)

Exercise 2.6 (continued)

For further practice on the constraints, categorize each of the following as an individual, environmental, or task constraint.

1. Having the flu
2. Running into the wind
3. Brushing your teeth with an electric toothbrush
4. Arthritic joints
5. Playing touch football
6. Hiking through rough terrain

Categorize each of the following as either a structural or functional constraint.

1. Lacking motivation
2. Recovering from a broken leg
3. Being 5-foot, 10-inches (178 cm) tall
4. Having poor muscular flexibility
5. Being mentally fatigued

in sport than young women in the United States because sport is less encouraged for females (Bhalla & Weiss, 2010). In the United States, women's participation in sport is rivaling that of men. This was not always the case, however. It was not until the passage of Title IX in 1972 that the gender gap in sport participation began to close. Prior to this educational amendment, women had far fewer opportunities for sport participation. Since 1972, there are more and more organizations promoting sport for women, with the Beijing Winter Olympics coming the closest to closing the gap.

SUMMARY

This chapter discussed the three main theoretical constructs that drive research in motor behavior: the information-processing theory, ecological approach, and dynamic systems approach. These perspectives differ not only in the way they define development and learning, but also in how they examine behavior. Some perspectives focus on age groups (e.g., the maturational period;

see chapter 1), whereas others compare age differences (information processing) or examine how movement transitions emerge (dynamic systems and ecological approaches).

In the information-processing theory, movement patterns are defined as generalized motor programs that include variables that cannot be modified (invariant features) and variables that can be modified (parameters). It is important for learners to vary the parameters in practice to enhance their schema as well as increase their adaptability. However, they should not practice the movement pattern if there is a change in an invariant feature, because doing so will encourage incorrect form. Because of the many options for adapting any movement pattern, skill production is controlled in many ways. In a broad sense, two control systems underlie movements: closed-loop control and open-loop control.

According to the ecological approach, perception and action are the same. We perceive objects as the actions they can afford us, and those perceptions and actions are guided by body-scaled ratios. Proponents of the dynamic systems approach contend that movement emerges as a function of the person, the task, and the environment. As individuals, we have our own unique structural and functional constraints, which are affected by changing task and environmental constraints. We encourage you to compare and contrast these theories and to examine development and learning from the theoretical perspective you find the most compelling.

> **ONLINE ACTIVITIES**

> The student material found in HK *Propel* includes exercises, labs, and videos to enhance learning and encourage practical application of important concepts.

LEARNING AIDS

Supplemental Activities

1. In this chapter you learned about closed- and open-loop control. Many tasks have some components that are controlled by open-loop control and some by closed-loop control.

   a. Take 15 playing cards and, to the best of your ability, stack them to make a pyramid like the one in the illustration. Try this five times and record how many cards were stacked before they fell for each attempt. Break down card stacking into three components: (a) adjusting the cards in your hands, (b) leaning the cards, and (c) releasing the cards. Label each as either open- or closed-loop control.

   b. Take a coin and practice spinning it on a table and trapping it in a vertical position with your index finger. Perform this task 20 times and record the number of successful spins and successful vertical traps. Then break the task into three components: (a) spinning the coin, (b) preparing to trap the coin, and (c) trapping the coin; label each as either open- or closed-loop control.

   c. Choose a sport-related motor skill and explain which components are controlled by closed-loop control and which are controlled by open-loop control.

   d. Choose an everyday activity and explain which components are controlled by closed-loop control and which are controlled by open-loop control.

2. Manipulating task and environmental constraints is an effective strategy for improving performance. Equipment can be changed so that it is appropriate for young learners or beginners. The rules can be adjusted so that learners can understand the basics without being overwhelmed. Activities can also be practiced in more predictable environments to enhance performance during skill acquisition.

   a. Choose an activity and discuss several ways you could manipulate the environment and task (including the rules, goals, and equipment) to increase successful performances in beginning learners.

   b. Discuss how you would progressively manipulate these constraints as the learners improve.

   c. When could manipulating these constraints be ineffective and potentially even detrimental to skill learning?

Glossary

affordances—The action possibilities of the environment and task in relation to the perceiver's own capabilities.

attractor—A preferred state of stability toward which a system spontaneously shifts (dynamic systems approach).

closed-loop control—A type of control system that provides the opportunity to make continuous corrections based on feedback received during the movement.

constraints—Boundaries that limit a person's movement capabilities.

constraints model—A model of behavior asserting that coordination is developed by changing constraints imposed by the interaction of the individual with the environment.

control parameters—Variables that induce a shift from the current attractor state to a new attractor state.

dynamic systems approach—A perspective that addresses the interplay of the environment, task, and individual on skilled movement. Movement is the result of a self-organization of many systems, owing to interactions across these constraints.

ecological approach—A motor development or learning perspective that rejects the hierarchical view of the brain as the ultimate controller of movement. This perspective stresses the role of the environment as it interacts with the individual to produce fluid movement.

environmental constraints—Constraints that are external to the mover.

functional constraints—Individual constraints imposed by psychological variables such as motivation, arousal, and intellect.

generalized motor program (GMP)—A representation of a pattern of movements that is modifiable to produce a movement outcome; enables the production of skilled movement in the information-processing theory.

individual constraints—Boundaries imposed by the organism itself. *Also see* structural constraints and functional constraints.

information-processing theory—One of the theoretical constructs of motor behavior; it proposes that the brain receives, processes, and interprets information to send signals to produce skilled coordinated movements, like how a computer functions.

invariant features—Variables that cannot be modified between attempts (including the sequence of movements, relative force, and relative timing).

open-loop control—A type of control system for error correction that produces rapid, discrete movements; it requires preplanning of the movement.

parameters—Features that can be modified during the execution of a movement pattern (including muscle selection, overall force, and overall duration).

perception—The act of attaching meaning to something.

phase shift—The change in a state that causes a shift or reorganization to a new attractor state.

physical environmental constraints—External conditions that can aid or hinder movement patterns (e.g., weather, temperature, lighting, floor surface, step height).

rate limiter—A control parameter that limits or hinders performance.

schemas—Rules or relationships developed through accumulated experiences within a generalized motor program.

self-organization—A system's ability to change state or acquire a new structure or pattern of movement.

sociocultural environmental constraints—Constraints imposed by social and cultural norms and pressures.

speed–accuracy trade-off—The tendency for accuracy to be compromised when speed is increased (e.g., many errors) or for speed to be sacrificed when one is focused on accuracy (e.g., movement is slowed down).

structural constraints—Individual constraints imposed by physical characteristics such as gender, height, weight, and body makeup.

task constraints—Constraints imposed by the task itself, including the goals of the movement, rules, and equipment.

UNDERSTANDING MOVEMENT CONTROL

CHAPTER OBJECTIVES

After reading this chapter, you should be able to do the following:

- Understand factors associated with movement preparation.
- Describe the factors that influence reaction time.
- Compare theories of attention and illustrate how arousal levels affect performance.
- Explain sensory contributions to movement and balance.
- Differentiate between short-term, long-term, and working memory.

Performance Under Fire

Sheila is still in a state of shock. Last night she witnessed a terrible car accident. The driver, two cars in front of her, drifted off the road, crashing into a tree. He was trapped in the car, and the engine was starting to smoke. After pulling onto the shoulder of the road and turning on her hazard lights, Sheila called 911. Within a few minutes, she heard sirens in the distance and saw the approach of flashing lights. A fire engine! From the sidelines, she watched, amazed at the speed and precision with which the firefighters worked once they arrived on scene. The driver was quickly and safely freed from the car, and other firefighters worked to contain the fire beginning to burn from the engine. Even now, it all seems like a blur. Sheila finds herself wondering how the firefighters were able to perform so well given the gravity of the situation. What if they had hesitated for even an instant? What if they had focused only on freeing the driver and ignored the smoke from the engine? What if . . . ?

Many of you have probably been in a situation like Sheila's—witnessing an incredible feat of motor performance that leaves you dumbfounded: a NASCAR driver passing another car with only inches between them, a soccer goalie making a save at a critical moment in the game, or an athletic training team responding in record time to a serious injury. However, the observable motor response is often only the tip of the iceberg. The processes under the surface that dictate the motor response are often more important than the execution.

Imagine being one of the firefighters in the preceding scenario. You arrive at the scene of a serious accident filled with twisted metal, smoke, an entrapped and possibly injured driver, and witnesses in various emotional states. Amid the chaos, you might find your heart rate begin to rise, your breathing rate increase, and your mind pulled in a hundred different directions. In this heightened physiological and psychological state, how can you pick out the most pertinent sensory information, determine the best course of action, and act accordingly, all in as little time as possible? What if you hesitate or fail to notice the smoke coming from the car's engine? These questions highlight some of the important considerations when preparing any motor response: reaction time, attention, arousal, and sensory contributions. We discuss these concepts in this chapter.

REACTION TIME

When someone is preparing a motor response, speed is often a critical factor. In some sport contexts, such as swimming and track, the speed at which the person reacts to the starting signal (see figure 3.1) could be the difference between first place and second place. For the firefighters in the opening scenario, the speed at which they can assess the scene and decide on a course of action could be the difference between whether the driver of the car lives or dies. This element of movement preparation is termed **reaction time (RT)**. It is the measure of the time between the presentation of a stimulus and the initiation of a motor response. Although the processes involved during RT are not directly observable, RT provides an indication of the speed at which one makes a decision; however, it does not take into account whether the decision was correct or appropriate. A related term, **movement time**, is the speed of the observable movement—that is, the time from the initiation of the movement until it has been completed. When combined, these two measures make up the individual's **response time** (see figure 3.1). Given the importance of RT in many movement-related situations, it is necessary to understand the factors that affect RT and how to use them effectively. These factors include the number of stimu-

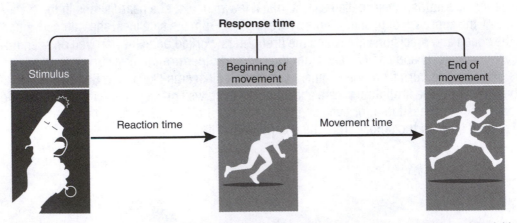

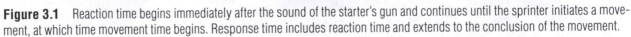

Figure 3.1   Reaction time begins immediately after the sound of the starter's gun and continues until the sprinter initiates a movement, at which time movement time begins. Response time includes reaction time and extends to the conclusion of the movement.

lus–response alternatives, the psychological refractory period, and stimulus–response compatibility.

Stimulus–Response Alternatives

The simplest decisions involve those in which a stimulus requires only one motor response. For example, when approaching a stop sign while driving, the only appropriate motor response is to hit the brakes and bring the car to a stop. The reaction time to such an event is termed **simple reaction time** (or **simple RT**). In such cases, when there is only one stimulus and one corresponding response option, human RT is relatively short. However, what happens to RT when the driver approaches a stoplight? In this situation, the driver now faces a choice of three stimulus–response (S–R) options: green light, go; yellow light, slow down or speed up; red light, stop. This increase in the number of S–R alternatives, or **choice reaction time** (or **choice RT**), has been shown to negatively affect RT. In a classic paper, W.E. Hick (1952), an experimental psychologist, found a logarithmic relationship between the number of S–R alternatives and choice RT. That is, as the number of S–R alternatives increases, RT increases at a constant rate. This finding was later termed **Hick's law**.

Hick's law helps explain the performance advantage from creating more choices for opponent players. Let's consider the triple option in American football. This is an offensive scheme that allows for three players to run the ball, thus increasing the number of S–R alternatives. This play increases the amount of uncertainty for the defensive players, which will likely increase their RT to the play. However, strategies can reduce the amount of uncertainty. Predicting a stimulus (**event anticipation**) or predicting when the stimulus might occur (**temporal anticipation**)—or both—can reduce the number of S–R alternatives. This is often achieved by noticing **precues** in the environment (e.g., hip angle) that telegraph

information pertinent to the situation. This, in turn, reduces the number of options that require a response. For example, the coaching staff might use scouting reports and game film in preparation for an upcoming game to identify the tendencies of the opposing offense during certain game situations to narrow down the number of defensive responses. Likewise, an athletic trainer might use mental practice to run through common injury scenarios prior to a game to prime her responses to specific stimuli.

Although anticipating correctly can help reduce RT, it can have the opposite effect if done incorrectly. For example, Brianna McNeal, 2016 Olympic gold medalist in the 100-meter hurdles, was disqualified during the first round of the 100-meter hurdles at the 2019 World Championships because of a false start; she had incorrectly anticipated the timing of the starting gun and moved too early.

Another way that individuals can reduce uncertainty in choice RT scenarios is by using **action plan profiles**. Action plan profiles are condition–action links (if this *condition* happens, then I do this *action*) developed due to increased knowledge and experience that serve as preplanned responses to specific situations in a choice RT scenario. This, essentially, reduces a choice RT scenario to a simple RT scenario, which decreases the time needed to prepare the motor response. For example, when a tennis player's opponent comes up to play at the net (condition), she can use her action plan profile to automatically select an offensive lob (action) as the motor response rather than spend extra time choosing a response from multiple options (e.g., passing shot, slice). Although action plan profiles are helpful for reducing uncertainty in a choice RT scenario, they are not always effective. For example, the tennis player in the previous example might notice that her opponent is very quick on the court but has a very weak backhand volley. As such, the tennis player decides to adjust her plan by modifying

TRY THIS

Ruler Test

Exercise 3.1

1. To examine the difference between simple reaction time and choice reaction time, break up into pairs. Each pair of students has two 12-inch (30 cm) rulers. Alternatively, you may use yard or meter sticks.

   a. *Simple reaction time:* One student (the experimenter) begins by holding a ruler vertically. The other student (the participant) places a thumb and forefinger at the bottom end of the ruler (at 0) without touching the ruler. The participant should leave approximately 1 inch (2.5 cm) of space between the thumb and the ruler and the finger and the ruler. The experimenter drops the ruler without warning, and the participant grasps it as quickly as possible (see figure 3.2). Record the number at the top of the position the participant grasps the ruler in the chart. Perform the experiment 10 times, then switch roles.

   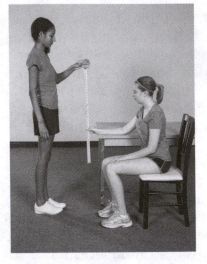

   Figure 3.2 The ruler test can be used with a yardstick as shown. This picture illustrates a student grasping the yardstick after the experimenter has released it.

   b. *Choice reaction time:* The experimenter holds two rulers vertically, and the participant positions thumbs and forefingers at the end of each ruler (at 0) as in the previous experiment. The experimenter randomly releases one of the rulers without warning. The participant grasps only the dropped ruler as quickly as possible. The participant may not grasp with both hands. If both hands grasp the rulers at the same time, the trial must be aborted. Record the value at the top of the position where the participant grasps the ruler into the chart, then switch roles.

Trial	Simple reaction time	Choice reaction time
1		
2		
3		
4		
5		
6		
7		
8		
9		
10		
Mean		

2. Compare your results for simple reaction time versus choice reaction time.

3. Did you find it difficult to close only one hand during the choice reaction time test?

4. Explain why you are not permitted to grasp with both hands during the choice reaction time test.

her response to the condition, based on her diagnosis of the opponent. Thus, the next time her opponent is at the net, she selects a deep passing shot down the backhand side, a more effective shot against her current opponent, rather than the response from her action plan profile. This updated plan is known as a **current event profile**.

Psychological Refractory Period

The way stimuli presented themselves can also affect RT. Often, stimuli requiring a response presented themselves at separate times. For example, during a double play in baseball, the shortstop moves toward second base when the batter hits a ground ball, receives the throw from the first or second baseman, tags the base, adjusts positioning toward first base away from the line of the runner, and completes the play with an accurate throw to the first baseman. However, when two stimuli that require different responses present themselves in quick succession, processing a response to the first stimulus delays the response to the second stimulus. This delay, termed the **psychological refractory period (PRP)**, causes a marked increase in RT to the second stimulus. This delay is further compounded with age; that is, the PRP tends to affect older adults more than younger adults (Allen et al., 1998). Researchers believe the PRP delay results from a narrowing of attention to a single channel in which only one stimulus can be processed at a time (Smith, 1967). If the time given between stimuli is not sufficient, an attentional bottleneck occurs (see the Attentional Capacity section later in this chapter).

The PRP helps explain why faking works (see figure 3.3). Consider a basketball game in which Jackie dribbles the ball down the court toward her team's hoop while Alyssa guards her. Jackie pretends to pass the ball to a teammate, which causes Alyssa to change her positioning. However, Jackie quickly pulls up for a jump shot. Because the PRP delayed Alyssa's reaction to the shot, she was not able to respond quickly enough to make a strong defensive play. Of course, the fake must be believable to work. If Jackie had not made a quality fake, Alyssa would likely not have been out of position because she would not have wasted time responding to it. The timing between the presentation of the two stimuli is also important. If the stimuli occur too close together, there is not enough time for the individual to perceive the initial stimulus or begin preparing a response to it before the second stimulus is introduced. Conversely, if the stimuli occur too far apart, then the attentional bottleneck resulting from perceiving and preparing responses to two stimuli is less likely to occur.

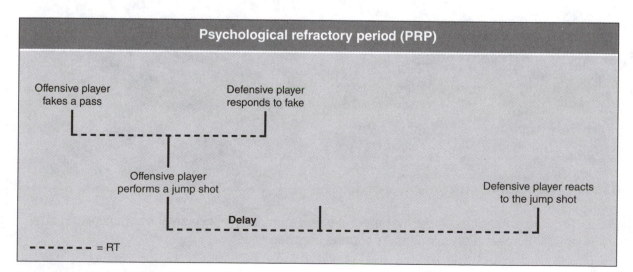

Figure 3.3   Time added by a psychological refractory period.

Stimulus–Response Compatibility

The degree of association between a stimulus and response can also affect RT, termed **stimulus–response (S–R) compatibility**. The greater the amount of association, the shorter the RT even in a choice RT scenario. As mentioned previously, a driver approaching a stoplight has three S–R alternatives. However, for experienced drivers, the colors red, yellow, and green are highly associated with the corresponding responses of stop, slow down, and go. As a result, RT is relatively short even though there are multiple S–R options. In a similar vein, many manufacturers have designed vehicle backup camera displays that include red, yellow, and green zones to indicate how close the vehicle is to an object. The intention is to decrease the amount of time needed to react to objects that are close to the rear of the vehicle. However, when a stimulus and response are not naturally associated with one another (i.e., S–R incompatibility), choice RT can increase. For example, a newer driver may respond more slowly when operating a vehicle in reverse because the front of the car moves opposite to the direction of the movements of the steering wheel.

ATTENTION

Attention is critical for effective decision making and motor performance. To fully understand how attention affects decision making and motor performance, we consider the three major characteristics: capacity, selectivity, and focus.

WHAT DO YOU THINK?

Exercise 3.2

1. Following are two images that illustrate various levels of stimulus–response compatibility. Describe the stimulus–response compatibility for each, including the stimulus and response and whether they are compatible.

    a. Stovetop

    b. Group exercise class

© Doug Collier

Bananastock

2. Provide another example that illustrates low stimulus–response compatibility and one that illustrates high stimulus–response compatibility.

Attentional Capacity

Most theories of attention propose that people have a **central limited capacity** when performing simultaneous activities (Magill & Anderson, 2013; Schmidt & Lee, 2011). In other words, the brain and central nervous system do not have an unlimited amount of space. If you have ever felt overloaded by visual and auditory information, you realize that you have limited attention. However, theories differ regarding the extent and location of the limits. **Single-channel filter theories** propose that we complete tasks in serial order and that a bottleneck occurs at that point in information processing wherein the system can process only one task at a time (see figure 3.4). If the bottleneck occurs while a person is identifying multiple stimuli in the environment, such as an air traffic controller, the person could not perform two tasks simultaneously without many errors. However, a task that requires identifying a specific environmental stimulus might be more easily accomplished along with a task that does not depend on stimulus detection, such as watching for a signal on a monitor while riding a stationary bike.

Consider a woman who is checking her social media account while talking to a friend and watching television. According to the single-channel theory, she can attend to only one thing at a time. Perhaps she reads one social media post, but at this time isn't processing what is happening on the television or her friend's conversation. Her attention can then shift to her friend's conversation, but this comes at the cost of reading the social media post. In this case, the woman can be thought of as task switching rather than multitasking because she cannot perform multiple tasks simultaneously.

Alternatively, Kahneman (1973) proposed a **central-resource capacity theory**. This is a more flexible system in which information-processing capacity can expand based on the individual, task, and situation. Kahneman asserted that attention requires cognitive effort. There is no particular bottleneck, but rather a more general pool of effort that can be strategically allocated to different activities. The person evaluates the amount of attention (e.g., cognitive effort) necessary to perform the tasks to determine whether she can do them simultaneously. The expansion and flexibility of the processing are limited, and at some critical point, performance of one or more of the tasks will be adversely affected.

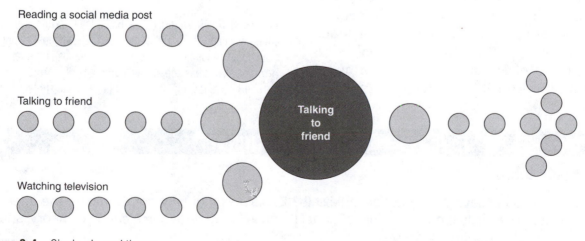

Reading a social media post

Talking to friend

Watching television

Figure 3.4   Single-channel theory.

Finally, **multiple-resource theories** contend that we have several attention mechanisms, each with limited capacity (Magill & Anderson, 2013). Wickens (1980, 1992) posited that the mechanisms might be modalities (e.g., movement and speech), stages of information processing (e.g., perception or decision making), or codes of processing information (e.g., verbal codes or spatial codes). Tasks that require a common mechanism are difficult to perform simultaneously, whereas those based on separate mechanisms can be performed simultaneously. This is like the central-resource theory, but each mechanism has its own capacity limitations. When people exceed their capacity, **interference** occurs, meaning that they cannot do both activities without compromising one of them. You can try this while walking with a friend. If you ask your friend to answer math questions and progressively increase the difficulty of the questions, you will likely notice that your friend will either slow down her walking pace, take longer to respond to the math questions, or make more math errors.

Attentional capacity is critical to understanding the importance of automaticity of performance. As some skills become automatized, people can attend to other aspects of the environment. For example, a basketball player must learn to dribble without looking at the ball before he can simultaneously dribble, run, view the positions of teammates and opponents, and contemplate his next move of either passing, shooting, or continuing to dribble (refer to figure 3.5a and 3.5b, for an illustration). In a study by Leavitt (1979), ice hockey players of different ages and experience levels skated for speed and performed one, two, or three simultaneous tasks, including visually identifying geometric shapes. The skating speed of

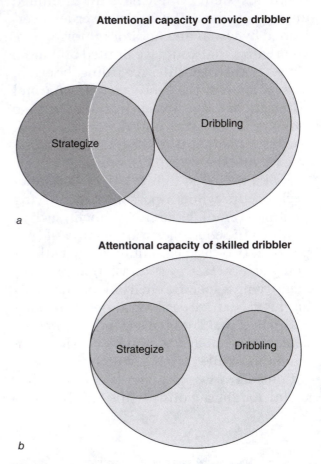

Figure 3.5 A young basketball player *(a)* uses a lot of attentional capacity to just dribble the ball. Even just raising his head could cause him to lose control of the ball (interference). However, skilled basketball players *(b)* can dribble running down the court while looking at the other players and strategizing.

WHAT DO YOU THINK?

Exercise 3.3

1. Do you believe that attention is flexible? Explain why or why not. Compare the attentional capacity theories: single-channel theories, central-resource capacity theory, and multiple-resource theories.

2. Consider the aforementioned theories of attention. How do they make you rethink how to teach your future students, patients, clients, or athletes?

young, less experienced players decreased more than that of older and more experienced players when they were required to stick handle with a puck while simultaneously performing other tasks. Years of playing had provided the older players with a greater degree of automaticity of skating and even stick handling so that they were minimally affected by a visual identification task of naming geometric shapes projected onto a screen.

Selective Attention

In any performance context, an abundance of information is available to the performer. This information can be either relevant or irrelevant depending on the situation. Consider a typist in an open office. What information is available to her? The words she is typing, the computer monitor, a ringing telephone, and colleagues' conversations are just a few examples. To perform her task well, she needs to be able to attend to the relevant information (e.g., words) while filtering out the irrelevant (e.g., ringing telephone). This ability is known as **selective attention**.

A classic research study on selective attention comes from a series of experiments on speech recognition (Cherry, 1953). The author sought to answer the cocktail party problem; that is, "How do we recognize what one person is saying when others are speaking at the same time?" (pp. 975-976). To investigate this question, the author used a shadowing task during which participants listened to two messages simultaneously, one in each ear. Participants were instructed to attend to only one message for later recall and to ignore the second message. The results indicated that participants had little to no trouble recalling the message while blocking out the other. Furthermore, very few participants could identify detailed characteristics about the rejected message, such as individual words, semantic meaning, and language. The findings from this research were later termed the cocktail party phenomenon.

Focus of Attention

Nideffer (1976) identified two dimensions along which attention can be focused: direction and width. *Direction* refers to the

---

TRY THIS

Are You Listening to Me?

Exercise 3.4

How good a listener are you? Are you so good that you can listen to two conversations at the same time? How about trying it? Break up into groups of three. One person is the listener, and the other two are the messengers. Each messenger plans a several-sentence message and delivers it into one of the listener's ears.

1. The first time around, the listener focuses on only one of the messages. Following the delivery of the message, the listener restates the message to the best of her or his ability. Then the listener recalls anything she or he can from the rejected message. How well was the listener able to recall each message?

2. The second time around, the messengers preplan new messages, and the listener tries to attend to both at the same time. How well was the listener able to recall each message this time?

3. Were you surprised by any of the results?

location of the focus. It can either be an **internal direction of focus** (within the person) or an **external direction of focus** (in the environment). *Width* refers to the amount or expanse of information attended to by the person. It can be either a **narrow width of focus** (attending to a specific cue) or a **broad width of focus** (attending to the larger context). When combined, four attentional styles emerge: internal broad, internal narrow, external broad, and external narrow. Each type of attentional focus can be used in any performance context. For example, a soccer player performing a free kick could use any of the attentional styles shown in figure 3.6.

Some attentional foci are more helpful than others, depending on their relevance to the task. For example, paying attention to the crowd is irrelevant (and often distracting) when performing a free kick during a soccer game. However, fixating on the formation of the wall has been shown to be effective for expert soccer players in free kick situations (Helsen & Pauwels, 1993).

Although a player could attend to only one of the attentional foci present during a performance situation, her attentional focus is likely to shift. For example, in the free kick scenario, a soccer player might first scan the field to get a complete picture of the situation (external broad), rehearse her role if the kick is recovered by the opposing team (internal broad), visualize the execution of her kick (internal narrow), and finally fixate on the formation of the wall just

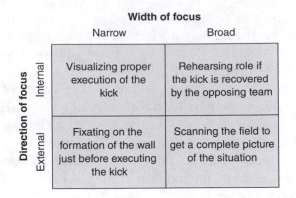

Figure 3.6 Attentional styles during a soccer free kick.

before executing the kick (external narrow). This shift in attentional focus is especially important when participating in many open skill sports. Because the environment is constantly in flux, a single attentional focus may prevent the performer from noticing all the relevant information available.

Attentional focus can also refer to how a person directs attention to the skill being performed. Under this view, an internal focus of attention occurs when the person attends to his body movements, whereas an external focus of attention occurs when he attends to the *effects* of his movements on the environment. For example, a basketball player attempting a free throw might focus on making sure his wrist flexes when he releases the ball. This is an internal focus of attention because he is attending to the movement of his wrist. In contrast, he might focus on making sure the ball rotates backward when he releases it. This is an external

---

WHAT DO YOU THINK?

Exercise 3.5

What kind of attentional focus shifts might occur for the following skills?

1. Rock climbing
2. Pitching a baseball
3. Assessing an injured athlete
4. Mountain biking

focus of attention because he is attending to the *effect* of the wrist flexion (i.e., the spin of the ball) rather than the movement itself. Additional examples are listed in table 3.1.

A large body of evidence (see Wulf, 2013, for a review) has demonstrated that an external focus of attention is more effective for motor learning and performance than an internal focus of attention. Wulf and colleagues (e.g., McNevin et al., 2003; Wulf et al., 2001) explained this effect using the **constrained action hypothesis**. They posit that an internal focus of attention constrains the motor system, which prevents

the motor program from running automatically, whereas an external focus of attention facilitates this automaticity. In recent years, Wulf and Lewthwaite (2010) extended this explanation with the **self-invoking trigger hypothesis**. They suggested that an internal focus of attention triggers people to engage in self-evaluation and self-regulatory processes to gain control over their thoughts and feelings. If the addition of these processes exceeds the individual's attentional capacity, automatic control of the motor program can become disrupted and lead to declines in motor performance.

Table 3.1   Research Examples Comparing Internal and External Attentional Focus

Task	Internal focus	External focus	Study
Ski simulator	Exert force on the outer foot.	Exert force on the outer wheels.	Wulf et al. (1998)
Soccer instep kick	Remember to kick the ball with the instep.	Remember to kick the ball with the shoelaces.	Wulf et al. (2003)
Biceps curl	Concentrate on the biceps muscles.	Concentrate on the curl bar.	Vance et al. (2004)
Golf pitch	Focus on the swinging motion of the arms.	Focus on the pendulum-like motion of the club.	Wulf & Su (2007)
Swimming: 16 m front crawl stroke	• Arms: Pull the hands back. • Legs: Push the insteps down.	• Arms: Push the water back. • Legs: Push the water down.	Freudheim et al. (2010)
Vertical jump	Concentrate on the tips of the fingers.	Concentrate on the rungs.	Wulf et al. (2010)

RESEARCH NOTES

Can Children Benefit From an External Focus?

Although most of the research on attentional focus has looked at adult populations, findings also support the external focus advantage with children. For example, Perreault and French (2015) had 10- to 12-year-olds learn a modified basketball free throw over two days while receiving either internal (e.g., "Line up your hand and eye with the basket.") or external (e.g., "Focus on a spot just above the rim.") attentional focus feedback following every third practice attempt.

Following practice, participants returned approximately 24 hours later for a retention test. The results indicated that the external focus group had significantly better scores than the internal focus group, illustrating the learning advantage associated with an external focus of attention. In addition, retrospective verbal reports from the participants following practice and retention provided support for the constrained action and self-invoking trigger hypotheses.

AROUSAL

Arousal is a term often used interchangeably with *anxiety*. Although related, these concepts have subtle, but distinct differences. **Arousal** is defined as "a general physiological and psychological activation, varying on a continuum from deep sleep to intense excitement," whereas **anxiety** is defined as "a negative emotional state in which feelings of nervousness, worry, and apprehension are associated with activation or arousal of the body" (Weinberg & Gould, 2015, p. 76). Thus, one who is anxious is also aroused; however, one who is aroused is not necessarily anxious.

The relationship between arousal and performance is often represented by the **inverted-*U* hypothesis** (Landers & Arent, 2010). As figure 3.7 illustrates, performance tends to increase as arousal increases, but only to a point. Once arousal surpasses the person's optimal arousal level, performance tends to drop off. The optimal arousal level largely depends on the person and the task being performed. Some people perform very well under high arousal conditions; however, others, especially those with **trait anxiety** (a predisposition for anxiety in threatening situations), perform better under low arousal

conditions. One's arousal level at any point in time is referred to as **state anxiety**. Even people with relatively low trait anxiety may experience very high state anxiety in certain situations, such as when taking an exam or performing in front of an audience. The complexity of the task can also affect the optimal arousal level. Generally, tasks that are highly complex are performed more effectively under low-arousal conditions (e.g., a chess game), whereas tasks that are low in complexity are performed more effectively under high-arousal conditions (e.g., a bench press).

The role arousal plays in performance can be explained using the **cue-utilization hypothesis** (Easterbrook, 1959). Recall that in any performance context there are numerous stimuli in the environment, both relevant and irrelevant, that one can attend to. Under optimal arousal conditions, a person can selectively attend to the relevant stimuli while blocking out or ignoring the irrelevant. However, under low arousal conditions, attention broadens, resulting in a focus on both relevant and irrelevant stimuli. For example, a volleyball player in a low-arousal situation (e.g., competing against low-skilled opponents) might start paying attention to irrelevant stimuli in the environment (e.g., fans in the stands or teammates on the sidelines). As a result, she might not direct her attention at all the relevant cues from her opponents, which ends up costing her team a point. Conversely, under high-arousal conditions, attention becomes overly narrowed, resulting in a lack of focus on all relevant stimuli. For example, the same volleyball player in a high-arousal situation (e.g., playing down a set) might miss important cues from her opponents (e.g., a poorly disguised tip) and not make it to the ball in time.

SENSORY CONTRIBUTIONS

Whether it's witnessing a traumatic accident (as with the example in the opening scenario of this chapter) or hearing oncoming

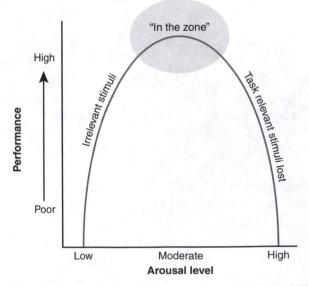

Figure 3.7 Effects of perceptual narrowing and the inverted-*U* hypothesis.

traffic approaching, sensory information influences every movement we make. Our movements are often in response to the visual information we receive. We see a pass in the air and move to intercept it; we see a pothole on the road and drive around it; or we see something interesting and move closer for a better look. It may not surprise you that vision is our predominant sensory system. In addition to the visual system, the somatosensory, auditory, and vestibular systems provide critical information about our balance and position in space. The following section provides a brief overview of these systems, focusing on their roles regarding balance and movement.

Exteroception

Exteroception provides perceptual information from environmental stimuli related to the position of the body, enabling individuals to adapt to the changing environment. Vision is the predominant source of exteroceptive information, with an estimated 70 percent of sensory receptors residing in the eyes (Marieb et al., 2017). Vision contributes information about the environment with respect to the position of the head. To perceive an image visually, light enters the eye and passes to a light-sensitive membrane, the retina, forming an image. The image is then converted into nerve signals by two types of light-sensitive photoreceptors—rods and cones. These cells differ in both their structure and functions:

Rods

- Are more numerous than cones
- Provide peripheral vision
- Detect movement
- Perceive shades of gray (night vision)

Cones

- Are fewer and denser than rods
- Enable acute vision (visual acuity)
- Operate best in bright lighting
- Perceive color

After the image is converted into nerve signals, these are transmitted from the eye through the optic tract to the visual cortex of the brain. The nerve signals are sent to the opposite side of the brain, crossing the optic chiasm (figure 3.8). Thus, the nerve signals from the right side of the visual field go to the left side of the visual cortex and vice versa. Finally, the brain interprets the nerve signals.

Visual acuity refers to the sharpness of vision and allows us to see images such as faces and words on a page, clearly. **Static visual acuity** is the ability to clearly see a stationary image and is mostly assessed using the Snellen eye chart (the chart that you commonly use when visiting your optometrist). **Dynamic visual acuity** is the ability to distinguish moving objects. Dynamic visual acuity is particularly important for athletes who must track an object or an opponent's position. Dynamic visual acuity develops at a later age than static visual acuity, reaching adult levels

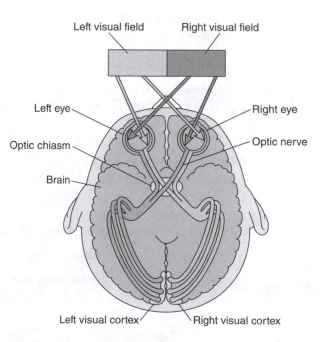

Figure 3.8   Light enters the eye through the pupil and moves to the retina, where a visual image is formed. Photoreceptors convert the image into nerve signals, which are sent through the optic nerve and cross over the optic chiasm to the visual cortex to be interpreted.

at around age 15 (Schrauf, Wist, & Ehrenstein, 1999). Girls tend to have poorer static and dynamic visual acuity than boys, which could affect sport performance, most notably in activities where a moving object must be tracked and is likely a factor in the reduced participation of girls in some sports (Gallahue et al., 2012).

Another source of exteroception is hearing, or audition. Auditory information is often overlooked as an important factor in skillful movement; however, it is critical to both learning a movement pattern and performing skillfully. One of the most common methods of teaching a motor skill is verbal instruction. Think about it. Have you ever been taught a motor skill without the use of verbal cues, or at least some form of verbal instruction? Skilled performers also often use auditory signals during an activity to react quickly, interact with their teammates, or as a frame of reference. For instance, a racquetball player may be helped regarding speed of the ball simply from hearing the sound of the opponent hitting the ball; a basketball makes different sounds depending on whether it hits the rim or the backboard or just the net (swish!); and the sound of a softball hitting the palm of the glove is different than the sound it makes when hitting the pocket. Sounds can indicate the rhythm of movements as well. The rhythmic movement of a golf swing can be heard. Devices have even been made to help golfers learn the timing and rhythm of the golf swing

RESEARCH NOTES

Dynamic Visual Acuity

Given the importance of seeing objects clearly and, even more importantly, tracking moving objects, dynamic visual acuity is often crucial for high-level performance. Although some research has indicated that athletes have better dynamic visual acuity than nonathletes (Hitzeman & Beckerman, 1993), it is difficult to determine whether the increased experience of practicing and performing in athletic events facilitates the development of dynamic visual acuity or if youth with more developed, or faster developing, dynamic visual acuity self-select to participate in high-level athletics. To better understand how static and dynamic visual acuity develop and how they develop differently in boys and girls, Kohmura and colleagues (2008) examined these in youth aged 8 to 17 years. The researchers found that dynamic visual acuity continued to develop until age 17 years, later than previously suggested by Schrauf and colleagues (1999). This study only included subjects up to 17 years of age, so it is possible that development continues beyond this age. A second study found an even later peak development, between ages 19 and 24 years in athletes (Yoo et al., 2009). Beyond athletics, these findings have important implications for such activities as driving and performing in combat situations.

WHAT DO YOU THINK?

Exercise 3.6

Dynamic visual acuity does not reach adult levels until age 15 years or later. What are some implications of this late development? Think of both sports and functional activities (that is, activities of daily living). Discuss not only what activities are affected, but also how functional constraints can intersect with the structural constraint of the development of dynamic visual acuity.

by listening to a music file composed from the rhythm of skilled golfers.

Proprioception

Proprioception provides information about the state of the body itself, including the sense of movement and the relationship of body parts to one another. Proprioception is supported by Golgi tendon organs, muscle spindles, joint receptors, cutaneous receptors, and the vestibular apparatus. Because of proprioception, when we move, we know where our hands, limbs, and feet are with respect to one another and relative to the physical environment without looking at them.

The **vestibular apparatus** found in the inner ear provides proprioceptive information by detecting head motion and the orientation of the head with respect to gravity, such as in a head tilt. The direction and rate of a spin is also provided by the semicircular canals. These three half-circle structures are oriented in three planes and filled with fluid to help us detect the direction and rotation of our movements. The vestibular system not only provides information about the head but is also a key contributor to the development of static and dynamic balance.

Joint receptors are in joint capsules and fire when the joint is in extreme positions, providing a protective function. **Muscle spindles** are embedded in muscle bellies and provide information about motion and joint positioning and are most active when the muscle is stretched. Muscle information is also provided by **Golgi tendon organs**, which are in the junction of the muscle and the tendon. The Golgi tendon organ responds to the intensity of the contraction and is most active when the muscle contracts. **Cutaneous receptors**, located in the skin, provide movement perception and, additionally, contribute to proprioception. Cutaneous receptors signal a variety of perceptual states such as temperature, pain, and pressure and are particularly important for our sense of touch. The highest concentration of cutaneous receptors in the body is in the fingertips, which is why we feel things much more acutely there than anywhere else on the body.

Poor proprioception has been linked to clumsiness in children (Li et al., 2015) and adolescents (Visser & Geuze, 2000). Proprioception is critical to performing skillfully and enables fluid movements by providing information about the relative positions of body parts to one another and in space, as well as the movements of the body (Haywood & Getchell, 2014). To fully develop proprioception, children must experience a wide variety of movement experiences. Today, many children lack such experiences because of safety concerns in urban environments, decreased skill levels, and relatedly an increasingly sedentary lifestyle. Children are spending less and less time playing outside and more time in passive activities such as watching television and playing video games. This reduction in physical activity increases with every year after age 5 years (Cooper et al., 2015), leading to a decrement in learning more complex motor skill skills. As you might surmise, these negative trends, among other important issues, are detrimental to proprioceptive development.

MEMORY

Memory, the ability to recall things, allows us to benefit from experience. When someone gives you a telephone number for later use, your first impulse may be to list it quickly in your cell phone directory or to write it on a piece of paper. If neither cell phone nor paper is available, you may rehearse the number several times with the hope of recalling it later; that is, you commit it to your memory. You use these three conscious strategies because of the failings of the memory system. This section outlines important ideas about how memory works and the role it plays in movement preparation.

Think about that phone number someone gave you. You need to dial it immediately, knowing that it will remain with you for only a few more seconds before you forget it. Older models of memory distinguished between short-term and long-term memory (e.g., Atkinson & Shiffrin, 1968). Using a computer analogy, these memory structures were described as the hardware of memory. Information moved from short-term to long-term memory via control processes such as rehearsal and practice. Control processes were akin to the software of memory. **Short-term memory** was used when you dialed the number immediately. If you rehearse the number frequently and use it often, the number eventually finds its way into **long-term memory**, a more permanent store. In terms of motor skills, long-term memory is reflected in the saying about never forgetting how to ride a bicycle. Older adults can and do ride bicycles, after not doing so for many years. How are they able to do this? Quite simply, the movement skills needed to ride a bike remain in the long-term memory store. Frequently used information often finds its way into long-term memory (see figure 3.9). Long-term memory contains past events and general knowledge. In terms of movement, knowledge includes the ability to perform physical skills such as swimming, bicycling, and skiing as well as declarative, procedural, and metacognitive knowledge (discussed in chapter 14). The capacity and duration of long-term memory are often considered unlimited, and long-term memory is relatively permanent.

A model of memory proposed by Baddeley (1986, 1995) has two structures: working memory and long-term memory. **Working memory** has similarities to short-term memory, but the term *working* underscores the more active role of the control processes beyond those typically ascribed to *short-term memory*. Working memory performs several functions, including temporarily storing recently presented material. It also retrieves information from long-term storage to solve problems, make decisions, and produce movement. Working memory is the structure that transfers information to long-term memory. We can think of working memory as a cognitive work space (Magill & Anderson, 2013). For example, just before a hitter comes to the plate, the second baseman might review the batter's hitting tendencies, stored in her long-term memory. She will then couple that information with knowledge that a *slow* runner is on first base, and review her options, keeping in

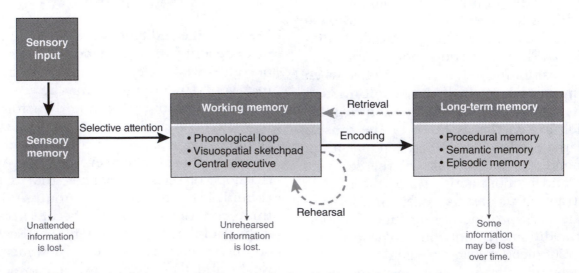

Figure 3.9 The process by which sensory input is eventually stored in long-term memory.
Adapted from Atkinson and Shiffrin (1968).

mind that the ball might be hit to her, away from her, sharply, or slowly. Many of these cognitive, memory-related activities are like the decision-making and attention processes previously described.

Working memory has been described in terms of both duration and capacity. Regarding duration, research by Adams and Dijkstra (1966) indicates that the maximum time is 20 seconds. In their work, Adams and Dijkstra required blindfolded participants to move the handle of an apparatus on a trackway until it was physically blocked. After a retention interval, the subjects tried to recall the movement by moving the handle back to the same point on the trackway. Results demonstrated that arm movements could be recalled very accurately if the retention interval was very short, but performance declined significantly in only 20 seconds.

It has long been argued that the capacity of working memory totals seven items, plus or minus two (Miller, 1956). Thus, depending on the difficulty of the content and the person, capacity is between five and nine. Adults can usually remember a series of seven numbers without too much effort, but beyond that, the memory system becomes severely challenged. When researchers asked young gymnasts (Ille & Cadopi, 1999) and dancers (Starkes et al., 1987) to recall a movement sequence, the participants showed limits of six items and eight items, respectively. Given that the subjects who were relatively experienced could only remember a few movements in the correct order, it is clear that practitioners should avoid lengthy sequential lists when teaching children movement sequences—or other things.

Working memory improves throughout childhood and, interestingly, is also associated with emotional intelligence. Emotional intelligence involves regulating emotion, performing under pressure, utilizing positive coping strategies, and being satisfied with performance. Athletes with higher emotional intelligence, the cognitive ability to control emotional behavior, have better working memory (Vaughan et al., 2021). These abilities are positively associated with working memory (such as remembering plays or a coach's instructions) while the negative influence of head injuries and concussions upon working memory should be noted. As you are likely aware, head injuries in athletics (including, but not limited to, football and soccer) are currently topics that are garnering significant attention, both in research and practice (Tsushima et al., 2019).

Still under debate in memory development research is the number of processes necessary for object recognition in children. Some suggest single-process models such that recognition is based upon the memory signal strength (Dunn, 2008; Wixted, 2007). Memory strength refers to the ability to remember items that have been examined as compared to items not examined, and this improves with age. Conversely, dual-process models assume that not only is memory strength important but also that it requires recollection, or conscious retrieval (Yonelinas, 2002). Developmentally, recognition develops at a later age, such as continuing from childhood through adolescence, than memory strength, which is typically developed around age 7 or 8 years (Ghetti & Lee, 2011; Koenig et al., 2015). This line of research is important in motor skill development because learners often learn not only the sequence of movements but also equipment considerations and rules. Memory strength, or familiarity, will be relatively weak in young children who may be first exposed to sports and easily confuse the equipment and rules in common activities such as tee ball and soccer. For example, they may wonder why throwing the ball in tee ball is encouraged but not even allowed in soccer.

TRY THIS

Short-Term Memory Test

Exercise 3.7

Search for and take a short-term memory test on the Internet.

1. Compare your results with the answers at the conclusion of the test. How did you perform? Were you able to remember more than the average person? Short-term memory is typically seven plus or minus two items. If you were able to remember more than the average, what are some strategies that you used? Explain.

2. Distinguish between short-term, long-term, and working memory.

3. What role does memory play in learning movements? How can you help students, athletes, patients, or clients remember movements?

SUMMARY

Many factors are involved in understanding movement control including reaction time, attention, arousal, sensory contributions, and memory. Speed is often a critical factor when preparing a motor response. This chapter discussed reaction time and the variables that affect it, including stimulus–response compatibility and the psychological refractory period. These factors are particularly evident in sport when a player is trying to gain an advantage over an opponent.

Attention and arousal are critical for effective decision making and motor performance. Although people have a limited attentional capacity, the capacity for performing a particular skill depends on the person's skill level. Highly skilled people require significantly less attentional capacity than novices; their skill frees up their attentional resources for dual tasks or strategies in sport contests. Attention is also selective, in that we choose what we pay attention to, as demonstrated in the cocktail party phenomenon.

Arousal is an important consideration for movement control because peak performance requires optimal levels of arousal. If arousal levels are too low, performers lack the focus necessary to perform well. In this case, they can be distracted by irrelevant stimuli such as sounds in the crowd. However, if arousal levels are too high, performers' attentional focus narrows and they can lose relevant information.

This chapter introduced sensory contributions to movement control including the visual, auditory, somatosensory, and vestibular systems. Each provides critical information for maintaining balance and movement control. The visual and auditory systems provide information about the environment, whereas the somatosensory and vestibular systems provide proprioceptive information. Through selective attention, sensory information is temporarily placed into short-term memory. This information is quickly lost unless it is rehearsed. If the information is rehearsed enough, it is placed into long-term memory. Information from long-term memory is retrieved by working memory to solve problems, make decisions, and produce movement.

> ONLINE ACTIVITIES

The student material found in HK*Propel* includes exercises, labs, and videos to enhance learning and encourage practical application of important concepts.

LEARNING AIDS

Supplemental Activities

1. Work with a partner and examine the effect of spinning on your vestibular system. Each of you should do one of the spinning activities.

   a. Person 1

      1. Rapidly spin 20 times with your eyes closed (or spin until you feel sufficiently dizzy); your partner can help, if needed.

      2. When you have finished spinning, open your eyes and turn toward your partner. Your partner will throw a ball to you from approximately 20 feet (6 m) away. Catch the ball and throw it back to your partner. Continue this for approximately four catches and throws. Discuss your results. How accurate were your tosses? Did you catch the ball every time?

      3. An accurate toss is one where the person can catch it without stepping or reaching. How accurate were the tosses and catches over time? Did they remain consistent?

   b. Person 2

      1. Rapidly spin 20 times with your eyes closed (or spin until you feel sufficiently dizzy); your partner can stand near you to help you if you feel too dizzy, if needed.

      2. When you have finished spinning, keep your eyes closed while your partner calls your name from approximately 10 feet (3 m) away. Try to walk as straight as possible toward your partner, who is calling your name. Describe the experience. Were you able to complete this task well—that is, did you walk in a straight line? Did you stumble?

      3. What is the main role of the vestibular system? Explain why you feel dizzy after spinning regarding the three sensory systems involved in balance: the visual, somatosensory, and vestibular systems.

2. Search YouTube for a video on selective attention tests (such as the original gorilla experiment). Many of these videos illustrate that we can be blind to visual information when selectively attending to something else, even if the visual information of interest is in the center of our visual field. This phenomenon has been demonstrated repeatedly, in many different contexts. Work with a small group of students in your class and design your own selective attention video.

Glossary

action plan profile—A preplanned movement in response to a context-specific situation based on prior knowledge and experience; often phrased as an if–then statement.

anxiety—An emotional response to a perceived threat; can involve cognitive concerns or physiological reactions.

arousal—A general state of activation or excitability.

broad width of focus—Attending to the larger context, such as scanning the field.

central limited capacity—A theory suggesting that human attention is limited because the central nervous system does not have endless space in which to process information.

central-resource capacity theory—Perspective on attention that is a more flexible system than the single-channel filter theories, in which information-processing capacity can expand based on the individual, task, and situation.

choice reaction time (choice RT)—Time needed to react when there is more than one stimulus.

constrained action hypothesis—Perspective on attentional focus that posited that an internal focus of attention constrains the motor system, which prevents the motor program from running automatically, whereas an external focus of attention facilitates this automaticity.

cue-utilization hypothesis—The hypothesis that the level of arousal influences attentional focus.

current event profile—A preplanned movement in response to a context specific situation based on current performance conditions.

cutaneous receptors—Located in the skin; provide proprioceptive information in regard to temperature, pain, and pressure.

dynamic visual acuity—The ability to distinguish moving objects.

event anticipation—Anticipating what the stimulus will be (e.g., anticipating what pitch the pitcher will pitch).

external direction of focus—Attentional focus that is directed in the environment, such as focusing on the putt.

exteroception—Sensory information regarding the external environment, enabling individuals to adapt to the changing environment.

Golgi tendon organs—Located at the junction of the muscle and the tendon; respond to the intensity of the muscular contraction, providing proprioceptive information.

Hick's law—A logarithmic relationship between the number of stimulus–response alternatives and reaction time, indicating that as the number of S–R alternatives increases, reaction time increases at a constant rate.

interference—A limitation on performance due to exceeding one's attentional capacity.

internal direction of focus—Attentional focus that is directed within the person, such as visualizing the movement.

inverted-*U* hypothesis—The idea that arousal and performance are related such that optimal performance is seen at a moderate level of arousal.

joint receptors—Located in the joint capsules; provide proprioceptive information regarding joint position and fire when the joint is in extreme positions to serve as a protective function.

long-term memory—Information that is retained in memory relatively permanently.

memory—The ability to recall things; allows us to benefit from experience.

movement time—The observable movement; that is, the time from the initiation of the movement until it has been completed.

multiple-resource theories—Perspectives of attention that suggest that humans have several attention mechanisms (e.g., modalities, stages of information processing, codes of processing information), each with a limited capacity.

muscle spindles—Located within the muscle belly; provide proprioceptive information about motion and joint positioning and are most active when the muscle is stretched.

narrow width of focus—Attending to specific cues in the environment, such as focusing on a specific player.

precues—Cues in the environment that provide information about the intentions of an individual in a motor performance context.

proprioception—Provides sensory information about the state of the body itself, including the sense of movements and the relationship of body parts to one another.

psychological refractory period (PRP)—Time delay that occurs when two stimuli occur in quick succession. The stimuli require different responses; processing a response to the first stimulus delays the response to the second stimulus.

reaction time (RT)—The measure of the time between the presentation of a stimulus and the initiation of a motor response.

response time—The measure of the time between the presentation of a stimulus and the completion of the movement response (reaction time plus movement time).

selective attention—The ability to focus on selected sensory information while ignoring irrelevant information.

self-invoking trigger hypothesis—A perspective on attentional focus that suggested an internal focus of attention triggers people to engage in self-evaluation and self-regulatory processes to gain control over thoughts and feelings.

short-term memory—Information that is only stored in memory for a relatively short period of time (typically 20-30 seconds).

simple reaction time (simple RT)—The time needed to react to a task with only one stimulus.

single-channel filter theories—Attention perspectives that propose a serial processing of tasks and the occurrence of a bottleneck at some point in information processing, a point at which the system can process only one task at a time.

state anxiety—Arousal level at a single point in time.

static visual acuity—The ability to clearly see a stationary image; commonly assessed using the Snellen eye chart.

stimulus–response (S–R) compatibility—The amount of association between a stimulus and response, which can also affect RT.

temporal anticipation—Anticipating when the stimulus will occur (e.g., when the pitcher will throw the pitch).

trait anxiety—Predisposition for anxiety in threatening situations.

vestibular apparatus—Located in the inner ear; provides proprioceptive information by detecting head motion and orientation of the head with respect to gravity (such as head tilt).

visual acuity—Sharpness of vision.

working memory—Performs an active role, including temporarily storing recently presented material, retrieving information from long-term memory storage to solve problems, making decisions, and producing movement.

SKILL CLASSIFICATION

CHAPTER OBJECTIVES

After reading this chapter, you should be able to do the following:

- Explain the importance of motor skill classification.
- Classify motor skills using sport skills, movement taxonomies, and single-dimensional classifications.
- Develop motor skill progressions using Gentile's multidimensional classification.
- Distinguish between motor skills and abilities.
- Understand Fleishman's taxonomy.
- Determine appropriate motor abilities for specific motor skills.

Becoming a Pro

Golfers are often not prepared for playing under the increased pressure and environmental conditions they may face during a match. However, professional golfers such as Tiger Woods must have exceptional focus even under intense pressure. Golfers do not become highly skilled professionals by practicing only in controlled environments. Earl Woods, Tiger's father, a Green Beret in the U.S. Army, learned to shoot a rifle during simulated war games rather than in controlled, predictable environments. When Tiger was a young child, Earl prepared him for unpredictable situations by distracting him during golf rounds. Tiger would also play under various weather conditions, day or night. At times, Earl would talk during Tiger's swing. These distractions taught him to tune out environmental influences, preparing him to play championship golf matches under unpredictable and often distracting circumstances.

Tiger Woods' story is only one example of how manipulating the environment can help learners perform better. Amateurs of any sport or recreational activity may believe that they simply choked under pressure, although there are ways to minimize this occurrence. Most often, amateurs do not have experience in stressful, competitive environments, whereas professionals are very familiar with varied conditions and pressure situations.

Children and adults who are occupational or physical therapy patients may notice that they perform better in the therapy setting than they do at home. To facilitate the transition from the clinic to home and continue the benefits of therapy outside of the facility, therapists often teach patients activities they can practice at home. For example, school occupational therapists help children with fine motor delays improve skills such as writing, typing, and cutting. To continue the improvements when school is not in session or when the therapist is not available, the therapist should encourage young clients to create art projects that require fine motor control, such as drawing, cutting, and painting, and to work on their writing or typing as a form of at-home occupational therapy. Classifications of motor skills are important for both physical educators and health professionals who design and implement motor skill programs, because certain practice designs are more appropriate for particular skill classifications.

SKILL CLASSIFICATION

Skills are the learned ability to bring about predetermined results with maximal certainty, often with a minimum outlay of time or energy (Knapp, 1963). Athletes or performers are considered **skillful** if they have achieved a criterion of excellence and are capable of performing at a high level most of the time. Motor skills have also been defined as activities that require a chain of sensory (vision, hearing, touch, smell), central (brain and nervous systems), and motor mechanisms whereby the performer is able to maintain constant control of the sensory input and in accordance with the goal of the movement (Argyle & Kendon, 1967). Physical activities can be classified into categories. Each activity is unique with respect to the structure of the task, task goals, and obstacles. Although physical activities have many unique qualities, there are also commonalities across activities, such that competency in one skill can lead to increased competence in another (i.e., positive transfer of learning).

Classifying skills is useful for teaching and learning. Practitioners who can appropriately classify skills are better able to adapt the learning experience to a changing environment, enabling better program design and maximizing motor learning. As discussed in chapters 17 through 21, practice sessions should be designed for specific skill classifications. The following sections examine motor skill classifications in terms of sport skills, movement taxonomies, single-dimensional classification, and multidimensional classification.

Sport Skills

Sport skills have been separated into three categories: cognitive, perceptual, and motor (Honeybourne, 2006). **Cognitive skills** refer to the intellectual skills of the mover. These are the skills that enable a performer to make decisions and solve problems. The cognitive skill of decision-making speed is critical for a quarterback in American football, who must make quick, effective decisions. **Perceptual skills** are those that involve interpreting and integrating sensory information to determine the best movement outcome. Attention and previous movement experiences also affect perceptual skills. For example, a soccer player assesses the position of defenders and teammates to determine whether to pass the ball to an open player or continue dribbling toward the goal. The speed and direction of the athlete's movements depend on the perceptual information she receives regarding the current situation. **Motor skills** are the physical elements that enable the movement. To put it simply, the activity could not be completed without the learned ability to coordinate the limbs to produce the action.

At young ages, basic skills provide the foundation for activities that require much more complicated sport-specific motor skills. These basic skills are termed **fundamental motor skills** and include activities such as overhand throwing, jumping, catching, kicking, and striking. By building a basis with these fundamental motor skills, people can perform a wide array of similar activities. For instance, a child who has learned how to jump, hop, and skip will be better able to perform more sport-specific activities such as the long jump, the high jump, and even the basketball layup. The fundamental skill of striking is useful in many sports, including hockey, golf, racket sports, softball, and baseball. Chapter 8 addresses the developmental progressions of several fundamental motor skills.

Movement Taxonomies

A **movement taxonomy** provides a framework for grouping motor skills into themes for teaching fundamental motor skills. **Taxonomies** are classifications of objects or events according to a common theme. In the developmental taxonomy, motor skills can be broken down into three groups: stability, locomotor skills, and manipulative skills.

Nonlocomotor Stability

Stability is the ability to maintain body position against the forces of gravity and other circumstances that increase the difficulty of the task (Gallahue et al., 2019). Gymnasts must be able to maintain body position while holding the body's entire weight upright between two rings or while completing a balance beam routine; figure skaters must be able to maintain a static position while gliding across the ice; and divers must be able to hold a vertical position while entering the water. Team sport athletes also must maintain stability, such as a pitcher in baseball holding a vertical position while winding up and throwing a baseball with both speed and accuracy or a hockey player shooting a slapshot. Maintaining stability is fundamental for not only most sport-related motor skills, but also many functional skills. It is also critical to maintain stability while reaching high for a can in a cupboard, getting dressed in the morning, or unexpectedly stepping onto ice.

Locomotor Skills

Locomotor skills are gross fundamental motor skills in which the goal of the movement is body transport. Locomotor skills cannot be developed separately from stability. The body must be stabilized before a proficient locomotor pattern can be performed. Body transport can occur when a person is moving from point *A* to point *B* or during sporting activities such as a racquetball match, a gymnastics routine, or a soccer game.

Typically developing infants progress through a developmental sequence of body transport. When infants are very young, they are not strong enough or coordinated enough to locomote using their feet, so they learn other methods for transporting their bodies from one point to another. Young infants begin body transport by learning how to roll over. This usually begins around three months of age, when most infants can roll from their backs or abdomens onto their sides. Infants then progress to using their arms and knees to transport their bodies by crawling (body drag) at six to eight months and by creeping (quadruped movement, abdomen off the floor) around age 8 to 10 months. After infants have increased their abdominal and leg strength as well as their coordination, they can pull to a standing position (seven to nine months), walk with assistance (9-10 months), and then finally perform bipedal walking alone (12-14 months). Infant motor milestones will be discussed in further depth in chapter 17.

Manipulative Skills

Manipulative skills use smaller muscle groups and enable people to explore the world, bringing objects closer and feeling their size and texture to identify them. Some physical activities are specifically geared toward the manipulation of objects (e.g., archery and marksmanship). In these tasks, even slight adjustments to the movement can compromise the performance outcome considerably.

Although tasks can be classified as manipulative or locomotor, they rarely occur as one or the other in complete isolation during recreation or sporting activities. Most advanced motor skills require the ability to control all three of the skill elements, whereas fundamental motor skills focus more on individual elements. For example, a basketball player is manipulating the basketball while also transporting the body closer to the basket; a bowler manipulates the bowling ball, adjusting the amount of spin and force at the release point, while also transporting the body closer to the pins; and even in billiards—while players are eyeing up the point of contact for the stick, they must also transport the body to that position. When designing a practice sequence or teaching a new skill, especially to a young child or someone with few movement experiences, a practitioner would do well to simplify the task by focusing on only one aspect of the movement at a time and to take each of the three developmental taxonomies into consideration. The sequence should begin with a stable task. As the performer increases in competence, more difficulty can be added, such as increased locomotion and manipulation of an implement. The following list presents an example of teaching a child how to kick a ball using the developmental taxonomy.

Developmental Taxonomy Progression for Kicking a Ball

Step 1: Kick a stationary ball into a goal while standing still.

Step 2: Take a step and kick a stationary ball into a goal.

Step 3: Run and kick a stationary ball into a goal.

Step 4: Dribble the ball and kick into a goal.

Step 5: Dribble the ball and kick into a goal that is being guarded.

Single-Dimensional Classification

The first step in learning a new motor skill is to understand the basic elements and sequence of the movements. Movements can be broken down into situations, including game strategies, rules, and goals. It is also important to break the activity down further into simple units—or the basic skills. In this section, skills are classified according to movement precision, environmental predictability, time constraint taxonomy, and the nature of the skill.

Movement Precision

Motor skills can be classified by the size of the muscle groups being used to produce the movement pattern and consequently the precision of the movement. Skills in which large muscle groups produce the movement, such as the quadriceps, hamstrings, and gluteus maximus, tend to be much larger, less precise movements. These motor skills are classified as **gross motor skills**. Skills in which precise movements are critical to perform with increased accuracy and control use smaller muscle groups and are categorized as **fine motor skills**. Dialing a phone number, playing the piano, and typing are skills that require precise movements of smaller muscle groups. This classification is important for developmental sequencing.

Children are generally less able to control smaller muscle groups and are thus taught activities that involve larger muscle groups, such as running and jumping, before they are taught how to coordinate their limbs to perform fine motor skills such as in drawing, writing, and playing games (e.g., jacks or marbles). Practitioners preparing motor skill programs for very young children should keep this concept in mind.

Environmental Predictability

Skills can also be classified according to the predictability of the environment. Skills used in a task that takes place in a stable environment in which objects or events are also stationary are considered **closed skills**. With closed skills, the performer's goal is to perform the movement correctly and then replicate the action; an example is performing a foul shot in basketball. Foul shots are not constrained by time or space, and the environment is stable. The shooter does not have to pay attention to defenders trying to steal the ball or block the shot, and the distance to the hoop and the height of the hoop remain stable. On the other hand, **open skills** occur in an environment in which objects, people, and events are constantly changing. These skills require that the mover be much more attentive to the environment, constantly monitoring the situation for changing conditions. A hockey slap shot is considered an open skill because the environment is highly unpredictable.

Skills classified according to the predictability of the environment occupy a continuum. It is very important to understand that *no skills are entirely closed*, because there are always some conditions, such as the pressure of a situation, motivation, or

time demands, that will change. However, for closed skills, the predictability is always much greater than it is for open skills. Bowling would be placed closer to the closed end of the continuum because the skill is completed inside a building, and the pins remain stationary for each frame. Gutters are the only obstacle, and they, too, remain stable. The only conditions that can vary are the number of pins that remain after each attempt and perhaps the amount of background noise, which is presumably much less than it is during a Division I collegiate American football game. Figure 4.1 provides several examples of motor skills on the open–closed continuum.

Golf is an example of a sport that is performed in a somewhat predictable environment compared to team sports. Golfers can benefit from practicing with added pressure or the element of surprise, such as in the example of Tiger Woods at the beginning of this chapter. Golf is often practiced in a very controlled and predictable facility (i.e., driving range), and then played in a much less predictable environment (i.e., golf course). Preparing the learning environment requires an understanding of the fundamental differences between game and motor tasks. This is also important for rehabilitation, because the clinical environment is much more controlled than the real world. Therapists must prepare their clients to function in unpredictable environments with changing surfaces of support including rough terrain, potholes, unexpected slippery surfaces, and unpredictable events.

An additional element of environmental predictability is **intertrial variability**, which refers to any change that occurs between trials (i.e., practice attempts). A

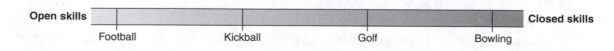
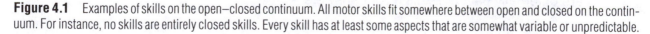

Figure 4.1   Examples of skills on the open–closed continuum. All motor skills fit somewhere between open and closed on the continuum. For instance, no skills are entirely closed skills. Every skill has at least some aspects that are somewhat variable or unpredictable.

skill with high intertrial variability has aspects that change with every performance attempt. Intertrial variability can be present in both open and closed skills. The closed skill of batting in tee ball has low intertrial variability, whereas a pitch in baseball has high intertrial variability. Each pitch is unique, requiring the batter to adapt to the changing conditions. The key to success in tee ball batting is consistency. Functional tasks can also have varying levels of intertrial variability. Walking up the stairs at home or across a room should have relatively low intertrial variability, whereas walking on the busy sidewalks of Manhattan would have high intertrial variability. Every day, a person's path would have to be different to avoid bumping into people or objects along the way.

Although open skills always include at least some intertrial variability, most closed skills have little to no intertrial variability. They are often performed in a stable environment in which most factors are predictable. In some closed skills, intertrial variability adds to the challenge of the task, as in golf. After each golf putt, the distance, angle, and position of the ball in relation to the hole is different. There are no defenders or other variable conditions except for the weather. The terrain may also change with differing obstructions (artificial) and impediments (natural) across the course. This variability adds to the complexity of the task, making it more challenging and interesting to the performer and the observer.

Time Constraint Taxonomy

The difficulty of a task can be determined by its pacing. Tasks with time constraints are less complex than tasks without them. **Self-paced tasks** are initiated by the mover (e.g., golf, darts, archery). Basketball players shooting foul shots often engage in preliminary routines prior to shooting. They can adopt a routine because the shot is not constrained by time; instead, accuracy is the key. Other skills do not have the luxury of self-pacing. A pitcher determines when to initiate the pitch, so the pitch is self-paced. The batter's movements are **externally paced tasks** because she is responding to the pitched ball. She does not have the luxury of swinging whenever she desires.

WHAT DO YOU THINK?

Exercise 4.1

1. Chris spends many hours a week practicing his golf swing at his local driving range, mastering techniques such as grip, posture, and the basics of the swing. Although he can perfect his swing on a practice tee, he experiences problems when transferring to a golf course. Why does he perform so well at the driving range yet have problems when playing on a course? Relate this example back to the Tiger Woods example in the beginning of this chapter.

2. What components (serve, return) in racket sports are self-paced and which are externally paced?

3. Name two games or sports that are entirely self-paced and two games or sports that are entirely externally paced. (Note that many team sports, which mostly call for open skills, have at least one self-paced skill, such as free throws or penalty shots.) Explain your answers.

4. Name two everyday or functional tasks that are self-paced and two functional tasks that are externally paced. Explain your answers.

Instead, she must swing when the ball reaches the plate, which is determined by the release, speed, and trajectory of the pitch. Performing a penalty kick in soccer is another example of a self-paced movement; however, the goalie's response is externally paced by the kicker. Most functional tasks and physical and occupational therapy treatments are internally paced, such as writing, brushing teeth, and performing muscle-strengthening exercises. Driving, on the other hand, is a combination of the two. You choose your speed, to some degree, and your route, but you must stop at red lights and wait for the green light before continuing while varying your speed based upon the traffic.

Nature of the Skill

A fourth method for defining skills is by the nature of the task. Fitts and Posner (1967) defined tasks by the beginning and end points of the movements. **A discrete motor skill** is one in which the beginning and end points are clearly defined. These movements are generally short in duration and have a distinct difference between their initiation and termination. A photograph taken during the beginning of the movement for a discrete skill would be qualitatively different from a photograph taken at the conclusion of the movement (see figure 4.2). The two photographs would illustrate undoubtedly different things. An observer would also easily be able to determine which photograph was taken at the beginning of the movement and which was taken at the end. Another key component of discrete skills is a period that must elapse before a subsequent movement must occur. For instance, a quarterback in American football must wait to receive a ball before passing. Some examples of discrete skills are throwing, kicking, punching, shooting, and catching.

Continuous motor skills do not have clearly defined beginning and ending points. These tasks are longer in duration, and the mover is in constant motion (Fitts & Posner, 1967). Continuous motor skills appear as repetitive movements. The movements are generally simple and are continuously repeated, as in running, swimming,

Figure 4.2   The movement (*a*) at the beginning of a throw is qualitatively different from that (*b*) at the end of the throw.

cross-country skiing, and bicycling. When looking at a photo of a child riding a bicycle, it is difficult to determine whether she is at the beginning or end of the movement. **Serial motor skills** are motor skills that include a series of discrete skills that must occur in a specific sequence. If the order of the movements can be altered, the task would not be classified as a serial task. The triple jump, consisting of an approach, hop, skip, and jump, is an example of a closed serial skill. If the sequence were altered to a hop, approach, jump, and skip, this combination would no longer be considered the triple jump. A basketball layup is an example of an open serial skill when performed in a game because defenders can alter the timing and position of the movement. Serial skills can be thought of as a string of beads. Each component can be performed separately as a discrete skill, such as catching, dribbling, jumping, and shooting. Serial skills require that the performer not only be skillful at the discrete skills independently, but also be able to transition from one movement to the next in the proper sequence.

Multidimensional Classification

Practitioners lead learners through a progression of movements to perform an open skill proficiently. It is best to place learners in a closed environment in which much of the task can be simplified and controlled before progressing to a more challenging and adaptable open environment. Gentile (2000) designed a classification system for gradual progressions from closed to open environments. **Gentile's taxonomy**, which is useful for individualizing motor skill progressions, uses two main categories to assist in program development: (a) the environmental context and (b) the action requirements. Gentile's classification system was developed for physical therapists but is widely used by physical educators, trainers, and coaches as well.

Environmental Context

The environmental context consists of two factors: (a) regulatory conditions and (b) intertrial variability. **Regulatory conditions** are the environmental factors specific to a particular skill or sport. For example, some of the regulatory conditions in soccer are the size of the field, the height and width of the goal, and the size and weight of the ball. These conditions typically are the same for any soccer game regardless of where it is played. Regulatory conditions standardize how a person must adapt to a given situation to produce a successful outcome.

Gentile (2000) classified regulatory conditions as either moving or stationary. Stationary regulatory conditions, such as the pins in bowling, require considerably less skill than moving regulatory conditions,

---

WHAT DO YOU THINK?

Exercise 4.2

Provide one example of each of the following classifications of skills and define each of your examples as either self-paced or externally paced.

1. Discrete open skill
2. Discrete closed skill
3. Continuous open skill
4. Continuous closed skill
5. Serial open skill
6. Serial closed skill

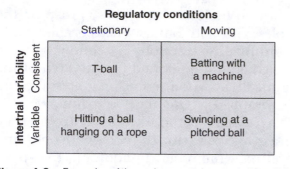

Figure 4.3   Examples of the environmental context of Gentile's (2000) multidimensional classification system.

such as the clay targets in skeet shooting. Stationary regulatory conditions in the absence of intertrial variability represent a closed skill, whereas moving regulatory conditions that include intertrial variability represent an open skill (Adams, 1999). Stationary regulatory conditions with intertrial variability require moderately closed skills. Figure 4.3 gives an example of a motor skill in each of the four categories. The complexity of tee ball is lower than that of batting with a pitching machine because the regulatory conditions are stable and there is no intertrial variability (i.e., the ball is in the same position for every attempt). A ball that is hanging on a rope will be in a different position every time, but the regulatory conditions are stationary. The most complex task is batting a pitched ball. The ball is moving, and the trials are variable.

Action Requirements

Gentile (2000) used two classifications to define the action requirements of a skill: body orientation and manipulation (figure 4.4). **Body orientation** is classified as either body transport (during sporting activities, such as a basketball layup or a triple jump) or body stability (as in archery). Body orientation is an important component in exercises used in therapy settings. Body transport activities include locomotor exercises (e.g., crawling, walking, and jumping), whereas body stability activities include many balance exercises. Activities that require body transport are more complex than activities

that can be completed in a stable body position. When someone must manipulate an object (e.g., racket, bat, or ball) or an opponent (e.g., in wrestling, boxing, or karate), the task is considered higher in complexity. The person must not only adjust or maintain body posture and position (or both) but also manipulate and control an implement (e.g., tennis ball) or a person (e.g., in judo).

Gentile's taxonomy combines the four classifications for the environmental context with the four classifications of the action requirements to create a 16-category system for classifying motor skills. Examples of motor skills for each category are depicted in figure 4.5. Motor skills become increasingly complex from the upper-left quadrant of the taxonomy to the lower-right quadrant. The push-up, in the first quadrant (upper left), is the task lowest in complexity. There is little variability in performing a push-up from trial to trial. When performing successive push-ups, the performer simply needs to repeat the previous movement until either reaching muscle failure or achieving a goal. No body transport or object manipulation is required. Throwing an American football pass, in the last quadrant (lower right), is considered highest in complexity. A quarterback must be able to anticipate the receiver's position and the time and location of the pass. A quarterback must also be able to adapt to various environmental conditions with each performance attempt while transporting his body and manipulating the ball.

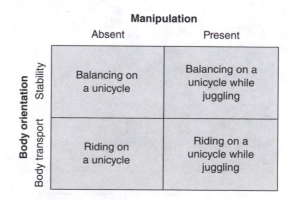

Figure 4.4   Examples of the action requirements of Gentile's (2000) multidimensional classification system.

Table 4.1 depicts progressions of one motor skill that illustrates how Gentile's taxonomy was designed to be used by practitioners. It is not expected that learners will move through each stage; rather, they will likely progress through several stages. Gentile's taxonomy allows for a variety of options including more progressions for learners who may need the slower progression to the whole motor skill in real time.

Gentile's taxonomy is particularly useful in therapy settings. By manipulating the environment or changing the task requirements, the activity can be progressed. For example, if the goal is to help a five-year-old child with left hemiplegic cerebral palsy climb a ladder to a slide, the task or the environment (or both) can be manipulated to create progressions to help the child succeed. One activity could be a stability task with a manipulation requirement in a closed environment; the child could stand in front of bilateral stationary upright poles and

work on maintaining a static grasp on the poles with both hands. The therapist could minimize distractions by conducting the sessions in a quiet and private area of the clinic. In addition, a nonslip material could be wrapped around the pole to improve grip. Progressions could include controlling the grasp and releasing the poles with one hand and then the other. In addition, the speed could be changed and the distractions could be increased (Kenyon & Blackinton, 2011).

Activities could be planned for all 16 categories for a particular motor skill; however, it is not likely to be necessary. A performer who can complete the movement pattern consistently and under variable conditions is prepared to begin at the ninth category, which is for a motor skill that requires moving and consistency, and does not involve body transport or object manipulation. If the motor skill is a closed skill, then the practice should be designed for only the first eight categories. Gentile's taxonomy

Action requirements

		No body transport or object manipulation	Object manipulation but no body transport	Body transport but no object manipulation	Both body transport and object manipulation
Closed skills	Stationary and consistent	Push-up	Decline sit-ups with a medicine ball	Triple jump	Javelin throw
Moderately closed skills	Stationary and variable	Balancing on one foot with different shoes on	Playing darts with darts	Completing an obstacle course	Salsa dancing in an empty dance studio
Moderately open skills	Moving and consistent	Sitting on an exercise ball	Striking a tennis ball from a ball machine	Running in the woods	Kicking a ball to an unguarded goal
Open skills	Moving and variable	Doing a push-up on an exercise ball	Skeet shooting	Dancing in a crowded club	Throwing a football pass

Environmental conditions / Increasing complexity / Increasing complexity

Figure 4.5 Examples of motor skills in each category of Gentile's (2000) multidimensional classification system. Note that this figure illustrates the classification of a variety of motor skills rather than progressions of one motor skill.

Table 4.1   Example of Gentile's Taxonomy for a Forehand Strike

		ACTION FUNCTION			
		BODY STABILITY		**BODY TRANSPORT**	
		No manipulation	**Manipulation**	**No manipulation**	**Manipulation**
ENVIRONMENTAL CONTEXT	**Stationary, no intertrial variability**	1. Practice body position for the reception of the ball.	2. Same as step 1, except hold a ball above the target hitting point with the other hand.	3. Carry out the entire forehand motion without the ball.	4. Same as step 2, except drop the ball into the hitting zone.
	Stationary, intertrial variability	5. Practice the reception of the point of contact position at different levels. The ball could bounce (low, medium, and high) in different directions across the court.	6. Same as step 5, except have the ball placed on a hitting tee and alter the level of the tee (low, medium, and high).	7. Carry out the entire forehand motion at different levels and approaches to achieve different directions. Move position around the court, stop and simulate the entire forehand motion.	8. Move to different locations in the court, stop and drop the ball into the hitting zone and hit a forehand from a static position in a planned direction.
	Motion, no intertrial variability	9. Position for forehand, in the return serve position. Learn distance from the baseline. Mimic the forehand as a partner runs through a serve.	10. The ball is thrown into the right service box, and the ball is caught. The ball is dropped into the hitting zone, and the ball is hit consistently to the left and right service box.	11. The ball is thrown short into the right service box. The player moves from a baseline spot into position to take the shot. See if they can get into position before the ball drops.	12. The ball is thrown short into the right service box. The player moves from a baseline spot into position to take the shot. Do this without returns and then add return pace.
	Motion, intertrial variability	13. The child starts at various positions on the court, based on possible inaccurate shots. A partner repositions based on the player's various positions. Run through the entire forehand motion again.	14. Same as step 13, except the player hits balls to three possible zones: left and right service boxes and between the service line and the baseline. The partner must adjust to each of the player's shot locations on the court.	15. The ball is hit over the net to the player. The player runs to position, readjusting when necessary for off-target shots. The partner adjusts to the player's new location, but no shot is made.	16. Same as step 15, except the ball is hit to one of the three zones: right and left service boxes and service box to baseline.

Reprinted from J. Rudd, L. O'Callaghan, and J. Williams, "Physical Education Pedagogies Built Upon Theories of Movement Learning: How Can Environmental Constraints Be Manipulated to Improve Children's Executive Function and Self-Regulation Skills?," *International Journal of Environmental Research and Public Health* 16 (2019): 1630. Distributed under the terms of the Creative Commons Attribution 4.0 International License (http://creativecommons.org/licenses/by/4.0/).

WHAT DO YOU THINK?

Exercise 4.3

Choose one motor skill and explain how you can modify the skill, the environment, or both to fit into 4 of the 16 categories in Gentile's multidimensional classification system. The motor skill can be related to a sport or be a therapeutic activity. Begin by selecting the most appropriate category for the motor skill you have selected and then work your way up the classification system by providing three examples of how to simplify the motor skill, allowing for increased success and progressions to improve the motor skill or therapeutic activity. Label how the skill would be classified according to the environmental context and action requirements.

enables an instructor to implement a precise skill progression appropriate for learners of all developmental levels to enable them to progress to their desired levels of difficulty.

SKILL VERSUS ABILITY

Abilities differ from skills in the sense that skills are learned, whereas abilities are a product of both learning and genetics (Fleishman, 1964). Skills describe a level of competence on a specific motor task, whereas abilities are part of a person's traits that affect the **capability** to become skillful when learning a new motor task. **Abilities** can be defined as genetically predetermined characteristics that affect movement performance, such as agility, coordination, strength, and flexibility. Abilities are enduring and, as such, are difficult to change in adults.

Early researchers in motor abilities hypothesized the existence of only one **general motor ability** (Brace, 1927). This hypothesis was based on observations of accomplished athletes who were adept at many athletic activities and were also able to quickly learn new and unfamiliar motor skills. You likely know athletes in your age group who fit this description (e.g., the star high school quarterback who also led the basketball team to state championships and held the school batting average record). It appears that many athletes can perform very skillfully across many motor skills.

Research examining individuals' performances across activities supports the notion that every motor skill requires very specific abilities for skillful performance and that each person has many independent abilities. This has been termed the **specificity hypothesis** (Henry, 1968). For example, abilities required for skilled race car driving include rate control, manual dexterity, stamina, control precision, and reaction time; a typist needs to have abilities in aiming and finger dexterity; a surgeon requires arm–hand steadiness and mul-

tilimb coordination; and a figure skater performing the triple axel requires abilities such as explosive strength, dynamic flexibility, gross body coordination, and multilimb coordination. These abilities were defined in Fleishman's (1962) taxonomy, which categorized abilities into either perceptual–motor abilities or physical proficiency abilities (see Fleishman's Taxonomy of Motor Abilities). Perceptual–motor abilities include 10 abilities each, which require a perceptual component such as visual or kinesthetic. Physical proficiency abilities include abilities associated with strength, speed, flexibility, endurance, and balance. Although it is doubtful that **Fleishman's taxonomy** is an exhaustive list of motor abilities, it does provide a framework for assessing individual differences.

Fleishman's Taxonomy of Motor Abilities

Perceptual–Motor Abilities

- *Control precision:* The ability to make highly controlled movements with larger muscle groups (e.g., hockey puck handling).
- *Rate control:* The ability to make continuous anticipatory adjustments in relation to a moving target (e.g., Formula 1 racing).
- *Aiming:* The ability to make accurate hand movements directed at small targets (e.g., texting).
- *Response orientation:* The ability to make quick decisions in the presence of multiple response options; also referred to as choice reaction time (e.g., playing quarterback in American football).
- *Reaction time:* The ability to react as quickly as possible to gain an advantage; also referred to as simple reaction time (e.g., sprinting).
- *Multilimb coordination:* The ability to coordinate movements of more than one limb simultaneously without moving the whole body (e.g., driving a car with a manual transmission).

TRY THIS

Assessing Motor Skills Using Gentile's Taxonomy

Exercise 4.4

Practice using Gentile's taxonomy by assessing either classmates or school-age children using either the example of Gentile's taxonomy in table 4.2 or the taxonomy you developed for exercise 4.3. Assess the first individual by starting at the lowest level of the taxonomy and progressing to more complex levels when the individual successfully completes each. Record the level and how the individual did for each level.

Assess another individual but begin midway on the taxonomy. Progress to more complex levels when the individual is successful or move to lower levels when the individual needs to improve on that level.

Table 4.2   Example of Modifying a Motor Skill Using Gentile's Taxonomy

Gentile's level	Describe movement pattern	Successful or needs improvement
Example: Body stability, no object manipulation, regulatory conditions stable and no intertrial variability.	Practicing stationary throwing motion without a ball.	Successful
Since the individual is successful, next increase difficulty of one or more of Gentile's levels: Example: Body transport, object manipulation, regulatory conditions stable and no intertrial variability.	Practicing throwing motion with a ball.	Successful
The individual is again successful, so again increase difficulty of one or more of Gentile's levels: Example: Body transport, object manipulation, regulatory conditions stable and intertrial variability.	Practicing throwing motion with a ball and taking a contralateral step. The goal of each throw is to hit various targets with the ball (intertrial variability).	Successful
The individual needs improvement, so decrease difficulty in one area: Example: Body transport, object manipulation, regulatory conditions stable and no intertrial variability.	Practicing throwing motion with a ball and taking a contralateral step while throwing at the same target on each attempt.	Needs improvement

1. Describe your experiences with this activity.
2. Were the progressions appropriate for the individuals you assessed? Why or why not?
3. Now that you have completed this activity, would you recommend any changes to the taxonomy levels?
4. When would it be most appropriate to use this taxonomy?
5. How would this taxonomy be used differently for a closed skill in comparison to an open skill?

- *Manual dexterity:* The ability to manipulate large objects with the hands (e.g., dribbling a basketball).
- *Finger dexterity:* The ability to manipulate small objects with the fingers (e.g., typing).
- *Arm–hand steadiness:* The ability to move the hand and fingers precisely without regard to strength or speed (e.g., performing surgery).
- *Wrist and finger speed:* The ability to move the fingers and wrist rapidly (e.g., speed stacking).

Physical Proficiency Abilities

- *Explosive strength:* The ability to exert maximal energy in one explosive act; commonly known as *power* (e.g., performing a standing long jump).
- *Static strength:* The ability to exert maximal force against an immovable or heavy object (e.g., playing defensive line in American football).
- *Trunk strength:* The ability to exert repeated strength using the core muscles (e.g., pole-vaulting).
- *Extent flexibility:* The ability to move the body through a large range of motion (e.g., practicing yoga).
- *Dynamic flexibility:* The ability to make repeated flexing movements (e.g., squat thrusts).
- *Speed of limb movement:* The ability to make fast, gross, and discrete limb movements without regard to accuracy (e.g., throwing a javelin).
- *Static balance:* The ability to maintain body equilibrium in one position (e.g., standing still on one foot).
- *Dynamic balance:* The ability to maintain balance while changing position (e.g., participating in gymnastics).

RESEARCH NOTES

What Abilities Most Influence Soccer Performance?

A research study was conducted to examine the motor abilities that most strongly influence technique and performance in soccer (Talović et al., 2009). Soccer was chosen because it is generally considered an aerobic sport because of the size of the field and the duration of the game (90 minutes). Yet soccer also has anaerobic elements, such as sprints and jumps. In the study, 88 participants between the ages of 12 and 14 years completed 18 activities demonstrating variables for motor abilities, such as foot tapping on the wall, body lift-ups from a lying position, and forward bends on the bench; two activities demonstrating variables for functional abilities, a 12-minute run and six 50-meter runs; and 15 activities demonstrating variables on soccer technique performance, such as inside-foot ball receiving, rolling dribbling, and heading.

The study question was, *What abilities most influence soccer performance?* The results revealed a strong influence of all the abilities as a whole, indicating that soccer is a complex sport that may require the interaction of many underlying abilities for highly proficient performance. Moving beyond this general finding, the authors examined each ability at a one-variant level and found that the most important abilities were multilimb and gross body coordination, dynamic strength, and explosive strength. These results indicate that physical proficiency abilities may be more influential on soccer technique performance than perceptual–motor abilities, specifically those related to strength, endurance, and coordination.

- *Balancing objects:* The ability to balance an external object (e.g., a circus clown balancing a stick on his nose).
- *Gross body coordination:* The ability to coordinate gross motor activity of the whole body (e.g., hurdling).
- *Stamina:* The ability to prolong exertions of the entire body; cardiorespiratory endurance (e.g., running a marathon).
- *Dynamic strength:* The ability to exert repeated force; also referred to as muscular endurance (e.g., kayaking).

An individual's abilities are shaped by biological and physiological factors (Fleishman, 1964). The composition of muscle tissue is certainly going to affect physical proficiency motor abilities such as strength, endurance, and flexibility. Physiological deficits in visual development would also limit perceptual–motor abilities, potentially affecting reaction time. Abilities are also affected by environmental factors. For example, children afforded formal education continue to develop their verbal and reasoning abilities throughout their academic years, just as children who participate in physical fitness–related or sport-related programs develop their motor abilities. The rate at which abilities develop varies across childhood and adolescence, both within individuals and across individuals. This is largely due to growth and maturation changes. The rate of development levels out between the ages of 18 and 22 years and then remains relatively stable throughout adulthood (Fleishman, 1964).

Occupational therapists often focus on improving motor abilities such as finger dexterity, arm–hand steadiness, and aiming, whereas physical therapists often focus on control precision, multilimb coordination, dynamic flexibility, and dynamic balance. Some clients have lost some ability due to injury, whereas others may have a developmental disability.

WHAT DO YOU THINK?

Exercise 4.5

1. Choose one motor skill (not a sport or a game) in which you consider yourself proficient. Refer to the list of Fleishman's taxonomy of motor abilities and choose five of the motor abilities that would be most important to perform skillfully at that motor skill. You can choose from either or both categories—perceptual-motor abilities and physical proficiency abilities—depending upon what abilities are most appropriate for the skill you have chosen. Then, for each motor ability, rank yourself from 1 (very low ability) to 5 (very high ability). Provide a brief explanation of how you chose your ranking for each ability.

2. Choose a motor skill at which you are not skillful. Name five of the motor abilities that would be most important to perform skillfully at that motor skill. For each motor ability, rank yourself from 1 (very low ability) to 5 (very high ability). Provide a brief explanation of how you chose your ranking for each ability.

3. Did you notice a difference between your general ranking for the motor skill in which you are proficient in comparison to your rankings for the motor skill in which you are not proficient?

4. Do you think your underlying abilities influence the sports and activities you choose to engage in? What about the sports and activities you generally avoid? Explain your answers.

SUMMARY

This chapter discussed skill classifications and motor abilities. Practitioners who use a multidimensional system, such as Gentile's, can individualize practice sessions for learners at various skill levels. By progressing through these stages, people can gradually increase the difficulty of the task until they are ready for the full complexity of the motor skill. Practitioners need to understand that a client can acquire motor skills only once she has the underlying abilities; however, she can have the underlying abilities but not be skillful in a particular motor skill.

> **> ONLINE ACTIVITIES**
>
> The student material found in HK*Propel* includes exercises, labs, and videos to enhance learning and encourage practical application of important concepts.

LEARNING AIDS

Supplemental Activities

1. Choose a motor skill that can be relearned or learned in physical therapy and a motor skill that can be learned in occupational therapy. Remember that physical therapy focuses on larger muscle group activities such as walking and balance, whereas occupational therapy works on smaller muscle group activities such as using the hands to eat or using scissors. Classify each motor skill and devise a list of several progressions to assist a client in improving each motor skill using Gentile's multidimensional classification.

2. Choose a motor skill in which you are skillful. Name five of Fleishman's underlying abilities that would be necessary to proficiently perform the motor skill.

3. Devise some assessments to be able to evaluate these abilities.

4. How effective do you think these assessments would be in identifying talent for this motor skill in youth? Would the assessment be effective for young adults? Why or why not?

5. Conduct a research search for talent identification finding two articles on the topic. Discuss your findings. What age groups were the studies examining? Did the talent identification examine abilities? If so, explain how. What were the conclusions of these studies?

Glossary

abilities—Genetically predetermined characteristics that affect movement performance such as agility, coordination, strength, and flexibility.

body orientation—Classified as either body transport (during sporting activities, such as a basketball layup or a triple jump) or body stability (as in archery).

capability—In regard to motor skill acquisition, a quality that implies that skilled behavior *may* occur if the conditions are favorable.

closed skills—Skills used in a task that is done in a stable environment in which objects or events are stationary.

cognitive skills—Intellectual skills that enable a performer to make decisions and solve problems.

continuous motor skills—Motor skills that do not have a clearly defined beginning or ending point because of their cyclical nature (e.g., running, swimming, juggling).

discrete motor skills—Motor skills that are short in duration and have clearly defined beginning and end points (e.g., throwing, catching, kicking).

externally paced tasks—Tasks performed in response to external stimuli (e.g., a batter responding to a pitch).

fine motor skills—Skills in which precise movements are critical for performing with increased accuracy and control and which use smaller muscle groups.

Fleishman's taxonomy—A classification system for motor skills that identifies the underlying motor abilities necessary to perform successfully.

fundamental motor skills—Basic motor skills (e.g., throwing, jumping, striking) that are typically acquired by around the age of seven.

general motor ability—An early hypothesis that there is only one motor ability.

Gentile's taxonomy—Motor skill taxonomy that uses two main categories—the environmental context and the action requirements—to assist practitioners with program development.

gross motor skills—Skills in which large muscle groups (e.g., quadriceps, hamstrings, gluteus maximus) produce the movement, which tends to be large and not very precise.

intertrial variability—Any change that occurs between trials (i.e., practice attempts).

locomotor skills—Gross motor skills with the goal of body transport.

manipulative skills—Motor skills that involve the manipulation of an object.

motor skills—Voluntary, goal-oriented physical elements that enable movement.

movement taxonomy—A framework for grouping motor skills into themes for teaching fundamental motor skills.

open skills—Skills performed in an environment in which objects, people, and events are constantly changing.

perceptual skills—The ability to interpret and integrate sensory information to determine the best movement outcome.

regulatory conditions—The environmental factors specific to a particular skill or sport.

self-paced tasks—Tasks initiated by the mover (e.g., in golf, darts, archery); also referred to as internally paced tasks.

serial motor skills—Motor skills that include a series of discrete skills that must occur in a specific sequence.

skill—The learned ability to bring about predetermined results with maximal certainty, often with minimal outlays of time or energy.

skillful—A criterion of excellence for performing a motor skill.

specificity hypothesis—The hypothesis by Henry that specific abilities are necessary to perform each motor skill proficiently.

stability—The ability to maintain body position against the forces of gravity and other circumstances that increase the difficulty of the task.

taxonomies—Classifications of objects or events according to a common theme.

5

STAGES OF SKILL ACQUISITION

After reading this chapter, you should be able to do the following:

- Compare and contrast three learning models—Fitts and Posner's, Gentile's, and Bernstein's. Generate a learner's behavioral characteristics for the stages of each learning model for specific motor skills.
- Prioritize the role of the practitioner according to each of the learning stages.

This Is Harder Than I Thought!

Finn is a very athletic 14-year-old who decided to pick up lacrosse, a new sport. Although he is a skilled athlete who has played a lot of sports, he had a lot of difficulty with stick handling, particularly cradling the ball when he sprinted. Nearly every time he sprinted, he dropped the ball. Even with many acquired skills from playing years of basketball, baseball, and American football, cradling was a new skill for Finn. He had to learn to twist his hand back and forth in a rocking motion, but not too hard. Finn also had to learn that if he cradled closer to his face, the ball was harder to steal. After a few weeks of practicing drills, Finn noticed a big improvement in his stick handling, and with his improved skill level came improved confidence and enjoyment of this new sport.

The example in the opening scenario is certainly not unique to Finn. Whether you are highly proficient at many motor skills or not, everyone progresses through a series of stages when learning a new motor skill. The models discussed in this chapter address the stages of learning and provide a framework for categorizing the skill level of the learner from novice to expert. These models enable practitioners to assess the level of the learner and more appropriately prepare practice sessions.

MOTOR LEARNING STAGES

Learners progress through a series of stages when improving motor skill competence, whether they are learning how to throw a ball, ride a unicycle, or type on a keyboard. By knowing and understanding the characteristics of each stage, practitioners are better prepared to meet learners' needs. Several models address the behavioral features of these stages and provide a unique perspective on them.

Fitts and Posner's Learning Stages

Fitts and Posner (1967) proposed a three-stage learning model (see the sidebar). Regardless of age or motor skill, all learners go through each of these stages when advancing from a novice level to an expert level. This model classifies the stages around behavioral changes that can be observed in the performer. Practitioners have distinct roles at each level of learning.

Cognitive Stage

During the first stage, the **cognitive stage**, the learner's main goal is to understand the basic components of the motor skill movement pattern. This stage is termed the *cognitive stage* because learners require a considerable amount of mental activity to understand the movement pattern and appropriately coordinate their limbs. Novice learners often mentally verbalize their movements (e.g., a dancer may count the beats of the steps, or a triple jumper may say, "Left, right, left, jump" to reinforce the movements until the pattern has been learned). During the cognitive stage, the learner is often easily confused and has many questions. If you were water-skiing for the first time, you might have questions, such as *How do I position my feet? Do I bend my knees? How fast do I stand up when I'm being pulled out of the water?* Although experienced water-skiers do not think about how to get out of the water, novice water-skiers must attend to the position of their body segments and the timing of their movements. Although attending to one's movements is a necessary process in learning any skill, it often causes movements to appear choppy and uncoordinated.

During the initial stages of learning, learners must attempt a number of techniques in a sort of trial-and-error process until they have achieved a certain level of success. It is not surprising, then, that the use of verbal instruction, feedback, modeling, and other teaching strategies is most effective during the cognitive stage. In addition to traditional forms of teaching, research studies have found that verbal instruction combined with passive movements (i.e., moving an individual through the movements) can be as effective in learning a new movement pattern as active movements (Bernardi et al., 2015). These findings are particularly significant for rehabilitation therapists, who often work with patients with limited mobility. It is during the cognitive stage that the largest gains in learning occur. Learners begin with very little knowledge of the motor skill and make rapid gains in performance as they learn the basics of the task.

Associative Stage

Once learners have a basic understanding of the task and have shown significant improvement in the movement pattern, they have progressed to the **associative stage** of learning. In this stage, the goal has shifted

FITTS AND POSNER'S LEARNING STAGES

Cognitive Stage (Beginner)

How do I produce this movement pattern?

Performer's Behavior

- Learning the fundamental movement patterns
- Engaging in high cognitive activity (attention to movement and self-talk)
- Exhibiting inconsistent performance
- Making many gross errors
- Experiencing the greatest performance improvements

Practitioner's Role

- Assisting the learner in understanding the movement pattern
- Using teaching strategies such as verbal instruction, modeling, and feedback, which are most effective during this stage

Associative Stage (Intermediate)

I've got it! Now, how do I get to the next level?

Performer's Behavior

- Refining the movement pattern
- Requiring fewer attentional demands
- Exhibiting more consistent performance
- Making fewer errors
- Making more gradual performance improvements

Practitioner's Role

- Designing practice
- Facilitating error detection and correction

Autonomous Stage (Advanced)

I'm on top! How do I stay here?

Performer's Behavior

- Experiencing a high level of skill proficiency
- Performing largely automatically
- Performing very consistently
- Making very few errors
- Focusing on strategies

Practitioner's Role

- Designing practice
- Refining performance
- Motivating the performer

from learning how to solve the movement problem to refining the movement. Performance improvements are more gradual than those observed during the cognitive stage. Learners perform more consistently and can focus on error detection and correction. Because they do not have to focus as much on the production of the movement, they can attend to other sources of information. The verbal component (self-talk) that was prominent in the cognitive stage is no longer present in the production of the movement pattern because self-talk is no longer necessary or beneficial to produce the movement pattern.

The role of the instructor shifts when the learner is in the associative stage—from instructing to designing appropriate and effective practice sessions (see chapters 18-21). The learner understands the basic movement pattern but still benefits from instructor feedback regarding errors and fine-tuning the movements.

Autonomous Stage

The final stage of learning in the Fitts and Posner model is the **autonomous stage**. To progress to the final stage, learners must practice for an extended period, often many years. Most people do not make it to the

---

RESEARCH NOTES

Are There Learning Stages to Mindfulness?

The importance of mindfulness in athletics has become increasingly prominent. Mindfulness is a mental skill of intentionally attending to moments in time and can be beneficial for reducing fear and helping athletes to focus (Birrer et al., 2012). Just as learners progress their skill of controlling a hockey puck or fielding a ground ball, they also progress in the development of mindfulness through stages, such as defined through the Fitts and Posner model (Kee, 2019). Early learners of mindfulness begin through attending mindfulness courses, reading books, or using web applications. Learners in the cognitive stages work on bringing their attention back when it wavers and being nonjudgmental and open, as well as regulating their levels of arousal. Similar to learning a new motor skill, mindfulness learners should focus on the basics of mindfulness so as to not become overwhelmed by too many instructions or concepts. Learners should take their time to understand the concepts, and, when possible, feedback should be given to help facilitate understanding. During the cognitive stage, learners acquire the capability to accept both positive and negative outcomes. Athletes should practice this concept while practicing their sport. For example, softball players can learn to accept the outcome of each swing and focus on the next swing, which enforces mindfulness and acceptance, while improving performance.

During the associative stage, the mindfulness skills practiced, such as acceptance and attention to breathing, will be much more familiar and require less instruction or feedback. Athletes in the associative stages should only need small reminders to apply mindfulness concepts and may even be using mindfulness practices during their daily life. At this point they have learned to suspend their judgment during negative circumstances, such as a bad pass or poor decision. By the time an individual has reached the autonomous stage for mindfulness, they are effortlessly using mindfulness practices in their daily life and their performances. The mindfulness skills are habitual, and the individual can optimize their focus upon tasks at hand (Kee, 2019).

WHAT DO YOU THINK?

Exercise 5.1

Choose a motor skill in which you are moderately to highly proficient. Discuss the behavioral aspects of the performance for someone in each of Fitts and Posner's three learning stages and develop strategies for instructing a learner in each stage (practitioner's role). An example is provided for the motor skill of juggling.

Juggling

Motor skill	BEHAVIORAL ASPECTS		
	Cognitive	**Associative**	**Autonomous**
Juggling	• Makes very few catches. • Uses self-talk. • Has to focus attention. • Does not know how to compensate for poor tosses. • Experiences fast improvement after the movement pattern is learned. • Visually tracks ball movements.	• Is confident. • Makes consistent tosses. • Makes many catches. • Shifts attention to the apex of the juggling trajectory. • Can detect errors but cannot always correct them while juggling.	• Is very confident. • Can perform multiple activities while juggling. • Can sustain the pattern for a long time.
	PRACTITIONER'S ROLE		

	• Demonstrate how to juggle.
	• Provide verbal instructions.
	• Discuss the juggling pattern and the movement of the limbs.
	• Answer questions.
	• Provide a lot of feedback.
		• Give feedback as requested.
		• Increase the challenges of the task (juggle under different conditions, focus on better control of the tosses, toss faster or slower).
		• Motivate the learner.
			• Further increase the challenge.
			  • Add distractions.
			  • Add a secondary task.
			  • Try a more difficult task (e.g., juggling with clubs or more balls).
			• Motivate the learner.

CHOSEN MOTOR SKILL

BEHAVIORAL ASPECTS		
Cognitive	**Associative**	**Autonomous**
PRACTITIONER'S ROLE		

autonomous stage of learning. During this stage, the performer is so skilled that the movement appears automatic, or without thought, and almost effortless, and he may even be able to perform an additional task at the same time, such as controlling the ball while driving down the court and making play decisions. In this stage, the mover can focus on decision-making strategies, which are critical for high-level performance in open skills such as wrestling and rugby. The autonomous stage is reserved for very skilled performers and is considered the highest skill level. Performers in the autonomous stage consistently perform very well and are confident in their performance capabilities.

Although performers who reach this stage may be at the top of their game, this does not mean that instructors no longer play an important role. Although the amount of improvement may not be visible, performers can continue to fine-tune their performances in the autonomous stage. It is also important for instructors to assist in the maintenance of the performer's level of skill. The instructor should focus on designing practice schedules and maintaining the motivation levels of the performers. Not only is it difficult to reach the top, but it is also challenging to stay there!

Bernstein's Learning Stages

Another view of the learning stages is based on the degrees of freedom problem. Bernstein (1967) identified the challenge of organizing a complex structure of joints and muscles to produce smooth, goal-oriented movement as the degrees of freedom problem. Degrees of freedom are the number of functional units required to solve a movement problem (see chapter 3). Degrees of freedom can be thought of as the number of possible solutions to a performance task. Keep in mind that very few movements involve only one body segment, and many movements require whole-body coordination. Using the notion of the degrees of freedom problem, Vereijken (1991) proposed a three-stage learning model using Bernstein's degrees of freedom.

• *Stage 1—freezing the limbs:* To perform a novel task, novices simplify the movement problem of having to control an overwhelming number of degrees of freedom by eliminating some of them. Novices do not understand the optimal method of managing these degrees of freedom to perform the new movement pattern, so they reduce these options to a more controllable number (Vereijken et al., 1992). Vereijken and colleagues

---

TRY THIS

Observational Skills

Exercise 5.2

Go to an open gym, court, or field and observe a game. Determine the various skill levels of the players. Describe specific behavioral characteristics of each of these players and categorize them into Fitts and Posner's stages. You may find that many or even all the athletes are categorized into the same stage (cognitive, associative, or autonomous stage); however, there is still a wide range of skills. For example, perhaps you feel that all the athletes on the junior varsity lacrosse team are all at the associative stage; however, there may still be much variation across their skill levels. Some athletes may be barely out of the cognitive stage while others may be approaching the autonomous stage. Discuss this variation of skill level as it pertains to the Fitts and Posner stage(s) exhibited by the players.

described this process as "freezing the limbs." This is accomplished by keeping certain joint angles rigid throughout the movement or by temporarily coupling multiple joints so that they move as one segment. Although freezing the degrees of freedom simplifies the task, the movement appears very rigid, and the novice's ability to adapt to any unexpected changes is poor. For example, a toddler only uses their arm to throw a ball overhand. They do not use their legs and trunk to assist them with the overhand throw as more advanced throwers do. Inexperienced throwers also eliminate the backswing. The throw is completed almost exclusively at the elbow joint.

To assist beginners during the freezing the limbs stage, practitioners should simplify the task. Doing so encourages learners to focus on fewer degrees of freedom and increases their opportunities for success. For example, it would be more effective to instruct unskilled soccer players to keep the ball in the air by hitting it with only one leg than to encourage them to control the ball in the air with both legs, chest, shoulders, and head. Clinicians should begin rehabilitation with exercises that require only one plane of motion, fewer joints, or both. As learners or patients improve, difficulty can increase by encouraging movements that require more degrees of freedom.

- *Stage 2—releasing the limbs:* As learners become more comfortable with the basic movement pattern, they can gradually release the constraints imposed on the degrees of freedom. This makes the movement appear more fluid and allows learners to gain more control over the production of the movement pattern. At this point, the degrees of freedom become incorporated into larger functional units of action, termed **coordinative structures**. Coordinative structures occur when separate movements combine into one larger movement. This combination, or coordinative structure, is self-organized and temporary (Bernstein, 1967). Coordinative structures are formed by constraining or limiting potential options (e.g., muscles and joints) appropriately for a particular movement pattern. For instance, pole-vaulters form coordinative structures to be able to swing the trail leg forward and row the arms down while also keeping both arms and the left leg straight. Some coordinative structures appear at birth, providing the groundwork for phylogenetic motor behaviors (e.g., grasping, walking) that will develop later with growth and maturation.

Once learners have gained a basic level of proficiency, they use significantly more degrees of freedom than when they began practicing the motor skill. Practitioners should continue to encourage learners to increase their range of motion and, depending on the skill, the speed of the movement as their movements become smoother and more controlled.

RESEARCH NOTES

You're Staying Too Still!

A surprising example of Bernstein's stages of learning was found in shooting. Given the clear importance of being still while shooting, it would be expected that elite shooters would exhibit fewer degrees of freedom than inexperienced shooters; however, this was not the case! A study completed several decades ago comparing novice and expert pistol shooters revealed that novices tightly locked the degrees of freedom in their arms, whereas experts did not show any locking of their upper limbs (Arutyunyan et al., 1968, 1969). Instead, expert pistol shooters use compensatory actions in the arm, allowing them to perform with more arm control, which resulted in less pistol motion. As suggested by Bernstein's learning model, the inexperienced shooters simplified the task by freezing their limbs.

• *Stage 3—exploiting the environment:* During the final stage of learning, the performer continues releasing degrees of freedom until all the degrees of freedom necessary to accomplish the task have been released. At this point, the performer is maximizing muscular efficiency using the optimal number of degrees of freedom and can exploit environmental passive forces (i.e., gravity or inertia). Learners at this stage are considered experts. At this stage, figure skaters can land impressive jumps, wide receivers in American football can make unbelievable catches while leaping into the air and avoiding defenders, and tennis players can maintain complete control of the flight patterns of the ball.

The main role of practitioners with learners in stage 3 is to design variable practice sessions that push them to continue extending their capabilities. Practitioners must keep the task interesting and fresh so that the learners stay motivated.

Evidence for Bernstein's Learning Stages

Researchers in one investigation examined degrees of freedom by teaching participants how to operate a ski simulator apparatus. Initially, the participants moved very rigidly, fixing their lower limb joints (Vereijken et al., 1992). This enabled them to move with relatively high frequency (quick movements) but low amplitude (small side-to-side movements). The cross correlations were very high between joints during the early stages of learning. With practice, the cross-correlations (couplings between joints) decreased, indicating that the degrees of freedom were being released. At this point, the participants were moving with more amplitude (covering more distance), but this came at the cost of frequency, meaning that they were unable to move back and forth at the same rate. As practice continued, the cross-correlations continued to decrease, and movement frequency continually increased until the performers were able to move with the same or greater frequency as in the initial practice trials while maintaining large movement amplitudes. These results indicate that learners initially freeze their degrees of freedom

to gain control over the movement. They do this because they are afraid of falling. As their confidence and familiarity with the task increases with practice, the number of degrees of freedom also increases. In 2018, the influence of practice using a ski simulator was again examined but this time with both skilled and novice downhill skiers over a period of seven days of practice (Dutt-Mazumder & Newell, 2018). The authors examined amplitude and frequency of movement using a ski simulator like the Vereijken and colleagues study (1992) previously discussed. The experienced skiers performed significantly better than the novice skiers; however, the performance gap decreased over practice. Of particular interest was the transition of the novice skiers observed. During the first practice session, all the skilled skiers moved in an antiphase pattern, while only some of the novice skiers performed in this fashion. With practice, the novice skiers transitioned from moving in phase to antiphase, which allowed them to move with more degrees of freedom, as expected when transitioning from Bernstein's first stage of learning to the second stage of learning. The effect of experience also declined with practice such that it is likely both groups would perform at nearly the same level with increased practice.

Another research study compared dominant limb movements with nondominant limb movements during handwriting to investigate whether there was a difference in the number of degrees of freedom involved in the two limbs (Newell & van Emmerik, 1989). Limb dominance provides an opportunity to compare the effect of skill acquisition within the same participant. The investigators found that the nondominant limb used fewer degrees of freedom than the dominant limb did. These findings provide more evidence in support of Bernstein's (1967) learning stages by demonstrating that the degrees of freedom were released in the more practiced, dominant limb as opposed to the nondominant limb. These results were observed through high correlations between the joints in the nondominant limb. The

WHAT DO YOU THINK?

Exercise 5.3

If you've ever watched people ice skate for the first time, you probably noticed how they stiffen their knees and move each leg as if it were a single segment. Their movements are very rigid and deliberate. Experienced ice skaters tend to move fluidly across the ice. Professional ice skaters can exploit the environment by propelling their bodies into the air, completing multiple turns, and landing smoothly.

Swimmers have also been found to reduce their degrees of freedom when learning to swim (refer to the following table). Rather than freely moving their arms and legs, novice swimmers often move their arms in a short downward-pushing motion and their legs in a bicycle pattern, causing them to produce more of a dog paddle than a fluid, advanced, formal stroke. Stiffening limb movements causes the body to be in an upright vertical position, preventing much forward propulsion.

Motor skill	Stage 1: freezing the limbs	Stage 2: releasing the limbs	Stage 3: exploiting the environment
Swimming	• Little to no arm or leg action occurs. • Arm action is a simple, short downward push. • Leg action is a circular bicycling action. • Overall, little to no forward propulsion occurs.	• Arm and leg action occurs. • Arms: Long push–pull motion • Legs: Bent-knee flutter kick • Overall: Rudimentary crawl	• Arms: Lift propulsion and bent elbow • Legs: Straight-leg flutter • Overall: Advanced crawl, rhythmic breathing

Think of two other activities in which Bernstein's learning stages are noticeably visible and add them to the table. Describe how the learner's movements appear in each of the three stages.

authors also evaluated the independence between multiple joints. Cross-correlations revealed the independence of two variables, with high cross-correlations indicating that the variables are highly interdependent. In this case, if one body segment moved, such as the shoulder, then another body segment, such as the elbow, from the same limb moved. When the participants were writing with the nondominant limb, they were freezing their degrees of freedom. In contrast, when they were writing with the dominant limb, each body segment moved independently.

Evidence Against Bernstein's Learning Stages

Although there is much support for Bernstein's learning stages, it is important to note that the effect of releasing degrees of freedom is task dependent, meaning that this effect is not found during the acquisition of all motor skills. The Bernstein learning stages have been challenged because they do not consider all influencing factors inherent in the performance of the motor skill (Newell & Vaillancourt, 2001). Newell and Liu (2021) have proposed that the task goal is important in determining the collective variable, which emerges early during skill learning when learners acquire new movement patterns. The collective variable is the variable that captures the main pattern of interactions among the muscles and joints involved in a movement pattern (Kelso, 1995). For example, the collective variable for walking is the ankle and hip coordination of one limb (Diedrich & Warren, 1995).

Completion of a motor skill occurs as the learner's characteristics (including structural constraints such as height and weight and functional constraints such as motivation and movement experience), the task (goals, equipment, rules), and the environment (physical and sociocultural) interact. It was proposed that the order of the learning stages depends on the task goal and the constraints of the person.

To examine how changing the constraints of the task affects the behaviors evident in the learning stages, researchers had participants practice maintaining balance on a moving platform that oscillated in an anteroposterior direction (Ko et al., 2003). In contrast to what happened in the study by Vereijken and colleagues (1992), participants produced large ranges of motion at all joints, including the neck, hips, knees, and ankles. With practice, rather than increasing their joint motion, the participants decreased it. The learners were gradually freezing the degrees of freedom that were not essential for the task. They also decreased motion in some degrees of freedom but not in others.

It appears that the participants were initially decreasing their degrees of freedom to find a new coordination mode, one that was more efficient and more stable (Newell et al., 1989). This new movement pattern would have a stronger attractor state (see chapter 2). Similar results were found in cellists: more skilled cellists used less elbow and wrist overall movement and less variability in comparison to novice cellists (Verrel et al., 2013). Higher skill in violin bowing was also associated with freezing degrees of freedom rather than releasing degrees of freedom, as Bernstein's learning model suggests (Konczak et al., 2009). The main suggestion from these research studies is that there are many ways to solve a move-

---

TRY THIS

Degrees of Freedom in Throwing

Exercise 5.4

Throw a ball 5 to 10 times with as much force as you can using your dominant hand. Then switch hands and throw 5 to 10 times with your nondominant hand. Most likely, you are not able to throw the ball as far or as fast with your nondominant hand, but what about the movement characteristics of your throws? Describe what was different about the kinematics of your throws with your dominant hand versus your nondominant hand. You may find it easier to observe the differences in a friend. When did your friend use more degrees of freedom (e.g., contralateral step, increased range of motion of the arm)? Explain why there is a difference in the number of degrees of freedom used in each arm to accomplish the same task. If possible, try using an app, such as Hudl Technique, to be able to view side-by-side video comparisons.

ment task. The most appropriate method for learning a new motor skill is determined by the interaction between the structural and functional constraints of the learner; the goals, equipment, and rules of the task; and the environmental constraints imposed on the learner.

Gentile's Learning Stages

Gentile (1972, 1987, 2000) proposed a two-stage learning model to help practitioners by not only describing the nature of the movement but also by providing instructional strategies for each learning stage.

Getting the Idea of the Movement Stage

The first stage of learning is termed the **getting the idea of the movement stage**, which is behaviorally like Fitts and Posner's cognitive stage of learning. During this stage the learner has two main goals: to understand the coordination required to perform the task and to determine the regulatory and nonregulatory conditions of the movement. Gentile used the term **regulatory conditions** to refer to conditions that provide relevant information for the performance of a motor skill. Regulatory conditions for the game of basketball include the ball (size and shape), surface of support (concrete slab or wood floor), the height and position of the hoop, the distance of the three-point line, and so on. To understand the basics of basketball, a learner must learn these important aspects. Individuals depend on the external environment to produce successful movements (Chow et al., 2008). Regulatory conditions for a simple motor skill, such as walking down the street, include the surface of support (concrete, ice, gravel), other pedestrians, and objects along the path. The more complex motor skill of hitting a baseball with a bat requires the player to contact the ball; to do this, the player must understand both the positional (spatial) and the time (temporal) characteristics of the ball (Gentile, 2000). There is a

much greater margin of error for a batter than for a walker. If the batter anticipates or misjudges the pitch, the bat will not make contact with the ball. The movement pattern executed by the batter depends on the spatial and temporal characteristics of the environment and the batter's spatial–temporal skills.

It is perhaps even more important for a learner to ignore nonrelevant cues, which Gentile refers to as **nonregulatory conditions**. Nonregulatory conditions distract learners from important relevant cues, preventing them from performing skillfully or accomplishing the goal of the task. Practitioners should emphasize the regulatory conditions during early skill acquisition to help learners avoid the acquisition of bad habits and to maximize learning during practice sessions. Learners who are easily distracted, especially children, should frequently be redirected toward the regulatory conditions. The learner must not only be able to selectively attend (refer to chapter 3) to the relevant cues (regulatory conditions) but also be able to ignore the irrelevant cues (nonregulatory conditions). A basketball player shooting a free throw must focus on the release of the ball and the rim of the basket while ignoring the sounds of the crowd screaming and stomping their feet on the bleachers. Most often, those distractions are not present during practice. The pedestrian needs to focus on oncoming traffic and traffic signals when crossing a busy street and avoid distractions from cell phone conversations, music, or other external noise. However, it is important for learners to practice under varying nonregulatory conditions to prepare for performances or real-world situations.

The practitioner's role during Gentile's getting the idea of the movement stage is to clearly and concisely teach the learner how to perform the movement pattern. The practitioner should emphasize the basics of the task (e.g., goals and objectives) through demonstrations and verbal instructions.

The learner's attention should be directed toward the relevant stimuli in the environment. For example, a batter should be told to focus on the pitcher's release point during the windup. Novice batters often alter their visual focus between the release point and the pitcher's head, whereas experts maintain a steady focus on the release point (Shank & Haywood, 1987). By focusing on the relevant stimulus (the release point), experts can accurately assess the pitch nearly 100 percent of the time, whereas novices who fluctuate between the head and the release point during the windup accurately identify only a little more than 50 percent of pitches. Altering their visual focus causes novices to miss critical components of the pitch, which decreases their chances of making contact with the ball.

Fixation and Diversification Stage

Once learners understand the basic movement pattern, they advance to the second learning stage, the fixation and diversification stage. The key element during this stage is refining the movement pattern (like what occurs in Fitts and Posner's associative stage) and maintaining consistent performance (similar to what occurs in Fitts and Posner's autonomous stage). Gentile separates the stage into two subcomponents (fixation and diversification), depending on the

predictability of the environment and the skill level of the performer (see figure 5.1).

- *Fixation:* When learning a closed skill, such as performing a power clean or performing a backflip, the focus should be on consistency. The learner must refine the movement by determining how to perform the motor skill most accurately and then reliably replicate the action time and time again. Learners who are performing a routine, as in gymnastics, figure skating, and dance, practice and refine the movements until they can consistently perform the movement sequence well. In rehabilitation settings, therapists first assist patients in performing exercises under very controlled settings. Gentile refers to this subcomponent as the **fixation stage** because learners are focusing on consistently reproducing a movement pattern. If, however, this was all they did, the performances would be very boring to watch.

- *Diversification:* Open skills, such as passing the puck to a teammate during a hockey game, or closed skills with intertrial variability such as golf or billiards progress to the subcomponent known as the **diversification stage** wherein they are practiced in unpredictable environments. Successful performers of open skills must be very adaptable. Because they cannot predict how the opposing team will respond to their plays, they must alter their responses as play unfolds.

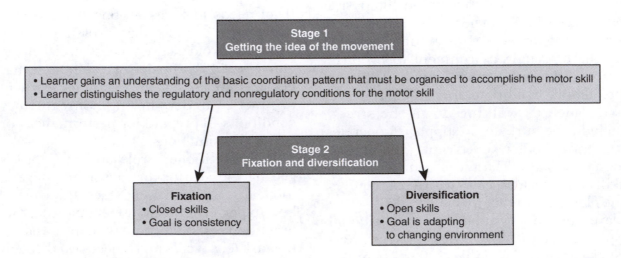

Figure 5.1 Gentile's two-stage learning model.

When learning an open skill, learners must focus on diversifying their movement pattern by practicing the motor skill under many conditions. When learning a closed motor skill, the main objective is consistency, or in Gentile's terms, fixation. The objective in open motor skills is adaptability, or in Gentile's terms, diversification. Learners who can perform a motor skill very consistently only under predictable conditions will not be prepared when the environment unexpectedly changes. They must be able to make decisions quickly and adapt their movement patterns to accommodate these changes. Patients undergoing physical or occupational therapy must not only learn how to perform the exercises in the controlled setting of the clinic, but more importantly, they must also learn how to adapt the exercises so they can adapt to daily activities that will be performed at home or in the community. Furthermore, the activities or motor skills they are learning or relearning must enable them to circumvent many obstacles and adjust to varying surfaces, slopes, and objects.

Once the learner has progressed to the second stage of learning, the fixation and diversification stage, instructional strategies should focus on refining the movement pattern until the learner can complete it consistently (i.e., fixation). The movement pattern should be practiced repeatedly under similar regulatory conditions, whereas nonregulatory conditions should be varied. For example, during a closed skill such as bowling, the regulatory conditions (i.e., length of lane, size of gutters, number of pins, size of pins) should not be changed, but the nonregulatory conditions (i.e., crowd noise, fatigue level, motivation level, number of pins remaining) should be changed.

If the motor skill is an open skill, the practitioner will advance to the subcomponent known as the diversification stage after, and only after, the learner is proficient at performing the motor skill consistently using the subcomponent known as the fixation stage. Again, the fixation strategy includes teaching under similar regulatory condi-

tions and variable nonregulatory conditions. Regardless of whether the motor skill is open or closed, instructional strategies are similar during stage 1, getting the idea of the movement, and then progress to stage 2, fixation and diversification. When practicing closed skills, the learner continues using the fixation strategy. For open skills or closed skills with intertrial variability, the practitioner should vary both the regulatory and nonregulatory conditions (diversification strategy) only after the learner can proficiently perform under stable regulatory conditions and variable nonregulatory conditions. For example, a punter in American football should be able to punt the ball consistently without defenders prior to trying to punt with defenders. The following is an example of teaching a learner how to shoot a basketball using Gentile's learning stages.

Stage 1: Getting the Idea of the Movement

Teach the goal of a basketball shot.

Provide a demonstration (use BEEF—balance, eyes on rim, elbow, follow-through).

Allow the learner to practice from the same position on the court repeatedly before moving to a different position.

Provide feedback regarding the shot (e.g., *Shoot with more arc, Increase the bend of your knees, Don't forget to follow through*).

Fixation Subcomponent of Stage 2

Vary practice conditions while remaining in a closed environment:

Practice shots without defenders at the foul line.

Practice when fatigued.

Practice under various motivation conditions.

Practice with crowd noise.

Practice under various levels of stress (e.g., provide incentives or punishments for missed shots, altering the importance of the shot).

Diversification Subcomponent of Stage 2

Vary practice conditions in an open environment (any of the following can be combined with any of the conditions in the stage 2 fixation subcomponent):

Add defenders.

Learn more plays.

Increase the pace of the game.

You may have asked yourself this question, "What about elite performers?" when reading about Gentile's learning model as it does focus predominantly on early learning. Although elite performers have progressed through all the stages, they are most certainly not done learning. Elite performers must continue practicing many long hours to polish their technique. They also need to practice to continuously refine their response to competitive pressure and maintain high motivation while also avoiding overtraining and burnout. Moreover, elite performers are expected to consistently perform at high levels while performing in varying contexts. Their motor skills became well established during the fixation and diversification stage; however, they must continue to refine their technique (Carson & Collins, 2011). Techniques and equipment design will continue to evolve to optimize performance, such as a change from a closed to a *V*-style position in ski jumpers or clap skates for speedskaters, which allow the blade of the skate to remain on the ice while the ankle joint extends. Although elite performers continue to enhance their performance, there is surprisingly limited research examining their technical advances in comparison to early skill learning research.

To provide a framework for elite performers to continue to advance their performance, the **five-A model** was developed. It includes these phases: (a) analysis; (b) awareness; (c) adjustment; (d) reautomation; and (e) assurance (Carson & Collins, 2011). A technique change can be driven by a move toward newer equipment, an adopted technique by competitors, or an injury. For

example, an Olympic weightlifter may use step 1, analysis, to recreate the position he held when he sustained an injury due to a long-term technical flaw. During step 1, the athlete could practice a new less injury-inducing technique with a broomstick. When progressing to step 2, awareness, he could practice both the new technique and the old technique with a lightly weighted bar to be able to feel the difference between the two techniques. Step 3, adjustment, can include learning more about the form and the injury as well as developing an imagery script and watching videos of the better techniques. Step 4, reautomation, would involve adding more weight and adjusting the imagery script. Weight would continually be added, and by step 5, the athlete would be practicing with competitive simulations and video feedback, which would be helpful for continued assurance. This five-step process could be applied to anyone refining their technique and could be implemented by coaches, teachers, or clinicians to either enhance an individual's performance or recover from an injury and learn safer movement patterns.

LINK TO DYNAMIC SYSTEMS APPROACH

The dynamic systems approach supports the changing dynamics and coordination patterns discussed in the three learning models. According to the dynamic systems approach (refer to chapter 2 for further information), learners begin producing a pattern of movement that is familiar to them, such as one from a similar motor skill (Zanone & Kelso, 1994). For instance, a skilled tennis player who has never played racquetball will likely swing at the racquetball with very little snap of the wrist. To control the ball in tennis, players are often initially taught to hit forehand and backhand with the whole arm from the shoulder. Because racquetball does not involve hitting the ball above a net into a court, the player can strategically hit the ball with great force against the wall.

Racquetball players can generate more force and power by snapping the elbow and wrist when swinging at the ball. Swinging with the whole arm is a coordination pattern that is well developed in tennis players. This pattern would work on a racquetball court, but not well. This coordination pattern would be a strong attractor state with a deep well for a tennis player. As the player practices and progresses with the new game of racquetball, she is likely to vary her swing to accommodate the changing constraints of the enclosed court and the different elastic properties of the ball and the strings of the racket. With practice and instruction, the learner's swing would transition from the initial preferred coordination pattern of swinging with the whole arm to a new attractor state of swinging with more elbow and wrist action.

It is important to consider prior movement experiences before instructing a new motor skill. Prior movement experiences will strongly influence the coordination patterns that a learner adopts, for better or worse. A practitioner should be aware of the learner's prior movement experiences and adjust teaching strategies accordingly to maximize the rate of learning.

PRACTICAL USE OF THE LEARNING MODELS

These three learning models provide a multilevel perspective on motor learning. An emphasis on the impact the environment has on the learning process is stressed in both Bernstein's learning stages and Gentile's learning stages. In Bernstein's learning model, the individual's perception is affected by the changing dynamics of the environment. Gentile emphasized that instruction should be designed based on the predictability of environmental influences. Fitts and Posner's learning model defined cognitive and behavior processes across the skill level of the performer. A practitioner who understands how the environment affects the learning process will be able to manipulate the environment to optimize learning.

With initial instruction, the focus should be on the individual constraints of the

---

WHAT DO YOU THINK?

Exercise 5.5

Refer to the tennis and racquetball example discussed in the section Link to Dynamic Systems Approach.

1. What is the rate limiter (this term was introduced in chapter 2) for the tennis player who is learning how to play racquetball?

2. For tennis:

   a. At what stage (using Fitts and Posner's learning model) would you classify the athlete? Explain why.

   b. What instructional strategies would be most appropriate for the athlete? (*Hint:* The instructional strategies should depend on the stage of learning for each motor skill.)

3. For racquetball:

   a. At what stage (using Fitts and Posner's learning model) would you classify the athlete? Explain why.

   b. What instructional strategies would be most appropriate for the athlete? (*Hint:* The instructional strategies should depend on the stage of learning for each motor skill.)

learner and then on the goal of the task. The practitioner should provide adequate instruction so learners can begin performing the movement task, with the goal of allowing them to explore movement options while attempting to produce the basic coordination pattern. During this time, movement errors can be seen as positive because learners are discovering the patterns of movement that work and discarding those that do not. Novice performers generally show rapid improvements in performance. This rate of improvement gradually tapers off with continuing practice.

Learners who can perform the basic movement pattern should then focus on refining their movements to increase their probability of success. Once they can consistently produce a movement pattern, they can focus on adapting the movement pattern. This enables the learner to perform under various internal conditions (e.g., fatigue levels, motivation levels, the importance of the outcome) and external conditions (e.g., crowd noise; the position, angle, and distance of the movement; the positions of other players).

These three models provide a background to the cognitive and physical components of the learning stages as well as instructional strategies appropriate for each stage. A practitioner who fully understands the learning process will have the skills necessary to properly manipulate the learning environment and the learner (Rose & Christina, 2006).

SUMMARY

Fitts and Posner (1967) developed a three-stage model for the acquisition of any motor skill. The first stage, the cognitive stage, is marked by many errors, inconsistencies, and self-talk. Once learners have learned the basic components of the task, they progress to the associative stage, in which the errors are fewer and less overt than in the cognitive stage. The final stage, which many people never reach, is the autonomous stage. Vereijken (1991) proposed a three-stage model from Bernstein's notion of the degrees of freedom problem. In the first stage, novices tend to freeze their limbs to simplify the movement. As learners progress, they increase the number of degrees of freedom, creating more fluid movements. When they have achieved a high level of proficiency, they have reached the third stage, exploitation of the environment.

The third learning model, proposed by Gentile (1972, 1987, 2000), was intended to provide instructional strategies to practitioners. During the first stage, the getting the idea of the movement stage, learners focus on the movement basics and regulatory cues. After they have acquired a basic concept of the movement pattern, they progress to the fixation and diversification stage. After achieving a high level of consistency by fixating on the same regulatory conditions, learners practice many movement modifications to prepare for unpredictable environments.

Each of these models contributes to our understanding of how people learn motor skills and helps the practitioner structure, design, and implement practice sessions with the goal of maximizing motor learning. By using a multilevel perspective, practitioners will have more tools to manipulate the environment to accommodate behavioral, cognitive, and physical changes in performers with increased skillfulness.

> **ONLINE ACTIVITIES**

The student material found in HK*Propel* includes exercises, labs, and videos to enhance learning and encourage practical application of important concepts.

LEARNING AIDS

Supplemental Activities

1. *Bernstein's learning stages:* YouTube has become a popular portal for searching for videos, from educational videos to cartoons to homemade videos. Many people, skillful or not, post videos of themselves performing. Search YouTube for three skill levels of soccer jugglers. Soccer juggling is an excellent example of Bernstein's learning stages because beginners generally limit their juggling to the use of only one leg, sometimes only the foot or the knee. As they increase their skill level, they begin to use more and more degrees of freedom by introducing more and more limb segments into their juggling.

   a. Were you able to find soccer jugglers you would classify as being in stages 1, 2, and 3 of Bernstein's learning stages? Explain your rationale for these classifications. Describe the jugglers' behavioral characteristics.

   b. Search for other motor skills (e.g., ice skating, throwing a ball, skateboarding) that you could classify into Bernstein's three learning stages. Describe how the performances fit into these classifications.

2. *Five-A model:* Examine a motor skill in which you have reached Gentile's diversification stage. Specifically, focus on how you could refine your technique by either using newer equipment or changing the movement pattern to be safer or more efficient. Discuss how you could use the five-A model to make this advanced change to your technique. Describe each step for the motor skill you chose.

Glossary

associative stage—The second stage in Fitts and Posner's learning model, in which the goal has shifted from solving the movement problem to refining the movement.

autonomous stage—The third and final stage in Fitts and Posner's learning model, in which the performer is at the highest level of motor skill proficiency.

cognitive stage—Fitts and Posner's first stage, in which the learner's main goal is to understand the basic components of the motor skill movement pattern.

coordinative structures—Structures that occur when the degrees of freedom become incorporated into larger functional units of action to preserve a certain posture or movement.

diversification stage—Subcomponent of Gentile's second stage of learning, in which open skills are practiced in unpredictable environments.

five-A model—A learning model that provides a framework for elite performers to continue to advance their performance through five steps: analysis, awareness, adjustment, reautomation, and assurance.

fixation stage—Subcomponent of Gentile's second stage of learning in which skills are practiced in a closed environment with a focus on consistency of the movement pattern.

getting the idea of the movement stage—Gentile's first stage of learning, like Fitts and Posner's cognitive stage of learning. During this stage, the learner has two main goals: (a) to understand the movement coordination required to perform the movement task, and (b) to determine the regulatory and nonregulatory conditions of the movement.

nonregulatory conditions—Factors, unrelated to the movement task, that can distract the learner from important relevant cues, preventing skillful performances.

regulatory conditions—Environmental conditions that provide relevant information for motor skill performance.

ASSESSING MOTOR LEARNING

CHAPTER OBJECTIVES

After reading this chapter, you should be able to do the following:

- Describe multiple indicators of motor learning.
- Generate and interpret performance curves and explain the limitations.
- Assess transfer of learning and support positive transfer.
- Calculate retention and transfer measures.

Ready to Hit the Water?

Ella is considering joining her university's rowing team next semester and has been training on her gym's indoor rowing machine (an ergometer—called an erg; see figure 6.1*a*) in anticipation of tryouts. From a peer with rowing experience, she has quickly learned the sequence of the stroke, driving with the legs, swinging the back open, and following through with the arms. Ella has also learned how to apply power on the erg as well as how to control her strokes per minute to be efficient no matter the length of her training. Ella's peer considers her scores and form on the erg to be impressive and thinks Ella is going to catch on quickly to rowing in a boat on the water (see figure 6.1*b*). This potential advantage would be considered positive transfer, meaning this experience using the erg benefited her rowing on the water. Would you expect there to be a benefit from Ella's knowledge of rowing on a machine on land, or would rowing in a boat on the water be too different for Ella to have an advantage?

Figure 6.1 Practicing on an (*a*) erg should positively transfer to (*b*) rowing on the water.

Many athletes train in different contexts under the assumption that the drills and training experiences will transfer to the new contexts of competitive performances, similar to Ella practicing on the erg before rowing on the water. Understanding how to maximize the benefits of practice sessions is critical because instructors, coaches, and therapists typically only have limited time with their learners. Training that does not result in positive transfer will not be an effective use of time. In the same regard, therapists must prescribe exercises that will positively transfer to natural settings.

Physical educators and health professionals are an essential component of childhood and adolescent motor development. Teachers, physical therapists, and coaches engage their students in fitness activities, sports, games, and other activities, teaching fundamental motor skills that are critical to motor development. Practitioners may assist delayed infants in learning to crawl; they may help children learn how to throw a ball, young athletes to serve a volleyball, or adults to bench press properly. It is not only important to properly instruct motor skills, but also to appropriately measure and assess learners' movement patterns to promote skill acquisition and transfer most effectively.

Understanding how to row on an erg will likely benefit Ella when she is learning how to row on the water. Previous movement experiences can greatly influence the performance of similar movement patterns— some in positive ways (positive transfer) and some in negative ways (negative transfer). This chapter discusses transfer of learning, including the types of transfer and how to foster positive transfer, in addition to how to assess motor performance and retention.

We can take many performance characteristics into consideration to determine whether students are learning motor skills, such as improved coordination patterns, increased consistency, and reduced mental and physical effort. These are all important in assessing performance, but the key to determining the level of learning attained is to assess the permanency of the motor skill. Think about an occupational therapist who is teaching a stroke patient how to brush her teeth or write her name again, or a physical therapist who is teaching a victim of a car accident how to walk again. What characteristics of the learner's performance assure the instructor that the learner is learning the movement and not simply showing improved performance? Just as math, science, and language teachers assess learning through examinations that cover the material, practitioners must administer retention tests to assess the learning of motor skills. Physical educators and movement clinicians assume that their students and clients have learned the material when they can perform at or near the same level as their previous performance following a break.

INDICATORS OF MOTOR SKILL LEARNING

Learning takes time, and practitioners must understand and accept this fact. Classrooms are based on the premise that the learning of some basic concepts will adequately prepare students for the next step in their careers, be that attending a university or starting a first professional job. Physical education classrooms assume that practicing basic movement patterns will transfer to other, more complex activities; sporting practices are centered on the assumption that drills will positively influence game-day performances; and therapists assume that exercises performed in the clinic will transfer to real-world settings. However, many factors must be addressed to ensure skill transfer. Motor learning is defined as a relatively permanent change in the capability to execute a motor skill due to practice or experience. This section discusses how motor learning is assessed and how to facilitate positive transfer and prolonged retention. The following are some movement characteristics that can indicate that motor learning has occurred:

- *Performance improvement:* Are observable performance changes shown across practice?
- *Consistency or stability:* Can the learner sustain a higher level of performance over time?
- *Persistence:* Can the learner perform the motor skill proficiently following a break in practice or performance?
- *Effort:* Is the learner performing with less physical or mental effort across practice?
- *Attention:* Does the learner require less attention to perform the motor skill?
- *Adaptability:* Can the learner adapt to changing environments or conditions with increased motor skill proficiency?

Performance Improvement

The most intuitive behavioral characteristic of learning a motor skill is **performance improvement**, which is defined as an overall increase in the performance outcome. Consider the discussion of performance and learning in chapter 1. Performance is the act of executing a motor skill at a particular time. Learning is the result of *permanent* changes, whereas performance is a temporary, *nonpermanent* change. Performance is observable, whereas learning is a construct. We can assume that someone has learned only after monitoring performance changes over time.

Performance improvement is the most common indicator of learning simply because it is the most obvious. We make inferences every day based on our observations; for example, we look for signs of a person's mood in their face. People often assume that someone is in a good mood because they are smiling, even though they may be sad or angry and smiling to hide their true feelings.

Although performance measures do not necessarily indicate motor learning at any point in time, assessing performance provides a good indicator of learning if it occurs across an extended period and the results are combined with other factors, such as consistency, persistence, and coordination stability. Depending on the performance measure, improvement may be marked by a decrease, as with error or speed. It is often assumed (although sometimes incorrectly) that people have learned when they exhibit significant performance gains. To assess whether motor learning has occurred, however, one must assess performance following a break in practice.

Improved performance may also result from the acquisition of bad habits. Learners can adopt bad habits when they are focusing on the outcome or product of the movement as opposed to the coordination patterns involved in moving skillfully. For example, when learning how to throw the discus, athletes must learn some movements that may feel unnatural to them until they become proficient. They must learn the rhythm of the throw, how to turn the lower body in a whipping motion with a relaxed upper body and with the lower body trailing. They must also keep their heels off the ground throughout the movement. It is important to note that, as with all motor skills, the precise technique and style of the throwing pattern is unique to every thrower, based on individual structural and functional constraints. Novices who are learning the throwing pattern may tend to tighten the upper body, which initially may allow them to throw farther because of the increased power behind the throw, but ultimately, this movement will prevent them from reaching their full potential. The more they practice this incorrect throwing pattern, the more difficulty they will have developing proper technique. A similar problem could result from continuing practice when they are ill or fatigued.

Because humans are competitive by nature, practitioners should eliminate movement outcomes when teaching novices the basic movement patterns. This will help prevent them from adopting unorthodox movement patterns or bad habits. To prevent a thrower from focusing on the outcome of her throw, such as the distance the object traveled, a practitioner could have her throw into a net. Basketball players could take practice shots on the wall, so they are focused on their form and not on whether they made the shot. Avoiding the formation of a bad habit is important, because, once formed, it can be very challenging to overcome. Using dynamic systems terminology (see chapter 2), bad habits result when the individual becomes trapped in a very deep and stable attractor state that has enabled the person to perform at an adequate level, even though other, more effective states should be discovered.

Performance Curves

Practitioners should not only evaluate learners' progress through subjective evaluations, but they should also obtain and record objective, quantitative performance measures over time. When deciding to quantify performance, the practitioner must first choose the performance measure that would be most appropriate to record. This decision is completely task dependent and may be driven by the resources available. For quantifying many motor skills, a measure of performance magnitude may be most appropriate, such as the distance of a throw, the height of a high jump, or the amount of weight bench pressed. Error is a good performance measure for motor skills in which the objective is accuracy. Instructors who have access to sufficient technology may be interested in quantifying the kinematics of the movement—for example, by measuring joint angle changes using high-speed video cameras and motion detectors. To assess the amount of effort required to perform the task, measuring heart rates throughout the performance may be useful. By quantifying performance, instructors can document performance changes over time and examine the effectiveness of their instructional techniques or strategies.

Performance curves can be generated by collecting a performance measure across time—for instance, the number of catches made each day in juggling or the number of foul shots made in each practice session. Figure 6.2 illustrates the maximal distance jumped per week for a long jumper. The distance jumped in feet is plotted on the y axis, and the weeks are plotted on the x axis. This allows the performer and instructor to see the gradual progress across the season.

Types of Performance Curves

There are four main types of performance curves (see figure 6.3). The most common, known as the **negatively accelerating curve**, illustrates a very rapid initial rate

---

WHAT DO YOU THINK?

Exercise 6.1

Refer to the Performance Improvement section.

1. Name a bad habit from the text example of the discus thrower in the cognitive stage of learning. Explain why this habit is bad and should be overcome.

2. Have you ever acquired a bad habit that you had to later overcome to move more proficiently? Describe this bad habit and how you overcame it. How long did it take you to eliminate the bad habit and move more proficiently?

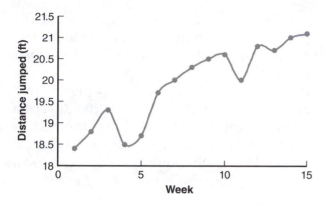

Figure 6.2 Fabricated performance curve of mean distance jumped in the long jump per week across 15 weeks.

of improvement followed by a gradual reduction in the rate of improvement. This rate of change is so common that it has been assigned a mathematical law known as the **power law of practice** (Newell & Rosenbloom, 1981; Snoddy, 1926). Negatively accelerating curves are common because

performance gains occur much more rapidly during early practice when a learner is essentially starting a motor skill from scratch. Initially, the learner experiences rapid improvements because there is much room for improvement; however, this rate of improvement is impossible to maintain. As the learner continues practicing, the room for improvement decreases, and further improvement becomes increasingly difficult to obtain.

A **positively accelerating curve** is illustrated by small initial gains, but this rate of improvement increases with every practice session. Learners may exhibit a positively accelerating curve when performing a challenging task such as juggling. Initially, learners may have difficulty improving, making only two to four catches per attempt. At some point, the learner will figure out the task and experience rapid gains in improvement. A

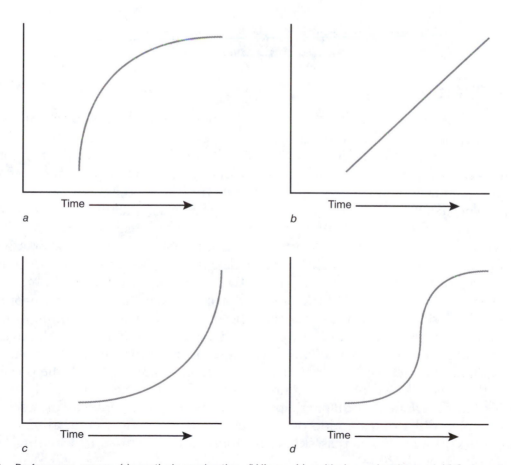

Figure 6.3 Performance curves: *(a)* negatively accelerating, *(b)* linear, *(c)* positively accelerating, and *(d)* S-shaped.

linear curve indicates that there is a direct relationship between the performance measure and time. A perfectly linear curve would be found for someone who shows the same gain in performance with every practice session or performance attempt. For example, a pitcher throws one mile per hour (two km/hr) faster each day of practice. The pitcher is improving at the same rate every day. On average, a person following a linear curve performs proportionately better each week. Finally, the **S-shaped curve** combines the rates of improvement found in the positively and negatively shaped curves. The learner initially takes some time to learn the motor skill. After some time, the learner experiences an aha moment and can perform the movement pattern much more successfully, like the positively accelerating curve. Performance then follows a gradual decline in the rate of improvement, like the negatively accelerating curve.

Keep in mind that the direction of the performance curve depends on the performance variable being measured. A thrower would be concerned with *increasing* the distance of the throw, but a sprinter would be concerned with *decreasing* the duration of the sprint. In the latter case, the performance curve would illustrate a downward trend. The same would be expected for a target shooter who is measuring error.

Limitations of Performance Curves

Although performance curves are a very useful, objective method of measuring and assessing performance, it is important to understand that performance curves represent only temporary effects. Because performance does not always indicate that learning has occurred, assessing learning through performance curves may falsely imply that someone has learned, even if the effects are not permanent. Performance

---

RESEARCH NOTES

Checkmate!

Many studies have exhibited the power law of practice; however, the generality of the power law of practice to complex skills has been in question (Howard, 2014). To address this, the power law's generality was examined over the development of a complex task, chess playing, over a period of 27 years among 387 participants, most of whom became grand masters at some point during this time. The objective of the study was to examine performance based on the amount of practice. Typically, practice is defined as performing a task. For this study, however, practice was playing Fédération Internationale des Échecs (FIDE)–rated games. FIDE-rated games are internationally rated chess games. Players increase their rating by defeating a player of higher ranking but can lose their rating when losing points. A FIDE rating is considered reliable after 25 games. The results revealed that the power law of practice was found for group data but not for individual data, meaning that the power law was only found when the results were averaged across all individuals. This is likely due to the high variability across the skill level of the participants. When examining individual data, there was an effect for skill level. The higher-skilled chess players improved with the power law; however, the lower-skilled players did not. It is possible that the results did not follow the power law of practice for all participants because of the complexity of the game of chess. Complex skills may develop on different time scales (Newell et al., 2006), and learning curves may vary across skills and individuals, such as in learning how to juggle (Haibach et al., 2004).

curves may also mask learning effects when there are no observable performance changes but the learner has gained some learning. For example, if several people are learning a difficult skill such as how to juggle, some may progress very rapidly initially (negatively accelerating curve), some may progress slowly at first and then improve rapidly (positively accelerating curve), and others may not ever show observable improvements. Those who are still averaging only two or three catches per attempt in juggling after many practice sessions may have learned the overall movement pattern of the hands in relation to the balls, a better technique to toss the balls through trial and error and observation, or both, even though their performance does not illustrate such learning. These people may have poorer eye–hand coordination, which would make the motor skill more challenging for them. They have gained some learning even though their performance curves appear flat.

It is important to understand that performance curves are limited by the performance measure. If there is a ceiling effect for the performance measure, then the performance curves may be flat. Ceiling effects often occur for simple tasks that are easily mastered. To reveal a more holistic picture of performance changes, practitioners should consider recording both product and process measures. For example, for a baseball throw, product measures such as speed

of the pitch (product) should be combined with an assessment of the thrower's arm movement, such as a looser arm movement as opposed to a stiff-arm movement (process).

Performance curves also provide only a limited perspective. For example, when averaging across participants, individual trends are often lost. An averaged performance curve may indicate that participants have learned a motor skill very quickly, when perhaps only one person has learned very quickly while the others showed a very small amount of improvement. Figure 6.4a shows a performance graph of the performances for four jugglers across 10 practice sessions. Juggler 1 progressed very quickly, whereas jugglers 2, 3, and 4 progressed at a much slower rate (and none of these three performed at nearly as high a level as juggler 1). It is difficult to even notice that juggler 4 became proficient with cascade juggling, averaging 15 catches by practice session 10. Although juggler 4's score doesn't compare to 250 catches, it does show that the juggler has acquired the basic coordination pattern of this complex motor skill. Examining figure 6.4a, we may infer that only one juggler learned the motor skill of juggling. Now look at figure 6.4b, which exhibits the mean performance across the four jugglers. If we examined only figure 6.4b, it would appear all jugglers most likely learned cascade juggling because the rates of learning are lost when performances are averaged across participants.

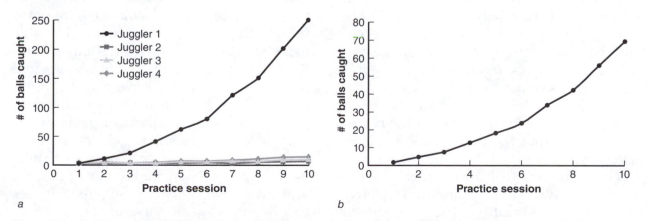

a

b

Figure 6.4   Performance curves: *(a)* individual performance curves for four jugglers and *(b)* mean performance across the four jugglers.

There are also limitations to averaging across trials for an individual's data. A graph that depicts only the average performance per session, as in figure 6.4a, does not provide any information about the consistency of an individual's performance. The consistency of an individual's performance provides important information regarding the learning process. As discussed in chapter 5, learners in the cognitive stage are inconsistent in comparison to learners in the associative and autonomous stages. Analyzing individual trials can also provide information regarding the effects of a warm-up decrement. A **warm-up decrement** is a reduction in performance resulting from a period of inactivity. These effects are generally short in duration. It is important to assess the amount of performance that is generally lost due to the warm-up decrement and the length of time or number of attempts required to overcome the warm-up decrement. This can be valuable information when people are preparing for a competition or event.

Consistency

The consistency of performance is another important indicator of motor skill learning. A consistent performer can sustain a higher level of performance over time. Although it is often assumed that consistency implies learning, this is not always the case. Let's refer to the definition of motor learning from chapter 1. Motor learning has been defined as the relatively permanent change in the learner's capability to execute a motor skill because of practice. Although the performance appears permanent because it is consistent, instructors must be careful not to use this as the only measure of motor learning. This is because it does not necessarily mean that the motor skill has been learned.

The consistency of a movement pattern from the dynamic systems perspective indicates the stability of the movement pattern—in other words, the depth of the

attractor well. Again, it is possible that the learner has adopted a bad habit and is consistently performing less skillfully because they have become trapped in a strong attractor state. Sometimes these attractor states can become *too* stable, making it very difficult to change a movement pattern. At this point, it is best for the instructor to force the learner out of the stable pattern. It will take time for the learner to become consistent with the new movement pattern; however, it is better to be inconsistently producing the desirable movement pattern than consistently performing the flawed movement pattern. Learners may feel uncomfortable producing a new movement pattern for a while, but it is important to encourage them to continue pushing through this potentially awkward stage. For example, body posture is a very important element in ballroom dance, and many dancers have poor body postures such as curved shoulders or a forward head position. The more a ballroom dancer has practiced with these bad habits, the more challenging they are to overcome. It is easy for dancers to focus on the steps and forget about maintaining their posture. When they are focusing on maintaining their posture, they are likely to mess up their steps or make other errors. Over time, the bad habit will be eliminated without detriment to the overall performance.

Persistence

Learning can also be measured by increased persistence in the performance of a motor skill. With practice, the learner will be able to perform following longer and longer durations of time without practice, as reflected in the saying, *It's like learning to ride a bike*. When initially learning a motor skill, people need to practice regularly; however, with increased practice, skill proficiency is maintained for longer periods of time, extending from days and weeks to months and even years. Of course, some losses can be expected because of forgetting or undergoing physical changes over time, but a sustained relative permanency should be present. This performance characteristic is central to the definition of motor learning (a relatively *permanent* change in the capability to perform a motor skill).

Effort

Another method of measuring performance or learning merges the field of exercise physiology with the field of motor learning by examining changes in skill acquisition by assessing effort (Lee & Carnahan, 2021). Energy expenditure is minimized as a function of skill acquisition (Sparrow & Newell, 1998). Experts perform challenging feats effortlessly. BMX bikers can complete phenomenal jumps; outfielders can leap into the air to make amazing catches; and dancers can complete incredible lifts in what appear to be effortless, seamless movements. Novice performers, on the other hand, can expend a lot of mental and physical effort to perform just a simple version of the coordination pattern. Many learners expend a great deal of energy producing an inefficient movement pattern because they have not learned the correct muscles to activate, the correct sequence for activating the muscles, or either. This causes them to exert much more effort than necessary to perform the task. Learners can become quickly fatigued and frustrated through this process.

Novice swimmers, young and old, initially attempt to swim with the body in a vertical position, which is very inefficient for swimming yet seemingly more comfortable for the inexperienced swimmer. This vertical positioning forces the swimmer to expend much energy to produce little if any forward propulsion. This can lead to frustration, and to increase forward propulsion, the swimmer will kick harder and use more arm motion. They exert a great deal of effort but only tire themselves out without gaining much forward motion, which frustrates them even more. With practice, swimmers become increasingly comfortable in the water, and their body positions gradually become more horizontal. This change enables them to produce more fluid motions with less overall energy expended.

Attention

The amount of conscious attention required to perform a motor skill decreases significantly with practice and skill level. Novices require focused attention on the overall mechanics of the movement. Because they are so focused on the coordination patterns

---

RESEARCH NOTES

Improving With Fewer Energy Requirements in Racewalking

To examine energy expenditures and perceived exertion when learning a new motor skill, researchers had seven participants engage in seven racewalking learning sessions on a motorized treadmill (Majed et al., 2012). Racewalking was chosen because it demands a lot of energy and is biomechanically constrained. Throughout the practice sessions, the speed of the treadmill was increased until the goal of a performance speed of 10 km/hr (6.2 mph) was reached. With practice, a reorganization of the movement patterns resulted in the racewalkers walking with progressively less variability across the practice sessions. These changes continued through the fourth practice session; however, improvements in energy expenditures and perceived exertion occurred throughout the practice sessions. The authors suggested that the trend of fewer energy expenditures occurred concurrently with a reorganization of the movement patterns.

of producing the movement, they cannot attend to game-playing strategies. Instead, they are focused on the technical components of the movement. With the development of skill, such as the progression from the cognitive stage to the associative stage (refer to chapter 5 for motor learning stages), the learners attend to the specifics of the movement pattern less and less. If they practice long enough to reach the autonomous stage, they can perform the skill with essentially no conscious attention devoted to the production of the movement pattern. This is termed **automaticity**. The following are the primary criteria of automaticity: (a) No processing capacity is required for the task; (b) the task is performed independently or without the performer's intentional control (involuntarily); and (c) the movement is not produced with consciousness or introspection (Neumann, 1984).

Because novices cannot perform the movement pattern efficiently and require much conscious attention when performing, their movements appear deliberate and choppy. Not only can experts produce the movement fluidly, but their attentional resources are also freed up, allowing them to focus on strategic elements of the game or task. For instance, a skilled soccer player does not have to focus on foot position and ball control; instead, she can focus on the positions of teammates and defenders as well as on strategies and game plays. By attending to these other game elements, the soccer player can respond quickly to changing environmental conditions.

Once automaticity is achieved, attention to the production of the movement pattern can have a negative impact on performance. Attention directed toward the production of a well-learned performance may interfere with the processes that have become automatic in a skilled performer, disrupting the production of the skilled movement (Wulf & Lewthwaite, 2016). Skilled performance is unconsciously controlled (Anderson, 1993; Fitts & Posner, 1967), whereas novice perfor-

mances are produced with a focus on declarative knowledge and the production of the coordination patterns. Drawing attention to the production of the movement pattern distracts an expert, disrupting the skillful performance. This is often referred to as paralysis by analysis and may explain why some skilled athletes choke under pressure. They may be able to perform very skillfully under most conditions, but under intense pressure they may shift their attention to the production of the movement, which distracts athletes just enough to degrade their performances.

Adaptability

Another method of assessing performance is to measure adaptability. **Adaptability** is the ability to make movement adjustments to fit the changing demands of the task and environmental conditions. The adaptability required for a particular movement is situation and skill dependent. For example, the catching ability of an outfielder will likely extend to catching other objects besides baseballs. A tennis player's experience with striking a ball with a racket will increase her ability to play other racket sports. Adaptability is especially critical for open skills, which test an individual's ability to adapt to constantly changing environmental demands, such as returning the ball with a forehand or backhand, at various positions on the court, with variable force, or some combination of these. Although closed skills do not require split-second adjustments necessarily, performers need to be adaptable in closed skills because every movement is variable. There are always at least some changes in the environment, the context of the movement itself (individual constraints), or the task.

People become increasingly adaptable with increased motor skill proficiency because they are now comfortable with the movement pattern and are no longer required to focus on internal processes.

TRY THIS

Can You Multitask?

Exercise 6.2

We do many activities without thinking, such as walking, taking a shower, and locking the door. You are probably also capable of doing some skillful activities automatically, such as typing on a keyboard, throwing a ball, or riding a bicycle. If you are a skilled typist, try typing while paying more attention to exactly what you're typing. It is likely that when you attended to your typing, you slowed down. Even breathing rate can be altered by focusing on breathing. Try counting your breaths. Did you feel as though you were controlling your breathing rate? Do you think you may have slowed down or sped up your breathing rate?

On the other hand, the benefit of performing a motor skill with little attention is that you can focus on other things; for example, you can talk while you are walking. What are some other examples of activities you can perform along with another functional task (i.e., multitasking)? Provide some sport-related examples.

They can alter their strategies for changing weather conditions, plays, or stressors, such as the importance of a game or situation.

PERFORMANCE AND LEARNING TESTS

Performance curves can provide a means to evaluate changes in performance measures over time. A simple method of measuring performance changes is to compare performance on a **pretest** (conducted prior to the practice session) with that on a **posttest** (conducted at the end of the practice session). This allows inferences of learning but does not reveal the persistence of the improved performance (i.e., retention). To assess the persistent capability to perform a motor skill, a retention test must be administered. A **retention test** is given following a break from practice. Assessing retention enables the practitioner to determine whether the change in skill level is temporary (performance) or permanent (learning). Effects that are temporary are unlikely to be reproduced following the **retention interval** (the amount of time between the last practice session or posttest and the retention test). The appropriate length of the retention interval depends on the duration and complexity of the motor skill and how often the motor skill is practiced. A motor skill that is practiced regularly, such as every day or even multiple times per day, could be assessed following a retention interval of only a day or two. A motor skill that is practiced less frequently will require a longer retention interval for adequate assessment of persistence. Very early motor learning research by Ebbinghaus (1913) on practice effects examined the effects of the length of a retention interval, finding that longer retention intervals lead to more forgetting; however, relearning is much quicker following this rest period (referred to as savings; Verhoeven & Newell, 2018).

It is important to understand the difference between learning and retention. Measures of performance during the acquisition phase allow inferences about learning, such as the mechanics, processes, and outcomes of learning (Rose & Christina, 2006). Measures of performance following a retention interval allow practitioners to make inferences about remembering and forgetting processes by assessing what was maintained or lost following the retention interval.

Another test that examines the permanence of motor skill acquisition is a transfer test. The difference between a transfer test and a retention test is that a retention test assesses performance on the same task following the break, whereas a transfer test assesses performance on a similar but different task following the break. **Transfer tests** measure the adaptability from the experience of one motor skill to a novel, related motor skill or performance situation. For example, a transfer test could examine how the experiences of Ella (refer to the beginning of this chapter) practicing on the erg transferred to rowing on water. This is an example of transfer of the same task using different equipment in a different environment. Transfer can also occur from related motor skills or sports, such as how snowboarding in the winter affects wakeboarding performance in the summer. A retention test would simply examine the person's snowboarding performance following a retention interval, but a transfer test would measure the performance on a similar motor skill (wakeboarding) following the retention interval. Table 6.1 provides a breakdown of the types of performance and learning tests.

Measuring Retention

The simplest way to measure retention is to measure **absolute retention**—the learner's performance immediately following the retention interval. This value is limited and does not provide information about how the learner did in comparison to prior performance levels.

Two other basic methods of measuring retention provide a comparative measure relative to performance during the original learning period. There are two main types of relative retention. The first is the difference score. To calculate the **difference score**, subtract the absolute retention score from the last score during the acquisition phase (original learning). This score is the change in performance following the retention interval. It represents the amount of performance that was lost or gained during a break. This score is somewhat limited because it does not reveal how much was lost relative to the change in the original learning. The **percentage score**, the most informative measure of retention, represents the percentage of performance that was lost or gained following the retention interval. To calculate the percentage score, divide the difference score by the change in original learning and then multiply by 100 percent. To calculate the change in original learning, subtract the performance on the first session or trial from the performance on the last session or trial of the original learning trials. In the example in figure 6.5, the participant is timed on how long he can track the movement. In this example, the absolute retention is 60 seconds because the learner's time on target was 60 seconds during the first trial following the retention interval of one week. To calculate the difference score (40 seconds), the absolute score (60 seconds)

Table 6.1 Performance and Learning Tests

Type of test	Definition	Measurement
Pretest	Test prior to practice of a motor skill	
Posttest	Test following practice of a motor skill	Performance (may or may not reveal learning)
Retention	Test following a retention interval; conditions are the same as in acquisition	Retention (remembering and forgetting)
Transfer	Test following a retention interval; conditions are different from but also like those in acquisition	Adaptability

was subtracted from the last score of the original session (100 seconds). To calculate the percentage score, the difference score (40 seconds) was divided by the change in original learning (100 seconds – 30 seconds) and multiplied by 100 percent. The percentage score is calculated as 57.14 percent, which can be interpreted to mean that 57.14 percent of the original improvement was lost over the retention interval, or conversely, 42.86 percent was retained.

Another useful retention measure is the **retention savings score**, which reflects how much time is required to return to the same level of performance compared to the time required to reach this level during the original practice sessions (see figure 6.5). During the original sessions, the learner took 10 sessions to reach a peak of 100 seconds. However, following the retention interval, the learner reached this same level in only three practice sessions. The retention savings score is the difference between these two values, so seven sessions were saved in reaching the same level of performance following the retention interval.

Types of Transfer

Previous movement experiences influence the ability to perform a new motor skill, just as the experience rowing on an erg likely helped Ella row on the water in the example at the beginning of this chapter. This is referred to as **transfer of learning**. The three types of transfer are positive, negative, and zero; the type depends on the direction of the transfer.

Positive transfer occurs when the learning of a previous motor skill enhances the performance of another motor skill (see figure 6.6). You may have experienced positive transfer if you were experienced with one racket sport and then tried to play a new racket sport. For example, a tennis player will likely experience an advantage when learning how to play pickleball because of the similarities in contacting a ball with a racket. Positive transfer is typically more for a beginner (cognitive stage) to a sport or activity than for an individual in the associative or autonomous stage. Skilled performers, on the other hand, often receive little benefit to performing other experiences because their level of performance is so high. The variations from another sport or activity are more likely to hinder than benefit their performance level.

When a previous movement experience hinders performance, **negative transfer** has occurred (see figure 6.7). Players who switch from baseball to softball can experience negative transfer because of the differences in tracking the ball following the pitch. In baseball, the ball is released high and then moves down because it is pitched overhand; in softball, pitchers use an underhand pitch,

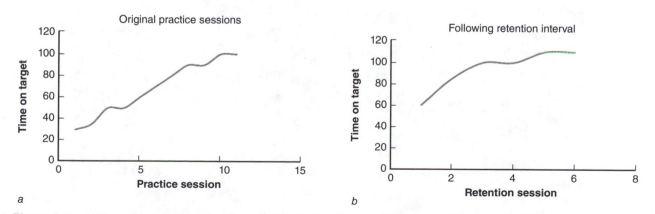

a   b

Figure 6.5 (a) Time on target was measured across 11 sessions. The goal of the task was to stay on target for as long as possible. (b) Following 11 sessions, the learner took one week off (retention interval) and then practiced for an additional 6 sessions.

WHAT DO YOU THINK?

Exercise 6.3

The data shown in this exercise are from a patient undergoing active rehabilitation of an injured rotator cuff. The main goal of the rehabilitation is to increase the patient's range of motion. The patient began physical therapy immediately following the injury. The original data are from the first three months of physical therapy. The patient then traveled for two weeks (retention interval) and returned to physical therapy.

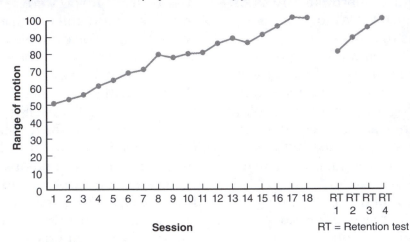

1. What is the absolute retention value?
2. Calculate the difference score.
3. Calculate the percentage score.
4. Calculate the retention savings score.
5. Interpret the results.

Figure 6.6 While the (a) tennis serve requires a racket and the (b) volleyball serve does not require any implement, positive transfer can occur from one to the other because they both are sport-specific skills of striking.

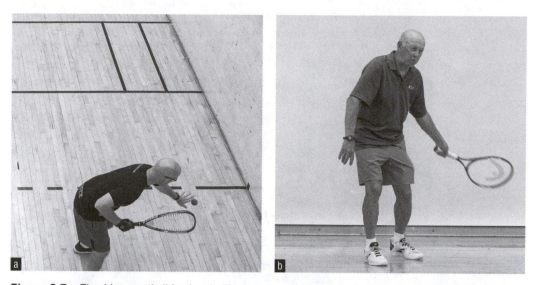

Figure 6.7   The *(a)* racquetball forehand will generally provide positive transfer to a *(b)* novice tennis player but may cause some negative transfer to a skilled tennis player due to the size of the ball and the court.

causing the ball to approach the plate from a low-to-high position. This previous experience could cause temporary negative transfer with batting when the player switches from softball back to baseball.

When the previous movement experience neither enhances nor hinders performance, then **zero transfer** has occurred. This happens when the two motor skills are unrelated, such as hurdling and fencing, or punting in American football and the backstroke in swimming.

Practitioners should be aware of learners' previous movement experiences because initial poor performance may be caused by negative transfer from prior experience in a similar skill. Luckily, when negative transfer does occur, as in batting in softball after prior experience with batting in baseball, it is generally temporary. On the other hand, learners often capitalize on previous movement experiences that provide positive transfer. In general, most transfer effects are small and positive. The amount of transfer depends upon the similarity of the tasks, with the more similar tasks or variations causing more transfer. Typically, the more movement experiences individuals have, the more likely they are to pick up new motor skills quickly (positive transfer).

Some of the strongest evidence for the persistence of negative transfer is found when learning a second language (Asher, 1964; Figueredo, 2006). The production of speech sounds necessary for speaking a particular language strongly influences how the person will produce the speech sounds for another language. This is why German and Chinese natives have very different accents in English. The negative transfer is causing nonnative speakers to have difficulty pronouncing certain sounds. For example, native Japanese speakers confuse the letter *l* with the letter *r*, so they often pronounce *salary* as *sarary* (Cook, 1997). French speakers have difficulty pronouncing *h*, saying *ouse* for *house* (Morris, 2001). These accents are so persistent that it is generally easy to determine the nationality of speakers simply from hearing their pronunciations. People who learn a second language can spend years or even decades speaking it while being immersed in the newer culture but still maintain their very distinct accents.

Transfer can also occur either proactively or retroactively (see figure 6.8). Learning that occurs because of a result of experience in a new motor skill to another motor skill in the future is termed **proactive transfer**. **Retroactive transfer** occurs when expe-

Proactive transfer

A skill learned in the past affects a skill being
learned or to be learned in the future

Retroactive transfer

Learning a new skill affects a previously learned skill

Figure 6.8 Proactive and retroactive transfer can cause either positive, negative, or zero transfer based upon the similarities of the motor skills and the skill level of the learners. In the proactive transfer example, hand–eye coordination in the tennis swing can positively transfer to the cricket swing for a beginner in cricket. In the retroactive example, golf practice in the middle of a baseball season may then negatively or positively affect a baseball player's baseball swing. Each of these examples is striking; however, there are nuances across each that can either improve or detract from their performance in the other motor skill.

Galina Barskaya/fotolia.com; iStockphoto/stuart hannagan; Photodisc/Getty Images

rience in a new motor skill affects performance of a previously learned motor skill (Hanseeuw et al., 2012). Proactive and retroactive transfer are transfer designs. The outcome of these designs can be either positive, negative, or zero transfer depending upon whether there was improvement, decline, or no change in the motor skill assessed. A snowboarder who tries wakeboarding in the summer and returns to snowboarding the following winter may experience retroactive transfer. Snowboarding is the motor skill the athlete focuses upon, but they were open to trying a similar activity, wakeboarding, during the off-season to see if it would affect their performance on snowboarding. This snowboarder may have experienced proactive transfer to wakeboarding due to their experience in snowboarding.

Transfer Tests

Sometimes practitioners want to assess the performer's adaptability of a motor skill. The ability to adapt quickly to unpredictable changes in the environment is especially important when performing open skills. Transfer tests (a method of assessing adaptability) are very similar to retention tests; however, rather than assessing performance on the same motor skill, they assess performance on a similar skill or a variation of the same skill following the retention interval. Examples are examining performance at different positions for a soccer player, such as playing midfield, defender, or forward, or learning to throw a different pitch in baseball. Transfer tests could also examine performance in an entirely new but similar sport, such as a learner who played racquetball for several months and then was tested

RESEARCH NOTES

Does Age Affect Proactive or Retroactive Transfer?

A research group investigated the transfer effects of age on proactive and retroactive transfer examining young adults, 18 to 30 years, and middle-aged adults, 50 to 65 years (Verneau et al., 2015). A sequential manual assembly task was used because the middle-aged group were part of manual assembly work. In this industry, it is important to be able to efficiently learn specific movement patterns. The task included assembling a product that required movements to occur in a fixed sequence. The second task was to assemble a similar product in which half the movements occurred in the same sequence. The researchers predicted that age would affect ability to learn the motor patterns, such that the young adults would perform in a more efficient pattern. They anticipated that the young adults would have increased proactive facilitation and reduced retroactive interference for the sequence learning. The researchers found proactive facilitation, meaning the participants benefited from learning the first motor sequence when performing the second motor sequence. Interestingly, the middle-aged adults only benefited in the portion of the sequence that was the same for both motor sequences. Regarding retroactive transfer, the impact of learning the second movement sequence upon performing the first motor sequence, the middle-aged adults performed with reduced accuracy, indicating negative transfer, while the young adults performed with sequence-specific positive transfer. The findings of this study indicate marked age differences in retroactive transfer in comparison to proactive transfer.

on squash. Both are racket sports played inside a court with four walls and a ceiling. The main difference between the the two is the size and elasticity of the balls and rackets. Squash balls are much smaller and less bouncy than racquetballs. When switching from racquetball to squash, racquetball players are generally quite surprised to find that they must move to the ball because it is not going to bounce to them.

Practitioners often make context changes in transfer tests rather than assessing different sports or games. For instance, a regulatory condition that can vary in some activities is the surface, as in American football (grass or artificial turf) or tennis (grass, clay, acrylic, or asphalt). Other regulatory conditions remain constant from location to location, such as the size of the field or court and the height and length of the net. A transfer test could assess tennis performance on a different surface. A transfer test could also assess performance under varying nonregulatory conditions, such as changing the importance of the situation. For instance, an athlete who is preparing for a competition should be tested while she is under increased emotional stress.

It is useful to assess performance with varying regulatory and nonregulatory conditions. This enables the practitioner to assess not only the adaptability of the learner, but also the stability of the performance. A learner should not be limited to performing skillfully during controlled conditions but should be able to adapt to changing situations and environmental conditions. This is important not only in physical education classes and sport but also in rehabilitation settings. The role of rehabilitation is to prepare patients to function outside of the rehabilitation clinic.

WHAT DO YOU THINK?

Exercise 6.4

1. Name two motor skills that you expect to produce positive transfer. Explain why you would expect experience in one of these skills to benefit the other skill.

2. Describe a drill or exercise that you expect to positively transfer to a competitive event or real-world context such as in a therapeutic situation. Again, explain why you expect the drill to benefit performance in that skill.

3. Describe a context or strategy that you expect to transfer from one sport to another. Explain how these strategies are similar and how they may differ in different sports. What aspects of these strategies do you expect to transfer?

RESEARCH NOTES

Transfer of Throwing Positions

Mount (1996) investigated the effect of transfer between throwing while sitting versus throwing while reclining. The task was to throw a dart to a target with a fixed elbow in an extended position. The prediction was that participants who practiced throwing the dart in one position would perform the skill in the same position better than those who practiced in a different position.

Forty right-handed female participants aged 20 to 34 participated in the study. The two conditions were sitting on a kneeling chair and reclining on a table at a 45-degree angle. Participants were randomly separated into four groups: Control group 1 used the chair during both the practice and transfer sessions; control group 2 used the table during both sessions; experimental group 1 practiced with the chair and tested with the table; and experimental group 2 practiced with the table and tested with the chair. Participants practiced four sets of five throws. Following the practice session, participants were given a five-minute break before completing four sets of five throws for the test.

Negative transfer occurred between the two positional conditions even though the task was the same. Mount's interpretation was that this negative transfer occurred because of a strong linkage between the first position learned and the movement of the arm. When the participants then switched positions, they had to adjust to the new body position. These results indicate the importance of taking body position into consideration prior to practicing a motor skill to avoid bad habits resulting in prolonged learning periods and poorer performances.

Rehabilitation specialists design movement activities with the expectation that they will help the person produce functional movement patterns. For example, when treating stroke patients with hemiplegia (paralysis on one half of the body), specialists should have the patients practice moving the paralyzed leg with many repetitions and a focus on task-relevant movements that include problem solving (Forrester et al., 2008). The movements should be generalizable to real-world environments by making them long lasting and meaningful regarding gait function.

Movements practiced diagonally are very beneficial for moving in everyday life and in sport (Voss et al., 1985). This is because diagonal movements are commonly produced to avoid obstacles. Although diagonal limb patterns may be beneficial, they are not used often in rehabilitation because it is simply more convenient for specialists to manipulate the limbs in a supine or sitting position (Mount, 1996). It is always important when designing an activity either for a sporting drill or for rehabilitation to focus on the similarities between the tasks. Tasks must be very similar to produce positive transfer.

Theories of Transfer

The **identical elements theory** asserts that the amount and direction of transfer depend on the number of identical elements between two motor skills (Thorndike, 1914). It would be expected, then, that transfer would occur if two motor skills involved similar equipment and movements, such as the example at the beginning of this chapter of the rower practicing on the erg before rowing on the water. Movements in board sports, such as snowboarding, wakeboarding, surfing, and skateboarding would be expected to transfer, whereas sports and games with similar strategies but very different movement patterns, such as American football and ultimate (flying disc), would be expected to have no transfer. Ultimate and American football are both outdoor sports played on a rectangular field with two end zones. The object is to keep passing the ball or disc until it gets into the end zone. In both sports, play begins with two teams lined up opposite each other. One main difference between the two sports is that in ultimate, the players may not run.

Although the movement patterns necessary to throw and catch a flying disc versus a football are very different, there are many similarities in the strategies and conceptual aspects of the two sports. According to the **transfer-appropriate processing theory**, movements or games that require similar cognitive processing can positively transfer (Bransford et al., 1979). Activities that require learners to engage in similar problem-solving strategies promote positive transfer. For instance, the strategy of faking an opponent is employed in many sports, such as basketball, hockey, and American football. A skilled basketball player will be much better at reading an opponent's intentions even in a different sport, such as hockey, than someone who has not had experiences with opponents, such as a gymnast or diver.

One common method of implementing transfer into instruction is to simplify the task using progressions; the expectation is that the simpler version will transfer to the more complex motor skill. For instance, preschoolers often first learn how to bat by using a tee. This allows them to learn the fundamental movement pattern without the temporal component of making contact with a moving ball, changing the motor skill from externally paced to self-paced. The spatial component of the motor skill is also less challenging because the ball is stationary, which changes the initiation of the skill to self-paced. Learners may then progress to batting a ball that is hung from a string, then a balloon or a large, light ball that is pitched, and finally a regular ball. It is expected that positive transfer occurs during each transition, enabling the child to learn how to bat quickly and safely. Skill progressions are often used for complex skills or activities that carry a risk of injury.

GAMES CLASSIFICATION FOR PROMOTING TRANSFER

Given the vast number of sporting activities, classification schemes are necessary to generalize similarities across games, thus increasing opportunities for positive transfer across games from the same classification. Physical educators do not have enough time to adequately teach all games, and they cannot offer an extensive variety of games. Also, students do not have enough time to become skillful in all activities. By classifying games, teachers can introduce one game from the classification group and then build on the students' understanding by adding a second game from the same classification. They can then compare the two games while also improving proficiency on similar skills (Werner & Almond, 1990).

A **game** is "any form of playful competition whose outcome is determined by physical skill, strategy or chance employed singly or in a combination" (Loy, 1968, p. 1). It is important to note from this definition that games arise out of play, are competitive, and require physical skill, strategy, or chance (Siedentop, 2012). Each game has its own defining set of rules and strategies. The rules that characterize the play of the game and how the game is won are the **primary rules** (Almond, 1986). Games can be modified to be developmentally appropriate. Rules that can be modified without changing the nature of the game are termed **secondary rules**. For example, National Basketball Association (NBA) regulations have extended the 3-point shot from 19 feet 9 inches (6 m) to 23 feet 6 inches (7.2 m). Changing this regulation has not changed the play of the game. However, it has made it more challenging for professional basketball players to score a 3-point basket. Other secondary rules in basketball include the size of the ball (women vs. men), the 3-second zone rule, and the 10-second half-court rule.

Classifying games became popular in the 1970s and 1980s, providing instructors with a framework for a more balanced curriculum based on the tactics of the games (Hopper & Bell, 1999). A problem-solving theme that used six criteria was employed: (a) the purpose of the game, (b) the initiation of the game, (c) the conclusion of the game, (d) game play rules, (e) skill requirements, and (f) game scoring (see table 6.2). In this section, we discuss games using Thorpe, Bunker, and Almond's (1986) games classification system. The five game categories are (a) target games, in which the goal is accuracy (e.g., golf and archery); (b) fielding and run-scoring games with the essential skills of throwing, striking, and receiving the ball (e.g., cricket and baseball); (c) net or wall games with the essential skills of striking and controlling the placement of the ball (e.g., tennis and volleyball); (d) invasion games, which require sending away, retrieving, and retaining the ball (e.g., basketball and American football); and (e) personal performance games, which are self-contests (e.g., track and field and gymnastics) (see table 6.3).

WHAT DO YOU THINK?

Exercise 6.5

1. Provide some examples of games in which you have modified the secondary rules. What did you modify and why?

2. Choose a game and discuss how you could modify secondary rules for one of the following:

    a. An older adult with some shoulder and wrist arthritis

    b. A child with a sensory impairment (such as a visual or hearing impairment)

    c. An elite athlete

Table 6.2 Classification Scheme for Game Categories

	Purpose	Start of game	End of game	Rules	Skills	Scoring
Target	Be the individual or team able to perform more accurately than the opponent.	One player or team initiates; then play occurs alternately from one side to the other.	All performers have had an equal number of attempts.	Regulate where and how the object is propelled and what defines accuracy.	Accuracy and control of the object.	Determined by a measure of accuracy.
Fielding	The batting team's aim is to score runs; the fielding team tries to get the batter out.	Opening pitch.	Each team has had a certain number of opportunities to score runs.	Include boundary restrictions on ball trajectory, batting, and pitching.	Temporal and spatial; fielding, catching, and throwing.	Number of runs.
Net or wall	Keep the ball in play and outsmart the opponent by positioning the ball such that it cannot be returned.	One player serves the ball either across a net or at a wall.	A certain score has been reached by one team.	Include contact with the net and boundary and serving violations.	Accuracy and control of the ball.	Points are scored when one team prevents opponents from returning the serve or hits. In some sports, only the serving team can score.
Invasion	Invade the opposing team's territory and score points.	Players on their own half of the field; play begins with players moving to the opponent's side.	A set amount of time has elapsed.	Include restrictions on body contact and ball handling.	Offensive skills and defensive skills.	Points scored by invading the other team's territory and scoring (shots, goals, touchdowns).
Personal performance	Often a self-contest in which the performer competes alone, striving for peak performance.	Initiated by the performer or by an external stimulus (e.g., starter's gun).	All performers have completed the activity.	Regulate the movement type and equipment used.	Specific skills for each activity, which requires specific equipment.	Each performance is ranked after the performer completes the activity.

Adapted from Werner and Almond (1990).

Invasion Games

In **invasion games**, players are divided into two opposing teams separated by sides on the playing field. During the game, the teams invade each other's territory. Invasion games can be subdivided into games that have a focused target, such as basketball and soccer, and games in which a line must be crossed to score (open end target), such as rugby and ultimate (Thorpe et al., 1986). The offensive goal of invasion games is to maintain possession of the ball and score, whereas the defensive objective is to obtain possession of the ball and defend the goal area to stop the other team from scoring. Taking the ball from the opponent serves two purposes: preventing the opponent from scoring and taking possession of the ball,

thus giving the team a chance to score. Play is broken down into timed segments. Invasion games are won by the team with the higher score at the conclusion of a set time. The final score indicates the team that was more successful at invading the opposing team's territory and scoring. These games have similar tactical problems; however, they differ in the task constraints imposed, including rules, equipment, and goals, as well as environmental regulations (e.g., terrain, weather, and indoor vs. outdoor play).

Net or Wall Games

Net or wall games are games in which the object of play is to serve or return the ball strategically so that the opponent is unable to sustain the play of the ball. These games

Table 6.3 Sports for Each Games Classification System Category and Type

Category	Type and examples
Invasion	Focused target • Basketball • Lacrosse • Ice hockey • Field hockey • Soccer • Water polo
	Open end target • Ultimate • American football • Rugby • Speedball
Net or wall	Divided court (net) • Volleyball • Tennis • Badminton • Table tennis
	Shared court (wall) • Racquetball • Handball • Squash
Target	Opposed • Croquet • Horseshoes • Shuffleboard
	Indirectly opposed • Archery • Bowling • Golf • Billiards
Fielding	Striking • Baseball • Cricket • Rounders • Softball
	Kicking • Kickball
Personal performance	Racing • Cycling • Track and field • Swimming
	Combative • Wrestling • Judo • Boxing
	Subjective performance • Gymnastics • Diving • X sports

separate opposing players by a net; or they may use a wall, and players alternate hitting. Players gain points each time they prevent their opponent from returning the ball (in some sports only the serving side can score). The contest ends when a certain number of points have been achieved by one player or team. One key component in skill proficiency in net or wall games is accuracy. The player must manipulate the speed and angle of the hit to control the ball position and the pace of the game. The ball must land within designated lines. Tactical understanding in net or wall games is to outsmart the opponent by placing shots where they cannot be returned, and the rules are geared toward boundary restrictions and serving. Most net or wall games use an implement to strike the ball (e.g., table tennis, badminton, and racquetball); however, some require use of the hand (e.g., volleyball and handball).

Target Games

Target games include activities during which performers compete without direct body contact or physical confrontation. The main goal of target games is accuracy. During target games, competitors wait until the activity has been completed by other performers before beginning their attempts (e.g., golf, archery, billiards). The focus of target games is self-testing. The winner is generally the performer with the highest score (except in golf).

Fielding Games

Fielding games are team games in which the contest begins with one team occupying positions throughout the field (the fielders) or with one player who throws the ball (pitcher) toward a player on the opposing team. Examples of fielding sports are softball, baseball, rounders, cricket, and kickball. All fielding games use a striking implement except for kickball. Players score points for their team by running counterclockwise around bases when batting or kicking. The offensive team strikes the ball into the defensive team's territory. The defensive team fields, throws, and catches the ball to prevent the offensive team from scoring runs. Generally, fielding games have no time restrictions. Instead, each team has a set number of opportunities to bat or kick and score runs. The team with the most runs wins the contest.

Personal Performance Games

There are many games in which participants attempt to outperform their opponents, exceed their personal best performance measures, or both. **Personal performance games** include racing activities such as cycling, running, and swimming; combative activities such as wrestling, judo, and boxing; and games with subjective performance measures such as diving and gymnastics. In recent decades many new performance games that are often referred to as X games (e.g., snowboarding and BMX biking) because of their extreme nature have emerged. Each requires different skills and equipment, in addition to much intrinsic motivation and drive, because the games challenge participants to compete not only against competitors but also against their own records.

Teaching Games for Transfer

When teaching games, the instructor should emphasize movement concepts, principles, and strategies that will transfer from one game to another in the same classification. Movement concepts are cognitive ideas, such as a particular pattern of movement (Rink, 1998). The concept of the pattern used in throwing a ball overhand would be expected to transfer to some extent to throwing other implements (e.g., a javelin) or to performing an overhand serve. When teaching a movement concept, the instructor should focus on key action words that can transfer from one situation to another.

When teaching learners how to strike, an instructor can provide many opportunities for striking an object, as well as focus on where to apply the force on the object and how this affects the trajectory. Learners should be able to apply the information learned from one experience (e.g., striking a ball with a bat) to another (e.g., striking a ball with a racket).

Movement skills can also transfer from one game to another in the same games classification. Movement tactics include stealing the ball in defensive play in invasion games and controlling the ball in net or wall games. Movement strategies—defined as how movement is used in cooperative and competitive relationships with others (Rink, 1998)—such as offensively faking defensive players to gain an advantage are similar in basketball and hockey. Zone defensives are similar for many invasion games as well. Movement concepts, tactics, and strategies transfer best when they are clearly explained, and learners are given a wide array of opportunities to apply them.

PROMOTING POSITIVE TRANSFER FOR ANY MOTOR SKILL

The first step in promoting positive transfer is to analyze the transfer task. A good practitioner analyzes skills when designing drills and activities. Positive transfer depends on the similarities between the two tasks. These similarities can be either in the fundamental movement pattern, as proposed by the identical elements theory, or in the strategies and concepts of the tasks, as asserted by the transfer-appropriate processing theory. Skills that involve striking have similar fundamental movement patterns. Someone who has experience with cricket will have an advantage in playing softball or baseball. Both skills have similar temporal and spatial elements. The bat must contact the ball at a specific time and position.

The strategic and conceptual components of the skills can also provide positive transfer. For instance, the fundamental movement patterns in kickball and baseball are very different and even require the use of different limbs. However, the strategies of the games are similar. In both, one team has possession of the ball (the fielding team) while the other team (the batting or kicking team) attempts to hit or kick it. Each side has a role that does not change until one team has acquired a certain number of outs. As noted earlier, games are classified according to similar strategies and concepts, so positive transfer would be expected for those who play multiple games in the same classification.

Knowing how to analyze motor skills effectively not only is important in designing practices but also can assist in maximizing positive transfer based on the learners' past experiences. Learners understand new skills more quickly when comparisons are made with skills they are familiar with. For instance, baseball and cricket have a similar defensive component that occurs in parallel with the offensive component of scoring runs. In baseball, the batter defends the strike zone, whereas in cricket, the batsman defends the wicket. Highlighting the differences can be just as beneficial to learners as pointing out the similarities. Some of the many differences between cricket and baseball include the terminology for similar positions, such as bowler versus pitcher, wicketkeeper versus catcher, and batsman versus batter. Another big difference between cricket and baseball is the batting stance. In cricket, the handle of the bat is held vertically with the end of the bat toward the ground; in baseball, the bat is held upward and cocked behind the head.

Comparing two motor skills or pointing out analogies between them can be helpful to learners. For example, when teaching how to swing a bat, an instructor can compare the lead arm position to that in throwing a disc. The back arm moves right through the movement with the elbow in, like the action of skipping a rock across a pond. The instructor must be sure that the learner has experience with the skill being compared to the new skill; if not, the comparison could be ineffective or even confuse the learner further.

Another factor that should be considered in promoting positive transfer is the learner's skill level. Novices gain more benefit from transfer than those at higher skill levels. For example, someone learning to play racquetball will gain more advantages from previous tennis experience than an experienced tennis player would from playing racquetball in the off-season. Learners in the associative or the autonomous stage benefit much less because they can produce the fundamental movement pattern and are now focusing on much more specific movements involved in the given motor skill. In these cases, some negative transfer may occur for higher level players if the previous movement experiences alter some of their techniques.

Before incorporating progressions or drills into a practice design, practitioners should examine the cost–benefit trade-off. This requires assessing how much practice is necessary to obtain positive transfer. The amount of practice that the transfer group required to gain the initial advantage should also be taken into consideration. If more practice was required for the transfer task than for the primary task alone, then the cost would outweigh the benefit.

SUMMARY

This chapter discussed how to measure and assess motor learning. The indicators of motor learning include consistency of performance, permanence of movement production, decreased effort, reduced attentional demands, and increased adaptability. Learners who have acquired the capability to perform a motor skill can consistently perform at a higher level. Their performance is also sustainable and permanent over long periods of time. Skilled learners can also perform the motor skill with less cognitive and physical effort than they could when they were initially learning the motor skill. They also need to devote less attention to the movement production, allowing them to focus on strategies rather than on producing the coordination pattern. Finally, improved performance can be measured by the adaptability of the learner, meaning that learners can perform similar and related motor skills at a higher level due to their experience with another task.

The true test of motor learning is sustained performance following a period away from regular practice, also known as a retention interval. Motor learning is a permanent change in the ability to produce a skilled movement, so if learners lose their ability to produce a particular movement pattern following the passage of time, the motor skill has not been learned. In this case, only performance (temporary) changes have occurred.

The chapter also discussed transfer of learning. Understanding transfer, includ-ing the types of transfer, how to measure transfer, and how to foster positive transfer, is of critical importance to practitioners in school, athletic, and rehabilitation settings. Educators in school settings must design activities that promote both the transfer and the retention of fundamental movement skills and sport-specific skills. Coaches must focus on drills that will positively transfer to the sport, preparing the athletes for competitive situations. Structuring the environment and the task so that they are as realistic as possible is critical for promoting transfer from the rehabilitation setting to patients' homes. The key points to take away about transfer are as follows:

- Transfer is generally small and positive.
- Transfer depends on the number of similarities between the two motor skills.
- Negative transfer is generally temporary.
- Previous movement experiences often provide some transfer.
- Most positive transfer effects are found in early acquisition.

> **ONLINE ACTIVITIES**

The student material found in HK*Propel* includes exercises, labs, and videos to enhance learning and encourage practical application of important concepts.

LEARNING AIDS

Supplemental Activities

1. Choose a motor skill that requires you to produce a movement pattern that you have not produced before (e.g., juggling, unicycling, speed stacking, standing on an exercise ball, playing footbag, or doing a handstand).

    a. Practice the skill every day for 10 days for a set time (e.g., five minutes per day). Record your performances every day.

    b. Following 10 days of practice, wait for a week (one-week retention interval) and then perform a retention test. Record your performance on the retention test. This score is your absolute retention score.

    c. Develop a performance curve exhibiting your performance changes across the 10-day practice sessions.

	Invasion	Net or wall	Target	Fielding	Personal performance
Number of games					
Percentage					

From P.S. Beach, M.E. Perreault, A.S. Brian, and D.H. Collier, *Motor Learning and Development*, 3rd ed. (Champaign, IL: Human Kinetics, 2024).

    d. Label the type of performance curve your scores represent.

    e. Calculate your retention scores, including the difference score, the percentage score, and the retention savings score.

    f. From the results of this exercise, did you *learn* the motor skill?

2. Using the following chart, list all of the games you have participated in for each of the classifications.

    a. Count the number of games you have participated in under each classification and write the number in the Number of games row. Divide these numbers by the total number of games in all columns and multiply by 100 to obtain percentages. Write these percentages in the percentage row.

    b. Do you participate in one classification of games more than the others? If yes, what interests you about these games?

    c. Which categories have you avoided to some extent? Why do you think you have avoided activities in these categories?

Glossary

absolute retention—The learner's performance immediately following the retention interval.

adaptability—The ability to make movement adjustments to fit the changing demands of the task and environmental conditions.

automaticity—The ability to perform a skill with essentially no conscious attention devoted to the production of the movement pattern.

difference score—A measure of relative retention calculated by subtracting the absolute retention score from the last score during the acquisition phase (original learning).

fielding games—Team games in which the contest begins with one team occupying positions throughout the field (the fielders), with one player who throws the ball (pitcher) toward a player on the opposing team.

game—Any form of playful competition whose outcome is determined by physical skill, strategy, or chance, employed singly or in combination.

identical elements theory—A theory on transfer that asserts that the amount and direction of transfer depend on the number of identical elements between two motor skills.

invasion games—Games in which players are divided into two opposing teams separated by sides on the playing field.

linear curve—A performance curve that indicates a direct relationship between the performance measure and time.

negatively accelerating curve—A performance curve that illustrates a very rapid initial rate of improvement followed by a gradual reduction in the rate of improvement.

negative transfer—Interference of previous experience on the performance of another motor skill.

net or wall games—Games in which the object of play is to serve or return the ball strategically so that the opponent is unable to sustain the play of the ball.

percentage score—A measure of relative retention calculated by dividing the difference score by the change in the original learning and then multiplying by 100 percent. This score is interpreted as the percentage of performance that was lost or gained following the retention interval.

performance improvement—An increase in the overall performance outcome.

personal performance games—Games in which individuals attempt to outperform their opponents, their personal best performance measures, or both.

positively accelerating curve—A performance curve that illustrates only small gains initially but an increasing rate of improvement with every practice session.

positive transfer—Enhanced learning of a motor skill because of the performance of another motor skill.

posttest—A test conducted at the end of the practice sessions.

power law of practice—A mathematical law describing a negatively accelerating rate of performance improvement.

pretest—A test conducted prior to the practice sessions.

primary rules—The rules that characterize the play of the game and how the game is won.

proactive transfer—Learning that occurs because of experience in a new motor skill to another motor skill in the future.

retention interval—The amount of time between the last practice session or posttest and the retention test.

retention savings score—A measurement of the amount of time required to return to a given level of performance compared to the time required to reach this level during the original practice sessions.

retention test—A performance test given following a break from practice.

retroactive transfer—Learning that occurs when experience in a new motor skill affects performance of a previously learned motor skill.

secondary rules—Rules that can be modified without changing the nature of the game.

S-shaped curve—A performance curve indicating that initial learning occurred at a positively accelerating rate for a set time and then continued to increase at a negatively accelerating rate.

target games—Games in which performers compete without direct body contact or physical confrontation.

transfer-appropriate processing theory—A theory on transfer asserting that movements or games requiring similar cognitive processing can positively transfer.

transfer of learning—The effect of a previous movement experience on performance in another task.

transfer tests—Tests that measure the adaptability between the practiced motor skill and a different, but related, motor skill or performance situation.

warm-up decrement—A reduction in performance because of a period of inactivity.

zero transfer—The lack of effect of a previous movement experience on performance in another task.

PART II

Life Span Physical Activity and Movement

This part presents an overview of physical activity and movement changes across the life span. Part I addressed some of the basic principles, terminology, and theoretical approaches in motor behavior; this part expands on this knowledge with a focus on growth and development. The discussion begins in chapter 7, which examines the reflexive behavior and spontaneous movements present during infancy. In the first year, the infant advances through a series of motor milestones from holding the head up to sitting up to creeping and eventually walking, to name a few. Because the way and the time infants progress through these motor milestones vary greatly, this chapter addresses both typical and atypical development. Chapter 8 offers an extensive discussion of the importance of fundamental movement skills that appear and are refined between the ages of two and six. The emphasis is on fundamental motor skills because they are essential to the healthy development of children in all domains. Practitioners need a solid understanding of how and when these fundamentals are achieved. Chapter 8 continues with a focus upon locomotor and stability skills, and chapter 9 continues this review with object control skills.

The developmental discussion then moves to the movement and physical activity of adults in chapter 10, from young to older adulthood. Also addressed are factors that affect adults' participation in physical activity. The exercise–aging cycle illustrates the detrimental effects of a sedentary lifestyle. Olympic and masters athletes' performances offer a window into how peak performance declines with advancing age, because performance changes in this demographic are less likely to be affected by chronic disease or long periods of physical inactivity and disuse. The chapter concludes with a summary of movement patterns in older adulthood, including locomotor patterns, fundamental movement patterns, and movements during functional activities. The final chapter (chapter 11) in part II discusses gross motor assessment, in which the importance of assessment and assessment considerations for individuals across the life span are discussed.

7

INFANT MOTOR DEVELOPMENT

CHAPTER OBJECTIVES

After reading this chapter, you should be able to do the following:

- Define the terms *neural plasticity* and *teratogens*.
- Identify healthy behaviors in pregnancy.
- Understand prenatal development and the factors that positively and negatively affect it.
- Explain the factors that interfere with early movements.
- Understand the important interactions of motor development, cognitive development, and affective development.
- Identify developmental disorders in infants.
- Appreciate how researchers and clinicians assess infant motor development.

Stunning Transformations!

When Luca was a newborn, his parents were tremendously excited—but more than a little nervous and apprehensive. Luca was so tiny and seemed to have trouble not only seeing things but also maintaining any control over his body at all. However, over his first year of life, Luca underwent a stunning transformation. He changed from being a dependent infant who struggled to maintain his balance (much less move around his environment) to a child who could locate a partially hidden toy in the corner of the room, trot right over (while avoiding the dog and dealing with the slippery floor), and smoothly and confidently grasp the item—and then put it in his pocket! How and at what point, and to what degree, these impressive perceptual and motor skills emerge during infancy is the focus of this chapter.

How developing infants move from a limited repertoire of motor behaviors to efficiently solving a vast number of movement tasks is becoming increasingly clear. This knowledge base is available to both scientists and practitioners as research tools (including, but not limited to, the ability to look deeply into the developing brain with precise imaging tools) become more and more advanced.

The development of motor skills in infancy has been answered historically from the vantage point of the maturation of the central nervous system (Gesell, 1946; McGraw, 1943; Shirley, 1931). Using a longitudinal approach (that is, observing an individual or group of individuals on multiple occasions over an extended period), these investigators were able to precisely catalog the appearance of phylogenetic movement skills common in developing children. Phylogenetic movement skills are those common to our species and, generally, are performed all over the world by people from all different cultures. Examples include walking, jumping, reaching, and grasping. These researchers assumed that the emerging skill set of the developing infant is tightly controlled by central nervous system maturation. Although this neuromaturational perspective of motor development continues to influence both scientific inquiry and clinical intervention, the theoretical approach referred to in this text as the dynamic systems approach (refer to chapter 2) moves away from the unicausal (the central nervous system) perspective of the neuromaturationists in explaining development. Instead of considering the brain—as interesting and important as it is—as the controller of development, proponents of this new approach believe that new and increasingly complex forms come from multiple developing subsystems that act within a specific physical and social context (Thelen, 1992). Thus, the quality of the emotional and physical environment is of great importance to optimizing development—motoric and otherwise.

Robust and varied early movement experiences in rich environments are crucial for healthy physical, cognitive, and affective development. Strongly related to the need for appropriate movement experiences is the important concept of **neural plasticity** (Sporns & Edelman, 1993), which posits that long-lasting, functional changes in the brain (primarily the neuronal pathways) are largely due to experience. Although this plasticity is present throughout the life span, it is particularly evident during infancy. This adaptive neural substrate change is based on not only novel, sustained experience, but also on individual adaptation (e.g., disease, trauma, injury).

These research-based observations regarding neuroplasticity point to the need for rich early movement experiences for all infants—including those who are typically developing and, maybe more importantly, those with identifiable disabilities. Unfortunately, vast inequities in many societies put infants at great risk. These risks are both intrinsic (such as having Down syndrome) and extrinsic (such as being exposed to cocaine prenatally or to lead-based paint as a toddler). Nutritional, movement-related, and linguistic inequities also abound. This chapter examines in some depth both the *why* and the *when* of infant development, for children without disabilities and those who are at risk of having a developmental disability.

PRENATAL DEVELOPMENT

At birth, an infant has already grown and developed at an astounding rate in a very short period. Although prenatal growth and development may be taken for granted, it is important to understand the many changes that occur and how this period of growth provides critical building blocks for normal development after birth. Prenatal age, often referred to as **gestational age**, begins the first day after the mother's last menstrual period. It may be confusing that conceptive age is only 38 weeks because the gestational age begins two weeks prior to conception. Due dates are typically estimated as 40 weeks after the gestational age begins.

Prenatal development begins with the fertilization of the female egg (ovum) by the male sperm (spermatozoon). At this point, the 23 chromosomes from the father combine with the 23 chromosomes from the mother to form a new cell with 46 chromosomes. The first prenatal period is referred to as the **germinal period**, which lasts approximately two weeks. During this period, the fertilized ovum (zygote) migrates along the fallopian tube into the uterus, which it reaches in three to four days. Throughout this migration, the number of cells increases rapidly. By 9 to 12 days from fertilization, the mass of cells (blastocyst) embeds itself into the endometrium in the wall of the uterus.

The second stage, known as the **embryonic period**, lasts for approximately six weeks. During this very critical period, cells that make up organs are defined through a process known as **organogenesis**. At around week 3, the central nervous system is one of the first systems to develop, with the heart following shortly after. Movement begins after the heart starts beating at a conceptive age of about four weeks. Other organs that develop during the embryonic stage include the limbs, eyes, ears, and palate. Around the end of the embryonic period, the embryo exhibits **myogenic movements**, which are not generated by the central nervous system or external stimulation.

The final stage of prenatal development is the **fetal period**, which begins at the completion of organ differentiation around week 8 and lasts until birth. During this period, the fetus continues to grow rapidly, and **neurogenic movements** appear at approximately 20 weeks postconception. Neurogenic movements are generated by the central nervous system. Exposure to environmental factors such as teratogens (discussed next) is less critical during the fetal stage because most of the major organs have differentiated and as such are not as susceptible to functional defects and minor congenital anomalies.

Teratogens

Prenatal development is a precarious period during which the fetus is influenced by both extrinsic and intrinsic factors experienced by the mother. The mother's nutrients, or lack thereof, physical activities, and the external environment (e.g., pollutants) all influence the growing fetus. At critical time periods of embryonic and fetal development, exposure to a **teratogen** (any agent that can cause defects or deformities) can be particularly harmful. Development is most vulnerable during the embryonic period; exposure to teratogens at this time can be harmful to the developing organs. Before examining specific teratogens, we want to clarify the difference between genetic abnormalities and environmental causes of congenital disorders. Genetic abnormalities are not the result of the environment; rather, they often result from chromosomal abnormalities, such as phenylketonuria, the product of an abnormal recessive autosomal gene (Piek, 2006).

A pregnant woman should avoid many environmental substances and events to limit any harmful exposure to her child. The obvious harmful substances are illegal drugs and cigarettes, but prescription medications should not be overlooked. A pregnant mom should discuss with her doctor both the risks of medications to her fetus and the risks to her of stopping any medication during the pregnancy. At times the risks to the mother from stopping a medication are greater than the risks to the fetus. Certain antidepressants increase the risk of developing heart defects, especially when taken during the first trimester. Antiepileptics increase the risk of neural tube defects, and antibiotics increase the risk of developing heart abnormalities (Lynch & Abel, 2015). In addition, pregestational diabetes (diabetes that develops in the mother prior to pregnancy) is linked to congenital heart disease when birth occurs during the mother's poor glycemic control (Jenkins et al., 2007).

Cigarette smoking during pregnancy can cause intrauterine growth restriction, preterm birth (Robinson et al., 2000), and health problems in childhood including short stature and obesity. This prevalence increases with the number of cigarettes smoked daily (Koshy et al., 2010). In addition to cigarette smoking, oxygen deprivation or exposure to other harmful events can cause embryonic or fetal damage, which is related to preterm birth.

Experts widely accept that alcohol is a teratogen that can cause fetal alcohol syndrome. Fetal alcohol syndrome is considered the leading preventable cause of birth defects and intellectual disability. Teratogenic harm from fetal exposure to alcohol during pregnancy may be found as soon as at birth and may lead to mental impairment throughout life (Addila, 2021). Although alcohol ingested during pregnancy is considered a teratogen, there is considerable confusion about the amount that is acceptable. The fetus does not process alcohol in the same manner as the pregnant mother, such that the alcohol is more concentrated in the fetus, preventing vital passage of nutrition and oxygen to the fetal organs (Hox et al., 2010). The effects of alcohol upon the fetus can cause a range of birth defects termed fetal alcohol spectrum disorder (Rothwell et al., 2010). As a result, many researchers suggest that the only safe amount of alcohol during pregnancy is no alcohol (Tracy, 2013).

Infectious maternal diseases, such as rubella, syphilis, HIV, and AIDS can cause anything from minor congenital abnormalities to spontaneous abortions (Piek, 2006). Risks of complications are increased for coronaviruses such as severe acute respiratory syndrome and Middle Eastern respiratory syndrome (Di Mascio et al., 2020); however, at the time of the publication of this edition, there are still many unknowns for risks for pregnancies with coronavirus disease 2019 (COVID-19; Wastnedge et al., 2021). At this time, the risks may be higher for severe COVID-19 in pregnant women than in the general population.

Healthy Pregnancy

A pregnant woman must make many positive behavioral choices because her behavior affects not only her body, but also, even more directly, the growing fetus inside her. Poor choices may have a profound effect on the areas currently developing in the fetus. In addition to avoiding teratogens, pregnant women must also eat well, including taking vitamins A, B_3, B_6, C, D, and folic acid, and maintain a physically active lifestyle throughout pregnancy.

To have a healthy pregnancy, a woman should have a healthy prepregnancy weight and gain weight appropriately throughout the pregnancy. Energy needs for a pregnant woman should be the same as her prepregnancy needs during the first trimester and should increase by 340 kcal and 452 kcal during the second and third trimesters, respectively. There are numerous benefits of physical activity during pregnancy, including reduced weight gain and instances of gestational diabetes, preeclampsia, preterm births, and low infant birth weights (ACOG Committee, 2020; Lee et al., 2020; Mottola et al., 2018). Although there are many benefits to exercising during pregnancy, many pregnant women either decrease their exercise levels or stop exercising (Nascimento et al., 2015). According to a systematic review on professional exercise recommendations, as many as half of pregnant women are not receiving any exercise guidelines during their prenatal care and about 15 percent are told to stop (Rudin et al., 2021). Physical activity should include either 150 minutes of moderate-intensity aerobic activity throughout the week or 30 minutes of moderate-intensity exercise most days of the week (Kaiser & Campbell, 2014). Physical activities should include a variety of aerobic (e.g., walking, biking, or swimming), resistance (light weights or body-weight exercises), flexibility (stretching), and neuro-motor (yoga) exercises throughout the week (Rudin et al., 2021).

SENSORY CAPABILITIES

The sensory capabilities of newborns have been widely studied; researchers have examined both the limitations and capabilities exhibited in this early period. The development of sensory capabilities during infancy greatly affects the child's movements and motor development. This section provides a brief description of vision, hearing, and proprioception from birth throughout infancy.

Vision

Although the visual system holds 70 percent of all sensory receptors, vision is the last sense to develop in infancy (Mercer, 1998). Structurally, the eye is completely intact at birth; however, all visual structures change following birth. The eye of a newborn is not smaller in overall size than the eye of

---

WHAT DO YOU THINK?

Exercise 7.1

Devise a list of teratogens, including some from the chapter and others not mentioned in the chapter. For each one, identify the potential effects on the fetus. Alcohol is provided as an example.

Teratogen	Effects
Alcohol	Birth defects, intellectual disabilities

Devise a list of healthy behaviors for pregnant women. Do a web search to find some not mentioned in the chapter. An example has been provided.

Healthy behavior	Benefits
400 mcg of folic acid daily	Helps to prevent birth defects of the brain and spinal cord

an adult, but the depth is shorter and the distance between the retina and the lens is less, causing farsightedness (difficulty seeing close objects). There is a rapid eyeball growth curve prenatally as well as during the first 18 months postnatally (Bremond-Gignac et al., 1994). Overall, eyeball growth rate decreases with age (Wong et al., 2010). The structure of the retina also changes rapidly over the first year. Retinas in newborns are thicker and the foveae are not well formed, making it difficult for them to see images clearly (Gabbard, 2021). Infants also have difficulty focusing on objects (they have astigmatisms) because of their weaker ciliary muscles.

Newborns have basic visual function shortly after birth and the visual capacity improves dramatically throughout the first year. At birth, infants can perceive color, and newborns as young as two days old can distinguish form (Frantz, 1963). Before this research, many believed that newborns several weeks or even months old did not have pattern vision. Infants can perceive depth around two to three months of age, but depth perception continues to improve throughout early childhood. Visual acuity slowly develops and improves across infancy and childhood beginning at around 20/400 at birth (Courage & Adams 1990). This means that a newborn sees at 20 feet (6 m) approximately what someone with 20/20 vision can see at 400 feet (122 m). Visual acuity continues to improve throughout childhood with adultlike levels typically being reached by ages 8 to 10 years (Drover et al., 2018).

Hearing

Infants have acute hearing, which begins prior to birth (Piek, 2006). By birth, most of the ear structures are developed (Timiras, 1972), except for the drum membrane, the ear canal, and the Eustachian tube. Infants can hear prior to and following birth and often turn their heads in the direction of sound. Infants under four months of age can differentiate both nonspeech sounds (Vouloumanos & Werker, 2004) and speech sounds (Eimas, 1975). By six months postnatally, infants can differentiate their native language from nonnative languages (Kuhl et al., 1992) and become increasingly interested in listening to their native language while they are beginning to understand that the sounds are associated with meaning.

Speech development is highly dependent upon sensory information. Children without disabilities mostly rely upon auditory information but also use visual information secondarily. Infants with hearing impairments must rely upon visual information for developing speech. Prior to birth, term fetuses already exhibit a preference for their

RESEARCH NOTES

What Can Infants Really See?

Examining vision capability in infants can be tricky. Clearly, they cannot respond verbally or explain what they can see. Thus, vision is often assessed by acclimating infants to visual scenes. The assumption is that spending more time gazing at one scene than at another indicates that they find it novel or interesting. Once infants have habituated to something, they will not gaze at it for very long. For example, to assess pattern vision, infants' length of gaze was examined for black and white patterns in comparison to plain colored surfaces. Infants two days old or older spend approximately twice as much time gazing at the patterns than at the plain surfaces (Frantz, 1963).

mother's voice in comparison to a female stranger (Kisilevsky et al., 2003). Newborns are already attuned to their native language such that they can distinguish between native and nonnative vowels (e.g., English *i* versus the Swedish *y*; Moon et al., 2013). By eight months of age, infants can distinguish many of the 800 global phenomes (Kuhl, 2010). A phenome is the basic sound of a language. To give context, each language has approximately 40 phenomes. Perhaps even more interestingly, infants by around the age of 10 to 12 months lose this ability to discriminate nonnative sounds that are not in their native language. For example, Japanese infants can discriminate the *r* and the *l* consonants, which are similarly pronounced in Japanese, at age eight months but lose this ability a couple of months later (Werker & Hensch, 2015).

Proprioception

Proprioception includes tactile, vestibular, and kinesthetic sensory information (Abernathy et al., 1996). Kinesthetic sense includes body and spatial awareness. Newborns have a highly developed sense of touch (Piek, 2006). It is also assumed that they can sense pain and temperature at least to some degree based on their responsiveness to medical procedures around the time of birth. The vestibular system, which is in the inner ear, is one of the most highly developed systems in newborns (Carmichael, 1946). The vestibular system assists in maintaining equilibrium by providing information about head position and movement. Little is known, however, about kinesthetic sense because of the difficulty of measuring this sense in infants.

EARLY MOVEMENTS

During the exciting and rapidly changing time of infancy, three relatively distinct types of movements occur. Although authors may use slightly different terminology, these movement types are (a) reflexive (some reflexes have been observed as early as the second or third month of fetal life until four months of age); (b) spontaneous, also referred to as rhythmical stereotypies (from 4 to 10 months of age, peaking between 6 and 10 months); and (c) voluntary (motor milestones), which appear and are generally refined between birth and two years of age.

Reflexive Movements

Reflexive movements (also called reflexive behaviors or reflexes) are thought to be automatic, involuntary responses to stimuli that are controlled at a subcortical level. That is, the higher brain centers are not involved in these movements. Generally, reflexive behaviors are broken down into three categories: primitive reflexes, postural reactions, and locomotor reflexes. It is hypothesized that **primitive reflexes** serve the functions of protection (e.g., the startle reflex) (see figure 7.1*a*) and securing nourishment (e.g., the sucking reflex) and disappear within a specific time frame. For example, the sucking reflex is present from birth to three months of age (see figure 7.1*b*). A particular reflex that is present beyond the typical point of disappearance may indicate an underlying neurological problem. For example, the persistence of primitive reflexes indicates delays in future motor ability as well as certain disabilities such as autism spectrum disorder (Chinello et al., 2018). In addition, a positive palmar grasp reflex at four months can indicate cerebral palsy in infants at six months (Handryastuti et al., 2018). The palmar grasp reflex is present at birth until approximately two months and is elicited by placing an object in the infant's palm. Infants react by grasping the object as well as contracting their arm and shoulder so much that the examiner can lift the infant off the ground by simply holding the object (Herring, 2020).

Postural reactions (e.g., the parachute reflex) serve to automatically maintain the

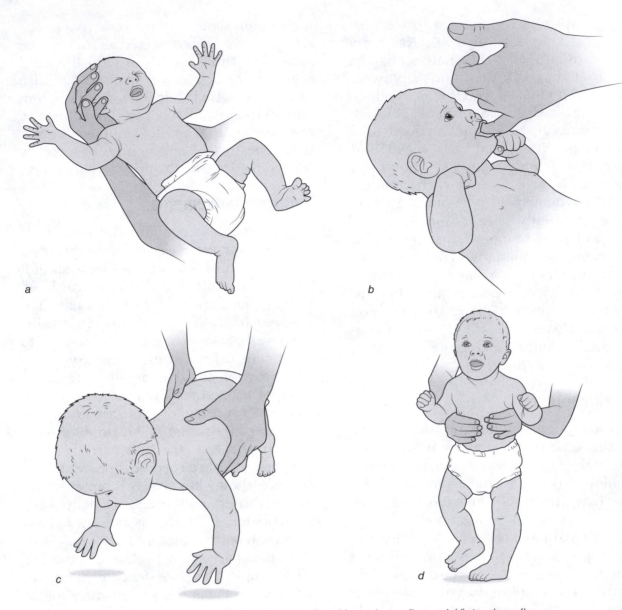

Figure 7.1 Examples of the (a) startle reflex, (b) sucking reflex, (c) parachute reflex, and (d) stepping reflex.

appropriate posture in a changing environment. The parachute reflex is an example of a postural reaction (see figure 7.1c). It is elicited when the infant is held in a vertical position and then suddenly lowered forward. The infant reacts by extending the arms and hands forward in a protective manner. **Locomotor reflexes** (e.g., the stepping reflex) are thought by some theorists (Thelen, 1995; Ulrich et al., 1992) (see figure 7.1d) to be precursors to voluntary locomotion and serve, at some level, as practice for these later motor milestones. Reflexive

behaviors are not voluntary but are critical to the initial survival and later development of the infant. The stepping movements typically disappear around two to three months of age unless trained daily. Without training there is a period of a couple of months in which there is no similar locomotor stepping movement pattern. This experience can expedite the onset of independent walking. Infants who have gone through a training period for stepping movements may walk up to four to six weeks earlier than untrained infants (Zelazo et al., 1972).

Spontaneous Movements

Although less often discussed than the earlier reflexive movements and the exciting motor milestones to come, spontaneous movements (rhythmical stereotypies) are frequently exhibited and are of great importance to the developing infant (see figure 7.2). If you've ever watched an infant kick his legs rhythmically, thrust his arms into the air, or extend his fingers, you have observed spontaneous movements. Although they do not appear to be goal directed, these seemingly random movements are thought to have a purpose for the developing infant. These movements of the arms and legs appear to have coordination patterns like those of later voluntary, goal-directed behavior. Research suggests that rhythmical stereotypies could be fundamental building blocks for the voluntary movement skills to come and indicate that motor behavior can also occur without a sensory stimulus.

Spontaneous movements begin prenatally and continue through the first couple of months of infancy. They are characterized by arm and leg movements that vary in both direction and duration (Hadders-Algra, 2000). Although limited variability in spontaneous movements might indicate a neurological deficit (Karch et al., 2012), the opposite holds true for voluntary, goal-directed movements. For these movements, reduced variation indicates good neurological function (Hadders-Algra, 2018). These initial, seemingly random and uncontrolled movements are critical features of brain development and serve to help the newborn explore.

Voluntary (Goal-Directed) Movements

Early voluntary movement skills are the motor milestones that mothers and fathers look forward to with great anticipation. Although it is quite exciting for parents to see their infant sit up unassisted for the first time, it is often even more exciting to see her take her first steps. These cortically controlled movements (contrasted with the subcortically controlled reflexes) follow a predictable sequence, although the skills may vary widely in terms of when they appear. Figure 7.3 shows the normative order in development and has been redrawn based on seminal work that was published many decades ago and is still generally accepted today (Newell et al., 2003).

Following a cephalocaudal direction, in terms of movement development, infants first control the head and then the upper body, which allows them, over time, to sit

Figure 7.2   Early rhythmic behavior is demonstrated by an infant (approximately five months of age) kicking in a supine position.

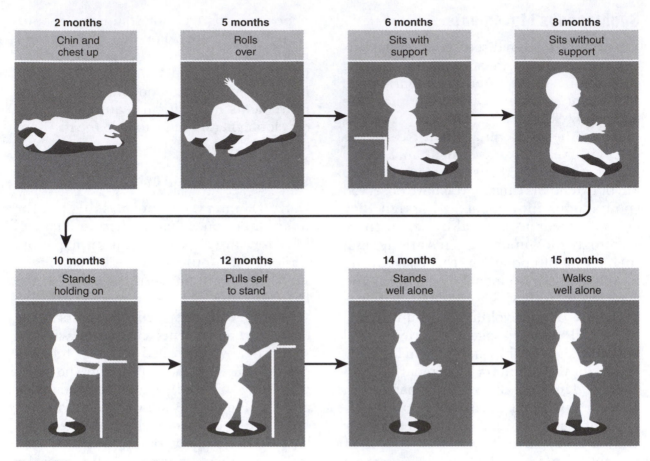

Figure 7.3   Infant motor milestone sequence.
Based on Shirley (1931).

unassisted. This is followed by independent standing as well as exploration of the environment through a variety of ambulatory patterns that include crawling, creeping, cruising, and walking. Development also takes place in a proximodistal direction, where control of the center of the body precedes control of extremities. Relatedly, hand and arm control are also critical accomplishments; during the first two years of life, undifferentiated and reflexive reaching becomes a relatively smooth and coordinated effort that leads to exploration of the environment through reaching, grasping, and, when appropriate, releasing the object of interest. To attain these critical motor milestones, the developing infant must have adequate postural control. The

following sections address the development of important motor milestones, including balance and stability.

Voluntary Head and Body Control

Although not frequently thought of as a motor milestone, adequate postural control of the head and trunk is fundamental to the attainment of an array of movement skills including, but not limited to, head control, sitting, standing, and a variety of locomotor patterns (crawling, creeping, cruising, and walking). With progressively more refined control of the body comes an improved ability to navigate and explore physical and social environments. Body control during infancy occurs sequentially, directionally, and cumulatively. This means that each movement is a building block to subsequent movements. As previously mentioned, development occurs in a cephalocaudal direction.

One of the first motor milestones to develop is the ability to lift the head while in a prone position. When considering the relatively large size of the infant's head in comparison to the body, one can appreciate the neck strength and coordination necessary to accomplish this task. An infant's head is approximately one fourth the size of the entire body. This is illustrated in figure 12.3 in chapter 12. Infants typically begin to lift the head while prone at around two months, but they cannot extend the neck while prone until three months. The ability to extend the neck enables the infant to visually scan the room, further advancing perceptual–motor development. It is not until approximately five months of age that an infant is able to raise the head while in a supine position (see figure 7.4).

The ability to control body movements continues to follow the cephalocaudal direction as the infant learns to control the upper body by first elevating the chest in addition to the head while in a prone position. This further increases the ability to view the world in a different way, while also increasing strength and coordination in the arms and chest and preparing the infant for future locomotor patterns. Young infants use this arm control to roll from a supine to a prone position, setting themselves up for crawling. Early rolling is more of a reflexive movement, rather than a sign of advanced motor development. Controlled rolling isn't typical until around six months of age. At this point, most infants can only roll from supine to prone and not prone to supine, which is generally acquired by around eight months.

Infants can sit with assistance at around the age of three months. They generally have enough neck and head control to remain in a supported sitting position. At three months, because lumbar control is quite weak, infants require additional support on the back and abdomen. Pillows have been developed to support young infants with sitting; however, if left alone, the infant may slide forward or sideways. Infants progress to being able to sit alone by holding something to support themselves at around five months and can sit with no support at around eight months.

Reaching and Grasping

A whole new world opens to an infant who can sit upright independently. Now their hands are free, enabling them to reach and grasp for objects. Once sitting, the infant has a new vantage point and can manipulate objects much more easily. Although

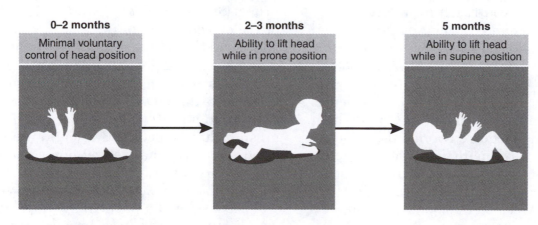

Figure 7.4   The typical progression of voluntary head control in early infancy.

RESEARCH NOTES

Does Culture Affect the Development of Sitting?

The age of developing the milestone of sitting without support varies greatly across different cultures. A study by Karasik and colleagues (2015) examined five-month-old infants at home doing daily activities from six countries across five continents. The differences in the percentages of infants who could support themselves in a sitting position was remarkable ranging from none (0 percent) of the Italian infants to nearly all (92 percent) of the Cameroonian infants! Only a small percentage of infants from the United States, South Korea, and Argentina were able to sit without support as well, ranging from 17 percent to 25 percent. Infants from Kenya also did quite well with two thirds of the infants sitting unsupported. Given these results, it is quite clear that there are some different cultural practices at play here. Infants in four of the countries spent very little time on the ground or on furniture not designed for infants, while infants from Cameroon and Kenya spent a large portion of their days on the floor or on adult furniture. Other researchers have noted similar differences in caregiving practices of newborns in African and Caribbean cultures, which can be rougher but encourage deliberate exercise for their infants. Caregivers in these regions begin training newborns and young infants to sit by propping them upright, encouraging the development of the postural muscles to support their body upright.

reaching and grasping may not appear to be as monumental a motor milestone as creeping or walking, these skills are challenging because they require incorporating haptic (exploration through touch) and visual perception with the motor control and coordination of the arms, wrists, and hands. In addition, these perceptual–motor experiences are also greatly affected by memory. Let's say that you reach for a large empty pot with two hands. When you grasp it, you realize that it is plastic rather than ceramic and requires only one hand to lift. You will likely then free up the other hand to grab something else. Following this experience, you remember that the empty pot is light and does not require two hands. Children and adults have many years of experience with a large variety of objects and can accurately prejudge the requirements necessary to grasp each object (e.g., one hand, two hands, different grasps).

Many studies have been conducted to better understand how infants change and improve their reaching and grasping as well as how they use visual and haptic information. Reaching and grasping emerge as a confluence of both intrinsic factors (i.e., the infant's age, experience, level of postural control, and exposure to risk conditions) and extrinsic factors (i.e., body position, physical properties of objects, spatial orientation of the object, speed of the object, and any additional load to the infant's arm or arms) (Campos et al., 2009). Through experience, infants learn to adjust their reach and grasp relative to the environmental properties. They learn how to preplan their reach and grasp including deciding when to use one hand versus two hands and how to adjust their grasp based on the object's size and shape (Gibson & Pick, 2000). Postural control is considered a particularly important rate limiter for reaching because infants have been found to reach and grasp at much earlier ages when placed in an appropriate posture.

Reaching and grasping develops rapidly over the course of the first eight months. Newborns have poor coordination and control in their arms and hands as well as poor visual acuity. They typically bring their hands toward objects with very jerky prereaching movements (Campos et al., 2008). Prereaching movements often appear as movements toward an object without a successful grasp. Prereaches consist of movements that include extending and flapping the arm that are not directed toward an object or arm movements that bring the hand to the mouth. Prior to four months, infants tend to move their hands closer to an object when they are visually fixated on the object than they do when they are not focusing on it (Von Hofsten, 1984). Often, they reach with clenched fists because they cannot open them. Typically, infants do not begin reaching with an open hand until four months. Prior to four months is considered phase I reaching, which is characterized by an inability to reach and grasp for objects.

Successful reaching generally begins to occur around the age of three to four months; it is defined at this point as being able to control the hand in such a way as to contact an object. Early successful reaching (referred to as phase II reaching) is characterized by much variation in movement velocity, amplitude, and duration. The next several months demonstrate improvement in reaching through progressively increased movement velocity and reduced corrections in movement kinematics (Hadders-Algra, 2018). At these early ages, vision plays a minimal role in reaching. After six months, the ability to reach improves at a slower pace but is marked by progressively straighter movement trajectories. However, infants as young as five to six months of age can differentiate their grip configurations based on the object's size relative to the size of their fingers and hands (Newell et al., 1993).

Think about the importance of manual dexterity in tasks such as writing, using hand tools, sewing, and cutting with scissors. While you can manipulate small objects and button a shirt easily, these fine motor skills are quite difficult to acquire. Infants typically cannot use a **precision grip** (finger and thumb grasp) until they are close to one year of age. Younger infants use what is termed a **power grip**, in which they grasp an object by supporting it with the palm of the hand and the undersurface of the fingers. Infants begin contacting objects and grasping them at around five or six months with this type of grip, but they have little control or ability to manipulate the object. As adults, we use visual information and memories from many previous experiences of manipulating objects to anticipate the type of grasp necessary prior to reaching for the object. We may need all our fingers and thumb if the object is large or awkward to pick up, but we use a precision grip for smaller objects. Likewise, we use one hand rather than two hands if the object is light enough. A timeline showing the development of grasping over the course of the first year of life is shown in figure 7.5.

The Three Cs of Locomotion

Locomotion is perhaps the most celebrated early motor milestone in infancy. Locomotor patterns in infancy typically begin with

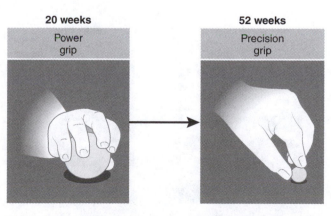

Figure 7.5   The development of grasping during infancy.

TRY THIS

Acquiring Manual Dexterity

Exercise 7.2

Lay out a few common objects that you have with you right now (e.g., a pencil, quarter, water bottle, textbook, laptop computer) and pick them up one at a time. Describe the grip you used for each and explain why you chose the grip you did for each object.

Now, describe how you would expect an eight-month-old infant to pick up each item. What rate limiters do you think would affect an eight-month-old who is picking up these objects?

crawling; however, there is considerable variation in how and when infants crawl. Although many people refer to crawling as any movement in which an infant locomotes on all fours, the first *C*, **crawling** includes only the prone progression in which the infant pulls the trunk forward by extending and flexing the forearms while the legs extend symmetrically and are passively dragged forward (Gesell & Ames, 1940). The second *C*, **creeping**, is forward progression on all fours with the belly off the ground. Indeed, *creeping* and *crawling* are frequently confused, and in general conversation (and even in some physical education textbooks), the terms are sometimes reversed. However, as motor developmentalists, we should be aware of and use the correct terminology. Crawling typically occurs around 34 weeks of age and progresses to an alternating arm motion. Parents tend to refer to this type of crawling as commando or the army crawl. Initially, crawling involves minimal leg involvement. Infants pull themselves forward in a sliding motion, and some push themselves backward. Some infants skip this milestone entirely and begin with creeping, which includes moving on all fours alternately with the belly and chest lifted off the ground. Creeping is typically exhibited by infants after nine months. Figure 7.6 shows the difference.

There is a wide variety of movement patterns that infants adopt to crawl. While some can coordinate their movements of alternating their arms and legs, many solve the problem in other ways, including moving in a homolateral pattern, meaning that the limbs on the same side move either forward or backward together, and others roll, shuffle their bum, or hitch one leg out (Adolph & Hoch, 2018). Infants who skip crawling

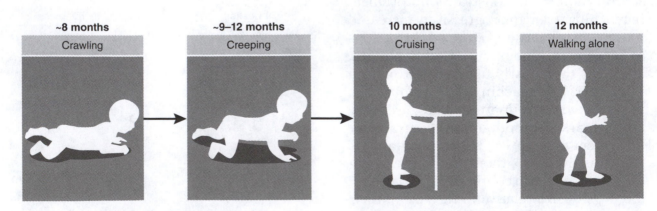

Figure 7.6   The typical early motor milestone locomotor progression for infants.

WHAT DO YOU THINK?

Exercise 7.3

1. What is the difference between crawling and creeping?
2. Describe several strategies for infants' early crawling movement patterns.
3. Describe several ways in which environmental changes can affect infants' locomotion patterns.
4. What rate limiters do you think are holding back infants from progressing from crawling to creeping?

may begin with contralateral creeping, in which the limbs on each side oppose one another (Piek, 2006). Keep in mind that there is much variability in crawling and creeping; some infants even skip crawling altogether, and a small percentage skip creeping. Although crawling and creeping are considered motor milestones, skipping one or the other is not an indication of abnormal development.

The third *C* is **cruising** (moving laterally while upright, using both arms for support), leading to the ultimate method of locomotion—walking. This tremendously exciting—and important—motor milestone is discussed in depth in chapter 8.

Although the order and approximate timing of these milestones has been carefully cataloged since the early 1900s (Gesell, 1946; McGraw, 1943), *how* the developing infant learns to control a rapidly changing body while learning new movement skills—in varied and often unpredictable environments—has been less examined. Adolph (2008) referred to this conundrum as a "learning to learn" issue. Based on work by Harlow (1949), Adolph posited that each new motor milestone (unassisted sitting, creeping on hands and knees, reaching and grasping, or walking) presents its own unique movement challenges for the infant to solve. Furthermore, these new challenges (often occurring in less predictable or novel environments) take place as the infant's body is undergoing rapid neurological and morphological change. So, as infants grow and simultaneously get more practice at a given skill (such as walking), they become more adept.

Interestingly, Adolph and Berger's research (2006) provides evidence that knowledge and ability gained in one posture do not transfer to a second. Briefly stated, they contended that because motor milestones such as independent sitting, crawling, creeping, and walking have different motoric and perceptual requirements, learning is specific to each milestone. This speaks against the widely held neuromaturational perspective (e.g., Gesell, 1946; Shirley, 1931) that each new motor milestone builds on the previous one—that is, what an infant learns while sitting transfers to crawling. In an investigation into how infants learn to navigate slopes, Adolph and colleagues (1997) concluded that the strategies that infants honed over time that were effective for creeping did not transfer to walking. That is, when learning this new locomotor pattern, the infant generally had to start from scratch. "In other words, *each* problem space [in this example, creeping and walking] has its own set of information-generating behaviors and its own learning curve" (Adolph, 2008, p. 214). Thus, as previously noted, the breadth, depth, and variety of movement experiences available to an infant—for each motor milestone—influence the rate and quality of motor development (Cintas, 1995). Infants are acquiring motor milestones in a continuously growing and changing body (Adolph & Hoch, 2018). Infants must learn how to adapt their movements to their changing body size and strength while also adjusting to temporary changes such as clothing or objects in their hands. For example, in the late 1800s when American infants mostly wore long dresses, they adopted rolling or hitched crawling with one leg out because their legs would get caught in their clothing (Trettien, 1900). Infants who are wearing bulkier clothing often roll or crawl at a later age than infants in warmer climates who can wear less clothing (Benson, 1993). Learning to move and acquire new motor milestones requires learning to adapt.

Although appropriate motor experiences are important for all developing infants, it is intuitively evident that they are crucial to infants who are at risk (Maitre et al., 2013). These include, but are not limited to, infants who come from low socioeconomic backgrounds as well as those with identifiable disabilities such as Down syndrome, cerebral palsy, autistic spectrum disorder, and developmental coordination disorder. Seminal work by Thelen and colleagues (Thelen, 1985; Thelen et al., 1991; Thelen et al., 1996) has emphasized the individuality of motor development. That is, as practitioners and researchers, we should attend to how individual babies solve individual movement problems "in their own unique ways" (Spencer et al., 2006, p. 1533). Tying this idea to the depth and variety of movement experiences previously mentioned, individual learners bring their own unique sets of skills to problems they are solving in real and changing environments.

Postural Control

Environments grow and change in many important ways as infants become capable of observing from different heights and angles, reaching for and grasping items of interest, and, before we know it, locomoting smoothly. Postural control (along with balance) is an excellent example of action systems and perceptual systems working in concert. Specifically, the visual and kinesthetic senses (with input from both the vestibular and proprioceptive systems) supply the sensory inputs required by the developing, active infant.

RESEARCH NOTES

How Should Babies Sleep?

A wide-ranging societal change with significant (and unexpected) negative ramifications for motor development involved American Academy of Pediatrics (AAP) guidelines issued in 1992. In this brief, it was strongly suggested that parents have their infants sleep in a supine, as opposed to prone, position to reduce the incidence of sudden infant death syndrome. This position statement was very effective in reducing the number of infant deaths; however, an unintended negative consequence was that, while awake, infants who slept in a supine position were placed in a prone position very infrequently (Monson et al., 2003; Salls et al., 2002). The result of infants being predominantly in a supine position in comparison to prone while awake delays motor milestones that require upper-body strength (rolling from prone to supine, tripod sitting, crawling, creeping, and pulling to stand). Because of a reduced ability to navigate and explore their environment, these delays are thought to have a deleterious effect on infants' intellectual and social development.

It is important to note that the term *postural control* is not universally understood or defined consistently (Pollock et al., 2000). We need a broadly accepted definition to understand the development and maintenance of postural control over the life span, as well as to determine whether developmental problems are the result of an identifiable disability (e.g., cerebral palsy or Down syndrome) or acquired through injury or disease. For our purposes, postural control involves (a) the ability to maintain the correct relationship between body segments and the environment or a specific task, or both; (b) the maintenance of stability, specifically, keeping the center of mass (center of gravity) within the person's base of support; (c) predictive (anticipatory) strategies that potentially involve an increase in muscular activity or a specific, voluntary movement prior to a predicted disturbance; and (d) reactive (compensatory) strategies, again potentially involving increased muscular activity or a voluntary movement (or both) in response to an unanticipated disturbance (also referred to as a perturbation).

As discussed earlier in the chapter, Thelen's developmental work within a dynamic systems context stressed the importance of individual differences regarding solving movement problems in ever-changing environments. In the same vein, Thelen, as well as her colleagues (Spencer et al., 2006; Ulrich & Ulrich, 1993), examined variability in motor responses both in each infant (intraindividual differences) and between individuals (interindividual differences). That is, across trials by a specific infant, one could expect, especially early in development, that the responses would be different. Given innate and acquired differences between infants, we would expect different solutions to the same movement problem depending on each infant's very personal characteristics. These empirically derived hypotheses apply to the development of movement abilities, including, of course, postural control. Dusing and Harbourne (2010) outlined several principles that address the complexity of developing postural control that are in accord with the dynamic systems perspective.

To summarize, although the route taken by a given infant may differ from that of the infant's peers, over the course of the first year, several significant postural achieve-

WHAT DO YOU THINK?

Exercise 7.4

1. What rate limiters are holding back an infant who can pull to a standing position with the assistance of a couch but cannot stand or walk independently?

2. What control parameters can help a toddler progress from walking with a wide stance to walking with a narrow stance?

3. Order the following motor milestones in a typical developmental order:
   a. Standing independently
   b. Holding the head up
   c. Creeping
   d. Crawling
   e. Pulling to stand
   f. Rolling over
   g. Sitting independently

ments have taken place. Although newborns do not appear to have much in the way of postural control, and their actions seem to be excessive, random, and nonfunctional, even at this point they are exploring movement possibilities and developing strategies that support looking around, reaching, and moving through their environments. Perception and action are working together in a bidirectional manner in which each informs the other. This allows developing infants to use visual, vestibular, and somatosensory information to adjust their rapidly changing bodies over a dynamic base of support that changes position frequently. As all behaviors do, the development of postural control results from the interaction of rapidly changing organismic constraints, the dynamic physical and emotional environment in which the child resides, and the movement task to be accomplished (Newell, 1986).

INFANTS AT RISK

Although differing one from another, infants who are at risk frequently have characteristics that significantly hinder the quality, quantity, and emergence of their movement skills. Interacting with the environment reflexively, using spontaneous movements, maintaining balance, reaching and grasping, and moving through space are not only important for their own sake, but they also directly affect learning in the social and intellectual domains. Therefore, the early and accurate identification of infants at risk for movement problems is of great importance. Except for infants with Down syndrome (who are often identified at birth and sometimes in utero), only infants who are severely affected are accurately diagnosed early in their lives. Thus, many at-risk infants are undiagnosed until they are much older, leading to a delay in the presentation of well-designed early intervention programs.

A particularly important reason for the early identification and, relatedly, early start to rehabilitative interventions con-

cerns infants' neural plasticity, as previously discussed in this chapter. Because neural plasticity is greatest during infancy and early childhood, this is the time frame during which therapeutic interventions are most likely to reap long-term developmental benefits (Maitre et al., 2013). As noted, many disabling conditions and environments negatively affect the development of movement skills, and the following section briefly examines three prevalent conditions: prematurity, cerebral palsy, and Down syndrome. Although the underlying etiologies (causes) of these three conditions generally differ, the principles underlying the interventions have much in common.

Prematurity

Prematurity (or being born preterm) is defined as being born at least three weeks before the due date, or before the start of the 37th week. Because the important growth and development of vital organ systems that take place outside the womb (in the extra-uterine environment) over the last weeks and months of pregnancy, prematurity often results in serious health complications as well as being the leading cause of infant death (Piek, 2006). Infants born prematurely have significantly higher rates of respiratory problems, feeding difficulties, hearing and vision impairments, developmental delays, and cerebral palsy than do those who are born at full term. In general, the more immature the preterm infant is, the more acute the problems will be. How an infant's organ systems respond to the extrauterine environment, along with the level of immediate medical care provided (generally, this occurs in a neonatal intensive care unit), has a significant influence on both short- and long-term health outcomes. Important secondary factors that influence the development of the infant born preterm include socioeconomic status and the educational, physical, and social environments within which the infant develops.

One might assume that given improved medical care, particularly in developed countries, the incidence of premature births would decrease. However, because of considerably more preterm births, there is a higher survival rate for very-low-birth-weight infants. As noted, the earlier the birth is, relative to full term, the more serious the health concerns will be. The terminology used when categorizing preterm births is as follows:

- *Late preterm:* Born between 34 and 36 weeks of pregnancy
- *Moderately preterm:* Born between 32 and 34 weeks of pregnancy
- *Very preterm:* Born at less than 32 weeks of pregnancy
- *Extremely preterm:* Born at or before 25 weeks of pregnancy

It should be noted that most preterm births are late preterm.

Clearly, reducing premature births is of paramount importance. The causes of prematurity and how these causes may intersect remain poorly understood. However, suggestions (Moore, 2003) have included poor nutrition, stress, hypoxia, fetal stress, changes in the mother's hormonal levels, and problems associated with upper genital tract infection. Although some risk factors are not changeable, interventions are possible with others. The movement abilities of infants born prematurely are often compromised, and more severe impairments are evident in those of lower birth weight or more pronounced prematurity, or both. Table 7.1 lists premature infant risk factors and prevention strategies.

Developmental differences in the movement domain associated with prematurity include hypotonia (low active and passive muscle tone), predominant extensor muscle tone resulting in difficulty acting against gravity, and reduced variability in spontaneous movements (Lenke, 2003). Regarding reflexive movements, primitive reflexes such as the asymmetrical tonic neck reflex, moro reflex, and palmar grasp reflex may be entirely absent or persist longer than normal. Along with frequently severe medical complications and reduced opportunities to move (given a severely restricted environment), movement abilities are often compromised because of extended time spent in the hospital (Lenke, 2003). This

Table 7.1   Risk Factors for Premature Birth and Prevention Strategies

Premature infant risk factor	Prevention strategies
Unplanned pregnancy	• Family planning education • Provision of appropriate contraception
Number of embryos implanted in assisted reproduction	Discussion between physician and families contemplating assisted reproduction
Young age at pregnancy	Comprehensive family planning education at community, state, and national levels
Weight at time of pregnancy	Encouragement and education regarding appropriate weight for height at every doctor's visit
General health status (hypertension, diabetes mellitus, clotting disorders, anemia)	• Treatment to ensure best health status prior to pregnancy • Under certain circumstances, consideration of pregnancy avoidance
Uterine fibroids	Treatment prior to pregnancy
Low income, life stress	• Individual support • Advocacy for education, employment, and community improvements
Cigarette smoking	• Assessment at every health visit • Referral for smoking cessation
Other substance abuse	Referral for substance abuse assistance

protracted time in the hospital results, not infrequently, in gross motor delays in head and trunk control.

Researchers have noted that a single delay or abnormal sign is not necessarily indicative of a significant movement or cognitive impairment; however, early assessment and careful observation are warranted. To a significant degree, the rate and quality of development are unpredictable (developmental lags and then catch-up periods are evident). Finally, when assessing motor development (including, but not limited to, motor milestones), parents and professionals must keep in mind the infant's corrected age (chronological age minus the number of weeks the infant was preterm). "Early [motor] differences may not always be indicative of an emerging deficit and may resolve, although some are associated with long-term problems and should be closely monitored" (Lenke, 2003, p. 105).

Cerebral Palsy

Of babies born prematurely, a considerable percentage (14.7 percent of infants born before 28 weeks of gestation; 6.2 percent of children born between 28 and 31 weeks of gestation) present with **cerebral palsy (CP)**, a serious neurodevelopmental condition. CP has been referred to as "a group of permanent disorders of the development of movement and posture, causing activity limitation, that are attributed to nonprogressive disturbances that occurred in the developing fetal or infant brain" (Rosenbaum et al., 2007, p. 9). Although experts in the field (Rosenbaum et al., 2007) have maintained that motor dysfunction is a critical and necessary feature of CP, they have argued persuasively that problems related to perception, sensation, communication, cognition, and behavior are often present. It is important to recognize that CP isn't a single disability but rather a group of neurodevelopmental disorders that, based on the severity, location, and timing of the insult to the brain, present somewhat unusual obstacles and challenges to different people. Furthermore, these challenges (motoric, cognitive, perceptual, communicative, and so on) may be more significant during one period of life than another.

Although CP does originate with some type of prenatal or perinatal insult, the environment (including, but not limited to, early intervention and familial support) plays a large role in the person's development. CP is generally identified before 18 months of age. Each infant requires individualized, multidimensional attention from a trained team of professionals, the parents, and, when appropriate, siblings. As noted, the underlying cause or set of causes (etiology) of CP varies; thus, it is important that approaches to remediation and education be determined based on the functional limitations (as well as strengths) of the infant as opposed to the medical diagnosis. This is not to say that certain empirically determined best practices for those who present with, for example, spasticity can't be very similar from one infant to another. However, professionals and parents should keep

---

WHAT DO YOU THINK?

Exercise 7.5

1. What types of conditions may be indicated by low muscle tone in a young infant?
2. How and when could low muscle tone be noticed in a young infant?
3. How might a delay in one motor milestone affect subsequent milestones?

in mind the unique characteristics of the child (referred to, from a dynamic systems perspective, as intrinsic dynamics) as well as the unique environment when determining an intervention. The type of intervention, as well as the people who administer it, will also likely change over time because the needs of the individual are not static. Although CP is a nonprogressive disorder of the brain, clear functional changes (in all the aforementioned domains) resulting from aging, learning activities, therapeutic intervention, and movement opportunities, among others, will occur.

The extent and accuracy of information available to accurately classify children thought to have CP vary significantly across the life span and geographic areas (for example, the availability of neuroimaging equipment, diagnostic specialists, and bio-chemical laboratories—as well as accurate historical data on the course of the preg-nancy—may be unavailable). Nonetheless, it is critical that classification information include, at the least, the age of the child, whatever historical information is available (e.g., maternal recall, systematic observation, clinical notes), and whether neuroim-aging or metabolic testing occurred.

The emphasis throughout this chapter has been on the individuality of developmental trajectories (i.e., the nonlinear transitions that develop over the course of their lives). However, people with a particular classifi-cation of CP demonstrate, in general, unique motor patterns and deficits. The severity, as well as the specific limbs involved, differs depending on the motor pathways affected by the lesion. Motor deficits have been cate-gorized based on (a) movement type (spastic-ity, ataxia, dyskinesia, and hypotonia; Evans & Alberman, 1985) and (b) the affected body part (Aicardi & Bax, 1992).

Regardless of the etiology or classifica-tion, it is essential to identify an infant as having CP as early as possible to begin the appropriate interventions. As noted earlier in this chapter, the developing brain is at its most malleable (that is, neural plasticity is most evident) early in life. Because of this neural plasticity, interventions begun at younger ages are more effective than those begun later. As we know, improved motor function has far-reaching, positive develop-mental consequences.

Down Syndrome

Down syndrome (DS), given its clear and unambiguous etiology, is one of the very few genetic disabilities that is identified soon after birth and results in moderate to severe intellectual disability (specifically, signifi-cant delays in speech, language production, auditory short-term memory, and nonverbal cognitive development) as well as delays in the onset of motor milestones and atypical motor skill acquisition (Angulo-Barroso et al., 2007). DS is the most common organic cause of intellectual disability: it occurs in approximately one in every 800 births in the United States.

Understanding the course of motor development as well as how infants with DS acquire stable and efficient basic move-ment skills not only lays the foundation for the more complex and socially valued movement abilities to follow but also enables developing infants to interact meaningfully with their environments. These movement skills have, as with all infants with and without identifiable disabilities, an import-ant role in the affective, intellectual, and communicative development of infants with DS. Although research with infants who develop atypically has been largely descrip-tive, chronicling behavioral differences and similarities with peers who develop nor-mally (Henderson, 1985), more recent work from a dynamic systems perspective has rigorously examined atypical development using sophisticated quantitative and qual-itative tools, at both individual and group levels of analysis.

Earlier researchers (Carr, 1970; Hogg & Moss, 1983) postulated that infants with DS acquire physical skills in the same sequence as their typically developing peers, albeit in a more extended fashion. However, evidence has been accumulating that suggests that infants with DS develop not only more slowly, but also in a qualitatively distinct fashion (Henderson, 1986; Lloyd et al., 2010; Ulrich et al., 1993). An example of unique movement solutions comes from Lydic and Steele's (1979) investigation, during which they queried parents about their infants' movement patterns. The results of the questionnaire confirmed the authors' observation that excessive external rotation and abduction of the hips resulted in the following atypical sitting and walking patterns: (a) when sitting, the infant's legs were frequently spread out at an extreme angle; (b) achievement of the sitting position from prone was accomplished by spreading the legs close to 180 degrees apart and then pushing up with the arms or head; and (c) walking was performed with a waddling gait and a wide base of support (a variety of arm movements were used in place of alternating swinging).

Subsequent research has identified a litany of qualitative and quantitative motor deficiencies in children with DS, including less frequent self-generated spontaneous movements, less frequent and lengthy general movements (e.g., gross movements involving the whole body), more low-intensity movement, and atypical and delayed gait. Physiological characteristics that would negatively affect motor development in infants and young children with DS include poor postural control and balance, low muscle tone and ligamentous laxity, lower cardiorespiratory fitness, a higher percentage of body fat, and a lower maximal heart rate (Angulo-Barroso et al., 2007; Lloyd et al., 2010). The physiological, sensory, cognitive, and morphological reasons for these significant barriers to skilled and frequent movement include a less efficient nervous system, smaller cerebellum, reduced hand size, visual and hearing problems, and reduced kinesthesia.

Some have suggested that increasing the activity level of self-generated spontaneous movements and general movements in children with DS would likely improve strength, endurance, and coordination and thus have a positive impact on the acquisition of motor milestones. Ulrich and Ulrich (1993) compared the spontaneous movements of typically developing infants with infants with DS and found that the quantity of spontaneous movements (particularly supine kicking) was significantly less in infants with DS than in their typically developing peers. Relatedly, a relative absence of these self-generated movements was discussed by Henderson in a 1985 review of movement skill development in infants with DS. She suggested that the delayed and abnormal trajectory regarding movement skills may be closely related to diminished exploratory behavior. She went on to suggest that a "form of self-perpetuating sensory-motor deprivation" occurs (Henderson, 1986, p. 74), resulting from this lack of exploratory behavior.

Interventions

We end this section with a critically important question that applies to all infants who are at risk of developmental delay including, but not limited to, those who are born prematurely, are at risk for CP, or have DS. Simply put, are there interventions that have proven efficacy? That is, how do we know they work? This is particularly challenging given the limited amount of research and the heterogeneity of the infants we're considering. Specific issues include identifying important outcomes; identifying the tools needed to accurately assess these outcomes; deciding (beyond choosing an appropriate theory-driven, data-based approach) how intense and frequent the sessions should be, who will carry out the interventions, and how those people will be trained; and finally, ensuring that the interventions are

WHAT DO YOU THINK?

Exercise 7.6

1. Describe the typical delays exhibited in children with Down syndrome and cerebral palsy.
2. How might early interventions be similar for each delay, and how might they differ?

carried out effectively and consistently. Because it is impossible to find a generic patient, and given that infants, regardless of their diagnoses, vary along the dimensions of intellect, attention, sensory impairment, and behavior, can we identify one intervention that can apply to all infants?

Over the past 25 years, Thelen and colleagues (Angulo-Barroso et al., 2007; Lloyd et al., 2010; Ulrich et al., 1993) have used a dynamic systems approach to inform therapeutic practice. A particular tenet of the dynamic systems approach posits that behavior is softly assembled. That is, the developing infant uses what is maturationally available at a given point in time, in a particular environment, to solve a specific movement task. By saying *maturationally available,* we are referring to individual characteristics (intrinsic dynamics).

Behavior is thought to be determined by the status of all the underlying systems (for walking, these would include muscular strength, dynamic balance, and motivation), so if one or more of these systems is compromised, the appearance or the quality (or both) of a given movement (in our example, walking) would be affected. Therefore, therapeutic interventions should be individually tailored to improve the functioning of one or more systems, should a given system prove to be ineffective. For example, if a child with CP solves the movement task of walking across the room with an awkward, inefficient gait that requires a lot of energy, this might be—probably would be—the best way for them to get from one place to another. Therefore, a targeted therapeutic intervention would identify the rate limiters (what, specifically, was hindering them) and work specifically on the issue at hand. Here, the intervention might involve increasing range of motion and muscular strength, leading to a more efficient gait pattern. We would, of course, keep a good eye on the program, collecting formative and summative data that would indicate whether the child is improving. If the answer is no, the next question would address whether we have the correct approach but are not implementing it properly, or whether we're not using the correct approach. At all times, our intervention must be individually tailored, thoughtful, and, to the extent possible, based on scientific findings.

SUMMARY

Infant development is a period of immense change. Newborns have minimal volitional control and quickly grow and develop to being able to manipulate objects with their hands and even locomote by the end of the first year. This chapter began by discussing the importance of healthy pregnancies and detailed the development of the embryo and fetus. Many factors affect development during the critical months in the womb. Pregnant women must avoid harmful substances and potentially dangerous situations that may have dramatic and lasting effects on their unborn children.

Infants change in how they respond to the environment as they progress from making mostly spontaneous and reflexive movements to making controlled volitional movements. Their senses improve dramatically throughout the first year; improved vision, hearing, and somatosensation enable them to respond to the environment in increasingly more meaningful ways. Infants can more efficiently reach and grasp objects because of improved vision and increased experiences. They learn when it is appropriate to use one hand versus two hands and begin to be able to use a precision grip for smaller objects. This grip becomes increasingly more important as they grow older and learn how to use crayons and later to write.

During the first year, the infant advances through a series of motor milestones including holding up the head, sitting up, creeping, and eventually walking. The way and the time in which each infant progresses through these motor milestones vary greatly. Most infants follow the progression discussed in this chapter; however, some advance more quickly than others. Slower progression through the motor milestones does not necessarily indicate developmental delays. The onset of motor milestones occurs due to both genetic and environmental factors. For example, infants who live in homes with slippery floors may learn to walk later, and those who are carried a lot are more likely to locomote at a later age. Infant personalities can also drive some of these changes. A particularly curious infant or an infant who has older siblings running around may be motivated to locomote earlier to be able to explore more of the environment.

This chapter also discussed infants who are at risk, including preterm infants and those with the identifiable disabilities of cerebral palsy and Down syndrome. Early identification of these disabilities is crucial to ensure an early start to rehabilitative interventions. Because neural plasticity is greatest during infancy and early childhood, therapeutic interventions undertaken at this time would be most likely to reap long-term benefits for the developing infant.

> ONLINE ACTIVITIES

The student material found in HK*Propel* includes exercises, labs, and videos to enhance learning and encourage practical application of important concepts.

LEARNING AIDS

Supplemental Activities

1. Develop an advertisement (brochure), front and back, providing prenatal information to pregnant women. Be sure to format it so that it folds like a brochure. You are free to choose any issue related to pregnancy and prenatal development for the brochure; anything from fetal alcohol syndrome to exercise and pregnancy is appropriate. Make the brochure appealing to the eye to catch people's attention and provide as much pertinent information as you can.

2. Interview someone close to you about their child's development as an infant.

   a. Describe the child and the person you interviewed. Did this child go through all the motor milestones? At what ages did the child go through each milestone? If the child did not go through all the milestones, what milestones were missed?

   b. If an infant skips a motor milestone, what might this tell us about how individual, environmental, and task constraints interact? Look up information on the Internet with regard to the skipping of motor milestones. Please cite your sources.

Glossary

cerebral palsy (CP)—A neuromuscular disorder that negatively affects coordination; typically, it is caused by external factors that prevent optimal brain development.

crawling—A prone progression in which the infant pulls the trunk forward by extending and flexing the forearms while the legs extend symmetrically and are passively dragged forward.

creeping—Forward progression on all fours with the belly off the ground.

cruising—Moving laterally while upright, using both arms and a stable object for support.

embryonic period—The second prenatal period, which lasts for the first six weeks.

fetal period—The final stage of prenatal development, which begins at the completion of organ differentiation at around week 8 and lasts until birth.

germinal period—The first prenatal period following conception, which lasts approximately two weeks.

gestational age—The prenatal age that begins the first day after the mother's last menstrual period.

locomotor reflexes—Reflexes that are thought to be precursors to voluntary locomotion and serve at some level as practice for these later motor milestones.

myogenic movements—Movements that are not generated by the central nervous system.

neural plasticity—The ability of the brain to change function because of either damage or experience.

neurogenic movements—Movements generated by the central nervous system.

organogenesis—The process by which cells are defined to make up organs.

postural reactions—Reflexes that automatically maintain the appropriate posture in a changing environment.

power grip—An early form of grasping in which the object is supported with the palm of the hand and the undersurface of the fingers.

precision grip—A finger and thumb grasp that is generally acquired around age 1.

primitive reflexes—Reflexes that serve the functions of protection and securing nourishment.

teratogen—Any agent that can cause defects or deformities in the fetus.

LOCOMOTOR AND STABILITY SKILLS IN CHILDHOOD

8

CHAPTER OBJECTIVES

After reading this chapter, you should be able to do the following:

- Define the term *fundamental motor skills.*
- Identify levels of competency in selected locomotor skills.
- List factors that facilitate the acquisition of locomotor skills.
- List factors that interfere with the development of locomotor skills.
- Understand the important interactions of motor development, cognitive development, and affective development.
- Appreciate how researchers study the emergence of fundamental motor skills.

Ayisha in Physical Education Class

Ayisha and her family had just arrived in the United States from Saudi Arabia, and she was getting used to many new experiences. When she attended her new school, she noticed both boys and girls playing an exciting game together in physical education class. That they played together was something new to see, and it looked like they really enjoyed the running, jumping, turning, and twisting that went on in the game. Although some of the children were a little quicker, others seemed to be able to jump higher. Ayisha found it interesting that being pretty good at one motor skill did not mean that a person was also good at a different motor skill. Also, no one seemed to care whether the students they teamed up with were excellent or not. They said nice things whether someone got away or was tagged. Although she had very few opportunities to run, jump, and twist in a game, she was looking forward to doing it a lot in the future.

As children begin to spend more time in school settings, moving well and playing competently, both independently and with their peers, have important short-term and long-term consequences. Indeed, developing movement competency has important psychological consequences regarding perceptions of competence, mastery, and persistence, along with a significantly greater likelihood of continued involvement in physical activity over the life span. Among other researchers, Seefeldt (1980), Clark and Metcalfe (2002), and Stodden and colleagues (2008) have proposed models that emphasize the importance of developing movement skill during the childhood years (ages 3-5) to successfully participate in an array of active childhood games and activities. The development of these foundational balance, locomotor, and object control skills (referred to as a "movement alphabet" by Goodway, 2015) will not only allow for positive, vigorous, and social activity but will also allow for participation in more complex games, sports, and individual movement pursuits, over the life span. Like Goodway's movement alphabet, the image of movement building blocks that establish a foundation for involvement in more complex activities is one that is frequently invoked (Barnett et al., 2020). Whether one is able, or is *unable*, to achieve a certain level of movement skill is thought to have a major impact on the number and quality of movement experiences over the life span, perceptions of movement competency, cardiorespiratory fitness, muscular strength, and muscular endurance (Lopes et al., 2017).

If, during these critical early years, children develop a solid foundation of locomotor, balance, and object control skills, they will be able to cross the hypothesized proficiency barrier (Brian et al., 2020; De Meester et al., 2018; Robinson et al., 2015; Seefeldt, 1980) allowing for an active and healthy future with all the associated health benefits. Conversely, poorly developed fundamental motor skills will result in an inability

to cross the proficiency barrier, leading to a negative spiral of disengagement (Goodway, 2015). Although the precipitous decline in activity levels and concomitant increase in obesity and other health-related markers is extremely complex and multiply determined, the effect of significantly decreased abilities in foundational movement skills cannot be overlooked (Brian et al., 2019; Robinson et al., 2015). Elsewhere in this text, important questions regarding the relationship between movement competency and health status; how to accurately assess movement competency over the life span; and the design and evaluation of movement programs for school-aged children, adolescents, and adults will be answered in depth. Additionally, these questions will be examined for all learners, including those who struggle motorically, behaviorally, socially, or cognitively as well as elite performers.

This chapter (focusing on locomotor and stability skills) and the following chapter (focusing on object control skills) will examine the essential fundamental motor skills, already alluded to, that should emerge over the first six years of life. Additionally, *why* these foundational skills do or do not emerge and the way this takes place will be discussed. How skilled and unskilled movement affects a child's development in the cognitive and social–affective domains will also be examined.

FUNDAMENTAL MOTOR SKILLS

Within the motor development community, there is currently an important discussion taking place regarding terminology related to movement competency (Logan et al., 2018; Newell, 2020). Over many years, different definitions and terminology have arisen. The terminology often depended on the dominant developmental theory, the discipline or subdiscipline examining a movement-related issue, or the cultural or geographical background of the researcher. Although this may seem like an overly scholarly debate, this lack of clarity and ambiguity have led to the same term being used to describe different phenomena as well as different terms being used to describe the same thing. Examples of terminology that have been ambiguous include *motor proficiency*, *motor performance*, *motor skill*, *motor ability*, and *motor coordination*. Logan and his colleagues (2018) have called for precisely describing the specific categories of skill that constitute the foundation for more complex and advanced skills. In this spirit, we will use the terminology proposed by Goodway and colleagues (2019) that is frequently found in the physical education and motor development literature (Logan et al., 2018) and includes, along with *object control*, *ball*, and *manipulative skills* (e.g., throw, catch, kick, roll, strike, and dribble); *locomotor skills* (e.g., walk, run, jump, hop, leap, gallop, slide, and skip); and *balance* and *stability skills* (e.g., body rolling, bending, stretching, swinging, turning, and twisting). Although earlier researchers have viewed balance and stability skills as underlying abilities required for skillful locomotion and object control, an alternative perspective gaining acceptance among researchers (Logan et al., 2018; Stodden et al., 2008) views these movement competencies as stand-alone skills. While we acknowledge the importance of balance and stability as they relate to competently running, jumping, throwing, catching, and kicking, we also can see the importance of such balance and stability skills as bending, twisting, and turning as required movements for sports such as gymnastics, diving, and synchronized swimming along with recreational activities (dance) and a large variety of activities of daily living.

During the first two years of life, an array of motor skills that allow children to interact with their environments in meaningful ways emerges. As examples, they can explore and act on their environments, somewhat capably, by walking in and around objects and by reaching for, grasping, manipulating, and then, if they feel like it, releasing the item. No longer are they prisoners of gravity; rather, they can maintain and change their postures while lying, sitting, standing, and moving. Although children two years of age or younger with typical development would not be considered *skillful* movers, they have progressed systematically, at a rapid rate, and have developed a repertoire of rudimentary movement abilities. At the age of two years, children interact with their physical and emotional worlds in a complex and bidirectional fashion. That is, they act upon and change their environments, while at the same time, their environments affect and change them. This time of rapid motor development has been studied extensively, with researchers examining not only movement competency, but also preverbal cognitive and affective development. In this work, observable motor behaviors act as a window into both cognition and social development (Kretch & Adolph, 2015; Soska et al., 2010; Yoshida & Smith, 2008). As we know, a picture—or in this case, an action—is worth a thousand words.

The last four decades have seen a rekindling of interest in the underlying processes that lead to developmental change in the motor domain. This renewed interest coincides with the advent of the ecological (Adolph, 2008; Cole et al., 2013; Newell, 1986) and dynamic systems (Spencer et al., 2011; Thelen, 1985; Thelen & Ulrich, 1991; Ulrich, 2010) approaches to how perception and action develop (and influence each other) over time. These related approaches to development have been discussed extensively in earlier chapters and provide the theoretical underpinnings as, in this chapter and the next, we explore the development of fundamental skills in early childhood. To recap briefly, from the ecological and dynamic systems perspectives, movement skill emerges and becomes refined over time through changes in individual structural and functional constraints as well as environmental and task-related constraints that are "imposed on the organism-environment system" (Savelsbergh et al., 2003, p. 6). One or more of these structural or functional constraints may act, at a particular point in developmental time, in a *rate-limiting* capacity, potentially inhibiting the emergence of new skills, slowing the development of existing skills, or even causing the person to regress (i.e., to return to a less skillful level). An example of regression due to an individual constraint can be observed in gymnast Aurelia Dobre. Before turning 15, Dobre was the world gymnastics champion, but she could not maintain her elite level of performance because of a combination of growth spurts and injury. She retired from international competition before she turned 19.

With respect to motor development, what takes place following infancy, as the child moves into early childhood? Whitall (2003) has observed that, regarding movement skill, the primary goal during early childhood changes from acquiring movement skills to becoming an adept and proficient mover. Between the ages of two and six years, new and important movement abilities may appear while existing skills become more refined, flexible, and functional. Physical education teachers, physical therapists, and movement scientists must be knowledgeable about (a) the fundamental motor skills that emerge during this period, (b) how researchers study these skills, (c) the factors that lead to skilled movement, (d) the factors that interfere with the development of skilled movement, (e) how to facilitate skill acquisition, and finally, (f) why fundamental skill development is important.

Breakdown of Fundamental Motor Skills

To best understand how, between two and six years of age, **fundamental motor skills** develop and why they are so important to the developing child, we must first be clear about the skills to which we are referring. As previously noted, fundamental motor skills are foundational (Brian et al., 2020), given their importance in the subsequent development of complex skill combinations used in sport, gymnastics, and dance, as well as in many activities of daily living.

WHAT DO YOU THINK?

Exercise 8.1

Can you identify two highly skilled athletes who, because of changes in rate limiters, regressed or became less skillful (that is, experienced a phase shift to a less competent level)? This regression could be due to injury, changes in body type (morphology), or changes in movement pattern (either planned or unplanned).

Athlete	Rate limiter	Phase shift

Fundamental motor skills can be divided into three general groupings: **stability skills** (also referred to as nonlocomotor skills), **locomotor skills**, and **object control skills** (also referred to as manipulative skills or ball skills). Following a brief overview of stability and locomotor skills, the remainder of this chapter will examine the development of locomotor skills in some depth. The following chapter will discuss object control skills.

The term *stability skills* refers to axial movements—that is, movements around the axis of the body such as bending, stretching, swinging, swaying, pushing, pulling, turning, and twisting. These movements are performed with little or no movement of the base of support. *Locomotor skills,* in comparison, transport a person from one place to another. Although human beings most commonly move by walking or running, locomotor activities also include jumping, hopping, galloping, and skipping.

These less common ways to move are, nevertheless, often used in sporting events and artistic endeavors (e.g., track and field, fencing, court games, combative activities, and dance).

As noted, a later section of the chapter will revisit locomotor skills and examine what research and practice have shown about how children become competent in their execution over developmental and chronological time. Although introduced at the beginning of the chapter, at this point we further consider why it is important for prospective teachers and therapists to understand the development of fundamental motor skills.

Importance of Understanding Fundamental Motor Skills

Researchers, practitioners, and social critics have addressed why the timely and appropriate acquisition of fundamental motor

---

WHAT DO YOU THINK?

Exercise 8.2

As children, adolescents, and adults become more skilled, they combine fundamental motor skills when they engage in recreational and sporting activities. For example, while doing a rhythmic gymnastics routine, the performer might, at a given point, leap into the air, land in a balanced fashion, and then spin (rotate), all while moving smoothly to music and artistically waving a 20-foot (6 m) ribbon. Identify two motor skills that involve axial and locomotor skills. These combinations could be used within a game context (e.g., a team game or a racket sport) or an individual pursuit (e.g., gymnastics, diving, cycling, or rock climbing).

Motor skill	Axial skills involved	Locomotor skills involved

skills is crucial to the cognitive, affective, and motoric development of young children. As noted earlier in this chapter, careful study of the development of physical skillfulness in young children offers a window into the advancement of perceptual, cognitive, and affective processes. There are also the practical and clinical reasons for careful study, given that a significant number of young children struggle with movement skills (Brian et al., 2019). Unfortunately, the number of unskilled young children—those who do not cross the proficiency barrier—is increasing at an alarming rate with dire health-related consequences (Brian et al., 2019; De Meester et al., 2018; Lopes et al., 2017). It makes intuitive sense that decrements in skill would be magnified by such factors as socioeconomic status, access to education, and geography.

Regarding fundamental motor skill acquisition, there is a strongly held belief that instruction is not needed; rather, children naturally acquire fundamental motor skills through maturation and free play. In other words, developmentally appropriate, thoughtfully designed movement programs are not necessary. This perspective is patently inaccurate. Although there is certainly an important role for less supervised movement experiences, the skillful teaching (including research-based design, implementation, and assessment) of fundamental motor skills is imperative (Brian et al., 2020; Goodway & Branta, 2003). The pedagogical approaches to movement skill instruction for preschool-aged children vary from directive to a student-centered, mastery-learning environment. However, what they have in common is close attention to developmental and chronological appropriateness, differentiated instruction, and a philosophical and practical orientation that hews closely to the dynamic systems or constraints model of motor development discussed at length within this book.

An understanding of the level of fundamental motor skill development that one should expect of children of a given chronological age as well as recognizing differences in how a given skill is performed (keeping in mind functional and structural constraints) helps in developing individualized, educative programs for students who struggle with movement skills. Clearly, along with the design and implementation of research-based educational interventions, the continued development and appropriate use of assessment tools with strong psychometric properties are of paramount importance. Discussion of movement programs along with the appropriate assessment of gross motor development is discussed in depth elsewhere in this text.

As noted elsewhere in the book, across all societal groups, people have become more sedentary over the past two decades, with a concomitant increase in obesity and the host of health risks that accompany obesity (Owen et al., 2010). Teasing out the relative contributions and interactions of diet and physical inactivity, genetic predispositions to obesity, and environmental and educational inequities remains challenging; however, that physical inactivity plays a significant role in reducing health has been established (Clark & Metcalf, 2002). An important task, therefore, is to identify the factors that are likely to maintain appropriate physical activity levels throughout the life span. An array of motor developmentalists (Goodway et al., 2019; Haywood & Getchell, 2020; Logan et al., 2018) have argued strongly that competency in fundamental motor skills is essential to remaining healthy and active over the course of one's life with both physical and psychological benefits. An array of scholars who are currently examining multiple facets of the development of movement skill have echoed Clark and Metcalfe's (2002) and Stodden's (2008) earlier observations that inadequate foundational stability, locomotor, and object control (manipulative) skills result in limited opportunities and interest in physical activity. As noted in this chapter, as children age, this increasingly prevalent lack of fundamental motor skill becomes increasingly detrimental across many important health indices.

To telescope into a typical day at recess or into a physical education setting, it becomes quickly evident that learners with poorly developed stability, locomotor, or manipulative skills are clearly at a disadvantage when it comes to taking part in games and movement activities. Before too long, the requirements of play become more demanding. Movements must be done more quickly; decisions regarding which pattern to use become more complicated; and the consequences of making the wrong play, or choosing the right play but making an error, become more important. It is little wonder that so many children stop moving. They see no reason to participate in activities that they are not good at and that lead to derision from peers, often in very public ways. When a student struggles with reading, a good teacher, likely, will not embarrass him by having him read aloud to his classmates. When it comes to physical activities, there often is no choice. In a high-stakes game of kickball at recess, when the ball comes to a child and bounces off her hands (likely, not for the first time), the result is public humiliation. The child sees no reason to endure this if she does not have to. In essence, for physical activity to become an integral part of life—with the concomitant physical, health-related, and psychological health benefits—the developing child needs a solid base of fundamental motor skills.

Within historical context, Gabbard (2012) noted that *how* children acquire and develop fundamental motor skills has likely been the most carefully studied area in motor development. Indeed, pioneering researchers such as Lolas Halverson and Marianne Roberton (Roberton & Halverson, 1984) have been intrigued with the apparent age-related changes in fundamental motor skills, as well as the components that make up these skills. Much early work focused on cataloging and assessing age-related (as well as sex-related) changes in fundamental motor skills from a quantitative, or *product*, perspective (that is, how fast, how far, or how high). This era was followed by examination of the qualitative, or *process*-related, changes in fundamental motor skills over time. Currently, approaches to motor skill assessment and programming have combined both the **quantitative changes** and the **qualitative changes** (Tamplain et al., 2019). Although exceptions certainly exist (often, due to structural constraints) it should be intuitively clear that if a child's form (i.e., the mechanics) is closer to a competent level of execution, the outcome will be better. As an example, if Juan is hopping on one leg in his physical education class and now can move the arm opposite to his swing leg forward and upward, at the same time as his swing leg moves forward and upward, he covers more distance in a balanced and powerful manner. This differs from when he had just begun to hop and his arms were stationary, held out and to the side.

In this example, the oppositional arm swing is much more efficient. However, viewing movement through our dynamic systems lens, the most effective and efficient pattern depends on the task to be solved (Newell, 2020). If Shanice, participating in Roslyn Elementary School's spring field day, performs the standing long jump by explosively swinging her arms forward and upward and then, in quick succession, extending her hips, knees, and ankles, she will jump as far as she can, which is the point of this contest. In other words, the task to be solved is jump far. If, on the other hand, Shanice was jumping up in the air to pluck a low-hanging apple from a tree, the explosive bilateral use of her arms would get in the way of her performance; she would be much better off smoothly raising just her right arm to get that apple. In this example, the two very different mechanics of the arm action were determined by the goal of the task. Jumping for distance was more successfully accomplished with explosive arm action, while jumping up to pluck the apple required the use of just one arm, smoothly and carefully extended. In this chapter and in chapter 9, we will use a three-stage system to classify the level of development for a given fundamental motor skill; the tiers are initial, emerging, and competent.

Whole-Body Approach Versus Component Approach

How researchers and practitioners examine qualitative changes in movement skills has been an area of debate over the past five decades. When Wild (1938) did her classic cross-sectional research on the overarm throw for force, she concluded that children move through relatively invariant stages of development for the entire body. In the preceding example of Juan hopping, if he were at an unskilled (initial) stage with respect to his leg action, he would also be at the initial stage with respect to his arm action.

Given our example of hopping, as Juan's performance improved qualitatively in the leg component, his performance would also improve in the arm components. Roberton and colleagues (Roberton, 1977; Roberton & Konczak, 2001), however, took issue with the **whole-body approach** to the development of fundamental motor skills. Their longitudinal and cross-sectional research indicated that rather than all components becoming qualitatively more advanced (that is, moving toward the mature form) at approximately the same time, different components improved at different times. Roberton referred to this perspective as the **component approach**. In this view, Juan's leg action, as he hopped as quickly as he could, might be at a competent level with strong pumping action of the swing leg transmitting power to the support leg, whereas his arm action—both arms held high and out to the side—might be at the ini-

---

WHAT DO YOU THINK?

Exercise 8.3

Consider a beginning gymnast who is just learning how to do a front handspring vault. Imagine her standing, nervously, as she is about to begin her run up. What does her front handspring vault look like? Now, imagine the legendary gymnast Simone Biles going way back to the basics and doing the same front handspring vault. What does her front handspring vault look like? In the following table, describe, in a qualitative manner, what each vault looks like. Describe this entire skill, but keep in mind all parts of the body—legs, torso, arms, and head.

	Qualitative description of a front handspring vault
Novice gymnast	
Expert gymnast	

tial level, often referred to by practitioners as an immature level.

As discussed earlier in the chapter, improved fundamental motor skills allow children to explore and act upon their environments in a progressively more adept fashion. These improvements coincide with concomitant gains in the intellectual and social arenas. The following section examines the development of several fundamental locomotor skills, specifically, walking, running, jumping, hopping, galloping, sliding, and skipping. A considerable body of research has been devoted to understanding and accurately examining the development (or lack of development) of fundamental locomotor skills; foundational knowledge in this area is critical if practitioners are to develop the skills necessary to work effectively with young children in the movement arena. As has been previously discussed, poorly developed fundamental motor skills have led to a wide array of health and psychosocial indicants (Brian et al., 2020).

LOCOMOTOR SKILLS

Locomotor skills have been described, simply, as movements that transport people from one physical location to another, and although their development would appear to be relatively automatic, they received considerable attention over the course of the 20th century. That this attention came from fields as diverse as biomechanics,

physical therapy, adapted physical education, and medicine suggests that efficiently moving through space may be a more complex undertaking than first meets the eye. Indeed, the developing child must commandeer a dizzying array of body systems (many that are changing rapidly) and use them in a controlled and coordinated way to navigate through changing physical environments. Four-year-old Marty might be walking along a level and firm pathway when suddenly, he encounters a steeply angled dip; the ground has also become spongier and less firm. If he doesn't speed up—that is, run downhill—he'll take a nasty fall. Suddenly, Marty must deal with a change in angle and surface characteristics. The need for a new locomotor pattern presents itself, and Marty quickly and efficiently adapts, changing his movement pattern from a calm walk to a somewhat frenzied run. Flexibility is needed because Marty must solve specific movement tasks that often require a range of skills. In this example, he had to adjust to sudden environmental and task constraints, changing his locomotor pattern from a walk to a very specific type of run (with a shortened stride length and his torso leaning backward). A little later that same day, Marty played a tag game where three task requirements were (a) looking out for others as he moved, (b) quickly changing direction, and (c) accelerating and decelerating.

When examined in more depth, the requirements for Marty to efficiently nav-

---

WHAT DO YOU THINK?

Exercise 8.4

Take a moment and think back to when you were developing fundamental motor skills. For some of them (e.g., running), it may be difficult to remember how and when you realized, *Hey, I'm pretty good at this!* But for others, such as hopping or jumping, you might have a stronger memory. As you look back, think about (a) how you knew you had mastered the skill and (b) how you arrived at that point. For example, was it by playing around with your friends in the driveway? Practicing with your mom? Playing on a travel team? Or was it through some other avenue?

igate from point *A* to point *B* and be successful at tag seem quite remarkable. As noted earlier, the development of efficient and effective locomotor skills takes place as a variety of constraints interact. A child's weight, height, and arm and leg length are undergoing radical changes, and, at the same time, societal values influence how motivated a child might or might not be (e.g., believing that boys don't skip). Thus, in dynamic systems terms, children develop a variety of forms of locomotion while also dealing with physical and cultural constraints that constantly change and interact.

In the following sections we examine the development of walking, running, jumping, hopping, galloping, sliding, and skipping during childhood.

Walking

Nearly a century ago, the eminent developmentalist Mary Shirley (1931) suggested that the emergence of independent walking was the most important, and certainly the most impressive, of the developmental milestones. Few parents who delight at their children's first uncertain steps would disagree. Although up to then, the child was able to locomote through the environment by crawling (moving on hands and stomach), creeping (moving on hands and knees), and cruising (moving sideways so both hands and feet can be used to aid balance), the arrival of independent walking freed up the hands to further explore the changing environment (Newell, 2020). Although walking is generally considered to be a highly automatic skill that, once learned, changes little over the course of our lives, this is not the case. As people's physical abilities change (e.g., with arthritis) or their confidence wavers (e.g., after a serious fall), their technique might change. Environmental variables also play a role. Vacationers walking on a sandy beach are likely to slow their pace, while heavy snow or slick ice will modify the cadence, trunk

angle, and the amount of force used. Logic would suggest that 36-year-old Charrise, dealing with early-onset arthritis of the hip and navigating an icy parking lot, would walk in a very different way than her cousin, 29-year-old Louis, who is physically fit and has perfect health. Other factors that can influence walking patterns are (a) moving while handling an object (e.g., dribbling a basketball); (b) performing activities that require a great deal of balance and stability (e.g., traversing a balance beam); and (c) walking with an external load (e.g., carrying a backpack) (Payne & Isaacs, 2016).

Several motor developmentalists (Haywood & Getchell, 2020; Wickstrom, 1983) have noted, with reference to walking, that what does remain constant over the life span is the underlying timing of the act. During walking, weight shifts from the left foot to the right, and one foot is always in contact with the ground. Generally, the initial contact of the foot occurs halfway through the gait cycle referred to as a 50 percent phasing between the legs. A gait cycle (also referred to as a walking cycle) is made up of a support phase and a swing phase. The swing phase begins when the toes of one foot (or the whole foot) leave the ground and ends when the heel of that foot (or the whole foot) returns to the ground. The support phase of the gait cycle takes place when one foot is in contact with the ground. Therefore, when one foot is in the swing phase, the other is in the support phase. When both feet are in contact with the ground, the walker is in the double-support phase. Although early walking has been called a precarious adventure (Wickstrom, 1983) featuring frequent falls, the young walker over the next two to six years becomes an accomplished mover whose gait resembles that of a mature adult. Figures 8.1 through 8.3 outline the whole-body approach for walking (Gabbard, 2012; Goodway et al., 2019; Haywood & Getchell, 2020; Payne & Isaacs, 2016; Wickstrom, 1983).

FIGURE 8.1

WHOLE-BODY APPROACH FOR WALKING—INITIAL STAGE

- The base of support is wide.
- Contact is flat footed.
- The toes point outward.
- Steps are short, quick, and rigid.
- No trunk rotation occurs.
- A single-knee lock pattern is used.

- The knee flexes at contact followed by rapid knee extension.
- Hip flexion is significant.
- The pelvis tilts forward slightly.
- The arms are in high guard position.
- The arms are rigid with little or no movement.

FIGURE 8.2

WHOLE-BODY APPROACH FOR WALKING—ELEMENTARY STAGE

- The base of support is narrower than in the initial stage.
- Toeing out occurs less frequently than in the initial stage.
- Pelvic rotation is increased from the initial stage.
- Heel strike becomes apparent.

- Stride length is increased from the initial stage.
- Hip flexion is reduced from the initial stage.
- The forward pelvic tilt is reduced from the initial stage.

FIGURE 8.3

WHOLE-BODY APPROACH FOR WALKING—COMPETENT STAGE

- The base of support is significantly narrower than in the earlier stages.
- Foot contact becomes heel–toe as opposed to flat footed.
- The single-knee lock pattern is replaced by a double-knee lock pattern.

- Step and stride lengths are increased from the earlier stages.
- Walking speed and step frequency are increased from the earlier stages.
- Oppositional arm swing is apparent.

Although the ability to perform an alternating movement pattern is present from birth (Thelen, 1985), the beginning walker must deal with the rate limiters of balance and strength. To move around the environment without falling too often, the developing walker must take short baby steps while using a wide stance with the toes pointing slightly outward. With the hands held in a high guard position to protect against falls, the beginning walker moves tentatively with little trunk rotation and lands on a flat foot. The pelvis tilts slightly, and the ankles are essentially locked. Although this walking pattern is, at one level of analysis, immature, it allows for relatively stable ambulation. What it does not allow for is efficient movement with the ability to change direction smoothly and quickly. There is, however, variability regarding when a baby becomes skillful. Examples abound of children as young as nine months of age walking (and even running) with a fluid, mature gait. Why

these infants are preternaturally skillful is up for debate; however, the ecological approach to development (Adolph, 2008) and the concept of what the environment affords could offer insight into this unusually early development. In addition to the important environmental affordances, Haywood and Getchell (2020, p. 71) have observed that proficient walking involves the person's "exploiting biomechanical principles as body dimensions change." As a more mature gait gradually emerges (generally by age 4 or 5), the following characteristics are seen (Gabbard, 2012; Haywood & Getchell, 2020):

- *Base of support and foot angle.* The dynamic base of support (i.e., the base of support during moving) is reduced to approximately the width of the person's trunk. This narrowing generally takes place four and a half months after independent walking begins, allowing for more efficient movement. Regarding foot angle, the beginning walker tends to move with the toes out (called toeing out). This pattern disappears at approximately the same time the base of support narrows, with the foot becoming aligned in a straight fore–aft position. Both the narrowing of the base of support and the disappearance of toeing out result in the application of forces in a forward–backward plane (Haywood & Getchell, 2020), a significantly more efficient movement pattern. In-toeing (commonly referred to as a pigeon-toed gait) is not a normal pattern and is seen infrequently.

- *Foot contact.* As walkers develop, they move from the flat footfall to a heel–toe pattern, resulting in an increased range of motion. Toe walking is often seen in young children and is not a cause for concern; however, if this pattern persists beyond three years of age, it should be examined.

- *Step and stride length.* Between ages 1 and 7, step and stride length almost double. This is due, for the most part, to significant increases in force and leg extension at push-off. Secondarily, children's stride length increases because of increased leg length.

- *Walking speed and step frequency.* As walking develops, speed increases while step frequency (steps per minute) decreases. Sutherland (1997) hypothesized that increased neuromuscular control in older walkers is primarily responsible for the decreased step frequency. It was posited that younger walkers lack the postural control to increase speed through longer strides and thus must take more frequent steps.

- *Double-knee lock.* As walking improves, children increase their range of motion through the double-knee lock pattern. The knee is extended at heel strike, flexed slightly as body weight shifts over the support leg, and extended once more at push-off.

- *Pelvic rotation.* By 14 months of age, pelvic rotation is apparent, allowing for full range of motion as well as oppositional movements of the upper and lower bodies.

- *Oppositional arm swing.* As noted earlier, beginning walkers have their arms in a high guard position with elbows slightly flexed and abducted. Over the ensuing months, this position is gradually replaced by a mechanically efficient oppositional arm swing. Initially, the arm swing may not be coordinated; the arms may sometimes come forward in unison. Over time, oppositional arm swing becomes established, and the opposite arm and leg move forward and backward at the same time. As this reciprocal movement is refined, the arm swing becomes relaxed, with slight movement at both the shoulder and the elbow.

As noted previously, the development of proficient walking not only allows children to explore their environment capably, but it also provides a stable and effective base for more advanced locomotor skills.

Running

Twelve-year-old Luc looked down at his watch and realized that dinner would be on the table in six minutes, and there was a long way to go before he got home. Walking would not get him there on time, and a light jog would not do it either. Even though the terrain was uneven, he launched into a smooth run. Luc made it to the dinner table with minutes to spare. Running has been characterized as an extension of walking, and certainly the two forms of locomotion have much in common—the reciprocal arm and leg action as well as the alternating leg action. However, there are clear differences; primary among these is that running does not have a double-support phase. Instead, there is a flight phase during which neither foot is in contact with the ground.

Luc's running wasn't always as smooth as on that evening. When he began to run (approximately seven months after beginning to walk independently), he had to develop enough strength to become airborne, as well as the balance to catch himself on one leg and maintain balance on that leg while moving forward. Thus, developing adequate strength and balance is imperative with these factors acting as *rate limiters* for the developing runner. Figures 8.4 through 8.6 present a hypothesized developmental sequence for running, including both leg and arm action (Gabbard, 2012; Goodway et al., 2019; Haywood & Getchell, 2020; Payne & Isaacs, 2016; Wickstrom, 1983).

As children mature physically (specifically, they gain in body size and strength as well as coordination) and get more practice, they demonstrate a concomitant improvement in both process and product measures related to running. Regarding product measures, children run more quickly and increase the amount of time spent in the flight phase. With respect to process measures, the following positive changes take place over developmental time, resulting in a proficient running pattern (Haywood & Getchell, 2020; Wickstrom, 1983):

- A slight forward lean is maintained throughout the stride.
- The arms swing in a synchronized pattern in opposition to the leg pattern, with the elbows held at approximately 90 degrees.
- The support foot contacts the ground

approximately under the center of gravity in a flat-footed fashion.

- The knee of the support leg bends slightly after the foot contacts the ground.
- The body moves forward and upward (into the nonsupport phase) through forceful extension of the support leg at the ankle, knee, and hip.
- The recovery knee moves forcefully to a high knee raise, while the lower leg simultaneously flexes, bringing the heel close to the buttock.
- Toeing out is eliminated, and the base of support is narrowed.
- Trunk rotation increases, leading to greater stride length as well as improved arm–leg opposition.

In typically developing children, learning to run proficiently occurs fairly automatically. However, when advanced maneuvers are introduced or required for a particular task (e.g., chasing, fleeing, changing direc-

FIGURE 8.4

WHOLE-BODY APPROACH FOR RUNNING—INITIAL STAGE

- The movements of the legs and feet are exaggerated.
- The flight period is minimal.
- Contact is generally flat footed (although some children run on tiptoes).

- The base of support is wide.
- The arms are held in either a middle or high guard position.
- The arms move to the sides as opposed to back and forth.

FIGURE 8.5

WHOLE-BODY APPROACH FOR RUNNING—ELEMENTARY STAGE

- Hip, knee, and ankle extension is increased from the initial stage at takeoff.
- The height of the forward knee is increased from the initial stage at takeoff.
- The length of the running stride is increased from the initial stage.

- The speed of running is increased from the initial stage.
- The flight period is increased from the initial stage.
- Horizontal arm swing is increased from the initial stage.

FIGURE 8.6

WHOLE-BODY APPROACH FOR RUNNING—COMPETENT STAGE

- The base of support is narrow.
- The length of running stride is increased further from the elementary stage.
- The application of force is greater than in the elementary stage.
- The trunk leans forward slightly.
- The arms move in a large arc, in opposition to the leg movements.

- The arms are bent at the elbows at approximately 90 degrees.
- The recovery knee is raised high and swings forward quickly.
- The support leg bends slightly at contact and subsequently extends quickly and completely from the initial stage.
- Horizontal arm swing is increased from the initial stage.

TRY THIS

Looking at the Quality of Your Running

Exercise 8.5

In a gymnasium or other open area, with a partner, set up a course that challenges your ability to change direction quickly and fluidly. Using plastic cones, set up a course so that you can run in a straight line for 10 feet (3 m), dodge to the left at a 45-degree angle, and run for 10 feet and then dodge right, again running for 10 feet. Following this, sprint back to the starting point. Each person will run this course at full speed five times. In each case, both the runner and the observer will write down the quantitative differences (that is, how quickly the course was run for each of the five trials) and the qualitative differences (that is, Was the individual able to change direction more smoothly and accurately as they had more practice?). Compare your partner's quantitative and qualitative observations with your own. Whose observations would you consider more accurate, and why?

tion quickly, accelerating, or decelerating), instructors should keep in mind both the developmental and chronological age of the learner.

Jumping

From the age of two, children begin to explore and develop ways of moving other than walking and running, and, importantly, a child who has mastered running has the essential ingredients needed to be a jumper. The family of jumps is a large one and includes leaping (a one-foot takeoff followed by a landing on the opposite foot), hopping (jumping from one foot to the same foot rhythmically), the vertical jump for height (a two-foot takeoff with a two-foot landing), and the standing long jump or horizontal jump for distance (a two-foot takeoff with a two-foot landing).

Developing competency in this assortment of jumps allowed Luc, whom we met in our previous running example, to not only speed along quickly and fluidly but also to keep his brand-new shoes dry by jumping over a narrow stream. As he got closer to home and recognized that he had time to spare, Luc gathered himself, jumped high in the air, and grabbed an apple from a tree. When Luc entered high school, all the jumping skills he had developed helped him

with the sports he enjoyed; he was proficient at hitting a volleyball, making a layup, and running the steeplechase.

Jumping is the fundamental motor skill of projecting the body into the air by the force generated by either one or both legs and then landing on one or both feet. It can be done in a forward, backward, or sideways direction. Although related to walking and running (the leap is an exaggerated running step), jumping is a more challenging movement skill for children to master. They need adequate strength to get the body into the air, postural control and coordination while in the air, and balance upon landing. When hopping, strength is particularly important because the one-foot-to-one-foot pattern is done repeatedly. Wickstrom (1983) observed that, beyond the significant physical requirements of jumping, there are confidence requirements. Jumping from heights, particularly, requires a certain level of bravery. In a very early investigation, Gutteridge (1939) noted that when children had to jump from a greater height than they were used to or were introduced to a new, challenging type of jump, they reverted to an earlier form of jumping. That is, an *affective* rate limiter (or functional constraint) resulted in a skill regression under certain circumstances.

TRY THIS

Does the Jumping Environment Affect the Quality of a Jump?

Exercise 8.6

As mentioned, Gutteridge's early work suggested that jumping from a high level resulted in children demonstrating a less mature level of jumping skill. He hypothesized that bravery (or a lack of bravery) was the reason for the change. With a gymnastics mat on the ground, jump down, five times, from a height of 30 inches. Following these five jumps, repeat the exercise without the gymnastics mat. Aim for a spot on the floor that is two feet away. Using a cell phone, have a partner record all your jumps. From a qualitative perspective, did your jumps with a mat on the floor vary one from another? If so, did you improve over the five jumps? If you did improve, why do you think that this was the case? Please answer the same questions for jumping without a mat. Finally, did the quality of your jumps differ, depending on whether you had a mat? If so, why?

Gutteridge's and Wickstrom's observations lead to an interesting question that motor developmentalists must answer. Regardless of the skill being considered, how do we measure improvement or regression? Although these questions will be answered in depth in chapter 11, here are three general approaches that are certainly not independent of each other (Barnett et al., 2020; Logan et al., 2018):

1. *Age norms:* Comparing when the person acquired a skill to when most people acquire the skill

2. *Quantitative measures:* Determining how much of something is present; for jumping, determining the height or the distance of the jump (also known as product measures)

3. *Qualitative measures:* Observing the pattern or form of the movement (also known as process measures)

Along with these three methods, Wickstrom and Wild's perspective that considers the affective qualities of courage and confidence should be considered. Although this is more difficult to evaluate objectively, how confident an individual is of her skill level has a considerable bearing on how well she performs.

With respect to the age at which preschool children typically learn types of jumps, early scholars in the area of motor development (Bayley, 1935; McCaskill & Wellman, 1938) determined approximate ages at which the skills are typically mastered (e.g., jump from a 12 ft [3.7 m] height with one foot ahead at 24 months; jump from a 12 ft [3.7 m] height with both feet at 34 months; jump over a rope 2-8 in. [5-20 cm] high with both feet at 41.5 months). Wickstrom (1983) stressed that these are approximate because of the wide range of scores observed. Given that people of all ages have changed in size and strength over the past century (referred to as a **secular trend**), it might be presumed that children born in the 21st century would, likely, achieve jumping landmarks (as well as other fundamental motor landmarks) at somewhat younger ages. However, the opposite scenario has come to pass with children becoming less capable. Work by Brian and her colleagues (2019) found that, instead of an improvement in fundamental motor skill, there has been a precipitous decline.

Skill development in children involves the gradual refinement of movement abilities over time. Indeed, researchers examining the acquisition of movement skill from a dynamic systems perspective have noted that children who refine their movement patterns appear better able to take advantage of the principles of motion. These observations clearly apply to the acquisition of jumping skill. With respect to the refinement of movement abilities over chronological time, Haywood and Getchell (2020) noted that even if beginning jumpers intend to perform a long jump, because of limitations in their form (the qualitative components of the jump), they end up doing a vertical jump. This is largely a result of posture that is too erect. By three years of age, however, the developing child can modify the trunk angle to perform either a vertical or a horizontal jump as desired (Clark et al., 1989).

Early jumps, for either height or distance, are characterized by a preparatory shallow crouch. That is, the hip, knees, and ankles are not flexed enough to generate a significant amount of force. Additionally, the legs remain slightly flexed at takeoff. Beginning jumpers often use a one-foot takeoff (also referred to as a step-out) and land with one foot touching down before the other. Because of the one-foot takeoff, the legs are frequently asymmetrical during flight. Adopting a two-foot takeoff, with an appropriate body lean, generally keeps the legs symmetrical and thus more aerodynamic during flight.

RESEARCH NOTES

Are Young Children Becoming Less Skilled?

It has been posited that developmental delay in the acquisition of fundamental motor skills has a profound effect on a wide range of health indices including, but not limited to, overweight, reduced activity levels, perceptions of competence, and an ability and willingness to engage in active structured and unstructured movement experiences. However, the current level of motor competency of young learners in the United States had not been carefully examined (Brian et al., 2019). Given the previously noted importance of developing movement competency, Brian and her colleagues (Brian et al., 2019) conducted a large-scale investigation that examined the motor proficiency of American children aged three to six years. Additionally, the authors looked at predictors of motor competency including socioeconomic status, race, sex, body mass index, and geographic region. Children from multiple states took part in the study and were assessed through the *Test of Gross Motor Development–Second Edition*. There were 580 children, including 296 girls. Unfortunately, but not unsurprisingly, the results were dire with 77 percent of the sample at risk for developmental delay. Although socioeconomic status, race, geographic region, and body mass index were neither protective nor negative, there were sex-related differences with girls being significantly less skilled in object control skills, specifically catching, kicking, rolling, dribbling, and striking. These sex differences were consistent with earlier findings. The authors of this study suggested that this extremely low level of movement skill competency in young children would likely limit their active play in an array of social contexts including, but not limited to, using playground equipment, taking part in childhood games, and playing sports. Brian and her colleagues argue that to reverse this secular decline, children must have (a) more opportunities to play and (b) structured movement experiences, during which fundamental motor skills are taught by trained movement specialists.

To this point, the discussion has concentrated on the lower body; however, the way the arms are used can help or hinder jumping. Beginning jumpers often demonstrate arm actions that are not beneficial for a long jump or vertical jump. These jumpers may use the arms asymmetrically, hold them stationary (at the sides), or hold them in a high guard position for protection in case of a fall.

Despite these inauspicious beginnings, the goal is that children should learn to jump effectively by the time they begin school. As noted earlier, this is not currently the case (Brian et al., 2020). Movement toward the competent jumps outlined earlier depends on the opportunity to practice in varied environments and on normal growth in size and strength. Although consistent quantitative changes in jump distance (average increases of 3-5 in. [7.6-12.7 cm] a year during the elementary years) and height (average increases of 2 in. [5 cm] per year during the elementary years) have been cataloged (DeOreo & Keogh, 1980), qualitative changes are more varied (Haywood & Getchell, 2020).

As discussed earlier and demonstrated for the skill of running in figures 8.4 through 8.6, researchers have presented changes in movement skill as developmental sequences that capture the qualitative changes in the critical features of a skill. Both the whole-body approach and the component approach identify the steps children go through as they move from inefficient movements to more skillful patterns. Figures 8.7 through 8.9 present developmental characteristics of the standing long jump, and figures 8.10 through 8.12 present developmental characteristics of the vertical jump, using the whole-body approach (Gabbard, 2012; Goodway et al., 2019; Haywood & Getchell, 2020; Payne & Isaacs, 2016; Wickstrom, 1983).

The standing long jump (also referred to as the horizontal jump and broad jump) and the vertical jump have much in common. Both have easily identifiable preparatory, takeoff, flight, and landing phases, and the takeoffs and landings are two footed. However, the standing long jump presents more movement challenges than the vertical jump does. Because the jumper is moving the body both upward and outward, the center of gravity must be slightly in front of the base of support at takeoff. Proficient jumping requires a takeoff angle of approximately 45 degrees. Because this is a challenge for developing jumpers, they frequently step out to maintain their balance. A second significant movement challenge for long jumpers is swinging their legs from behind the center of gravity (at takeoff) forward and under the trunk in preparation for landing. Because the vertical jump does not require the body to tip forward or the legs to swing forward, it is an easier jump to perform and master than the long jump.

Hopping

A hop is defined as taking off and landing on the same foot. As discussed earlier, this movement requires considerable strength and balance. The proficient hopper demonstrates the following characteristics (Haywood & Getchell, 2020, p. 88):

- The swing leg leads the hip.
- The support leg extends fully.
- The arms move in opposition to the legs.
- The support leg flexes at landing to absorb the force of the landing and to prepare for extension at the next takeoff.

Both a component developmental sequence (Halverson & Williams, 1985) and a whole-body developmental sequence (Goodway et al., 2019) have been developed for the hop. Figures 8.13 through 8.15 present a whole-body sequence (Gabbard, 2012; Goodway et al., 2019; Haywood & Getchell, 2020; Payne & Isaacs, 2016; Wickstrom, 1983).

FIGURE 8.7

WHOLE-BODY APPROACH FOR THE STANDING LONG JUMP—INITIAL STAGE

- The preparatory crouch is limited and inconsistent.
- The trunk lean is less than 30 degrees.
- Extension of the hips and knees at takeoff and during flight is minimal.
- Arm swing is minimal and ineffective (the arms are held rigidly at the sides with elbows flexed or arms held in winged position).

- Legs are positioned asymmetrically during flight.
- Vertical force is generally greater than horizontal force, leading to an upward rather than a forward jump.
- An inability to flex the hips and knees during the jump leads to an abrupt landing.

FIGURE 8.8

WHOLE-BODY APPROACH FOR THE STANDING LONG JUMP—ELEMENTARY STAGE

- The preparatory crouch becomes deeper and more consistent than in the initial stage.
- The extension of the hips and knees is increased from the initial stage.
- Forward swing of the arms (in the anteroposterior plane) is increased from the initial stage.

- Total-body extension at takeoff is increased from the initial stage.
- Thigh flexion during flight is increased from the initial stage.

FIGURE 8.9

WHOLE-BODY APPROACH FOR THE STANDING LONG JUMP—COMPETENT STAGE

- The preparatory crouch is deep with flexion of the hips, knees, and ankles.
- Trunk lean is at least 30 degrees.
- The arms are swung backward simultaneously in a smooth fashion.
- The heels come off the ground before knee extension.
- There is a rapid and vigorous extension at takeoff of the hips and knees in the direction of travel.

- The arms vigorously swing forward and upward.
- Both knees are flexed, and the thighs are brought forward, parallel to the ground, during flight.
- The lower legs swing forward for a two-foot landing.

FIGURE 8.10

WHOLE-BODY APPROACH FOR VERTICAL JUMPING—INITIAL STAGE

- Form is variable and unpredictable.
- The preparatory crouch is limited and inconsistent.
- The legs are not fully extended at takeoff.
- There is very quick flexion of the hips and knees (the legs are tucked under the body).

- The arms and shoulders are elevated sideways.
- The head flexes forward.

FIGURE 8.11

WHOLE-BODY APPROACH FOR VERTICAL JUMPING—ELEMENTARY STAGE

- The form becomes less variable and more predictable than in the initial stage.
- The preparatory crouch becomes deeper (with increased knee bend).
- A two-foot takeoff takes place.

- The arms are used to aid in flight and balance, but often unequally.
- The body does not extend completely during flight.

FIGURE 8.12

WHOLE-BODY APPROACH FOR VERTICAL JUMPING—COMPETENT STAGE

- There is a deep preparatory crouch with flexion of the hips, knees, and ankles.
- The hips, knees, and ankles extend completely upon takeoff.
- There is very quick flexion of the hips and knees (the legs are tucked under the body).
- The arms are swung forward and upward.

- One hand continues up while the other comes down, resulting in an effective tipping of the shoulder girdle near the peak of the jump.
- The head flexes backward.
- The trunk extends at the crest of the reach.
- Landing is on the balls of the feet with the hips and knees flexed.

FIGURE 8.13

WHOLE-BODY APPROACH FOR HOPPING—INITIAL STAGE

- Forward movement is minimal.
- Elevation is minimal.
- Movement is jerky.
- The support leg is lifted by flexion rather than by forceful extension.

- The nonsupport (swing) leg is generally held high and is largely inactive.
- Arm action is minimal or inconsistent.
- The arms are held in the high guard position and to the sides for balance.
- Landings are flat footed.

FIGURE 8.14

WHOLE-BODY APPROACH FOR HOPPING—ELEMENTARY STAGE

- Forward movement is increased from the initial stage.
- Elevation is increased from the initial stage.
- The support leg is lifted by minimal knee and ankle extension because of slight body lean.

- The nonsupport (swing) leg moves forward and upward.
- The arms begin to be used (bilaterally) for thrust rather than for balance.

FIGURE 8.15

WHOLE-BODY APPROACH FOR HOPPING—COMPETENT STAGE

- Weight is transferred smoothly, upon landing, to the ball of the foot of the support leg before the ankle and knee extend.

- The support leg reaches almost full extension upon takeoff.

- The swing leg leads the movement, pumping up and down.

- The pumping action of the swing leg increases such that, when viewed from the side, it passes behind the support leg.

- The arm opposite the swing leg moves upward and forward in synchrony with the upward and forward movement of the swing leg.

- The other arm moves in a direction opposite that of the swing leg.

- Vigorous swinging action may not be present unless there are speed or distance requirements, or both.

Galloping, Sliding, and Skipping— Combining Movements

Galloping, sliding, and skipping are complicated movement patterns that combine two or more previously mastered locomotor skills. These skills include stepping, hopping, and leaping (Haywood & Getchell, 2020). Referred to as combination skills (Goodway et al., 2019), the complexity of these three fundamental locomotor skills leads to their emergence later in childhood, after the acquisition of the single-motor pattern skills that they are based upon (Payne & Isaacs, 2016).

The asynchronous patterns of galloping and sliding develop before skipping, with galloping being the first of the three to be mastered. Except for the body orientation (in galloping, the body is front facing, while sliding is performed sideways, thus being more challenging for the mover) these patterns are very similar. In both galloping and sliding, the motor patterns include (a) a rhythmic step forward, followed by (b) a leap-step on the other foot (Roberton & Halverson, 1984). To efficiently gallop and slide, the child must have (a) adequate dynamic balance, (b) leg strength, (c) coordination, and (d) the ability to maintain an asymmetrical, rhythmic pattern. Haywood and Getchell (2020) and Goodway and colleagues (2019) have noted that an adequate strength-to-weight ratio affects the performance of the gallop and slide, particularly during the leap (flight) phase of the movement. Both the gallop and slide are used in a variety of folk dances, while effectively sliding is a foundational skill in an array of sports, including but not limited to tennis (moving along the baseline), basketball (guarding an opponent), and baseball and softball (taking a lead). Proficient gallopers and sliders demonstrate (a) smooth, fluid, and rhythmical action; (b) a trail leg that lands adjacent to or slightly behind the lead leg; (c) feet that remain close to the surface; (d) knees that are slightly bent; and (e) an ability to lead with either leg. Conversely, beginning gallopers and sliders demonstrate a choppy pattern with the trail (rear) leg crossing in front of the front leg, while the rear leg is in the air. Additionally, the beginner has a preferred lead leg and demonstrates a look of deep concentration as they attempt these movements. This cognitive experience (Goodway et al., 2019) suggests a need to pay a lot of attention to the task leading to the lack of fluidity previously mentioned.

As noted, of these three skills, skipping is by far the most complicated (Payne & Isaacs, 2016) and is not, generally, mastered until the student is between six and seven years of age (with girls demonstrating mastery approximately six or seven months before boys). Haubenstricker, Seefeldt, and Branta (1983) found that by age 5 years, only a little more than 50 percent of children were able to skip. Unlike galloping and sliding, skipping is a synchronous skill, with each leg performing the same, relatively complicated pattern. Specifically, skipping requires a step and a hop on one leg before these movements are then repeated on the other leg. One can see that performing dual tasks, instead of just one task, on a given leg asks considerably more of a young mover than performing a single task, as with galloping or sliding. Like galloping and sliding, prerequisite movement skills include dynamic balance, such that the mover can move smoothly, keeping their body over their base of support; leg strength; and multilimb coordination. Proficient skippers move smoothly with a rhythmical weight transfer on each leg. Additionally, the legs stay close to the ground with minimal vertical displacement. The arms are not used for force production and swing in opposition to the legs.

As with galloping and sliding, skipping makes significant demands on the cardiovascular system, while in terms of functional skills, skipping is found in an array of international folk dances. Developmentalist Alan Burton has suggested that, regardless of its functional utility, a skipping child captures a certain happy innocence. This unbridled joy can also be seen with Charles Schulz's depiction of Snoopy doing his happy dance. We are pretty sure that Snoopy was skipping.

SUMMARY

Learning fundamental motor skills is essential to the healthy development of children and, given a strong movement foundation, they will have the skill set—and the confidence—to be physically active on their own, with their families, and with their peers. Whether the child ultimately decides to participate in formalized athletic events or is content to play more recreationally is, of course, up to the child. What is evident, though, is that carefully designed movement environments and progressive educational experiences that are well thought out are essential to ensure early and sustained success. This chapter laid a solid foundation for understanding how and when these fundamentals are achieved, with particular attention to locomotor skills. Practitioners can take the concepts presented and build on them through practical experiences and focused research.

> **ONLINE ACTIVITIES**

The student material found in HK*Propel* includes exercises, labs, and videos to enhance learning and encourage practical application of important concepts.

LEARNING AIDS

Supplemental Activities

1. It is imperative that you be able to accurately assess how skillfully a person moves through space. Accurate assessment requires frequent well-thought-out observations. From the Internet (YouTube or another video-sharing website), access video clips of novice and expert runners (one of each) and assess their competency. Watch each video clip at least five times. Use the following checklist to complete the assignment.

	Novice Age: Gender:	Expert Age: Gender:
Base of support		
Length of running stride		
Application of force by support leg		
Arms held in middle guard position		
Arms swung backward and forward together (bilateral arm swing)		
Arms swung forward and back in an opposition pattern		

From P.S. Beach, M.E. Perreault, A.S. Brian, and D.H. Collier, *Motor Learning and Development*, 3rd ed. (Champaign, IL: Human Kinetics, 2024).

2. For this activity, watch 7- to 8-year-old gymnasts and 9- to 11-year-old gymnasts. Using YouTube, locate two female gymnasts who are within the 7- to 8-year-old group and two female gymnasts who are within the 9- to 11-year-old group. If possible, choose two 7-year-olds and two 11-year-olds. Watch the athletes in an array of gymnastics activities (e.g., vault, floor routines) and compare and contrast the four gymnasts.

   a. Did you observe differences in the competency between the older and younger gymnasts?

   b. If there were differences, why do you think that this was the case? Was this solely a psychomotor issue or did affective or cognitive factors play a role?

   c. Do you think that you became more proficient at assessing gymnastics as you gained more experience observing?

   d. Are there ways by which you could improve your observational skills?

Glossary

component approach—The perspective that learners' component body parts move toward the advanced form at potentially different times.

fundamental motor skills—Fundamental motor skills are foundational abilities that are required for the subsequent development of complex skill combinations used in sport, gymnastics, and dance, as well as in many activities of daily living. They are divided into three general groupings: stability skills (also referred to as nonlocomotor skills), locomotor skills, and object control skills (also referred to as manipulative skills or ball skills).

locomotor skills—Skills that involve moving from one place to the next.

object control skills—Skills that involve controlling implements and objects such as balls, hoops, bats, and ribbons by hand, by foot, or with any other part of the body.

qualitative changes—Process-related changes in skills over time.

quantitative changes—Product-related changes in skills over time.

secular trend—A change in an ability or skill over successive generations.

stability skills—Movements around the axis of the body (e.g., bending, stretching, swinging, swaying, pushing, pulling, turning, twisting) that are done with little or no movement of the base of support.

whole-body approach—The perspective that learners move through relatively invariant stages of movement skill development in which all body components move toward the advanced form at approximately the same time.

9

OBJECT CONTROL SKILLS IN CHILDHOOD

CHAPTER OBJECTIVES

After reading this chapter, you should be able to do the following:

- Define the term *object control skills.*
- Identify levels of competency in object control skills.
- List factors that facilitate the acquisition of object control skills.
- List factors that interfere with the development of object control skills.
- List factors that may contribute to differences in object control skill performance between girls and boys.

Back to Ayisha in Physical Education Class

Remember in chapter 8 that Ayisha had just moved to the United States and received her first experiences in physical education. Ayisha is starting to really enjoy physical education, and this week, she is learning a new sport: softball. People don't play softball in Saudi Arabia, so Ayisha has no experience with batting a ball, overhand throwing, or even catching. At first, Ayisha is really scared. Ayisha's physical education teacher smartly pairs Ayisha with Sara. Sara has played softball for years and even coaches children's softball in their community. Sara teaches Ayisha how to catch first so that she is no longer afraid of the ball. Sara uses a soft yarn ball first and then progresses up to eventually throwing with an actual softball. Ayisha figures out how to catch quickly and is now ready to move on to learning more parts of the game.

The authors wish to thank Layne Case for her contribution to this chapter.

As noted in chapter 8, it is very important to have opportunities to engage in motor skills throughout development. As young children begin to sit, move well, and ambulate independently, their hands, arms, legs, and feet are free to move around their environment and help them explore. With more experience, a new type of motor skill, commonly known as **object control skills**, will begin to emerge. As children begin to spend more time in school and within their community, both independently and with their peers, opportunities for object control skill instruction and repetition become important. Object control skills, including those softball-related skills that Ayisha had never experienced before, do not typically develop through maturation or during unstructured free play. Instead, structured opportunities for children to practice object control skills are necessary for children to become proficient in this domain. If children cannot proficiently perform these skills, they may not gain adequate access to physical activity, leaving them to miss opportunities for other positive health and developmental outcomes. This chapter discusses object control skills, their importance for childhood and throughout the course of life, and how they develop. We also address the differences we may see in object control skill performance, including between girls and boys.

DEVELOPMENT OF OBJECT CONTROL SKILLS

During the first two years of life, children become motivated to explore their environments independently. Their motor skills develop rapidly as they begin to interact with their surroundings, reaching for, grasping, and manipulating items around them. At the age of two, children have the basic patterns needed for locomotion and object manipulation. Through increased exploration and practice, eye–hand and eye–foot coordination begin to develop and tremendously improve, and, over time, motor patterns begin to progress into the foundational building blocks of more complex, context-specific skills that will be used for sports and physical activities later in life. This period in which children develop fundamental motor patterns, including object control skills, is studied extensively and in diverse ways. For many children, acquisition of object control skills is observed rapidly. However, trends from recent decades are showing noticeable and considerable differences in motor skill patterns between children with varied learning, social, and environmental experiences, and, potentially, from current and previous generations. Researchers interested in object control skill development have developed unique and innovative experiments that shed light on these differences and lay the foundation for effective and targeted intervention.

As we consider these differences in object control skill performance that promote intervention, remembering the underlying processes that researchers theorize to lead to developmental change in the motor domain is important and must stay consistent. The ecological and dynamic systems approaches to motor development have been discussed extensively in other chapters and provide the underlying theoretical and conceptual frameworks that encourage us to understand the development and acquisition of fundamental motor skills in early childhood and throughout life. In summary, according to the ecological and dynamic systems perspectives, human movement skill results and develops over time from interactions between individual, task, or environmental constraints. While new skills emerge from these constraints, any or all these constraints can also act as rate limiters that inhibit or minimize the development of new skills or reverse existing skills to a less skillful level. Considering Ayisha, for example, when she was learning to play

WHAT DO YOU THINK?

Exercise 9.1

Can you identify two instances in which you or an athlete you know, because of changes in rate limiters, regressed or became less skillful with the performance of a particular object control skill? In other words, because of this change, you experienced a phase shift to a less competent performance level. This regression could be due to injury, changes in body type (morphology), changes in equipment, changes in movement pattern (either planned or unplanned), or other factors.

Object control skill	Rate limiter	Phase shift

softball, her fear of catching the larger, dense softball limited her from practicing to catch. Instead, using a softer yarn ball to first practice to catch allowed her to develop that skill.

Breakdown of Object Control Skills

Object control skills include an array of abilities: overarm and underarm throwing, rolling, striking, heading, kicking, punting, catching, and trapping. If we examine object control skills more closely, several issues become apparent. First, they can involve, primarily, either the upper body (arms or head) or the lower body; second, they can also involve either imparting force to an object and moving it away from the body or positioning a part of the body in front of an oncoming object to deflect or stop it. Goodway and colleagues (2020) referred to these actions as propulsive and absorptive,

respectively. A third issue involves the use of an implement to either impart force to an object or absorb the force of an object. Examples of implements are rackets, bats, and gloves. Obviously, the use of implements depends on the person's skill level, the rules of the game, or both.

Importance of Understanding Object Control Skills

Across all societal groups, people have become more sedentary with a concomitant increase in obesity and the host of health risks that accompany obesity (Owen et al., 2010). An important priority within several research domains related to public health, therefore, has been placed on examining the relative contributions of healthy lifestyle factors, including diet and physical activity, toward increasing overall health.

WHAT DO YOU THINK?

Exercise 9.2

As children and adults become more skilled, they combine fundamental motor skills while engaging in sporting activities. For example, while fielding a ground ball during a softball game, a right-handed player has to slide to her right (locomotor skill), bend and turn her body as she prepares to field the ball (axial movements), field the ball with a backhand motion (object control skill), and then throw the ball to first base (object control skill). Identify two motor skills that involve axial, locomotor, and object control skills. A person could use these combinations within a game context (e.g., a team game or a racket sport) or an individual pursuit (e.g., cycling or rock climbing).

Motor skill	Axial skill(s) involved	Object control skill(s) involved	Locomotor skills involved
Fielding a ground ball	Bending and turning your body in preparation	Fielding the ball, throwing the ball	Sliding to the left or right

Of particular interest is the identification of factors that are likely to support adequate physical activity levels in childhood and throughout the life span. Over time, many motor behaviorists (Clark & Metcalfe, 2002; Goodway et al., 2020; Haywood & Getchell, 2019; Payne & Isaacs, 2020) have strongly argued that competence in fundamental motor skills, including locomotor and object control skills, is essential to remaining physically active over the course of our lives. Clark and Metcalfe (2002) noted that an inability to perform fundamental locomotor and object control skills results in limited opportunities for physical activity as children age, because prerequisite skills are not adequately developed.

Researchers have addressed why the early and appropriate acquisition of object control skills is crucial for positive developmental trajectories throughout life. In 2009, Barnett and colleagues longitudinally examined the relationship between childhood motor skill proficiency and adolescent physical activity among a sample of Australian children. Trends from their data support proficiency in object control skills but not locomotor skills as a significant predictor of time spent in both moderately vigorous and organized (e.g., instructor-led, somewhat structured training) physical activity in adolescence. Moreover, adolescents who were proficient in object control skills as children demonstrated an increased probability of participation in any vigorous physical activity. An important strategy for promoting continued and long-term participation in physical activity, therefore, may be to develop fundamental motor skill interventions that pay specific attention to object control skills for children.

Interestingly, Barnett and colleagues' (2009) longitudinal investigation also suggests that boys and girls have similar likelihoods of participating in vigorous activity as adolescents, assuming similar levels of object control proficiency as children. This is promising evidence that supports the importance of object control skill intervention. However, over time, researchers and practitioners have consistently noted the differences in fundamental motor skill proficiency observed between young boys and young girls. Data trends from longitudinal and systematic review research suggest that while girls often perform locomotor skills with similar or higher proficiency, girls tend to demonstrate lower levels of object control skill proficiency compared to boys (Barnett et al., 2010; Bolger et al., 2021). This predictive relationship between childhood object control proficiency and adolescent physical activity therefore further accentuates the need for girls to have targeted experiences to develop object control skill proficiency. Without such experiences, substantial gender-specific differences in fundamental motor performance will remain, and girls may be excluded from the benefits associated with object control skill proficiency throughout life.

When children can walk in and around the immediate environment independently and with some fluidity, their hands and feet are suddenly available to explore even more thoroughly. Suddenly, they can impart force to an object and watch it move through the environment. They can also receive objects projected toward them. Object control skills (also referred to as ball skills or manipulative skills) generally involve a combination of at least two movements and are performed in concert with other types of movements. For example, in striking a ball with a bat, stepping, turning, swinging, and stretching occur. Object control skills include overarm throwing, catching with one or both hands,

---

WHAT DO YOU THINK?

Exercise 9.3

Consider a soccer player who is just learning the game. Imagine him standing in front of the goalie trying to score on a penalty kick. What does the kick look like? Now imagine the legendary Lionel Messi or another soccer superstar. What does his penalty kick look like? In the following table, describe in a qualitative manner what each kick looks like. Describe the whole kick, but keep in mind all parts of the body—legs, torso, arms, and head.

	Qualitative description of a penalty kick
Novice kicker	
Expert kicker	

and kicking and striking objects (with or without an implement). This section discusses the development of the ballistic skills of overarm throwing, kicking, and striking.

Overarm Throwing

Objects can be thrown in a variety of ways, including, but not limited to, underhand, sidearm, and overarm (also referred to as overhand). The pattern chosen has much to do with the task to be performed, that is (a) what the thrower hopes to accomplish and (b) specific constraints of the task as defined by the size, shape, and weight of the implement to be thrown (e.g., a regulation-size American football versus a basketball) as well as the rules of the game. From a biomechanical (technique) perspective, the three throws have much in common. In this section we concentrate on the overarm throw because it is frequently used in sports (e.g., softball, European handball, and American football) and has been extensively studied over the past 80 years (Halverson et al., 1982; Roberton & Konczak, 2001; Thomas et al., 2010; Wild, 1938).

As with all fundamental motor skills, overarm throwing can be examined in several ways. Researchers who use a quantitative or product approach focus on such outcomes as ball velocity, distance thrown, and accuracy. Since Wild's initial work in 1938, researchers have also looked at throwing using a qualitative or process approach. Haywood and Getchell (2019)

persuasively argued for the usefulness of rigorously examining the quality of the movement. Coaches, parents, and physical education teachers will be of most use to developing throwers by becoming skilled at (a) assessing how they throw and (b) setting up tasks and environments so that throwing improves and learners are engaged in and excited about the activities.

Children first demonstrate a rudimentary overarm throw when they are approximately six months of age and in a sitting position (Eckert, 1987). Although most children demonstrate a competent overarm throwing pattern by six years of age, a significant number remain unskilled into adulthood (this is particularly true of girls, an observation that has garnered a large amount of research attention since the 1980s).

A study by Halverson and colleagues (1982) supports observations that many children remain unskilled throwers well into middle childhood and early adolescence and that many more girls than boys remain unskilled. The authors observed the development of overarm throwing in a sample of both boys and girls from kindergarten through ninth grade. Using this longitudinal approach, the authors noted that by the seventh grade, 80 percent of males had reached the competent level of upper arm action, whereas only 29 percent of females had done so.

Some hypothesized that with the advent of Title IX law in the United States, the gap

---

WHAT DO YOU THINK?

Exercise 9.4

Take a moment and think back to when you were developing object control skills. For some of them (e.g., kicking), it may be difficult to remember how and when you realized, *Hey, I'm pretty good at this!* But for others, such as catching a ball with one hand, you might have a stronger memory of finally getting it right. As you look back, think about (a) how you knew you had mastered the skill and (b) how you arrived at that point. For example, was it by playing around with your friends in the driveway? Practicing with your siblings after school? Playing on a sports team? Or was it through some other avenue?

between boys and girls would narrow; however, work by Runion and colleagues (2003) on throw velocity suggests that qualitative and quantitative differences between the sexes remain. Gender-based differences in object control skill performance, including overarm throw, similarly continue to be observed within normative motor skill assessment. For example, following the revision of the *Test of Gross Motor Development–Second Edition* (TGMD-2; Ulrich, 2000) to the *Test of Gross Motor Development–Third Edition* (TGMD-3; Ulrich, 2019), gender-based differences in object control or ball skill performance remained across test versions, maintaining the need for separate, male-versus-female normative data for the TGMD-3 ball (but not locomotor) skills subtest (Field et al., 2020). Furthermore, examinations of the relative contributions of each of the six (TGMD-2) and seven (TGMD-3) skill scores to the overall object control or ball skill subtest scores revealed that overhand throw scores strongly undercontributed to the overall subtest score among girls across test versions. The undercontribution of overhand throwing was consistent for girls both in comparison to other subtest skills and with boys' scores, reinforcing the importance of gender-based normative data for object control skills. See chapter 11 for a further description of the TGMD-3.

Title IX has, however, led to significant increases in female sport participation, and thus opportunities to practice overarm throwing. In an investigation done in 2011, Petranek and Barton examined the overarm throwing patterns of 13- and 14-year-old female softball players who took part in highly competitive play. As would be expected, they were significantly more skilled than girls who were not engaged in high-level, organized athletics. However, the authors found that despite frequent practice in overarm throwing, boys (from Germany and the United States) who had not engaged in systematic throwing practice were still better than their female counterparts in both qualitative and quantitative measures. The authors suggested that "practice when combined with genetics and evolution may afford boys the ability to exhibit more advanced throwing patterns with greater ball velocities than girls" (p. 227). It was further suggested that the precise spatial and temporal qualities of advanced throwers should be further examined, along with the quality of the throwing practice and the specific training approaches used in baseball and softball.

Despite the potential cultural explanations of the gender discrepancy in object control skills, trends from recent research support the potential for quality fundamental motor skills (FMS) intervention to minimize this gap. Sheehan and colleagues (2020) examined the effect of an all-girl, six-week, physical education intervention on the ball skills subtest of the TGMD-3 among girls aged eight to nine years. The intervention included daily 35-minute sessions of targeted object control skill practice during their typical school-based physical education classes. While girls received specific object control skill programming, their boy classmates resumed their usual physical education activities as scheduled. At baseline (prior to intervention), boys demonstrated significantly higher object control skill performance than the girls. Postintervention, however, girls improved their scores, and the gender difference in scores was no longer statistically significant, highlighting that targeted intervention may reduce the variance observed between girls and boys. Unfortunately, when children were tested again six weeks after the intervention, the gender difference returned. These data are nonetheless promising because they support the long-standing recommendations for focused object control skill intervention for girls (Barnett et al., 2010; Bolger et al., 2021; Taunton Miedema et al., 2021). Physical education teachers should support girls in their classrooms by carefully and intentionally planning activities that target object control skills.

RESEARCH NOTES

Can the Throwing Gap Be Narrowed?

That most girls throw, well, like girls has been an insult thrown around (pun intended) for many years. Regardless of whether researchers have focused on distance and velocity (Atwater, 1979; Thomas & French, 1985) or the biomechanical properties of the throw (Atwater, 1979; Thomas & Marzke, 1992), females have lagged way behind their male counterparts. These stark differences are evident long before puberty, when physiological differences between the sexes are much less pronounced. So, this begs the questions, *Why such a big difference?* and *Can the throwing gap between the sexes be narrowed?*

Thomas and colleagues (2010) hypothesized that the very different cultural expectations of men and women—over the centuries—have contributed significantly to differences in throwing ability. Specifically, men have been the hunter-gatherers, while women have been the primary food producers. Thus, men had to be able to throw weapons of one sort or another, whereas women didn't. This is an interesting hypothesis, but it is difficult to prove. However, if the researchers could locate a culture in which both men and women were responsible for hunting, they could, to a degree, test this hypothesis. Aboriginal Australians fit this description: the historical record suggested that women, historically, threw for defense and hunting alongside the men (Clarke, 2003). Thomas and colleagues (2010) found that Aboriginal boys tested on the overarm throw had velocities and biomechanical properties that were similar to their counterparts in the United States, Germany, Japan, and Thailand (where the previous research had been done). However, the Aboriginal girls threw with significantly greater velocity than girls in the United States, Germany, Japan, and Thailand. Additionally, Aboriginal boys and girls were more similar with respect to the velocity and biomechanical properties of their throws compared to children from the United States. None of the Aboriginal boys and girls received any special training, and yet the girls were more skilled than their peers in other countries. Could the results be due to different societal expectations, or is there another explanation (maybe one that could lead to the phrase *throwing like a girl* being considered a compliment)?

Irrespective of sex differences, the route to a competent throwing pattern appears to be a lengthy one, and considerable variability in movement patterns is a consistent observation. By being aware of the elements involved in a competent throw, practitioners and parents can become more attuned to what is missing in less efficient attempts. As presented in chapter 8, changes in throwing proficiency can be cataloged using either a component or a whole-body approach. Both approaches precisely delineate changes in competency as the developing child moves toward throwing proficiency. Figures 9.1 through 9.3 present the hypothesized whole-body developmental sequence for the overarm throw for distance (Gabbard, 2021; Goodway et al., 2020; Haywood & Getchell, 2019; Payne & Isaacs, 2020; Wickstrom, 1983).

Kicking

Like throwing, kicking imparts force to an object. However, the kicker strikes the object as opposed to hurling it. To kick competently, a person must have adequate perceptual abilities along with eye–foot coordination. As with throwing, children kick in a few ways. Goodway and colleagues (2020) postulated that the kick is chosen

FIGURE 9.1

WHOLE-BODY APPROACH FOR THE OVERARM THROW FOR DISTANCE—INITIAL STAGE

- The throw tends to result from arm action only.
- No preparatory backswing occurs; rather, the hand is brought back with the elbow up.
- The throw is completed by releasing the ball following elbow extension.
- Follow-through, if present, occurs in a forward direction.

- There is either little or no trunk action; if trunk action takes place, it does so in a forward–backward direction.
- The body weight may shift slightly to the rear to maintain balance.
- No step is taken.

FIGURE 9.2

WHOLE-BODY APPROACH FOR THE OVERARM THROW FOR DISTANCE—ELEMENTARY STAGE

- The trunk and shoulders rotate toward the throwing side to prepare for the throw.
- A sideways and backward swing of the arm then brings the ball to a position behind the head with the elbow flexed.
- The arm is swung forward, high over the shoulder.

- The forearm extends before the ball is released.
- A forward shift in body weight is evident.
- An ipsilateral (same-side) step is taken during the throw.

FIGURE 9.3

WHOLE-BODY APPROACH FOR THE OVERARM THROW FOR DISTANCE—INITIAL STAGE

- The body pivots to the throwing side with the weight on the foot of the throwing side.
- The throwing arm swings back in a circular, downward direction.
- The elbow of the nonthrowing arm is raised for balance.
- The elbow of the throwing arm is bent at approximately a right angle.
- A long, contralateral (opposite-side) step is taken in the direction of the target.

- There is differentiated trunk rotation; that is, the pelvis begins to rotate before the upper spine in the initiation of trunk rotation.
- The throwing elbow moves forward horizontally as it extends.
- The forearm lags when the shoulders are front facing.
- The ball is released just forward of the head; at this point, the arm is extended at the elbow.
- The arm follows through across the body after ball release.

TRY THIS

Looking at the Quality of Your Throwing

Exercise 9.5

Stand 20 feet (6 m) from a target located at head height. Using an overarm throwing for distance technique, throw a tennis ball at the target 10 times with your dominant hand, keeping track of the number of times you hit the target. Think about how you are throwing—that is, the quality of the throw. Now, throw the tennis ball 10 times with your nondominant hand, again keeping track of how many times you hit the target and the quality of the throw. Then write down the differences you experienced both quantitatively (how many times you hit the target) and qualitatively. Having done this exercise yourself, have a partner observe you doing it. Compare your partner's qualitative observations with your own. Which observations would you consider more accurate. Why?

based on the desired trajectory and how high the ball is when contacted. These authors also noted that the type of kick chosen is influenced by the force of the ball, when received, and (as frequently noted in this text) the desired outcome—the task at hand. Another consideration in the playing of a sport, as mentioned with reference to the throw, is the techniques the rules allow. For example, in soccer, the goaltender may hold the ball in the hands, drop it, and then kick it; other players may not contact the ball with the hands, which means that a different type of kicking technique is necessary.

As with the other fundamental motor skills, an advanced kick has certain critical features. In this section we consider the placekick, a kick that occurs when the ball is either on the ground or on a kicking tee.

As in throwing, inefficient kickers do not sequence their actions; rather, the kick is a single action, and the force imparted to the ball is inadequate. The action is more of a push, with the kicking leg often remaining bent on contact. The development of kicking skill has not been carefully examined regarding the qualitative changes needed for proficiency. Given that only 10 percent of the 9.5- to 10-year-olds studied by Haubenstricker and colleagues (1983) were competent kickers, it appears that a more careful examination of developmental changes in this fundamental motor skill is imperative. Initial work has been done on the validation of a whole-body developmental sequence for placekicking (Seefeldt & Haubenstricker, 1975). Figures 9.4 through 9.6 show the hypothesized whole-body developmental sequence for placekicking (Gabbard, 2021; Goodway et al., 2020; Haywood & Getchell, 2019; Payne & Isaacs, 2020; Wickstrom, 1983).

Striking

Striking, a skill used in many sporting activities, has many configurations. It can

FIGURE 9.4

WHOLE-BODY APPROACH FOR PLACEKICKING—INITIAL STAGE

- The action is a simple pushing of the ball with the foot.
- The motion of the kicking leg is straight and perpendicular.
- Range of motion is very limited; backswing and follow-through are minimal.
- The nonkicking leg does not step forward.
- The trunk remains upright with no rotation present; there is limited movement of the upper body.
- The knee of the kicking leg is often bent at contact.
- The arms are held out to the sides to aid in the maintenance of balance.

FIGURE 9.5

WHOLE-BODY APPROACH FOR PLACEKICKING—ELEMENTARY STAGE

- Range of motion of the kicking leg (backswing and follow-through) increases at the hip and knee.
- The kicker takes one or more deliberate steps while approaching the ball.
- The kicker tends to start farther behind the ball than in the initial stage and move the body forward into the kick.

- The support leg is placed slightly to the side of the ball.
- The kicking leg is in a cocked position and tends to remain bent throughout the kick.
- The kicking leg often retracts after completing the kick; that is, follow-through is minimal.
- Compensatory trunk lean and arm opposition increase from the initial stage.

FIGURE 9.6

WHOLE-BODY APPROACH FOR PLACEKICKING—COMPETENT STAGE

- Following one or more deliberate steps, the kicker becomes airborne immediately before contacting the ball, allowing appropriate hip hyperextension and knee flexion.
- The trunk is rotated to the side, and the knee of the kicking leg is flexed.
- The knee of the kicking leg extends rapidly just prior to contacting the ball.

- The arms are used in opposition to the legs during the kick.
- The trunk bends at the waist during follow-through.
- Forward momentum is sufficient; the kicker either hops on the support leg or scissors the legs while in the air, thus allowing a landing on the kicking foot.

TRY THIS

Do You Have What It Takes to Kick Like a Pro?

Exercise 9.6

As you did with throwing, stand 20 feet (6 m) from a target located at head height. Kick a soccer ball with your dominant leg at the target 10 times, keeping track of the number of times you hit the target. Think about how you are kicking—that is, the quality of the kick. Now, kick the soccer ball 10 times with your nondominant leg, again keeping track of how many times you hit the target and the quality of the kick. Then write down the differences you experienced both quantitatively and qualitatively. Please repeat and have a partner observe you doing the same thing. Compare your partner's qualitative observations with your own. Which observations would you consider more accurate, and why?

be done with an implement (e.g., bat, racket, golf club) or with a body part (e.g., head, hand, foot). It can be performed in a variety of orientations—swinging a bat sidearm, spiking a volleyball overhand, or driving a golf ball underhand. Striking can also be done with either one or two hands (e.g., a one-handed backhand or a two-handed backhand in tennis). With such an array of orientations, implements, and sporting activities, one would think that this fundamental motor skill would have been studied extensively. It has not.

Haywood and Getchell (2019) suggested that the relative lack of research may be a result of the difficulty of the task. Indeed, the perceptual judgments needed to make effective contact with a projectile, often a moving one, are tremendously complex. As many frustrated golfers know, even contacting a ball that isn't moving at all can be more than a little difficult.

Nevertheless, because the developing child lacks the ability to strike a moving object, teachers and researchers adapt the task by making the ball stationary. As the child becomes more adept, a slowly moving ball with a smooth trajectory can be used. The size and shape of the ball can be modified, as can the length and weight of the

striking implement. As with jumping for height and jumping for distance, different configurations for striking (e.g., overarm, sidearm) have certain features in common, such as early strikers using an upward or downward chopping motion (as opposed to more accomplished strikers striking in a horizontal plane). With increased practice, the swing usually becomes more fluid as learners incorporate more degrees of freedom into their movement patterns. This more accomplished movement pattern may include taking a contralateral step, adding a backswing, rotating the hips and trunk, and developing a coordinated wrist snap (Payne & Isaacs, 2020).

Although the research base for striking is sparse, Seefeldt and Haubenstricker (1975) hypothesized a whole-body developmental sequence for striking with a bat. This sequence, although not validated, provides practitioners with fundamental and important information regarding the development of competent striking. Figures 9.7 through 9.9 present a hypothesized whole-body developmental sequence for sidearm striking (Gabbard, 2021; Goodway et al., 2020; Haywood & Getchell, 2019; Payne & Isaacs, 2020; Wickstrom, 1983).

FIGURE 9.7

WHOLE-BODY APPROACH FOR SIDEARM STRIKING—INITIAL STAGE

- Early attempts to strike are like the inefficient throwing motion; the racket is swung using a vertical (chopping) motion.
- The motion is from back to front with a slight bend at the waist.
- The striker flexes and extends the forearm to chop at the ball, while the trunk directly faces the direction of the tossed ball.

- The trunk and legs are minimally involved, and the feet are generally stationary.
- There is minimal or no weight transfer.
- The arms are held rigidly, with little or no wrist snap.

FIGURE 9.8

WHOLE-BODY APPROACH FOR SIDEARM STRIKING—ELEMENTARY STAGE

- The striker stands sideways to the ball.
- The striker transfers his weight from the rear foot to the front foot by taking a step forward.
- Differentiated (hip, then shoulder) rotation is apparent.

- The plane of the swing changes from vertical (a chop), to oblique, to horizontal.
- The elbows are held away from the sides, allowing for arm extension before contact, which results in increased force production.

FIGURE 9.9

WHOLE-BODY APPROACH FOR SIDEARM STRIKING—COMPETENT STAGE

- The trunk is turned to the side in anticipation of a thrown ball.
- The weight is shifted to the back foot, and the trunk and hips subsequently rotate before ball contact.
- The striker uses a full range of motion and strikes the ball in the horizontal plane.

- The weight shifts to the forward foot at contact.
- The arms are relaxed.

SUMMARY

Acquiring fundamental motor skills is essential to the healthy development of children. Children given a strong movement foundation will have the skill set—and the confidence—to be physically active on their own, with their families, and with their peers. Whether the child decides to participate in formalized athletic events or is content to play recreationally is of course up to the child. What is evident, though, is that carefully designed movement environments and progressive educational experiences that are well thought out are essential to ensure early and sustained success. This chapter laid a solid foundation for understanding how and when these fundamentals are achieved. Practitioners can take the concepts presented and build on them through practical experiences, focused research, or a combination of the two.

> ONLINE ACTIVITIES

The student material found in HK*Propel* includes exercises, labs, and videos to enhance learning and encourage practical application of important concepts.

LEARNING AIDS

Supplemental Activities

1. It is imperative that you can accurately and qualitatively assess how skillfully a person moves through space. Accurate assessment requires frequent well-thought-out observations. From the Internet (YouTube or another video-sharing website), access video clips of novice and expert runners (one of each) and assess their proficiency. Watch each video clip at least five times. Use the following checklist in completing the assignment.

	Novice Age: Gender:	Expert Age: Gender:
Leg action Step 1: Minimal flight		
Step 2: Crossover swing		
Step 3: Direct projection		
Arm action Step 1: Middle guard		
Step 2: Oblique arm swing		
Step 3: Opposition, sagittal		

From P.S. Beach, M.E. Perreault, A.S. Brian, and D.H. Collier, *Motor Learning and Development*, 3rd ed. (Champaign, IL: Human Kinetics, 2024).

   a. Were some components more difficult to observe than others?

   b. Did the observations become easier the more you viewed the video clip?

   c. Was it easier to rate the expert runner? Why or why not?

2. For this activity, watch six 11-year-old (elementary-age) students playing either soccer or softball. Get permission and then go to a local sports complex, recreational facility, or school. Choose two male players and two female players and watch them throughout the contest. Using the whole-body approach as outlined in this chapter, assess the proficiency level of the four players you chose. If you are watching soccer, assess kicking; if you are watching softball, assess the overarm throw. As best you can, choose a boy and a girl who are relatively unskilled and a boy and a girl who are relatively skilled.

   a. Did you observe differences in the proficiency levels between boys and girls?

   b. If so, why do you think this was the case? If there were no sex differences, why not?

   c. Do you feel you became more competent at assessing kicking or throwing as you gained more experience observing?

Glossary

object control skills—Skills that involve controlling implements and objects such as balls, hoops, bats, and ribbons by hand, by foot, or with any other part of the body.

MOVEMENT IN ADULTHOOD

After reading this chapter, you should be able to do the following:

- Define *aging*, contrasting biological and chronological aging.
- Explain the exercise–aging cycle.
- Explain Kirschenbaum's five-step model of self-regulation.
- Compare peak athletic performance for various sports and activities.
- Discuss how peak performance changes from young to older adulthood.
- Describe how movement patterns change from young to older adulthood in locomotor skills, object control skills, and functional activities.

Never Limit Yourself

Martina Navratilova marveled the world with her remarkable tennis skills and ability to seemingly defy not only aging but also cancer. In 2006, at almost 50 years old, Martina won the U.S. Open mixed doubles championship and won the senior doubles Wimbledon title only days after completing radiation treatment for breast cancer at the age of 53. She was quoted as saying to ESPN, "You can do great things regardless of your age if you just believe and, you know, go for it," when she won the U.S. Open. She also said, "Don't get limited by people that say, 'No, you can't do that because you're too old or because you're heavy or you're not an athlete.' Whatever your limitations might be, don't let them define you. I didn't let it define me" (DeSimone, 2006). Being able to stay at the top of her game at an age at which most people consider themselves decades past their prime, Martina is a true testament of successful aging.

Adults advance through many stages throughout life, and these stages affect not only the activities they are involved in but also how they move. Young adults are at their physical peak, yet some avoid an active lifestyle for various reasons. Older adults, on the other hand, can avoid many age-related declines by maintaining a healthy and active lifestyle.

Some older adults are becoming increasingly physically active, participating in physical recreation activities, fitness activities, and even competitive sports. Every year, more seniors, both male and female, compete in races and triathlons, play golf and tennis, and join gyms and fitness groups. Some older adults are going extreme, competing in marathons and even Ironman triathlons. The Ironman is an ultimate testament to physical human capabilities, with a 2.4-mile (3.9 km) swim, a 112-mile (180 km) bike ride, and a 26.2-mile (42 km) run. In a period of 10 years, the number of Ironman competitors at Kona (on the Big Island of Hawaii) over the age of 70 increased threefold, from only 11 in 1997 to 37 in 2007. Now, more than ever, adults are aware of the importance of physical activity and the role fitness plays in their lives. With today's medical advances, changing technology, and increased focus on the benefits of good nutrition and physical activity, we can only expect this trend to continue.

This chapter discusses movement from young adulthood through older adulthood. We discuss peak athletic performance for both younger and older adults, as well as changing movement patterns in the areas of locomotor skills, object control skills, and functional activities.

AGING

In the minds of many, the term *aging* refers to declining physical function. Aging is thought of as something that occurs in older adulthood. However, in its simplest terms, aging can be defined as the number of time units over which an organism has existed following birth (Spirduso et al., 2005). When aging is defined this way, it becomes synonymous with time. The biological changes associated with infancy and childhood are referred to as developmental, whereas the changes that occur because of declining functional systems are referred to as aging (Spirduso et al., 2005). Because aging does not have a definitive onset, it is helpful to define **aging** as a progressive process leading to physical and mental functional decline, increased risk of disease, and eventually death (Jia et al., 2017).

Although we all age, we do not all age in the same way. We age differently and at varying rates. Functional impairments cannot be predicted because so many factors affect how we age, such as environmental, lifestyle, and cultural factors, as well as heredity. Individual differences are even greater for older adults than they are for young adults or children, allowing for wide variability. Older adults range from the frail elderly to masters athletes competing in marathons. An impressive example is Fauja Singh, who, at the age of 81, became serious about running and began running marathons at the age of 89. At the age of 94, he had run seven marathons and was picked up by the Adidas "Impossible Is Nothing" campaign, along with David Beckham (retired soccer player who played for England's national team, Manchester United; Real Madrid; and the L.A. Galaxy) and Jonny Wilkinson (retired English rugby player known as one of the world's best). Singh completed in his last long-distance competitive race (10 km) in Hong Kong at the age of 101, which he completed in 1 hour, 32 minutes, and 28 seconds.

In general, when we refer to a person's age, we are referring to **chronological age**. This is simply the number of years the person has been alive. This age does not account for any biological or health factors, such as the person's overall well-being, fitness level, or health. **Biological aging** refers to the physiological adaptations that occur within the body due to the passage of time. Chronological age is one of the most important risk factors for morbidity, yet people at the same chronological age often have markedly different biological aging states. For example, a very active, healthy man may have a very low biological age in comparison to his chronological age. The situation could be the opposite in an overweight sedentary person who smokes and drinks.

Currently, there is a debate in the literature on the most accurate way to assess biological age. Some assessments of biological age include those that focus on one measure or score, such as metabolic age based on urinary metabolism (Hertel et al., 2016) or the degree of gray or white hairs as a risk factor for coronary artery disease (Kocaman et al., 2012). Other assessments of biological age are complicated because biological systems age at different rates. For example, Comfort's biological age index (1979) includes anthropometric measures (e.g., body mass, graying of hair), physiological scores (e.g., vital capacity, tidal volume, blood volume, heart size, grip strength), bone and connective tissue integrity (e.g., skin elasticity, nail calcium, osteoporotic index), sensory tests (e.g., audiometry, visual acuity), biochemical data (e.g., serum cholesterol, copper, albumin, elastase, and RNAase), cellular characteristics, intelligence tests, and psychomotor tests (e.g., reaction time and light extinction tests).

Although a thorough biological aging examination is complex, one should take biological age, rather than chronological age, into consideration when assessing a person's fitness, whether the purpose relates to fitness for a job, an exercise program, or skill learning (Jia et al., 2017). Active older adults have outperformed sedentary young adults on many fitness tests. For example, consider the incredible fitness level of Jack LaLanne, the well-known father of fitness who died in 2011 at the age of 96. At age 90, Jack still performed better than an average 30-year-old (an age group who should be in their prime) on physical fitness tests. Jack's enthusiasm for fitness and his incredible athleticism across his long life are a testament to the possibility of really pushing the aging envelope, enabling people to maintain their fitness levels decades past young adulthood.

PHYSICAL ACTIVITY

Note in table 1.2 in chapter 1 that young adulthood generally includes the period from the early third decade to the beginning of the fifth decade (ages 21-40). Middle adulthood is classified as the fifth through sixth decades (approximately 41-60 years). It is during young adulthood and halfway through adulthood that both biological function and physical performance are at their peak (Shephard, 2008). Unfortunately, a sedentary lifestyle remains common for older adults (Harvey et al., 2015). Although there is general agreement that physical activity is important for adults of all ages, it is not quite as clear how active older adults need to be, what types of activity are most important as people age, and how to encourage older adults to become or continue to be physically active (Macera et al., 2015).

During middle-aged adulthood (ages 41-60), physical activity levels tend to decline further in most people as women go through menopause and men experience a reduction in sex hormones (Hackney, 2021). See chapter 13 for further information on changes in hormones with age. Physically active adults in the United States over the age of 55 most commonly participate in walking, gardening, cycling, golf, and aerobics (DiPietro et al., 1993). Not until adults reach retirement age (young-old adults, ages 61-74) is there an increase in physical activity; most physically active people at this point take up walking, swimming, cycling, and dancing (Stephens & Craig, 1990). It is important to note that these activities are nearly all outdoor activities, so weather conditions can affect ability to participate in these activities. It should also be noted that many of these activities are not only outdoors but also social activities. While outdoor and social activities are very important and beneficial to older adults, leaving the home and socializing became quite challenging during the COVID-19 pandemic. The ability to maintain activity became significantly more difficult, as older adults were at a higher risk of COVID-19 infection. However, they also have a higher likelihood of becoming further sedentary (Goethals et al., 2020). According to the 2007 Behavioral Risk Factor Surveillance System of the U.S. Centers for Disease Control and Prevention (CDC), Americans over the age of 65 have the highest prevalence of physical inactivity; 23.7 percent are inactive, and 32.7 percent take part in no leisure-time physical activity (CDC, 2015). These percentages increased to 28 percent in 2016 with inactivity levels 30 percent higher for individuals with a chronic disease. Hispanics, African Americans, and adults with lower levels of education also were more likely to be physically inactive (Errata, 2016). Moreover, a review of studies published in 1981 to 2014 revealed that adults over 60 years old spend 5.3-9.4 hours of their waking day engaged in sedentary behavior (Harvey et al., 2015).

Physical activity levels decline again during old adulthood (ages 75-99) and beyond as many adults develop physical disabilities. Approximately 65.4 percent of males and 69.6 percent of females have two or more chronic diseases between the ages of 65 and 74 according to 2015 data by the CDC. Black, non-Hispanic older adults have the highest prevalence of two or more chronic diseases (71.1 percent) and Hispanic older adults have the lowest prevalence (63.6 percent; CDC, 2015). Developing chronic diseases in older adulthood, such as cancer, heart disease, or diabetes, can significantly affect their ability to participate in physical activities and even daily activities (Burns et al., 2017).

Physical Activity Recommendations

The current public health recommendation in the United States is to participate in moderate-intensity aerobic physical activity for at least 150 minutes per week or vigorous-intensity physical activity for 75 minutes per week. For additional benefits, adults should engage in physical activity beyond these minimums and incorporate muscle-strengthening activities that are moderate or high in intensity, involving all major muscle groups, two or more days per week (U.S. Department of Health and Human Services, 2018). According to the 2018 U.S. Department of Health and Human Services physical activity guidelines, older adults can do three things to improve their physical activity levels: increase aerobic activity, increase muscle-strengthening activity, and reduce sedentary, or sitting, behavior (Macera et al., 2015).

Approximately one in five (21.3 percent) American adults over the age of 18 met the current and age-adjusted U.S. federal physical activity guidelines for aerobic and resistance activities in 2014 (Blackwell & Clarke, 2018). Figure 10.1 illustrates the aerobic and muscle-strengthening activities in Americans from age 18 to over 85. Furthermore, the percentage of adults over the age of 25 who met the physical activity guideline levels was proportional to their levels of education. Only 6.9 percent had less than a high school education, 12.9 percent had a high school diploma or equivalent, 19.8 percent had some university education, 20.1 percent had an associate degree, 29.1 percent had a four-year university degree, and 31.3 percent had an advanced degree.

Barriers to Physical Activity

One of the greatest factors affecting exercise adherence is the person's *intention* to exercise. According to the **theory of planned behavior**, attitudes toward a behavior depend on (a) the belief that the behavior

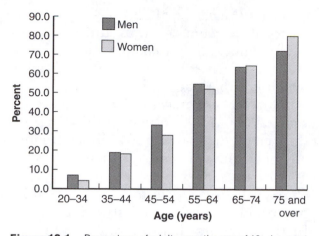

Figure 10.1 Percentage of adults over the age of 18 who meet the U.S. federal physical activity guidelines.

Data from *National Health Interview Survey (NHIS)*, (Hyattsville, MD: National Center for Health Statistics, 2014).

will produce a specified outcome and (b) the person's desire to attain the specified outcome (Ajzen, 1985). Adults who do not place much value and importance on exercise are much less likely to adhere to a regular exercise program (Motalebi et al., 2014). Intention is the main determinant of behavior because it reflects both motivation and willingness (Ajzen, 1991; Kosma, 2012). Intention comprises three concepts: (a) the attitude toward the behavior, (b) perceived social pressures about the behavior, and (c) perceived behavioral control (White et al., 2012). Someone who has a positive attitude toward exercise, perceived social pressures, and behavioral control will have a much higher intention to exercise than someone who does not. Researchers have discovered a negative relationship between age and exercise intention in older adults (Yardley et al., 2007). This is likely the result of decreasing positive attitudes toward exercise with age and a reduced belief in the ability to perform exercises in this population. Because older adults tend not to meet physical activity related guidelines, improving their attitudes toward physical activity—and therefore their intention to exercise—is critical for improving exercise behavior (Hausenblas et al., 1997).

Although in some Eastern cultures aging is revered, in the Western Hemisphere, aging is often associated with many negative stereotypes. Stereotyping people based on aging has become so common that it is referred to as **ageism**. Like racism (stereotyping based on a person's race) and sexism (stereotyping associated with a person's sex), ageism can have a severely negative impact on people. Older adults can be discriminated against for jobs and social activities. Ageism can also have a negative effect on older adults' participation in physical activities, because they are assumed to be less fit than younger adults and less able to perform physical activities. In light of these attitudes, it is not surprising that many adults progressively limit their physical activity levels. When adults buy into these negative attitudes, they often decrease their involvement in physical activity, and the attitudes turn into a self-fulfilling prophecy (Berger & McInman, 1993). Decreasing physical activity levels based on age is referred to as **age grading**.

Participation in physical activity often begins to decline as young adults approach middle adulthood and face increasing responsibilities with finances and growing families (Payne & Isaacs, 2016). The barriers to exercise most reported by adults are the same for both exercisers and nonexercisers (e.g., lack of time, laziness, and work responsibilities). Given these similarities, it is likely that they are *perceived* barriers (i.e., personal priorities) rather than *actual* barriers. Adults who place a higher priority on exercise or do not perceive the barriers to be insurmountable are much more likely to continue exercising despite them. Adults who do not make exercise a priority may be using these external barriers to avoid a physically active lifestyle (Valois et al., 1986).

Women participate in less physical activity and report more barriers to participating in physical activity than men do (Stephens & Craig, 1990). When walking, women reported more environmental concerns such as heavy traffic, unattended dogs, and lack of safety than men did. Single parents find it particularly difficult to fit exercise into their schedules. Retired adults have more free time but often limit participation in physical activity because of reduced financial means, limited means of transportation, and an apprehension about starting after so many years of not participating.

As adults age, many further decrease their involvement in exercise-related activities. Barriers to exercise in older adults, not surprisingly, are different because older adults no longer have the time constraints of work and raising children; however, many have physical limitations. In the over-65 age group, the most common barriers reported by nonexercisers were fear of falling, laziness, and lack of motivation, whereas the barriers reported by exercisers were time constraints, physical ailments, and laziness (Lees et al., 2005). A study of older adults who were afraid of falling found that in addition to a lack of motivation, they reported reduced health status, bad experiences with exercise, and other environmental factors (Lindgren De Groot & Fagerström, 2011). Barriers reported by older adults also differ based on socioeconomic status. Those of higher socioeconomic status reported time, facilities, and transport as the three biggest barriers to physical activity; those of lower socioeconomic status reported health conditions, neighborhood safety (including fear of crime), and facilities as their three biggest barriers (Gray et al., 2016).

Poor physical health is the most common reason for lack of participation in physical activity in older adults (Baert et al., 2011). In 2012, 35.9 percent of older Americans reported a disability, and 23.1 percent reported difficulty with walking or climbing stairs or both (U.S. Department of Health and Human Services, Administration for Community Living, 2015). Common disabilities affecting physical activity participation are reduced mobility, pain, sensory deficits, cognitive impairments, and other medical problems (Macera et al., 2015). Approximately 25 to 50 percent of community-dwelling older adults and up to 80 percent of nursing home residents experience physical disability, which is either caused by or results in pain (AGS Panel on Persistent Pain in Older Persons, 2002). Adults often find dealing with their changing bodies and abilities emotionally difficult, which affects their self-esteem and increases anxiety and stress. These changes cause people to become even less interested in physical activity, which in turn further impairs them physiologically. This phenomenon is known as the exercise–aging cycle (Berger & Hecht, 1989) (see figure 10.2).

Creating a successful exercise program requires an understanding of the greatest barriers to exercise. If practitioners focus older adults' attention on the benefits of exercise and reduce their perceptions of exercise barriers, older adults are more likely to maintain a physically active lifestyle (Rhodes et al., 1999).

SELF-REGULATION IN PHYSICAL ACTIVITY

Self-regulation is a complex process in which individuals engage in voluntary goal-directed behaviors over time and context by initiating, monitoring, sustaining, and achieving certain thoughts, feelings, and behaviors (Weiss & Gould, 2015). All adults, regardless of age, health, or fitness level, need self-regulatory skills. For example, these skills are important for the inactive adult who is trying to initiate and adhere to an exercise program as well as for the injured adult who is going through rehabilitation.

Self-Regulation Process

Adults self-regulate their behavior in both exercise and sport through management of short- and long-term goals. Individuals who decide to start an exercise program, improve their skills, or recover from an injury through a rehabilitation program go through a series

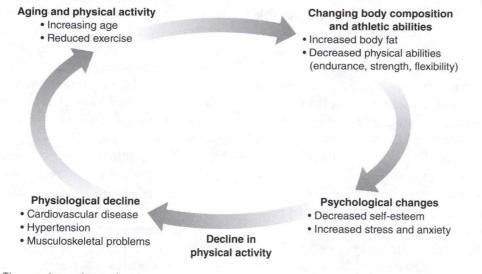

Figure 10.2   The exercise–aging cycle.
Adapted from Berger and Hecht (1989).

WHAT DO YOU THINK?

Exercise 10.1

For each of the following examples, list several possible barriers to exercise and strategies for removing these barriers.

1. A 25-year-old woman with little previous movement experience who does not exercise
   a. Barriers:
   b. Strategies:
2. A 44-year-old man who played a lot of sports in high school and at university but has not exercised or participated in sports since then
   a. Barriers:
   b. Strategies:
3. A 70-year-old woman who exhibits interest in going to the gym but is intimidated by all the equipment
   a. Barriers:
   b. Strategies:

of steps, as depicted in Kirschenbaum's (1984) self-regulation process, to achieve the necessary self-regulation skills. To facilitate self-regulation skills in their students, patients, or athletes, practitioners need to understand these steps.

Kirschenbaum (1984) developed a five-stage model of self-regulation (see figure 10.3). The first stage is the **problem identification stage**. During this stage, adults must not only identify the problem, such as a need to improve their softball skills or to start an exercise program, but also decide whether the change is possible and worth the effort. During stage 1, the person must be willing to take responsibility for solving the problem. Stage 2 is the **commitment stage**. To commit, the person must be willing to make the sacrifices necessary to persevere through the process.

Once a commitment has been made, the person moves to the **execution stage**, which is the active stage of behavioral change. During this stage, the person must develop self-expectancies for success through goal setting and continually self-evaluate and self-monitor their performance with respect to these goals. In addition to goal setting, they should plan ways to reinforce continued improvement and potentially even punishment for deviating from goal attainment. An athlete trying to improve his swim for triathlons might set a goal to swim 40 minutes, four times per week, or to decrease his swim time by 10 percent by the next competition. He could log when he swims and the duration and distance of each swim. If he meets his goals, he could reward himself by buying new gear or an athletic watch. In therapy settings, physical and occupational therapists work closely with patients during the execution phase by developing goals with them and continually evaluating their progress.

Stage 1: Problem identification
Sierra needs to improve her golf drive.

Stage 2: Commitment
Sierra is willing to make the sacrifices necessary to relearn how to perform a drive in golf.

Stage 3: Execution
Sierra sets goals and monitors her progress.

Stage 4: Environmental management
Alternative practice locations are found for possible inclement weather.

Stage 5: Generalization
Goals are reevaluated. Sierra may now focus on other aspects of her game.

Figure 10.3 Kirschenbaum's five-stage model of self-regulation.

The fourth stage is the **environmental management stage**. In this stage, adults prepare strategies to deal with potential environmental or social barriers to attaining their goals. The triathlete may schedule some practices in open water but have an indoor pool option as a backup during inclement weather. Social barriers could also affect performances or practices. For instance, someone who relies on a friend for moral support to exercise could lose motivation when her friend decides to cancel a workout session. Having backup plans, such as other people to walk with or group exercise classes to participate in, could keep unforeseen changes from affecting an exercise routine. Therapists must also help patients set up their home environments, providing them with the knowledge and equipment they need to continue their treatments at home.

Stage 5 is the **generalization stage**, during which people focus on sustaining their efforts for long periods of time. They may change some of their goals. For instance, the triathlete may notice that his swim times have improved, but he needs to focus on his run. Or he may want to increase his strength and thus begin a weightlifting program. A woman who has successfully adhered to her exercise program may want to shift her focus to improving her diet while continuing her exercise program. Therapists may help patients develop at-home plans to continue their treatments after completing their rehabilitation programs.

The five stages in Kirschenbaum's (1984) model emphasize the importance of self-monitoring in self-regulation. People must continually evaluate their performances and progress toward their goals. Self-regulation is also strongly influenced by personality styles and dispositions. Optimistic people with high self-esteem are much more stable and likely to continue self-regulatory behavior, whereas pessimistic people with low self-esteem are more likely to see changing social and environmental con-

WHAT DO YOU THINK?

Exercise 10.2

1. How would a recreational runner likely differ in self-regulatory strategies from a competitive runner?
2. What self-regulatory skills would you encourage a recreational runner to focus on?
3. What are some self-regulatory skills you use in either fitness, recreational activities, or competitive sports?

ditions as barriers to continuing with the program (Waschall & Kernis, 1996).

Self-Regulation Strategies

Although there are many self-regulation strategies, the most used are self-monitoring, goal setting, self-talk, and imagery (Weiss & Gould, 2015). Self-monitoring and goal setting are critical skills in self-regulation because they keep people focused on attaining their performance goals (Massey et al., 2015). We are almost constantly engaging in some form of self-talk. Therefore, regulating self-talk has a strong influence on all our behaviors, from sport performance to social situations. Imagery can also be a powerful form of self-regulation that can help us improve performance and control emotion.

Self-Monitoring

Self-monitoring is the systematic observation of oneself (Kirschenbaum, 1987). Methods of self-monitoring include recording behaviors or performances and making self-observations. Performances can also be self-monitored using tangible items, such as putting a nickel in a jar for every mistake. The purpose of self-monitoring is to become more aware of one's behaviors, which can improve performance and decrease anxiety and boost confidence (Crews et al., 2000). Self-monitoring can be either positive (e.g., recording successful performances) or negative (e.g., recording poor performances). Research has shown that positive

self-monitoring is beneficial for difficult tasks because it enhances the performer's expectancies and improves performance. On the other hand, well-learned and simple tasks benefit more from negative self-monitoring, such as focusing on failures and mistakes (Kirschenbaum, 1987).

Goal Setting

Perhaps the most critical self-regulation skill is goal setting. Setting goals focuses the learner's attention on attaining a set level of proficiency. It is especially important to set specific and measurable goals that must be achieved by a predetermined time (e.g., decreasing 5 km running time by 10 percent in the next six weeks). Goals that either are not specific or cannot be measured are ineffective. Goal setting is further discussed in chapter 18.

Self-Talk

Another useful self-regulation skill is the management of self-talk. Considering that people engage in a lot of self-talk every day, it is not surprising that managing self-talk can assist in regulating behavior. Athletes may say to themselves, *I can't do this, I am the worst player,* or *I'm going to mess this up.* On the flip side, positive self-talk can improve confidence, increase motivation, correct bad habits, and focus attention (Williams & Leffingwell, 1996). Most skilled athletes have learned how to manage their self-talk, even to the point of changing negative thoughts to positive thoughts, as Bjorn

Borg did in the following example at the Wimbledon final against John McEnroe in 1980, a match that has often been referred to as legendary:

> As [Bjorn] Borg took his position for the fifth set, he said to himself, "This is terrible. I'm going to lose." But then thought, "If you lose a match like this, the Wimbledon final, after all those chances, you will not forget it for a long, long time. That could be very hard." It was his serve to start the last set. He lost the first two points. "But then," Borg recalls, "I say to myself, 'I have to forget. I have to keep trying, try to win'." He served the next point and won. And again and again. (Deford, 1980)

The mind can have a very powerful influence on performance. Negative thoughts can not only prevent improvement but can also be the downfall of even the most skilled athletes. Maintaining positive thinking and clearing the mind can provide an athletic advantage. Managing self-talk can divert people from negative, unproductive thoughts and guide them toward positive thoughts. Self-talk management strategies include stopping self-talk that is negative or irrational; changing negative self-talk to positive self-talk; internally reasoning to counter negative self-talk; and reframing, which is changing one's perspective on the situation (Zinsser et al., 2001).

Imagery

Imagery, the visualization or cognitive rehearsal of a movement, has been found to be a very effective self-regulatory skill and performance enhancer. It provides additional rehearsal of the movement pattern and can be implemented as part of a regular practice schedule. Imagery can be either internal (i.e., viewing through your own eyes) or external (imagining you are an external observer watching yourself). Imagery training directs attention to the movement, promotes self-monitoring, and assists with positive self-reinforcement (Kirschenbaum, 1987). Chapter 19 addresses imagery (or mental practice) in more detail and provides basic guidelines for effective imagery training.

PEAK ATHLETIC PERFORMANCE

One of the most intriguing issues in human motor development is the connection between chronological age and physical performance. In general, research on highly skilled athletes indicates that peak athletic performance occurs between the ages of 25 and 35 (Gabbard, 2021). It is certainly rare for either a 12-year-old or a 75-year-old to break a world record. The main limiting factor for the 12-year-old or the 75-year-old is not motivation or behavior; rather, it is biological (Schulz & Curnow, 1988). During adolescence, many growth and developmental changes are still occurring, and the systems are not capable of working together for maximal function until early adulthood. On the other end of the spectrum, the biological capacity of older adults is declining, limiting their physiological capacity and peak performance. Refer to chapter 13 for more on age-related physiologic changes throughout adulthood.

The simplest way to measure the age of peak athletic performance in humans is to compare the ages of world record holders (Hill, 1925). Most sport records (e.g., in running, swimming, cycling, and weightlifting) are achieved by people in their late 20s or early 30s (Kenney et al., 2015). This suggests that humans are in their physical prime during this age range.

The age of peak athletic performance depends on the most important physiological element of the sport (Shephard, 2008). In gymnastics, the key element is the ratio of strength to body mass. This becomes a large structural constraint for females when they become young adults, because they gain fat

TRY THIS

Imagery Training

Exercise 10.3

Imagery Process

1. *Visualizing simple objects:* The ability to visualize images and scenes takes time and practice. When you first attempt imagery, it is best to simply practice visualizing stationary objects. For instance, look closely at an object in the room, at its size, shape, color, and texture. Now close your eyes and try to visualize the object. Try to remember all the details you noticed with your eyes open. Then open your eyes and compare your image with the object. Were you able to easily visualize this object? Were there details that you missed? Next, try visualizing an object in another room without looking at it first. After visualizing the object, go into that room and compare your image with the object. Did your visualization closely resemble the object?

2. *Visualizing yourself completing daily activities:* The next step in imagery training is to practice controlling images of your movements in the environment. It is best to start with simple activities, such as your morning routine. Close your eyes and imagine yourself lying in your bed. If you use an alarm, hear your alarm sound. What does it sound like? How does your body react to the alarm? Then follow your normal morning routine in your mind. What do you do next? Be sure to include all your senses. What does your shampoo smell like? How does the water feel on your skin? Can you hear the sound of the shower?

3. *Visualizing yourself in a competitive event:* Once you can control images in a simple environment, you can practice imagery for a more complex environment, such as a competitive event. During this practice, begin by imagining the entire scene before the competition even begins. What are the sights, sounds, and smells? Now move into imagining the entire event. Try to control the outcome. It is important that you visualize yourself performing well, because this will increase your confidence and motivation. If you find yourself having trouble controlling the images, or if you are visualizing poor performances, go back and practice visualizing simple objects and movements. Imagery is a learned skill and developing it may take some practice.

Questions

1. How vivid were your images? Which details seemed the most vivid? Which aspects of the object, routine, or event were not part of the image?
2. Did you incorporate all your senses (sight, sound, smell, and touch)?
3. Were you able to control your movements and the outcome in the competitive event?
4. Did you use internal imagery, external imagery, or both?

in the breasts and hips. This may explain in part why so many female gymnasts reach their peak prior to puberty. In aerobic activities, such as swimming and running, the average velocities for 100-meter and 10-kilometer runs and the 100-meter front crawl decrease by a rate of about 1 percent per year after the age of 25. The rates of decline are approximately the same for both sprints and distance performances. Muscular strength generally increases up to approximately age 25 to 35 and decreases by a rate of about 1.8 percent per year thereafter.

TRY THIS

Peak Performance

Exercise 10.4

Work in a small group of two to four people. Divide up the following sports: gymnastics, swimming, running, baseball, wrestling, boxing, tennis, and golf. Search for the peak performance age for each sport for both males and females. You can further divide up the sports (e.g., divide running into sprinting and long=distance running) or add to this list. Write the sport in the appropriate box for age and sex. Shot put and diving are included as examples.

Age	Male	Female
17		
18		
19		
20		
21		Diving
22	Diving	
23		
24		
25		
26		Shot put
27		
28		
29	Shot put	
30		
31		

Performances in Olympic Events

The ages of peak athletic performances in track and field events range in the lower to mid-20s; women reach their peak approximately one year sooner than men in most events (Schultz & Curnow, 1988). For running events, the average age for peak athletic performance tends to depend on the distance of the run. According to a systematic review on age of peak competitive performance, there was a trend for the duration of the event and age at peak performance, which was found for both sexes (Allen & Hopkins, 2015). Peak performances at younger ages were found for shorter duration events such as sprints and events requiring explosive power, ranging from swimming sprints

peak age around 20 years (best times of 2 to 15 minutes) to ultracycling with a peak age of about 39 years (best times of about 28 hours). Peak ages were similar for men and women.

The mean ages for peak performances in sprints are younger than for distance running, ranging from a mean age of 22 for the 100- and 200-meter sprints to 27 for the 5,000 and 10,000 meters and the marathon. Interestingly, this trend was not observed in swimming events. The mean age for peak athletic performance was 20 for men and 18 for women. The age remained the same for men regardless of the swimming event. For women, the age was younger for longer swim distances, which is opposite the trend for running events. This is well illustrated by the world record–breaking performances in 1987 by Janet Evans at the age of 15 in the 400-, 800-, and 1,500-meter freestyle.

Surprisingly, the age of peak athletic performances from the standpoint of gold medals and world records changed very little across a period of 90 years (Schulz & Curnow, 1988), even though the performances themselves improved quite dramatically. For example, the age of the 1,500-meter gold medalist in 1896 was 22, and 90 years later the gold medalist was 24 years old; yet, a 37.8 percent improvement was seen in the men's marathon over this 90-year period. In 1896, the fastest marathon time was 2:58:50; it decreased dramatically to 2:11:03 in 1980. The greatest percentage of improvement was in the men's shot put—an increase of 90 percent! Although there were huge improvements across this period, performances have stabilized in more recent years.

With the vast improvements in training programs, equipment, technology, diet, and other factors, it is not surprising that elite performance has improved quite significantly. Yet, it is surprising that the age at which elite peak performance occurs has not changed. The simple fact that the age of peak athletic performance remained consistent over a century regardless of all these large scientific advancements leads to the assumption that the major factor affecting age at peak athletic performance is biological. The only exception to the stability of age at optimal performance is golf. Schulz and Curnow (1988) suggested that the higher age variability at elite levels seen in complex tasks is affected by variables additional to the biological factors that strongly affect motor skills and that rely heavily on endurance, strength, or both. Biological developmental factors do not seem to affect skills with a higher cognitive component. World chess champions tend to be significantly older than track and field athletes, with a mean age of 38. Similarly, productivity in the arts and sciences does not peak until the late 30s to early 40s (Belsky, 1984).

Performances in Selected Sports

Assessing the age of peak athletic performance in a sport such as baseball is more complicated than it is in track and field or swimming because of the complexity of the game and the large number of performance measurements compiled. To assess the age of peak athletic performance in baseball, Schulz and Curnow (1988) analyzed 10 categories for nonpitchers (runs, hits, doubles, triples, home runs, RBIs, walks, strikeouts, stolen bases, and batting average) and six categories for pitchers (wins, win–loss percentage, strikeouts, earned run average, shutouts, and saves). Although many categories were assessed, the mean age of peak athletic performance remained very consistent at age 27 to 28. Broken down more specifically, peak ages in baseball ranged from on-base percentage, which peaks at age 30, to pitcher's strikeouts, which peak at age 23.5 years, which is typically the age at which Major Leaguers begin their careers. Due to the reliance upon pitch speed requiring muscular and tendon strength, it is not surprising getting strikeouts is the first skill to deteriorate. Although the ability to strike batters out deteriorates quickly, a pitcher's ability to prevent walks does not peak for another nine years, at age 32.5 (Bradbury, 2009).

To examine the age at peak athletic performance for two other complex games, tennis and golf, the age of the number one–ranking athlete per year was recorded. In tennis, the mean age was 25 for men and 24 for women. Mean ages for golfers were significantly higher, at approximately 33; women averaged one year younger than men. A trend toward younger golf champions began in the late 1960s with Jack Nicklaus and certainly continued with the golf sensation Tiger Woods and more recently Rory McIlroy. In 1997, at the age of 21, Woods became the youngest Masters winner, won three other PGA events, and achieved the number-one world ranking all within 42 weeks of becoming a pro. Nicklaus, Woods, and McIlroy each won three majors by the age of 25.

WHAT DO YOU THINK?

Exercise 10.5

Given that the age of peak athletic performance remained consistent over a period of 90 years, even though performance improved substantially (sometimes as much as 90 percent), we can conclude that there are biological limitations to performing at a peak level. Using this information for a sport of your choice, answer the following questions:

1. How could you use this information to maximize the performance of an athlete who is above the mean age for peak athletic performance for this sport?

2. Would you use this information to help you identify talent (i.e., would you use age as a factor when selecting your team and athletes)? Why or why not?

Performance Changes in Older Adults

In general, regardless of sport or activity, performance declines tend to occur at a slow to moderate rate between 30 and 50 years of age, followed by a steeper performance decline from 50 to 60 years. After age 70, the reduction in performance is significant (Bernard et al., 2009; Reider, 2008). A sharp decline in athletic performance at the age of 70 has been found in masters athletes in running events, both sprints and endurance (Wright & Perricelli, 2008), weightlifting (Meltzer, 1994), and swimming (Donato et al., 2003). Most performances follow these trends with few exceptions. One of the rare exceptions is the ultramarathon (100 km), wherein performances improve until age 30, but do not improve again until age 49 for men and age 54 for women (Knechtle et al., 2012).

After ages 60 or 70, people find it significantly more difficult to perform at the levels they have previously. It is as if these older adults are pushing a boulder up a hill that is getting steeper and steeper (Reider, 2008) as they fight with age-related physiological changes, such as decreasing muscle mass, reduced size of type II muscle fibers, lower maximal oxygen volumes and heart rates, and stiffening connective tissues (refer to chapter 13). It is important for rehabilitation specialists and geriatric instructors to be aware of this sharp decline in older adults. Although the decline is inevitable, interventions, such as endurance training and strength training, can help older adults maximize their functional potential.

MOVEMENT PATTERNS

Age-related declines in strength, flexibility, and processing speed all contribute to changing movement patterns in older adults (refer to chapter 13). Older adults are also much more likely to have secondary factors, such as disease or injury, that can compound age-related movement changes. This section focuses on the factors affecting healthy aging in relation to locomotor skills (running and jumping), object control skills (throwing and striking), and functional activities (driving, handwriting, and typing).

Changes in Locomotor Skills

Changes in gait have been associated with the aging process. Reduced gait speed is one of the most significant changes seen in healthy older adults, who walk on average 20 percent more slowly than young adults (Spirduso et al., 2005). Surprisingly, the reduction in gait speed is not the result of decreased stride frequency (the number of strides per unit of time); rather, it is largely the result of reduced stride length (the distance traveled between right-foot contacts). A reduced stride length negatively affects many other aspects of the gait, resulting in

RESEARCH NOTES

Senior Athletic Track and Field Performances

To examine age-related changes in peak athletic performance among elite senior athletes, researchers looked at track and field Olympians over the age of 50 who participated in the 2001 National Senior Olympic Games (Wright & Perricelli, 2008). Examining elite athletes provides a clearer picture of age-related peak performance changes because these are less likely to be affected by chronic disease or long periods of physical inactivity and disuse. Age-related changes were determined from the mean winning performance times in various track and field events, and age and sex differences were compared. Performance times significantly increased for both sprints and endurance events for both males and females. Performances declined slowly until the age of 75 and then declined dramatically. Men declined at a similar rate in both sprints and endurance events, whereas women declined at a higher rate in sprints than in endurance events.

Senior elite athletes provide an excellent example of what the aging human body can achieve. They demonstrate that aging alone should not prevent people from participating in physical activity or from competing in high-level contests. Even though significant declines in peak athletic performance occur, most notably beyond the age of 75, these athletes are delaying the onset of chronic disease and are maintaining a high sense of both physical and mental well-being.

reduced joint rotation in the lower extremities, increased double-support time (time during which both feet are in contact with the ground), reduced arm swing, and a more flat-footed contact with the ground (Elble, 1997).

These age-related changes in gait should not be taken lightly because impaired gait places adults at a higher risk of accidental falls (Saftari & Kwon, 2018). Accidental falls occur in 30 percent of adults over age 65 and 50 percent of adults over the age of 80. The likelihood of falling again also increases with each fall. Locomotion becomes even more challenging when older adults are facing obstacles, such as stepping up over a curb or stepping around a chair (Steffen et al., 2002) or during dual tasks, such as walking while talking (Beurskens & Bock, 2012). Every day we avoid many obstacles without even noticing ourselves doing it. However, the ability to negotiate many different obstacles while traveling from point *A* to point *B* is an important component of independent living. To compensate for age-related changes in gait,

some adults walk with increased toeing out (Murray et al., 1970) to provide more stability, they walk slower, and they pick up their feet higher to avoid tripping over obstacles.

Many factors contribute to age-related changes in gait, including muscular weakness in the hip abductors, hip extensors, knee extensors, plantar flexors, and dorsiflexors, as well as sensory impairments in the visual, somatosensory, and vestibular systems. Spirduso and colleagues (2005) found 10 age-related gait changes:

Temporal and Distance Variables

1. Decreased velocity
2. Decreased step length (distance traveled of alternate feet)
3. Decreased step frequency (walking cadence)
4. Decreased stride length (distance traveled of same foot)
5. Increased stride width (distance between the two feet)

6. Increased stance phase (begins when the first foot contacts the ground)
7. Increased time in double support (time when both feet are in contact with the ground)
8. Decreased time in the swing phase (begins as the foot leaves the ground)

Kinematic Variables

1. Flatter foot–floor pattern
2. Reduced arm swing

The causes of gait changes may not be limited to physiological age-related changes. Evidence supports the possibility that many older adults alter their gait because they are afraid of falling. Older adults adopt a safer gait by taking shorter steps, with more time in double stance, to decrease their risk of falling. Willmott (1986) proposed this after finding that older adults walked significantly faster on carpet than on vinyl flooring.

Running

The movement pattern characteristics (kinematics) of older adults up to age 80 have been found to be the same as those of female university track athletes (Adrian & Cooper, 1995). However, few similarities were seen in the sprinting kinematics of older females and young athletes. Young athletes use longer strides and generate more force through greater flexion and extension, which enables them to take fewer strides. It is also not surprising that older adults show a steady decline in both jogging and running speeds in comparison to young adults (Nelson, 1981).

Jumping

Research on jumping has revealed age-related differences in the kinematics of vertical jumping. Young adult males (18-year-olds) were compared with males in their mid-60s on vertical jumping (Wang, 2008). The older men had significantly less strength in the knee and hip, which can affect the ability to perform other activities of daily living.

During the jump, the older men exhibited less hip flexion and extension than the young adults but showed no differences in their knees. The decreased hip joint angles enabled them to maintain hip angular stiffness. Joint angular stiffness increases joint stability by resisting sudden angular displacements of the hip (Flanagan & Harrison, 2007), which can damage cartilage and ligaments (Butler et al., 2003). Similarly, Haguenauer and colleagues (2005) examined adults between ages 79 and 100 years, finding reduced jump height, which was attributed to decreased range of motion. However, the participants in this group not only decreased hip and ankle flexion, but they also reduced flexion in the knee. The reduced range of motion and a decrease in explosive force caused the decrease in overall jump height of about 28 centimeters in the older adults.

One factor that likely affects jumping ability in older adults is little to no high-intensity exercise. High-intensity exercise can provide a lot of physiological and functional benefits. Recently, assisted jumping has been hypothesized to be an effective, safe, and easy modality for older adults to incorporate higher-intensity jumping into their workouts leading to increased lower body strength and power output and ultimately decreasing their fall risk (Tufano, 2019).

Changes in Object Control Skills

Unfortunately, studies on movement patterns in adults are limited (Lorson et al., 2013; Williams et al., 1998). Most research studies have instead focused on functional activities such as walking, running, and rising from a seated to a standing position. Research on movements using maximal force is also quite limited; most studies have focused on performing the movements at preferred speeds. Although research is limited in this area, this section discusses object control movement patterns in older adulthood for throwing and striking.

TRY THIS

Mall Walkers

Exercise 10.6

Take a trip to a mall or a downtown street or other location where many people are walking around in a leisurely fashion. Notice the kinematic, temporal, and distance variables of the people walking. Compare two adults in each of the following age groups: young adults (20 to 40 years), middle-aged adults (40 to 60 years), and older adults (over 60 years). Use the chart to take qualitative notes on gait-related variables to describe each of their walking patterns.

	Young adults		Middle-aged adults		Older adults	
	1	2	1	2	1	2
Velocity (slow, moderate, or fast)						
Step length (distance traveled by alternate feet) (short, medium, long)						
Step frequency (walking cadence) (slow, moderate, or fast)						
Stride length (distance traveled by the same foot) (short, medium, long)						
Stride width (distance between the two feet) (narrow, moderate, or wide)						
Time in double support (time when both feet are in contact with the ground) (minimal, moderate, much)						
Arm swing (minimal, moderate, much)						
Other observations						

What variables other than age may cause some of the differences in gait that you observed?

Throwing

A hypothetical life span developmental trajectory was developed for the progression of throwing patterns from middle adolescence to young adulthood, and then the regression to middle-aged adulthood (Lorson et al., 2013). Researchers used the developmental sequence for the overarm throw for force divided into categories for each of four body segment actions: trunk, humerus, forearm, and foot action (Roberton & Halverson,

1984). Age-related differences are more pronounced in males than females, but this gap decreases with age. This sex-related difference is likely attributable to larger developmental improvements in males than females (Lorson et al., 2013).

A further regression in the developmental sequence for throwing was found in adults over the age of 70 (Williams et al., 1990, 1991). Very few older adults threw with developmentally advanced actions for any of the body segments. Older adults also threw with reduced range of motion and took smaller steps. Only 11.4 percent of participants were in the most advanced stage of humerus action (humerus lag), and none of the participants were in the most advanced stage of the forearm action (delayed forearm lag). Similar results were found in the advanced stage of the trunk action component (0 percent of the older adults exhibited differentiated trunk rotation), and only 3.5 percent of participants were in the advanced stage of the foot action (contralateral long step). Sex differences were also reported: women threw with significantly fewer developmentally advanced actions of the forearm and humerus than men (Williams et al., 1991).

When the throwing velocities of the older adults were compared with those of children and adolescents by Halverson and colleagues (1982), the older adults' speeds were comparable to those of third-grade children (see figure 10.4). Throwing velocities were higher for males than for females in all age groups, which is likely due to the more advanced movement patterns produced by the males. The developmental level of movement patterns has been found to predict ball velocities in children (Roberton & Konczak, 2001).

Striking

The fundamental movement pattern of striking is a coincident timing skill that requires a person to contact a ball by manipulating an object such as a racket, bat, or club. Striking skills can vary quite considerably. The planes of motion—overhand (e.g., tennis serve), sidearm (e.g., batting), and underhand (e.g., golf)—vary from sport to sport, as do the size and elasticity of the ball and the implement (e.g., tennis racket, baseball bat, or golf club).

Slower extension velocities have been found in the striking patterns of executing the tennis backhand and batting in older adults (Klinger et al., 1980) but not in the golf swing for a short shot (Jagacinski et al., 1997). Although no differences were found between young and older adults in the tempo of the golf swing or the overall speed of the swing, marked group differences were observed in the rhythm of the swing, or the speeding up and slowing down within a shot. The older adults reached their peak downswing force earlier than the young adults did. Young adults reached this peak just prior to contacting the ball. These results may indicate that older adults have reduced control during the swing compared to young adults. The older adults also exerted more effort, although most of them performed as well as the young adults.

Research suggests that age-related effects on movement performances, such as decision-making and movement times can be reduced in active adults (Horníková et al., 2018). In general, active older adults can maintain their movement patterns at a level

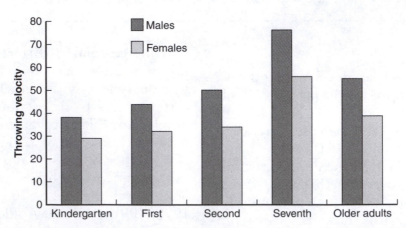

Figure 10.4 Overhand throwing velocities (feet per second) for children in kindergarten through seventh grade and older adults.
Data from Williams, Haywood, and VanSant (1991).

RESEARCH NOTES

Maybe Older Adults Aren't So Bad at Throwing

Williams and colleagues (1998) conducted a longitudinal study on overhand throwing in adults between the ages of 62 and 77. Over a period of seven years, eight older adults were videotaped from the sagittal plane (side view) as they threw a tennis ball. The results indicated that many of the age-related differences found in older adults may be the result of the study design, because previous studies on overarm throwing were cohort studies, comparing people of different ages rather than the same people across time. The developmental levels were the same across the seven years 90 percent of the time, which indicates that only small changes in the coordination patterns occurred in the participants during this period. The older adults coordinated their movements similarly to younger throwers except for the control of the overarm throw, the amount of trunk rotation, and the range of shoulder motion. The changes seen in movement control are likely the result of factors such as chronic disuse (Spirduso et al., 2005), osteoarthritis, and losses in balance (Thapa et al., 1994).

The researchers also found that older adults coordinated their backswings differently than younger throwers. Due to the different movement patterns performed by the older adults during the backswing, two new steps were added to the developmental sequence (levels 3 and 5):

Level 1: No backswing

Level 2: Elbow and humeral flexion

Level 3: Humeral lateral rotation

Level 4: Circular, upward backswing

Level 5: Shortcut circular, downward backswing

Level 6: Circular, downward backswing

The older adults threw using these two new steps more than any other preparatory backswing step. These movements are likely adaptations resulting from changes in the range of motion at the shoulder.

like that achieved during young adulthood. Movement speed and range of motion are affected to a lesser degree in active adults than in inactive adults.

Changes in Functional Activities

Given the many physical changes that accompany aging, it is important to understand how these changes affect older adults' abilities to perform functional tasks such as driving, handwriting, and typing. These activities are very important for quality of life and independence. Older adults who lose the ability to drive become dependent on either public transportation or friends and family for transportation. Public transportation can be limited for adults who do not reside in metropolitan areas, forcing them to rely on others to drive them. Handwriting and typing are also important everyday functional tasks and are strong indicators of cognitive and physical declines.

Driving

The primary mode of transportation for older adults in the United States is driving; however, drivers continue driving an average of 11 years for women and 6 years for men beyond an age in which they can safely drive (Foley et al., 2002). "Driving an automobile is a source of independence, freedom, socialization, and self-esteem for many older individuals" (Johnson, 2003, p. 34). Driving provides an increased quality of life for many adults, allowing them to pursue activities they could not if they were unable to drive. Policy makers often suggest public transportation as the solution; however, older adults do not perceive public transportation as a viable alternative to driving. Transitioning from driving to nondriving can be quite difficult (Dickerson et al., 2019). Some older adults do not have access to public transportation, some don't like using it, and some cannot physically walk the distance necessary to access the system (Donorfio et al., 2008).

The number of drivers over the age of 70 is increasing as the baby boomer generation joins this age group and as people are living longer. Not only are there more drivers over the age of 70, but it is also expected that older drivers will dramatically increase their driving miles (Castro et al., 2005). With the growing older population and increased mileage, the number of vehicle fatalities in adults over 65 years in the United States increased 19.9 percent from 2007 to 2016 and is expected to increase 30 percent by 2030 (National Highway Traffic Safety Administration, 2017). In general, older adults are safer drivers and are less likely to be involved in accidents than younger adults. Yet, because of their physical declines, older adults involved in accidents are much more likely to sustain serious injuries or die (Braver & Trempel, 2003).

Older adults are generally aware of their functional declines, both physical (i.e., eyesight, hearing, reflexes, and neck or shoulder mobility) and psychological (i.e., confidence, enjoyment, ability to concentrate, trust of other drivers, independence, and ability to drive in stressful environments). Because of this heightened awareness in relation to driving abilities, they tend to compensate with strategies, such as an increased awareness of their performance, the driving behaviors of other drivers, their vehicle, and road rules (Donorfio et al., 2008). Driving shifts from an activity that is largely automatic to a chore, requiring more planning and increased concentration and cautiousness.

Policy making for older adults is challenging. Older drivers often have physical declines, but positive alterations in their driving behaviors allow them to drive more safely than younger adults. Older adults are also quite variable, so rating driving ability solely based on age would not be judicious. Some older adults can drive competently in their 90s, whereas others show significant impairment in their 60s or 70s.

Medical conditions that are more prevalent in older adults have been associated with increased accident risk (Marshall, 2008). Cardiovascular disease, cerebrovascular disease, depression, diabetes, medication use, musculoskeletal disorders, and visual deficit have been shown to cause a slight to moderate increase in crash risk. Alcohol abuse and dependence, dementia, epilepsy, schizophrenia, and sleep apnea, on the other hand, are associated with a moderate to high increase in crash risk. The accident risk fluctuates according to the severity of the condition, which varies considerably across individuals.

One factor that may be as important to (if not more important than) driving safety as medical conditions, sensory limitations, and cognitive declines is the ability to self-assess changes affecting driving skills (Meng & Siren, 2012). Older adults who are more cognizant of these changes are more likely to compensate for them by avoiding night driving, driving more slowly, or not driving long distances. In addition, many

---

WHAT DO YOU THINK?

Exercise 10.7

What are the implications of aging for driving? What declines could affect driving ability? Do you believe that drivers should be assessed or lose their driving privileges (or both) after they reach a certain age? If so, at what age? If not, why not? Weigh the pros and cons of implementing a policy on the cessation of driving in older adults. Think about the physical, psychological, and cognitive changes in older adults. Also, consider the effects of driving cessation on older adults (e.g., emotional effects, impact on social life).

---

advances have been made to cars, including backup cameras, adaptive headlights, and even auto-pilot, which help older adults continue driving.

Handwriting and Typing

Fine motor control such as is required for handwriting and typing is one of the greatest age-related declines in motor control (Martinez-Valdes & De Nunzio, 2021). These deficits are typically observed in adults over the age of 60 but can be observable as early as age 50 (Diermayr et al., 2011). Fine motor control is a predictor of functional dependency and as such is particularly important to maintain an independent lifestyle (Martinez-Valdes & De Nunzio, 2021).

The importance of handwriting, although reduced since the onset of computers and handheld devices such as iPads and cell phones, is one of the most common daily activities, necessary for both professional and leisure activities. Handwriting is a complex activity involving eye–hand coordination, dexterity, motor planning, visual and kinesthetic perception, and manual skills (Tseng & Cermak, 1993). Moreover, many years are needed to acquire the skill. Hand function has been found to decrease with increasing age because of reduced physical activity levels and neuromuscular decline in hand strength, speed, and coordination (Cole et al., 1999).

Older adults often report having no impairment in handwriting, but research has shown that they write significantly slower and with less pressure than young adults (Rosenblum & Werner, 2005). The decreased pressure is likely due to decreased hand strength (Fried et al., 1991), including reduced finger-pinch strength and finger-pinch posture (Ranganathan et al., 2001). Decreased handwriting speed was not simply the result of slower movements; also noted was increased air time—the time during writing in which the pen or pencil is not making marks on the paper (Rosenblum & Werner, 2005). Unlike other tasks requiring muscular strength, no sex differences were found with age for handwriting (Rosenblum & Werner, 2005).

In today's digital age, communication consists largely of typing and texting on computers or small screens, such as phones and tablets. Currently, there is limited research examining the effect of age on the ability to type. Kalman and colleagues (2015) compared young adults (21-31 years) to older adults (65-83 years) on typing measures, such as speed and self-corrections. The younger adults spent less time typing and used the Delete key more often than the older adults. The number of typing errors increased in the older adults as they increased their speed. Interestingly, the older adults spent more of their total time typing (70 percent compared to 50 percent in younger adults) and less time editing and correcting. These results may be due to a cohort effect, in that they grew up in an era when much more time was spent writing than typing. On the other hand, these results could be due to age-related changes, such as a decline in motor skills, timing, or sequencing, or a combination of both a cohort and an aging effect.

SUMMARY

Aging refers to the physical changes that occur across time. Chronological age is the most used indicator of age; however, this age marker is limiting, because adults can vary markedly in physiological adaptations and physical function. Two people can be the same chronological age but decades apart in biological age. On the other hand, there is a strong connection between chronological age and peak athletic performance. The age of peak athletic performance is between 25 and 35 years with very few exceptions. Even following vast improvements in technology, training programs, and nutrition that have resulted in dramatically improved performances in all sports, the age at which elite performances are achieved has remained consistent. Performance declines can be minimized by continuing to practice the sport, although large performance declines tend to occur after the age of 75 regardless of the sport or activity.

Current public health recommendations in the United States are for adults to maintain moderate-intensity physical activity for a minimum of 150 minutes per week, yet many adults are insufficiently physically active. Aging stereotypes and age grading contribute to negative stereotypes of older adults and seriously affect physical activity participation. This often leads to the exercise–aging cycle of decreased function because of decreased physical activity, leading to further decreased function, and so on. Adults who continue to be physically active have been found to maintain many of their physical capabilities, including physical performance, functional activities, and independence.

Driving provides a means of independence and freedom for adults and is considered an important component in the maintenance of enhanced quality of life for many seniors. Although many age-related physiological declines result in diminished driving capability, some adults continue to safely drive into their 90s and beyond.

❯ ONLINE ACTIVITIES

The student material found in HK*Propel* includes exercises, labs, and videos to enhance learning and encourage practical application of important concepts.

LEARNING AIDS

Supplemental Activities

1. How much time have you spent with an older adult—not your grandmother, grandfather, or another older relative, but an unrelated older adult? Unless you work with older adults, you likely haven't had an extended conversation with one. For this supplemental activity, visit a senior center or an assisted-living facility and spend some time with an older adult. Ask about the physical activities the person participated in as a child, an adolescent, a young adult, a middle-aged adult, and an older adult. Ask why the person participated in those activities and why they may have dropped out of certain activities or taken up different activities as an older person.

2. Choose a sport.

  a. Search for the record performances in that sport across time (e.g., the records for the sport in the 1930s, 1950s, 1970s, 1990s, and today).

    1. How have records changed?

    2. Did they change significantly more during one period than during others?

    3. What may have caused this more significant change in the sport?

    4. Why do you think performances are better now than they were in previous decades (e.g., new techniques, technological advances, diet changes)?

  b. Now, search for record performance times across ages (e.g., 20s, 30s, 40s, 50s, 60s, 70s). Graph the performance changes across these ages. Discuss your findings.

Glossary

age grading—Decreasing physical activity levels based on age.

ageism—Stereotyping someone based on age.

aging—A process or group of processes occurring in living organisms that, with the passage of time, lead to a loss of adaptability, functional impairment, and eventually death.

biological aging—The physiological adaptations that occur within the body due to the passage of time.

chronological age—The number of years a person has been alive.

commitment stage—Stage 2 of Kirschenbaum's (1984) five-stage model of self-regulation. To commit, the person must be willing to make the sacrifices necessary to persevere through the process.

environmental management stage—Stage 4 of Kirschenbaum's self-regulation process, in which adults prepare strategies to deal with environmental or social barriers that may prevent them from attaining their goals.

execution stage—Stage 3 of Kirschenbaum's self-regulation process, the active stage of behavioral change. During this stage, the person develops self-expectancies for success through goal setting.

generalization stage—Stage 5 of Kirschenbaum's self-regulation process, in which people focus on sustaining their efforts for long periods of time.

imagery—The visualization or cognitive rehearsal of a movement has been found to be a very effective self-regulatory skill and performance enhancer.

problem identification stage—Stage 1 of Kirschenbaum's self-regulation process, in which adults identify the problem and must decide whether the change is possible and worth the effort.

theory of planned behavior—A theory that attitudes toward a behavior depend on two factors: (a) the belief that the behavior will produce a specified outcome and (b) the person's desire to attain the specified outcome.

ASSESSMENT OF GROSS MOTOR DEVELOPMENT

CHAPTER OBJECTIVES

After reading this chapter, you should be able to do the following:

- Describe the connection between assessment and evaluation.
- Compare and contrast the five categories of assessment—formative versus summative, formal versus informal, normative versus criterion, component versus whole body, and process versus product.
- Explain the function of age with assessment.
- Understand the role of assessment for different types of practitioners.
- Compare several motor competence assessments and understand how to administer them.

Is It Developmentally Appropriate? How Do I Know?

Henry is new to Lake Murray Elementary School. Henry is 11 years old and is excited to start his new physical education class; it is his favorite! Henry really loves to run around, but he has very little experience playing games that require ball skills. During his first day of physical education, the teacher, Ms. Feeny, paid close attention to Henry. The children were in the middle of a throwing and catching unit. Henry steps with his right foot, then throws with his right hand; he has a hard time hitting the targets. While playing catch with Josie, Henry was hit in the face with the foam ball and struggled to use his hands on most trials. After class, Henry's face changed from a big smile to a somber expression. At home, Henry's mother asked how school and physical education went. Henry said he did not want to go back. Ms. Feeny contacted Henry's mother asking her if she (Ms. Feeny) could conduct a formal, norm-referenced gross motor skill assessment and evaluation of Henry. Henry's mother agreed.

The example in the opening scenario was an informal assessment of Henry in a naturalistic setting. Henry's performance is not unique; however, his physical education teacher made the right call. Assessment and the resultant evaluation are vital components of creating developmentally appropriate programming in physical education, adapted physical education, sport settings, and rehabilitation settings. The assessment strategies discussed in this chapter support practitioners with placement decisions in schools; provide evaluations of program effectiveness in school, sport, and rehabilitation settings; and offer flexible solutions to variable scenarios. Those working with children with and without disabilities must be able to understand the present level of performance, how performance changes across time, and how to evaluate assessment results for assisting with decision-making processes. This chapter also examines assessment types based upon procedure and outcome.

MOTOR PERFORMANCE VERSUS DEVELOPMENT

Motor development refers to the changes in motor behavior across the life span and the processes that underlie these changes (Clark & Whitall, 1989). One must embrace the notion that motor development is a construct and much more than just a score on a test (Barnett et al., 2016). Assessment opens the window into motor development as, technically, one cannot assess motor development in any one particular time. Rather, a singular gross motor assessment only captures motor performance (Getchell et al., 2019; Tamplain et al., 2019). To truly measure motor development, one must assess the same person across multiple time points (Getchell et al., 2019) and consider the factors that affect change (Clark & Whitall, 1989). For example, when a physical therapist evaluates the motor

skills of a four-year-old child, that is their actual motor performance at that specific time. Conversely, if the physical therapist evaluates the same child every six months across the next three years and plots their scores on a chart, the changes in motor skill across time provide an indication of motor development (e.g., changes across time) rather than just motor performance (e.g., the evaluation at one specific time). Factors that affect change in motor development are discussed throughout this book and are beyond the scope of this chapter. Please keep in mind that repeated measures are paramount for assessing motor development throughout our exploration of concepts within this chapter.

CATEGORIES OF ASSESSMENT

Assessment refers to the procedure through which assessors compile information on the processes of movement and/or the resultant products of movement (Rink, 2014). **Evaluation** refers to the use of the information collected from the assessment to make a judgment regarding one's performance at that time (Rink, 2014). Assessment and evaluation are not mutually exclusive. Assessment data alone have no subjective qualities, and evaluations are purely opinion without actual data. Thus, assessment and evaluation go hand in hand, and there are numerous types of assessments, which vary based upon desired purpose (Rink, 2014).

Process Versus Product Assessments

Typically, when assessing gross motor development, assessors are interested in either the process or product of movement and sometimes a combination of both. **Process assessments** refer to the collection of information regarding the *components* of a particular skill or the entire movement pattern as a collective regarding the *whole body* (see chapters 8 and 9 for more description). Process assessments focus on the qualitative aspects of components of a movement pattern (True et al., 2017). For example, stepping with opposition represents a component of throwing a ball. Stepping ipsilaterally, with no trunk rotation, an upward-initiated windup, and a follow-through that does not cross the midlines, as a collective, represents a whole-body evaluation of throwing.

Typically, process-oriented assessments struggle with ceiling effects. **Ceiling effects** are a type of inaccuracy with a measurement where performers can produce higher outcomes than the assessment will measure. Thus, assessments that are prone to ceiling effects struggle to discriminate between skilled performers. In contrast, **product assessments** include the outcome of the movement compiled quantitatively (True et al., 2017). With that same throwing task,

product assessments could include measures on the speed of the throw, number of times hitting a target, distance of the throw, and more. Sometimes, product measures suffer from floor effects. **Floor effects** are the opposite of ceiling effects in that they fail to provide a low enough metric to accurately capture the performance. For example, radar guns might only register speeds of at least 10 miles per hour. If a child throws slower than 10 miles per hour, the speed will not register, representing an inaccurate measurement. To avoid floor and ceiling effects, Logan and colleagues (2017) recommend assessing both processes and products of skills to capture a more comprehensive picture of motor performance.

WHAT DO YOU THINK?

Exercise 11.1

Choose two motor skills. Create a process and a product assessment for each skill. With the process, assess the whole body of movement and one individual component (e.g., trunk action). An example is provided for the motor skill of throwing. Also, refer to chapters 8 and 9 on whole-body assessments.

Throwing

Motor skill	TYPES OF ASSESSMENTS		
	Product	**Component**	**Whole body**
Throwing	• What was the maximum speed in miles per hour out of five throws? • How many times did the ball hit the target on the wall?	**Legs** *Step 1:* No step *Step 2:* Ipsilateral step *Step 3:* Contralateral step **Windup** *Step 1:* No windup *Step 2:* Upward initiated *Step 3:* Downward initiated **Trunk rotation** *Step 1:* None *Step 2:* Blocked *Step 3:* Segmented **Follow-through** *Step 1:* Not past the shoulder *Step 2:* Ipsilateral and past the shoulder *Step 3:* Contralateral	**Elementary** No step, no windup, follow-through not past the shoulder **Emerging** Ipsilateral step, upward-initiated windup, ipsilateral follow-through Contralateral step, upward-initiated windup, no trunk rotation, ipsilateral follow-through **Competent** Contralateral step, downward-initiated windup, segmented trunk rotation, and contralateral follow-through

RESEARCH NOTES

Is It the Process or the Product?

In 2017, Logan and colleagues compared performances on process- and product-oriented assessments of gross motor skills across childhood. In general, the product-oriented assessments were better at detecting advanced skills but were vulnerable to floor effects. For example, some radar guns can only detect speeds over 10 miles per hour. Many young children fail to throw a ball over 10 miles per hour. However, there are qualitative differences between them (e.g., one steps and other one does not step). Thus, the product measure was stuck in the floor and could not detect the difference between the two. The component-oriented developmental sequences, on the other hand, were better at detecting lower skilled individuals but suffered from ceiling effects. For example, the component approach would detect the difference between a young child who steps and one who does not. However, a young child who steps with opposition, has trunk rotation, and follows through to the opposite hip would score the same as a professional baseball pitcher. Thus, process-oriented assessments can hit the ceiling because assessors cannot detect differences between moderate and highly skilled movers. The authors recommend using both product- and process-oriented assessments to avoid floor and ceiling effects when evaluating motor skills.

Classification of Assessments

In rehabilitation settings, it is important to establish a baseline, or present level of performance, prior to any therapy, training, or treatment. Without establishing a baseline, a physical therapist would not have any indication of the extent to which exercises improve outcomes. In school settings, understanding the present level of performance can serve as a baseline so that teachers can design tasks that are developmentally appropriate meeting the needs of all learners. Baseline assessments are also referred to as **formative assessments**. Formative assessments occur either at the beginning or the middle of a unit or treatment schedule. Often, formative assessment is used for setting goals, evaluating progress, and evaluating the procedures within a unit or treatment schedule. **Summative assessment**, on the other hand, always occurs at the end of a unit or treatment schedule. Typically, physical therapists report baseline evaluations to justify the need for physical therapy, midpoint evaluations to under-

stand if the selected treatment options are working, and summative evaluations to discharge a patient. Similarly, in school settings, adapted physical educators could use baseline evaluation to qualify a student for adapted physical education and set individualized education plan goals, midpoint formative assessments to evaluate progress, and summative evaluations to determine adequate yearly progress and provide recommendations for the following year.

Typically, baseline and summative evaluations are **formal assessments**, while midpoint (formative) evaluations are **informal assessments**. When teachers, physical therapists, and researchers conduct *formal assessments*, they typically do so to report the evaluation to an outside agency (e.g., for research purposes, to qualify a student for adapted physical education, for insurance to approve physical therapy, etc.). Standardized assessments include indicators of its psychometric properties. **Psychometric properties** refer to the extent to which the results are both *valid* and *reliable*. **Validity** globally refers to the extent to which an assessment captures the construct it is purported to measure. **Reliability**, on the other hand, refers to the extent to which results of an assessment occur, as intended, consistently.

Figure 11.1 is a classic, visual representation to help us better understand reliability and validity. Figure 11.1 includes four dart boards, and the holes represent markers where darts landed. In scenario A, the darts hit the same spot consistently (despite a slight skew to the top left); thus the darts were reliable. However, the goal of the darts was to hit the bull's-eye. Given that the darts never hit the intended goal, they were not valid. Thus, this scenario in A can be interpreted as reliable, but not valid. Scenario B is slightly different. Here, the dart throws are all over the board. Thus, the throws were not reliable. However, all throws did land within the confines of the dart board without any skewing; thus, to some extent, the throws were valid. Scenario B is an example of a valid but unreliable set of throws. Scenario C is ideal. The goal was to hit the bull's-eye and to do so consistently. As you can see, all darts hit the bull's-eye; thus, the thrower was both valid and reliable. Scenario D is the worst-case scenario. The thrower never hit the bull's-eye, and throws were skewed to the top. Thus, scenario D is neither valid nor reliable.

Formal Assessments

Several formal assessments exist to examine the gross motor development of children. Most formal assessments incorporate the component approach and include psycho-

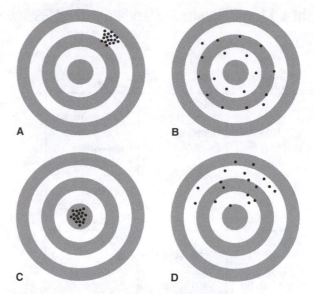

Figure 11.1 Validity and reliability examples.

Adapted from Pie Tutors, "Reliability and Validity: The Dartboard Analogy," YouTube video, 4:08, https://www.youtube.com/watch?app=desktop&v=UKU7hEOd4SU.

metrics of their validity and reliability. Table 11.1 highlights a few examples.

The cheapest and arguably simplest test to administer is the TGMD-3. The TGMD-3 includes process and product assessments and can be used formally, informally, and in many environments (e.g., physical education or clinical settings). Table 11.2 breaks out the use of the TGMD-3.

Standardized assessments, like the TGMD-3, are typically required for formal evaluations because their data are considered trustworthy due to their previously vetted psychometric properties. However, data from standardized assessments are only acceptable if the assessor always follows standardized procedures and protocols. In addition, it is critical to establish

---

WHAT DO YOU THINK?

Exercise 11.2

Can you be reliably bad?

1. Explain figure 11.1 in terms of validity and reliability?
2. Create or discuss two examples for each bull's-eye that relates to your field.

Table 11.1   Common Standardized Assessments

Test	Age	Construct	Norm-referenced testing for United States	Number of skills	Cost of equipment needed	Time to administer per subject
Test of Gross Motor Development–Third Edition (TGMD-3; Ulrich, 2019)	3 years, 0 months-11 years, 11 months	• Gross motor performance—if assessed only at baseline • Motor development—if assessed across multiple time points	X	13; 6 locomotor skills; 7 ball skills	Under $200 USD; typical equipment like tennis balls, plastic paddles, plastic bat, batting tee, playground ball, etc.	15-20 minutes
Körperkoordinationstest Für Kinder (KTK) (Kiphard & Schilling, 1974)	5 years, 0 months-14 years, 11 months	Motor coordination		4; all locomotor or stability	More than $1,500 USD; specialized equipment; manual *(not available in English)*	20 minutes
Bruininks-Oseretsky Test of Motor Proficiency	4 years-21 years	Gross and fine motor performance; includes separate stability skills and aspects of fitness; can also be repeated for development assessment	X	• Five; 22 (subscales to complete form) • 14 on the brief form selected from the 22 on the complete form. • Subscales include: • Manual dexterity—5 items; bilateral coordination—5 items; running speed and agility—5 items; upper limb coordination—7 items.	$1,000 or more USD, most equipment is included.	15 (short form); 60 minutes (complete battery)
Peabody Developmental Motor Screening Test (PDMS-2) (Folio & Fewell, 2000)	0-6 years, 11 months	Gross and fine motor performance; includes separate stability skills; can be repeated for development performance	X	• Reflexes—8 items • Stationary—30 items • Locomotion—89 items • Object manipulation—24 items • Grasping—26 items • Visual-motor integration—72 items*	$500 or more USD	20-60 minutes
Movement Assessment Battery for Children–Second Edition (M-ABC-2; Henderson et al., 2007)	4 years-12 years	Gross and fine motor performance; includes separate stability skills; can be repeated for development assessment	X	8 skills for manual dexterity, ball skills, and static or dynamic balance.	$1,100 or more USD. Includes all equipment.	20-30 minutes

*Numbers of actual items vary by participant because the subscale stops when a participant fails to meet the criteria for any given subscale.

Table 11.2 Various Uses of the TGMD-3

Motor skill	Formal, formative, or process	Informal, formative, or product	Formal, summative, or process and product
Test of Gross Motor Development–Third Edition (TGMD-3)	TGMD-3, conducted during week 3 of the school year	Tally sheets for how many times the ball hits the target, conducted at the beginning of the year	• TGMD-3, conducted during the last week of the school year • Throwing speed in miles per hour as assessed by a radar gun

rater reliability either for yourself (intrarater, or within the individual) or among multiple raters (interrater, or between individuals). Both **intrarater reliability** and **interrater reliability** are important to reduce bias within evaluations. Within a school or a rehabilitation setting, intrarater reliability may be the only option. In a research setting, it is critical to include both intrarater and interrater reliability so that readers may deem the results trustworthy. Often, researchers will include a **double-blind rater** to ensure their data are of the highest quality. Double-blind raters do not know *when* the assessment occurred and to *which* group the participant belonged. Double-blind raters are typically not necessary in school or rehabilitation settings. Can you see how double-blind raters might be necessary in a research study?

Establishing Rater Reliability

As noted previously in the study conducted by Palmer and Brian (2016), scoring assessment trials can be difficult, leading to inconsistencies in evaluations. If data or scores from assessments are not reliable, they can differentially affect desired outcomes. Typically, minimally accepted agreements among raters are 80 percent to 120 percent when using **average agreement** (see table 11.3). Average agreement is the agreement based upon the total score and not each individual trial. **Absolute agreement** refers to exact agreement with scoring of each trial, one at a time. Of course, absolute agreement is very challenging to obtain. With two raters you can calculate interrater reliability using the following formula: smaller amount/larger amount × 100. With multiple

RESEARCH NOTES

Do All Teachers Agree?

In 2016, Palmer and Brian evaluated the variability in coding the TGMD-2 among teachers who were new to the assessment and experts in motor development research. All participants received the same training as the experts. While watching videos, teachers were able to agree with the experts for the skills of kicking and galloping. However, the biggest struggles for the teachers were scoring the dribble, throw, slide, and jump. Scoring differences ranged from 14 to 195 percent. Interestingly, the researchers were harsher scorers than the teachers; teachers tended to score the children higher than the researchers. Maybe the teachers see the good in the children, whereas the researchers do not know the children. Regardless, rater reliability matters!

WHAT DO YOU THINK?

Exercise 11.3

Think of two other skills and create formal or informal, summative or formative, and process or product assessments similar to throwing and balance in the bottom rows of the table.

Motor skill	Formal, formative, or process	Informal, formative, or product	Formal, summative, or process and product
Throwing	TGMD-3 conducted during week 3 of the school year	Tally sheets for how many times the ball hits the target, conducted at the beginning of the year	• TGMD-3 conducted during the last week of the school year • Throwing speed in miles per hour as assessed by a radar gun
Static balance	M-ABC-2 conducted when the patient arrives to the physical therapy clinic	Time how long the patient can stand on one leg during their third, fifth, and seventh visits.	• M-ABC-2 conducted during the patient's last visit. • Count how long the patient can stand on one leg. • Denote how many times the patient "wobbles" during the balance test.

raters, you first establish the **gold standard rater** (e.g., the person who is most likely conducting the training or the person who most closely matched any training videos or a prototype example score). Afterward, use the formula gold standard/rater no. × 100 and repeat for all raters. Then, take the average of all raters (see table 11.4).

Evaluating Normative Versus Criterion References

Now that we better understand the relationship between assessment and evaluation, let's interpret our scores to create an evaluation. Most assessments result with scores in a raw form. **Raw scores** are simply the unaltered results from an assessment. Altered scores include adjustments for age or sex, including transformations into standard scores. Standard scores are exactly that, standardized for ease with interpretation against a normative reference. Generally, normative reference, or norm reference, refers to the extent to which a person compares with others of the same age and sex in similar locations. Certain assessments, like

Table 11.3 Calculating Agreement

	Rater 1	Rater 2	Absolute agreement
Trial 1	2	4	0
2	1	2	0
3	3	3	1
4	1	0	0
Total	7	9	1
	Average agreement = 7/9 = 0.78 × 100 = 78%		Absolute agreement = 1/4 = 25%

Table 11.4 Calculating Rater Reliability

	Gold standard	Rater 1	Rater 2
Trial 1	2	3	2
2	3	4	4
3	3	2	3
4	2	2	4
Sum	10	11	13
% Agreement with gold standard		91%	77%
% Team agreement	91 + 77/2 = 84%		

TRY THIS

Scoring the Assessment

Exercise 11.4

Go to an open gym, court, or field and observe the people playing a pickup game. Try to find the most skilled and least skilled players. Assess the highest and the lowest skilled players using at least three components of their skill (refer to chapters 8 and 9 for the whole-body approach). Compare and contrast the difficulty with evaluating process-oriented components between high- and low-skilled individuals. Was this difficult to do with the naked eye? Repeat with friends, recording on your smartphone with your friends' permission. Compare and contrast the difficulty with live scoring versus scoring from a video. Repeat the entire scenario with product measures or using the whole-body approach from the video bank on HK*Propel*.

---

the TGMD-3 (Ulrich, 2020; see table 11.5), establish national (and sometimes international) norms that are helpful for creating a **norm-referenced assessment** allowing assessors to easily interpret the data. Standardized outcomes of norm-referenced testing include the following: standard scores, percentile ranks, and age-based equivalents. Standardized assessments come with manuals that include conversion tables. One must translate the raw scores into standard scores using these conversion tables. From there, standard scores can then translate into percentile ranks and age-based equivalents.

Percentile ranks represent the percentage of people in the same location (national, state, or local) who score higher than, lower than, or similar to the participant. For example, if your participant scores in the fifth percentile, that is interpreted as 95 percent of the population (same age, same sex, same location) scored equal or better than they did, and 5 percent of the population scored equal or lower than they did. Raw scores can also be interpreted as age equivalents. Age equivalents are derived from the median scores of the reference sample for that particular age and sex. Administrators can take the raw score of their participant and, based upon their age and sex, compare it to the normative reference to gauge the extent to which their participant is ahead, behind, or on par with same-aged peers.

Motor development is age related, not age dependent. Although norm-referenced assessments develop their criterion reference based upon age, it is merely a statistical suggestion and a baseline from which to start. Age should not be the only predictor or criterion because all people are individuals and develop differently. Some children are behind; some are advanced, and that information should be used to create developmentally appropriate programming to maximize desired outcomes for all. Remember, motor skills do not naturally emerge as if they were a birthday present (Clark, 2007). Rather, motor skills are age related and are the result of the interaction of individual characteristics performing certain tasks within their given environment (remember Newell's constraints in chapter 2). Please interpret age-based norm references with caution since other factors, such as culture, can influence motor development.

Norm references are based upon a standard set by large, nationally represented assessments. The criterion for a norm reference is nationally derived standard scores. However, there are other forms of criterion-referenced testing where you set the standard from which to compare results. In general, when the standard for comparison is self-selected by either the administrator or the participant, we typically refer to this as a **criterion reference** (see table 11.6). Examples include goal setting, class averages, and more.

Table 11.5 Examples of Normative References From TGMD-3

Participant	Age	Sex	Raw score	Percentile rank	Standard score	Age equivalent
Norm	6 years, 0 months-6 years, 5 months	Female	29-34	50th	10	6 years, 6 months
No. 1	6 years, 5 months	Female	14	5th	5	3 years, 0 months
No. 2	6 years, 2 months	Female	40	84th	13	8 years, 6 months

Adapted from Ulrich (2019).

Table 11.6 Examples of Normative Versus Criterion References

	Running	Weight training	Rehabilitation
Criterion reference	To beat your personal best time by one minute	To increase weight by 10% each week	To increase range of motion by 1° each day
Normative reference	To meet the age-based average one-mile running time for 14-year-old girls in the United States	To bench press the amount of weight that falls in the intermediate class for peers my age and sex	To be back to full range of motion for my age, sex, height, and weight

WHAT DO YOU THINK?

Exercise 11.5

See tables 11.3 through 11.6 for interpreting and translating raw scores into norms, common assessments, and samples of norm versus criterion references.

1. How would you evaluate the scores from participant no. 1 in the example in table 11.5? Participant no. 2? What recommendations would you make for each for your areas of interest (e.g., adapted physical education, rehabilitation). Can you link these to the concepts of rater reliability including the use of a double-blind rater? Based upon your recommendations, can you explain the implications of (a) a double-blind rater, (b) a rater who overestimates scores, or (c) a rater who underestimates scores?

2. Based upon your field of choice, which assessments do you think you would use for your setting and why?

3. Think of a common outcome you assess in your field. Can you find national norms for that variable based upon age and sex? Create a criterion-referenced goal and a norm-referenced goal. Can you link these to the concepts of rater reliability including the use of a double-blind rater. Does it matter for your field?

RESEARCH NOTES

A Secular Decline in Gross Motor Development?

In chapter 8, we learned that a secular trend is one where population-based measures change across time. In 2019, Brian and colleagues evaluated the present levels of gross motor skills in American preschoolers. Based upon the TGMD, Brian and colleagues found that the raw scores composing the 50th percentile were substantially lower than the raw scores from 2000 (TGMD-2) and 1985 (TGMD-1). Given that norm references comprise scores from a sample representing the population at the time, Brian and colleagues report a concern that new normative references may *normalize* developmental delay by lowering the raw score criterion used to calculate percentile ranks. Sadly, 77 percent of the children within their sample scored at or below the 25th percentile, suggesting that developmental delay may be the new norm. What should we do?

SUMMARY

Assessment and evaluation are interdependent terms necessary for program creation and evaluation and for understanding learners, clients, and participants. Although many gross motor assessments rely upon age as their criterion, motor development remains age related, not age dependent.

Assessments vary based on whether the administrator assesses the process of movement or its resultant products. Process assessments can vary based upon evaluating individual components or the whole body of movement. Sometimes assessments include aspects of both process and product measures. To avoid floor and ceiling effects, assessors should consider using both process and product measures for their participants to result in the most qualitative snapshot of motor performance.

Evaluations of assessments can be based on either a norm reference or a criterion reference and can be in either formal or informal settings. Technically, norm-referenced testing should only occur in formal settings following all standardized procedures within the assessment manual. To evaluate all scores, raters should establish intra- or interrater reliability at or above 80 percent with a gold standard. Double-blind coders are ideal but not always practical. Practitioners should consider establishing a baseline, informally assessing in the middle, and concluding with a summative assessment to show program effectiveness and to design developmentally appropriate tasks based upon the present level of performance of your participants.

> ## › ONLINE ACTIVITIES

The student material found in HK*Propel* includes exercises, labs, and videos to enhance learning and encourage practical application of important concepts.

LEARNING AIDS

Supplemental Activities

1. How reliable were you? Let's refer to exercise 11.3. With three peers, establish a rotation of one person completing a skill and two people simultaneously scoring the skill. Conduct all scoring live (no video camera) and repeat until everyone has completed the skill and rated the other peers. Repeat again, but this time using your camera on your smartphone (only with everyone's permission). Compare and contrast reliability results.

2. Fill in the chart below:

Live	Rater 1	Rater 2	Rater 3
Trial 1	Score =	Score =	Participant
Trial 2	Score =	Participant	Score =
Trial 3	Participant	Score =	Score =
% agreement			
Video	Rater 1	Rater 2	Rater 3
Trial 1	Score =	Score =	Participant
Trial 2	Score =	Participant	Score =
Trial 3	Participant	Score =	Score =
% agreement			
% agreement difference video—live			

3. Search the Internet for training videos for each of the standardized assessments listed in this chapter.

    a. What can you find?

    b. Can you get reliable with their gold standard?

Glossary

absolute agreement—Exact agreement with scoring of each trial, one at a time.

assessment—Refers to the procedure through which assessors compile information on the processes of movement or the resultant products of movement.

average agreement—The agreement based upon the total score and not each individual trial.

ceiling effects—A type of inaccuracy with a measurement where performers can produce higher outcomes than the assessment will measure.

criterion reference—Standard for comparison that is self-selected by either the administrator or the participant.

double-blind rater—Rater who scores assessments and is blinded to both condition (experimental, control) and time (pretest, midpoint, posttest).

evaluation—Refers to the use of the information collected from the assessment to make a judgment regarding one's performance at that time.

floor effects—Effects that fail to provide a low enough metric to accurately capture the performance. The opposite of *ceiling effects*.

formal assessments—Assessments that include criterion references based upon norms that are conducted following standardized procedures.

formative assessments—Assessments that occur either at the beginning or the middle of a unit or treatment schedule.

gold standard rater—The rater whose scores set the standard for others to match.

informal assessments—Assessments that require no standardization procedures can occur in authentic settings and are often used for providing information regarding program effectiveness. They usually occur in the middle of a unit or a treatment schedule.

interrater reliability—The extent to which multiple raters similarly score the same participants.

intrarater reliability—The extent to which a rater can produce similar results for the same participant multiple times.

norm-referenced assessment—Test that measures the extent to which a person compares with others of the same age and sex in similar locations. Also known as norm-referenced test and norm-referenced evaluation.

percentile ranks—Represent the percentage of people in the same location (national, state, or local) who score higher than, lower than, or similar to the participant.

process assessments—The collection of information regarding the *components* of a particular skill or the entire movement pattern as a collective regarding the *whole body*. Process assessments focus on the qualitative aspects of components of a movement pattern.

product assessments—Includes the outcome of the movement compiled quantitatively.

psychometric properties—The extent to which the results are both *valid* and *reliable*.

raw scores—The unaltered results from an assessment.

reliability—The extent to which results of an assessment occur, as intended, consistently.

summative assessment—Always occurs at the end of a unit or treatment schedule.

validity—The extent to which an assessment captures the construct it is purported to measure.

PART III

Individual and Environmental Constraints

This part emphasizes individual and environmental constraints across the life span. Individual structural constraints—physical growth and the changing dynamics of the body systems—are explored in chapters 12 and 13. The focus in chapter 12 is on structural factors that constrain or promote the acquisition and performance of both fundamental and skillful movements. It also provides a discussion of how structural constraints may interact with functional factors, tasks, and the environment. We then turn to age-related changes in the body systems during adulthood in chapter 13, with a primary focus on normal age-related changes; we also include a discussion of secondary aging.

To many people, the term *aging* is synonymous with time, but even though everyone does age, we do not age the same. Environmental factors and behavioral lifestyle factors play a large role in our health and well-being, and these effects compound every year. Because people age so differently, assumptions about an individual's physiological function based solely on a simple measure of age with respect to time, or chronological age, are not very accurate. Because of this high variability in motor behavior across adulthood, this part of the book focuses on primary aging—that is, age-related changes that are not due to disease or poor behavioral practices, such as obesity, smoking, and sedentary lifestyles.

The discussion then turns to individual functional constraints and how they interact with tasks and environmental constraints. Chapter 14 addresses knowledge and cognitive development. Learners have different abilities regarding cognition, knowledge, attention, memory—abilities that affect them in motor learning and performance situations. Chapter 15 focuses on psychosocial and affective development. Psychological and affective constraints, such as self-esteem, motivation, and emotion, change over time and are heavily influenced by the individual's social environment.

We then extend the examination of environmental constraints in chapter 16 to sociocultural influences on movement behavior. This chapter includes both physical (e.g., geographic location) and social (e.g., gender norms) environmental constraints that can influence an individual's opportunities and access to movement experiences. A strong understanding about how individual and environmental constraints and their interaction affect movement and how they change across the life span will help readers appreciate the individual differences in a class of children, adolescents, or adults. This understanding and appreciation will better enable readers to design developmentally appropriate programs as discussed in part IV.

12

PHYSICAL DEVELOPMENT

CHAPTER OBJECTIVES

After reading this chapter, you should be able to do the following:

- Analyze the role of genes and the environment in motor learning and development.
- Discuss distance and velocity curves as well as relative growth.
- Examine key developmental changes in the skeletal, nervous, endocrine, and adipose systems.
- Understand the developmental changes in three sensory systems.

Systems, Many Systems!

Ethan is a very tall eight-year-old boy. At 56 inches, he is over 99 percent of the height growth curve for boys his age, meaning that he is taller than nearly all boys his age. Although height is typically viewed as beneficial for most sports, there are also many challenges, particularly during growth. With a height advantage of up to a foot over some of Ethan's competitors, there is also the added concern of his inflicting injury if he were to play too defensively. After several years of being told by his parents and sometimes coaches to tone it down, now a few years later he has adopted an opposite approach and plays perhaps too cautiously.

Size differences, while apparent in children, typically become even more exaggerated through puberty and adolescence. During this time, teens will transition through many growth and maturational changes that will affect many aspects of their lives from height to strength. Unfortunately, just as there is much variation in height, the timing of these transitions is also quite variable. As Ethan and his teammates continue to grow and mature, their individual differences will become increasingly variable and will not only affect their height, strength, and flexibility, but will also interact with functional constraints resulting in adjustments such as his adopting a more cautious approach to his game. The human body is a wonderful combination of many interacting systems, and each plays a role in development, sometimes exerting more influence at specific times.

As the dynamic systems and ecological approaches predict, intrinsic dynamics are constraints that affect observable motor patterns and the learning or refinement of motor skills. We hinted in chapter 2 that a person's size and shape are important constraints, but we did not explain developmental changes in height, weight, or physique—nor did we describe other structural differences such as bone growth and development, muscular development, and sensory changes such as in vision and spatial awareness. This chapter explains how both genetic and environmental factors may affect motor learning and development. We also discuss important and fascinating growth changes in height and weight and outline the developmental changes in systems—the skeletal, nervous, endocrine, and adipose systems, as well as the sensory systems of vision, audition, and kinesthesis. All these systems function as constraints to learning and development. Chapters 14 and 15 deal with the functional constraints of learners that would further help Ethan understand the vast differences on his soccer team.

Have you ever seen a young child with a basketball in hand, looking up, up, up at a distant hoop? There is motivation to throw that basketball, but also the realization that size and strength are not quite there for a successful toss. Growth in height and gains in strength are important structural constraints in children and adolescents. Other examples of structural constraints are spinal cord damage that restricts or eliminates lower limb movement, and hearing or visual impairments limiting sensory information of an approaching ball or defender. Individuals with disabilities live full and independent lives but often perform tasks in unique ways and use adaptive equipment or techniques such as wheelchairs, hearing aids, sign language, canes, or a guide dog.

NATURE AND NURTURE

We are amazed by truly exceptional performances, whether they be Beethoven or Mozart in music or Simone Biles or Lionel Messi in sport. Because their brilliance seems to defy the notion that their achievements are the result of practice and learning, we often explain their excellence as the result of some inborn talent or gift. Recent research identifying specific genes in deoxyribonucleic acid may have resulted in the illusion that it is only a matter of time before one or more genes are linked to exceptionality. Ericsson (2007) suggested that the complete genetic account of superior abilities is exceedingly complex and that an environmental perspective of extensive practice is better able to account for exceptional abilities. The relative contribution of genes (nature) and environment (nurture) to individual differences that we observe in everyday life has been the topic of one of the most energetic scientific debates for over 140 years (Baker & Davids, 2007).

There is much to be learned about the role of genetic constraints in living organisms. Genetic factors are almost the sole determinant of characteristics such as height, blood type, and hair color in humans. Genes largely control the timing of growth, such as the onset of the adolescent growth spurt and loss of muscular strength later in life. However, growth can be significantly affected by extrinsic factors, and poor prenatal nutrition, drugs, or exposure to X-rays can negatively affect the growing embryo or fetus. Healthy behaviors such as good nutrition and exercise, on the other hand, can positively affect growth and development across the life span. Therefore, motor learning and development most certainly are affected by both genetic and environmental constraints, but the precise manner of their interplay is not well known. Usually, we simply read about the interaction of genes and experience as contributing to sport performance or academic learning, as if this fully explains the relationship. There is some truth to this idea, but the interaction is exceedingly complex and influenced by one's theoretical viewpoint of genetic action (Davids & Baker, 2007).

The impact of genes and extrinsic influences on human behavior is often studied with **monozygotic twins** and **dizygotic twins** (Klissouras et al., 2007). Human beings receive genes randomly from both parents, which results in a unique genetic makeup, or genotype. Monozygotic (identical) twins have identical genotypes, whereas dizygotic (fraternal) twins share half their genes like ordinary siblings. Occasionally, twin research provides one of the monozygotic twins with some special treatment to determine the impact of heredity or environment in producing the phenotype—that is, an observable characteristic or behavior such as height, personality, or fitness. Because these twins are genetically identical, a positive impact from the special treatment suggests that the characteristic or phenotype is modifiable by the environment (e.g., gain in $\dot{V}O_2$max or motor skills). Thus, the characteristic or phenotype is not completely determined by the genotype. Twin studies also include situations in which monozygotic twins are reared apart. In this case it is assumed that the life experiences of the two twins are different. If they have a similar phenotype after many years apart, it is usually concluded that the phenotype was largely determined by genes rather than environment.

Nature–nurture research attempts to explain differences in individuals in a population as a function of genetics, extrinsic factors, or both; it cannot explain how much of your weight is controlled by your genes or your exercise and your eating habits,

nor can it predict how much improvement you might expect as a function of training or practice. It can only explain differences in a group of people. Suppose 40 students were requested to practice a juggling task until each person reached a criterion of 10 consecutive tosses without dropping a ball. Assume that an average of 200 trials (attempts) were required to reach that criterion. The quickest individual in the group needed 150 trials, and the slowest required 250 trials to be able to juggle 10 consecutive catches. Genetic research attempts to explain how much of the 100-trial difference in the group of 40 is due to genetic factors. A statistic called **heritability** can be calculated (see Klissouras et al., 2007, for more details and other estimates of genetic influence). A heritability score close to one is interpreted as a strong genetic influence in producing differences between individuals, but it has no meaning for the abilities of an individual. A high heritability score of nine-tenths does not mean that an individual's $\dot{V}O_2$max score is due to 90 percent genetic and 10 percent training factors. Nor should such a high score be interpreted as suggesting that the environment has almost no impact. The 0.9 does mean that "after individuals have reached the upper limits of their $\dot{V}O_2$max, with appropriate training, there will still be wide interindividual variability which is genetic in origin" (Klissouras et al., 2007, p. 52).

Heritability scores are often quite high for physical fitness measures, body mass index, physique, height, and somatotype, as well as personality and cognitive abilities (Klissouras et al., 2007). Investigations have explored individual differences in motor learning, but the studies are fewer and the overall findings remain mixed. Fox and colleagues (1996) used both monozygotic and dizygotic twins reared apart to investigate individual differences in motor performance in a

RESEARCH NOTES

A Classic Nature–Nurture Study in Motor Development

McGraw (1935) conducted an early and classic longitudinal study on the impact of environment on the acquisition of motor skills—specifically, to determine whether a stimulating and challenging movement environment would alter motor development. Twins Johnny and Jimmy were involved in the research for several years. McGraw began observing them soon after birth, but Johnny began receiving stimulation and practice on several motor activities at about one year that were not offered to Jimmy. At various times Johnny was exposed to climbing, jumping, riding a tricycle, swimming, jumping, and roller skating. If motor development is fixed and determined largely by the maturation of the central nervous system, as most theorists at that time believed, the extra exposure and practice received by Johnny should not have had any positive influence on his acquisition of motor skills. Nature would have scored a point over nurture. Support for the impact of nurturing by practice in a stimulating environment would have resulted if Johnny's motor development had exceeded that of Jimmy. Unfortunately, the results of the study were equivocal. In some movement skills, such as climbing, Johnny demonstrated superiority over Jimmy, which supported the nurture perspective. In other activities no differences were found between the twins, supporting a nature explanation. Of course, this type of twin research requires monozygotic twins, which unfortunately was not the case, because it was later revealed that Johnny and Jimmy were dizygotic twins. This fact may have influenced the results of McGraw's research.

tracking task for 75 trials. They concluded that performance differences between individuals did reflect genetic influence. It is important to remember that the authors did not discount the role of practice; they asserted simply that there is a significant genetic impact on the outcome of practice. Marisi (1977) also used the pursuit rotor task with twins but found that the genetic influence diminished over trials. Generally, these findings support the impact of genetic factors on motor learning and are consistent with the views of Klissouras, Bouchard, and their colleagues (Bouchard et al., 1999; Klissouras et al., 2007).

In the domain of musical talent, Howe and colleagues (1998) concluded that "individual differences in some special abilities may indeed have partly genetic origins" (p. 407). Thus, they accepted the notion that genetic endowment can constrain

ultimate skill level, acting as a ceiling of performance. Geladas and colleagues (2007) stated: "It seems that training will never erase individual differences that are due to innate abilities. Training can exert its . . . profound effect only within the fixed limits of heredity" (p. 125). Thus training and practice, true environmental factors, are considered critical even if genetics determines a ceiling of performance. It is important to remember that these statements say nothing about the extent of improvement or the ultimate level of performance for a specific individual. Parents, teachers, and therapists can justifiably remain optimistic about the motor learning of each child and adolescent.

Ericsson (2003, 2007, 2013, 2016) advanced an opposing viewpoint of expert performance. He acknowledged that genes are important in developing physiological adaptations of the body and nervous system, but he maintained that they place no limits on the performance of healthy people. He argued that genetic differences in innate talent cannot explain the remarkable improvement of individuals in training research because "the DNA stored in the nucleus of each cell of a person is the same before and after training" (Ericsson, 2007, p. 6).

Deliberate practice is a proposed theoretic explanation. **Deliberate practice** is specific practice requiring much effort without an immediate reward; performance improvement is the motivation, and it is not necessarily enjoyable. Through the lengthy process of deliberate practice and the accompanying changes in cognitive activity, any healthy person can become an expert. To state this differently, deliberate practice, rather than genetic endowment, can explain differences between individuals who have access to the instruction, training, and social support necessary to reach high levels of achievement. Most people do not become experts, in part because they cannot sustain the intensity and effort of the required practice. The only exceptions to the deliberate practice hypothesis acknowledged by Ericsson are height and body size. Neither has been shown to be influenced by training and practice. Therefore, these can be viewed as influenced primarily by genes. The deliberate practice account of expertise, including what constitutes practice and how to measure it, is an issue of some current debate (e.g., Ericsson, 2013, 2016; Macnamara et al., 2016; Tucker & Collins, 2012). Chapter 19 will examine variables of practice, including types of practice and scheduling practice, in depth.

Galton made the distinction between nature and nurture in 1874 as an explanation for individual differences. Thus began the nature–nurture debate in science. Much of the debate has centered on which one is more important for a specific domain, such as movements skills. Some scientists have expressed frustration over this debate because the two are inextricably linked so that it is impossible to distinguish what is nature and what is nurture (Baker & Davids, 2007). Kimble (1993, as cited by Baker & Davids, 2007) suggested that trying to determine whether individual differences in behavior are caused by heredity or environment is like asking whether the area of a rectangle is determined more by its width or its length. Genetic and environmental forces influence each other, are interactive in producing behavior, and must be studied together to understand human development (Kail & Cavanaugh, 2016; Shulman, 2016). Although the precise impact of genes and environment on skill acquisition is not clear, there is certainly no evidence of a physical skill acquisition gene (Davids & Baker, 2007). Individual differences in motor learning and development are no doubt influenced by many genes interacting with many extrinsic factors, including types of practice, amount of practice, social support mechanisms, motivation, personal value beliefs, and cultural influences.

Although many current theories of development and learning adopt a genetic–environment interaction perspective, the dynamic systems approach minimizes the privileged status of genetic influence on conceptual grounds (Thelen & Smith, 1994). According to this argument, a key issue in development is the respective impact of many systems, and genes are only one system. The continued search for the genetic impact may be slowing the search for more important explanations of development.

PHYSICAL GROWTH AND MATURATION

The size and shape of children and adolescents change as they grow, and these structural realities affect how they coordinate their movements and learn motor skills. Most certainly, a small child will throw a 7-inch (18 cm) playground ball with two hands because the ball is almost impossible to balance on one hand, whereas a teenager (with a larger hand) may use a one-handed throw. Older adults might change how they perform physical skills because of loss of strength or arthritis. Thus, motor performance and learning are affected by changes during growth and aging in the skeletal, muscular, and nervous systems.

The rate of physical growth in the first year of life is remarkable. A newborn who is 7.5 pounds and 20 inches long (3.4 kg and

---

RESEARCH NOTES

Are Elite Athletes Born or Built?

The nature–nurture argument is particularly interesting for high-level sports development programs. There is much research to support that elite athletes are blessed with a larger share of genetic potential that is then developed through much deliberate practice, but it is difficult to determine whether nature or nurture prevails. Georgiades and colleagues (2017) examined two centuries of experimental research on the nature–nurture argument to determine whether elite athletes are built or made. Twin model heritability studies have enabled the genetic and environmental factors that contribute to complex traits and have even enabled gene identification for elite performance. From the massive amount of literature on the topic, it appears that nature does have an advantage over nurture; however, nurture is still a strong variable in elite performance. The authors stated that the research indicates that to be a truly elite-level athlete, the individual must not only train hard but have the born ability for high level performance.

TRY THIS

Does Athleticism Run in a Family?

Exercise 12.1

Let's look at the complexity of heritability a bit further. Find a person in your class (maybe yourself) who has achieved a reasonably high level of athletic success (e.g., university or high school varsity). Was this person's mom or dad athletic at a young age? Or perhaps an aunt or uncle? Was it in the same sport as the person in your class? Are physical characteristics such as height important in this sport?

WHAT DO YOU THINK?

Exercise 12.2

1. Has the previous section of the chapter challenged your views of instruction in physical education? Is it fair to view students as naturally talented? Explain.
2. Pick two sports. Describe how students' skill level in these sports may be influenced by both nature and nurture.

51 cm) at birth may grow to be 22.5 pounds and 30 inches long (10.2 kg and 76 cm) by her first birthday. This represents a 200 percent gain in weight and a 50 percent gain in height. Never again does the body change so much in a year. In fact, if the **rate of change** in the first year after birth continued until age 20, this person would be 1,150 feet tall (350 m) and weigh nearly 50 million pounds (22.7 million kg) (Krogman, 1972). In addition to much growth over the first year, many new motor skills are acquired, such as sitting, standing, crawling, and walking. These milestones are particularly impressive considering the child must coordinate her rapidly growing body with the changing tasks and environmental constraints she faces.

Growth Curves

Stature (height) growth curves for males and females are shown in figure 12.1*a* and 12.1*b*. Other common body-size measures in growth research are weight; sitting height; leg length; limb and head circumferences; and breadth of shoulders, hips, and knees (Malina et al., 2004). The pattern of change for height and weight is called a **sigmoid curve** after the Greek letter for *s*. The rapid change after birth and again at adolescence makes the sigmoid shape curvilinear rather than straight. Because the values on the *y* axis are accumulated heights, this type of curve is also called a **distance curve**. These curves also include **percentile** rankings. The 50th percentile is the average for the age group; half the children score above this height or weight and half score below it. A child who falls at the 75th percentile is taller at this age than 75 percent of his chronological-age peers.

These growth charts show whether a particular person is short, tall, light, or heavy for his age. A group of adolescents of the same age can vary greatly in height and weight. A parent may be concerned if a child is at the 50th percentile for height but at the 80th percentile for weight, suggesting extra

weight for that height. Pediatricians monitor the extremes of stature and weight as possible indicators of growth pathology. A toddler could be relatively short for her age because of genetic factors, a growth problem, or a dietary deficiency (Preedy, 2012). Additional assessment would be required to determine the reason. Much to the disappointment of parents of a big newborn child, perhaps, size at birth is not an accurate predictor of final height or weight. However, predicting adult height is an important tool for practitioners as well as understanding bone growth and maturation (Thodberg et al., 2012). There is much variation in growth rates in children and they do not always follow a universal growth curve; however, by age 2 or 3 years, children tend to remain in their percentile position compared to others (Malina et al., 2004). Thus, a boy at four years of age who is at the 90th percentile for height (taller than 90 percent of the four-year-old boys) is likely to be a tall adult, and a boy at the 30th percentile will likely be shorter than the typical adult male when he reaches his full height. This relative stability in growth can be used for clinical evaluation because a child would not be expected to be at the 80th percentile at one age and the 30th at a subsequent age. Such dramatic changes might indicate unhealthy growth and be cause to seek further assessment.

Distance curves show only the extent of growth and hide whether children are growing fast one year and slower the next. The sigmoid distance curves are created by averaging the heights of many children, and they also hide the dramatic changes that can occur in an individual. Notice that the **velocity curve** for height shown in figure 12.2 looks very different from the distance curve for height. A velocity curve describes *change* in height (centimeters per year) over 18 years. Think of centimeters per year like miles per hour. A change from 60 to 40 miles per hour is described as decelerating, or slowing down. Forward movement is still occurring, just more slowly. The same

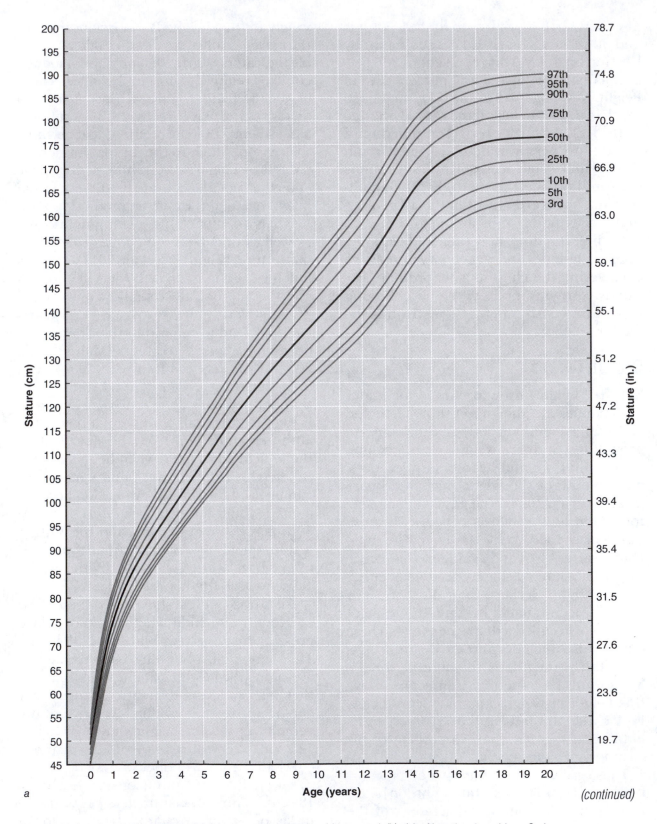

a   *(continued)*

Figure 12.1 Stature (standing height) by age percentiles for *(a)* boys and *(b)* girls. Note the sigmoid, or *S*-shape, curves.

Adapted from "Clinical Growth Charts," National Center for Health Statistics, last modified June 16, 2017, www.cdc.gov/growthcharts/clinical_charts.htm#Set1.

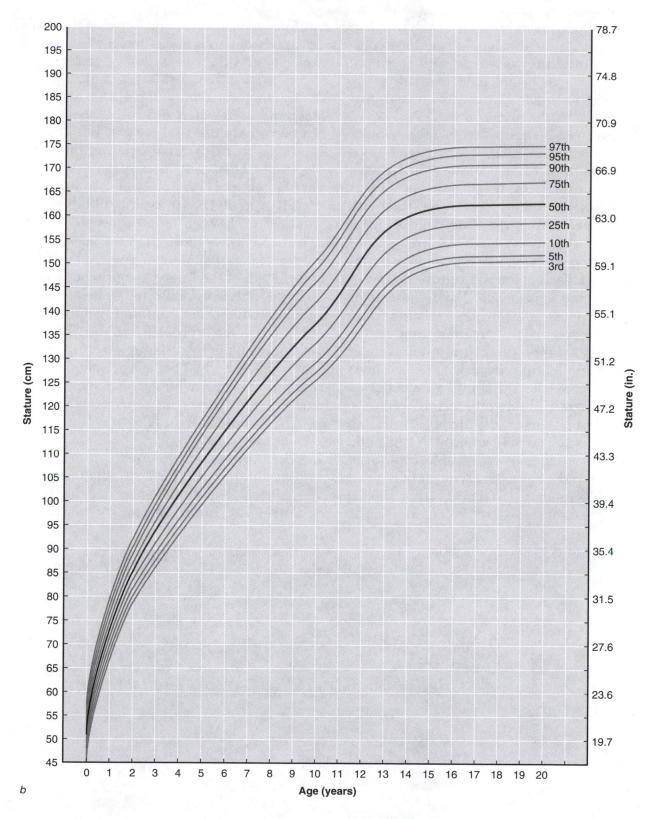

b

Figure 12.1 *(continued)*

change happens in height over the first five years; each year less height is gained compared to the previous year, and therefore the velocity of height gain is *decelerating*. The person is getting taller each year, just not as fast as the previous year.

Figure 12.2 shows that height velocity continues to slow slightly from age 5 until the initiation of the adolescent growth spurt, at which time height gain accelerates for about two years. Notice that the **peak height velocity** is the time when gain in height is the fastest since the first year of life. The peak height velocity corresponds to the dramatic change in stature that most adolescents experience. For females this may be three and two-fifths inches (8.6 cm) per year; for males, three and nine-tenths inches (10 cm) per year. It is small wonder that some children experience some awkwardness as they attempt to incorporate rapidly growing limbs into their movements. The velocity curves also demonstrate that girls enter the adolescent growth spurt and puberty about two years before boys, at ages 10 and 12 years, respectively (Ong et al., 2009). As shown in figure 12.2, girls also stop growing two years before boys. The

difference in adult height between the sexes is largely due to females' lower peak height velocity and their cessation of growth two years prior to males (Malina et al., 2004).

The motor learning of children and adolescents is affected not only by changes in overall stature and weight, but also by changes in **body proportions** or form. Figure 12.3 demonstrates postnatal changes in body proportions, a phenomenon called **relative growth**. In essence, body parts and tissues have different rates of growth. The head grows more than the legs during prenatal months. At birth, the head is about one fourth of the infant's length, but it contributes only one eighth to the height of an adult. A child is not a miniature adult. One of the movement problems of the first year of life is balancing a large head on a relatively small body. The legs are about three eighths of height at birth and one half when growth terminates. In other words, from birth to adulthood, the legs grow faster than the head.

Thus, although obviously taller than young children, adults have a distinctly different form. Newell (1984) argued that these changes are biomechanical constraints

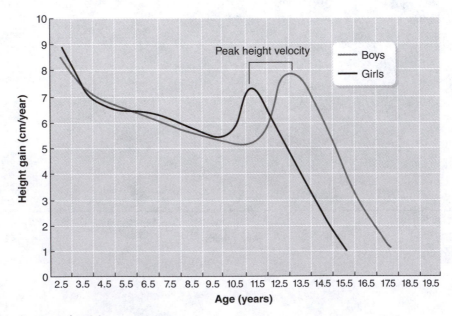

Figure 12.2 Velocity curves for stature.

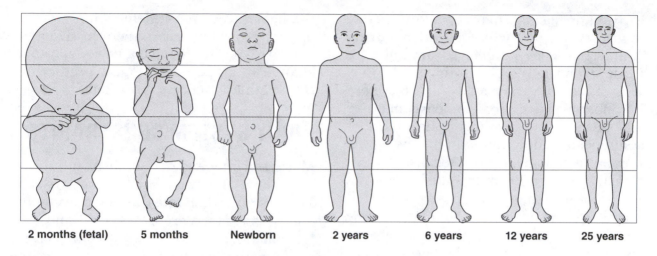

| 2 months (fetal) | 5 months | Newborn | 2 years | 6 years | 12 years | 25 years |

Figure 12.3 Changes in body form: relative growth.

RESEARCH NOTES

Why Are the Dutch So Tall?

The Dutch are the tallest people in the world. Perhaps more interesting than who are the tallest people in the world is how they became the tallest, which is a story of human plasticity over many generations (Bogin, 1998). In the mid-1800s, Americans were the tallest males in the world at an average 5 feet 6 inches (168 cm), whereas the Dutch stood at 5 feet, 4 inches (163 cm). At the turn of the 21st century, Dutch men averaged 5 feet, 10 inches (178 cm), whereas the typical American man was 5 feet, 8 inches (173 cm). Bogin argued that over the last 150 years, the Dutch profited in stature from societal changes that include purifying drinking water, installing sewer systems, regulating the safety of food, and providing public health care and food to children. The Dutch children responded to the changing environment by growing taller. Although these changes are available to many Americans, those who are poor often lack adequate housing, sanitation, and health care. This scenario demonstrates the plasticity of stature over generations if people's life conditions improve, showing that height, although influenced almost completely by the genes inherited from parents, can change over generations.

that affect coordination. As children grow, their movement patterns must include a constantly changing body shape. In some cases, performance is affected. For example, as elite female gymnasts progress through puberty, they may not maintain sufficient strength to compensate for their longer and heavier limbs, resulting in a decline in skill.

Limitations to Growth Curves

Distance and velocity curves describe average patterns of change, but individuals have unique timing of these events. This is illustrated clearly by those who mature early and late. The initiation of the adolescent growth spurt may differ by several years. An early-maturing male may begin to accelerate in growth at age 9, while his late-maturing counterpart may be delayed until age 15. Peak strength velocity follows within a year of peak height velocity, and therefore it is not surprising that the early maturer will be taller and stronger than most of his peers for a few years despite being the same chronological age. Because stature and strength are structural constraints, the early maturer may be more coordinated than her same-aged peers and hence enjoy an athletic advantage. Early maturing adolescents may ultimately be shorter than their later maturing peers if they terminate growth earlier and therefore do not grow for as many years. It is not uncommon for athletically talented children who mature early to be very successful as a 12-year-old (girl) or 14-year-old (boy), yet lose relative placement in their peer group when peers mature. Early maturers do not suddenly become poorly coordinated or uninterested; the later maturing athletes simply catch up and possibly surpass them in size and strength. In this adolescent period of rapid change in size and strength, predicting future athletic success is difficult.

BODY SYSTEM CONSTRAINTS

Motor learning and development can theoretically be constrained by any body system. The systems that most affect movement and performance are the skeletal, muscular, cardiovascular, nervous, endocrine, adipose, and sensory systems. Just as with relative growth, as shown in figure 12.3, these systems do not change at a constant rate. The developing child and adolescent must learn to incorporate changing limb size, muscle mass, and visual capabilities into new and old movement patterns. Once again, the changes described next underscore the notion that children are not miniature adults.

TRY THIS

The Early Maturer

Exercise 12.3

Assume that a female is 59.1 inches (150 cm) tall. Look at figure 12.1b. How old is the girl if 59.1 inches (150 cm) inches places her at the 90th percentile? How old is she if 59.1 inches (150 cm) places her at the 50th percentile? The 5th percentile? Those three ages represent quite a wide range. Which of the ages leads you to believe she is an early maturer? What other information is necessary to support your prediction?

WHAT DO YOU THINK?

Exercise 12.4

1. How will the age at which a person experiences a growth spurt influence his performance in sport? What other factors (e.g., cognitive, psychological, or social) must be considered?
2. Compare growth differences and similarities across the sexes from birth to adulthood.

Skeletal System

The skeleton is the structural support system of the body and provides a lever for muscles, enabling movement. Large developmental changes occur in bone size and structure from birth through adolescence, as previously discussed. Bone changes do not end following the cessation of growth during late adolescence. Bone is a living and growing tissue. Old bone is removed (in a process called resorption) while new bone is continually being formed. Through this process termed remodeling, an entire skeleton is replaced every 10 years. During childhood, bone building occurs at a much faster rate than bone resorption, allowing for increases in bone size to occur. Throughout childhood, physical activity is particularly important for increasing bone strength through increased bone mass and structure (Dias Quiterio et al., 2011). Unfortunately, over half of children are not active enough to fully achieve the benefits of physical activity upon bone health. To maximize bone health, it is important to not only consider frequency of physical activity, but also the mechanical load upon the bones during physical activity. When considering bone health, walking 60 minutes seven times per week would provide the same bone health benefits as running 30 minutes for three times per week or jumping for 10 minutes two times per week, according to equations by Turner and Robling (2003). This indicates the specificity of effects necessary to plan the most appropriate physical activity programs to improve or maximize bone health.

Our previous discussion of stature dealt with the typical development of the skeletal system, but difficulties with skeletal growth can occur. **Osgood-Schlatter disease** is a painful disruption in the growth of the upper shinbone where the patellar tendon attaches. **Legg-Calvé-Perthes disease** is an irritation of the femur where it inserts into the hip. These are childhood problems that restrict weight-bearing activities and make movement painful. Also, people who have limb amputations perform some movements in unique ways to compensate for the loss of the limb.

Muscular System

The muscular system follows a sigmoid growth curve like that for weight. Muscle mass becomes a relatively larger component of overall body weight with development. It is about 25 percent of total body weight at birth, and by maturity is up to 54 percent for men and 45 percent for women. It has been suggested that a critical level of strength is an important rate limiter for independent walking (Ulrich et al., 2001). This helps explain why heavier babies might not walk as early as leaner babies (more strength is needed to move a larger mass). Strength is important for many motor skills and is influenced by the amount of muscle mass, maturation, and the recruitment of muscle fibers, as well as extrinsic factors such as nutrition and exercise.

Strength

A growth in muscle mass can occur through an increase in the number of muscle fibers (**hyperplasia**) or through an increase in the relative size, or volume, of the muscle fibers (**hypertrophy**). Muscle fibers increase by both hyperplasia and hypertrophy prenatally and for a short time postnatally. Then, muscle mass can be increased only by hypertrophy. Sex differences in muscle mass are small until adolescence, when both sexes experience a rapid gain in muscle mass. However, the spurt in muscle mass continues in girls only until age 13 years, whereas in boys the rapid increase continues until age 17 years (Malina, 1978). Following maturity, muscle mass can be changed only through hypertrophy (increase in size of muscle fibers) or through atrophy (decrease in size of muscle fibers) (Gollnick et al., 1981). Muscle fibers increase in both diameter and length during growth and development. Increases in muscle length occur in conjunction with increases in bone length, whereas increases in the diameter of a muscle fiber result from physical activity (Malina & Bouchard, 1991).

Flexibility

Flexibility is the ability to move body parts through a range of motion without strain (Gabbard, 2012). Flexibility is necessary to perform well athletically and prevent muscular injury, as well as to perform activities of daily living from dressing oneself to climbing in and out of a car. The sit and reach test is one of the most commonly used measures of flexibility. This test assesses the flexibility of the hamstrings, low back, and hip flexors.

Flexibility peaks around age 15 years (Sermaxhaj et al., 2021) with males peaking about two years earlier than females (Clarke, 1975). Females tend to be more flexible than males from the age of five through adulthood (Haubenstricker et al., 1997). The sex differences have been attributed to body size and composition, hormone levels, and physical activities (Gabbard, 2012). Females also participate in physical activities that promote increased range of motion (e.g., dance and gymnastics) more often than males. People with larger body sizes generally have poorer flexibility (Bataweel & Ibrahim, 2020).

Flexibility changes occur at specific joints rather than across the body as a whole and are greatly affected by physical activity. Flexibility should be developed from a young age and continue throughout the life span to benefit both fitness and functionality. Flexibility not only improves performance in dance and gymnastics, but also in team sports such as football. Football players who are more flexible perform better in speed, jumping, and agility tests (Garcia-Pinillos et al., 2015).

Cardiovascular System

Heart rate is a simple and convenient measure of cardiac effort at rest, during moderate exercise (submaximal heart rate), and during maximal effort (maximal heart rate). Heart rate provides an indicator of both cardiac output (amount of blood pumped) and maximal oxygen consumption. On average, resting heart rate decreases with age (van den Berg et al., 2018). At birth,

---

WHAT DO YOU THINK?

Exercise 12.5

Discuss how strength can be a rate limiter for the following.

1. A four-month-old infant learning to crawl
2. An eight-year-old baseball batter

WHAT DO YOU THINK?

Exercise 12.6

Females participate in physical activities that promote flexibility more often than males do. Why do you think that is? List several strategies to encourage male students (of all ages) to increase their flexibility.

resting heart rate is very high, averaging 140 beats per minute. By age 2 years, it has decreased to about 105 beats per minute, and by age 20 years, it is approximately 66 beats per minute. The increase in heart rate in infancy and childhood is a physiological compensation for a smaller heart size. With a smaller heart, the stroke volume (volume of blood pumped during each contraction) is decreased. To compensate, the heart rate increases. For this same reason, females average about five beats per minute more than males.

$\dot{V}O_2$max is considered the best measure of aerobic capacity and cardiorespiratory fitness. $\dot{V}O_2$max is the maximal amount of oxygen that can be transported and used during exercise. Endurance performance and $\dot{V}O_2$max are highly correlated (Joyner, 1993); however, this does not mean that a person's $\dot{V}O_2$max is set. $\dot{V}O_2$max can be greatly increased with endurance training. Athletes' $\dot{V}O_2$max increases as they can run farther and faster because $\dot{V}O_2$max is determined by the maximal amount of oxygen that is required. Someone who is running fast requires more oxygen than someone who is running slowly. This increase continues until the runner cannot run any faster. Some highly trained competitive athletes have reached as much as eight liters per minute. In general, $\dot{V}O_2$max increases for both boys and girls at the same rate throughout childhood. At age 12, boys and girls have similar $\dot{V}O_2$max measures. Girls continue to increase their $\dot{V}O_2$max until about age 14 years, and boys continue to increase their $\dot{V}O_2$max until age 18 years (Gabbard, 2012). The increase in $\dot{V}O_2$max in boys is a result of continued growth through a later age.

Nervous System

The nervous system undergoes change throughout life. As many as 100 billion neurons are formed, most by the third or fourth prenatal week. Later in the prenatal period and early in the first postnatal year, the neurons fire and establish **synapses** (connections) with other neurons. At birth the brain is 25 percent of its adult weight, and by the time the person is five years old, it is 90 percent (Keogh & Sugden, 1985; Piek, 2006). Infants have the major fibers and folding patterns of the cerebral cortex in the adult locations. Researchers formerly believed that brain development is completed by early childhood. Although during this early period there is more rapid development of the number of neurons, which may continue until the person is six years old (Piek, 2006), learning and life experiences alter the nervous system throughout life, because the development of the brain continues through early adulthood or beyond (Ashtari & Cyckowski, 2012). The postnatal period and adolescence are particularly active periods of not only physical growth but also brain development. There are two primary tissues of the brain: gray and white matter (see figure 12.4). Gray matter makes up approximately 40 percent of the brain at adulthood and is made up of neuronal cell bodies. White matter is made up of bundles that connect the gray matter, making up approximately 60 percent of the brain. The gray matter fully develops by around 20 years old, while the white matter continues to develop and peaks much later, in middle adulthood.

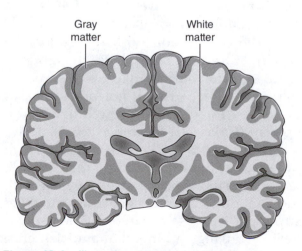

Figure 12.4 Illustration of gray and white matter.

When learning new motor skills, synapses are formed between motor and sensory neurons. In fact, one account of motor control proposed that muscle synergies (the synchrony of motor neurons) produce coordinated movement patterns. Practicing new motor skills results in hundreds of thousands of new groups of synapses. Neuromotor difficulties can severely affect coordination, for example, in someone with cerebral palsy. In this case, an extrinsic factor such as loss of oxygen to the developing brain, prenatally or during birth, may damage brain tissue needed in coordination. Severe malnutrition can also keep the brain from functioning optimally.

Endocrine System

The **endocrine system** controls the hormones in body tissue. For example, **pituitary** growth hormones and **thyroid** hormones are largely responsible for skeletal growth. In some cases, shorter stature may be related to a deficiency of these hormones and may be a structural constraint. Hormones from the testicles or ovaries and adrenal glands, primarily estrogen and androgens (e.g., testosterone), are responsible for the growth spurt and for epiphyseal fusion of the long bones, which terminates growth.

Physical activity during childhood is not only important for well-being but is also critical for physiological growth particularly with the interaction with the endocrine system. Children should be engaging in regular, brief but intense exercise bouts that will induce growth hormone releases necessary for physical growth and development (Galassetti & Pablico, 2012). Active children and adolescents benefit from physical exertion through measurable growth hormone peaks resulting in growth modulation. Researchers have asserted that sufficient exercise during critical growth periods during childhood and adolescence is particularly important for physiological development (Cooper et al., 2004).

Adipose System

Adipose tissue, the connective tissue in which fat is stored, develops rapidly during the last three months of pregnancy. Babies born prematurely often have a skinny appearance because they have not remained long enough in the womb during this important period of adipose tissue formation. As figure 12.5 demonstrates, adipose tissue continues to develop rapidly during the first 6 to 12 postnatal months (Malina et al., 2004), when fat constitutes as much as 30 percent of body weight. The age-related changes in fat-free mass resemble the sigmoid curves of height and weight.

When adipose tissue is expressed as a percentage of body weight, there is a decline in both sexes after a peak at about age 1 year until the adolescent growth spurt. However, if body fat is expressed as an absolute value in pounds or kilograms, adipose tissue continues to develop from 12 months to 20 years. The absolute amount of adiposity increases during childhood and

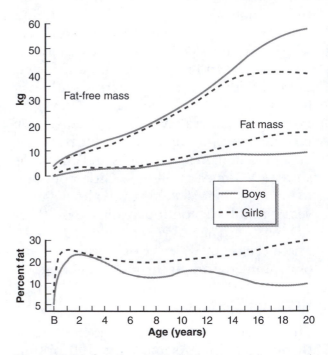

Figure 12.5 Growth curves for fat-free mass, fat mass, and relative fatness derived from measurements of total body water.

Reprinted by permission from R.M. Malina, C. Bouchard, and O. Bar-Or, *Growth, Maturation, and Physical Activity*, 2nd ed. (Champaign, IL: Human Kinetics, 2004), 113. Data from Malina (1989); Malina, Bouchard, and Beunen (1988).

adolescence, like skeletal or muscular tissue, but this is simply because children and adolescents are still growing. Compare a 50-pound (23 kg) child to one at 100 pounds (45 kg). We would expect the 100-pound child to have more adipose tissue than the 50-pound child because of the difference in weight. The average adult female possesses about 70 percent of the fat-free mass of her male counterpart, largely because males at adulthood are taller than females and gained more muscle mass during adolescence than females.

Currently, there is an epidemic of childhood obesity in developed and developing countries caused in part by physical inactivity. Obesity is associated with many health issues but is also a structural constraint during performance because greater energy expenditure is necessary to move the additional weight. Obesity is associated with sedentary behaviors, and perhaps not surprisingly, there is evidence that obesity is associated with poor motor skills (Marshall & Bouffard, 1994, 1997). Malina and colleagues (2004) concluded that after six years of age, the fattest children have a higher risk of remaining fat until adolescence and adulthood than their peers. Variation is large, and some people are fat as children and not as adults, whereas some lean children become fat in adolescence or adulthood.

Sensory Systems

Many developmental changes occur in the sensory systems. Sensory system development is of particular importance to motor development and motor learning because of the many implications for skillful performance. Movement depends on and is intricately related to perception. Our movements are based on what we see, hear, and feel. A child's sensory development can greatly affect how she performs. Practitioners should take developmental changes in vision, audition, and kinesthesis into consideration when designing programs.

Equipment and tasks should be modified according to not only the physical capabilities of children or adolescents, but also their perceptual capabilities.

Vision

Among the many visual functions, we focus only on those of particular importance to moving skillfully: visual acuity (see chapter 3 for more detail), visuomotor coordination, depth perception, and figure–ground perception. Visual acuity is sharpness of vision, allowing us to see an image clearly, such as a face or words on a page. There are two types of visual acuity, static and dynamic. Static visual acuity is the ability to clearly see an image that is stationary; it is most assessed using the Snellen eye chart. Normal vision is considered 20/20, meaning that the image can be clearly seen from 20 feet (6 m) away. At birth, visual acuity is approximately 20/400, meaning that the newborn can distinguish at 20 feet (6 m) what people with normal vision can see at 400 feet (122 m). Newborns can clearly see images only if they are less than 1.5 feet (46 cm) away (Kellman & Arterberry, 1998). Furthermore, newborns can not only differentiate face and nonface objects, but they can also show a preference for their mother's face over other female faces within only hours of birth (Bushnell, 2001). Visual acuity continues to improve rapidly throughout the first year and then continues to improve at a slower rate to a 20/20 rating by the age of 10 years (Williams, 1983).

The perception of motion is a particularly important factor in motor development and motor learning. Infants can visually perceive motion at birth, but they cannot perceive the direction of motion until approximately eight weeks of age (Wattam-Bell, 1996). **Visuomotor coordination**, the ability to visually track a moving object and guide the body or limbs (or both) to intercept the object, improves with the infant's active exploration of the environment (e.g., playing with the hands and toys and eventually throwing). One of the reasons young children have difficulty catching is underdeveloped visuomotor coordination. Children cannot accurately track a moving object, such as a tossed ball, until the age of five or six years (Morris, 1980). Parents often throw balls with a high arc to children to give them more time to prepare for a catch; however, it is even more challenging for children to catch a ball thrown in a high arc because they cannot visually track objects in two planes until they are eight or nine years old. Movement perception continues to develop until approximately age 12 years (Williams, 1983). Visual tracking continues to improve until age 20 years, and optimal visual tracking is often maintained through age 50 years (Maruta et al., 2017).

These are only a few of the developmental changes in vision. It is also important to consider that children have difficulty separating an object from the background. The ability to do this is referred to as **figure–ground perception**. Figure–ground perception improves through childhood and adolescence until approximately age 18 years. The ability to distinguish the object from its surroundings is of critical importance to many sports and activities. A ball that is not easily discernible apart from the environment is much less likely to be caught or struck. **Depth perception**, the ability to see in three dimensions, is also a critical component in intercepting an object. Depth perception arises partly from the **retinal disparity** of the two eyes. Because the eyes are in different locations, they see images at different visual angles.

The development of depth perception is affected by the development of visual acuity because depth perception depends on the clarity of the image to each eye, allowing a better comparison. Many factors affect the perception of the depth of an approaching ball, such as the ball's size, color, speed, and trajectory (Payne & Isaacs, 2008). A child must be able to clearly distinguish the ball from the background and use all depth cues to make a catch.

Audition

Children can locate sound effectively by the age of three years. The ability to localize sound continues to improve through the teens. Sound localization is especially important in sporting contexts, such as knowing the location of an oncoming ball hitting a wall in racquetball or the position of other players relative to one another in invasion sports. Localizing sound is also very important for driving; it allows drivers to react after hearing sirens, horns, or other sounds.

Differentiating sound is also an important component of sensory development, particularly for speech development. Young children can differentiate similar speech sounds, such as b and d. Differentiating b and d becomes quite important when learning to read and write. A child who cannot discern the difference may have difficulty spelling or pronouncing words with these letters because they cannot hear the difference. The ability to differentiate similar sounds amid noisy background sounds is particularly challenging for children.

WHAT DO YOU THINK?

Exercise 12.7

Provide an example of how vision can be a rate limiter for the following populations based on visual development.

1. A four-month-old infant learning to crawl
2. An eight-year-old male baseball batter

Improvements in the ability to discriminate speech sounds in noisy environments continue through late childhood (Neuman & Hochberg, 1983). The ability to ignore background noise while attending to sounds is called **auditory figure–ground perception**. Although some children appear to have more difficulty with figure–ground perception than others do, it is not well known how figure–ground perception changes during childhood because research in this area has been minimal.

Proprioception

The kinesthetic system provides us with our sense of proprioception and is supported by muscles, tendons, joints, and skin receptors, as well as the inner ear and eyes. Proprioceptively, some of the most important aspects to develop are body awareness and spatial awareness.

Body awareness is an individual's sense of the body, such as knowledge of the different body parts, and body image. Body awareness includes being able to locate body parts, knowing the movement of the body parts, and knowing how to efficiently move the body parts. The development of body awareness begins at birth and continues through childhood. Infants are born with an unconscious sense that enables them to orient themselves toward pleasant sensory experiences. The initial discovery of their own hands can be very exciting. Infants often spend much time simply staring at their hands, opening them, closing them, and watching them move closer and farther away. This discovery becomes even more exciting when infants shake a rattle. They are beginning to understand the relationship of their movements to other objects, as well as the placement of their body parts

WHAT DO YOU THINK?

Exercise 12.8

Choose two activities. As an instructor, how would you include auditory information to enhance learning? Would this change if you were instructing children versus adolescents? Explain.

RESEARCH NOTES

Even Babies Know Bad Dancing!

Moving to music is a universal behavior found across cultures and genders. A joy for moving to sound is not learned but is innate in human nature. It is likely you have even seen a niece or nephew dancing to tunes or viewed funny videos of babies busting a move to a new song on social media. Although moving to music is universal, it was not known how babies observe and perceive other dancers. Hannon and colleagues (2017) examined how music audiovisual perception develops across infancy by habituating infants to a video of a dancer followed by presenting matched and mismatched audiovisuals, meaning the audio did not match the timing of the movements. Differences were found between the younger and older infants indicating that musical audiovisual synchrony develops in infants around 8 to 12 months. So keep in mind that if you are dancing in front of a crawling infant, you may be judged if you cannot keep a beat.

with respect to other body parts. Through active exploration, older infants learn how to propel themselves by understanding the relationship between their feet and leg movements and the ground. Preschoolers (three- to four-year-olds) continue to develop their body awareness through active experiences in relation to their own bodies, as seen in the following story.

While they are eating a snack together, four-year-old Joseph's teacher says to him, "You have the longest eyelashes!" Looking straight ahead, Joseph asks, "Do they reach all the way out to the juice pitcher?" The teacher laughs and replies, "Not that far." Curious, Joseph wonders aloud, "Then how far?" Spontaneously, he holds up his finger and moves it slowly toward his eye until he feels it gently touch his lashes. Delighted with his experiment, he shares, "Now I can see and feel how far!" Later, Joseph and his friends have more fun checking out their eyelash lengths in a mirror (Poole et al., 2006).

Joseph not only further developed his body awareness, but he also gained a better sense of distance and size. By comparing the feeling of his eyelashes with the image he saw in the mirror, he also gained a better understanding of the link between visual and kinesthetic perception. When instructing young children, practitioners should help young children become more aware of their bodies by asking them where their body parts are located and what their body parts do.

Spatial awareness is the awareness of the size of the body and the position of the body in relation to people and objects. Toddlers are very interested in spatial concepts. A favorite activity of toddlers is to place small objects into containers and take them out again. They learn about size and dimensions by filling open containers with smaller objects. Toddlers are also gaining a sense of **object permanence**, which is the concept that an object still exists even if it can no longer be seen. They learn that the ball they put in a box is still inside the box even if the lid has been placed on top. Because children learn spatial awareness through active exploration, they need a wide variety of experiences in manipulating objects and interacting with other children and adults. Preschoolers relate the positioning of objects to their own personal space. At this age, children are very **egocentric**, meaning that they perceive the world only in terms of themselves. By age 5 or 6 years, children learn spatial orientation and the words associated with orientation, such as *near* and *far, left* and *right,* and *front* and *back* (Poole et al., 2006). Children learn much better through active experiences than through observation or verbal instruction. By the age of six, children are less egocentric, and their spatial awareness is much more established. They also have a stronger sense of personal space and can locate objects relative to other objects and general space. Activities that encourage various movements through space, such as obstacle courses, are especially helpful for young children.

WHAT DO YOU THINK?

Exercise 12.9

1. Describe activities that could help children develop kinesthetic perception.
2. How is spatial awareness important in sport?
3. How is spatial awareness important for firefighting or driving?

SUMMARY

Most of us go through changes in movement skills if exposed to experiences and environments that encourage motor development (Clark, 2007). This chapter explored some of the structural factors that constrain (i.e., promote or limit) the acquisition of and forms of these movements. With this information, Ethan (the tall, young soccer player from the chapter-opening scenario) can appreciate the vast range of structural differences on his soccer team. Not only do parents and coaches need to understand how structural constraints interact with functional factors (the focus of chapters 14 through 16), tasks, and the environment, but these are also critical components for therapists and other practitioners to understand as well. For example, we can understand the difficulty many youngsters have with catching if we know that tracking and movement perception are rather late to develop.

The structural systems we have described change at very different rates; for example, the rapid growth in stature during the first year of life decelerates in subsequent years until the growth spurt of puberty. The endocrine system is rather quiet until puberty, when its influence on skeletal and muscle tissue becomes dramatic. Although systems change at different rates, change among individuals is extremely variable as well. Our discussion of early and late maturers underscores this fact. The discussion of relative growth (both in stature and percentage of muscle mass) from birth to adolescence reminds us that structural changes provide challenges and new opportunities for coordination, and that children are not miniature adults. Finally, differences in structure between the sexes are generally minimal until puberty. Thus, motor development and learning differences between girls and boys prior to adolescence are likely influenced largely by environment constraints.

› ONLINE ACTIVITIES

The student material found in HK*Propel* includes exercises, labs, and videos to enhance learning and encourage practical application of important concepts.

LEARNING AIDS

Supplemental Activities

1. It seems that almost weekly we read about a new research study that indicates that more and more children are becoming obese. This is a significant challenge for our society and for the professions associated with kinesiology and physical education. Practitioners should keep up to date on statistics such as those on obesity. Search the website of the U.S. Centers for Disease Control and Prevention in Atlanta to find the most recent statistics and recommendations for physical activity. Discuss the current statistics and recommendations. Do you think these recommendations are adequate? Explain why or why not.

2. Are athletic injuries in developing children and adolescents detrimental to growth? Are some sports (e.g., American football and long-distance running) associated with injuries to such an extent that parents or professionals should restrict kids from playing them? Search the Internet for information on this topic and report your findings.

Glossary

auditory figure–ground perception—The ability to ignore background noise while attending to sounds (e.g., in a conversation).

body awareness—A sense of the body in space, including the ability to locate body parts, knowing the movement of body parts, and knowing how to efficiently move body parts.

body proportions—The relationships of body parts in terms of size.

deliberate practice—Specific practice requiring much effort without an immediate reward; performance improvement is the motivation, and it is not necessarily enjoyable.

depth perception—The ability to see in three dimensions.

distance curve—The extent of growth in terms of height and weight.

dizygotic twins—Twins who develop from two separate ova and therefore share no more genes than typical siblings do.

egocentric—The inability to view the world from a perspective other than one's own.

endocrine system—The body system that controls the hormones of body tissue.

figure–ground perception—The ability to distinguish an object from its surroundings.

heritability—A statistic that can be calculated to estimate genetic influences in producing differences in individuals.

hyperplasia—An increase in the number of muscle units such as muscle fibers or neurons.

hypertrophy—An increase in the relative size or volume of muscle fibers or neurons.

Legg-Calvé-Perthes disease—An irritation of the femur where it inserts into the hip.

monozygotic twins—Twins who develop from a single fertilized ovum and therefore have identical genotypes.

object permanence—An awareness that an object exists even if removed from sight.

Osgood-Schlatter disease—A disruption in growth of the upper shinbone where the patellar tendon attaches.

peak height velocity—The period during adolescence in which height gain is fastest.

percentile—A relative rank or position on a scale; the percentage of a distribution that is equal to or below that position.

pituitary—A gland that secretes the hormones responsible for skeletal growth.

rate of change—The speed at which a variable changes over time.

relative growth—Postnatal changes in body proportions.

retinal disparity—Differences in the two retinal images produced by the eyes due to the different positions of the eyes in the head.

sigmoid curve—An S-shaped pattern of change—for example, for height and weight.

spatial awareness—Awareness of the size of the body and the position of the body in relationship to people and objects.

synapses—Gaps between two nerve cells in which a nerve impulse is transmitted.

thyroid—A gland that secretes the hormones responsible for skeletal growth.

velocity curve—A curve that describes change per unit of time, such as height in centimeters per year.

visuomotor coordination—The ability to visually track a moving object and guide the body, the limbs, or both, to intercept the object.

13

PHYSICAL AGING

After reading this chapter, you should be able to do the following:

- Describe peak physiological function.
- Explain age-related changes in the skeletal, muscular, nervous, cardiovascular, and sensory systems.
- Compare the effects of a physically active lifestyle and a sedentary lifestyle in each of these systems.
- Understand the effects of normal aging on aerobic capacity and body composition, as well as any benefits of a physically active lifestyle on each.

Am I Getting Old?

Yasmine was noticing that she was getting headaches from reading. She always had perfect vision, but she wondered if this was this a sign that she was experiencing age-related vision acuity decline. She also noticed that she had been turning her music up a little more than she used to. Could her hearing decline be related to working in a loud environment, or is this a common age-related decline? In addition, Yasmine certainly cannot miss the undeniable increases in her running times. She was running five miles at a 7:50-minute-per-mile pace and lately has been lucky to run five miles at a 9-minute pace. Is this decline due to weight gain? Reduced frequency of running? Or have her speed and endurance declined due to age-related changes in her muscular and skeletal systems? What about memory lapses? Yasmine headed to the grocery store but was delayed because she could not remember where she had put her keys. She looked in the usual places—her purse, the key holder, coat pockets, counters; it turned out they were upstairs on her nightstand. She must have absentmindedly carried them upstairs. When Yasmine arrived at the grocery store, she ran into an old friend. They carried on a conversation, but she could not remember the man's name or how she knew him. Could Yasmine also be experiencing age-related cognitive declines, or was this just a typical memory lapse that can occur with anyone? Yasmine is certainly not an older adult at age 42, but could she be experiencing the expected age-related declines in various body systems, or might something more serious be going on?

Experiences of occasional short-term memory loss can occur at any age. You have likely had one, or even all, of the experiences mentioned: not remembering where you put an object, not recognizing an acquaintance, or forgetting what you intended to purchase at the grocery store. These experiences are certainly irritating and they beg the question, how does age affect memory? Should we expect to forget more and more, or is this a sign of something else, such as dementia?

With age, humans experience many declines, including cognitive function, cardiorespiratory function, muscular strength, and movement speed, to name a few. This chapter discusses these, as well as other age-related body system changes, including those of the skeletal, muscular, cardiovascular, nervous, endocrine, and sensory systems. Although many age-related declines are associated with aging (**primary aging**), older adults have discovered that by maintaining an active and healthy lifestyle, they are able to not only avoid some secondary aging changes, but also reduce many age-related declines. **Secondary aging** refers to changes that are the result of disease or environmental effects. Although primary aging changes can be expected in everyone, as a function of age, secondary aging is not inevitable. Examples of primary aging are mild memory losses and slower central nervous system responses; a serious and debilitating example of secondary aging is emphysema resulting from years of smoking.

Much research indicates that physically active older adults can maintain much of their function for years longer than their sedentary counterparts, allowing them to experience a higher quality of life into old adulthood, with reduced secondary diseases and improved physical and cognitive function. Considering the importance of physical activity and exercise with regard to physical aging, terms should be clearly defined. **Physical activity** includes any bodily movement produced by skeletal muscle requiring energy expenditure above resting rate, and **exercise** is a subcategory of physical activity that includes planned, purposeful movement to improve or maintain one or more physical fitness components. Both involve energy expenditure that is above resting state, but exercise is a more planned and rigorous form of physical activity (Harridge & Lazarus, 2017). All practitioners who work with older adults should understand the effects physical activity and aging have on the physiological systems, their impact on movement, and the effects of physically active lifestyles on physiological systems.

Human peak physiological function occurs between the ages of 25 and 30 years (McArdle et al., 2001). It is during these years of peak physiological function that the greatest sex differences are found. Women mature earlier and reach their peak physiological function between the ages of 22 years and 25 years; men mature later, reaching peak function between the ages of 28 and 30 years (Gabbard, 2021). Peak athletic performance parallels peak physiological function because muscular strength, cardiorespiratory efficiency, and reaction time are at their maximum.

How people move and learn motor skills is greatly affected by the changes occurring in their body systems. Chapter 12 discussed the development of body systems from birth through adolescence. Changes in body systems do not stop following growth and maturation. Profound age-related changes occur in the body systems across the life span. When aging is combined with environmental and behavioral factors, such as diet and physical activity or living in an area with poor air quality, even more variability is found across individuals of the same age and sex. When designing programs to improve function, structural constraints are among the most important factors to consider. Practitioners must understand

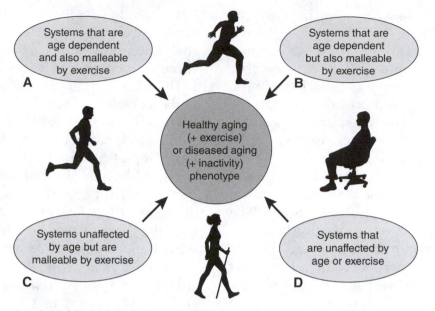

Figure 13.1 Categories of physiological regulation during aging.
Adapted from Lazarus, Lord, and Harridge (2019).

how aging affects both these systems and movement. They must also understand the wide variability across adults. Because adults vary considerably (more than children and adolescents do), individualizing their rehabilitation or exercise programs is essential.

Physical activity is a vital component to secondary aging. Research comparing exercisers with nonexercisers has revealed the broad variation of physical aging, which occurs not only within, but also across physiological systems (Lazarus et al., 2019). A model that includes four categories of physiologic regulation of aging with exercise has been devised: (a) age-dependent, activity-independent systems (primary aging); (b) age and exercise dependent; (c) exercise dependent and age independent; and (d) age and exercise independent. See figure 13.1. In this chapter, we will explore the impact of age-related changes and exercise, specifically examining the skeletal, muscular, cardiovascular, nervous, and endocrine systems and how behavioral function and physical activity affect physical aging of each system.

SKELETAL SYSTEM

Bone health in adulthood is determined by **peak bone mass** (the highest bone mass) and the age-related rate of bone loss (Spirduso et al., 2005). As discussed in chapter 12, physical activities undertaken during adolescence and young adulthood help determine the size and strength of bones. Those who participate in more resistance training activities or activities that require much physical stress and load (e.g., weightlifters and powerlifters) develop stronger and thicker bones than endurance athletes (e.g., runners, swimmers, and cyclists). Increased bone density has been found in those who take part in all types of resistance training (Bemben & Bemben, 2011). Conversely, because swimming is not a weight-bearing activity, swimmers often have weaker, less dense bones than runners (Nillsson & Westlin, 1971). Bone health acquired during youth and young adulthood provide lifelong benefits, and it has been suggested that denser bones may delay the onset of microfractures in older adulthood (Schultheis, 1991).

Peak bone mass occurs in the early 20s for men and mid-30s for women (Boisvert-Vigneault & Dionne, 2021) with women generally attaining a peak bone mass that is 10 percent below men's peak bone mass. This higher bone mineral density in men continues across the life span. The sex differences in bone mass increase in midlife, with perimenopausal women losing bone mass at a higher rate than men, followed by a decelerated loss for 10 years postmenopause (Hunter & Sambrook, 2000). The most important factor influencing bone loss in women is menopause; however, there is much variability across women. Bone loss increases from an average of 0.7 to 1 percent loss per year to between 2 and 3 percent loss per year after menopause over a 5- to 10-year period. During menopause, women can lose between 30 and 50 percent of their bone mineral density; the rate of bone loss can vary greatly across individuals with some experiencing very rapid bone loss (Reeve et al., 1999). Men and women lose bone mineral density at about the same rate by age 65 years. Bone loss then increases in both men and women during old adulthood, between the 9th and 10th decades (Spirduso et al., 2005).

Osteoporosis

As bone mineral density decreases with age, bones become so weak that they may fracture from mild falls or even coughing. Fractures, especially hip fractures, in adulthood can seriously hamper an independent lifestyle. The threat of bone fractures increases even further for those with **osteoporosis**, a crippling disease that results from low bone mass and poor structural bone quality. With specific regard to the vertebrae, damage may result in a stooped posture that affects the execution of well-learned skills. Regarding motivation, a person with osteoporosis may be reluctant to learn new motor skills or use former motor skills for fear of falling and fracturing a limb.

Women have a higher risk of microfractures and osteoporosis than men because of their lower bone mineral density. One out of three women over 50 years of age and one in five men over 50 years of age, worldwide, will experience a fracture because of osteoporosis (Kanis et al., 2000) with thin-framed women and women under 127 pounds (58 kg) being at an increased risk of osteoporosis. Although the risk of osteoporosis increases with age, the disease can occur at any age (Spirduso et al., 2005). Ethnicity has also been linked to osteoporosis risk with Caucasian and Asian women being at highest risk, while African American women are at lowest risk (Nam et al., 2013). Importantly, many of the risk factors for osteoporosis are modifiable. Refer to the lists of modifiable and nonmodifiable risk factors for osteoporosis.

Nonmodifiable Risk Factors for Osteoporosis

- *Sex:* Women have a higher risk.
- *Age:* Bones become thinner and weaker with age.
- *Body size:* Thin-framed women are at highest risk.
- *Ethnicity:* Caucasian and Asian women are at highest risk.
- *Family history:* Heredity can increase risk.

Modifiable Risk Factors for Osteoporosis

- *Lifestyle:* Increased weight-bearing physical activity decreases risk.
- *Calcium and vitamin D:* Increased calcium and vitamin D intake decreases risk.
- *Sex hormones:* Low estrogen or low testosterone levels can increase risk.
- *Medications:* Glucocorticoids and some anticonvulsants can lead to loss of bone density.

- *Anorexia:* Serious reductions in food intake and body weight increase risk.
- *Cigarette smoking:* Smoking increases risk.
- *Excessive alcohol intake:* Alcohol consumption increases risk.

Adapted from "Osteoporosis Overview," National Institutes of Health, Osteoporosis and Related Bone Diseases National Resource Center, last modified October, 2019, www.niams.nih.gov/Health_Info/Bone/Osteoporosis/overview.asp#c.

Participating in regular load-bearing exercise, such as resistance training and running can decrease or even reverse bone mineral loss even throughout older adulthood (Boisvert-Vigneault & Dionne, 2021). Older adults with low bone density should be advised by their physicians, regarding appropriate exercise, as their risks for fragility fractures are higher. Fragility fractures occur most commonly in the lumbar spine, neck, or forearm and can cause long-lasting pain and discomfort. Older adults at risk should choose low-risk activities that put less strain on the joints and bones (such as yoga, tai chi, and Pilates) and avoid high-impact and heavy-resistance training exercises. Taking in 1,500 milligrams of calcium per day can also help decrease bone loss.

Body Stature

With age, there is a general trend toward a decrease in standing height (Shephard, 1997), beginning around the age of 40, with women losing height at a faster rate than men. A cross-sectional study (i.e., a study of different people at different ages) showed that men aged 80 years and older were on average 4.9 centimeters shorter, and women over 80 years were about 5.7 centimeters shorter than young adults (National Center for Health Statistics, 2021). Losses in height accelerate after age 70, to an average of under one tenth of an inch (2 mm) per year in both sexes (Svänborg et al., 1991). Decreases in height largely result from a progressive compression of the intervertebral discs (Shephard, 1997). This compression shortens the spine and can cause curvature of the upper spine (**kyphosis**) (see figure 13.2). Kyphosis can also be the result of years of poor posture, weak back muscles, osteoporosis, and osteoarthritis of the vertebrae. **Osteoarthritis** is a degenerative joint disease that can affect any joint but most often affects the hips, vertebrae, feet, and knees. Arthritis cripples millions of Americans, impairing their ability to move fluidly and comfortably and affects 49.6 percent of adults over the age of 65 years (Barbour et al., 2017). Fortunately, many of the symptoms of arthritis can be controlled through non-weight-bearing exercise such as swimming and cycling, flexibility training, and light resistance training (Van Norman, 1995).

WHAT DO YOU THINK?

Exercise 13.1

1. Devise a list of exercises that could prevent age-related bone density loss.
2. Refer to your list and indicate which activities would be low, moderate, or high risk for injury or bone fracture in an older adult with lower bone density and possible risk of osteoporosis.

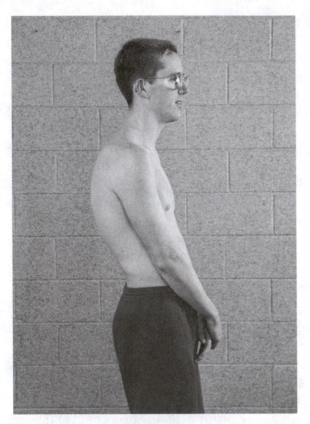

Figure 13.2   An example of early kyphosis, which can continue to develop into a much more curved spine if not corrected.

MUSCULAR SYSTEM

The muscular system works in concert with the skeletal system to allow the body to move. Large changes in body composition occur in adulthood, resulting in a progressive loss of lean body mass. The loss of lean body mass results more from an increase in body fat than from a reduction in muscle mass. Losses in muscle mass are small until around the age of 50 years, after which they accelerate. People can avoid much of this loss in muscle mass by maintaining moderate to high physical activity levels and good nutrition (Boisvert-Vigneault & Dionne, 2021).

Strength

Maximal strength correlates with muscular cross-sectional area, which is largest during the 20s and then plateaus until a decline starts around age 45 to 55 years (Jackson et al., 2012). Strength generally begins to decline at the age of 40 years but can begin earlier in sedentary people. A loss of between 30 and 50 percent of skeletal muscle mass occurs between the ages of 40 and 80 years, thus contributing to a decline in motor performance (Akima et al., 2001). Subsequent declines in strength and power generally parallel the rate of skeletal muscle mass decline, but often are greater (Bassey et al., 1992; Goodpaster et al., 2006). Increases in muscle weakness and fatigability also result from decreased muscle mass (Faulkner & Brooks, 1995) with declines in maximal strength being greater in the legs than in the arms (Jackson et al., 2012). It has been suggested that this may be attributed to reduced use of the legs with age.

WHAT DO YOU THINK?

Exercise 13.2

Suppose you are an instructor or clinician working with an 82-year-old woman who has osteoarthritis in her knees and ankles. She is also frail and relatively sedentary.

1. What exercises might you prescribe? Explain why you chose these exercises. What exercises should this woman avoid? What are some warnings (signs and symptoms) for a frail woman with osteoarthritis?

2. Explain why developing a program for someone with both osteoporosis and osteoarthritis would be particularly challenging.

Most adults experience a reduction in muscle mass because of heredity, intergenerational lifestyle, nutrition, socioeconomic factors, and other factors (Lazarus & Harridge, 2010), but the biggest factor is lack of adequate physical activity (Blair, 2009). Because the number of muscle fibers decreases around the age of 50 years, losses in muscle mass at younger ages occur because of a sedentary lifestyle (Faulkner et al., 2007). Age-related muscle tissue loss (**sarcopenia**) is the amount of muscle loss that will occur regardless of physical activity levels and other factors. Sarcopenia is differentiated with loss of muscle mass due to disuse, which is termed **atrophy**. Loss of muscle mass is one of the biggest factors contributing to loss of muscular power and strength.

The changes in muscle mass are related to the muscle fiber type. While there appears to be an age-related decline in fast-twitch, or type II fibers, slow-twitch, type I fibers can be maintained with a physically active lifestyle even through old age (Snijders et al., 2009). **Slow-twitch fibers** have a slower contraction–relaxation cycle than fast-twitch fibers do and are best suited for endurance activities. **Fast-twitch fibers**, with their much quicker contraction–relaxation cycle, are better suited for short-duration, high-intensity activities such as sprinting and powerlifting. Although a loss of fast-twitch fibers appears inevitable, the amount and rate of decline are greatly affected by the frequency and intensity of physical activity. Older adults benefit from a reduction in the rate of decline, but they also experience hypertrophy in the muscle fibers that remain (Lexell, 1995). The type II fibers tend to decrease, while the type I fibers are maintained. This tendency remains even with frequent and intense physical activity (Shephard, 1998).

Although sarcopenia is associated with loss of strength, the loss of muscle mass only represents 6 to 10 percent of age-related loss of muscular strength (Delmonico et al., 2009). The term **dynapenia** describes the age-related loss of muscle strength and muscle power (Clark & Manini, 2008). The loss of muscular strength in older adults can be quite significant, affecting their ability to maintain independence (dos Santos et al., 2017). Activities many people take for granted such as carrying a bag of groceries, climbing steps, or even opening a medicine bottle can be very challenging for an older adult with significant losses in strength (Shephard, 1991). Losses in muscular strength are exacerbated by long-term physical inactivity, which leads to frailty. **Frailty** is characterized by severe limitations in mobility, strength, balance, and endurance, resulting from weak and highly fatigable muscles and is often due to a long-term, inactive, lifestyle (Faulkner et al., 2007). Reversing this condition is often difficult. Frailty results from a long-term inactive lifestyle, and when combined with genetic factors, disease, injury, or aging (or some combination of these), it causes muscular atrophy, decreased strength, and increased fatigability (see figure 13.3). Frail people experience impaired mobility and balance and are at an increased risk

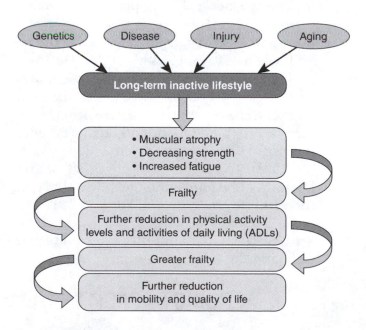

Figure 13.3 Downward spiral of physical inactivity leading to frailty and reduced mobility.

of falls. With declining fitness, health, and quality of life, the frail elderly often spiral downward, participating in less physical activity. This further reduces their strength and mobility, continually worsening their condition by limiting their physical activity and activities of daily living even more. By further limiting their physical activity, they experience more muscle wasting (atrophy), resulting in a worsening condition as well as serious psychological ramifications including anxiety and depression.

Flexibility

The elasticity of the tendons and ligaments and the condition of the synovial fluid enable smooth body and limb movements (Gabbard, 2012). With age, flexibility decreases as cross-linkages between collagen fibrils develop and synovial fluid degrades. The cross-linkages reduce the elasticity of the tendons, ligaments, and joint capsules (Shephard, 1998). Females experience a more gradual per-year decline in flexibility than men (0.6 vs. 0.8 percent) (Baptista de Oliveira Medeiros et al., 2013). Reductions in flexibility accelerate at a faster rate following middle age; adults lose approximately 3 to 4 inches (8-10 cm) of flexibility of the low back, hips, and hamstrings as assessed by the sit and reach test (Shephard, 2008). Declines in flexibility are joint specific; shoulder and trunk flexibility declines at a faster rate than knee and elbow flexibility. These differences may be attributed to individualistic activity patterns (Baptista de Oliveira Medeiros et al., 2013). To mitigate the aging effects on flexibility, the joints must be taken through their full range of motion. Yoga and stretching exercises (done when muscles are warm) are beneficial in maintaining flexibility and reducing the effects of aging.

AEROBIC CAPACITY

The strongest predictor of independent living and mortality risk is cardiovascular and respiratory fitness (Paterson & War-burton, 2010). Although there is a progressive age-related decline in aerobic capacity found in adults from age 25 to 65 years, age-related losses in aerobic capacity accelerate at the age of 70 and are like declines found in strength (Shephard, 1998). Adults between the ages of 55 and 85 declined aerobically, on average, 16 percent per decade; as would be expected, individuals who were healthy and independent declined the least (Cunningham et al., 1997). It is difficult to separate age-related losses in function from changes due to other factors such as reduced regular physical activity and the intensity of physical activity bouts. Although it has been suggested that aerobic capacity can be maintained with regular intense training (Kasch et al., 1988), most research has found this to be only a short-lived training response. Following the initial training response, the rate of age-related declines in aerobic power follows a pattern like that in nontraining people (Shephard, 1998). Some of the factors of an age-related decline in aerobic power are maximal aerobic capacity, lactate threshold, and exercise economy.

Maximal Aerobic Capacity

Maximal aerobic capacity, often referred to as $\dot{V}O_2$max, begins to decline following young adulthood. Although $\dot{V}O_2$max is highly correlated with endurance, the decline in $\dot{V}O_2$max throughout adulthood tends to be greater than the decline in performance. Endurance training can increase $\dot{V}O_2$max by 5 to 20 percent in children and adults (Gabbard, 2012). Typically, the $\dot{V}O_2$max decline is approximately 10 percent per decade, after age 40 years (Pogliaghi & Murias, 2021). One would expect endurance-trained older athletes to experience a decreased rate of decline compared to sedentary people, yet recent studies have not found this to be true. Longitudinal studies have indicated that endurance-trained older women decline at twice the rate of sedentary women (Eskurza et al., 2002), but endurance-trained and sedentary men decline at the same rate (Wilson & Tanaka, 2000). Greater declines in endurance-trained men than in sedentary men have been found but have been related to a reduction in training (Pimentel et al., 2003). Keep in mind that these comparisons are with individuals' $\dot{V}O_2$max at an earlier age, not with that of the average younger adult, so the endurance-trained adults had more $\dot{V}O_2$max to lose than sedentary adults because of their higher initial levels. Also, many of the older women had significantly reduced their training volume, which would decrease their $\dot{V}O_2$max. Declines in the rate of $\dot{V}O_2$max are similar in endurance-trained and sedentary adults, but the endurance-trained adults have a much higher $\dot{V}O_2$max because they start at a much higher level. This initially higher $\dot{V}O_2$max can be critical in maintaining cardiovascular fitness above the functional thresholds to avoid becoming dependent (Pogliaghi & Murias, 2021).

Sex differences in the $\dot{V}O_2$max of adults are quite large, due to lean body mass and overall body weight differences across the sexes. Men generally have a $\dot{V}O_2$max that is 40 to 60 percent greater than that of women (Hyde & Gengenbach, 2007). An untrained male averages approximately three and a half liters per minute, whereas an untrained female averages about half of that, at two liters per minute. Intervention research on endurance exercise has shown improvements of 20 percent after 6 to 12 months of training with some studies showing similar improvements in as little as 12 weeks of training (Pogliaghi & Murias, 2021).

Lactate Threshold

Aerobic performance can also be determined by **lactate threshold**, which occurs at the exercise intensity at which blood lactate begins to accumulate significantly above baseline levels in the bloodstream (Tanaka & Seals, 2003). Lactate threshold declines with increasing age, resulting in reduced overall performance. Although reductions in endurance performance are largely affected by the declining lactate threshold in young and middle-aged adults, reduced endurance performance in older adulthood is more affected by reductions in $\dot{V}O_2$max (Evans et al., 1995).

Exercise Economy

The oxygen cost of exercise at a particular velocity is known as **exercise economy** (Tanaka & Seals, 2003) and is a strong indicator of endurance ability (Morgan & Craig, 1992). Although only a few studies have addressed the effects of age on exercise economy, aging does not appear to have a negative effect. Thus, the reductions in endurance performance found with aging are likely largely the result of declines in $\dot{V}O_2$max and lactate threshold.

CARDIOVASCULAR SYSTEM

The cardiovascular system declines by approximately 30 percent between the ages of 30 and 70 years (Spirduso et al., 2005). Most age-related cardiovascular changes are not evident while at rest, except for

WHAT DO YOU THINK?

Exercise 13.3

1. Define *maximal aerobic capacity*, *lactate threshold*, and *exercise economy*.
2. Which is the strongest indicator of endurance ability?
3. Which is most affected by aging?
4. What types of activities increase aerobic capacity?

blood pressure (Pogliaghi & Murias, 2021); however, postural changes, or engaging in exercise, will quickly induce cardiovascular changes such as increased heart rate. Heart rate, most notably heart rate during maximal exertion (maximal heart rate), decreases across the lifetime. Declines in stroke volume are also seen with aging. Increases in arteriovenous oxygen difference occur in older adults, although little difference is found in older adults who exercise regularly. Furthermore, blood pressure tends to increase in older adults. Note that these changes occur in healthy adults. Some people will exhibit some form of cardiovascular disease resulting from heredity or lifestyle behaviors. It is important to evaluate cardiorespiratory fitness level prior to involvement in a fitness program or teaching a motor skill, because the assessed level will greatly affect the person's ability to perform aerobic exercise.

Heart Rate

Heart rate is one of the most used measures of response to exercise because of the relative ease of measurement and is particularly important because it is a major determinant of cardiac output and maximal oxygen consumption (Gabbard, 2012). Measurements can be taken at various points from resting heart rate to maximal heart rate (measurement taken when people are exerting themselves to their maximal oxygen uptake).

Resting heart rate exhibits only small changes with age throughout adulthood (Fagard et al., 1993), while heart rates during submaximal exercise tend to be lower in older adults than in young adults (Sachs et al., 1985). This is because one's heart rate not only increases at a faster rate in young adulthood, but it also continues to increase to higher levels than older adults' heart rate during submaximal exercise (Paterson et al., 1989). The largest age-related change in heart rate is found during maximal physical effort. A simple and common formula for computing maximal heart rate is to subtract a person's age in years from 220 beats per minute. Therefore, a 50-year-old's maximal heart rate would be 170 beats per minute. Although a maximal heart rate of around 190 beats per minute would be expected for a 30-year-old, this formula does not always hold for fit and healthy older adults. Some older adults have been found to reach maximal heart rates of 20 beats per minute higher than would be expected based on the given formula (Dempsey & Seals, 1995). It is suggested that this commonly used equation underestimates heart rate maximum in individuals over the age of 40 years; therefore, new equations separated for sex were developed. These formulas provide a better estimate for both women and older adults (Tanaka et al., 2001).

Men: Predicted HRmax = 209.6 – (0.72 × age)

Women: Predicted HRmax = 207.2 – (0.65 × age)

Stroke Volume

Stroke volume is the amount of blood pumped through one ventricle of the heart during one contraction. It should be noted that not all the blood is pumped out during a contraction, with approximately one third of the blood remaining in the left ventricle. Stroke volume depends on the size of the heart, the duration of the contraction, preload (the amount of ventricle stretching prior to the contraction), and afterload (aortic pressure during the contraction). In general, men tend to have higher stroke volumes than women because their hearts are larger. Stroke volume can be increased through aerobic training, which can also provide the benefits of lower resting heart rates.

The human heart is quite flexible, allowing heart volume to be well maintained until older adulthood (Shephard, 1997). Older adults can have higher stroke volumes than younger adults during submaximal exercise; however, increased stroke volume is difficult for older adults to maintain when exercise intensity nears maximal effort (Niinimaa & Shephard, 1978). As older adults approach maximal effort, many actually exhibit declines in stroke volume, whereas young adults exhibit a gradual increase in stroke volume when approaching maximal effort (Tate et al., 1994).

Arteriovenous Oxygen Difference

Arteriovenous oxygen difference is the difference in oxygen content between arterial and venous blood. The mean arteriovenous oxygen difference determines the volume of oxygen that is transported to the tissues following a contraction. Arteriovenous oxygen difference is typically at 4.5 mL · 100 mL · min at rest and increases to 16 mL · 100 mL · min at maximum physical capacity (Rowell, 1993). Physically active men can sustain the arteriovenous oxygen difference during rest and submaximal exercise, whereas the largest arteriovenous oxygen differences are found in sedentary women, up to 50 milliliters per liter greater than their physically active counterparts (Dempsey & Seals, 1995). In very healthy and fit older adults, the maximal arterio-

venous oxygen difference can remain the same, but it generally decreases by approximately 20 milliliters per liter (Shephard, 1998). This change is due, in part, to a larger distribution of the cardiac output to the skin and internal organs, with age (Shephard, 1993).

Blood Pressure

A blood pressure reading is a combination of the pressure from the contraction of the left ventricle forcing blood into the aorta (systolic) and the brief relaxation of the ventricle that follows (diastolic). A healthy blood pressure for a young or middle-aged adult is typically 120/80 (Saxon et al., 2010). Blood pressure fluctuates throughout the day as a result of physiological and psychological changes. The American College of Sports Medicine recently redefined the threshold for high blood pressure (hypertension) to a systolic reading of over 130 millimeters of mercury (mmHg) or a diastolic reading of 80 mmHg or higher (Riebe et al., 2018). Recommendations may vary for people with different conditions; however, changes are common with age (see figure 13.4). Early treatment of prehypertension is highly recommended to prevent serious health complications (Hernandez, 2008).

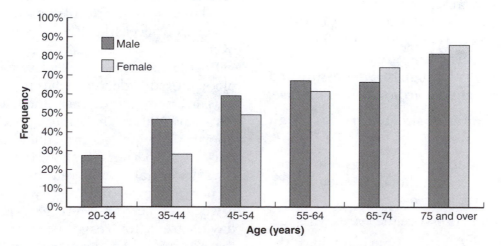

Figure 13.4   Rates of hypertension in males and females over the age of 20 in the United States, 2015 to 2018.

Data from National Center for Health Statistics. Health, United States, 2019: Table 22. Hyattsville, MD. 2021. Available from: https://www.cdc.gov/nchs/hus/contents2019.htm.

Older adults are more prone to orthostatic hypotension (postural low blood pressure) (Shephard, 1997). Orthostatic hypotension induces dizziness, confusion, and sometimes fainting (Fagard et al., 1993). Orthostatic hypotension is due, in part, to the fact that older adults are less able to respond to changes in body position or heat than young adults are. Sharp drops in blood pressure can occur when an older adult moves from a lying position to standing or when stepping out of a swimming pool. These drops in blood pressure may also occur following an exercise bout.

Clinical hypertension affects two thirds of adults over the age of 65 (National Center for Health Statistics, 2021) with blood pressure rising as much as 35 mmHg or more across a life span (Kannel et al., 1980). This rise is generally found in people living in developed countries; indigenous community dwellers show little to no increase in hypertension across age (DeStefano et al., 1979). This cultural change is largely attributed to lifestyle differences between urban community dwellers and many Indigenous people, such as the Navajo and the Pacific Islanders, who live in rural areas. Some behavioral factors have been found to increase blood pressure, including sedentary lifestyles, excessive body weight, and sodium intake; conversely, other behavioral factors can decrease blood pressure, including the intake of omega-3 fatty acids (Saxon et al., 2010). The following are lists of both nonmodifiable and modifiable risk factors for high blood pressure and the development of cardiovascular disease.

Nonmodifiable Risk Factors for High Blood Pressure

- *Gender:* Men are at higher risk in young and middle adulthood; women have a higher risk after age 55.
- *Age:* Blood pressure increases with age.
- *Ethnicity:* African Americans have the highest incidence.
- *Family history:* Heredity can increase risk.
- *Diabetes:* This poses a higher risk.

Modifiable Risk Factors for High Blood Pressure

- *Lifestyle:* Regular exercise reduces risk.
- *Sodium intake:* Excessive sodium intake increases risk.
- *Obesity:* Maintaining a healthy weight reduces risk.
- *Lipids and cholesterol:* Reducing lipids and cholesterol in the diet reduces risk.
- *Stress:* Stress reduction is beneficial.
- *Cigarette smoking:* Smoking increases risk.
- *Alcohol intake:* Excessive alcohol consumption increases risk.

Adapted from Saxon et al. (2010).

Blood pressure tends to increase during physical exercise, regardless of age, with increases being even larger for people with higher resting blood pressures (Zerzawy, 1987). Elderly men have averaged 37 mmHg higher blood pressure than young adults, and elderly women have averaged 26 mmHg higher (Shephard, 1997). Continued regular or vigorous exercise (or both) can decrease resting, submaximal, and maximal blood pressure in older adults, bringing them down to a level like that of young adults over time.

Regular, systematic exercise can reduce blood pressure, decrease the risk of developing cardiovascular disease, and lower weight (Bradley, 2007). The American College of Sports Medicine recommends that individuals with hypertension should exercise most days a week at a moderate intensity (40 to 65 percent of maximum), five to seven days a week for aerobic exercise, two to three days a week for resistance training and two to three days per week for flexibility. Exercise duration should be between 30 and

---

WHAT DO YOU THINK?

Exercise 13.4

Suppose you are an instructor or clinician working with a 72-year-old man with hypertension with arthritis in his knees and hips. Your client was an athlete as a young adult but did not continue a physically active lifestyle beyond his 30s. He held a sedentary job for 40 years and has been obese for about 30 years.

What exercises might you prescribe for this man? Explain why you chose these exercises. What exercises should he avoid? What are some warnings (signs and symptoms) for an obese hypertensive older adult with arthritis?

---

60 minutes, with the option of beginning with several 10-minute bouts dispersed throughout the day (Riebe et al., 2018). Weight training is also favorable; however, high resistance with few repetitions should be replaced with lower resistance and more repetitions. People with hypertension should not participate in high-intensity exercise, because it will increase blood pressure and could place them at risk for cardiac problems (Hagberg, 1988). It is very important to encourage breathing during weight training (some people tend to hold their breath) to avoid further increases in blood pressure (Van Norman, 1995).

NERVOUS SYSTEM

The central nervous system is composed of the brain and the spinal cord. There are approximately 100 billion neurons in the brain, giving rise to a very complex neuronal network. A neuron consists of a cell body, axon, and dendrite, and with age, the dendrites and axons gradually degrade. The brain also experiences a gradual loss in the number of neurons (thousands each day). These changes contribute to the reduced size and weight of the brain. Structurally, older adults have less gray matter volume than younger adults (Salat et al., 2004). Gray matter enables all functions and is important for movement, memory, and emotion. Losses in the prefrontal cortex and the primary motor and somatosensory cortices affect the planning of complex movements, movement execution, and proprioceptive feedback. In older adults, gray matter is often reduced in the cerebellum and basal ganglia, which affect both the ability to learn new motor skills and to maintain performance on previously learned movements (Raz et al., 2005). On a positive note, the functional changes due to age such as memory are more minor than the structural age-related changes described.

The brain can recover from many of these declines through a process called neural plasticity. Plasticity refers to the brain's ability to rewire itself to compensate for the aforementioned changes (also discussed in chapter 7). The brain restructures itself based on past experiences and what it learns. Neuronal connections increase in areas of the brain that receive information more frequently than areas of the brain that are used less frequently. For instance, a soccer player would have more of their cortex devoted to the feet, and a violinist would have more of their cortex devoted to the fingers. Neural plasticity can occur at any age but is most adaptable during childhood. You've likely heard of the phrase that small children's brains are like sponges. This phrase is derived from the ability of young children to absorb and adapt more readily than adults. Although the incredible ability of the brain to adapt does decline with age, it can be strengthened through both cognitive and physical activity. Exposing older adults to new and challenging motor skills may improve their motor learning in such areas as dancing, painting, playing a new sport, or learning a musical instrument (Martinez-Valdes & De Nunzio, 2021).

Aging is associated with an increase in abnormal formations in the brain such as neurofibrillary tangles and senile plaques. **Neurofibrillary tangles** occur when the fibers of a neuron become twisted with one another. These tangles can lead to the death of the neuron and are thought to contribute to the slowing of central nervous system responsiveness. **Senile plaques** form on the outside of neurons and have been related to memory loss. Plaques and tangles are found, to some degree, in most adults over the age of 80 years (Saxon et al., 2010), while plaques and tangles are often found in adults with dementia (Gant et al., 2018).

That older adults require more time to learn motor skills than young adults do could partly be the result of structural and functional changes to the motor cortex, basal ganglia, and cerebellum. These changes cause older adults to rely more upon cognitive processes such as attention and executive function (Martinez-Valdes & De Nunzio, 2021). Older adults activate more areas of the brain when executing the same motor skills when compared to younger adults (Heuninckx et al., 2008). It has been suggested that this increased activation may be a compensatory function to make up for some of the sensory losses older adults have experienced. Functional losses occur in both long-term and short-term memory in older adults (Lee, 2010), which may further explain increased brain activation required to perform motor skills. Age-related cognitive losses can be slowed down by maintaining moderate physical activity levels and keeping the mind sharp through mental activities such as word puzzles, reading, and writing.

Brain games, such as sudoku, crossword puzzles, or online memory games, have become a popular tool in recent years with advertising targeting young children and older adults. Although there is some research to support the benefits of brain games (Nouchi et al., 2012), others claim that the benefit is merely a placebo effect (Foroughi et al., 2016). Although some companies are facing federal regulations regarding the efficacy of their products, brain games continue to be quite popular. Although they are not as catchy, there are many brain game activities that people can do without having to purchase products (see the activities in exercise 13.5).

ENDOCRINE SYSTEM

The endocrine system plays an important role in maintaining homeostasis by signaling hormones through an integrated system of organs that include the pineal gland, pituitary gland, thyroid gland, thymus, adrenal gland, pancreas, ovary, and testes. The endocrine system influences metabolism, tissue function, growth, and mood regulation. The endocrine system also affects energy production and cognitive activity. These functions undergo changes during the aging process; however, the endocrine system also adapts to these changes as they occur (Hashizume et al., 2006).

Age-related changes in the endocrine system include declining thyroid function, decreasing gonadal hormone levels, and declining neural and hormonal control systems (Shephard, 1997). The thyroid hormone has a role in increasing basal metabolic rate and thermoregulation in extended cold exposure. Changes in basal metabolic rate across a lifetime are more greatly affected by a decrease in lean body mass than by changes in the thyroid.

Gonadal hormone changes can increase muscular atrophy and osteoporosis. The key sex steroid category for women is estrogens and, secondarily, progesterone. For men it is testosterone with males having a tenfold increase in testosterone levels in comparison to females (Sowers et al., 2001). The

An Idle Mind Is the Devil's Plaything

The benefits of neural plasticity may be best evidenced by a longitudinal study on the effects of aging and brain health conducted on a group of 678 nuns in Mankato, Minnesota, in the United States (Snowdon, 2003). Snowdon studied nuns because they are a homogeneous population. Nuns have very little or no drug or alcohol use, live in similar environments, and have similar reproductive histories. This group is also interesting because, on average, they live much longer than the general population, many into their 90s and 100s. Not only do the nuns live longer, but they also suffer dementia at a much lower rate, and those who do suffer dementia generally have milder cases than the average population. **Dementia** is defined as a substantial loss in cognitive ability above normal age-related declines.

After following these nuns for many years, Snowdon hypothesized that the reason for their prolonged length and quality of life was their belief that they must continue to be both physically and mentally active throughout their lives (Ratey, 2001). The nuns continued to challenge themselves mentally even beyond their 90s, keeping their minds actively engaged with puzzles, debates, weekly seminars, vocabulary quizzes, and daily journal writing; some even continued working into their late 90s. Sister Matthia, featured in *National Geographic* at the age of 103 years of age, was one of the first nuns to participate in Snowdon's study and became a model for healthy aging. Her postmortem neuropathological evaluation revealed that she had no signs of brain pathologies, which is rare for someone over the age of 90 (Snowdon, 2003).

Snowdon posited that the education level of the nuns and the jobs they held greatly affected both their brain health and their length of life. The nuns with university degrees who continued to challenge themselves lived longer and had less dementia than the nuns who held less intellectually challenging positions such as housecleaning and food preparation. Those who continually challenged themselves mentally had more neural connections, enabling them to recover from disease and stay healthier and active longer (Ratey, 2001).

most known age-related change is menopause, leading to the loss of ovarian follicles because of reduced female sex hormones. Menopause typically occurs at around 45 years of age in females. Symptoms of menopause include hot flashes, mood swings, insomnia, weight gain, depression, and osteoporosis (Hackney, 2021). While women experience menopause, men go through age-related hormone declines, referred to as andropause. Although much loss in testosterone is due to age, males can also experience loss due to decreases in physical activity levels. Active older men can increase their testosterone levels through training (Hayes et al., 2013).

Hormonal regulatory systems also play an important role in the maintenance of homeostasis during exercise. Hormones are particularly important during vigorous exercise, affecting cardiovascular regulation in warm environments, fuel mobilization, and the synthesis of new protein (Shephard, 1997). The role of the endocrine system during aging has been studied extensively because of its effect on other systems and its relationship to quality of life. There are genetic factors that have been associated

---

TRY THIS

Brain Exercises

Exercise 13.5

Simple activities that cause a mental conflict or require the opposing sides of the body to perform opposite or different activities are mentally challenging. The following are exercises designed to integrate both sides of the brain while providing challenging movements for the whole body. With practice, they become easier. Try each of these activities seated or standing.

1. Repeatedly say the word *yes* while turning your head back and forth from left to right (as if you were saying no).
2. Say the word *no* while nodding your head up and down.
3. Swing your arms up and down while at the same time shaking your head no and saying the word *yes*.
4. Move your arms forward and backward while nodding your head up and down and saying the word *no*.
5. Move one of your shoulders up and down while moving the other one forward and backward.
6. Move your shoulders in circles going in opposite directions.
7. Move one shoulder in a circle while moving the other shoulder forward and backward.
8. Do regular jumping jacks; then switch to jumping with the feet apart and the arms together.
9. Try alternating from feet apart and arms together to feet together and arms together.

Were you surprised at the difficulty of some of these simple activities? You probably required more time to adjust to each change. Can you think of other activities that would challenge the brain?

---

with longevity and have been found to protect against age-dependent diseases and to promote exceptional health in later years (Barzilai & Gabriely, 2010). Physical activity and exercise are effective stimulants to the endocrine system and have been found to induce positive hormonal changes. The effect of physical activity and the endocrine system are so strongly linked that it is difficult to separate the age-related declines of the endocrine system from declines in physical activity levels (Hackney, 2021).

BODY COMPOSITION

Body weight tends to increase in adults until the age of 60 and decrease thereafter. In the United States, the mean weight of women in their 60s (the age at which they are at peak weight) is four and three-tenths pounds (2 kg) greater than that of women in their 20s; men in their 50s (the age at which they are at peak weight) is 4.9 pounds (2.2 kg) heavier than men in their 20s (National Center for Health Statistics, 2021). The increase in body weight is largely due to an increase in fat mass. In conjunction with the increase in fat mass with age is a redistribution of body fat. With age, body fat tends to be redistributed from the limbs to the abdominal area (Spirduso et al., 2005). Intra-abdominal fat accumulation begins in the 20s and increases through the 60s (Schwartz, 1990). Abdominal obesity (an apple-shaped body) is associated with a high risk for cardiovascular disease.

While fat mass increases with age, fat-free mass decreases with age. Fat-free mass, including the nonfat components of the body such as organs, muscle, bone, and skin, peaks in the 20s and 30s and then gradually declines. The decline in fat-free mass is largely attributed to muscle atrophy or wasting of the muscle. Decreases in fat-free mass are a result of reduced physical activity, osteopenia (bone loss), hormonal changes, and diet changes (Spirduso et al., 2005).

Exercise is the best defense against negative, age-related changes in body composition. Physical activity can increase muscle mass while decreasing fat mass, increasing resting metabolism, and improving mood state. Although dieting, in addition to physical activity, is preferred, replacing physical activity with dieting alone is detrimental. Dieting alone often leads to a loss in body mass because of decreased muscle mass, a reduction in resting metabolism, and a depressed mood state (Shephard, 1997).

SENSORY SYSTEM

Movement is profoundly affected by the ability to receive and interpret sensory information. How we move is determined by our response to the sensory information we receive. Infants who are blind take significantly longer to crawl, stand, and walk because, among other rate limiters, they lack the incentive that infants with vision are provided (Fazzi et al., 2002). Similarly, older adults who have progressive vision loss tend to walk more slowly, taking deliberate steps. Sensory losses begin in the 30s, and, although these losses generally do not affect everyday function until older adulthood, they do affect athletic performances. Although humans also receive sensory information from the senses of smell and taste, it is vision, audition, and proprioception that are essential to proficient motor performance.

Visual System

With age, many anatomical and physiological changes occur in the visual system. Age-related changes, some of which begin in the 20s, result in reduced function, which can negatively affect skillful performance and the learning of new motor skills. Additionally, changes in vision can have an impact on independent living in older adults who have increased difficulty with visual cues affecting driving ability and walking across a street without assistance, among other things.

Physiological and Anatomical Changes

The many age-related physiological and anatomical changes in vision include modifications of the cornea, iris, lens, and retina. With age, the cornea increases in thickness, resulting in decreased corneal sensitivity (Millodot, 1977), which may cause more tearing of the eye. The iris also undergoes many changes, including decreased thickness, increased rigidity, and reduced pigmentation, causing a degraded retinal image because of an increased amount of stray light (Weale, 1963). The pupil begins decreasing in size during the teenage years, which keeps more light out of the eye, while the lens grows throughout life and begins to become less flexible in adulthood. Changes in the lens reduce visual accommodation and the ability to focus clearly on close objects. **Accommodation** is the process that enables the eye to adjust and focus to produce a clear image. The retina also increases in thickness, affecting **peripheral vision** (vision outside of the center of gaze). The rods and cones experience age-related changes that affect vision in light and darkness, as well as color sensitivity. Changes also occur in the primary visual cortex, the area of the brain responsible for interpreting visual images. Table 13.1 lists age-related structural and functional changes in several of the main structures of the eye.

Table 13.1   Age-Related Changes in Vision

Eye structure	Structural changes	Functional changes
Cornea	Thicker and less curved	Increased sensitivity to glare; reduced refractive ability and more prone to astigmatism
Anterior chamber	Decreased size	Can lead to glaucoma
Iris	Pigmentation changes	Faded eye color
Pupil	Decreased diameter	Sensitivity
Lens	Thicker, denser, and less elastic	Impaired refractive ability and changes in color vision; cataracts can develop
Retina	Loss of rods and cones	Reduced adaptation to light and dark

Functional Changes

Functional changes result from the many anatomical and physiological age-related changes in the eye. Young adults are quite good at discriminating colors; they can see differences in up to 100,000 colors (Garzia & Trick, 1992). With age, color and brightness sensitivity declines, affecting the eye's ability to adapt to changing levels of light and dark. Older adults may find it particularly challenging to find open seats in a dark theater because it takes longer for their eyes to adjust.

One of the most common measures of vision is the Snellen chart, which is used to assess visual acuity (the sharpness of vision) by having people identify high-contrast letters of various sizes. Visual acuity decreases with advanced age (Saxon et al., 2010) and although it is the most common method of assessing vision, contrast sensitivity provides a better overall assessment (Garzia & Trick, 1992). **Contrast sensitivity** is the amount of contrast necessary to discriminate between an image and its background. Contrast sensitivity, which peaks at age 20 years and declines thereafter, is an important factor in many motor skills. A person who needs a lot of time to detect the position of a ball as it comes toward them will likely not contact it.

Eye movement control also declines with age, causing further difficulty with tracking moving objects and **visual search** (the act of directing attention toward important cues in the environment). Visual search is an important factor in moving skillfully because skilled performers' decision-making abilities and reaction times depend on their search strategies. Effective visual search strategies can be developed with instruction and feedback directing the learner to the most important cues. For example, experts tend to fixate on the most important aspect of the movement, whereas novices tend to alter their visual focus. **Fixation** is the focusing of visual attention on an object. By looking at unimportant cues, people often miss important information. Shank and Haywood (1987) found that during the windup of a baseball pitch, skilled baseball batters fixated on the release point, whereas novice batters alternated between the release point and the pitcher's head. Skilled batters were able to identify the correct pitch nearly 100 percent of the time, whereas novice batters identified the correct pitch only 60 percent of the time. It is important to focus on the critical cues, such as the release point, but it is just as important to ignore irrelevant cues such as the head (Coker, 2013). With age, visual search can become increasingly difficult, not only compromising skillful performance, but also affecting everyday activities such as identifying street signs and locating house numbers.

Older adults begin to have trouble with driving and mobility. Driving at night can be particularly challenging for an older adult because of increased problems with glare and night vision. The issue of driving in old adulthood has stirred up a lot of controversy, given that driving provides the primary mode of transportation for most Americans and provides a sense of independence to the older adult. Although driving ability is a complex motor skill, dependent on many factors including attentional focus, coordination, reaction time, processing speed, and sensory information, vision is one of the most important factors affecting driving performance. Loss of peripheral vision is particularly important (Linton, 2007). Research has revealed that twice as many older drivers with peripheral deficits experienced accidents and conviction rates than did older drivers without peripheral field deficits. Dynamic visual acuity (clearly seeing an object while it is moving) is also a risk factor for driving accidents in older adults (Owsley & Ball, 1993).

Auditory System

Hearing losses generally begin in the mid-30s but can occur earlier or be exacerbated by an overexposure to noise. Hearing loss that occurs from noise is called noise-induced hearing loss. Losses of higher-pitch tones are very common, particularly due to noise exposure, and begin to occur in adults as early as age 18 years. This loss, termed **presbycusis**, occurs due to hardening auditory nerve cells. High-pitched cell phone ring tones, such as the mosquito ring tone Teen Buzz, have been designed specifically for teenagers; most adults over the age of 20 years (including their teachers) cannot hear them.

Females tend to have markedly better hearing than males beginning at the age of 40 years (Schieber, 1992). This difference may be due, in part, to increased environmental noise in many male-dominated occupations. Hearing loss continues in both males and females throughout middle and older adulthood with many older adults

---

TRY THIS

Vision Screening

Exercise 13.6

The Amsler grid screening test is used to detect diseases of the retina such as macular degeneration. Macular degeneration causes a loss of vision in the central visual field due to damage to the retina. This loss can make facial recognition or reading nearly impossible. When taking the following test, wear glasses or contacts if that's what you typically do.

1. Perform an Internet search for the Amsler grid screening test and print out a copy of the grid. Hold the grid at eye level, approximately 15 inches (38 cm) away from your eyes.
2. Look at the dot in the center of the grid.
3. While maintaining your gaze, cover your right eye and continue to look at the dot.
4. Repeat this test covering the left eye.

Did you notice any changes, such as the dot disappearing or the squares blurring or changing shape? A *yes* answer to any of these questions could indicate damage to the retina and possible macular degeneration, a serious condition that could result in legal blindness if not treated.

experiencing an inability to hear high-pitch tones and some lower pitch tones. This makes it increasingly difficult to maintain conversations in noisy environments. Although age-related hearing losses are not life threatening, they do negatively affect quality of life. Hearing impairments can affect the ability to respond to auditory signals of danger but, more frequently negatively affect daily communication with family members, friends, and coworkers. Inappropriately, older adults with hearing impairments are sometimes even treated as if they have an intellectual disability or are demonstrating early signs of dementia (Saxon et al., 2010). When communicating with someone with a hearing impairment, at any age, speak face-to-face so that the person can clearly see you, speak slowly, and enunciate. Do not shout, and if you have a high-pitched voice, try to lower the pitch of your voice.

Somatosensory System

The somatosensory system provides information on touch, pressure, pain, and body positioning. Age-related declines occur in proprioceptors, impairing these functions. Proprioception, also known as kinesthetic perception, is the perception of the body and limb position and movements in space and has both a conscious and unconscious component. Proprioceptors also enable a conscious awareness of joint and body positioning. Proprioceptors function to protect overstretched joint capsules as well as enable posture at the unconscious levels, which occurs as you are sitting at your desk or standing. You typically are not consciously aware or thinking about maintaining your upright posture.

The vestibular system, located in the middle ear, provides proprioceptive information regarding head position and movement. Reduced vestibular function, which negatively affects balance, begins in the 30s with deficits potentially causing dizziness and **vertigo**. Vertigo is a balance disorder with signs and symptoms that can vary from dizziness and vomiting to difficulty standing and walking. A progressive loss of sensitivity to pain and temperature may also occur with age (Kenshalo, 1977) along with a reduction in tactile sensitivity, the lower extremities being more affected than the upper extremities (Corso, 1987). This loss of tactile sensitivity is due to an age-related decline in the number of touch receptors in the skin. With declines in vestibular function and proprioceptors in the lower extremities, balance is perhaps the most critical functional decline of the somatosensory system because it leads to an increase in fall risk. Physical activity is critical to improve fitness and proprioceptive function. Among other benefits, improved fitness and proprioceptive function will reduce the risk of falling, which poses a major health threat to older adults (Ferlinc et al., 2019).

SUMMARY

Aging is a unique experience for everyone and is affected by genetic factors, behavioral lifestyle, and past experiences. These factors interact, causing us all to age qualitatively differently and at different rates. Not only do adults age differently from one another, but their physiological systems also age at different rates too. For example, someone may experience a faster rate of decline in the cardiovascular system while a second person may have a quicker decline in the endocrine or nervous system.

This chapter outlined age-related changes in the skeletal, muscular, cardiovascular, nervous, endocrine, and sensory systems. These physiological changes are due to healthy aging (primary aging) and are not the result of disease or the effects of the environment (secondary aging). Although a physically active lifestyle can slow or delay many age-related declines, these declines are inevitable. The rate of decline in many areas increases at the age of 75 when healthy, physically active adults experience similar rates of decline; however, active, healthy older adults are starting at higher levels than their sedentary peers, which enables them to maintain their physical function much longer.

Maintaining a physically active lifestyle is a key ingredient in sustaining a high quality of life. Regardless of age, a physically active lifestyle reduces the risk of many secondary diseases, decreases the symptoms of secondary diseases, and improves physical and cognitive function. Clinicians, physical educators, fitness instructors, and coaches who work with older adults must understand the effects of aging on the physiological systems and the impact these changes have on movement. Because variability across individuals in older populations is much higher than in children and adolescents, it is perhaps even more important to individualize programs.

> **❯ ONLINE ACTIVITIES**
>
> The student material found in HK*Propel* includes exercises, labs, and videos to enhance learning and encourage practical application of important concepts.

LEARNING AIDS

Supplemental Activities

1. Primary aging includes age-related declines as a function of healthy aging, whereas secondary aging is the result of disease or environmental effects. For each of the systems discussed in this chapter, list several examples of primary aging and secondary aging.

	Primary aging	Secondary aging
Skeletal system		
Muscular system		
Cardiovascular system		
Nervous system		
Endocrine system		
Sensory system		

From P.S. Beach, M.E. Perreault, A.S. Brian, and D.H. Collier, *Motor Learning and Development*, 3rd ed. (Champaign, IL: Human Kinetics, 2024).

2. Research one of the following conditions: osteoporosis, arthritis, cardiovascular disease, hypertension, or stroke. In an essay, describe this condition and how it differs from primary aging (age-related changes that are not due to disease or poor behavioral practices such as smoking, a sedentary lifestyle, or obesity). Explain whether and how this condition could be prevented through behavioral changes.

Glossary

accommodation—Related to vision, the process that enables the eye to adjust and focus, producing a clearer image.

arteriovenous oxygen difference—The difference in oxygen content between arterial and venous blood.

atrophy—Muscle mass loss due to disuse.

contrast sensitivity—The amount of contrast necessary to discriminate between an image and its background.

dementia—A substantial loss in cognitive ability above normal age-related declines.

dynapenia—The age-related loss of muscle strength and muscle power.

exercise—A subcategory of physical activity that includes planned purposeful movement to improve or maintain one or more physical fitness components.

exercise economy—The oxygen cost of exercising at a particular velocity.

fast-twitch fibers—Muscle fibers that have a quick contraction–relaxation cycle and are well suited for short-duration, high-intensity activities such as sprinting and powerlifting.

fixation—The focusing of visual attention on an object.

frailty—A condition in which a person exhibits severe limitations in mobility, strength, balance, and endurance, resulting from weak and highly fatigable muscles following a long-term inactive lifestyle.

kyphosis—Curvature of the upper spine; can be the result of years of poor posture, weak back muscles, senile osteoporosis, or osteoarthritis of the vertebrae.

lactate threshold—The exercise intensity at which blood lactate begins to accumulate significantly above the baseline levels in the bloodstream.

neurofibrillary tangles—Neural fibers that are twisted together.

osteoarthritis—A degenerative joint disease that affects approximately 80 percent of adults over the age of 65; can cause pain and stiffness in the joint.

osteoporosis—A crippling disease resulting from low bone mass and poor structural bone quality; increases the threat of bone fractures.

peak bone mass—The highest bone mass acquired prior to the age of 30.

peripheral vision—Vision outside of the center of gaze.

physical activity—Any bodily movement produced by skeletal muscle requiring energy expenditure above resting rate.

presbycusis—Age-related hearing loss.

primary aging—Age-related declines associated with healthy aging.

sarcopenia—Age-related muscle tissue loss that occurs regardless of physical activity levels and other factors.

secondary aging—Changes that are the result of disease or environmental effects (e.g., emphysema or Alzheimer's disease).

senile plaques—Masses that form on the outside of neurons and have been related to memory loss.

slow-twitch fibers—Muscle fibers that have a slower contraction–relaxation cycle than fast-twitch fibers and are best suited for endurance activities such as long-distance running and swimming.

stroke volume—The volume of blood pumped through one ventricle during one contraction.

vertigo—A balance disorder with signs and symptoms that can vary from dizziness and vomiting to difficulty standing and walking.

visual search—The act of directing attention toward important cues in the environment.

14

KNOWLEDGE AND COGNITIVE CONSTRAINTS

CHAPTER OBJECTIVES

After reading this chapter, you should be able to do the following:

- Discuss the ways declarative, procedural, and metacognitive knowledge and skill execution differ.
- Explain Piaget's four stages of cognitive development.
- Describe the developmental relationship between knowing and doing.
- Understand the development of attention and information processing.
- Describe the relationship between memory and knowledge.
- Discuss strategies to improve memory for movements.

Form and Function

When Nya met her summer recreation group of 12-year-olds for the first time, she noticed wide differences in body size and shape. These were among the structural constraints discussed in chapter 12. She directed a couple of basketball activities and observed the expected differences in skill level. Then she asked some questions about basketball rules and strategies and was overwhelmed with the range of basketball knowledge in her group. Two of the children could articulate subtle differences in offensive strategies, while a couple of others were unaware that five players from each team were on the court at the same time! In high school, Nya made the varsity team and remembered that her teammates differed widely in their knowledge of the game and other "smart" things such as attending to important cues during the game and remembering the coach's instructions. One of Nya's teammates could recall a lengthy sequence of plays with remarkable accuracy and insight while most of the other players were not quite so sharp. How does cognition relate to basketball knowledge and basketball skill? More specifically for Nya, what changes in skill and knowledge about the game of basketball might she expect over the summer in this diverse group of 12-year-olds?

It is not surprising that many 12-year-olds will not comprehend the subtle aspects of instruction or team play. Sport-specific knowledge will likely assist performance, and some keen youngsters acquire an almost encyclopedic knowledge of their favorite sports. Moreover, some children develop the ability to understand, think, and conceptualize more quickly than others, which has advantages for both learning and performance. Likewise, those that are better able to attend to detail and focus on two things at the same time will likely have an advantage when performing physical skills. Finally, although it may not have occurred to you that we have a memory of movement, the ability of older people to ride a bicycle, after not doing so for many years, suggests that we do. Awareness of these factors should help Nya understand the skill and learning differences in her group of 12-year-olds. This chapter explores the developmental changes in functional constraints that affect the learning of physical skills, including changes in knowledge acquisition, cognitive development, attention, processing speed, and memory.

KNOWLEDGE CONSTRAINTS

Influential papers by Chase and Simon (1973) and Chi (1978) prompted an exploration of knowledge and its relationship to memory and development. Chase and Simon asked expert and nonexpert chess players to look at a chess board and remember the positions of the chess pieces. The pieces were then removed, and the participants were instructed to replace them in their original positions. Not surprisingly, the chess experts remembered the positions of the pieces better than the nonexperts did. However, this excellent memory was apparent *only* when the chess pieces represented patterns seen in a game. When the chess pieces were randomly placed on the board, the experts could not recall their positions any better than the nonexperts.

Interestingly, the experts did not have any advantage in basic abilities or mental "hardware" (Ericsson, 2003); however, their extensive knowledge of the game of chess was responsible for their remarkable memory of actual chess patterns. This result has been replicated in studies wherein expert athletes recalled patterns of game play in basketball, volleyball, and field hockey more effectively than sport novices (Starkes & Allard, 1991).

Chi (1978) extended this thinking about the role of knowledge by challenging the long-held assumption that the memory of adults always exceeds that of children. She used the previously discussed chess task and demonstrated that children who were chess experts could recall more chess positions than could adults who were novices in chess. Children can outperform adults when their knowledge is more extensive. This work supported the impact of domain-specific knowledge (regardless of age) on memory and led researchers to compare experts and novices in a wide range of areas, such as chess, sport and refereeing, music, and science, to gain insight into knowledge development and performance (Starkes & Ericsson, 2003). In this section, we focus on how knowledge acts as a constraint on physical activity and sport with specific emphasis on types of knowledge (see table 14.1) and knowledge development.

Types of Knowledge

Declarative knowledge is factual and conceptual information stored in memory that can influence the development and execution of skilled movement (Wall et al., 2007). Factual knowledge includes knowing the difference between a softball (which is not soft) and a Nerf ball (which is soft) or between an underhand throw and an overhead throw. Factual knowledge begins to develop in preschool through experience and facilitated by language. Conceptual knowledge developed by athletes and sport enthusiasts involves knowledge of the rules, equipment, and tac-

Table 14.1   Knowledge Influences on Movement Performance

Type of knowledge	Description
Declarative knowledge	Factual knowledge stored in memory: *My ball landed in the sand trap, so I'd better switch to my sand wedge on the next shot.*
Procedural knowledge	Knowledge underlying action such as decision making: *If the ball rolls slowly to me at third base and the runner on first base is fast and has a good lead, I will throw to first base instead of second to get the sure out.*
Metacognitive knowledge	A higher level of declarative knowledge about how one learns: *I really want to make this team, but my attention can wander, so I'd better place myself in the front of the other players where I can see the coach.*
Metacognitive skills	A higher level of procedural knowledge about how one performs: *I am not doing very well in this race now, but I will not stay with the leaders because I think they are going too fast and I know my strength is the final kick.*

tics of the game. This is affected by cultural norms. As examples, Canadians often have extensive knowledge of ice hockey, and the British have extensive knowledge of cricket. Declarative knowledge is often assessed using written or verbal tests.

Procedural knowledge is knowing how to do something. It underlies an action and includes anticipation, decision making, and response selection (Wall et al., 2007). Catching a ball is influenced by perceptual knowledge of the trajectory, speed, and size of the ball; cues from the thrower; and the position of the catcher in relation to the environment. Experts pick up cues earlier than nonexperts do for perceptual processing (Abernethy, 1991; Wall et al., 2007), while children from 5 to 12 years old show improvement in the use of cues to predict the direction of a ball (Lefebvre & Reid, 1998). Ste-Marie (1999) found that expert gymnastic judges were able to use perceptual information to anticipate future gymnastics elements better than novice judges. Moreover, the experts were able to make more accurate judgments for gymnastics elements that were anticipated correctly. French and Thomas (1987) studied decision making in basketball with an observation instrument that recorded whether the child shot, passed, or dribbled after receiving the ball; French and colleagues (1995) conducted a similar study in baseball. Both studies found that children with more expertise in their sport had better

skill execution and made better game decisions than those with less expertise.

The relationships between movement execution, declarative knowledge, and procedural knowledge are complicated. In chess, declarative knowledge is information about the game quite different from playing the game. One would assess procedural knowledge by having people play the game to determine the extent of their knowledge of how to play. In chess, researchers are not typically concerned with the act of reaching and grasping the chess pieces and moving them to a new location; however, movement scientists are very much interested in the act of reaching and grasping, not just declarative and procedural knowledge. Although some argue that procedural knowledge is synonymous with skill execution, it is wise to differentiate between movement execution, declarative knowledge, and procedural knowledge (e.g., French & Thomas, 1987; Kourtessis & Reid, 1997). If you have ever decided to execute a particular movement (procedural) but failed to accomplish it (execution)—that is, you didn't do what you meant to do—then you understand the distinction between procedural knowledge and movement execution.

Meta is a prefix that refers to a higher level. In the context of knowledge, it is a higher level of understanding knowledge. It is not just *more* knowledge but personal reflection on one's knowledge, awareness of how one acquires knowledge, and awareness of one's strengths and weaknesses. University students demonstrate **metacognitive knowledge** when they realize that they must study in a quiet environment to do well on a test, or when they find it easier to learn subject A than subject B. Wall and colleagues (2007) distinguished between metacognitive knowledge (a higher level of declarative knowledge) and **metacognitive skill** (a higher level of procedural knowledge). A swimmer may know that her kick in the breaststroke is fine but that she needs more work on her arm action; this is an example of metacognitive knowledge about action. With development, metacognitive knowledge becomes more "organized, coherent, and accessible" (Wall et al., 2007, p. 267). While metacognitive knowledge is an awareness of one's own strengths and weaknesses, metacognitive skills are especially important in selecting and planning goal-directed actions. Much of what we describe later as self-regulation could be viewed as metacognitive skills. A budding athlete who intentionally continues to problem solve to push his personal performance limits is demonstrating metacognitive, or self-regulatory, skill.

Knowledge Development

The development of knowledge typically progresses in the following order: declarative, procedural, and metacognitive (Brown, 1975, 1978; Wall et al., 1985). As children acquire language in the preschool years, they demonstrate factual (declarative) knowledge of early movements. Evidence of declarative knowledge and procedural knowledge then emerges. However, these knowledge types are related to specific actions (i.e., domain-specific knowledge); thus, the extent of knowledge is based largely on experience rather than age. One of the children in the recreation program mentioned at the beginning of this chapter might have extensive procedural and declarative knowledge of basketball from playing the game frequently. Therefore, just like the young chess experts in Chi's (1978) experiment who could remember the placement of pieces better than the novice adults could, the young basketball player may have more declarative and procedural knowledge of basketball—not only beyond that of her age peers, but also beyond that of her teacher. Metacognitive knowledge is the last to develop and requires abstract thinking as well as much experience.

Perhaps it is not surprising that sport-specific declarative, procedural, and metacognitive knowledge is better developed in people who participate extensively in a specific sport. We would expect that people who play baseball will know more about the game than those who do not. But what

---

TRY THIS

Exploring Types of Knowledge

Exercise 14.1

Establish a group with one or two of your classmates. In your group, pick a sport or physical activity you feel quite knowledgeable about. Your first task is to list examples of declarative knowledge, procedural knowledge, metacognitive knowledge, and metacognitive skill that are important to your sport or activity. For procedural knowledge, focus on decision making rather than skill execution. Second, identify professional players, or other highly skilled individuals, who are recognized as particularly strong in one of the types of knowledge.

about the armchair quarterback who might have much declarative knowledge about the game of American football but limited to no playing ability? Knowing and doing are obviously related, but precisely how they intersect and how they change over time is not clear. The relationship between knowing and doing is quite complex because knowledge and performance are dynamic, ever-changing factors.

Kourtessis and Reid (1997) supported the idea that children might learn appropriate actions before attaining the ability to execute them. They demonstrated that fundamental knowledge of catching preceded actual performance. In contrast, French and colleagues (1995) showed that in baseball players who were 7 to 10 years of age, skill contributed to expertise more than decision-making skills, possibly because baseball is a low-strategy sport. If sport experts have more declarative knowledge than novices, is it simply because the experts have more experience with the sport, or because they have more skill?

RESEARCH NOTES

Basketball Skills and Knowledge

French and Thomas (1987) published two studies that explored knowing and doing in basketball. In the first study, they examined declarative knowledge, skill development, and expertise. The participants were basketball players in two age groups: 8 to 10 and 11 to 12. Their coaches completed a questionnaire, rating each player's basketball ability, with the top third of each age group designated as experts and the bottom third as novices. All players completed a 50-item multiple-choice declarative knowledge test along with a test of basketball skills (dribbling, shooting, etc.). In addition, an observational instrument was used during games to assess control, decision making, and execution. Control referred to whether the player made a successful or unsuccessful catch. Decision making involved whether the player held the ball, passed, shot, or dribbled. Execution related to the success of the decision. The findings showed that the experts in both groups had better shooting skill and basketball knowledge and made more correct decisions than the novices did. The authors concluded that "development of sport-specific declarative knowledge is related to the development of cognitive decision-making skills or procedural knowledge, whereas development of shooting skill and dribbling skill are related to motor execution components of control and execution" (French & Thomas, 1987, p. 24).

The second study explored change in declarative knowledge, skills, and basketball performance (using an observational instrument) of 31 players in an 8- to 10-year-old youth basketball league over a seven-week season. The study also included a control group of 16 children with no prior basketball experience from middle school physical education classes. Basketball knowledge, cognitive decision making, and control components of performance improved; however, performance on the skills test did not change significantly, nor did the execution component of performance. Because cognitive knowledge and decision making improved, the authors concluded that "children are learning what to do in certain basketball situations faster than they are acquiring the motor skills to carry out the action" (French & Thomas, 1987, p. 30).

Williams and Davids (1998) tried to distinguish between **game experience** and **skills** by comparing high-skilled soccer players, low-skilled soccer players, and spectators with a physical disability who had never played the game but reported having watched hundreds of games. Arguably, the latter group had much experience with the game but minimal skill. Overall, the results showed that the high-skilled players had the most extensive declarative knowledge about soccer, suggesting that playing the sport was an important factor in developing declarative knowledge. Declarative knowledge is part of skill rather than only a by-product of experience. The relationship between knowing and doing is not simple, and at times an individual might know a lot about a given activity but have little or no actual skill to perform it. However, more research is needed to determine the best combination of knowledge and motor instruction.

Another aspect of the relationship between knowing and doing is the role of knowledge that accompanies skill acquisition. Experts have asserted for many years that well-learned skills become automatic, and we might assume that the impact of explicit knowledge would diminish or change with such automaticity. Stanley and Krakauer (2013) contended that even highly skilled performers continue to use knowledge as they seek new and improved actions to guide their performances. Knowledge is important for continued improvement and is used by elite athletes in practice sessions and preperformance routines in closed-skilled sports (Toner, 2014). Knowledge is also a critical dimension of sport education models (e.g., Hastie et al., 2013).

COGNITIVE CONSTRAINTS

Cognition refers to the mental processes involved in thinking and acquiring new knowledge. These processes serve several important roles; they help individuals attend to and understand relevant information in the environment that is important for decision making and motor performance; they also help acquire knowledge from past experience that will be needed in the future. For example, a patient undergoing rehabilitation for an injury will need to actively attend to his physical therapist while the physical therapist is explaining the different exercises of his program; otherwise, he may not be able to recall the exercises later when performing them at home. Likewise, a soccer goalie must understand that it is important to focus on the hip angle of an opposing player setting up a shot; otherwise, she may not be able to effectively anticipate which direction the opponent will kick the ball. The following sections focus on the development of cognition as well as life span changes in our ability to process, attend to, and recall information.

Cognitive Development

Jean Piaget was a brilliant Swiss child psychologist who published his first paper at age 10 and received his doctorate at 21 (Crain, 1985). His passion was examining the origin of knowledge, which led to his developmental studies of children's thinking. Experimentally, he observed youngsters in spontaneous activities and discussed with them their logic in arriving at, often, wrong answers. Younger children's thinking

---

WHAT DO YOU THINK?

Exercise 14.2

How do students' declarative knowledge, procedural knowledge, and metacognitive knowledge influence their ability to learn motor skills?

was not wrong, but it was quite different from the thinking of those who were more mature. In addition, Piaget recorded in detail and interpreted the activities of his three children. His widely discussed theory of cognitive development emerged from this body of work.

Piaget proposed four general stages of cognitive development (see table 14.2) to describe the qualitatively different ways children and adolescents think from birth to maturity (Crain, 1985; Ginsburg & Opper, 1969; Piaget, 1976; Shaffer, 1999). He suggested that children develop structures called **schemes** (or schema) for thoughts and action. The schemes are the result of children's actively constructing an understanding of the world based on their experiences (Shaffer, 1999). Because cognitive experiences early in life are movement based, motor development and cognitive development interact in important ways. The four stages of cognitive development proposed by Piaget are as follows: sensorimotor (zero to two years), preoperational (two to seven years), concrete operational (7-11 years), and formal operational (11 years and beyond).

In the first month of Piaget's **sensorimotor stage**, schemes are based on reflexes. By one month of age, children learn to self-initiate a movement like a reflex; for example, sucking in anticipation of a nipple. This is referred to as a sucking scheme. By four months, infants repeat actions they enjoy, such as bringing a hand into view to watch it. These actions occur very close to the body. In this early developmental period, infants learn that their actions affect their own bodies. From 4 to 10 months, this cause-and-effect link is extended outside the body; for example, the infant realizes that shaking a rattle results in a unique sound and that other actions, such as throwing food against the wall, get an interesting reaction from her parents. By one year of age, children are experimenting with a host of actions that produce many fascinating outcomes. A rattle can be seen, reached for, grasped, and shaken. Children also become aware that an object removed from vision still exists (object permanence). They find the object by thoughtfully searching around barriers and under coverings. By two years of age, children demonstrate a time lag before acting on a problem. Although the outcome remains a motor act, a thought process appears to precede the action. Of course, by age 2, children understand many words and requests (receptive language) and have been experimenting with expressive language, such has pointing at an object of interest, for almost a year.

Piaget's **preoperational stage** is characterized using symbols, such as images and words. Language can reconstruct a previous event, explain the present, or predict the future. Children at this stage initiate pretend play and develop logical thinking through action. In most cases, however, children at this age are not logical thinkers the way adults are. In Piaget's famous experiment on **conservation of liquids**, children were presented with two identical glasses

Table 14.2 Piaget's Four Stages of Cognitive Development

Stage and age	Description
Sensorimotor (zero to two years)	Sensory experience and movement coordinate to act on the world and generate knowledge.
Preoperational (two to seven years)	Thinking is symbolic but egocentric and often illogical from an adult perspective.
Concrete operational (7-11 years)	Thinking is logical but restricted to events experienced, seen, or heard.
Formal operational (11 years and beyond)	Logical thinking can now extend to ideas and hypotheses.

that contained the same amount of water (Crain, 1985). When water from one glass was placed into a taller glass, the children were asked which glass had the most water. They often responded that the taller glass had more water, suggesting that their logic was based on only one dimension—in this case, height.

It is not surprising that parents, therapists, and teachers who attempt to use adult logic with children are met with minimal understanding. In social situations, children are often egocentric in their thinking until quite late in the preoperational stage. *Egocentric* does not imply selfishness, but rather, that children are unable to view the world from a perspective other than their own. Thus, it makes little sense to the child to spread out on a playing field in the hope that someone will pass him the ball, or even to wait his turn on a playground. The child who tells the teacher on a Monday morning that her parents had a big fight during the weekend over the time she should go to bed cannot understand that sharing the story with the teacher is not desirable from the viewpoint of her parents. This stage is also the time when children move from **parallel play** (playing alongside peers but not interacting) to **cooperative play** (sharing a goal with other children, such as building a sandcastle).

Children in Piaget's **concrete operational stage** are more logical in their thinking regarding *real* objects or events based on their experience. They can master the conservation of liquid problem as well as other conservation problems; for example, they are aware that objects have more than one dimension. In sport, children at this stage can begin to think strategically about an opponent's intentions and the actions they need to perform to counter their opponents' tactics (Payne & Isaacs, 2008). They also develop a less egocentric view of the world during this period, because they find that they must adopt the perspective of others if they want to be understood. Thus, they

consider what they are saying and the needs of the listener. Rules of games that were unchangeable and determined by adults now can be viewed as plastic—modifiable to suit the needs of *all* individuals involved.

Piaget's **formal operational stage** begins at approximately age 11 and continues until adulthood. Understanding and thinking are no longer restricted to concrete objects; rather, the individual can deal with abstractions. In the conservation of liquid problem, children understand that water can be repoured into the original glass, and they know the outcome without performing the action. Arriving at the formal operational stage affects a wide array of cognitions, in areas from science to sport to the social values held by the individual. Those at the formal operational stage can deal with science problems systematically by exploring a wide variety of possibilities and hypotheses. In terms of sport, in a defensive situation, a player can picture the oncoming opponent's options and decide on an appropriate defensive strategy.

Formal operations allow adolescents to examine their future, as it relates to their aspirations. In relation to this thinking, they can begin to set longer-term goals and, importantly, recognize that certain actions are needed to achieve these goals. In the context of social development, prior to the formal operational stage, a child might brag about their parents being athletic and rich. During the formal operational stage, concepts of honesty, thoughtfulness, and integrity develop, positively affecting what the individual tells others. Some aspects of egocentrism may reappear while adolescents ponder the vast array of life's possibilities. Eventually, experience and adultlike thinking allow older adolescents to assess their own limits and cognitive abilities more accurately.

Piaget's theory helps us appreciate the cognitive functioning of children and adolescents. Regarding the nature-versus-nurture discussion, Piaget advocated neither a strict maturational nor a strict environmental position. Rather than viewing knowledge as something to be provided by teachers or parents, he believed that true learning comes from active discovery. Therefore, materials of interest to children are critical and should be tailored to their stage of cognitive development. The ages associated with Piaget's four stages vary because children of the same age often differ in terms of their development. Some of the 12-year-old children described at the beginning of the chapter may still be functioning in the concrete operational stage, whereas others may be well into formal operations. Thus, students in this group may vary a great deal in how they think and view the social and academic worlds.

Attention

Humans are limited in the amount of information they can process at one time. This is referred to as attentional capacity (see chapter 3 for more information on attention). If people try to process more information than they are able, interference occurs. When someone attempts to perform two activities at the same time (e.g., juggling while unicycling or holding a conversation while walking), interference will occur if attentional capacity is exceeded.

Interference can be either structural or cognitive. When an individual's physical structure limits actions, **structural interference** has occurred. Humans have only two hands, which limits the number of activities they can do at any given time. For example, typing while catching a ball would cause structural interference. In this example, the performance of one of the two activities would be impaired, most likely the typing. The person would have to briefly stop typing to catch and toss the ball before resuming their work. Vision is another structural limitation because we can focus on only one thing at a time. In a softball game, an outfielder cannot see the positioning of the runner if she is focusing on catching the fly ball above her. These limitations are not the result of attentional capacity; rather, they are limitations imposed by our physical bodies.

Given these structural limitations, when multiple activities are performed, any decrement that occurs is the result of limited central capacity, or **cognitive interference**. Attentional capacity, although limited, is flexible. With practice and increasing skill, the attention necessary to perform a particular skill can decrease. You may have observed that older adults often slow down when they are engaged in conversation. Most young adults can hold conversations while walking without interference, but if one task becomes increasingly difficult (e.g., answering a difficult question), even young adults' attentional capacities may be exceeded. This can cause them to either slow down or take longer to answer the question.

Attention is also selective. Selective attention is the ability to focus on selected sensory information while ignoring irrelevant

---

WHAT DO YOU THINK?

Exercise 14.3

Movement development and cognitive development are interacting processes. How might a child's stage of cognitive development influence his movement abilities in the following situations?

1. Playing a game of soccer with modified rules
2. Playing defense in basketball or hockey

information (Määttä et al., 2005). Selective attention can be either intentional or incidental (Eimer et al., 1996). We can choose to attend to something (intentional attention), such as reading a paper, holding a conversation, or learning to juggle, but our attention can then unexpectedly be directed to something else (incidental attention), such as a text message alert, our name being called, or the sound of a referee's whistle.

Development of Attention

The ability to manage attentional resources develops with age; thus, there would seem to be little doubt that children are less able than adults to perform simultaneous tasks. In other words, attention (from a capacity viewpoint) is greater in adults than in children. The intriguing developmental question is, *why* are adults more capable? The simple explanation is that overall capacity increases with age. A person is analogous to a container that changes over time, from a pint to a gallon. This capacity-increase view has generally not received much support (Thomas et al., 1993); rather, it is more likely, as Wickens and Benel (1982) concluded, that automation and deployment of attention skills explain developmental changes. Automation is the autonomous phase of learning described by Fitts and Posner (1967). It is the point at which motor skills can be executed with almost no attention. Because this occurs after considerable practice, automation is not determined solely by age or maturation but also by experience with the task. For example, excellent downhill skiers, young or old, likely require thoughtful attention only when they find themselves suddenly on dangerous terrain. Attention skills are strategies employed during the learning and performance of

WHAT DO YOU THINK?

Exercise 14.4

Looking at the illustration, list all the activities that the multitasker is completing. Give two examples of structural and cognitive interference that are affecting his performance on one or more of these tasks at any given time.

© Copyright Bonnie Mincu, Certified ADHD Coach. Bonnie Mincu is the founder of www.ThrivewithADD.com, a website of resources for Attention Deficit Disorder Adults. (Illustrator: Peter Fasolino, www.pfasolino.com).

tasks that improve with age and experience. For instance, children's memories improve when they intentionally engage in rehearsal strategies, such as rehearsing a telephone number presented to them verbally.

Newborns demonstrate some selective attention (Reynolds et al., 2013). Fantz (1963, 1964) showed that newborns systematically stop looking at repeatedly presented stimuli (1963) and that they look longer (suggesting preference) at patterned rather than at unpatterned forms (1964). This suggests early perceptual processing of visual information. By three months, there is rapid neurological development of the retina and visual pathways to the cortex, permitting expansion of the visual field, increased eye movements, and the ability to sustain attention for 5 to 10 seconds. By six months, infants can orient and focus on most environmental stimuli and are attracted to complex visual forms such as a caregiver (Reynolds et al., 2013). There are pronounced individual differences in the amount of time infants spend attending to visual stimuli. At 24, 36, and 48 months of age, those who spent less time attending to events (short lookers) were superior to those who spent more time attending to events on tasks of inhibition, memory, and cognitive flexibility (Cuevas & Bell, 2014). The researchers hypothesized that the short lookers were, likely, more efficient information processors.

As the brain (particularly the prefrontal cortex) develops during the second decade of life, the ability to control selective attention and inhibit the processing of irrelevant stimuli continues to improve (Wetzel, 2014). Selective attention is important for information processing and required for learning, thinking, remembering, and gaining competence in the world. Atypical development of selective attention is linked to disorders, such as ADHD (Atkinson & Braddick, 2012; Wetzel, 2014).

Thomas and colleagues (1993) reviewed the development of selective attention regarding motor skills. Ross (1976, as cited by Thomas et al., 1993) described overexclusive, overinclusive, and selective attention. Children five or six years of age are likely to be overexclusive; that is, they attend to a limited number of cues regardless of the importance of the task. Between about 6 and 11 years of age, children become overinclusive, directing attention to the complete display rather than focusing on task-relevant cues. Children older than 11 begin to selectively attend to the task-important cues and ignore the task-irrelevant cues. This is consistent with recent models of selective attention (Atkinson & Braddick, 2012; Wetzel, 2014).

Intentional attention declines with increasing age due to age-related reductions in attentional capacity (Van Gerven & Guerreiro, 2016). Envision an older woman engaged in an unfamiliar task, such as browsing the Internet. While searching for information, she is continuously bombarded with pop-ups and advertisements. Dealing with these distractions is likely challenging. Perhaps in addition to the many distractions on her computer, she is also in a noisy coffee shop with people coming and going, coffee grinding, conversations happening, and possibly even some background music. For this woman, a simple Internet search may become an overwhelming challenge.

Because of their reduced attentional capacity, older adults have been referred to as cognitive misers because they tend to focus specifically on one component of a task while ignoring others (Hess et al., 1998). You may have noticed this in an older adult, such as your grandfather, to whom you had to repeat a message multiple times when he was focused on another task, such as reading a newspaper or watching television. Older adults are even more impaired in their auditory selective attention (i.e., focusing on voices or music) when there is a visual distraction (Van Gerven & Guerreiro, 2016).

Focusing on one task while ignoring others is a compensation mechanism. Older adults realize they have fewer cognitive resources than they had when they were younger and must focus only on the most relevant information. Their ability to attend is also affected by other factors, such as the time of day; their abilities are significantly worse in the morning than in the afternoon (Lustig & Meck, 2001). For instance, older adults may perform worse in a morning game of tennis than in an afternoon game because they are more easily distracted in the morning when they attend to irrelevant cues rather than focus on the relevant ones, such as the ball speed and spin, the position of the opponent, and the angle of the hit.

Arousal and Attention

A strong relationship exists between arousal and attention. This is explained by the cue-utilization hypothesis (Easterbrook, 1959). (See chapter 3 for further information on arousal and attention.) This hypothesis states that attentional focus progressively decreases with increasing levels of arousal.

With low arousal levels, attentional focus is very broad. This is detrimental because it causes people to be easily distracted. For example, a cornerback in American football with a very broad attentional focus could be easily distracted by players on the sidelines, the crowd, or other environmental noise (irrelevant stimuli) rather than the movements and positions of the quarterback and receiver (relevant stimuli). As arousal levels increase, attentional focus becomes progressively narrower. At a moderate arousal level, irrelevant cues are ignored, and the person can solely focus on task-relevant stimuli. Some refer to this as being in the zone. If arousal levels continue to increase, attentional focus will become too narrow, and relevant cues will be lost. The cornerback whose arousal levels are too high may miss a cue from the quarterback, preventing him from blocking a pass. This progressive reduction in attentional focus is termed **perceptual narrowing**.

RESEARCH NOTES

Can Older Adults Improve Their Attentional Capacities With Training?

Older adults perform significantly worse in dual tasks (performing two tasks concurrently) than young adults do. This is not surprising given that older adults have significantly reduced attentional capacities, including selective attention and divided attention (i.e., the ability to attend to more than one sensory input at a time; Verhaeghen et al., 2003). Bherer and colleagues (2008) investigated whether training would improve older adults' performances in dual tasks. A total of 88 adults (44 younger and 44 older) performed a task involving two visual tasks (color discrimination [yellow or green] and letter discrimination [B or C]) and two motor responses. Participants were given one of three instructions on how to prioritize their responses: (a) respond to the color first; (b) respond as fast as you can on both tasks; (c) respond to the letter first. Each instruction was given twice per session. The results revealed that both younger and older adults significantly improved their performances on the dual tasks. Both groups also performed well on a slightly different task, indicating that this training program was generalizable. The authors suggested that cognitive plasticity (changes in the organization of the brain as a result of experience) in attentional capacity is possible at any age through training.

The cue-utilization hypothesis can explain the inverted-*U* hypothesis regarding performance and arousal levels. When the arousal level is too low, the person is distracted by irrelevant stimuli. Attention becomes progressively narrower with increased arousal. Performance initially improves with increasing arousal because irrelevant cues are being eliminated, helping the performer to focus on the relevant cues and not be distracted by irrelevant cues. Performance peaks at a moderate level of arousal. (The optimal level of arousal is task dependent.) If the arousal level continues to increase, the performer will begin to miss relevant cues. When the arousal level becomes too high, performance is degraded because the person's perception is too narrow to include all the necessary task-relevant cues. Once task-relevant cues begin to be eliminated, performance worsens.

Age-related differences are found with increases in arousal. Studies have shown that young, middle-aged, and older adults exhibit parallel higher arousal levels when performing in competitive events than relaxed settings as measured by heart rates and subjective anxiety ratings (Molander & Bäckman, 1989, 1994). Although the young adults performed similarly or even better with increased arousal levels, middle-aged and older adults performed significantly worse during competitive events than during training (Molander & Bäckman, 1994). These effects may be task or skill dependent, however, because less competitive anxiety has been reported in more skilled amateur golfers competing at a World Amateur Golf championship than in skilled golfers. The more skilled golfers also reported greater use of psychological skills such as imagery, positive self-talk, and goal setting, as well as less worry and negative thinking than the less skilled golfers did (Bert et al., 2010).

Molander and Bäckman (1994) examined the effect of age and increased arousal in miniature golf. Young adults performed well in competitive environments, whereas middle-aged and older adults performed significantly worse. Even though all age groups showed a similar increase in arousal levels from training sessions to competition, the middle-aged and older adults may have experienced declines in their performance because they had higher arousal levels during training than the younger adults had. It is possible that they were already in the zone during training, and so further increases in arousal led to performance declines (Molander & Bäckman, 1994). When their arousal levels increased even more during the competitive events, they were losing task-relevant stimuli. Since the young adults had lower arousal levels during training, the increase in arousal levels may have either kept them in the zone or brought them up to the zone.

The results of this study (Molander & Bäckman, 1994) also indicate that age-related changes in performance because of stress (arousal levels) occur during middle age and that no more declines occur in older age. The authors explained that this change may be due to a shift from an external attentional focus in young adulthood to an internal (self-reflective) attentional focus. Middle-aged and older adults reported being distracted more than the younger adults and spent significantly less time concentrating prior to swinging. This is especially surprising given that miniature golf is a self-paced motor skill wherein there is no pressure to initiate the swing early. Furthermore, although the young adults increased their concentration time in increasingly stressful situations, middle-aged and older adults decreased their concentration time. This may also be explained by a reduction in attentional capacity under stressful conditions with increasing age.

Information-Processing Speed

Information-processing speed also shows clear developmental trends. In a simple reaction time experiment, participants remove a finger from a response key when a light comes on. Adults outperform children, or, to put this more positively, children improve with age. In a more complex situation called choice reaction time, the finger is lifted from the key and moved to a second response key under two or more lights. Removing the finger from the initial response key is the same act in both simple and choice reaction time, yet choice reaction time is longer than simple reaction time presumably because the decision to move to a specific response key is processed before the lifting of the finger. Hick (1952) demonstrated that reaction time increases as more choices are presented (see chapter 3). Choice reaction time improves with age and, at higher loads of information, is particularly slower in children than in adults (Keogh & Sugden, 1985). Information-processing speed also improves with age on tasks involving feedback processing and decision making (Thomas et al., 1993). Thus, overall, children process information more slowly and less efficiently than adults.

As in the case of attention, the intriguing question is *why* are children slower on information-processing tasks? It is unlikely that children have slower nerve impulse conduction speed or motor capacity than adults (Thomas et al., 1993). Central information-processing mechanisms may account for the age difference in processing speed. Keogh and Sugden (1985) suggested that this may occur in any part of the processing chain (e.g., perception, recognition, decision making). More research is necessary to determine whether the slower reactions of children are due to slower perception of stimuli or slower decision making. It is also possible that children lack task-specific strategies and knowledge, which reduces their speed of processing (Thomas et al., 1993). Finally, several noncentral factors might be involved, such as attentiveness, incentive, and practice. Perhaps children do not perform as well as adults on such speed tasks because they are not attentive enough during testing, lack motivation to perform well, or do not have as much experience.

Memory

Memory, defined as the ability to recall things, was introduced in chapter 3, where we discussed short-term, working, and long-term memory. For over 100 years there has been research and speculation about memory development (Schneider & Ornstein, 2015). Knowledge of children's memory, especially strategies, such as rehearsal for encoding information, received a boost from Flavell's research in the 1960s (e.g., Flavell et al., 1966; Flavell et al., 1970). Strategies are defined as goal-directed and mentally effortful processes that enhance the acquisition and retrieval of information (Bjorklund & Douglas, 1997). Flavell and others demonstrated that strategies develop with age and that memory performance was closely aligned with the use of strategies. Older elementary school–aged children have shown themselves to be more intentional than younger children in recalling information; they actively used strategies, such as rehearsal, elaboration, and organization, to remember. Strategies become more complex with age and contribute to age-related memory performance differences (Schneider & Ornstein, 2015). Researchers have also discovered that a significant contributor to memory devel-

---

WHAT DO YOU THINK?

Exercise 14.5

How does the development of processing speed make you rethink teaching students?

opment is the knowledge of how one's own memory works. In this section we describe more fully the relationship between memory and knowledge, memory for movements, and age-related changes in memory.

Memory and Knowledge

Because long-term memory represents our personal knowledge, memory and knowledge have been categorized in several similar ways. While Piaget believed that understanding, knowledge, and memory were inseparable, Tulving (1985, 2002) distinguished between **episodic memory** and **semantic memory**. Episodic memory refers to remembering personal events, going back in time, such as your first day at university. You might recall details of your feelings, your parents' reactions, the people you met, and your first class. Semantic memory refers to general knowledge built from life experiences and learning. Semantic memory includes everything from the concept of school to the name of the current United States president. Tulving (1985) also included procedural knowledge—that is, knowing how to do something. He viewed motor skills as a form of procedural knowledge that allows us to achieve goals in our environment, not just talk about what to do. We noted earlier that skilled movement should be differentiated from procedural knowledge of that skilled movement.

Developmental psychologist Ann Brown (1975) described memory as three types of knowledge: knowing, knowing how to know, and knowing about knowing. **Knowing** is our knowledge base, which others have called semantic memory or declarative knowledge. From a developmental perspective, younger children are not expected to perform as well on memory recall tasks as older children, because the younger ones have less detailed knowledge that they can relate to the new information. When practitioners build links with previous knowledge, learners benefit. For example, a practitioner

might say, "Remember how you learned to step forward when throwing a ball? With the football, you have to do the same thing."

Knowing how to know refers to control processes and strategies used for deliberate learning. These activities move information or action from working memory to long-term memory. Strategies include rehearsing information, naming (attaching a verbal label to stimuli), grouping information (e.g., tennis instructors may suggest you scratch your back with the racket rather than provide a lengthy list of actions), and searching long-term memory. Knowledge acquisition depends on strategic learning, according to Brown (1975). Her research demonstrated that young children, and those with intellectual disabilities, must learn to use strategies and become more active learners. Therefore, games that intentionally teach strategies, such as how to get open to receive a pass in a football game, are important. Likewise, the common reminder when teaching the breaststroke—*arms, legs, glide*—specifies the important coordination sequences and is a strategy learners can, subsequently, use on their own.

Finally, **knowing about knowing**, also referred to as metamemory or metacognition (Flavell, 1979), is the knowledge of how our personal memory functions, which improves with age. For example, if young children are asked if they can recall a list of 14 foods provided verbally, they are likely to say yes; however, adolescents know that 14 items exceeds their working memory capacity (seven plus or minus two). Teenagers know more about how memory works, realizing that they can recall a list of 14 items only if they use a memory strategy, such as writing the list on paper or grouping similar food items into categories (e.g., fruits, vegetables, and grains). In a movement context, a person with excellent metamemory might know that she needs to read about a skill to learn the verbal labels to gain some declarative knowledge. Next, she would need to practice alone to get the idea of the movements and rehearse the declarative knowledge. Finally, she would seek out a teacher to provide feedback after some practice attempts. Others might know that they learn best by going to an instructor at the beginning. *Knowing how to know* develops after *knowing about knowing* and *knowing*.

Memory Strategies

Memory for movements may be assisted by visual imagery, verbal labels, rehearsal, intention to remember, and subjective organization (Magill, 2007). First, memory is influenced by the **meaningfulness** of the movement. Here, we are not referring to meaningfulness in a motivational context, such as how important the movement is to the person. Rather, we are referring to the similarity of new movements to previously learned movements. A meaningful movement is one that the learner can relate to because the new movement is like a movement that is already known. Meaningfulness can be assisted by **visual imagery** and/or **verbal labels**. For example, a swimming instructor could provide an image of picking an apple from a tree, bringing the apple down, and putting it into a basket rather than a detailed description of the biomechanics of the arm pull of the sidestroke. In a similar vein, if a new movement skill is like a previously learned skill, the instructor can provide that link for learners. For example, if a tennis coach is working with a skilled volleyball player, he might point out the similarities between the serve and an overhand volleyball serve.

Verbal labels can also improve meaningfulness. Winther and Thomas (1981) and Weiss (1983) showed that children as young as five years old can benefit from relevant labels. Verbal instructions for movements that include labels that match something well known are also effective, such as *Move your arm to the 2 o'clock position*. Magill (2007) offered four reasons images and verbal labels are effective: (a) they reduce the complexity of verbal instructions needed to describe all movements, (b) they make abstract movements more concrete, (c) they focus on the intended outcome of the movements rather than the movements themselves, and (d) they help in movement planning by using memories of previously learned movements. Verbal labels, also called verbal cues, are discussed further in chapter 18.

Most children begin to use rehearsal strategies between five and seven years of age and become more efficient and intentional in their use over the childhood and early adolescence years (Ornstein & Naus, 1978). The conscious rehearsal of movements is also developmental (Reid, 1980b; Sugden, 1978). Generally, young children do not spontaneously rehearse, but when they are instructed to use a memory strategy, performance usually improves. When presented with a sequence of movements to remember, five- and seven-year-olds who were taught to rehearse a subset of movements, rather than each movement separately, improved more than those who did not receive instruction (Gallagher & Thomas, 1984).

Liu and Jensen (2011) had 5- to 7-year-olds and 8- to 10-year-olds practice cycling on a stationery ergometer at three cadences (60, 80, 100 rpms). Following practice, they were told to reproduce each cadence and then asked how they remembered. The older children were superior to the younger children in terms of pedaling at the three cadences and used more strategies to remember. In a second experiment, the children with the most errors were assigned to either an experimental or a control group. The experimental group was instructed to count with a metronome beat while pedaling while the control group was instructed to remember how fast they pedaled. The metronome strategy resulted in more accuracy recalling cadences than the control group. Memory strategy instruction is also effective for those with intellectual and learning disabilities (Hoover & Wade, 1985; Reid, 1980a).

Another way to help memory for movements is to tell learners, explicitly, that they will be required to remember a particular movement, or series of movements. For example, they will be told, *OK folks, remember this sliding action because tomorrow, we will use it in an exciting folk dance*. Although incidental memory (nonintentional recall) occurs, knowing that a test of memory will happen later often promotes the use of intentional memory strategies. Memory can also be enhanced by allowing participants to develop **subjective organization**, that is, the arrangement of information into memorable parts. This is particularly useful in remembering a series of movements in sequence, such as dance steps or gymnastics moves. When faced with a sequence of movements, novices are likely to only see a long list of individual movements (Magill, 2007). For example, if there are 20 movements, the novice quickly becomes overwhelmed. With practice, two or three separate movements could be organized into one, thus reducing the number of movements to remember from 20 to 7, or even fewer. Because experts often group a sequence of 20 into fewer parts, it is no wonder they can remember all the movements more easily than novices. Their knowledge of dance and their use of subjective organization make remembering the steps easier because they really do have less to remember. In a study by Starkes and colleagues (1987), expert dancers recalled the eight steps of a sequence almost perfectly, whereas novices recalled about half correctly. Like the findings with chess players (Chase & Simon, 1973), when the dance sequences did not conform to typical and expected dance sequences, the experts were no better able to recall the sequences than the novices.

TRY THIS

I Know That I Remember . . . but How?

Exercise 14.6

We don't often think about memory for movements we perform; however, vision, the vestibular apparatus, and kinesthesis permit us to replicate movements we have experienced. Pair up with a classmate. One pair from the class should volunteer to go to the front of the class and do a quick demonstration that proves we can replicate previously experienced movements. One student stands facing the class with eyes closed. His partner lifts one of his arms to form an angle (45 or 90 degrees) to the side of the body, then lowers the arm and asks him to return to the previous angle. The angle will not be perfect, but it will approximate the angle experienced.

After you have seen the demonstration, face your partner, with each of you at a desk. Place your elbow and forearm on the desk so that your forearm crosses your chest. Close your eyes. Your partner will now slowly move your hand around in an arc with the elbow as a pivot point (really, a curvilinear path of the hand). After 20 seconds, your partner asks you to go back to the same spot. Your partner should select five distances to move your arm, such as 30, 60, 90, 120, and 150 degrees. Thus, there will be five trials consisting of (a) a movement, (b) 20-second pause, and (c) replicating the movement. After five trials, switch positions.

After each person has had five trials, discuss with your partner your strategies for remembering the movements. Did you use any of these strategies: visual imagery, verbal labels, rehearsal, intention to remember, or subjective organization? Did you use techniques other than these?

RESEARCH NOTES

Rehearsal of Movements by Children

Gallagher and Thomas (1984) used four participant age groups (approximate ages were 5, 7, 11, and 19) in a study examining movement rehearsal. The experimenters compared three rehearsal conditions: mature, childlike, and self-determined. The participants were required to grasp a handle that supported an arm and to move the handle in different angle and distance combinations. Specifically, the angles were parallel, 15 degrees, and 30 degrees, and the distances were 10 to 45 centimeters (4 to 16 in.). The experimenters determined the distances and angles. Essentially, participants made an initial movement that was constrained by the experimenter, remained at the end location, and then returned to the starting point and independently moved the handle to the end location once again. In other words, they tried to remember the first movement and reproduce it in the recall trial. The differences between the end location on the recall trial and the initial trial is considered an error (of one magnitude or another) in such motor memory studies. This is an example of a positioning task, typical of much of the research from that era.

Participants were presented with a series of eight movements to recall, but in any order they chose. The childlike rehearsal condition, considered passive, involved remaining at each of the eight movements for eight seconds. The mature, or adultlike, condition was more active; participants remained at the first movement end location for eight seconds. At the end of the second movement, they remained for three seconds, but then moved to the first end location for three seconds followed by the second location for an additional two seconds. Subsequent new movements were rehearsed for two seconds and the previous two movements for two seconds each, followed by two seconds at the new movement. Thus, rehearsal was more active than in the passive childlike condition, but rehearsal time was a constant eight seconds. The self-determined condition had participants move to the end point of a movement for two seconds and allowed them to use the remaining six seconds any way they wished. The results showed that the youngest children remembered the eight movements as well as the 7- and 11-year-old children did when forced to rehearse like adults. In addition, participants using the mature strategy tended to recall movements from short to long, whereas those in the childlike rehearsal group were more likely to recall in random order. Thus, imposing an organizational strategy was effective. Overall, active rehearsal was shown to be important in the recall of movements.

Age-Related Changes in Memory

Older adults often complain of memory changes with advancing age (Vestergren & Nilsson, 2011); however, objective measures of memory indicate that only some types of memory decline with age (Nyberg et al., 2012). Some of the changes associated with age-related memory declines were more strongly associated with mood rather than with age (Mowla et al., 2007). In addition, not all areas of memory decline at the same rate. Procedural memory, the type of memory that enables the acquisition and performance of motor skills, shows little change with age. This is likely because procedural memory is largely automatic and cannot be verbalized (Luo & Craik, 2008). In general, semantic memory also holds up well with age; however, certain things, such as names, can become hard to recall. The greatest age-related decline in memory is found in episodic memory, such as remembering personal experiences.

Recall and recognition are both long-term memory processes, but only one is affected by aging. **Recall** refers to retrieving long-term memories with very few cues, which requires much conscious effort. **Recognition** requires both conscious and unconscious processes and is considered easier than recall because it provides environmental support (Craik, 1986). An example of recognition is choosing a word from a list rather than remembering it without any cues. An intense memory search is not required for recognition, but it can be for recall. Memory tasks that are strategic or effortful are more difficult for older adults, such as *recalling* a particular word, a person's name, or items on a grocery list (Zelinski & Kennison, 2001). However, older adults are very good at *recognizing* items or names.

Adults can use many strategies to improve long-term memory.

• *Group it:* People can memorize up to about seven items well. The key to memorizing larger amounts of information is to group, or chunk, items. For instance, if you have a grocery list, group the vegetables, the meats, and the dairy. It is much easier to remember 15 items if you know you have five in each of the three categories. It's also much easier to remember a phone number if you are already familiar with the area code.

• *Repeat, repeat, repeat:* For information to move from working memory to long-term memory, it must be rehearsed, which is why it is so easy to forget the name of a person you just met. If someone says her name but you do not repeat it in your head or back to her, it will likely be lost. By simply repeating the name in your head once or twice or associating it with a sentence or something or someone familiar, you will be much more likely to remember it.

• *Make a jingle:* If you can make a tune out of the information or associate it with a familiar tune, you are much more likely to retain the information. For instance, if you have just met someone and know a song with the person's name in the title, you will probably not forget the name if you sing the song in your head. Think about it. You probably still sing the alphabet song when you need to alphabetize something!

• *Concentrate:* If nothing else, simply concentrate when you are receiving the information. It's a no-brainer that if you are not focused, you are simply not going to remember.

SUMMARY

This chapter outlined several functional constraints related to thinking and learning that help describe a person at a specific point in time. Learners have different abilities in knowledge, cognition, attention, processing speed, and memory that affect them in motor learning and performance situations. Being familiar with these constraints can help anyone interested in understanding the individual differences in a class of children or adolescents or in a fitness program for older adults. Same-age peers, no matter the age of the individuals, vary widely in both knowledge and cogni-

---

WHAT DO YOU THINK?

Exercise 14.7

What are some memory strategies you use when preparing for an exam? Are they effective?

tion. Some people have acquired several intentional memory strategies, and some have not. Constraints in attention are also influential. To complicate matters even more, the functional constraints described in this chapter change over developmental time for a given individual.

Children are less mature learners than adults. As children develop, their knowledge base increases; attention to relevant cues becomes more precise; skills become more automatized; decisions are made more quickly; and learning is more strategic and intentional. Thus, the wide individual differences noted by most instructors in a class of 30 individuals results from both structural and functional constraints that change over time due to growth, development, and learning. The diversity of the recreation class of 12-year-olds described at the beginning of this chapter can now be understood in a new light. These learners will differ in many areas that will influence their attention, skill, enjoyment, and learning.

> **ONLINE ACTIVITIES**

> The student material found in HK*Propel* includes exercises, labs, and videos to enhance learning and encourage practical application of important concepts.

LEARNING AIDS

Supplemental Activities

1. Arrange an interview with an accomplished occupational therapist, physical therapist, or athletic trainer. Ask this person to reflect on declarative knowledge, procedural knowledge, metacognitive skills, and metacognitive knowledge. Your interviewee might not use these terms per se, but can they see their daily work reflected in this conceptualization of knowledge? Do some areas of their work not fit into the knowledge perspective presented in this chapter?

2. There are many popular books on memory and how to improve it. Find one and see what it suggests. Are the strategies consistent with the information presented in this chapter? Are some different?

Glossary

cognitive interference—A decrease in performance because of exceeding one's attentional capacity due to a limitation in central capacity.

concrete operational stage—Piaget's third stage (ages 7-11) of intellectual development, in which children develop logical thinking that is restricted to events or things experienced, seen, or heard.

conservation of liquids—Piaget's experiment demonstrating that, unlike that of adults, children's logic is based on one dimension.

cooperative play—Play in which children strive to achieve the same goal.

declarative knowledge—Factual and conceptual information about knowledge stored in memory.

episodic memory—Memories that are associated with personal experiences and are related to a specific time; the ability to remember personal events.

formal operational stage—Piaget's fourth stage (age 11 or higher) of intellectual development, in which children develop logical thinking.

game experience—Knowing about a sport (i.e., declarative knowledge) without necessarily knowing how to perform the skills involved in playing the sport (i.e., procedural knowledge).

knowing—A person's base of knowledge.

knowing about knowing—Knowledge of how personal memory functions; also known as metamemory or metacognition.

knowing how to know—The use of control processes and strategies for deliberate learning.

meaningfulness—The degree to which a new movement relates to previous movements or knowledge.

memory—The ability to recall things from experience.

metacognitive knowledge—A higher level of declarative knowledge that includes an awareness of one's own strengths and weaknesses.

metacognitive skill—A higher level of procedural knowledge that is particularly important in selecting and planning goal-directed learning.

parallel play—Playing alongside peers but not really interacting.

perceptual narrowing—A progressive reduction in attentional focus with an increased level of arousal.

preoperational stage—Piaget's second stage (ages 2-7) of intellectual development, which is characterized by symbolic but egocentric thinking.

procedural knowledge—Knowledge of how to do something; this type of knowledge underlies an action and includes anticipation and prediction, decision making, and response-selection aspects of information processing.

recall—The retrieval of long-term memories with very few cues.

recognition—The identification of familiar objects, situations, or people.

schemes—Structures developed by children for thoughts and action, resulting from actively constructing understandings of the world based on their experience.

semantic memory—The ability to remember general knowledge built from life experiences and learning.

sensorimotor stage—Piaget's first stage (ages 0-2) of intellectual development, in which children coordinate sensory experience and movement to act on the world and generate knowledge.

skills—Learned abilities to bring about predetermined results with maximal certainty, often with a minimal outlay of time, energy, or both.

structural interference—Interference that occurs due to a physical structure.

subjective organization—The arrangement of information into memorable parts.

verbal labels—Words used to describe a part of a skill to improve memory.

visual imagery—Images stimulated by memory.

PSYCHOSOCIAL AND AFFECTIVE CONSTRAINTS

15

CHAPTER OBJECTIVES

After reading this chapter, you should be able to do the following:

- Discuss the developmental changes in Erikson's stages of psychosocial development.
- Discuss the developmental changes of self-representation based on Harter's stages.
- Discuss the development of perceived competence and its relationship with physical activity.
- Explain how self-efficacy develops and how professionals can promote it.
- Describe self-determined motivation and explain how it develops.
- Discuss the relationship between emotional development and physical activity.
- Describe self-regulation and its relationship to physical activity.

Quality Over Quantity

Kyla is an elite-level gymnast who trains with and competes for a local gym, where she possesses the highest difficulty score among any of her peers on the gym's team. Last year, she was consistently her gym's highest scorer and helped lead the gym to their first medal on the national stage. This year, a new elite-level gymnast, Shea, moved into the area and joined the gym's elite team, and quickly proved herself to be a talented, high-scoring, all-around gymnast. Before the first meet of the season, the team's coach had all the gymnasts compete in a mock meet with real judges to see where they stood. Though her difficulty scores were much lower than Kyla's, Shea won the mock meet with a significant margin due to high-execution scores. Confused by the discrepancy between her difficulty scores and meet results, Kyla asked her coach for feedback. The team's coach explained that while Kyla had the ability to perform more difficult and higher scoring skills than her peers, she did not execute her skills consistently during her event, and it appeared that sometimes she gave up and loosely performed significantly less difficult skills after making a minor mistake.

Once she saw that Shea was uncatchable in the last event of the rotation, it appeared Kyla gave up altogether. In reflection, Kyla recalled that Shea is always the first to arrive at practice and the last to leave. She appears driven and confident in her abilities, and she monitors her performances through postpractice journaling. Perhaps these attributes make up for lower difficulty scores in the form of higher and more consistent execution scores.

Participating in a sport is certainly influenced by structure (chapter 12) and functional constraints, such as cognition, knowledge, attention, and memory (chapter 14). However, it is also influenced by how people view themselves, how competent they perceive themselves to be as athletes, the extent of their motivation to become better players, their awareness of emotional factors in this quest, and their ability to regulate much of their learning. These thoughts and feelings are largely shaped by psychological factors, such as motivation, that have strong social and emotional influences that change over time. These powerful forces and experiences influenced Shea's approach and focus on gymnastics. This chapter outlines many psychosocial and affective functional constraints that influence an individual's motor behavior, such as self-esteem, perceived competence, self-efficacy, self-determined motivation, and self-regulation.

PSYCHOSOCIAL CONSTRAINTS

How we come to view ourselves is largely affected by our social experiences. We live in a social world from birth. Our initial interactions with our immediate caregivers are followed by interactions with extended family members, friends of our parents, and eventually our own friends and schoolmates. These increasingly extensive social networks influence our uniqueness, sense of self, and how well we manage in the world. We explore these psychosocial influences more completely in this section.

Erikson's Psychosocial Development Theory

Erik Erikson was born out of wedlock in 1902 in Europe and was abandoned by his father at birth. He became an artist, teacher, and psychoanalyst and eventually fled Europe for the United States when the Nazis gained power. He received an appointment at Harvard Medical School and went on to practice childhood psychoanalysis in Boston. Although he had studied Freudian psychoanalysis, he was also greatly influenced by work with Native American communities in South Dakota and California, civil rights groups, and combat soldiers (Crain, 1985; Shaffer, 1999). His views of psychosocial development became more social and more culturally influenced than Freud's. Erikson also stressed that children are active explorers of their world rather than simply passive reactors to biological urges; his research and experience culminated in 1950 with the first edition of his classic text, *Childhood and Society*.

Erikson adopted a life-span perspective in his work, which was unusual for the mid-20th century; his eight life stages extended into adulthood and old age. Each stage was viewed from the standpoint of a psychosocial crisis or conflict that had to be resolved to move to the next stage. Erikson (1963) described the stages very well and influenced thinking about social and emotional development as well as **self-esteem**. However, he has been criticized for not explaining the experiences that might resolve the

Table 15.1 Erikson's Psychosocial Stages of Development

Approximate age	Psychosocial conflict
Birth to 1 year	Basic trust versus mistrust
1 to 3 years	Autonomy versus shame and doubt
3 to 6 years	Initiative versus guilt
6 to 12 years	Industry versus inferiority
12 to 20 years	Identity versus role confusion
20 to 40 years	Intimacy versus isolation
40 to 65 years	Generativity versus stagnation
65 and over	Ego integrity versus despair

Adapted from E.H. Erikson, *Childhood and Society*, 2nd ed. (New York: W.W. Norton, 1963), 263-269.

conflicts and promote development (Shaffer, 1999). An overview of the stages of Erikson's psychosocial development theory are in table 15.1 and described in the following sections.

Basic Trust Versus Mistrust (Birth to One Year Old)

Basic trust by infants emerges from interactions with primary caregivers. Infants of parents who attend to feeding, cleaning, and comforting them learn to expect consistency and predictability in the world. The reliability and sameness of parent action produces a feeling of trust. Erikson (1963) claimed that "the infant's first social achievement . . . is his willingness to let the mother out of sight without undue anxiety or rage, because she has an inner certainty as well as outer predictability" (p. 247). An unreliable parent fosters a general sense of mistrust. However, some experience with mistrust can strengthen the understanding of trust because babies must also learn to trust themselves. Erikson suggested that babies may have an urge to bite while teething, but a grasp of the nipple rather than a bite is a sign of their trustworthiness. As they develop a sense of being trustworthy, infants form a sense of "being 'all right,' of being oneself" (p. 249). The social impact of self-concept begins very early in life.

Autonomy Versus Shame and Doubt (One to Three Years Old)

The basic conflict in this stage is to become autonomous in action but within social regulations. Children from one to three years of age learn to stand on their own two feet (literally and figuratively), dress and feed themselves, and express their needs and wants with language. Their explorations of the world and growing independence are sources of cognitive development (see the discussion of Piaget in chapter 14) and awareness of social and cultural expectations. A 12-month-old will make a mess as she tries to feed herself, and parents are likely to accept messiness as part of the process of gaining autonomy. By the time a child is age 3, however, parents are likely to insist on some degree of tidiness during eating; this is an early social regulation that is imposed on the child. Social expectations should not be acquired through shame and doubt. Shame is the conscious feeling that one is exposed and does not look good to others, and doubt refers to a sense of loss of personal control. Parents are primary social agents who should attempt to carefully guide the learning of social behaviors without promoting lasting shame and doubt. They must understand that "from a sense of self-control without loss of self-esteem comes a lasting sense of good will and pride" (Erikson, 1963, p. 254).

Initiative Versus Guilt (Three to Six Years Old)

At age 3, enjoyment of new physical and mental powers propels the child to action. Behaviors can be goal directed and very imaginative. As the child makes plans and tries to realize them, some plans come into conflict with others because the consequences of the actions are often unknown to the child and certainly not considered. There might be physically aggressive acts toward siblings or parents, as well as infantile jealousy and rivalry for parental attention. This may produce guilt. In other cases, the initial plan is beyond the child's capacities, and his autonomy is challenged by failure. As in the previous stage, the child must learn social regulations but now is ready, with the assistance of parents and siblings, to accept these as internal guides through self-observation, self-control, and self-punishment.

Industry Versus Inferiority (6-12 Years Old)

This stage occurs in the elementary school years when teachers and peers become important socializing agents. Children learn to win recognition by producing things in the wider context of school. The need to produce mobilizes them beyond play to acquire cognitive skills, such as reading and writing, as well as social skills appropriate to their culture. They learn to cooperate with others to achieve shared goals. Although Erikson did not mention physical skills, fundamental motor skills and game performance are valued in Western cultures and are sources of self-assuredness. In school, children are able to compare themselves to peers as never before. The danger is that a feeling of inferiority may result such that the child "considers himself doomed to mediocrity or inadequacy" (Erikson, 1963, p. 260). Teachers and coaches can contribute to resolving this conflict by truly valuing all students, encouraging a focus on personal improvement rather than comparison to others, and counseling those who are struggling to find niches of skilled performance.

Identity Versus Role Confusion (12-20 Years Old)

This stage of adolescence is characterized largely by a new search for ego identity (Who am I?) in the social world (Erikson, 1963; Shaffer, 1999). The crisis that must be resolved is role identity versus role confusion. This conflict occurs in the context of a rapidly changing body and sexual awakening. Erikson contended that adolescents seek a new sense of continuity and sameness related primarily to social and occupational identities. Peer influence is significant, and teenagers worry about meeting others' expectations and the career roles they will assume as adults. Their ego identity is a social matter because they wonder about how others perceive them and about their social role in a larger social world. The conflict of ego identity is resolved in part by identifying with others who appeal to them, celebrating personal accomplishments, and accepting their uniqueness in terms of strengths and weaknesses.

Intimacy Versus Isolation (19-40 Years Old)

Erikson believed that during young adulthood, people focus on exploring personal relationships. At this stage of life, it is vital for people to form personal and committed relationships. Young adulthood is a transitional period in which people acquire more responsibilities and liberties than they had during childhood and early adolescence; they move out of their parents' homes and start making their own decisions. This experience is often quite liberating and allows young adults to better understand who they are as individuals and how they fit with and influence other people.

Young adults also form relationships through group recreational and sporting experiences. Those who cannot work cooperatively on a team may feel a sense of isolation, whereas those who can develop relationships with a team or group members will likely feel a greater sense of intimacy. Keep in mind that Erikson's psychosocial stages are like building blocks. One must be in place before the next one is formed. People must form their own identities during adolescence (stage 5) before they can develop intimate relationships. Young adults who have not developed a strong sense of self often have less committed relationships and are likely to feel lonely and isolated.

Generativity Versus Stagnation (40-65 Years Old)

Erikson believed that during adulthood, people's focus shifts to their career and family. Adults during this stage are less interested in their own problems and more interested in how they can affect future generations by nurturing their own children, helping other children through education or other support systems, or having a positive influence on society. Adults interested in movement and physical activity may focus on improving society by increasing physical fitness or by passing on to their peers or even future generations the self-fulfillment of involvement in recreation and sport. Adults who shift their concentration from self-interests to the interests of others during this stage feel fulfilled because they have contributed to future generations in their local communities or globally. Successful adults experience feelings of usefulness and accomplishment, whereas adults who fail during this stage often have a shallow sense of self. Self-absorbed adults experience increased difficulties dealing with their changing capabilities through middle and old adulthood.

Integrity Versus Despair (65 Years and Older)

The final Erikson psychosocial stage occurs during late adulthood. This stage is marked by reflecting on one's life. Successful adults in this stage can reflect with a sense of fulfillment, whereas adults who fail at this stage experience much regret, which leaves them feeling bitterness and despair. Adults who reflect on their life with a feeling of accomplishment and sense of satisfaction attain a sense of integrity. Successful adults at this stage also gain a sense of wisdom that reaches beyond their own lives. In the movement domain, those who are successful can adapt their movements to their changing capabilities, enabling them to sustain an independent lifestyle. Rather than feeling despair about their declining function, they maintain an active lifestyle, continuing to walk, swim, play tennis, or stay involved in other recreational or sport activities. This allows them a much greater sense of freedom and enjoyment of life. Adults who sustain active lifestyles have accepted their changing physical capabilities and maintain their competence rather than feeling despair about their declining physical bodies. Those who feel despair often limit their physical activities, which results in further physical decline.

Several themes are apparent in Erikson's model of psychosocial development: trust, competency, autonomy, acceptance, self-concept, self-control, and social regulation. Although Erikson quite appropriately underscored the adolescent conflict of self-identity, the development of a sense of self begins much earlier and is explained more completely by Harter's (1999) descriptions of change in self-representation during childhood and adolescence.

Harter's Self-Representation Stages

Harter (1999) viewed the development of self as a cognitive and social process that is thus influenced by the interaction of our own thinking and evaluation of ourselves and feedback from others in a young person's life, such as caregivers, siblings, peers, teachers, and coaches. Harter acknowledged the distinctions between self-descriptions (what I am) and self-evaluations (how good I am) but contended that most research focuses on self-evaluations. The more common terms for self-evaluation are *self-esteem* and *self-worth* (Harter, 1999; Shaffer, 1999). Harter's six descriptive stages are very early childhood, early to middle childhood, middle to late childhood, early adolescence, middle adolescence, and late adolescence.

Very Early Childhood

Very young children focus on the physical aspects of self, such as the color of their hair. They know their favorite foods and the color of their house. They are likely to view themselves, for example, as good jumpers or runners, but they do not generalize this to viewing themselves as good athletes or good at sports. They do not have a judgment of overall self-esteem and do not differentiate competence domains such as academic, social, and physical appearance. When they are aware of specific behaviors (e.g., jumping or speaking), they are usually unrealistically positive about themselves.

Early to Middle Childhood

As children enter school in early childhood, they continue to overestimate their abilities and remain positive about themselves (LeGear et al., 2012), in part because they are not comparing themselves with others. They do not distinguish between ability and effort; for example, they might think, *If I am working hard, I must be a good swimmer.* During this stage, they do become aware that others are evaluating them and that some can perform better than others. They also understand that they can be good in several domains and are capable of personal comparisons over time. They might say to themselves, *Last year I couldn't swim the length of the pool, but now I can.*

Middle to Late Childhood

As children move toward later childhood, they can differentiate between additional competence domains such as academic, athletic, social, physical appearance, and behavior. With the aid of language and increased cognitive functioning, they are now aware of social comparisons as they interact with others in school and sport environments. They know others have an opinion of them, which influences their self-esteem positively if they know others have positive opinions of them. They understand competence within domains; that is, they can be a good swimmer but a poor baseball player. At this point children have a more balanced and accurate view of themselves. A global evaluation of self-esteem begins to emerge, such as, *Overall, I am a talented person.*

Early Adolescence

In early adolescence, domains of self continue to expand and include competence with romantic partners, close friends, and work. Children in this stage become concerned about how others view them. They may have multiple selves; for example, "cheerful and rowdy with friends, depressed and sarcastic with parents" (Harter, 1999, p. 62). However, they do not give these seemingly inconsistent descriptions of the self much thought. In addition, they are very sensitive to the opinions and standards of people in different contexts.

Middle Adolescence

Middle adolescents make even finer discriminations that include self with close friends, self with a group of friends, and self with mother versus self with father. They continue to realize that their behavior and feelings can be quite different with each group (e.g., tolerant with friends but depressed with parents). A sport example is an increased self-awareness of competence in basketball that suggests being outstanding in dribbling and shooting, but average in passing and decision making. Adolescents at this stage remain greatly occupied by what others, particularly peers, think of them. Some believe that they will not be popular if they are too studious. As in Erikson's identity and role confusion stage, adolescents struggle with different levels of self-worth in different domains, potential conflict and confusion from perceptions of self versus others, and discrepancies between real and ideal self-concepts.

Late Adolescence

Finally, late adolescence is characterized by a clearer sense of direction as personal beliefs, values, and standards are internalized. Older adolescents better understand their strengths, weaknesses, and potential and are less influenced by the opinions of others. They may realize they are ethical, desire independence, and are generally optimistic. Some conflict with parents may remain if parents' expectations and future hopes conflict with their own. Self-knowledge becomes internally rather than externally driven.

Perceived Competence

The development of self-representation deals with emerging self-esteem and related competence in various domains. The young toddler demonstrates an intrinsic interest in mastery of his world by spending hours playing with blocks, stacking them, lining them up, or placing them into and taking them out of a container. As success is achieved, feelings of competence and control develop.

Harter (1978) formalized these observations into a model of competence motivation. Recent research has demonstrated that perceptions of physical competence are important in physical activity involvement (Babic et al., 2014; Bai et al., 2015; Seabra et al., 2012), leisure participation in adolescence (Leversen et al., 2012), and enjoyment of physical education (Cairney et al., 2012) and it is one of the reasons children participate in sport (Bailey et al., 2013).

Competence motivation represents the fundamental desire of humans to be competent. This desire leads to participation in a domain (e.g., physical activities or a specific sport); such participation is referred to more formally as mastery attempts. Optimal challenges should exist; those that are difficult but realistic with respect to improvement with practice are preferred over those that are too hard or too easy. People who are very low in competence motivation may choose not to be involved (i.e., make no attempts at mastery) and remain inactive. Low perceived competence is related to reasons children drop out of sport programs (Balish et al., 2014). If a person is successful in a mastery attempt, an increase in perceptions of competence and control should result, as should an increase in positive affect, such as pride and happiness. When significant others, such as parents and peers, approve of and reinforce such mastery attempts,

---

TRY THIS

Guess the Stage

Exercise 15.1

Age is not always a perfect predictor of behavior or thinking. However, let's play a game about the self-representation stages. Pair up with a classmate; both of you should have access to the descriptions of Harter's six stages of self-representation. One person makes a self-statement that represents one of the time periods. The other person has to determine which stage is represented by the statement. The two can debate the answer because a single statement could arguably fall into two or more stages. Try three statements each.

perceptions of competence and control are enhanced as well. One of the consequences of heightened self-perceptions is the seeking of further mastery attempts with effort and persistence For example, *If I believe I am improving in an activity valued by Mom, Dad, and myself, I will tend to practice more with considerable enjoyment and persist in achieving my goals in the face of a setback.*

Weiss and Williams (2004) offered an overview of some of the critical developmental changes related to competence motivation. Competence domains are increasingly differentiated as children develop, which is consistent with the changes in self-representation discussed earlier. Toddlers have no sense of general self-esteem, but they can recognize skill in specific activities, such as being a good jumper. School-aged children are aware of competence in social, academic, and athletic domains and begin to view themselves with a general sense of self-esteem. Older adolescents add domains, such as romantic involvement and employment, to those recognized at younger ages.

Developmental changes in perceived competence are also affected by the level and accuracy of perceived competence as well as information sources used to judge competence (Weiss & Williams, 2004). Level and accuracy of perceived competence relate to whether perceptions are high or low (level) and the relationship between perceived and actual competence (accuracy). Preschool-aged children are notoriously inaccurate in their perceptions of competence, but they become more realistic by the end of elementary school. By ages 4 through 8, children's perceived competence may reflect actual competence (Barnett et al., 2015).

Perceived competence in academic areas generally increases with age, but research is equivocal with respect to perceived physical competence. Some studies show a positive increase with age while others show a decline, and some demonstrate stability over childhood and adolescence.

Among the reasons offered by Weiss and Williams (2004) for these contradictions are the public nature of physical performance and the unusual transition pattern through sport levels. Unlike most academic performances, physical skills can be viewed by anyone. As one practices in the gymnasium, performance is a public exercise. Moving through academic levels is standardized for all ages, such as moving from middle school to high school. Transition through sport levels, however, depends largely on skill as well as a willingness to devote more time to the activity. Three 11-year-old boys may be playing at three different levels of soccer (e.g., recreation, select, or travel). Thus, their comparison groups are very different, which may influence perceived competence.

Developmental changes in perceived competence may also be due to changes in information sources used to judge competence. Information sources include parent feedback, coach evaluation, peer comparison and evaluation, spectator feedback, performance statistics, and skill improvement (Weiss & Williams, 2004). Children under 10 years of age tend to rely on their parents, game outcomes, and spectator feedback. Even among 10- and 11-year-olds, parental encouragement and modeling have been shown to have a positive impact on physical activity and perceived competence (Maatta et al., 2014). Ten- to fifteen-year-olds use peer comparison, evaluation of peers, and coach feedback more frequently than younger athletes (Weiss & Williams, 2004). Older adolescents (aged 16-18) report greater use of self-referenced information, such as skill improvement and attraction to the sport, than younger adolescents. This is consistent with the development of self-representation discussed earlier as well as Harter's (1978) assertion that self-regulation (self-judgment, self-goals, and self-reinforcement) develops over time when parents and coaches encourage mastery performance and independence in learning.

RESEARCH NOTES

Does Perceived Motor Competence Influence Physical Activity?

De Meester and colleagues (2016) conducted a study to examine the influence of actual and perceived motor competence on adolescents' motivation for physical education and participation in physical activity and organized sport. Participants (n = 215; M age = 13.64 years, SD = 0.58) completed questionnaires on their physical activity levels, sport participation, motivation for physical education, and perceived motor competence. They were also assessed on actual motor competence using a body coordination test. The researchers first examined the relationship between actual and perceived motor competence and found four profiles among the participants: (a) low—accurate estimation, (b) low—overestimation, (c) average—accurate estimation, and (d) average—overestimation. Next, the researchers investigated the relationship of these profiles with motivation for physical education, physical activity levels, and organized sport participation. They found that participants with a low—accurate estimation profile had less motivation for physical education and lower levels of physical activity than those with a low—overestimation profile. Similarly, those with an average—accurate estimation profile were less motivated for physical education than those with an average—overestimation profile. Interestingly, those with a low—overestimation profile did not differ from those with an average—overestimation profile on motivation for physical education, physical activity levels, or organized sport participation. These findings suggest that increasing perceived motor competence in adolescents even among those with low actual motor competence is important for increasing motivation and participation in physical activity.

Self-Determined Motivation

Motivation to learn and participate in physical activity is obviously important. It influences whether people even begin an activity and how long they persist. As noted in the discussion of competence motivation, preschoolers and young children engage in play seemingly for no other reason than the sheer joy of participating. The two-year-old may play with pots and pans for hours, stacking, banging, and rearranging. Piaget's theory would argue that the children are learning important cause-and-effect relationships, linking language to actions, and creating and refining action schemes of exploring objects with the hands or the perceptual schemes of circles and rectangles. Harter (1978) suggested that they are motivated to influence their environment and develop perceptions of competence. The notion of competence was also central to the thinking of Deci and colleagues (Deci & Flaste, 1995; Deci & Ryan, 1985; Ryan & Deci, 2000), who were fascinated with such behavior of young children and proposed self-determination theory as an explanation. The theory has been expanded as a hierarchical model of intrinsic and extrinsic motivation by Vallerand (1997, 2007).

Self-determination theory includes three types of motivation:

1. **Intrinsically motivated behaviors** provide pleasure and satisfaction from participating, in the absence of

material rewards or constraints. A long-distance runner who enjoys the peace and tranquility of the outdoors is intrinsically motivated.

2. **Extrinsically motivated behaviors** provide a means to an end and are not engaged in for their own sake. Extrinsic motivation explains a host of behaviors, from completing additional fitness workouts to make a team, competing in a running event to earn a medal, or engaging in rehabilitation exercises to please a partner. If the behavior is extrinsic but valued by the person, and outcomes are viewed as positive, it is referred to as **self-determined extrinsic motivation**. If the behavior is based on avoiding negative consequences, it is called **non-self-determined extrinsic motivation**.

3. **Amotivation** is present when people do not see any relationship between outcomes and actions. In other words, people feel that whatever they do, nothing positive will result, so why should they bother? We certainly do not want children or adolescents to be amotivated toward physical activity.

Self-determination theory postulates that humans have basic needs to feel **competent**, **autonomous**, and connected with other people (i.e., **relatedness**). When these needs are met, psychological health is promoted; but when they are not met, psychological health is undermined (Vallerand, 2007). People engage in activities to satisfy these needs. For example, children who spend hours in free play do it of their own accord (autonomy); they gradually become more skilled at tasks (competent) and particularly enjoy the time when parents join in (relatedness). To the extent that play satisfies these three needs, it is considered intrinsically motivated behavior. Maintaining a learning environment that emphasizes play and fun will likely keep children motivated to participate and learn new skills. On the other hand, consider a child who begins snow skiing because he is told he must (i.e., no autonomy), whose initial attempts result in frequent falls and embarrassment (i.e., no competence), and who sees no one in the future with whom to ski (no relatedness). Without some intervention in the form of excellent instruction and support, this child is destined to become a dropout because his needs are not being met, and a state of amotivation may result.

When children and adolescents are sampling activities and sports, a strong emphasis on intrinsic motivation is desirable. Coaches and teachers should offer a choice of activities, encourage achievable goal setting, emphasize personal improvement, and provide positive feedback. These ideas are explored further in chapters 18, 19, and 20. Of course, people can participate for both intrinsic and extrinsic reasons. For example, someone can feel competent and really want that team jacket. If extrinsic reasons dominate as children become older, the chances of their dropping out of sport increase. Côté and colleagues (2003) reported that highly skilled sport experts recall early practice activities connected with fun and experimenting with new ways of solving movement problems. Thus, practitioners and parents should be very careful not to turn fun practice into dreadful work for children.

Motivation is also important for older adults. Dacey and colleagues (2008) found that the amount of physical activity older adults engage in is affected by their type of motivation for exercise. Intrinsic and self-determined extrinsic motivation were positively correlated with increased physical activity. Self-determined extrinsic motivators included health and fitness, stress management, and social–emotional benefits. Weight management and appearance were considered non-self-determined extrinsic motivators because they reflect a desire to attain social approval or enhance the ego. The results of this study revealed that appearance and weight management did not discriminate well between activity levels, and appearance became less important with advancing age. This suggests that weight management and appearance are least likely to induce long-term behavior change. Better motivators for older adults to increase physical activity levels could include the social benefits of a game of tennis with a friend or a group exercise class, or the fitness benefits of increasing flexibility through stretching exercises.

Self-determination motivation theory is used in many areas related to kinesiology. The needs of autonomy and competence predict exercise behaviors, and intrinsic motivation is associated with long-term adherence to exercise (Teixeira et al., 2012). In pedagogy, Sun and Chen (2010) promoted self-determination practices that lead to physical competence and relatedness with others but acknowledged some conflict with satisfying the need of autonomy in an institutional environment. They wondered whether students in physical education can be fully autonomous and how much autonomy is required to enhance learning. Van den Berghe and colleagues (2014) located 74 self-determination studies in physical education and recommended the usefulness of the theory to guide practice as well as the need for future research. Moreover, Sanli and colleagues (2013) reviewed 26 studies in motor learning and medical training and found at least one aspect of practice was controlled by the learner. The advantages of self-controlled learning are well documented and discussed later in this chapter. Sanli and colleagues (2013) proposed that feelings of autonomy and competence are the likely reasons for the beneficial learning effects of self-control.

WHAT DO YOU THINK?

Exercise 15.2

Classify the following individuals according to their type of motivation toward physical activity (amotivation, non-self-determined extrinsic motivation, self-determined extrinsic motivation, intrinsic motivation). Three examples are given. After you have classified each of them, devise an example of a person who would fit the fourth type of motivation.

1. Sandeep is a 68-year-old man who has recently started an exercise program that includes resistance training, cardio workouts, and stretching. He began the exercise program to maintain his functionality and reduce age-related physical declines.
2. Anya is a highly active 22-year-old who exercises six or seven times per week and regularly competes in local and regional running events. She thoroughly enjoys the highs she feels from both her workouts and the competitions.
3. Jose is a 10-year-old who recently joined a youth soccer league. Although he prefers skateboarding, he joined the league to appease his father, a former collegiate soccer player.

WHAT DO YOU THINK?

Exercise 15.3

1. Name specific ways to facilitate self-determination in students or clients.
2. How can self-determination theory assist in understanding clients who do not want to engage in rehabilitation exercises?
3. Provide examples of times you were intrinsically motivated, extrinsically motivated, and amotivated to engage in physical activity. How did you feel in each of these situations from the viewpoints of relatedness, competence, and autonomy?

Self-Efficacy

Bandura (1997) defined perceived **self-efficacy** as "beliefs in one's capabilities to organize and execute the courses of action required to produce given attainments" (p. 3). It is a belief that you can accomplish a specific task. Can you jump over that high jump pole at 6 feet (1.8 m)? Self-efficacy beliefs such as *I can high jump 6 feet [1.8 m]* are more specific than perceived competence beliefs like *In general, I am good at track and field compared to my peers.* Adults can distinguish these beliefs from each other (Rodgers et al., 2014). Bandura argued that there is little incentive to engage in an activity without the belief that you can achieve desired outcomes. Children with higher self-efficacy do seem to participate more in physical activity than those with lower self-efficacy (Chase, 2001). When self-efficacy is defined as confidence in the ability to be physically active in specific situations, it becomes the most consistently identified psychosocial determinant of physical activity in children, adolescents, and adults (Bauman et al., 2012). It is good to believe you can accomplish a task. One of the authors of this text admits that a 6-foot (1.8 m) jump is beyond his capabilities, and this lack of self-efficacy is motivation to remain on the couch rather than to jump.

Infants have little sense of who they are and must learn that their actions have consequences. Piaget's position (discussed in chapter 14) is that in the first four months of life, infants begin to recognize that they are controlling the hands in front of their eyes. A few months later, these same hands can grasp and throw. The sense of self continues to improve as children understand language and realize that others refer to them by a specific name. From ages 8 to 14, children may experience a decrease in their self-efficacy for sport and physical education as they become more accurate in their perceptions (Chase, 2001). As children age, parents and family members, followed by peers and then school activities, have major impacts on their sense of personal capabilities. Bandura listed four sources of self-efficacy: past mastery experiences (successful actions, which increase self-efficacy), vicarious experiences (viewing others and comparing oneself to them, which may enhance or diminish self-efficacy), verbal persuasion (having others express faith in one's abilities), and physiological and affective states (personal judgments of **arousal**, fatigue, and mood states).

Much of the research on self-efficacy and movement behavior has occurred in the sport domain. Feltz and colleagues (2008) provided practitioners with five techniques to increase self-efficacy in young novice athletes (see table 15.2). This reference also provides additional ideas for more advanced athletes and teams.

Table 15.2   Promoting Self-Efficacy in Novice Athletes

Technique	Description
Instructional strategies and performance aids	Break down skills, modify equipment, use physical guidance and performance aids to ensure some initial success. Gradually remove aids so that learners take some ownership for success.
Feedback	Give feedback based on personal skill acquisition, not in comparison to others. Provide realistic verbal persuasion about ability.
Modeling	Use peer models to convey skill, attitudes, and behaviors (see chapter 13).
Imagery	Encourage imaging or rehearsing successful performance once learners have developed the concept of the movement.
Goal setting	Establish specific, measurable, and realistic goals. This provides objective evidence of increased competence on a specific task (see chapter 18).

Based on Feltz, Short, and Sullivan (2008).

WHAT DO YOU THINK?

Exercise 15.4

How can you assist older adults in developing self-efficacy to help increase adherence to an exercise program?

Self-efficacy is also an important factor when people adopt an exercise program (McAuley, 1992). According to Bandura's **social cognitive theory**, self-efficacy determines (a) whether the person is even going to attempt a task, (b) how persistent the person will be amid challenges, and (c) the outcome (either successful maintenance of an exercise program or failure to adhere to the program). Adults with higher self-efficacy typically engage in physical activity longer than those with lower self-efficacy (Litt et al., 2002). Older adults have significantly lower self-efficacy than young adults have, perhaps because they perceive that they have reduced control in exercise situations (Dishman, 1994) and are afraid of injury (Stephens & Craig, 1990). Self-efficacy is such a positive mediator for physical activity that it can reverse common barriers to exercise. In a study of older Filipino adults living in Hawaii, lack of health became a motivator to exercise (Ceria-Ulep et al., 2011).

AFFECTIVE CONSTRAINTS

A newborn is not likely to have a sense of self separate from the environment; however, Piaget demonstrated that infants in the first two months of life begin to repeat pleasurable acts centered on their own bodies and to understand that they are responsible for some of the events that fascinate them (Shaffer, 1999). Their social world is primarily limited to immediate family members, and their crying as early as seven to nine months when held by strangers suggests that they distinguish between friendly and unknown people. They can recognize themselves in

a mirror by 18 months, and by 2 or 3 years may issue self-concept statements such as, "I am a big boy, not a baby" (Shaffer, 1999). The impact of their social world is powerfully demonstrated by the emergence of language early in the second year of life. Yet they may remain egocentric thinkers until the end of the preoperational stage (ages 2-7), unable to imagine that their worldview is different from others' worldviews. As a result, they have difficulty realizing that others in their world have different needs and desires from their own. As outlined in the sections on self-representation and perceived competence, children are affected by an increasing number of social agents over time that change in their relative impact; they develop a sense of self-esteem that can be strongly affected by physical competence; and they develop a repertoire of emotional reactions. We turn next to these functional constraints.

Emotional Development and Physical Activity

Participating in physical activities and sport competitions is often a significant emotional experience—pride, anger, satisfaction, and happiness can be experienced and expressed (Crocker et al., 2004). The model of competence motivation suggests that positive affect is an outcome of success at challenging activities and is related to competence motivation. Young athletes must also learn to control and express emotions that are socially appropriate and regulate them for optimal performance (Crocker et al., 2004).

In the first six months of life, if not earlier, children demonstrate primary emotions, such as interest, distress, anger, fear, joy, sadness, and surprise (Shaffer, 1999). Later, in the second year, they may display guilt, pride, envy, and embarrassment. Yet despite the honesty of a young infant's emotions, each society has "**emotional display rules**" (Shaffer, 1999, p. 394) that determine the circumstances under which emotions should or should not be expressed. Subsequently, infants and toddlers begin to learn how to regulate their emotions, which is called emotional self-regulation (Garner & Waajid, 2012). A strategy adopted from age 2 to 6 is closing the eyes to control an unpleasant emotional arousal, such as when looking at a scary shark. Learning to control one's emotions may become context specific with development, because all athletes realize that controlling their emotions is critical to performance (Crocker et al., 2004; Tamminen & Crocker, 2013).

Another important aspect of emotional development is recognizing the emotions of others, which facilitates social interaction. Preschool children learn to correctly interpret facial features, a skill that is called emotional knowledge (Garner & Waajid, 2012). Family conversations about emotions can help children deal with their feelings and to become aware of others. Children aged 3 and over begin to show awareness, and by age 5 can offer reasons a playmate is happy or sad. It may not be until age 6 or later that children understand that people can experience more than one emotion at a time.

Emotional knowledge and self-regulation are important skills to develop as children interact with others, as these skills are related to educational and social outcomes in preschoolers (Garner & Waajid, 2012). It appears that all children, from 5 to 18 years of age, make affective judgments about engaging in physical activities (Nasuti & Rhodes, 2013). Perhaps not surprisingly, pleasure and enjoyment are common emotions they seek from participation in physical activity. Physical activity programs are sometimes recommended as venues in which to learn positive emotional responses. Lubans and colleagues (2012) found evidence for improved emotional and social functioning in at-risk youth because of participating in outdoor education, sport, or fitness programs. The authors added that a bias on the part of the respondents might have contributed to the positive findings.

Attributions

Attribution theory (Weiner, 1985) has implications for understanding emotion and motivation in achievement situations (Crocker et al., 2004). According to Weiner, emotion is a function of the outcome of achievement attempts (i.e., success or failure) and people's attributions for the outcomes. Attributions are explanations of why things turned out as they did. Common attributions are personal ability, effort, task difficulty, and luck; in sport, they also include teamwork, injury, and referee decisions. For example, an athlete may experience happiness due to winning a game (outcome) as well as crediting the win to the time she spent in extra practice sessions (attribution).

Weiner (1985) suggested that causal attributions have three dimensions: locus of control, stability, and control. Locus of control can be internal or external—the former referring to causes related to one's own behavior (e.g., mental toughness) and the latter to causes that are beyond one's personal control (e.g., a lucky bounce or a teammate's play). Stability refers to attributions or factors influencing outcomes that are either stable from situation to situation (e.g., ability) or unstable (e.g., luck and effort). Effort is considered unstable because someone can try very hard and expend considerable energy one day but be much less involved on another day. The control factor refers to whether people perceive that they control the factors influencing outcomes (e.g., a belief that hard work and a personal trainer can help them make the team) or consider the results uncontrollable, such as, *Nothing I can do will influence my success.*

According to Seligman (1975), people who believe there is no relationship between effort and outcome (i.e., success or failure is unrelated to whatever they do) have developed learned helplessness. The person has minimal motivation to engage in the activity, but if forced to do so, he or she experiences **anxiety** and frustration. Learned helplessness may be domain specific. For example, a child who initially struggles to ride a bike, despite her best effort, because her legs aren't strong enough to push the pedals may give up on future attempts even when she gains necessary leg strength. Teachers and coaches can help learners by creating experiences that enhance success, even small successes, and encouraging them to take credit for the outcome, such as by pointing out improved times in track. Horn (1987) also recommended emphasizing improvement with effort and practice, goal setting, and accurate feedback.

In general, positive emotions, such as joy and pride, occur due to success in a valued activity that is attributed to personal factors (Crocker et al., 2004). Consistent with the competence motivation model of Harter, the positive affect resulting from success enhances competence motivation. Differentiating between ability, effort, luck, and task difficulty and hence making accurate attributions is developmental. Five-year-olds see no difference between effort and ability. By seven years of age, some children can make causal explanations in some situations (Caprara et al., 1997). Even at 11 years, children are limited in knowledge, the ability to process information, and reasoning (Crocker et al., 2004; see also the discussion of information processing in chapter 14). Although clear developmental trends have not been identified (Crocker et al., 2004; Haywood & Getchell, 2014), attributions in achievement situations emerge more clearly and are more accurate during adolescence.

SELF-REGULATION

Guidance and feedback from therapists, teachers, and coaches are important for those in rehabilitation, recreation, and sport settings. However, learning and performing motor skills also occur through self-regulation—that is, practice and play without formal instruction. This begins at a young age when infants and preschoolers learn that their actions can affect the environment and that they can learn new skills by watching others. As a student, have you ever decided to read or study for 60 minutes before taking a break to check your social media account? If so, you have engaged in two dimensions of self-regulation: goal setting (60 minutes) and self-reinforcement (checking social media). As a fitness enthusiast, have you recorded your times on 10-kilometer runs over a season or listed the dates and durations of your workouts? These are examples of self-monitoring.

Zimmerman (2000) suggested that self-regulation is an inherently human endeavor because it helps us adapt to our environment. Although it is similar to metacognition (knowledge of one's mental processes), self-regulation also includes knowledge of one's motivation (self-motivation beliefs) and emotional reactions. More formally, self-regulation "refers to the self-generated thoughts, feelings, and actions that are planned and cyclically adapted to the attainment of personal goals" (Zimmerman, 2000, p. 14). People must set goals for self-regulation to function. They must then plan thoughts, feelings, and behaviors to attain those goals while also monitoring them along the way and changing them as necessary if they get off course. Self-regulation is thus an attractive concept in motor learning and development. For example, a runner might set a specific time for a long race. However, during the race she realizes that she feels great and the humidity is low and thus decides to increase her goal and shoot for a personal best.

Zimmerman proposed a three-phase cyclical model of self-regulation: *forethought* leads to *performance or volitional control*, which leads to *self-reflection*. Self-reflection then leads right back to forethought as greater self-regulation becomes possible. In a movement context, the participant plans an action (forethought), executes it (volitional control), and reflects on its success (self-reflection) (see figure 15.1). The self-reflection processes provide information for the forethought phase of the next trial for a discrete motor skill such as batting a ball or later in the activity for a continuous motor skill, such as swimming.

Forethought ("Plans an action" in figure 15.1) consists of task analysis and self-motivation beliefs. **Task analysis** includes setting personal goals for achievement and creating general strategies for achieving those goals. **Self-motivation beliefs** refer to the person's valuing of the activity, degree of intrinsic interest in the activity, degree of self-efficacy or belief in the ability to achieve the goal, and expectation of the outcome or awareness of the benefits that will occur if the goal is attained.

Performance control and **volitional control** ("Executes it" in figure 15.1) are the self-regulation strategies applied during learning or performance that include self-control and self-observation.

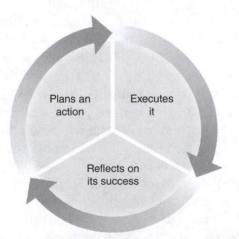

Figure 15.1 Three-phase cyclical model of self-regulation.

Adapted from *Self-Regulated Learning: From Teaching to Self-Reflective Practice*, edited by D.H. Schunk and B.J. Zimmerman (New York: Guilford Press, 1998).

Self-control includes self-instruction, such as reminding yourself while swimming a length that the left arm must come farther out of the water or focusing on your own motivation when you realize you might be attending to the noise of the crowd cheering for your opponents. Also included in self-control is the imagery of performance or imagining yourself performing an action, which is a common technique used by divers and gymnasts just prior to performance. Self-control also includes task strategies that can be altered during the game or event. **Self-observation** guides progress toward a goal, particularly self-recording of task-relevant events, such as the percentage of successful free throws during a basketball season, the types of food consumed during training, or independent steps accomplished in rehabilitation. Self-experimentation is a self-observation activity in which a new approach to performance or learning is attempted long enough to be able to perform a fair evaluation.

The final part of the cyclical self-regulation process is **self-reflection** ("Reflects on its success" in figure 15.1), which occurs at some point following a trial, a set of trials, a game, or a season. Self-reflection includes self-judgment and self-reaction. Self-judgment is when the person assesses the degree to which the goals were achieved. Also included in self-judgment are causal attributions, that is, explanations for why goals were met or not met as discussed earlier in the chapter. Questions might be *What did you think led most to goal success? Did you exert sufficient effort?* and *Did you try to accomplish the task without enough coaching?* Finally, self-reaction refers to being aware of one's degree of overall self-satisfaction. Even if the goal was not attained, a self-reflective person might ask herself, *Am I satisfied with my performance, with what I learned, and with the effort I expended?*

Is self-regulation important for learning and performance? Researchers have found that experts are more likely to engage in self-regulation than novices (Cleary & Zimmerman, 2001; Kitsantas & Zimmerman, 1998). Singer (2002) suggested that self-regulation is just as important as skill in performance. Self-regulation is sometimes called self-control in motor learning studies. These studies reveal advantages in skill learning when learners control aspects of practice (Sanli et al., 2013), such as when to receive knowledge of results (Chiviacowsky & Wulf, 2005; Janelle et al., 1997), the delivery of augmented feedback (Aiken et al., 2012), task difficulty (Andrieux et al., 2016), the relative timing of a movement sequence (Wu & Magill, 2011), physical guidance (Wulf & Toole, 1999), the amount of practice (Post et al., 2011), the amount of practice in a fixed time period (Post et al., 2014), and blocked versus random practice (Keetch & Lee, 2007). Even choices about the color of practice golf balls augmented skill learning (Lewthwaite et al., 2015). The importance of self-regulatory skills is not limited to athletic adults trying to improve or maintain their skills. All adults, regardless of age, health, or fitness level, need self-regulatory skills. For example, these skills are also important for the inactive adult who is trying to initiate and adhere to an exercise program or for the injured adult who is going through rehabilitation.

Self-controlled motor learning also extends to children. For example, 10-year-olds allowed to determine when they would receive knowledge of their results on a non-dominant hand throwing task performed better than children who received an equal number of feedback trials that they did not specifically request (Chiviacowsky et al., 2008). The children tended to request feedback after good trials, and the authors suggested that feedback after poor trials may be ineffective and that self-selected feedback appears to have a motivational influence. As Sanli and colleagues (2013) suggested, the positive impact of self-controlled learning might be due to facilitating feelings of autonomy and competence. There is also evidence that novices and those with learning difficulties show few signs of self-directed learning (Lloyd et al., 2006; Zimmerman, 2000), which suggests that self-regulation is very important in the learning process. However, it is encouraging to note that self-regulation appears to improve with instruction, including of those with a disability (Jokic et al., 2013; Kitsantas & Zimmerman, 1998; Zimmerman & Kitsantas, 1997).

How does self-regulation develop? There is not much research available on this question, but a developmental model from Zimmerman (2000) has proved helpful. The four developmental levels are observation (observing and listening to proficient models for major features of the skill), emulation (mimicking the model's style and skill with social assistance), self-control (mastering the skill of a model in structured settings), and self-regulation (adapting the use of the skill across changing environments and interpersonal states).

Observation, the first level in the development of self-regulation, includes witnessing

---

TRY THIS

Self-Regulate Your Studies

Exercise 15.5

In groups of two or three, review the strategies in each of the three phases of self-regulation and discuss how you might apply these strategies to improve your studying behaviors. The identified strategies can be ones you currently use or consider using in the future.

RESEARCH NOTES

Self-Regulation and Developmental Coordination Disorder

Lloyd and colleagues (2006) explored self-regulation in children with and without developmental coordination disorder (DCD). Developmental coordination disorder is a formal diagnostic term for those who have considerable difficulty performing movement skills at age-expected levels that is not due to factors such as cerebral palsy or intellectual disability. Some authors have described these individuals as awkward or clumsy. Developmental coordination disorder is associated with low self-concept and withdrawal from physical activity. The authors postulated that DCD might be related to poor self-regulation. Therefore, they compared a group of 10 boys without DCD to 10 boys with DCD. The mean age of the boys was 11.5 years old. The investigators used two tasks: a sport-specific problem-solving task of shooting indoors at a hockey net with a rubber puck and an educational problem-solving task of peg solitaire in which to goal was to remove all wooden pegs from the holes on the board by jumping over a peg and then picking it up. Participants were taught to use a think-aloud verbal report in which they articulated their thought processes during the activity. Their thoughts were transcribed and then categorized into self-regulation categories such as goals, knowledge, monitoring, emotion, and evaluation. Among the salient results was the finding that the boys with DCD expressed less knowledge about the shooting task, had fewer error correction plans, and had more total emotion and negative emotion and 25 percent had fewer action plans. On the peg solitaire task, the only difference was less planning ahead by the boys with DCD. The authors concluded that the results were consistent with a self-regulation deficit in children with DCD and that, apart from planning, the difficulties did not appear on nonmotor tasks.

skills of peers or older children or hearing about them from teachers. These are largely vicarious experiences that provide an image of the skills and awareness of rewards received by models. Thus, children may be motivated to engage in the activity (e.g., jumping down from a height, skiing, or roller skating) and will maintain some persistence during initial learning trials. Observational learning is described more fully in chapter 18. **Emulation**, the second level, refers to adopting a model's style of skill rather than mimicking exact response components. Thus, the learner performs a skill but in his own unique way and using self-regulatory skills. The motivated four-year-old will ice skate at the rink with a more upright posture than a skilled skater and with minimal glide on the skates.

This style maintains stability, but with practice, the body lean and glide increase. As we will see in chapter 18, research has demonstrated that children who fear water can benefit from exposure to models by emulating their coping strategies (Weiss et al., 1998). According to Zimmerman (2000), this produces sensorimotor feedback and internal standards of correct performance that are necessary for the next two steps. This process is like the creation of a generalized motor program, which has a recall dimension for initiating movements but also a recognition dimension for evaluating the movement based on expected sensory consequences.

Self-control, the third level of self-regulation development, refers to the use of one's own strategy as a planned and self-monitored process. At this level, people practice by themselves without a model present. Their personal representation or image of the skill is their guide, and their motivation is largely self-rewards and personal reactions to attaining standards. Hence, they may go to the gym and shoot at the basketball hoop while focusing on how they are performing (e.g., placement of feet, arms, and hands or how many baskets they get). The highest level is **self-regulation**, in which skills can be adapted to changing environmental demands (e.g., a hostile crowd, rain during a track meet) and interpersonal states. At this level, people need not focus on how they are performing but on their performance outcomes, such as how many of their shots are successful. With experience at this level, self-efficacy and self-motivation toward mastery should increase.

Research with motor and other skills has demonstrated that students can be taught more effective self-regulation and that they do progress through the four levels (Kitsantas & Zimmerman, 1998; Zimmerman & Kitsantas, 1997, 1999). Kolovelonis and colleagues (2012) used emulation and self-control instruction with fifth- and sixth-graders who were learning basketball dribbling. The success of the self-regulation groups in comparison to control groups provided support for the developmental model and evidence that self-regulation is amenable to instruction. Self-regulation must become a more prominent research topic in motor development for a clearer development picture to emerge.

The use of self-regulation processes, much like the development of expertise and knowledge, is primarily task dependent. The following recommendations may enhance self-regulation by children and adolescents (in part from Petlichkoff, 2004):

- Instructors should promote self-observation, which includes self-monitoring progress toward a goal and monitoring behavioral outcomes and processes such as cognitive strategies generated internally and available from models.
- Students should set process goals before outcome goals. This means focusing on skill improvement rather than a specific outcome such as 10 points in a game.
- When skills become automatic, students should shift to outcome goals that are within reach.
- To assist in self-judgment processes, teachers should expose learners to peer coping models rather than expert models (see chapter 18) and encourage them to focus on personal improvement (self-comparison) rather than comparing themselves to peers, which should help increase self-efficacy.

WHAT DO YOU THINK?

Exercise 15.6

1. Define the term *self-regulation* in your own words. Provide at least three examples of times when you used self-regulation to succeed in a sport or physical activity.

2. Imagine that you are teaching an elementary school physical education class. Provide specific examples of how you could help your students develop self-regulation. Now imagine that you are teaching a high school physical education class. How would you facilitate self-regulation among these students? Do your ideas differ for these two groups? Explain.

3. If you are an occupational or physical therapist, how might you include self-regulation in your interventions?

- Teachers, coaches, and parents should model self-regulatory strategies such as self-instruction and goal setting.
- Teachers should demonstrate and promote problem solving for tasks that have more than one movement solution, such as guarding an opponent one-on-one or executing an offensive two-on-one situation.
- Instructors should encourage self-reinforcement.
- Instructors should discuss attributions of success and failure with learners. What influenced the outcome? What can be done immediately to counteract a failure? What factors should be considered in the longer term?

SUMMARY

This chapter outlined several functional individual constraints that people bring with them to motor learning and performance situations. The constraints included psychosocial and affective constraints as well as those having to do with self-regulation. The psychosocial model of Erikson (1963) outlined the development of autonomy, initiation, and identity while simultaneously coming to terms with social expectations and regulations. Identity, or self-representation, was also the focus of Harter's description of self-esteem. There are many individual differences in the timing and ultimate level of achievement of Erikson's and Harter's phases, and thus people demonstrate considerable heterogeneity regarding perceptions of self.

Perceptions of competence affect physical activity, but researchers have recently argued that actual competence in motor skills is the most important factor leading to physical activity (Robinson et al., 2015; Stodden et al., 2008). Based on experiences with a host of social agents and environmental factors, self-efficacy and intrinsic motivation vary across the life span, and both affect performance. In a physical activity context, some learners show behaviors consistent with seeking competence motivation experiences and intrinsic motivation, while others have little interest in learning or participating in physical activity because their previous experiences and social influences have been negative. Finally, self-regulation represents a host of strategies that learners can adopt to self-direct learning. When learners are allowed to control aspects of practice, learning is frequently enhanced.

Kyla is the gymnast with the high-difficulty routines who does not execute as well as Shea, who has less difficult routines (see the chapter-opening scenario). Can you see some reasons for this difference? Despite the lower difficulty of her routines, Shea likely possesses a stronger sense of self, higher perceived competence and self-efficacy, and greater intrinsic motivation for the sport than Kyla does. Moreover, Shea is almost assuredly engaged in self-regulation of her practices. Overall, Kyla possesses the physical ability to compete at a higher level, but not the functional ones to excel.

> **ONLINE ACTIVITIES**

The student material found in HK*Propel* includes exercises, labs, and videos to enhance learning and encourage practical application of important concepts.

LEARNING AIDS

Supplemental Activities

1. Spend some time talking to an elementary school–aged child—a younger sibling, a cousin, or the child across the street. Ask the child to describe him- or herself. See which age period of self-representation most closely matches your interviewee's comments. Then, talk with an older person, perhaps an adolescent, to confirm development in self-representation.

2. Self-determination is a major motivational theory as described in this chapter. But it has other meanings. Search the Internet for pre–20th-century philosophical interpretations of self-determination; then find political meanings of self-determination that were important in the early 20th century.

Glossary

amotivation—Lack of any motivation; present when a person does not see any relationship between outcomes and actions.

anxiety—An emotional response to perceived threat; can involve cognitive concerns or physiological reactions.

arousal—A general state of activation or excitability.

autonomous—Engaging in a task by free will, without external influence from others; autonomy is one of three basic needs according to self-determination theory.

competent—Having the ability to realize success in a domain; competence is one of three basic needs according to self-determination theory.

emotional display rules—Socially defined circumstances in which emotions should or should not be expressed.

emulation—The adoption of a model's style of skill rather than imitating an exact response; Zimmerman's second level in the development of self-regulation.

extrinsically motivated behaviors—Behaviors engaged in as a means to an end and not for their own sake.

forethought—The phase of Zimmerman's cyclical model of self-regulation that involves planning an action; it consists of task analysis and self-motivation beliefs.

intrinsically motivated behaviors—Behaviors that provide pleasure and satisfaction from participation in the absence of material rewards or constraints.

non-self-determined extrinsic motivation—Motivation toward a behavior based on avoiding immediate negative consequences.

observation—Witnessing the skills of peers or older children or hearing about them from others; Zimmerman's first level in the development of self-regulation.

performance control—The phase in Zimmerman's cyclical model of self-regulation that involves self-control and self-observation.

relatedness—Being connected with other people; one of three basic needs in self-determination theory.

self-control—The use of personal strategies as a planned and self-monitored process; Zimmerman's third level in the development of self-regulation.

self-determination—A theory of motivation proposing that the basic needs of competence, autonomy, and relatedness drive people to action.

self-determined extrinsic motivation—Motivation based on extrinsic rewards.

self-efficacy—(a) The belief in personal capabilities to successfully execute the action required to achieve identified goals. (b) The belief that one can successfully perform a desired behavior given various instrumental barriers.

self-esteem—A self-evaluation of competency, successfulness, and worthiness.

self-motivation beliefs—The perceived value of an activity, the degree of intrinsic interest in the activity, the degree of self-efficacy or the belief in the ability to achieve the goal, and the expectation of the outcome or the awareness of the benefits that will occur if the goal is attained.

self-observation—The process that guides personal progress toward a goal, particularly self-recording.

self-reflection—The phase of Zimmerman's cyclical model of self-regulation that involves reflecting on the success of an action; it consists of self-judgment and self-reaction.

self-regulation—(a) "Self-generated thoughts, feelings, and actions that are planned and cyclically adapted to the attainment of personal goals" (Zimmerman, 2000, p. 14), or informally, the ability to practice and play without formal instruction. (b) A complex process whereby athletes or exercisers engage in voluntary goal-directed behaviors over time and context by initiating, monitoring, sustaining, and achieving certain thoughts, feelings, and behaviors (Weiss, 2004, p. 385).

social cognitive theory—A theory asserting that self-efficacy determines (a) whether someone is even going to attempt a task, (b) how persistent the person will be amid challenges, and (c) the outcome (either successful maintenance of an exercise program or failure to adhere to the program).

task analysis—The process of setting personal goals for achievement and creating general strategies for achieving those goals.

volitional control—A phase of Zimmerman's cyclical model of self-regulation; includes self-regulation strategies such as self-control and self-observation that can be applied during learning or performance.

SOCIOCULTURAL CONSTRAINTS

CHAPTER OBJECTIVES

After reading this chapter, you should be able to do the following:

- Differentiate between sex, gender identity, gender expression, and sexual orientation.
- Explain how gender-based stereotypes affect motor development.
- Describe racial stacking and tasking and why they occur in sport.
- Understand cultural influences on participation in sport and physical activity.
- Explain how disability can act as a sociocultural constraint on motor development.
- Describe how societal views on aging can affect physical activity engagement in older adults.

Fish out of Water

Elena, a recent college graduate, recently moved from South Florida to New Hampshire after accepting a job offer. While in Florida, Elena participated in a year-round tennis league with several of her friends and hoped to continue playing in her new state. However, she found it difficult to find anyone to play with in New Hampshire. Instead, most of her new coworkers spent their leisure time hiking, skiing, rock climbing, or mountain biking. Since Elena had little to no experience with any of these activities, she often refused invitations from her coworkers and, instead, continued to search for a tennis partner. However, after a few months of failed attempts to do so, she became frustrated with her newly acquired sedentary lifestyle and accepted an invitation to hike a nearby mountain with a couple of her coworkers. Although she struggled with some of the terrain and had to fight off black flies, Elena enjoyed the experience and decided that it might be time to embrace the leisure lifestyle of her new community.

A major tenet of motor development is that one's motor behavior changes with changes in constraints. Elena's shift from an avid tennis player to novice hiker was due largely to a change in location. Although the physical elements of the environment likely played a role (i.e., trading beaches and sun for mountains and snow), they cannot fully explain the change in motor behavior, because tennis courts are available in communities across the United States, including indoor courts to use during the winter months. Instead, it is more likely that her coworkers had a greater influence on her decision to start hiking due to their positive attitude toward and engagement in outdoor adventure activities. The influence of her coworkers is an example of a **sociocultural constraint**, which is an environmental constraint within Newell's model. Sociocultural constraints are socially and culturally constructed attitudes, beliefs, and stereotypes that can either encourage or discourage motor behavior. This chapter will explore five major types of sociocultural constraints and their impact on motor development: gender, race, cultural background, disability, and aging.

GENDER

Before we begin our discussion of gender as a sociocultural constraint, it is important that we understand the relevant terms. *Gender* is a term often used interchangeably with *sex*; however, these constructs are not synonymous. **Sex** is a classification based on biological determinants of reproduction. An individual who has XX chromosomes and develops a uterus, vagina, and ovaries is classified as female, while an individual who has XY chromosomes and develops a penis and testes is classified as male. **Gender**, on the other hand, is based on socially constructed roles, behavior, and norms associated with being male or female. For example, in Western culture, traditional views on gender would suggest that a child

who likes to wear dresses, practice ballet, and play with dolls is feminine, while a child who likes to wear a baseball cap, practice football, and play with trucks is masculine. An individual's perception of their gender is termed **gender identity**. Gender identity can be the same (cisgender) or different (transgender) from an individual's sex. For example, a biological male can identify as female, while a biological female can also identify as female. Moreover, gender identity has expanded beyond the dichotomy of male and female to include individuals who identify as both genders (gender fluid) or neither gender (genderqueer or nonbinary). The outward portrayal of an individual's gender through behavior, clothing, or other outward characteristics is termed **gender expression**. As with gender identity, gender expression can be the same as or different from one's sex. For example, a biological female who identifies as nonbinary may wear androgynous clothing. Moreover, some transgender individuals choose to change their physical appearance with hormone therapy or gender confirming surgery to better match their gender identity. Related to gender, **sexual orientation** is the romantic, physical, or emotional attraction to the same gender (lesbian or gay), opposite gender (straight), or multiple genders (bisexual or pansexual). Sexual orientation should not be confused with gender identity. For example, a biological male who identifies as female can be straight, gay, or bisexual.

Gender Typing and Stereotypes

The concept of gender is important to consider as a sociocultural constraint within motor development. As we learned in chapter 9, gender differences in motor competence for many fundamental motor skills are present in early childhood and continue to widen throughout development without intervention. For example, boys tend to have better endurance and ball skills, while girls have greater flexibility and fine motor skills (Thomas & French, 1985). One sociocultural explanation for gender differences in motor competence is **stereotype threat** (Steele & Arson, 1995). This theory proposes that individuals act in accordance with cultural stereotypes when they encounter a situation where they may be at risk of confirming negative stereotypes about their social group. Individuals do not need to adopt the stereotype; rather, the mere presence of the stereotype is enough to elicit changes in motor performance. For example, competitive female soccer players took longer to perform a soccer dribbling task after they read an article about the inferiority of female soccer players than when they read an article about the popularity of soccer (Hermann & Vollmeyer, 2016). Research using golf tasks has shown that stereotype threat also affects men and boys (Beilock et al., 2006). Interestingly, Chalabaev and colleagues (2008) found evidence that an additional mechanism may account for gender differences in motor performance in lieu of stereotype threat. In their study, negative stereotypes increased performance of the outgroup gender (i.e., the gender not associated with the negative stereotypes) on a balance task rather than decreasing performance of the in-group gender. This phenomenon is termed **stereotype lift**.

Another explanation for motor performance differences is **gender typing**, the internalization of gender-specific roles and behaviors derived from cultural norms that coincide with an individual's sex. These gender-specific roles and behavior are often based on gender stereotypes present in sport. Metheny (1965), one of the early researchers in this area, developed a classification system for socially acceptable sports for women and girls based on his work. Sports considered *inappropriate* for female athletes require bodily contact with an opponent, significant bodily force against a heavy object, and significant or sustained bodily projection through space. Sports considered *generally appropriate* for female athletes require force against a light object and assisted projection of the body through space that is aesthetically pleasing. Sports considered *completely appropriate* for female athletes require no bodily contact with an opponent, minimal force against a light object, and aesthetically pleasing bodily projection through space. Based on these guidelines, it would be acceptable for girls to participate in individual sports with an emphasis on aesthetics, such as gymnastics and swimming, and avoid competitive contact sports, such as basketball and hockey. Although Metheny's work was conducted over 50 years ago, recent research has found that these stereotypes, unfortunately, persist across a range of ages (Plaza et al., 2017).

Several theories address why gender typing occurs in physical activity. Bem's (1981) *gender schema theory* proposes that children develop a cognitive system for organizing and perceiving gender-based information that becomes integrated into their self-concept. This cognitive system, or schema, is learned from the society or culture in which they live. Thus, when individuals encounter an event, such as participating in a sport, the choice to do so will likely depend on how the sport fits their schema for their gender. Another theory that explains gender typing within physical activity is Eccles and colleagues' (1983) *expectancy-value model*. Within this model, an individual's choice to participate in an activity relies on their perception of two factors: performance expectations and subjective value of the activity. Since these factors are influenced by perception rather than reality, gender-based stereotypes developed from the social environment can affect an individual's choice. For example, a boy, given the choice between football and gymnastics, will likely see more subjective value in football because of its masculine qualities and see more potential for success despite having little actual success in the past.

Gender typing begins at a very young age. Knowledge of gender roles and behavior can develop as early as two years (Ruble &

Martin, 1998). Early gender typing is often manifested in gender-specific toy selection (Todd et al., 2018; see figure 16.1) and play behavior (Rose & Smith, 2018) that begins in toddlers and strengthens in preschool and elementary school. These early experiences can have a significant influence on the development of early motor skills, especially for girls, because more active play is often encouraged for boys. Gender-typed toys are often designed and marketed in ways that appeal to one gender or the other. Feminine toys tend to be aesthetically attractive and focus on nurturing or domestic activities, while masculine toys focus on movement, aggression, or violence (Cherney, 2018). In addition to encouraging gender stereotypes, these gender-specific toys often promote different skills. For example, feminine toys have been shown to promote verbal and social skills, while masculine toys promote spatial awareness and manipulative skills (Cherney, 2018). However, recent legislation in California (Gender Neutral Retail Departments, 2021) may help to reduce gender-specific toy marketing. Starting in 2024, large retailers located in the state will be required to include nongendered toy sections or areas within their stores regardless of the toy's original gendered packaging; otherwise, the retailer will face financial penalties.

Gender differences in play behavior are also evident. Although girls and boys both prefer same-gender play groups, girls tend to play in small groups, while boys tend to play in larger groups (Rose & Smith, 2018). Moreover, girls participate in more cooperative play while boys prefer rough-and-tumble play. As children get older, gender typing still exists, which can steer children and youth toward gender-specific activities (Riemer & Visio, 2003). Unfortunately, gender typing limits opportunities to develop a large repertoire of fundamental motor skills. For example, "masculine" sports such as football and baseball promote the development of object control skills, while "feminine" activities such as dance and gymnastics promote locomotor skills. As we learned in chapter 8, timely development of fundamental motor skills is critical for continued participation in physical activity.

Language choices, based on gender stereotypes, can also affect participation in sport and physical activity (Garcia, 2011). A well-known example of stereotypic language is the phrase *you throw like a girl*. This statement implies that girls cannot throw well and is usually targeted at men and boys to denigrate their throwing competence. This stereotype not only perpetuates an inaccurate stereotype regarding female

Figure 16.1 Gendered toys.

Adapted from E. Liederman, "Consumers Don't See Gender as Binary, So Why Are Toys Still Pink and Blue?," *Adweek*, last modified September 30, 2020, www.adweek.com/brand-marketing/consumers-dont-see-gender-as-binary-so-why-are-toys-still-pink-and-blue/.

WHAT DO YOU THINK?

Exercise 16.1

What types of toys did you play with as a child? Would you consider them feminine, masculine, or gender neutral? How did these toys influence your play behavior?

throwing competence (girls can throw well when given adequate opportunities), but it may also discourage girls from participating in activities that require throwing, thus limiting the continued development of this important fundamental motor skill. Another language-based stereotype that affects motor development is referring to a girl as a *tomboy*. This term is often associated with girls who have a more masculine gender expression and is used to denigrate their athleticism. Although some girls, particularly those who identify as male or gender fluid, may not be bothered by the term, but others may view the term as an insult and become less inclined to participate in sport. A third derogatory phrase is *that's so gay*. This statement implies that the activity or behavior in question is effeminate or worthless and reflects negatively toward a lesbian or gay sexual orientation. The use of this phrase perpetuates a negative and inaccurate view of gay and lesbian people as well as denigrating the activity being discussed. Educators and coaches should discourage the use of these phrases, because they have the potential to negatively affect an individual's self-worth, perceived competence, and engagement in physical activity.

Gender-Based Policy

Although individuals within a social environment (e.g., parents, peers, practitioners) can contribute significantly to gender-based constraints and, more precisely, limitations on motor development, formalized policies within a given community can also play a role—for better or worse. One major gender-based policy in the United States that had a significant impact on female physical activity participation was the introduction of Title IX. Title IX, as part of the 1972 Education Amendments to the Civil Rights Act of 1964, mandates that "No person in the United States shall, on the basis of sex, be excluded from participation in, be denied the benefits of, or be subjected to discrimination under any educational program or activity receiving financial assistance." Although this policy has a significantly broader reach, Title IX is often thought of within the context of sports. Specifically, this law ensures equitable access to sports, scholarships, and resources (e.g., equipment, facilities, and publicity) for male and female athletes within public school settings.

A common misconception is that equitable access to sport means that male and female athletes are provided with the same number of sports; however, this is not the case. In fact, there are three ways to satisfy the requirements of Title IX, referred to as the *three-part* or *three-prong test*. The school only needs to meet the requirements of one part of the test to comply with the law. The first part, *proportionality*, requires that the number of opportunities provided to male and female athletes be proportional to their enrollment in the school. For example, if 55 percent of the school's population is female, they should be provided with 55 percent of the sport opportunities. The second part, *history and continuing practice*, requires that the school continues to expand sport opportunities for the less represented sex. The last part, *full and effective accommodation*, requires that sport opportunities match the interest of the underrepresented sex. For example, if female students are interested in sports not currently offered at the school

RESEARCH NOTES

Gender Stereotypes and Object Control Skills in Children

Research consistently demonstrates that boys tend to be more proficient at object control skills (throwing, kicking, striking) than girls. One potential explanation for these differences is early development of gender-based stereotypes that may influence motor development of these skills. Although the influence of gender stereotypes on motor performance has been found in adults (Hively & El-Alayli, 2014), limited research exists on children. However, a recent study sheds some light on this matter. Miedema and colleagues (2021) investigated gender stereotypes of object control skills in preschool boys and girls to determine whether those stereotypes related to their object control skill performance. Participants were 40 boys and 44 girls (*M* age = 4.6 years old, *SD* = 0.58) from a Head Start program. They completed the object control scale from the *Test of Gross Motor Development–Second Edition* and an adapted version of the Children's Occupations, Activities, and Traits Measure. Like previous research, the girls in the study had significantly lower object control skill performance than boys. More interestingly, the results revealed a significant negative relationship between gender stereotypes for object control skills and object control skill performance for girls; that is, as gender stereotypes increased, object control skill performance decreased. However, the same relationship was not observed for boys. Thus, preliminary evidence suggests that some gender stereotypes may affect genders differently and interventions should target motor skills as well as gender stereotypes.

(e.g., golf or lacrosse), the school should add those sports to the athletic program.

Since its implementation, Title IX has had a profound effect on female sport participation. For example, female high school sport participation rates have grown by over 1,000 percent from 1971 to 2019 and the ratio of female to male participation has grown from 2 in 25 in 1971-1972 to 3 in 4 in 2018-2019 (National Federation of State High School Associations, 2019). Moreover, evidence suggests that the increased participation rates of female athletes because of Title IX are associated with increased levels of physical activity and a decreased chance of female obesity (Kaestner & Xu, 2006, 2010). Despite these positive developments, not all public education settings are in full compliance with Title IX. For example, historically Black colleges and universities and those located in the South tend to have large gaps in proportionality of

athlete numbers and expenditures (Yanus & O'Connor, 2016). Lack of full compliance is problematic because it slows the growth of sport participation and the physical activity levels of female students within these populations and areas, which tend to have higher reported rates of obesity when compared to other races and regions in the United States (Centers for Disease Control and Prevention, 2021).

Another issue related to Title IX concerns how protections are implemented under the definition of *sex*. More specifically, does sex extend to gender identity? This is particularly important for transgender athletes, because they often experience barriers to sport participation, such as noninclusive environments as well as discriminatory sport policies (Jones et al., 2017). Moreover, there has been a significant increase in state legislation that places restrictions on transgender individuals, especially youth, from participating in sports that align with their gender identity (Krishnakumar, 2021). Supporters of this legislation claim that transgender athletes, especially transgender females, have a physical advantage in female sports despite evidence to support it (Chen, 2022). However, recent developments at the federal level may change this current trajectory. In February 2021, the House of Representatives passed the Equality Act (2021), which "prohibits discrimination based on sex, sexual orientation, and gender identity in areas including public accommodations and facilities, education, federal funding, employment, housing, credit, and the jury system." The Equality Act applies to locations that provide recreation and exercise as well as any building that provides shared facilities, such as locker rooms. If enacted into law, this policy change could have important implications for transgender athletes by increasing sport opportunities and providing more inclusive environments.

RESEARCH NOTES

Acceptance of Transgender Athletes

Given the controversy regarding transgender athlete participation in competitive sport, a recent study by Tanimoto and Miwa (2021) examined factors that may influence the acceptance of transgender athletes in sporting events. The researchers recruited student-athletes from a Japanese university. They chose this sample to provide a different cultural perspective from Western societies on transgender issues. Of the 548 participants initially recruited, 373 responded to a questionnaire that measured four constructs: (a) acceptance of transgender athletes' participation, (b) belief in a just world, (c) athletic identity, and (d) transphobia. The findings indicated that trans men were more accepted than trans women and that transgender athletes who underwent hormone treatment, especially transgender women, were more accepted than those who did not. The greater acceptance of transgender women who received hormone treatment is likely due to the perception that testosterone is responsible for any physical advantage that transgender women may have in sport. Another finding was that acceptance of transgender athletes was dependent on the level of the event. Transgendered athletes were more accepted in children's and unofficial events than the more prestigious national and international events. The participants' large discrepancy in transgender athlete acceptance between recreational and competitive events may be due to their perceptions of winning as a form of social status and desire to maintain a level playing field. The researchers also found that individuals with a weaker athletic identity and a strong belief in a just world were more accepting of transgender athletes while those with a stronger athletic identity and strong belief in a just world were less accepting. Thus, it appears participants with a strong athletic identity view the inclusion of transgender athletes as a threat to fair play while those with a weaker athletic identity view the inclusion of transgender athletes as a form of social justice. Finally, individuals with higher levels of transphobia were less accepting of transgender athletes as those with lower levels of transphobia. Although this finding was expected, the impact of transphobia on acceptance was not more substantial than the other variables. The authors suggest this may be due to the East Asian cultural practice of viewing information holistically rather than analytically as in Western cultures.

RACE

Race is another sociocultural constraint that has important implications for motor development. Like sex and gender, the terms *race* and *ethnicity* are often used interchangeably with the distinction between them often being blurred. Thus, it is important to have a clear understanding of these terms before we begin our discussion. **Race** is a classification system based on an individual's physical characteristics (e.g., skin color, facial form) indicative of historical ancestry, while **ethnicity** refers to the individual's social group that shares common cultural elements, such as traditions, language, and religion. Although race is linked to biology and ethnicity to culture, they are both socially constructed ways of classifying individuals into groups. Classification is usually determined through self-identification. For example, an individual born in the United States might identify as Caucasian based on her skin color and French Canadian based on her cultural heritage. When race is measured (as with the United States census) it is commonly divided into five categories: American Indian or Alaska Native, Asian, Black or African American, Native Hawaiian or other Pacific Islander, and White. However, measures of ethnicity are often limited to a distinction between *Hispanic or Latino* and *not Hispanic or Latino*.

Within sport and physical activity contexts, participation levels often differ based on race and ethnicity. The 2020 Racial and Gender Report Card (Lapchick, 2020) reveals some clear racial disparities within professional and collegiate sport. At the professional level, Black athletes are overrepresented in basketball and football. In the National Basketball Association, 74.2 percent of the players were Black athletes, 16.9 percent were White athletes, and 2.2 percent were Hispanic athletes. In the National Football League, the figures were 57.5 percent Black athletes, 24.9 percent White athletes, and 0.4 percent Hispanic athletes. Conversely, White athletes are overrepresented in baseball and soccer; 62.3 percent of Major League Baseball players were White athletes, 28.1 percent were Hispanic athletes, and 7.6 percent were Black athletes. In Major League Soccer, 39.9 percent were White athletes, 30.4 percent were Hispanic athletes, and 22.4 percent were Black athletes. There are similar trends at the collegiate level; however, some of the discrepancies are greater or lesser than those at the professional level. For example, Division I men's basketball has more Black athletes, but to a *lesser* degree than the National Basketball Association (53.2 percent Black athletes, 25.5 percent White athletes, and 2.2 percent Hispanic athletes) while men's baseball has more White athletes but to a *greater* degree than Major League Baseball (71.4 percent White athletes, 10.9 percent Hispanic athletes, and 4.4 percent Black athletes).

Racial Stereotypes

One potential reason for racial differences in sport and physical activity participation is racial stereotypes—commonly accepted beliefs about a racial group. Racial stereotypes for athletes are often derived from explanations for their success and failure (Stone et al., 1999), with much of the focus on White and Black athletes. As early as the 1800s, scientists, practitioners, and sportswriters speculated as to why some Black athletes outperformed White athletes in sports traditionally dominated by the latter, such as boxing and cycling (Wiggins, 1997). In line with the nature–nurture debate, some explanations concerned unique biological traits, such as temperament and innate athletic ability, while others focused on environmental factors, such as training and resilience. Conversely, White athletes' success was primarily attributed to superior intelligence. Unfortunately, racial stereotypes have persisted over time and are often reinforced within the sport media.

For example, telecasts of the 2000 Olympics attributed the success of Black athletes to their innate talent while the success of White athletes was largely chalked up to their commitment (Billings & Eastman, 2002). Moreover, research suggests that repeated exposure to inaccurate racial stereotypes through the media increases an individual's implicit bias (Kobach & Potter, 2013).

Racial stereotypes have been shown to affect motor performance for White and Black athletes due to stereotype threat. Recall from our discussion on gender that stereotype threat happens when an individual acts in a way that confirms a stereotype due to a cognitive fixation on the stereotype. For example, a White athlete may perform poorly on a motor task when athletic ability, rather than intelligence, is emphasized because he becomes overly concerned with the stereotype that Black athletes are more athletic. Stone and colleagues (1999) used a golf task to examine stereotype threat with White and Black college students. In this investigation, White participants who were told that success with the golf task was suggestive of natural athletic ability performed significantly worse than those who were told that success was indicative of sport intelligence. Conversely, Black participants who were told that success with the golf task reflected sport intelligence performed significantly worse than those who were told success suggested natural athletic ability. In addition to affecting motor performance, stereotype threat has also been shown to affect the way individuals approach a sport or physical activity. In a study by Stone (2002), White athletes who were told that success at a golf task was indicative of natural athletic ability practiced less often than those who were told that success was suggestive of sport intelligence. This self-handicapping behavior could be a reason for poorer performance on motor tasks.

Racial Stacking and Tasking

Another explanation for racial differences in sport and physical activity participation is **racial stacking**. Stacking is the overrepresentation of a racial or ethnic group in specific roles or positions within sport or physical activity contexts. Historically, stacking results in a higher proportion of White athletes in central positions while minority athletes occupy more peripheral positions. Stacking has been documented in several sports and generally becomes more pronounced at higher levels of performance (e.g., moving from the high school level to the collegiate level). In baseball, White players are often overrepresented as pitchers and catchers, while Black players are overrepresented in the outfield. For example, Margolis and Piliavin (1999) found that 80 percent of Major League Baseball catchers in their study were White, while almost half of the outfielders were Black. Likewise, in collegiate football, Siler (2019) found that White football players are more represented in the central positions of quarterback,

---

TRY THIS

Racial Stereotypes in the Media

Exercise 16.2

Watch a sporting event or read a sport news article and record how the commentators or sportswriters discuss athletes of different races. What kind of language was used to describe athletes of different races? Were there any trends? Did anything surprise you? Did the descriptions of the athletes align with any racial stereotypes? Did you notice any new stereotypes?

offensive line, and tight end, while Black players are overrepresented in peripheral positions of defensive back and running back. Similar trends were found in women's collegiate volleyball, wherein Black players were overrepresented in the hitter position and underrepresented in the setter position (Eitzen & Furst, 1989).

Several explanations have been proposed to account for stacking within sport and physical activity contexts. An early idea called *sport centrality* (Loy & McElvogue, 1970) asserts that stacking results from deselecting minorities from central positions that require decision making and leadership skills. Since White athletes are believed to be more intelligent and, thus, better suited to central positions, minority players are left to occupy peripheral positions. Another explanation is the *outcome control hypothesis* (Edwards, 1973), which posits that stacking is based on how crucial the position is to the outcome of the game. Under this hypothesis, the more vital the position is to the outcome, the more likely it is to be occupied by White athletes. For example, kickers in American football and relief pitchers in baseball, key players at important times during game play, are commonly occupied by White athletes. A final explanation is *self-stacking* wherein minority athletes self-select stereotyped positions. This could occur to outperform the majority group to make a team or because they believe that opportunities only exist in certain positions. For example, a Black baseball player may choose to play in the outfield because he feels that those are the only positions available to him.

Stacking is not unique to the United States. In British cricket, Asian minorities are overrepresented in the batter positions, while Black minorities are overrepresented in the bowler position (Malcolm, 1997). In Australia, Aboriginal rugby players are overrepresented in peripheral positions, such as wing and center, rather than central positions, such as hooker, prop, and halfback (Hallinan, 1991). Coaches indicated that Aboriginal positions required more speed and quickness than non-Aboriginal positions, while non-Aboriginal positions required more leadership and cognitive abilities. These stereotypical perspectives mimic those found when examining Black and White player positions in the United States. Likewise, in postapartheid South Africa, on rugby teams, White players are more likely to occupy central positions, while minorities tend to occupy peripheral positions (Cros, 2013). The South African government has attempted to increase representation of non-White players on many of their national sport teams through a quota system, which has similarities to affirmative action in the United States. However, there has been much debate about the use of quotas to end racial segregation in sport. Those who support quotas argue that they are necessary to ensure players have equal opportunities to make the national team, while those who oppose contend that player selection should be based solely on merit and change in racial equity should come from the grassroots efforts.

Although stacking still exists, some positions have become more racially diverse. For example, Coleman and Scott (2018) found a

---

WHAT DO YOU THINK?

Exercise 16.3

Do you think quotas should be used to reduce racial segregation in sport? Why or why not? What are some additional ways to encourage racial equity within sport?

0.47 percent yearly increase in Black quarterbacks in the National Football League between 1990 and 2016. Even so, racial stereotypes that can affect a player's performance persist. One way this has occurred is through **racial tasking**. Racial tasking is when players in the same position are instructed or coached to perform different tasks based on their race. In football, racial tasking has been documented within the quarterback position. Specifically, Bopp and Sagas (2014) found that White quarterbacks tend to pass the ball more than Black quarterbacks, while Black quarterbacks tend to run the ball more than White quarterbacks. This likely occurs due to the idea that pass attempts require more mental prowess (e.g., reading the field) while rush attempts require more physicality, which aligns with the racial stereotypes for White and Black players discussed earlier. The deemphasis on passing by instructors and coaches for Black quarterbacks limits their opportunities to develop strategic and decision-making skills that are vital for the quarterback position, which may affect how well they progress at the sport.

CULTURAL BACKGROUND

Sport and physical activity participation varies across the world. For example, adults in Africa have the highest participation rates in running, netball, tennis, cycling, and stair climbing, while adults in Europe participate most in soccer, running, swimming, resistance training, and cycling (Hulteen et al., 2017). This worldwide variation is also evident with adolescents. Adolescents in the Americas participate the most in soccer, bowling, baseball, swimming, and volleyball, while those in the Western Pacific countries (e.g., Australia, New Zealand, and China) participate most in running, swimming, walking, cycling, and basketball (Hulteen et al., 2017). Soccer (referred to as football by most countries outside of North America) is the most popular sport with a global following of 4 billion people. Although it is played throughout the world, its popularity is largely concentrated in Europe, Africa, and Central and South America (World Atlas, 2021). Similarly, the popularity of cricket, the second most popular sport with 2.5 billion fans, stems mainly from the United Kingdom, India, Pakistan, and Australia. Even within a single country, sport and physical activity participation rates vary by region. In the United States, soccer participation is higher for high school girls who live in eastern states while volleyball tends to dominate the Midwest and western states (National Federation of State High School Associations, 2019).

What accounts for the differences in popularity and participation rates both regionally and globally? One explanation for these differences is geographic location. Some areas naturally afford more opportunities than others. For example, someone who lives in Brazil will have ample opportunities to participate in beach volleyball and swimming because the country has more than 4,500 miles of coastline; however, there are virtually no opportunities to participate in winter sports, such as hockey or cross-country skiing. Similarly, a person who lives in the Blue Ridge Mountains in the United States will have greater opportunities for mountain biking and hiking than a person who lives on the plains of the Midwest. Although the physical characteristics of a location can influence involvement in sport and physical activity, participation is often driven by characteristics of the community, such as availability of facilities and resources as well as its values and religion.

Facilities and Resources

The quantity and quality of facilities and resources available in a community can affect how often one engages in sport and physical activity. In a review of 43 studies, Limstrand (2008) found that adolescents with greater access to sport facilities and equipment in their community were more likely to participate in physical activity. Thus, if one lives in a community with limited or no facilities or equipment, engagement in sports and activities *requiring* these will be minimal. For example, a poorly funded school system with limited equipment for children to use during physical education will likely limit the development of motor competence for some motor skills, particularly object control skills (e.g., catching, throwing, striking, and kicking). Limstrand (2008) also found that adolescents were more physically active when their community offered sufficient sidewalks and made cycling safe and easy. Thus, walkable and bike friendly communities will likely have more individuals who walk, run, and bike, both for transportation and recreation, than communities that do not have the same infrastructure. However, the influence of facility access on participation may depend on the context. For example, a study in Germany found that female adolescents were more likely to engage in indoor sports when they lived in closer proximity to gyms; however, proximity to indoor pools and tennis courts did not influence participation in water sports or tennis (Reimers et al., 2014). Thus, access to facilities alone does not guarantee participation, because many other factors contribute to one's physical activity choices.

Access to opportunities for sport and physical activity is also affected by an individual's **socioeconomic status** (SES). This term refers to one's social class or standing based on the individual's education, occupation, and income. An individual with a high school diploma who works a minimum wage job would be considered at a lower SES than an individual with a graduate degree who works at a high-paying, white-collar job. SES often accounts for inequities in access to resources, including sport and physical activity opportunities, as well as issues related to privilege and power. Ice hockey, for example, requires access to an ice rink, which often has fees, and expensive, specialized equipment (e.g., skates, pads, hockey sticks). Conversely, soccer only requires a ball and an open area to play.

Gordon-Larsen and colleagues (2006) found that individuals who live in lower-SES communities in the United States were less likely to have access to physical activity and recreation facilities than those who live in higher-SES communities. This inequity was the case even for facilities that were expected to be distributed equitably (e.g., parks, YMCAs). Moreover, they found that this inequity in access to facilities was tied to differences in health-related behaviors and obesity rates. Similar results have been found in Australia (Eime et al., 2015), Canada (Pan et al., 2009), Italy (Federico et al., 2013), and the Netherlands (Kamphuis et al., 2007).

Values and Religion

Another explanation for differences in participation rates regionally and globally is common cultural traditions, such as values and religion, shared by an individual's social group. These traditions can have a strong influence on one's physical activity behavior. For example, a sport or physical activity can be tremendously important to a country's national identity. This is true of

---

WHAT DO YOU THINK?

Exercise 16.4

How many sport and recreational facilities were available to you growing up? Were they close by or far away? How do you think these might have influenced your physical activity behavior?

rugby in New Zealand. Rugby is not only the most popular sport in the country, with over 500 clubs and 100,000 players, but New Zealand's professional men's team, the All Blacks, has also dominated international play with a winning record of over 77 percent from 1903 to 2019 along with three Rugby World Cups. Some important cultural traditions of New Zealand are also interwoven within the sport of rugby by way of the haka, a pregame ritual performed by the All Blacks (see figure 16.2). The haka is rooted in Maori culture and consists of a ceremonial dance or challenge with chanting, rhythmic movements, and exaggerated facial expressions used to convey cultural pride, strength, and identity. This display of Maori culture within the sport further reinforces the influence of rugby on New Zealander identity.

Cultural traditions can also be represented in a community's everyday way of life. For example, cycling is a common practice throughout the Netherlands. According to the Netherlands Institute for Transport Policy Analysis (Harms & Kansen, 2018), approximately a quarter of Dutch residents use a bicycle daily while less than half of the population uses a car. In Amsterdam, bike ownership far outpaces car ownership; in fact, there are more bikes in Amsterdam than people! This is in stark contrast to the United States, where over 90 percent of households own at least one vehicle and more than 70 percent of commuters travel by car (U.S. Department of Transportation, 2020). These stark differences are likely because within the Netherlands, cycling is ingrained into their culture, while in the United States, cycling is viewed more as a subculture or hipster trend reserved for the elite. Moreover, the Netherlands has a superior infrastructure designed to support cyclists with an abundance of bike lanes and parking areas. Although some areas of the United States are becoming more bike friendly, especially in western states (e.g., Washington and Oregon), there has not been a significant culture shift nationwide toward bicycle use.

Cultural traditions in the form of religious practices can also strongly affect physical activity behavior. Despite a desire to participate in sport and recreation (Abdul Razak et al., 2010), Muslim women are often not afforded the accommodations needed to

Figure 16.2 All Blacks performing the haka.

Phil Walter/Getty Images

engage in physical activity while still meeting their religious obligations. Specific examples include the need to wear a head covering (e.g., hijab) and modest clothing while engaged in physical activity. For example, in 2011, the Iranian women's soccer team was disqualified from a qualification game for the 2012 Olympics for wearing conservative uniforms that aligned with their religious practices because they violated Federation Internationale de Football Association regulations. In 2014, the association overturned this rule and now allows head coverings for religious reasons during game play. Head coverings, however, can also present practical challenges while one is engaged in physical activity, and some activities don't lend themselves well to modest clothing (e.g., swimming). However, recent product developments have attempted to resolve some of these practical issues for Muslim women so that they can more easily engage in physical activity. These products include a sports hijab, which is more secure and breathable than a traditional hijab (see figure 16.3), and a burkini, which is a full-body swimsuit that covers everything but the face, hands, and feet.

DISABILITY

In terms of motor development, we often think of disability within the framework of individual constraints, both structural and functional; however, when looking at the achievement of functional leisure skills, meaningful physical activity, and motor skill improvement, the environment must also be considered. This includes the physical, the sociocultural, the instructional, and, importantly, the political environment. Generally, the views of disability in the society in which one lives has a significant influence on their movement opportunities. For example, policy changes at the global and local levels have had a positive impact on disability rights related to sport and recreation. One of the most significant influences at the global level is the United Nations' Convention on the Rights of Persons with Disabilities (2006). This is an international treaty that outlines the rights of individuals with disabilities and the obligations of state parties to implement and monitor measures to ensure that these rights are being upheld. Currently, all but seven state parties have signed or ratified the treaty. Article 30 of

svetikd/E+/Getty Images

Figure 16.3   Athlete wearing a sports hijab.

the treaty stipulates that individuals with disabilities must be afforded opportunities for equal participation in recreation, leisure, and sporting activities. This includes promoting and encouraging participation in physical activity as well as ensuring access to venues, activities, services, and resources.

Beyond article 30 of the convention, individual countries have implemented their own laws and policies. For example, the United States passed the Individuals with Disabilities Education Act (2004), which guarantees that children with disabilities have access to appropriate services. These services include providing physical education in the least restrictive environment, meaning that children should be in a learning environment with their typically developing peers whenever possible. In Canada, the Policy on Sport for Persons with a Disability was implemented in 2006 to aid in the elimination of barriers for individuals with disabilities to participate in sport and physical activity. More recently, the Accessible Canada Act received royal assent in 2019, which aims to make Canada more inclusive for individuals with disabilities.

In addition to laws and policy, greater visibility of disability sports has helped to increase awareness and support for the inclusion of individuals with disabilities in sport and physical activity. This is especially evident with the increased media coverage and spectatorship of the Paralympic Games. The United States Olympic Committee has recently made efforts to increase the status and support of the Paralympics and its athletes. In 2018, the board voted unanimously to increase the monetary award for medal winners to equal that of Olympic medal winners. Moreover, in 2019, the organization officially changed its name to the United States Olympic and Paralympic Committee to demonstrate their full commitment to the Paralympics. The Paralympics have also been influential on China's attitude toward, and inclusion of, individuals with disabilities when Beijing hosted the 2008 Olympic and Paralympic Games. Prior to hosting the games, China was not very accommodating toward individuals with disabilities; however, after receiving the host bid, the Chinese government passed new accessibility legislation and spent more than $150 million over seven years to improve the accessibility of its infrastructure.

However, events surrounding the Paralympics have not always been positive. For example, the former Soviet Union refused to host the 1980 Paralympics because, according to a Soviet official, the country did not have any disabled individuals. Luckily, an alternative bid to host the games was granted, and the Paralympics took place in Arnhem, Netherlands. More recently, the 2016 Paralympic Games in Rio de Janeiro were almost canceled because the planning committee used money allocated for the Paralympics to fund the Olympics. Fortunately, alternative funding was secured by a last-minute government bailout that allowed the games to take place. However, the deleterious actions of the high-level Brazilian officials demonstrate a significant level of societal prejudice toward the Paralympics and their athletes. Social prejudice and discrimination toward individuals with disabilities (minority group) in favor of those who are typically developing (majority group) is known as **ableism** (Wolbring, 2012). There are many forms of ableism, from the overt to the unintentional. These include failure to provide appropriate accommodations, making a joke at the expense of someone with a disability, and using pejorative phrases (e.g., "the blind leading the blind").

At a more local level, there are many environmental constraints within the community that can affect participation of individuals with disabilities in sport and physical activity. One often-cited example is access to appropriate programs and facilities (Shields et al., 2012). As discussed previously, access is important for *everyone* to engage in sport and physical activity; however, for individuals with disabilities, access includes both *availability* and *accessibility*. For example, a child with a disability may live within walking distance of a playground, but if that playground is not accessible for the child (e.g., only stairs available to access upper levels of a play area), then the child does not have the opportunity to participate. However, sport and recreation programs that use inclusive practices increase opportunities for individuals with disabilities to participate. Effective programs also need instructors who are knowledgeable and accepting of inclusive practices. Lack of skilled instructors, or instructors willing to learn, can lead to intentional and unintentional exclusion. For example, a physical education teacher may exclude a student with autism from a lesson because she doesn't know how to handle his inappropriate outbursts or lack of social engagement with classmates.

Equal access to programs and facilities can be achieved for all individuals using **universal design**. Universal design involves the creation of products and environments that are accessible to everyone regardless of age, gender, or ability (see figure 16.4). For example, ramps can be used on play-grounds instead of stairs so that someone in a wheelchair could use it as well as someone who can ambulate independently. Likewise, a soccer program can use bright colored uniforms and bell balls to accommodate an individual with low vision as well as those that are typically sighted. Universal design also applies to instruction. For example, instructors could provide differentiated instruction appropriate to the needs of all individuals and make efforts to reduce excess noise and distractions. When stake-holders use principles of universal design for both programs and facilities, they create an environment that provides opportunities for individuals with disabilities to meaningfully engage in sport and physical activity.

Social support is another important environmental constraint that affects participation in sport and physical activity for individuals with disabilities (Shields et al., 2012). Although social support is important for all individuals, it is often mentioned as both a facilitator and barrier to physical activity for individuals with disabilities. Social support comes from many sources, including parents, friends, peers, teachers,

Photos courtesy of Landscape Structures.

Figure 16.4 Accessible play equipment.

and coaches. Parents are the main source of social support during early childhood, because they are usually the primary caregivers during this time. Parents often create the first opportunities for physical activity that are crucial for the development of fundamental motor skills. Without skilled parental support, children with disabilities often lag even further behind their typically developing peers on motor competence. When children reach adolescence, friends and peers become an important source of social support. Individuals with disabilities who have friends and peers that participate with them and provide support and targeted praise are more likely to participate in physical activity while those who are teased, ostracized, or bullied will be much less likely to be physically active. The teacher or coach is also an important source of social support. Not only can they provide direct support to the individual with a disability, but they can also create an inclusive and supportive environment that can affect the attitudes of everyone involved.

AGING

Sociocultural influences on physical activity behaviors continue across the life span. Prior to adulthood, the primary socialization occurs in home and school settings. The dominant socializing influences during adulthood include the media, significant others, friends, and community members, including instructors and health professionals (Gabbard, 2012). Physical activity and sport participation are also largely affected by life cycle changes, including marriage, the birth of children, career, retirement, and other transitions (Mihalik et al., 1989).

Most people attain peak physical performance during young adulthood. Many continually test their physical abilities during this stage. On the other hand, many adults do not engage in adequate physical activity because they believe they are already healthy and are not concerned with the lifelong benefits of physical activity. Once this attitude is established, it can be difficult to overcome, especially as people begin to decline physically (Gabbard, 2012). As they approach middle adulthood, around the age of 35 to 40, many people become increasingly concerned about their physical abilities and appearance. One of the main causes of these heightened concerns is the media, which often emphasize youth, beauty, and vitality. On a positive note, the media have also flooded society with educational information on healthy behaviors through advertisements, websites, and community medical organizations. The increased promotion of healthy behaviors and the focus on youthful appearance have had a very positive impact on young and middle-aged adults' attitudes toward physical activity. Now more than ever, people are realizing the benefits of a physically active lifestyle, including decreased risks for cardiovascular disease, high cholesterol, high blood pressure, and type 2 diabetes.

Unfortunately, ageism (i.e., the stereotyping of older adults based on their age) still exists today. One sign of it is decreased expectations of older adults professionally, physically, and cognitively. These negative perceptions devalue older adults, often affecting their opportunities, choices, and lifestyles. Someone who is expected to become increasingly sedentary with age is likely to fulfill that prophecy.

Social Theories of Aging

There are two main theories of aging: activity theory and disengagement theory. **Activity theory** suggests that adults who maintain social interactions and active lifestyles can not only maintain their life satisfaction but may also increase it (Rook, 2000; Schaie & Willis, 1991). **Disengagement theory** asserts that older adults must gradually withdraw from society by participating in fewer activities and decreasing their personal relationships. Disengagement theory suggests that older adults need to separate themselves from society to maintain their integrity by accepting their changing status and physical decline. Because participation in physical activity often involves social interaction, increased physical activity would be considered counterproductive according to the disengagement theory because it asserts that older adults need to *decrease* personal relationships. Activity theory, however, suggests that active and productive lifestyles are necessary to sustain happy and satisfying lives. Physical activity often involves social interaction, helping older adults to remain attached rather than detaching from society (Gallahue et al., 2012). Activity theory also asserts that adults should continue their roles throughout life. If they discontinue a particular activity—for example, when they retire—they should find other activities to replace it.

Social Support

Perceived social support of family, friends, and community members is a significant factor in young adults' (Darlow & Xu, 2011) and older adults' exercise adherence (Chogahara et al., 1998). Perceived social support is the anticipation of help from one's social network. This may be different from the actual social support received. Most research in the area of social support focuses on the benefits of perceived social support rather than actual received social support (Rackow et al., 2014).

WHAT DO YOU THINK?

Exercise 16.5

Using the following chart, write down the three biggest socializing agents that affected your physical activity participation, with 1 being the most important. Consider parents, teachers, coaches, peers, the media, significant others, and community members (doctors, medical professionals, instructors). Discuss your primary socializing agents during your childhood and adolescence, and those who most influence you now. Then try to predict who will be your biggest sociocultural influences 30 years from now.

	Childhood	Adolescence	Currently	In 30 years
1.				
2.				
3.				

Compare these socializing agents.

1. How did they change as you grew older?
2. Do you think your answers are typical of those of others in your generation? Explain.
3. Would you expect socializing agents to have been different 100 years ago? Explain your answer.
4. Do you expect socializing agents to be different in future generations?

Those who provide social support and affect a person's adherence to a healthy lifestyle, including physical activity, are termed **socializing agents**. Socializing agents change across the life span: parents are the primary socializing agents for infants and children, and peers become the primary socializing agents for adults. When compared to younger adults, older adults generally have poorer social networks (Stephens & Craig, 1990). Ageism may contribute to reduced social support from family members, and peers are often less active themselves. Given the decreased support of older adults, physical activities that involve social interaction may be most helpful.

RESEARCH NOTES

My Friend Laura

Social networks are unquestionably important for helping older adults adhere to exercise programs. However, as previously mentioned, many older adults do not receive much, if any, social support. Many live alone and are isolated from society. Given the ubiquitous presence of technology today, it is not surprising that computer-animated images have been designed to motivate adults to increase their daily physical activity. These computer-animated images, termed relational agents, are also designed to build long-term social–emotional relationships with them.

Bickmore and colleagues (2005) conducted a two-month study with 21 adults between the ages of 62 and 84 to see whether a relational agent would increase the daily number of steps walked. The relational agent had conversations with the participants, encouraged them to be physically active, and discussed their progress. The results revealed that the relational agent, Laura, increased the older adults' physical activity levels. According to some of the participants, not only did Laura motivate them to increase their physical activity, but they also formed a social bond with her. The relational agent "may be an ideal platform to provide an effective automated health educator with unbounded patience and empathy for . . . patients" (Bickmore et al., 2005, p. 733).

The following is part of a sample conversation between a user (*U*) and the relational agent (*A*):

A: Hello, Bertha. Great to see you.

U: Hi, Laura.

A: How are you feeling today?

U: I'm not feeling so great.

A: I am sorry to hear that. Tell me more about how you are feeling.

U: I'm tired.

A: How tired are you feeling?

U: I'm pretty beat.

A: Good grief, I hope you're not getting sick. Can you get some rest soon?

U: I think so.

A: That is great. I hope you come back feeling refreshed.

U: Me too!

A: So, are you from the East Coast originally?

Older adults with mutual interests in particular activities may be able to encourage each other to continue participating. Adults who live in active neighborhoods in which people are outside walking and gardening may be more inclined to be active themselves. Day-to-day interactions with neighbors can complement other social networks such as family and friends (Gardner, 2011).

SUMMARY

Sociocultural constraints can have a profound impact on motor development. Societal and cultural influences related to gender, race, cultural background, disability, and aging can influence the likelihood that one will have access to, and participate in, sport and physical activity. Thus, it is important that practitioners are aware of these constraints and how they might affect the motor competence and physical activity behavior of the individuals they are working with.

Societal views concerning gender can affect physical activity participation and motor competence through stereotype threat and gender typing. Boys tend to be socialized into masculine sports that require manipulative skills, while girls are encouraged to engage in feminine activities that focus on aesthetic and locomotor skills. Notably, Title IX has had a significant influence on increasing opportunities for female sport participation. Societal views surrounding race and ethnicity have also been influential when it comes to participation patterns within sport. Racial stereotypes that White athletes are intelligent while Black athletes are naturally athletic often result in racial stacking, wherein White athletes are placed in central positions while Black athletes are assigned to the periphery. Moreover, White and Black athletes in the same position are often instructed to perform tasks differently based on these stereotypes.

An individual's cultural background can affect physical activity behavior. Access, both physically and financially, to appropriate facilities and resources is often associated with participation levels in sport and physical activity; however, this may be context dependent. Cultural values are also influential, especially when a sport is part of cultural identity or ingrained within society. Moreover, religious practices within a culture may place certain constraints on how one can engage in physical activity. Disability, although individually determined, also has a significant sociocultural component, because societal views on disability can limit or enable opportunities. Laws and policies have increased disability rights at both global and local levels and include access to sport, recreation, and physical education, and increased visibility of parasports has helped to increase awareness and support. Additionally, the use of universal design can help reduce or eliminate barriers for individuals with disabilities to participate meaningfully in sport and physical activity. Finally, societal views on aging as well as social support can greatly influence physical activity engagement in older adults. Thus, it is important to encourage and provide social opportunities for older adults to participate in physical activity to support their health and overall well-being.

> **ONLINE ACTIVITIES**

The student material found in HK*Propel* includes exercises, labs, and videos to enhance learning and encourage practical application of important concepts.

LEARNING AIDS

Supplemental Activities

1. *Racial stacking:* Choose a professional team sport (e.g., basketball or baseball). Divide the positions of the sport into two categories: central and peripheral. For example, in baseball, the catcher, pitcher, and infielders could be categorized as central, while the outfielders could be categorized as peripheral. Next, select a sample of three teams and look up the website for each. Write the name of each team in the first column of the following table. Next, use the team rosters and player bios to determine how many athletes from the majority and minority group are represented in each position category. Finally, calculate the sum for each column and record it in the table. Based on the findings from your sample, does racial stacking exist in the team sport you selected? Use evidence from your data and content from the chapter to support your claim. How do you explain the findings within the context of the current social and cultural environment?

Team	CENTRAL POSITIONS		PERIPHERAL POSITIONS	
	Majority	Minority	Majority	Minority
Total				

From P.S. Beach, M.E. Perreault, A.S. Brian, and D.H. Collier, *Motor Learning and Development*, 3rd ed. (Champaign, IL: Human Kinetics, 2024).

2. *Universal design:* Visit a local park or playground. Make a list of each area of the park or piece of equipment on the playground. Next, determine how accessible each item on your list is based on the principles of universal design. Rate the accessibility on a 5-point Likert scale (1—very poor, 2—poor, 3—fair, 4—good, and 5—excellent) and provide justification for your ratings. For each item on your list that was rated below a 4, provide suggestions for improving the accessibility.

Glossary

ableism—Social prejudice and discrimination of individuals with disabilities (minority group) in favor of those who are typically developing (majority group).

activity theory—A social theory on aging that suggests that adults who maintain social interactions and active lives can not only maintain life satisfaction, but also perhaps even increase it.

disengagement theory—A social theory on aging that asserts that older adults must separate themselves from society to maintain their integrity by accepting their changing status and physical decline.

ethnicity—The social group to which an individual belongs that shares common cultural elements, such as traditions, language, and religion.

gender—Socially constructed roles, behavior, and norms associated with being male or female.

gender expression—The outward portrayal of an individual's gender through behavior, clothing, or other characteristics.

gender identity—The internal concept of one's gender.

gender typing—The internalization of gender-specific roles and behaviors derived from cultural norms that coincide with an individual's sex.

race—A classification system based on an individual's physical characteristics (e.g., skin color, facial form) indicative of historical ancestry.

racial stacking—The overrepresentation of a racial or ethnic group in specific roles or positions within sport or physical activity contexts.

racial tasking—Situation in which players in the same position are instructed or coached to perform different tasks based on their race.

sex—A method of classification based on biological determinants of reproduction.

sexual orientation—The romantic, physical, or emotional attraction to the same gender, opposite gender, or multiple genders.

socializing agents—(1) People who affect someone's adherence to a healthy lifestyle including physical activity. (2) People who influence the development of someone's social role, such as parents, teachers, and coaches. One of the major elements of the socialization process.

sociocultural constraint—Socially and culturally constructed attitudes, beliefs, and stereotypes that can either encourage or discourage motor behavior.

socioeconomic status—An individual's social class or standing based on education, occupation, and income.

stereotype lift—A performance increase that results from an in-group when they are aware of negative stereotypes about an out-group.

stereotype threat—A situational dilemma that occurs when individuals act in accordance with cultural stereotypes when at risk of confirming negative stereotypes about their social group.

universal design—The creation of products and environments that are accessible to everyone regardless of age, gender, or ability.

PART IV

Designing Developmentally Appropriate Programs

Now that you understand the foundational concepts in motor learning and motor development and have explored life span changes including structural and functional constraints from infancy to older adulthood, you are ready to learn how to design developmentally appropriate programs. In part IV, we strongly encourage you to use the knowledge you have gained to individualize programs for each learner.

It is quite clear that practice is essential for acquiring a motor skill, but the amount of practice that is necessary and how it should be organized are probably much less obvious. Part IV explores key factors in arranging both physical and mental practice. Scheduling practice is a complex topic. Variables such as age, experience, and the type of skill affect whether a particular form of practice will accelerate learning. We consider when and how to use variable, part, and whole practice and also discuss the distribution of practice. Next, we consider feedback. Feedback helps performers execute the proper movement patterns, motivates them, and reinforces successful performances. It is perhaps obvious that feedback is critical when people are learning a new motor skill, especially a complex one, but as with practice, many considerations come into play. Each of these issues is examined, including the type, frequency, and timing of feedback.

As a practitioner, you must learn how to manipulate constraints to encourage the appropriate movement patterns in your learners. Before implementing a program, you will have to make many instructional decisions, including what teaching style to use, how to optimize motivation, and how to develop tactical skills and decision making. Part IV begins by examining developmental models of instruction (chapter 17). Then we explore those prepractice variables that affect performance and learning: goal setting, demonstrations, verbal instruction, directing attention, and physical guidance (chapter 18). Of course, this is only the beginning of your role as a practitioner. You must also arrange physical practice (chapter 19) and provide appropriate feedback (chapter 20).

Part IV concludes with program design (chapter 21) to show you how what you learned in this book can be applied in practice. The labs for this chapter include case studies that present real-life situations on a variety of topics ranging from physical education and adapted physical education to the instruction of older adults and rehabilitation.

DEVELOPMENTAL MODELS FOR INSTRUCTION

CHAPTER OBJECTIVES

After reading this chapter, you should be able to do the following:

- Understand the potential impact of the proficiency barrier on the development of future motor skills.
- Describe how motor skills progress through each period of the mountain of motor development.
- Explain the developmental relationship between motor competence and physical activity.
- Explain the difference between free play, deliberate play, structured practice, and deliberate practice.
- Describe how multiple outcomes can be achieved using applied sport development models.
- Understand the importance of early sport diversification on future physical activity behavior.
- Explain how developmental models inform instructional decisions made by practitioners.

Putting the Cart Before the Horse

Yasmina is the newest volunteer coach for a U5 coed soccer program through a local recreation center. Having played soccer in college, she feels up to the task. During a brief coaches training workshop prior to the beginning of the season, the recreation director explains that each team will practice for 15 minutes while the remaining 45 minutes will consist of small-sided games between teams. At first, Yasmina thought this sounded like a great idea because the players would get more game experience. However, during the first practice, she noticed that this approach was problematic. Instead of playing a game, many of the kids chased the ball around, kicked it out of bounds, or stared off into space. She also noticed several kids sitting out or socializing with friends instead of participating. At the next coaches meeting, she brought this issue up to the director and suggested that more time be spent on instruction. The director shrugged her off stating, "They don't need to be taught how to run and kick; kids develop these things naturally."

As illustrated in the chapter-opening scenario, there is a misconception that maturation drives infant and child motor skill development (Clark, 2007). Although it may appear that a child has developed a new motor skill overnight, such as running, jumping, kicking, or catching, these skills do not magically appear; rather, motor skills must be taught and practiced (Drost et al., 2015). Children move the way they do because of individual and environmental constraints (Newell, 1984, 1986). Humans sit upright because of the biomechanical constraints of the human body and the gravitational forces imposed on the body. If gravitational forces were removed (as in outer space), it is unlikely that infants would acquire the ability to sit upright. Humans are born with preadapted motor behaviors that predispose reflexes and actions (e.g., grasp reflex, rolling over); nonetheless, these behaviors are either reinforced or modified by constraints in the environment. For example, an infant is more likely to practice crawling when enticed with a favorite toy or encouragement by a parent. These preadapted motor behaviors prepare the infant to acquire basic motor skills that, generally, develop during the first year of life. As noted, the acquisition of motor skills does not occur through maturation alone; rather, these skills are honed by adapting to changing constraints and through a learning process (Clark, 2007). As typically developing infants continue to grow, they will use these developmental skills to perform increasingly complex and sport-specific skills.

MOTOR DEVELOPMENT MODELS

Practitioners are an important environmental constraint within the learning process, because they often take on the primary instructional role when individuals acquire and refine motor skills. An important consideration when planning instruction is determining an individual's needs at specific points in time. To determine this, a developmental lens is useful. Motor development models provide guidance for instruction by specifying the progression of motor skills across time. Thus, an understanding of how motor skill needs change during different stages of development will help ensure that practitioners know what types of motor skills to focus on to ensure a positive trajectory toward physical activity engagement.

Hierarchy of Motor Proficiency

Vern Seefeldt (1980) proposed an early motor development framework to understand the progression of motor proficiency from birth to adulthood. The model is conceptualized as a pyramid broken up into a hierarchy of four developmental levels (see figure 17.1).

The first level, **reflexes-reactions**, is at the base of the pyramid. These skills emerge during the neonatal period and consist of infant reflexes and early motor milestones. The next level is **fundamental motor skills**, which occurs during early childhood. These consist of foundational skills used in a variety of sports and physical activities. Seefeldt (1980) placed these skills into three categories: locomotor (e.g., run, jump, and hop), nonlocomotor (e.g., turn, bend, and twist), and projection and reception of objects (e.g., throw, kick, and catch). At this point, children typically pass a **proficiency barrier**, meaning they have exceeded a threshold of motor skill proficiency in fundamental motor skills necessary to progress to more complex motor skills (Seefeldt, 1980). Again, it should be noted that fundamental motor skills do not develop naturally but are the result of many constraints that influence their development (Newell, 1984, 1986). Movement experiences during early childhood are critical to the development of fundamental motor skills (Stodden & Goodway, 2007; Stodden et al., 2008). Without appropriate exposure and instruction, not

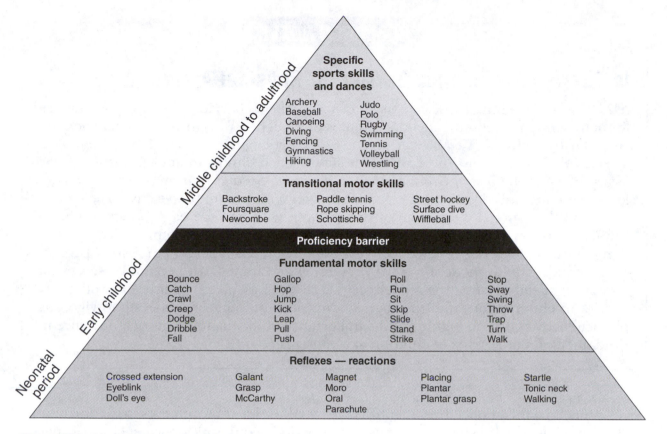

Figure 17.1   Hierarchy of motor proficiency.

Adapted by permission from V. Seefeldt, "Developmental Motor Patterns: Implications for Elementary School Physical Education," in *Psychology of Motor Behavior and Sport*, edited by C. Nadeau, W. Holliwell, K. Newell, and G. Roberts (Champaign, IL: Human Kinetics, 1980), 314-323.

every child will pass the proficiency barrier at the desired time. Those who don't may be delayed in their future development of related motor skills.

Following the proficiency barrier, the last two developmental levels occur during middle childhood to adulthood. The first is **transitional motor skills**. These consist of skills that aid the transition between fundamental motor skills and specialized motor skills used in sport and physical activity. For example, a child learns how to adapt the fundamental motor skills of striking and throwing to a recreational game (e.g., Wiffle ball) before using them in a sport context (e.g., baseball or softball). The final level of the pyramid is **specific sport skills and dances**, which represents the attainment of motor proficiency in a specific context, such as volleyball, tennis, or wrestling. As

individuals progress up the hierarchy and attain greater motor proficiency, they are afforded more opportunities to participate in physical activity. For example, a child with proficiency in the fundamental motor skill of throwing is more likely to achieve success in activities that utilize that skill (e.g., football or softball) than a child who does not. This, in turn, will influence how likely the child will continue to participate in these activities in the future. Thus, it is vital that practitioners differentiate instruction of motor skills based on relevant developmental periods to ensure proper progression toward motor skill competence.

Mountain of Motor Development

Clark and Metcalfe (2002) developed a more contemporary life span view of motor skill

RESEARCH NOTES

Is There a Proficiency Barrier for Physical Activity?

A 2018 study examined whether there is a proficiency barrier of motor competence for achieving the recommended 60 minutes of moderate to vigorous physical activity each day by children (De Meester et al., 2018). Participants consisted of 326 children ages 7 to 12 years from three different states. Each child's motor competence was assessed using the *Test of Gross Motor Development–Second Edition*. Physical activity levels were measured with an accelerometer over a minimum of five days. The results indicated that only 11.69 percent of the children with low scores (8th percentile) on the *Test of Gross Motor Development–Second Edition* met the recommended amount of moderate to vigorous physical activity. Conversely, 25.45 percent and 40.74 percent of the children with moderate (43rd percentile) and high (75th percentile) scores on the test, respectively, met the guidelines. These findings suggest there is a proficiency barrier in children for attaining the recommended amount of moderate to vigorous physical activity, which highlights the importance of increasing motor competence in fundamental motor skills in children at a young age.

development. In this model, they identified periods during which typical patterns of motor skill development occur in a particular order (see figure 17.2). Clark and Metcalfe (2002) labeled this model the mountain of motor development because each period builds on the previous period. This model breaks down motor skill development into five periods that occur over the life span. Although there are some similarities between the mountain of motor development and Seefeldt's hierarchy of motor proficiency, there are some distinct differences as well.

The base of the mountain is the **prenatal period**, which consists of the last two trimesters of pregnancy during which the fetus moves quite a bit. The initial stage, the **reflexive period**, occurs after birth and lasts approximately two weeks. As suggested by the title of the period, movements are reflexive, because the newborn adjusts to many sensory changes such as bright lights and sounds. Following the first two weeks, the **preadapted period** begins. During this period, infants start interacting with the environment by making

goal-directed movements. Also during this period, motor milestones, such as sitting up, standing, crawling, and walking, predominate. When the infant can independently walk and self-feed—that is, perform the two fundamental skills necessary for basic survival—the infant will have progressed to the **fundamental motor patterns** period. Fundamental motor patterns, like Seefeldt's fundamental motor skills, are foundational movements, such as throwing, catching, hopping, and jumping, that form a base for more complex, sport-specific movement patterns. These patterns are, generally, well developed around the age of seven (Clark & Metcalfe, 2002; Gallahue et al., 2012).

Once children achieve a certain level of proficiency in fundamental motor patterns, they begin to refine and adapt them into movements specific for sports or physical activities as well as develop and maintain physical fitness (Stodden et al., 2013). For example, a striking pattern may be modified for racket sports or golf while a sliding pattern may be modified for a dance sequence. This period of refinement and adaptation of fundamental motor patterns is termed

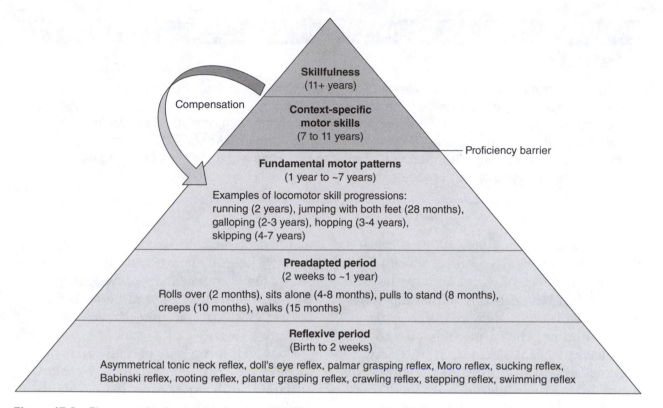

Figure 17.2 The mountain of motor development. *Note:* These ages are approximations. Each person is unique and progresses at his own rate.

Adapted by permission from J.E. Clark and J.M. Metcalfe, "The Mountain of Motor Development: A Metaphor," in *Motor Development: Research and Reviews*, vol. 2, edited by J.E. Clark and J.H. Humphrey (Reston, VA: National Association for Sport and Physical Education, 2002), 163-190.

the **context-specific motor skills period**. The period at the peak of the mountain is the **skillfulness period**. This period does not separate people of different skill levels (junior varsity, varsity, university, professional). To reach this period, a person needs to be skilled at a particular movement. Importantly, skillfulness varies between motor skills because not all people are skillful in a wide variety of motor skills. For example, a baseball player may be very good at batting, catching, fielding, and throwing but may not be a skillful swimmer or gymnast. As such, there is no single peak on the mountain as in Seefeldt's hierarchy; instead, there are many peaks of varying heights depending on the person's skillfulness in each activity (Goodway et al., 2012). Those who aspire to reach the highest possible peak of the mountain must recognize that this is a long and demanding journey. Unique to the mountain of motor development is the **compensation period**, which individuals can enter at any point in the model due to declines in motor skill competence from injury, aging, or other setbacks. A full recovery from an injury may culminate with a return to the former level of skillfulness. However, biological changes resulting from permanent injuries or aging effects may cause the person to remain at a lower position on the mountain.

Developmental Trajectories Model

Stodden and colleagues (2008) proposed a developmental model to describe the relationship of motor skill competence to physical activity and health. It has been known for many years that regular physical activity is positively linked to health-related benefits including reduced body weight and obesity.

WHAT DO YOU THINK?

Exercise 17.1

A recent commentary by Karl Newell (2020) has challenged the traditional notion of what defines a fundamental motor skill. He suggests that a fundamental motor skill would need to meet three specific criteria: (a) uniqueness of movement or outcome, (b) universality of function to human movement, and (c) generalizability to many motor skills. Given these criteria, what would you consider a fundamental motor skill? How would this new conceptualization fit within motor development models described previously?

Stodden and colleagues (2008) proposed that being physically skilled should lead to more frequent physical activity, but the relationship between physical competence and physical activity may change over developmental time. They argued that the contribution of physical skill to physical activity and health had not received the emphasis warranted. Much has been learned about how to measure physical activity and its relationship to health, but with little focus on the impact of good or poor performance on physical activity.

Within their model, Stodden and colleagues (2008) propose four interacting factors: motor competence, perceived motor competence, health-related fitness, and physical activity. They suggested that the relationship between motor competence and physical activity strengthens over developmental time. In early childhood (ages 2-5), physical activity influences motor competence. Parents, available environments, and socioeconomic status promote physical activity, which should lead to the acquisition of fundamental motor skills and other motor skills important in a culture (e.g., swimming). However, because physical activity is so strongly influenced by parents at this age, motor competence and physical activity are only weakly related. In middle childhood (ages 6-9) and later childhood (ages 10-13), physical activity and motor competence should become more strongly related because those with moderate or greater skill are more able to participate in physical activities, games, dance, and sport. Those who are less able in motor competence engage in less physical activity. By late elementary or middle school ages, motor skill competence drives physical activity levels.

Young children may perceive themselves to be quite competent if they are actively engaged and expending effort (Harter, 1999). They do not judge themselves accurately or in comparison to others. Thus, in early childhood the relationship between actual physical competence and perceived physical competence is quite low (Stodden et al., 2008). During middle childhood, opportunities for social comparison and cognitive growth have increased, resulting in more accurate comparisons to peers. At this point, perceived physical competence is more closely related to actual physical competence. Stodden and colleagues (2008) predicted that less skilled youngsters will become less active because they view activities as difficult. They begin to opt out of physical activity because it is not enjoyable. This is termed a negative spiral of disengagement, which even further reduces physical competence, perceived competence, and physical activity. In contrast, skilled youngsters become more active during middle childhood because they experience fun and rewards from participating; this is termed a positive spiral of engagement. More activity across the elementary school years should augment physical competence, perceived competence, and physical activity.

The positive or negative spirals of engagement or disengagement affect physical fitness from middle childhood through adolescence. Quite simply, those who are more physically skilled are more physically active and thus able to realize greater health-related fitness. Also, children who are more physically fit can engage in physical activity for longer periods of time and thus continue to progress in the development of movement skills. For those with lower levels of physical skills, lower levels of physical fitness are predicted. These children and youth have difficulty persisting in physical activities, which limits their gains in motor competence.

Obesity is both a product of Stodden and colleagues' (2008) four factors interacting and a mediating variable. Obesity is predicted because of the spiral of disengagement and associated low levels of physical and perceived motor competence that result in reduced physical activity levels and health-related fitness. However, obesity is also a mediating variable because heavier children have difficulty performing motor skills, are less likely to be physically active, and experience less success when they attempt physical activities.

The postulates of Stodden and colleagues (2008) place new emphasis on the role of physical competence in perceived physical competence, physical activity, physical fitness, and obesity, which is a major health issue around the world. Much research has been generated on issues related to the four factors, how they interact over developmental time, and their predictions regarding health (e.g., Barnett et al., 2015; Holfelder & Schott, 2014; Lloyd et al., 2014; Lubans et al., 2010; Robinson, 2010; Stodden et al., 2014). Although more research is needed, considerable support currently exists for the model and its predictions regarding the importance of skillfulness in promoting physically active lifestyles (Robinson et al., 2015).

Implications for Instruction

Using the motor development models described earlier in this chapter, there are some clear guidelines for practitioners. First, it is important to monitor the development of reflexes and motor milestones in infants. Although we know the timing of these can somewhat vary between individuals (see chapter 7), large delays or nonappearance may be a sign of underlying issues that require early intervention. During early childhood, physical fitness should be fostered along with instruction and interventions targeting the acquisition and refinement of fundamental motor skills. Since fundamental motor skills form the foundation for many other context-specific skills, it is important that children develop proficiency in a wide variety of locomotor, nonlocomotor, and object control skills. The timing of the development of these skills is also critical to ensure that children pass Seefeldt's (1980) proficiency barrier. Without these fundamental motor skills, there is an increased likelihood that children will not obtain recommended levels of physical activity (Stodden et al., 2008).

Once a strong foundation in fundamental motor skills has been achieved, practitioners can progress their instruction toward adaptation and application of these skills to specific contexts using modified or full-scale activities and games. For example, locomotor skills, such as running and sliding, can be practiced on an agility course that is set up to simulate conditions of a game. Likewise, ball skills, such as throwing, can be applied to learning a service motion in volleyball or tennis. Depending on the context, practitioners may then choose to further develop these context-specific skills for learners to participate at high levels of competition by shifting the focus to other aspects of instruction, such as game tactics and mental toughness. Practitioners should also be aware of ways to modify instruction if an individual experiences an injury or other setback. During these times, it is critical that the focus of instruction be based on where the individual is in the recovery process.

SPORT DEVELOPMENT MODELS

A common goal in physical education and sport programs is to create physically literate individuals that become lifelong participants in physical activity. However, individuals often have different goals when it comes to their participation in physical activity. Some may choose to participate in recreational activities that are more social in nature, such as a running group or bowling league, while others may choose to pursue competition at high levels, such as collegiate or professional sport. For this reason, sport development models can be a useful tool for practitioners. These models contain elements of the motor development models discussed previously, but offer different trajectories for physical activity participation, such as fitness, recreation, and competition. They also offer more specific guidelines on implementation that consider many individual, task, and environmental constraints that affect motor development at different time periods.

Developmental Model of Sport Participation

Côté (1999) and colleagues (Côté et al., 2003, 2007; Côté et al., 2009) proposed the developmental model of sport participation. The model was inspired by Bloom (1985), whose pioneering research in science, art, and athletics determined the antecedents of experts' high level of skill. It appears that sport experts progress toward excellence in much the same way as musicians, chess players, and scholars (Janelle & Hillman, 2003), but they require 3,000 to 4,000 hours of practice rather than the 10,000 hours often cited as

necessary for expertise in other domains. Like Bloom, Côté and colleagues (2003) identified three phases of development: the **sampling years** (ages 6-12), the **specializing years** (ages 13-15), and the **investment years** (age 16 and older).

The sampling years are characterized by exposure to many fundamental motor skills (see chapters 8 and 9) and a wide range of sports with an emphasis on fun and excitement. In the specializing years, the adolescent begins to spend more time on one or two sporting activities. Skill development takes on a higher priority than during the sampling years, but fun remains a critical component. Côté and colleagues (2003) suggested that the activities pursued at this point are a function of "positive experiences with a coach, encouragement from an older sibling, success, and simple enjoyment of the activity" (p. 93). Adolescents who move into the investment years want to achieve elite levels of performance. The foci are strategy, competition, and skill development within a context of deliberate practice directed and assisted by a teacher or coach.

Côté and colleagues (2003) proposed that the sampling, specializing, and investment years in sport are anchored in the concepts of **free play**, **deliberate play**, **structured practice**, and **deliberate practice**. Table 17.1 provides a comparison of these four types of physical activity participation across six dimensions. Children move from the free play of infancy and early childhood to deliberate play, in which some rules are established and monitored by children or adults. The concept of free play was intentionally included to incorporate play as conceived by Piaget and other developmentalists (see chapter 14). During deliberate play, children engage in unstructured movement activities, such as small-sided, informal games, but may self-govern by creating or modifying the rules. From deliberate play, children may elect to participate in the structured practice of a sport in which skill improvement assumes a higher priority

Table 17.1   Comparison of Free Play, Deliberate Play, Structured Practice, and Deliberate Practice Activities

	DIMENSIONS			
	Free play	**Deliberate play**	**Structured practice**	**Deliberate practice**
Goal	Fun	Fun	Improve performance	Improve performance
Perspective	Process (means)	Process (experimentation)	Outcome (ends)	Outcome (ends)
Monitored	Not monitored	Loosely monitored	Monitored	Carefully monitored
Correction	No correction	No focus on immediate correction	Focus on correction (often through discovery learning)	Focus on immediate correction
Gratification	Immediate	Immediate	Immediate and delayed	Delayed
Sources of enjoyment	Inherent	Predominantly inherent	Predominantly extrinsic	Extrinsic

Reprinted by permission from J. Côté, J. Baker, and B. Abernethy, "Play to Practice: A Developmental Framework for the Acquisition of Expertise in Team Sports," in *Expert Performance in Sports: Advances in Research on Sport Expertise*, edited by J.L. Starkes and K.A. Ericsson (Champaign, IL: Human Kinetics, 2003), 95.

than in deliberate play. Finally, some highly motivated adolescents move to deliberate practice. Often monitored by a teacher or coach, deliberate practice is highly structured, demanding, and purposeful, wherein performance improvement is the primary goal.

Long-Term Athlete Development Model

A more applied sport development framework is the long-term athlete development (LTAD) model (Balyi et al., 2013). The LTAD model was developed by researchers in Canada and is a commonly used framework for Canadian youth sport development programs. Although this model has also been used in other countries, USA Hockey has been the only sport organization in the United States to utilize it. The LTAD model has seven stages: (a) active start, (b) FUNda-mentals, (c) learn to train, (d) train to train, (e) train to compete, (f) train to win, and (g) active for life. Although there are suggested age ranges for each stage, the stages are designed around an individual's growth and maturation characteristics instead of chronological age. The stages within the LTAD model lead to three specific outcomes: physical literacy, sport excellence, and lifelong physical activity.

Physical Literacy Outcome

The first outcome in the LTAD model is physical literacy and includes the first three stages—active start, FUNdamentals, and learn to train. Physical literacy focuses on individuals obtaining foundational skills that can be applied and adapted across a variety of physical activity contexts. This is like the fundamental and context-specific motor skills in the motor development models described earlier in this chapter.

WHAT DO YOU THINK?

Exercise 17.2

Does the developmental model of sport participation reflect your experiences? Do you think it is a helpful model to adopt to reduce the criticisms of youth sport regarding too much emphasis on winning, too much stress, and athlete burnout?

The first stage of the LTAD model, active start, occurs during the developmental period of birth to age 6 for both sexes. During this stage, children begin to develop fundamental motor skills through play rather than structured activities to encourage enjoyment during physical activity. Because caregivers are the primary socializing agents during this developmental period, it is important that they model good physical activity behavior to set a positive example for their child.

The second stage of the LTAD model is FUNdamentals. Due to small developmental differences between sexes, this stage occurs at ages 6 to 8 years in girls and ages 6 to 9 years in boys. During this stage, children expand on the fundamental motor skills they developed during the active start stage to include a larger variety of both locomotor and ball skills. At this stage, the development of agility, balance, coordination, and speed (referred to as the ABCs) is also introduced. The third stage of the LTAD model is learn to train. This stage occurs at ages 8 to 12 years for girls and ages 9 to 14 years for boys. During the learn-to-train stage, children adapt their fundamental motor skills to more context-specific skills. The authors (Balyi et al., 2013) note that this is the last step for achieving the outcome of physical literacy; therefore, it is important that children learn a large repertoire of skills that can be used across many different contexts and should be encouraged to participate in a variety of different sports and physical activities throughout the year. At the learn-to-train stage, it is also important to introduce basic decision-making and psychological skills, such as goal setting, used in physical activity contexts.

Sport Excellence Outcome

The second outcome in the LTAD model is sport excellence; it includes the train-to-train, train-to-compete, and train-to-win stages. Sport excellence focuses on training methods to increase proficiency in context-specific skills, tactical knowledge, and psychological skills needed to successfully compete at high levels. The fourth stage of the LTAD model is train to train. This stage is considered one of the most important in the model, because it occurs during puberty for both sexes, which is marked by many changes in individual and environmental constraints (see chapters 12, 14, and 15). During the train-to-train stage, individuals focus on gaining further proficiency in context-specific motor skills. This stage is often when individuals begin narrowing the sports or physical activities they participate in; however, specialization in a single sport is discouraged. At the train-to-train stage, it is also important to continue the development of decision-making skills, tactical knowledge, and psychological skills.

The fifth stage of the LTAD model is train to compete. Although this stage is presumed to occur at ages 15 years and older for girls and 16 years and older for boys, the timing is influenced by individual constraints, such as maturational timing and motor competence. During the train-to-compete stage, individuals begin to specialize in a single sport or physical activity and engage in focused training to further develop proficiency in context-specific technical, tactical, and playing skills. In this stage, further engagement in psychological skills training is also encouraged for individuals to handle high-pressure situations. The sixth and final

---

WHAT DO YOU THINK?

Exercise 17.3

What are some ways that a parent or caregiver could encourage play behavior in the home?

stage of the LTAD model for achieving the outcome of sport excellence is train to win. This stage occurs at age 18 years for females and 19 years for males. During this stage, individuals engage in intense, context-specific training to further improve their technical, tactical, and psychological skills. At the train-to-win stage, training should become more individualized to optimize the individual's chances of achieving success at a high level.

Lifelong Physical Activity Outcome

The third outcome of the LTAD model is lifelong physical activity, which includes the active-for-life stage. This outcome focuses on continued engagement in physical activity across the life span. Although active for life is the final stage of the LTAD model, it does not focus on a specific developmental period; instead, it can begin at any time after physical literacy has been achieved. Within this stage, there are three options for continued engagement in physical activity that are based on the specific goals of the individual. The first option, competitive for life, is suited for individuals who want to continue participating in lower level competitive events. Someone who chooses this option might participate in 5K running events or a recreational soccer league. The second option, fit for life, is suited for individuals who are interested in participating in a wide variety of physical activities. Someone who chooses this option might participate in activities such as yoga and cross-country skiing. The last option, sport and physical activity leaders, is suited for individuals who intend to work in physical activity settings. Someone who chooses this option might coach a youth sport team or teach physical education at a high school.

Foundations, Talent, Elite, and Mastery Model

An applied, practitioner driven sport development framework is the foundations,

talent, elite, and mastery (FTEM) model. A multidisciplinary team at the Australian Institute of Sport developed this model, which is based on both theoretical principles and applied experiences (Gulbin et al., 2013). The elements of the acronym listed represent four macro phases of sport development. Within the macro phases, there are 10 micro phases. The foundations phase includes three micro phases: F1—learning and acquisition of basic movement, F2—extension and refinement of movement, and F3—sport-specific commitment or competition. The talent phase includes four micro phases: T1—demonstration of potential, T2—verification, T3—practicing and achieving, and T4—breakthrough and reward. The elite phase includes two micro phases: E1—representation and E2—success; and the mastery phase includes one: M1—sustained success. Unique to the FTEM model is a lack of age-specific recommendations for each phase. This was done intentionally to accommodate several individual, task, and environmental constraints that might affect when one enters a particular phase. Although the model appears linear, individuals can move around it at various points during their lives. Like the LTAD model, the phases within the FTEM model lead toward three specific outcomes: active lifestyle, sport participation, and sport excellence.

Foundations Phase

Foundations is the first macro phase of the FTEM model. The focus of this phase is to build foundational skills that allow the individual the ability to lead an active lifestyle or participate in sport. There are three micro phases within foundations. The first micro phase is F1, learning and acquisition of basic movement foundations. During F1, individuals are exposed to a variety of movement opportunities to develop fundamental locomotor and object control skills, which can be used across a variety of contexts. The next micro phase is F2, extension and refinement of movement foundations.

During F2, the individual builds on the skills learned during F1 by participating in diverse movement experiences in both formal and informal settings. The key transition between F1 and F2 is moving from free play environments to instructional settings (e.g., physical education, youth sport) to improve fundamental motor skills.

At the end of F2, individuals have achieved a level of physical literacy that will allow them to lead an active lifestyle. However, some individuals may choose to progress further to participate in organized school or recreational sports and physical activities. When this is the case, individuals progress to micro phase F3, sport-specific commitment or competition. During F3, individuals commit to a sport or physical activity and focus on developing context-specific skills. Formalized training and engagement in competition is also characteristic of this phase. Individuals may choose to stay in the phase for various amounts of time depending on their individual goals. For example, one person may choose to stay in this phase for the rest of their life while another may choose to pursue higher levels of training and proceed to the talent macro phase.

Talent Phase

Talent is the second macro phase of the FTEM model. The focus of this phase is to identify individuals deemed talented and develop their potential. Talent is often delimited to an individual's genetics alone; however, this model factors in both individual and environmental influences. There are four micro phases within the talent phase. The first micro phase is T1, demonstration of high-performance potential. During T1, individuals demonstrate some level of talent in one or more domains (e.g., skill proficiency, fitness, or mental toughness) that is indicative of future success at an elite level. The talent identification process is varied and complex and can include both formal and informal methods. For example, the National Football League scouting combine is a formal assessment of American collegiate football players' physical and mental

---

TRY THIS

Talent Identification

Exercise 17.4

Talent identification methods are often varied. Common methods include physical, cognitive, and psychological assessments. Pair up with a classmate and choose a sport or physical activity you are both familiar with. Individually, make a list of specific measures that you would use to identify someone who would be best suited for that sport or activity. Organize your list into categories using the chart below.

Physical	Cognitive	Psychological

Compare your responses with your partner. What was similar? What was different? Was one category represented more than the others? What might this indicate about the process of talent identification?

ability that coaches and other stakeholders use to identify potential athletes to draft for their teams. However, it is important to note that talent identification is often unreliable (Johnston et al., 2018) and can also overlook late maturers as well as children with a younger relative age (Goncalves et al., 2012).

The second micro phase is T2, talent verification. During T2, coaches and other stakeholders further subjectively confirm an individual's talent. This often takes place in more ecologically valid environments, such as games and practices. Practitioners often use intuition or prior experience as a basis for evaluation and look at additional characteristics, such as coachability, motivation, and commitment. Once talent has been confirmed, the individual enters micro phase T3, practicing and achieving. During T3, individuals engage in high-level sport-specific training to meet specific outcomes. During this phase, individuals can become susceptible to resource constraints, such as access to proper equipment, facilities, and coaching, that could lead to dropout or underachievement. The final micro phase is T4, breakthrough and reward. During T4, individuals participate in high-level competitive events to gain notice by relevant stakeholders. This phase is usually marked by the attainment of a college athletic scholarship, sponsorship, or position on a professional or high-level team or organization.

Elite and Mastery Phases

Elite and Mastery are the third and fourth macro phases of the FTEM model. The focus of these phases is to distinguish between different levels of elite performers. There are two micro phases within the elite phase. Individuals in micro phase E1, senior elite representation, are characterized by their *participation* in international competitions, such as the Olympic Games, while those in micro phase E2, senior elite success, are characterized by their *achievement* in international competitions, such as winning a medal at the Olympic Games. Individuals in the mastery phase, sustained elite success or mastery, are characterized with their achievement in international competitions over a sustained period of time. For example, Michael Phelps would be considered a mastery athlete due to his record of 28 medals over five Olympic Games. Although these phases provide some useful guidelines for distinguishing between levels of elite performance, the metrics used to determine these differences can often be context dependent. Thus, it is important to consider sport-specific considerations and competition formats when making these determinations.

Implications for Instruction

Overall, the sport development models described in this chapter focus largely on the idea of early **sport diversification**—when a child participates in a variety of movement activities during childhood to develop a large variety of fundamental motor skills. This contrasts early **sport specialization** wherein a child receives focused training in one sport or physical activity from a young age. Although early sport specialization has been shown to contribute to high levels of performance at an early age and beneficial

---

WHAT DO YOU THINK?

Exercise 17.5

Choose a sport or physical activity you are familiar with. How would you differentiate between phases E1, E2, and M for someone in that sport or activity? Provide an example of someone who would meet your criteria for each of these phases.

RESEARCH NOTES

Athlete Development in Parasport

Do parasport athletes follow the same developmental pathways as able-bodied athletes? In a recent study, Patatas and colleagues (2020) interviewed 32 individuals from the Brazilian Paralympic Committee representing five parasports: para-athletics, paraswimming, parapowerlifting, wheelchair basketball, and goalball. The interviews included several open-ended questions focused on understanding the career development of parasport athletes. The results of the study revealed six developmental phases:

1. *Attraction:* First contact with parasport (e.g., recruitment, rehabilitation, recreation); individuals with continental impairment start earlier than those with acquired impairment; deliberate play and sport sampling encouraged

2. *Retention:* A need for accessible facilities and appropriate instruction; shorter than other phases

3. *Competition:* Occurs early in one's athletic career often while the athlete is still in earlier phases; talent identification occurs most often during competition

4. *Talent identification and development:* Talented athletes identified and receive high-quality training by skill instructors; no specific talent identification process for parasport athletes; can occur very quickly

5. *Elite:* Regular participation in high-level competition; slow transition to elite phase due to severity and type of impairment can (e.g., limited opportunities, lack of access to quality coaches); faster transition to elite level and lengthened career with limited number of parasport opportunities

6. *Retirement:* Voluntary or involuntary transition out of parasport (e.g., progression of impairment); education and psychological preparation for transition important

Like the FTEM model, the phases for parasport athlete development do not have age boundaries. Instead, transition between phases is contingent on developmental and competition benchmarks.

to athletes in sports with an early age of peak performance (e.g., gymnastics), it often leads to an increased risk of injuries, burnout, and dropout (Goodway & Robinson, 2015). Moreover, early sport specialization does not necessarily predict later attainment of elite-level performance. Thus, sport specialization should not be promoted until later adolescence when the individual has gained adequate physical literacy.

Within these models, early diversification is promoted by engagement in deliberate play and structured play activities until the teenage years when specialization and deliberate practice may be desirable for some individuals. A consensus statement on youth athletic development from the International Olympic Committee (Bergeron et al., 2015) concurs that a variety of age-appropriate physical activities (i.e., diversification) in early development is associated with continued involvement in more intense activities later in life, elite performance, and continued participation in sport. In other words, diversification does not detract from elite performance in later years if that becomes a personal goal and is less likely to be linked to sport dropout and other negative aspects of youth sport noted previously. Diversification is also associated with intrinsic motivation, self-regulation, positive well-being, and long-term sport involvement. Using sport development models as a framework for youth sport organization and philosophy, coupled with parent and coach education, may go a long way to support the children and youth who entered sport in the first place to improve physical competence, enjoy social acceptance, and have fun (Weiss & Williams, 2004). In addition, it may reduce the negative aspects of youth sport (e.g., stress and dropout) while advancing the positive.

The multiple pathways within the sport development models share features with three types of environments proposed by Wall and colleagues (2007) to promote a greater depth of knowledge and performance in physical activity. These three environments (instructional, practice, and competitive) capture the additional challenges and social pressure experienced when moving from an environment for novices to one for athletes. "The instructional, practice, and competitive environments can be viewed as a continuum; seeing them this way underscores the need to recognize and assess the performance capabilities of learners in different performance environments" (Wall et al., 2007, p. 270).

An **instructional environment** is a relatively closed and supportive environment that provides instruction, feedback, and encouragement to explore movement options. Such instructional learning environments are typically present in physical education, which provides ample practice opportunities. Students are encouraged to move to progressively more difficult tasks and environmental conditions. A **practice environment** is more demanding because more emphasis is on the proper execution of specific skills under increasingly demanding space and time constraints. A practitioner controls the practice session by determining the number of players involved, the player roles, the equipment, and the space. In competitive environments, the performance expectations and social pressure increase as individuals or teams compete against each other. The performance expectations are lower in younger recreational settings than in older and more elite settings, where expectations can be very high. Aspects of deliberate practice may be present in elite contexts with older participants. Recall that deliberate practice includes more control by the coach, the goal of improving performance, and more effort in practice. Competitive environments can include the stress of evaluative fans, and outcomes may be linked to social prestige and future opportunities in the sport.

SUMMARY

Motor development models provide a useful framework for understanding how motor skills progress during different developmental periods, which can be used by practitioners to inform instructional content. There are many similarities across models including a focus on acquiring a variety of fundamental motor skills in early childhood followed by a progression toward context-specific skills that can be used to participate in sport and recreational activities. However, each model has some unique differences. Seefeldt's (1980) hierarchy of motor proficiency emphasizes a proficiency barrier during early childhood, wherein children must achieve a threshold of proficiency in fundamental motor skills before they can go on to learn more context-specific skills. Clark and Metcalfe's (2002) mountain of motor development includes a compensation stage that considers declines in competence due to injury or other setbacks. Stodden and colleagues (2008) emphasize the relationship between fundamental motor skills and physical activity at different developmental periods as well as the contributions of perceived physical competence, physical fitness, and obesity.

Like motor development models, sport development models provide a developmental lens for understanding motor skill progression that can be useful for practitioners. However, these models consider multiple outcomes for physical activity participation: active lifestyle, recreational sport, and high-level sport. Across models, there is an emphasis on building fundamental motor skills through early sport diversification to lead an active lifestyle. This is evident in Côté s sampling period of the developmental model of sport participation, the physical literacy outcome of the LTAD model, and the foundations phase of the FTEM model.

Sport specialization is not emphasized until later in the models for individuals seeking to become elite-level performers.

Overall, the models presented in this chapter provide practitioners with useful guidelines that can be used when designing instruction or program curricula. This includes an early focus on gaining competency in a variety of fundamental and context-specific motor skills so that learners can engage in lifelong physical activity. Practitioners can then change focus based on the goals of their learners to achieve other outcomes, such as competitive sport.

> **ONLINE ACTIVITIES**

The student material found in HK*Propel* includes exercises, labs, and videos to enhance learning and encourage practical application of important concepts.

LEARNING AIDS

Supplemental Activities

1. Choose two motor skills you would describe yourself as skillful in. Working backward down the mountain of motor development, explain what prior skills and experiences led you to achieve your level of proficiency. Start by defining how the motor skill is performed skillfully. For example, an experienced basketball player can perform a layup even when faced with a defender or increased game pressure, whereas a novice basketball player is unable to dribble to the basket and shoot. The novice must focus on the fundamental motor skill (e.g., dribbling or jumping). Work backward and describe the underlying motor skills and patterns required for your selected skills from the preadapted period to the skillfulness period.

   a. At what age did you become skillful?

   b. What context-specific skills that were critical to developing the level of skill you have now did you practice at an earlier age?

   c. Step back to fundamental motor skills. What fundamental motor skills were critical? Why?

   d. Ask your parents whether they did anything during the preadapted period that may have helped you advance your manipulative skills, postural skills, and locomotor skills.

   e. Use this information to fill out the following chart.

Motor skill	Skillfulness	Context-specific motor skills	Fundamental motor skills	Preadapted period
Basketball layup	Right, left, jump, shoot; pattern is performed well in spite of external influences (e.g., defenders)	• Basketball shooting • Stepping and shooting	• Jumping • Dribbling	• Pull to stand • Stand alone • Walk with and then without assistance

From P.S. Beach, M.E. Perreault, A.S. Brian, and D.H. Collier, *Motor Learning and Development*, 3rd ed. (Champaign, IL: Human Kinetics, 2024).

2. Arrange an interview with an accomplished athlete. Ask your interviewee about her early years in the sport. Did she participate in many activities before specializing in her current sport? At what age did she begin specializing in her current sport? How does her experience fit within the sport development models?

Glossary

compensation period—A period from Clark's mountain of motor development, which involves an adaptation to the environment as a result of an injury or declines resulting from aging.

context-specific motor skills period—A period of refinement of fundamental motor patterns in which performers learn movements specific to sports or other movement forms; from Clark's mountain of motor development.

deliberate play—Activities in which some rules are established and monitored by children or adults.

deliberate practice—Activities designed to improve current levels of performance; they require much effort and are not necessarily enjoyable.

free play—Activities engaged in exclusively for intrinsic reasons, often during infancy and early childhood.

fundamental motor patterns—Basic movements such as throwing, catching, hopping, and jumping that form a base for more complex sport-specific movement patterns.

fundamental motor skills—Developmental level of the hierarchy of motor proficiency that consists of foundational motor skills needed for the development of more context-specific motor skills.

instructional environment—A closed and supportive environment that includes ample instruction, feedback, and encouragement to help learners explore movement options.

investment years—The years characterized by achieving elite levels of performance. The foci are strategy, competition, and skill development within a context of deliberate practice directed and assisted by a coach.

practice environment—An instructor-controlled learning environment that emphasizes the proper execution of specific skills under increasingly more demanding space and time constraints.

preadapted period—The mountain of motor development period in which infants start interacting with the environment by engaging in phylogenetic motor behaviors such as sitting up, standing, crawling, and walking.

prenatal period—The mountain of motor development period consisting of the last two trimesters of pregnancy in which the fetus moves quite a bit.

proficiency barrier—A hypothetical barrier used to describe a threshold of motor skill proficiency.

reflexes-reactions—Developmental level of the hierarchy of motor proficiency that consists of infant reflexes and motor milestones.

reflexive period—The mountain of motor development period following birth and lasting two weeks, during which the newborn adjusts to sensory input such as bright lights and sounds.

sampling years—The years characterized by exposure to many fundamental motor skills and a wide range of sports with an emphasis on fun and excitement.

skillfulness period—The period at the peak of the mountain of motor development in which a learner has acquired a high level of skill proficiency. This period does not distinguish between levels of performance, such as university and professional athletes.

specializing years—The years during which people spend significant time on one or two sporting activities. Skill development takes on a higher priority than during the sampling years, but fun remains a critical component.

specific sport skills and dances—Developmental level of the hierarchy of motor proficiency that consists of context-specific motor skills.

sport diversification—Participation in a variety of movement experiences to develop a greater repertoire of fundamental motor skills.

sport specialization—Intense training in a single sport or physical activity to achieve elite-level performance.

structured practice—Activities in which skill performance assumes a higher priority than in deliberate play.

transitional motor skills—Developmental level of the hierarchy of motor proficiency that consists of motor skills that aid the transition between fundamental motor skills and context-specific motor skills.

PREPRACTICE CONSIDERATIONS

After reading this chapter, you should be able to do the following:

- Describe three types of goals and principles of goal setting.
- Explain when demonstrations are effective, when they are not, and why.
- List the pros and cons of expert and learning models.
- Discuss the relationships between verbal instruction and both implicit and explicit learning.
- Describe guidelines for using verbal cues.
- Discuss attention in terms of being broad or narrow and external or internal.

Challenging Traditional Thinking

Angel is a physical education teacher and a coach of a sixth-grade girls' golf team at her middle school. Because golf is new to many physical education students, she knows she will have to use demonstrations frequently. Her golfers are also in her physical education class; Angel reflects and wonders if she should ask her golfers to provide demonstrations too. She remembers from her time in the physical education teacher education program that young learners may better receive peers than adults. What if the golfers' demonstration is incorrect? Correct practice is critical; but Angel also knows that if students see a demonstration and do not think they can do it, they might quit before they try. What should Angel do?

This chapter explores several prepractice variables that affect performance and learning. Prepractice refers to actions of instructors, therapists, and coaches immediately prior to physical practice rather than more general issues of structuring the environment. Prepractice actions include goal setting, demonstrations, verbal instruction, directing attention, and physical guidance. Of course, the role of the instructor does not end here. It also includes arranging physical practice and deciding how to provide feedback during or after physical practice. Somewhat surprisingly, there is little scientific consensus about the role of prepractice information such as demonstrations and verbal instruction in motor learning (Fagundes et al., 2013; Ferrari et al., 2018; Hodges & Franks, 2002). Thus, physical education (Rink, 2014; Siedentop & Tannehill, 2000), motor learning (e.g., Magill & Anderson, 2021), and sport coaching textbooks (Purdy, 2017) often present contradictory information.

GOAL SETTING

Theories of motor learning and self-regulation assume that learners are goal directed—that they want to achieve something. As we saw in chapter 8, the purpose of free play and recess is fun, and as adults we do not want to turn child's play into anything else by inserting goals of achievement. We can modify the environment to present activity challenges and encourage exploration by supporting and interacting with children, but we should allow their natural sense of fun and intrinsic motivation to flourish while they play. However, free play and recess alone are not enough to support motor learning. In structured practice or deliberate practice, as opposed to free play, the situation changes, and performance improvement becomes more important. In these situations, goal setting is likely to enhance performance and learning. Goal setting has also become an important treat-

ment component in those who have had a stroke (Alanko et al., 2019) and those with cerebral palsy (Bayón et al., 2018).

In practice situations, instructors often tend to encourage students to do their best. At first glance, this seems sensible, because the instructor knows that a goal for the whole class or team (e.g., perform 15 push-ups or 10 throws that hit a target) will result in some students failing and others barely being challenged. If the whole class is watching and waiting on students to finish their repetitions, the students might feel embarrassed by being on display. In a class or team setting, goals should be time based (rather than trial based) and individualized to avoid being on display. It is critical to understand what goal setting is and which goals are most appropriate for the learner.

Goal setting is a self-regulatory skill that allows people to monitor progress toward a self-determined goal (Zimmerman, 2000). Instructors and therapists should encourage goal setting because people tend to commit to goals they set for themselves. In general, goals are most effective when they are specific, attainable, challenging, and realistic (Gould, 2006). Goals direct attention to important elements of the skill, produce greater effort and persistence, promote new learning strategies, and influence psychological characteristics such as confidence and anxiety (Gould & Chung, 2004). As adults age, goals remain motivational and affected by self-efficacy but become attenuated when ability declines (West et al., 2013).

The types of goals are outcome goals, performance goals, and process goals (Schmidt & Lee, 2020). **Outcome goals** emphasize the results of performance, often in comparison to others. An example would be, *I want to be first*. Such goals may provide direction, but outcomes are often beyond the person's control; someone else might win because of outstanding but unexpected performance. **Performance goals** focus on improvement relative to one's own performance, whereas **process goals** specifically emphasize aspects of skill execution or selected strategies. (See table 18.1 for examples.) Weinberg and Gould (2011) recommended setting specific, moderately difficult goals to which the person is committed. Goals should be realistic and used for practice and competition and for the short and long term. Moreover, goals should be recorded and periodically evaluated. Interestingly, for athletes from Generation Z (those born in or after 1996), Gould and colleagues (2020) suggest setting daily process goals to make the long-term goal seem more attainable.

Most early research in goal setting compared the instructions *Do your best* or *Give it 100 percent* to more specific and challenging but achievable goals in industrial settings (e.g., Locke & Latham, 1985). The results showed clearly that specific, challenging, and achievable goals were superior to vague goals such as *Do your best*. Similar comparisons between *Do your best* and more specific personal goals have been made in sport and exercise psychology research (see the review by Kyllo & Landers, 1995). The findings are like those in industrial settings but not quite as dramatic in sport. Schmidt and Lee (2020) speculated that in *Do your best* sport situations, people may secretly set their own goals, thus overshadowing the experimenter's manipulations. They also pointed out that most of the goal-set-

ting research has ignored the difference between performance and learning, except for Boyce's research (1992). The task was rifle shooting, and Boyce used three groups. Those in the first group were encouraged to do their best; those in the second group were encouraged to set specific but individual goals; and those in the third group were given individual goals set by the experimenter and based on previous performance. Those in the *Do your best* group performed better than those in the other groups only during the first practice session, whereas the specific goal-setting procedures in the other two groups were equally effective during performance and retention. Perhaps goal setting has a positive impact on both performance and learning.

A study of self-regulated dart throwing by adolescent girls showed some evidence that process goals lead to more improvement than performance goals do (Kitsantas & Zimmerman, 1998; Zimmerman & Kitsantas, 1996); however, setting process goals and then shifting to performance goals resulted in the highest performance (Zimmerman & Kitsantas, 1997). In younger children, the results of goal setting have been equivocal. A study by Kolovelonis, Goudas, and Dermitzaki (2011) showed no difference between performance and process goals with 11-year-olds, but youngsters who

Table 18.1   Examples of Outcome Goals, Performance Goals, and Process Goals

Activity	Outcome goals	Performance goals	Process goals
Basketball	Win the district championship.	Increase foul shot percentage from 50% to 70%.	Don't look at the teammate to whom you are passing the ball.
Cross country running	Finish in the top three at the state championship meet.	Improve time on state championship course by 10%.	Lean forward on the downhill to take advantage of the momentum of the hill.
Golf	Qualify for regional championship.	Score under 85 in practice rounds.	Concentrate on a smooth putt and ignore the crowd.
Folk dancing	Make no errors with the 10-step sequence and win the community dance-off.	Improve from three to seven correctly sequenced moves.	Maintain a straight back and keep the head up during the do-si-do move.
Therapy	Walk more steps each day than your spouse.	Improve from three steps with crutches to 10 yards without crutches.	Concentrate on a heel landing and improve toe takeoff with the injured foot.

WHAT DO YOU THINK?

Exercise 18.1

1. Pick two activities. Provide examples of outcome goals, performance goals, and process goals. Use table 18.1 as a guide if necessary.

2. Goal setting is clearly essential to learning and performance. Would your approach to goal setting differ depending on (a) the task and (b) the age of your students or clients? Explain.

self-recorded had superior performances. In a subsequent study (Kolovelonis et al., 2012) with children of the same age, those who used self-talk with either performance or process goals outperformed those in a goals-only group and those in a control group. Goal-setting research has not frequently compared groups of different ages, and hence few developmental trends have been noted. Practitioners might wish to encourage individual goal setting but to check goals periodically to ensure that they are realistic. More research into development and goal setting is clearly needed.

DEMONSTRATIONS

Demonstrations, modeling, and *observational learning* are terms often used interchangeably. These activities are so common in physical activity instruction and therapy that we do not give them much thought. The term *demonstration* is more closely aligned to motor learning and instruction, whereas *modeling* and *observational learning* are terms more frequently used in the context of social learning and sport psychology. In any case, practitioners often demonstrate a skill such as a forward roll, provide some verbal cues, and then send the class or team off to practice it. The notion that a picture is worth a thousand words seems true for learning motor skills.

In addition to demonstrations by the instructor, video clips of good performers and even photos of correct actions may be used (Schmidt & Lee, 2020). Under certain circumstances, demonstrations are effective in teaching motor skills (Hodges & Franks, 2002; McCullagh & Weiss, 2001; Schmidt & Lee, 2020; Scully & Newell, 1985). However, we seldom ask how different task goals or task types might make demonstrations effective or ineffective, who should perform demonstrations, what learners are supposed to see in demonstrations, or how demonstrations affect learning. We turn to these topics now.

Demonstrations and models may serve three functions (Weiss et al., 1993). The first is to *help learners acquire new skills,* such as a forward roll, or new behaviors, such as returning equipment to its proper storage spot. This is the focus of this section. The second function is to *elicit already learned behaviors,* such as going out for a walk or cheering for your team. The third function is to *reduce avoidance behavior* such as fear by using models that manipulate psychological factors such as self-confidence, motivation, and anxiety.

Effectiveness of Demonstrations

A demonstration provides a visual template, or model, of a desired movement pattern (Hodges & Franks, 2002) and can inform the learner about the nature of the task and its requirements. If a task is very simple and the learner has previous knowledge of the criteria for performance, a demonstration may have no impact (Newell, 1981). How simple the task is depends on both the task itself and the skills of the learner. Tasks such as dance steps or gymnastics actions might not require a demonstration of the individual skills, but if they need to be sequenced in a particular order, a demonstration may convey such cognitive information (Hodges & Franks, 2002).

Whether a demonstration of more complex tasks is effective likely depends on the task goal and the measurements of effectiveness used. In closed skills, the movement form is often the primary learning goal. In gymnastics, synchronized swimming, diving, and figure skating, how one performs is critical to success. Demonstrations may help learners acquire new patterns of coordination because they must practice the pattern or technique repeatedly until performance is automatic (see table 18.2).

A meta-analysis compared results from observational studies using movement form measures and movement outcome measures (Ashford et al., 2006). Meta-analysis is a mathematical technique that standardizes findings from many studies. As you might imagine, one researcher may use a basketball shooting task and another may use a badminton task; it is difficult to combine such studies quantitatively. Meta-analysis transforms the results from different tasks into a standard result called an effect size (ES). The ESs from each study can then be combined to determine an overall effect of the treatment—in this case, the difference between using demonstrations and not using demonstrations during practice. Combined with statistical significance, the ES provides a quantitative snapshot of treatment effects. Many researchers use Cohen's

Table 18.2 Effectiveness and Ineffectiveness of Demonstrations

Demonstration may be effective when . . .	Demonstration may not be more effective than other types of information when . . .
• The person is acquiring a new pattern of coordination. • The person requires a template of the movement pattern. • The person is learning a movement sequence. • The person is learning strategies and decision making. • The person is learning to cope with difficult emotional situations.	• The task is simple. • The person already knows the task and its requirements. • The new task involves a change in parameters. • The outcome is more important than how the movement is performed. • The outcome is clear and performance feedback is available.

TRY THIS

Focus, Focus

Exercise 18.2

Demonstrations are usually helpful when learners are acquiring new coordination patterns. Pair up with another student and crumple up a piece of paper to throw. One person demonstrates a throw, and the other person observes and then tries to copy the demonstrator. As you learned in chapter 4, a hop for distance with speed involves pumping the support leg, arm swings, keeping the foot on the support leg behind the torso, and so on. The demonstrator should perform one aspect of the hop in a unique way (e.g., keep the pumping leg in front of the body or put the hands above the head without moving them) to demonstrate a new pattern of coordination. After a couple of demonstrations, the other person tries to replicate the new hop. Discuss whether the observer was successful and how the demonstration could be enhanced. Did you find it easy, moderately difficult, or very difficult to replicate the hopping pattern of your partner? Why?

recommended interpretation of ES: an ES of 0.80 or higher is a large difference, an ES of 0.50 or higher is a moderate difference, and an ES of 0.20 is a small difference.

Ashford and colleagues (2006) measured how the model performed the task (i.e., form). Outcome measures included accuracy (or error) scores. A moderately large effect size (0.77) was reported for form; that is, practices with demonstrations were more effective than practices without demonstrations when form was measured. A significant but smaller effect size (0.17) resulted with outcome measures. That is, practices with demonstrations were still superior to practices without demonstrations, but not to the same degree when assessed with movement technique.

It appears that in the early phase of learning, movement technique is more sensitive to the influence of demonstrations than is the outcome of the movement. To state this simply, initial learning is associated with learning how to assemble the movement pattern, but its effect on outcome is not as obvious. People must learn how to perform before their movement pattern has an effect on the outcome. Movement dynamics were also more sensitive to the impact of demonstrations than movement outcomes for serial, continuous, and discrete tasks (Ashford et al., 2006). Attention to the end of the movement form (e.g., the hand and forearm in a basketball set shot) may be particularly helpful (Breslin et al., 2009). Early in the learning of a new movement, several demonstrations are likely necessary to begin building the template, followed by practice with additional demonstrations thoughtfully interspersed (see Weeks & Anderson, 2000). If the task is an old pattern of coordination and learners are required to perform new parameter characteristics (e.g., the same pattern faster), demonstrations may be no more effective than other forms of instruction (Magill & Anderson, 2021).

With open skills, the primary goal is the movement outcome (not the process by which the movement is accomplished). The successful basketball pass to a teammate is the desired outcome, but the movement form of the pass (i.e., how it was executed) is much less important. With many open skills, as discussed in chapter 4, variability in practice is desirable. There is less need for demonstrations that replicate the solutions of others and a greater need to emphasize discovering novel tactical solutions. Williams and Hodges (2005) contended that demonstrations may be no more effective than verbal descriptions when the goal is problem solving, because the outcome does not depend on replicating a specific movement pattern or technique. When instructors believe that a demonstration is needed in open skills, they should combine it with the outcome effect. This provides information for learners to use as they solve problems and determine how their actions relate to results. Williams and Hodges also recommended that instructors use verbal instruction expressing the intended outcome of the skill before offering a demonstration, such as *Can you pass the basketball from out of bounds to the high post area?* A demonstration can then be used to guide the learning process.

Hodges and Franks (2002) described several of their motor learning studies involving novel bimanual movements, such as those that might be found in juggling or playing musical instruments. In these situations, they concluded that "movement demonstrations and instructions relating to the movement of the limbs convey little useful information in the early stage of acquisition, if information about goal attainment is available through feedback" (p. 805). Thus, if the desired outcome is clear and performance feedback is available, demonstrations may not be necessary. Of course, bimanual movements are only one class of movements.

Demonstrations and video presentations may help learners develop strategies and decision making based on perceptual information. Martens, Burwitz, and Zuckerman (1976) used the task of trying to move a ball placed on top of two rods up an incline by manipulating the distance between the rods. The ball could fall into any of eight holes beneath the rods, and the hole at the end of the incline earned the highest score possible. Two approaches were modeled. A creep strategy involved slowly adjusting the rods, which produced consistent but moderate success. A ballistic strategy involved moving the rods very rapidly, which resulted in variable levels of achievement but very high scores when successful. Observers tended to replicate the strategy they had observed.

Weeks (1992) argued that most observational research had studied internally paced skills such as locomotor skill sequences or serial arm movements and suggested that more open, externally paced tasks should shed light on the impact of observation on perceptual processing and decision making in more complex tasks. In a coincident timing task, participants had to displace a barrier at the same time the final light was illuminated on a runway of lights. Three modeling groups were created. One group received modeling that focused on the perceptual demands of the task, and a second group received modeling that focused on the motor demands of the task. The perceptual modeling participants used 10 observations of the runway lights to assist in timing the arm action to the lights, although their hands had to remain on their knees during the prepractice observations. Motor modeling participants received 10 demonstrations of a person hitting the barrier. A third group received both motor and perceptual models, and a fourth group received no prepractice modeling. Groups in perceptual modeling conditions performed better than those in only motor task modeling conditions, which suggests that perceptual demands can be modeled and that they are very important in externally paced activities. Weeks recommended that instructors of externally paced tasks such as batting and ground strokes

in racket sports include training on the perceptual characteristics of ball flight. Thus, demonstrations may help learners focus on relevant perceptual cues and strategies of action.

Another line of research used video-recorded models of children coping with difficult situations (McCullagh & Weiss, 2001; Weiss et al., 1998). This represents the third function of modeling noted earlier—reducing avoidance behaviors. One approach is to show models exhibiting negative cognition, affect, and behavior while they perform in difficult or fear-evoking situations such as learning to swim. Over repeated trials, the models verbalize more positive thoughts and improve their performance. For example, statements that change from *I can't do this* to *I can do this* convey a shift from lower to higher self-confidence (Weiss et al., 1998). The models demonstrate how they are learning to cope through problem solving and the impact on their motivation. This has the potential to influence self-confidence and motivation.

Wrisberg and Pein (2002) explored the self-regulation of how often to view a demonstration of a badminton long serve by novice university students. One group watched a video of a model prior to each practice attempt, one group chose when to see the video, and one group never saw the video. The first two groups acquired the correct form of the serve and retained that form better than the group that did not see the video did. The group with the option of requesting when to see the video requested it only 9.8 percent of the time, primarily during the first half of the trials on the first day. This suggests that demonstrations may be most effective for novices early in learning. The motor learning benefits of learners controlling when and how often they view a demonstration (Wulf et al., 2005) has also been supported. Self-regulation of demonstrations may be an effective practice for promoting learning. Whether these findings would be the same for children must await further research.

RESEARCH NOTES

Observational Learning and Anxiety

Weiss and colleagues (1998) investigated the impact of observational learning on swimming performance and the psychological responses of children who were fearful of swimming. Twenty-four children (average age of 6.2 years) participated. They were matched on age and swim lesson experience and then randomly assigned to one of three model types: control, peer mastery, and peer coping. The control group watched cartoons on days of the swimming lessons, but the cartoons provided no information on swimming. The peer mastery group observed a video of a similar-age peer who verbalized positively and was technically correct in swimming. The peer coping group video showed a peer who expressed increasingly positive comments and showed gradual improvement in swimming. Three days of swimming lessons were used, and the researchers evaluated the children's swimming skills, fear of swimming, and swimming self-efficacy, in addition to producing field notes. The coping and mastery groups were superior in swimming performance, were higher in self-efficacy, and showed more change in fear compared to the control group. Coping models had a stronger effect on self-efficacy than mastery models did. Thus, the use of modeling may help young learners deal with movements involving some inherent degree of fear and produce change in associated psychological variables.

Performance of Demonstrations

Professionally created videos of top athletes performing the perfect throw or swing create the impression that an expert, or at least a very skilled person, should be performing the demonstration. This makes sense if the goal is to present the ideal movement pattern that all learners should mimic. These expert models often enjoy high status, and their demonstrations are often accompanied by verbal cues and explicit highlights of the correct technique (Darden, 1997). Consistent with the formation of a perceptual trace, or template, to which performance will be compared to detect errors, it is often assumed that more frequent expert demonstrations will create stronger blueprints. However, chapter 11 highlighted the value of using variability in practice and promoting problem solving and questioned whether a gold standard of movement patterns actually exists. These ideas are at odds with the logic of having all learners mimic one movement pattern and raise the question of the necessity of an expert model. In fact, there is some consensus that demonstrations by unskilled people may be more effective than those by experts (Darden, 1997; Hodges & Franks, 2002; McCullagh & Weiss, 2001; Ste-Marie et al., 2012). Of course, learners should have some idea about the correct movement pattern and understand that what they are observing contains errors.

Learning models have been shown to be as effective as expert models and, in some cases, more effective for learning (e.g., Lee & White, 1990). A **learning model** is a novice who practices the skill and receives feedback from an instructor or coach. The demonstration is of the model trying to acquire the task, receiving feedback, and then using the feedback to construct the next performance effort. By definition, a learning model demonstrates variability in performance. Learners might identify with the learning model because of similarity in status (both are learning) and realize that the demonstrated skill level is within their reach. It seems that learning can occur from watching others make errors (Domuracki et al., 2015). In addition, 10-year-olds learning a five-skill trampoline routine benefited more from a video of themselves than from verbal instructions alone (Ste-Marie et al., 2011).

It is also possible that what is being modeled is not the movement pattern per se but a process of problem solving. Andrieux and Proteau (2013, 2014) showed that both novice and expert models together are more effective than either alone, likely because more cognitive effort is expended in acquiring the skill through identifying a standard (expert model), witnessing the errors of a novice (learning model), and learning how to avoid those errors. In summary, there are motivational, attention, and learning explanations for the beneficial impact of learning models or mixed models.

Learning models could be incorporated into a class using reciprocal teaching or learning groups in which all students are both observers and models in a problem-solving activity. Magill & Anderson (2021) also recommended presenting a checklist of key aspects of the skill to the pairs or groups to guide observation and feedback.

Theoretical Explanations of Demonstrations

Thus far we have discussed several demonstration issues: when demonstrations are effective, who should perform demonstrations, and what the learner is viewing. Under some circumstances, demonstrations are very important. But questions of *when*, *who*, and *what* do not deal with how or why demonstrations are effective. *How* and *why* are theoretical questions. We now look at motor learning, social learning, and ecological theories to see how each explains why demonstrations are helpful to learners.

Motor Learning Theories

Demonstrations are a part of classic theories of skill acquisition, including the closed-loop theory of motor control (Adams, 1971) and schema theory (Schmidt, 1975). In Adams' closed-loop theory, a perceptual trace, or template, of the movement develops with practice. Sensory feedback during subsequent movements can be compared to the perceptual trace to ensure correct execution. A second memory trace that initiates the movement was also posited. The second trace was proposed because the same perceptual trace could not initiate and evaluate the correctness of a response. Schema theory is an open-loop account of motor control. Not unlike Adams, Schmidt postulated two types of schemas: a recall schema for response production and a rec-

---

WHAT DO YOU THINK?

Exercise 18.3

This section has probably made you realize that using demonstrations effectively is much more complex than you previously thought. Describe how you could use demonstrations to teach the following:

1. Students who are being introduced to the standing long jump for the first time

2. Students who are learning to dive

3. A student with a hearing impairment

ognition schema for response evaluation. If a template of movement already exists (that is, the perceptual trace of Adams and the recall schema of Schmidt), then a demonstration will likely refine the template to which feedback during movement execution will be compared (Hodges & Franks, 2002). For example, if a throwing schema exists, the demonstration will provide information about the specific type of throw, its force, and its direction. If the movement template is not established and the task is novel, the demonstrations may help learners engage in cognitive processes like those that occur in physical practice (Blandin & Proteau, 2000).

The stages of motor learning, according to Gentile (1972) and Fitts and Posner (1967), are discussed in chapter 5. Each provides some insight into how movement templates might be established in the early stages. Fitts and Posner called their first stage cognitive because the learner attends to cues and feedback to develop an executive program. In both these theories, a demonstration may present the idea of the movement and the cues that are necessary for initial learning of the movement skill.

Social Learning Theory

Social learning (Bandura 1986, 1997) theory is perhaps the most detailed account of demonstrations, although *modeling* and *observational learning* are preferred terms. Bandura's original focus was the social learning of behaviors rather than motor skills. He contended that people learn most about their social world through observation and that practice is not essential for developing social or cognitive behaviors. This makes sense for simple responses that are already in people's repertoires, such as a sequence of movements. If the movements can already be accomplished, the activity becomes more cognitive than motoric (Hodges & Franks, 2002). A demonstration of the sequence might help at the beginning of the learning process.

Bandura (1986, 1997) asserted that modeling is information processing with four subprocesses that transfer, or code, information from the model into a template of correctness to which future movements are compared. The first subprocess is attention to the modeling. This is affected by the observer's cognitive capabilities and arousal level. Attention is also influenced by characteristics of the modeled event (e.g., its complexity). For complex movement patterns, the observer should focus on relevant cues via verbal directives or alternating good and poor performances. Retention, the second subprocess, involves reformulating the event into a memory representation. It is assumed to be an abstraction of the event and likely verbal or visual, depending on the task. The third subprocess is production. As McCullagh and Weiss (2001) pointed out, this was not well developed in Bandura's original writings because he was concerned with explaining social behaviors that might be dichotomous (i.e., either performed or not). Motor learning specialists are concerned with movement quality and demonstrations may convey spatial and timing aspects of importance. The final information-processing subprocess is motivation, given that the person must be motivated to exhibit the behavior. Reinforcement of observed models or actions by the observer enhances the motivation of the observer to reproduce the action demonstrated. These four processes are developmental; the first three are cognitively oriented, and the fourth is motivation oriented (Weiss et al., 1993). Observation learning is therefore expected to improve with age because of critical developmental changes in attention, retention, production, and motivation.

Ecological Perspectives

As we have discussed in several chapters, practice from the ecological theoretical viewpoint is designed to enable the learner to explore the perceptual–motor landscape and to assemble functional coordination patterns that offer solutions to movement problems. Movement variability is highly valued, and demonstrations that highlight variability rather than one ideal movement pattern should be effective. The ecological perspective views perception as direct. Ecological researchers try to determine what information is available and useful for the learner in demonstrations without cognitive interpretations and transformation of information as put forth by Bandura (1986, 1997). Ecological researchers place more emphasis on the information learners glean from a demonstration than on how the information should be presented (Hodges & Franks, 2002). Observers may be sensitive to the relative motions of movements, which can be used to assemble coordination patterns (Scully & Newell, 1985).

Support for the ecological perspective and the information gleaned from demonstrations comes from research using point-light displays (e.g., Williams, 1989). A point-light display is a video from a motion analysis system showing dots of light placed at a person's joints. Williams provided a point-light display of a throwing motion with dots placed on the wrist, elbow, and shoulder. The observer saw the movement of only the dots, not the arm or ball. Almost 90 percent of children and adults reported seeing a throwing action after four trials. Thus, observers may attend to information about the relationships of limb components in the movement pattern. In ecological terms, the relationships of limb components in the movement pattern are invariant relative motions (Scully & Newell, 1985). Recall from chapter 2 that invariant features include the sequence of action, relative timing, and relative force. The sequence of movements such as the rotation of the trunk, the backswing of the arm, and the step with the contralateral foot, followed by forward rotation, was apparently conveyed to the adults and children by the moving dots.

Magill and Anderson (2021) reviewed similar studies of walking patterns in which people distinguished individual gaits based on unique relative motions rather than a single factor such as walking velocity. It seems that learners do perceive and use invariant relative motions in observational learning (Magill & Anderson, 2021). However, the movements used in most of this research were rather common and well practiced, such as throwing, walking, and running. It is not yet clear how instructors might help learners focus on the relative motions of skills that are not yet mastered or are very novel, because the perception of the invariant relative motions is likely learned without consciousness.

Learning From Demonstrations

What learners see in a demonstration is likely influenced by the nature of the task. In addition, the interpretation is influenced by the theory behind the research. Demonstrations can lead to learners' acquiring movement strategies, spatial information, and temporal information. Strategies might include task-specific approaches such as the creeping and ballistic movements described by Martens and colleagues (1976) or throwing a basketball from the foul line with one or two hands. More general problem-solving skills suggested by learning model research would be exemplified by a student receiving teacher feedback about the front crawl and then saying to herself, *I have to raise my elbow higher during recovery*. Martens and colleagues indicated that modeling of coping strategies led to performance improvement but also to enhanced psychological function such as self-efficacy. These coping strategies helped learners acquire a more positive psychological approach.

Spatial information can also be picked up, as shown in a series of studies on learning sign language through modeling (Carroll & Bandura, 1990). Relative motion also involves spatial and temporal information about body parts moving in relation to each other or to the environment, and strong evidence suggests that learners are aware of this information (Ashford et al., 2006). Temporal information (i.e., information about the timing of movements) has been demonstrated in several studies (Magill & Anderson, 2021). Think of the instructor who claps his hands in the rhythm of a skipping motion that young students happily try to imitate. This research presents auditory information about movement timing or rhythm and has led to gains in rhythmic timing of movement sequences as might occur in dance.

Mirror neurons in the premotor cortex were discovered in the 1990s (Lago-Rodriguez et al., 2014). As part of the motor system, these unique neurons fire both when an action is observed and when it is performed. An infant may grasp a cup and view its mom grasping the same or a very similar cup. The mirror neurons fire in both situations; hence, observing a movement may strengthen the neuronal path of action. Mirror neurons have been proposed as the neurological link between the observation of movement and the creation of motor commands (Lago-Rodriguez et al., 2014; Ste-Marie et al., 2012).

Developmental Considerations in Demonstrations

Functional constraints are developmental in that they improve with age, experience, and knowledge of the task. Adults, adolescents, and those with sport-specific knowledge are more likely to use self-regulated learning strategies and have access to other capacities that have resulted from years of experience dealing with educational and movement challenges. These functional constraints, coupled with structural constraints, give adults and adolescents an advantage over children when faced with unfamiliar tasks. Experienced observers are more likely to

produce closer approximations of a model early in learning. As Ashford and colleagues (2007) stated, "Adults can adapt existing coordination tendencies but in a way that results in the acquisition of a new coordination pattern suited to the goals of a task" (p. 548). McCullagh and Weiss (2001) provided the corollary that motor skill instruction for children under 12 years of age should facilitate task-relevant attention such as *Try not to look at the ball when you're dribbling;* strategies such as *Watch me. After I kick the ball to a teammate, I run quickly to a spot where I can receive a pass;* and knowledge such as *Let me show you an offside.* These factors must be considered in observational learning.

McCullagh and Weiss (2001), in a detailed review of studies that shed light on children's ability to benefit from models, underscored the point that the effectiveness of models is multifaceted: it depends on the age of the observer; how performance is measured; and whether acquisition, retention, or transfer is assessed. We have also discussed that the impact of demonstrations is affected by the type of task and task goals. Therefore, developmental generalizations to guide practice are difficult to generate. With children four or five years of age, a show-and-tell model can be effective for teaching a sequence of movements (Weiss, 1983). Show and tell is a demonstration and explanation of what should be done and is helpful for children who do not spontaneously attend to task-relevant cues, such as stepping forward with the foot opposite the throwing arm. It may also use verbal rehearsal strategies for remembering the order of events (e.g., *arms, legs, glide* for the breaststroke). In an obstacle course task, children were encouraged to use verbal self-instruction by thinking aloud—that is, saying phrases such as *Jump and clap* and *Jump-jump* that matched the activity (Weiss, 1983). Older children may benefit from show and tell but not more than from a visual demonstration without suggested rehearsal strategies. With novel tasks requiring new patterns of coordination, such as juggling, Meaney (1994) showed that both children and adults benefited from verbal rehearsal and cues combined with a demonstration, whereas adults improved following only the visual demonstration. The adults' physical performances were better than those of the children, and the adults used more strategies. These studies support the premise that the cognitive developmental level of children should be considered with demonstrations, and that children benefit from instruction focused on relevant cues and from engaging in intentional memory strategies.

Wiese-Bjornstal and Weiss (1992) showed that girls as young as seven to nine years old could watch a demonstration of a softball fast pitch and recognize a correct model from one of four video alternatives, could engage in verbal cues like the model, and could show some of the model's form (e.g., stride length, release body angle). Having learners restate the main points about a demonstration and verbal cues following show and tell would be good teaching practice. Watching the model more frequently and engaging in more practice resulted in better recognition of the correct form and in performances that resembled the model's. Self-regulation and observational learning research also supports the cognitive–developmental changes that occur during childhood and the influence on demonstrations. Younger children from five to seven years of age may benefit more than older children from verbal cueing and rehearsal strategies used along with a demonstration, because the older children already possess the language skills to use strategies spontaneously (Ste-Marie et al., 2012). The older children (11 years old) appeared to have greater awareness of their own learning, as evidenced by the fact that they requested more observations of a model than younger children did (eight years old) when rehearsing a dance sequence (Cadopi et al., 1995). The older children also used more verbal self-instruction, which is a self-regulated strategy.

Bouffard and Dunn (1993) explored whether developmental differences existed in children's use of self-regulation while learning the movement sequences of American Sign Language. They compared children 6 and 7 years old to children 9 and 10 years old; both groups had unlimited time and unlimited trials of watching a tape with the American Sign Language sequence. The length of the sequence was one and a half times longer than an estimated memory span for each child. When each child thought he had learned the sequence, he rang a bell, which signaled the researchers to enter the testing room to watch the child perform the sequence. Thus, this study explored what children do spontaneously in response to a demonstration without any guidance from the teacher. The older children displayed better recall of the sequences than the younger children did. In addition, the older children watched the demonstration videos more frequently than the younger ones did, and they used more strategies for learning the sequences (e.g., miming the gestures and rehearsing movements). Further, the 9- and 10-year-olds used more instances of language, indicating that they monitored their own learning more frequently. It appears that models can assist in self-regulation development and that older children spontaneously use self-regulation more often than younger children do.

A final developmental factor regarding modeling is the tendency for children to focus on task goals rather than movement form during demonstrations. Earlier, we stated that movement dynamics (approximation of the movement form) are more sensitive to the impact of demonstrations than movement outcomes (outcome performance such as accuracy or time) earlier in skill acquisition for serial, continuous, and discrete tasks (Ashford et al., 2006). It seems that developmental factors affect this generalization. Ashford and colleagues (2007) conducted a meta-analysis of 55 studies that

RESEARCH NOTES

Tailoring Observation and Demonstrations to the Learner

Ste-Marie and colleagues (2020) reviewed the observational intervention (e.g., demonstration) literature in hopes of providing evidence-based recommendations for practitioners. Since 2011, 42 researchers studied observational learning and found intervention to be effective for a wide variety of populations in diverse settings. Although scholars have researched demonstrations and their effectiveness with motor learning for decades, clarity regarding several specific aspects of demonstration is needed. For example, should demonstration occur before, during, or after practice? The types of models (video; picture; live peer or adult; cartoon; mastery, or coping) we should use and how much control we should provide to the learner (e.g., self-regulation) remain questions for the authors, because they suggest more research is needed. For now, Ste-Marie and colleagues (2020) suggest that practitioners have the choice in picking models but recommend variability with presentation. Specifically, they suggest that more than one demonstration by different sources may be beneficial. Multiple sources with varying presentations may promote problem-solving skills, which may also increase observers staying on task because the demonstration would be more interesting. Additionally, the benefits of viewing demonstrations from multiple angles and with varying speeds also remain inconclusive. Finally, the authors conclude that although some clarity exists, much more research is needed to provide evidence-based recommendations. Thus, practitioners should choose the demonstration strategies that they feel best fit their situation.

compared children and adults regarding their awareness of movement dynamics, movement outcome, or both, in demonstrations. The ES of movement dynamics for adults (0.80) was larger than that for children (0.24) when demonstrations were compared to practice-only conditions. This indicates that adults benefited more than children from demonstration and practice, compared to practice without demonstration, when measures of movement form were employed in the research. In fact, although the ES for the children was positive (0.24), it was not significant. The opposite was found for measures of movement outcome: the ES for adults was negligible (–0.02), and that for children was more substantial (0.48). In other words, children seem to benefit more from demonstrations when assessed on movement outcome, thus adding a developmental caveat to the earlier generalization that initial learning is associated with learn-

ing how to assemble the movement patterns. Children seem to be more aware than adults of movement outcomes than of movement form in demonstrations. Thus, therapists and instructors should feel comfortable using demonstrations with an emphasis on movement outcomes with children.

Although modeling can facilitate the acquisition of closed skills, the magnitude of the effect depends on age and the measure used to quantify learning. Children can discern and benefit from movement form, but they tend to focus on movement outcome. The extent to which instruction can focus children from movement outcome to movement form remains unknown. Hence, teachers and coaches should be sensitive to their students' and athletes' natural tendencies and help them focus on movement form if they believe that the youngsters possess the necessary cognitive functioning, attention, knowledge, self-regulation, and memory.

WHAT DO YOU THINK?

Exercise 18.4

Review what you learned about cognitive functioning, attention, knowledge, self-regulation, and memory. How do these act as constraints for children who are engaging in observational learning? What structural constraints should be considered?

VERBAL INSTRUCTION

Verbal instruction is a frequent and expected prepractice element that is often used in conjunction with demonstrations. Verbalization and demonstrations may provide redundant cues, but they may also provide different information to learners (Huff & Schwan, 2012; McCullagh & Weiss, 2001). Instructions could be in written form such as a task card, but more often they are spoken. Verbal instructions and cues are assumed to facilitate learning and to establish safe practice settings; however, they must be brief, such as *Bend your knees*. Magill and Anderson (2021) recommended presenting only one or two instructions about what to do because learners must remember the instructions and then perform the skill. Instructors should not exceed their charges' attentional capacity. This is particularly important for novice learners and children.

Verbal information conveys the nature of task requirements, just as demonstrations do (Lee et al., 2001). Examples include the correct and consistent movement form of a closed skill such as a dive, the creation of a smooth sequence of movements in the correct order in learning to stand independently while recovering from an accident, or the movement outcome goal of a successful pass to a teammate in an open sport. More specifically, Schmidt and Lee (2005) indicated that verbal information provides an initial orientation to a new skill, an overall idea or image of a movement, a means of recognizing one's own errors (e.g., checking the wrist on a follow-through), details of how to hold an apparatus or implement, information on where and how to move in a game, cues that are most important (e.g., the seams of a baseball), and the results performers should try to achieve (see the section called Goal Setting earlier in this chapter). A verbal phrase may simplify a rather complex movement in the tennis serve, such as *Scratch your back with the racket*. It may also reinforce the order of movements in the breaststroke (*arms, legs, glide*). Instructors may also promote the transfer of related, previously learned movements and strategies through verbal means. Feelings that should be expected from a movement can also be conveyed. For example, *If you are stretching properly, you should feel a slight pull in the calf muscle*.

Implicit and Explicit Learning

The examples in the previous paragraph underscore the many instances in which clear instructions would appear to be important in skill acquisition. Yet, there is not a great deal of research supporting these common purposes and outcomes of verbal instruction with respect to motor learning beyond specifying the task requirements, such as speed, accuracy, or both; movement form; or movement outcome (Hodges & Franks, 2002; Lee et al., 2001). In fact, research suggests that in some situations verbal instruction may not be helpful beyond personal practice and may be detrimental to learning. Some of this research deals with **explicit learning** and **implicit learning**.

Gentile (1998) extended the cognitive learning distinction between explicit and implicit learning to motor learning. The term *explicit* refers to conscious awareness of such factors as goal attainment and developing the relationship between the learner and the task. The aim of verbal instructions is to help learners become explicitly aware of some aspects of the skill. For example, *The goal of this skill is to . . .* or *Hold the ball with your fingers along the stitching.* This is like declarative knowledge. Implicit learning is not conscious and likely deals with issues such as force production. For example, consider a young toddler who is offered a tricycle and initially cannot contract and relax the appropriate muscle groups at the correct time and order, and with the appropriate force, to move the vehicle. She does learn to cycle but is not aware of how she does it. Even adults are unaware of the physical principles that govern bicycle riding, and they can have a hard time explaining how to tie shoelaces. Much motor learning is implicit, and knowing mechanical principles is not likely to assist such learning.

Hodges and Franks (2002) proposed that tasks with high perceptual–motor demands or complex response requirements would benefit less from explicit instructions. Some experimental support exists for this proposal (e.g., Farrow & Abernethy, 2002; Sanchez & Reber, 2013). Farrow and Abernethy (2002) manipulated the amount of time participants viewed a tennis ball after a serve. The participants were asked to predict whether the ball would fall to their forehand or backhand. The implicit instruction group received no information about the server's action and the direction of the ball. The explicit instruction group received specific information through videos, verbal and written information, and feedback during practice trials. Not surprisingly, those in the explicit group were able to write more rules and strategies that were important for returning serves than those in the implicit group were. The two groups performed equally well in predicting the direction of the ball, but the implicit group

had an advantage at ball contact (i.e., when no ball flight was evident). It seems that those in the implicit group used the anticipatory information to predict the direction without conscious awareness and without advanced cues.

Green and Flowers (1991) showed the potential detrimental effect of verbal information in a study in which participants had to manipulate a joystick to catch a ball that moved across a monitor. An explicit instruction group received information about expected pathways and their probability. The implicit group received no information other than the goal of the game. During 800 trials, those in the group that received explicit instruction performed more poorly than those in the implicit group, presumably because those in the explicit group devoted more attention to remembering the rule and looking for its occurrence, which disrupted their performance. It seems that instructors should use verbal instructions cautiously when a task has a high degree of perceptual input (e.g., video games) and involves complex responses (e.g., catching a ball that is thrown fast).

Several studies have used a ski simulator task to explore explicit and implicit motor learning, as well as discovery learning. The participants' goal is usually to move the platform as far to the left and right as possible for a specified time and with a constant cycle time (e.g., for 60 seconds; each cycle takes 3 seconds).

In a study by Wulf and Weigelt (1997), one group—based on previous research on participants who demonstrated high performance—was given explicit instructions to exert force once they moved beyond the center of the simulator platform. The second group was told only the goal of the activity—in this case, to move the platform as far to the left and right as possible for 90 seconds, with each cycle taking 2 seconds. This group was considered a discovery or implicit learning group. On performance and transfer tasks, the discovery group

---

Can You Make Walking Explicit?

Exercise 18.5

Create groups of two or three. Walking is an activity that we do regularly, and university students have had many years of practice. Create two columns on a sheet of paper, one labeled *Explicit* and one *Implicit*. For the first phase of this activity, the group lists explicit information about how to walk. This will be a bit of a challenge because you have had so many years of practice with this task. After you generate some explicit knowledge, walk around for a few minutes, and see if you can add to the explicit list and begin to identify implicit factors. Select a sport skill and repeat the exercise.

---

performed better. These participants apparently learned the technique (exert force once beyond the center) in an implicit manner.

Many studies have used the ski simulating apparatus as well as other complex motor tasks to explore the impact of both demonstrations and verbal instruction compared to discovery learning (see Hodges & Franks, 2002; Lee et al., 2001). In general, the results support the effectiveness of allowing learners to discover how best to achieve task goals. Instructions may interfere with learning if attention is misdirected by either demonstrations or verbal instruction. Of course, this assumes that the task goal is understood and that performance feedback of some form is present in the learning situation. This research usually included novice adult learners, but even with fourth- and fifth-grade children learning a soccer loft kick, discovery learning has been shown to be more effective than explicit instructions (Gredin & Williams, 2016).

Ringenbach and Lantero (2005) extended this line of thinking regarding self-discovery. They asked typically developing children and adults, as well as adults with Down syndrome, to draw circles with both hands. First, in an exploratory phase, participants performed the task any way they wished. Then the three groups were instructed to draw the circles either symmetrically (in-phase) or asymmetrically (antiphase).

Adults without a disability responded without problems. However, the children and the adults with Down syndrome, who had performed symmetrically in the exploratory, or self-selected phase, performed less symmetrically when they were requested to perform symmetrically. This demonstrates that even with children and people with an intellectual disability, self-selected or exploratory instructions may be best.

Verbal Cues

Coaches, instructors, and therapists commonly use **verbal cues**. They are brief and concise phrases that direct attention to regulatory conditions in the environment, prompt key skill components, or initiate activity (Magill & Anderson, 2021; Ste-Marie et al., 2012). The classic phrase *Look at the ball* directs attention; *Bend your knees* focuses on a skill component; and *Ready, set, go!* prompts activity. Magill and Anderson (2021) offered the following suggestions for using verbal cues to enhance their effectiveness. Cues should be one to three words in length, be easily related to aspects of the skill, be used only for the most critical elements, not interfere with performance, be rehearsed by the learner, and direct shifts of attention and the rhythm of movement sequences.

WHAT DO YOU THINK?

Exercise 18.6

1. Choose two skills. Describe how you could implement verbal instruction to facilitate student learning. Provide examples of verbal cues.

2. Can you recall instances when an instructor, perhaps even your professor in this course, seemed to go on and on verbally, and finally you said, "So *that's* what you mean?" What made this difficult? Was it simply too much detail, or was the goal of the activity unclear?

DIRECTING ATTENTION AND PROVIDING GUIDANCE

One of the uses of verbal cues is to direct attention. Previously presented research warned that explicitly directing attention to optimal or correct coordination of the limbs may not facilitate learning and may even be detrimental. How can we help learners focus on their bodies or the environment to promote skill acquisition, and what are the developmental implications? As mentioned in chapter 11, one of the concepts of attention is **visually searching** for environmental cues necessary for performance (Magill & Anderson, 2021; Schmidt & Lee, 2020). Attention may be broad or narrow and external or internal, as discussed in chapter 14.

An external focus produces greater accuracy, consistency, and efficiency in learning compared to an internal focus. This is consistent with the positive view of discovery learning and the potential detrimental effects of incorrect attentional focus via demonstrations and verbal instructions regarding coordination patterns. Unlike some variables in motor learning, the superiority of an external focus exists for both performance and learning (Wulf, 2013).

The external focus viewpoint is a rather robust finding for novice and experienced learners alike (Wulf, 2013). Research with children has provided unambiguous support for external focus on a soccer throwing task (Wulf et al., 2010) and with target throwing (Avila et al., 2012). External focus superiority also extends to children with attention-deficit/hyperactivity disorder (Saemi et al., 2013) and intellectual disabilities (Chiviacowsky et al., 2012). It seems reasonable for instructors to consider using some internal focus with children.

Visual selective attention (often called a visual cue) refers to directing visual attention to environmental information to help people prepare for and perform an action (Magill & Anderson, 2021). Important visual cues to guide movements are available in central vision (where the eyes focus) and peripherally. Much evidence suggests that experienced or expert performers in competitive sports are better able to attend to cues than less experienced or novice performers are, and that they pick up the cues earlier, thus enabling them to anticipate their opponents' movements and prepare their own responses. The cues depend on the situation. While waiting for the serve in tennis, experts watched for cues in the few seconds prior to the opponent initiating the serve, particularly in the head, shoulder, and trunk regions (Goulet et al., 1989). Experi-

---

WHAT DO YOU THINK?

Exercise 18.7

Much research over the past 20 years has demonstrated the superiority of an external focus for learners. As a future teacher, coach, or therapist, identify five skills and list the external and internal cues that might be used in teaching them.

---

enced players in soccer attended more to the hip region of an opponent in one-on-one situations than less experienced players did (Williams & Davids, 1998).

Lefebvre and Reid (1998) asked boys and girls aged 6 to 12, with and without coordination difficulties, to watch a video and predict whether the ball thrown by a child would land to the left, to the right, or in front of the catcher. The older children were more effective predictors with less visual information available; boys were generally more effective than girls; and those without coordination problems were more effective than those with coordination problems. The authors concluded that experience is a significant factor in the development of attention to early cues. Because the cues are quite specific to the activity context, instructors can assist by directing learners' attention to relevant cues as well as providing sufficient practice to use such cues (Magill & Anderson, 2021). Video-based visual search programs have also shown some promise as a teaching tool (e.g., Williams et al., 2004).

SUMMARY

This chapter would provide Angel, the physical educator and golf coach featured in the chapter-opening scenario, with some guidance about factors to consider prior to teaching her students. Goal setting, demonstrations, verbalizations, attention directing, and physical guidance have been used effectively to promote performance and learning. Demonstrations and verbalizations are advantageous when there is a need to explain a task goal, outline a movement sequence, promote the use of strategies, deal with a fearful learning situation, or point out an important cue. If the task goal is outcome oriented in a team sport, too many demonstrations and words might detract from the processing of team tactics. Demonstrations and verbalizations as means to acquire patterns of coordination with closed skills may best be described as overrated, assuming that the task goal is known and performance feedback is available. Implicit learning characterizes much motor learning. Angel can feel comfortable using carefully placed demonstrations, sometimes in concert with player demonstrations, and verbal cues to guide action and attention. She was correct in her questions but there are solutions!

> **ONLINE ACTIVITIES**

The student material found in HK*Propel* includes exercises, labs, and videos to enhance learning and encourage practical application of important concepts.

LEARNING AIDS

Supplemental Activities

1. Sometimes, practitioners receive conflicting information about whether they should demonstrate common errors or not. Interview current or former athletes of any sport of your choice. Report on what the athletes say regarding how they feel about seeing common errors in demonstrations. See if you can find any common themes. Can you resolve the areas of disagreement?

2. Can you watch a demonstration and listen to instructions? Clearly, demonstrations are important, but effectiveness is predicated on learners paying attention. Pick a novel task and demonstrate it to three to five people. Have each person take a turn but each time add more verbal language and distractions (add music, have an observer talk, etc.). Make notes about your observation. Are you watching the movement or listening? What distracts you? Ask your peers to do the same and then compare notes. See if you can find a consensus.

Glossary

explicit learning—The conscious awareness of learning a task.

goal setting—A self-regulatory skill that allows people to monitor progress toward a self-determined goal. Goals should be specific, attainable, challenging, and realistic.

implicit learning—Learning without consciousness.

learning model—A model who demonstrates variability in performance. In physical education, this usually refers to a novice who practices the skill and receives feedback from an instructor.

outcome goals—Goals that focus on the results of performance in comparison to others.

performance goals—Goals that focus on improvement relative to one's own performance.

process goals—Goals that focus on aspects of skill acquisition.

verbal cues—Brief and concise phrases used by teachers, coaches, and therapists to direct attention to regulatory conditions in the environment, prompt key skill components, or initiate activity.

visually searching—An aspect of attention that involves detecting the environmental cues necessary for performance.

PRACTICE

CHAPTER OBJECTIVES

After reading this chapter, you should be able to do the following:

- Discuss deliberate versus naïve practice.
- Understand the benefits of the contextual interference effect and be able to effectively implement variable practice.
- Appropriately design blocked, serial, and random practice as well as distribution of practice.
- Explain when it is appropriate to use part practice and whole practice and their respective challenges for transferring to real-life learning situations.
- Design practice sessions with the appropriate type of part practice based upon the learner and type of motor skill.
- Discuss mental practice and imagery and how they may enhance learning and performance and explain how instructors can mass or distribute practice.

Optimal Practice for Maximal Results

Benny is an eighth-grade student who loves to participate in cross country running and lacrosse. Recently, Benny lost his right leg just above the knee in a fluke accident. Benny is very disheartened because he is struggling to walk with his new prosthetic leg. However, Benny's coaches believe that he can, with proper practice, learn to not only walk but also to run. However, to learn to run again, Benny will need physical therapy. Both of Benny's coaches are concerned that if Benny does not see measurable progress, that he may not believe he will ever play sports again. Benny's parents agree that Benny needs to maximize his time with his new physical therapist and then collaborate with his coaches to best support his learning to most quickly get him back into the games. All stakeholders should consult to figure out the most effective practice designs for Benny.

This chapter focuses on many types of practice or how practice can be organized, including variable practice, distribution of practice, part versus whole practice, and mental practice. The learner, instructor, parent, or therapist can manipulate the types of practice to augment learning most effectively. We provide the scientific support behind each type of practice and address issues regarding practice organization that might be relevant to Benny. Variables such as age, experience, and type of skill affect whether a particular form of practice accelerates learning compared to another.

To learn lacrosse, downhill skiing, or how to use new prostheses, you need to practice. But how much practice is necessary and how practice should be organized are more complicated questions. Is it just a matter of repeating movements many times to become skilled, such as practicing running with a new prosthesis repeatedly? If the lacrosse skills of cradling, shooting, and passing need to be improved, should you focus on one skill for a considerable time before practicing the next skill? What advice can we give the coach who has her soccer team practice run drills repeatedly, only to see the players incapable of executing the skills in a real game?

Research findings relevant to practitioners sometimes depend on the type of task involved. The practice organization literature therefore has included discussions of findings from laboratories using controlled conditions versus real-life tasks and situations. These studies, among others, have led to several general conclusions, including the following:

- Early improvement in skill acquisition is generally very large and becomes smaller with additional practice.
- All things being equal, more learning will occur with more practice (e.g., see chapter 6—Assessing Motor Learning).
- Plateaus in performance may occur during skill acquisition.

- Improved performance, however minute, may be apparent after many years of practice.
- Motor learning is enhanced when learners control aspects of the practice.

Deliberate practice involves activities designed to improve performance that require much effort and are not necessarily enjoyable. However, athletes have often reported enjoyment while making deliberate attempts to improve performance (Deakin & Cobley, 2003). Thus, deliberate practice can be a confusing term. Fortunately, in a 2019 meta-analysis, Ericsson and Harwell clarify the definition of deliberate practice and contrast it to similar terms. The authors specify four criteria for determining deliberate practice:

1. It involves individualized training by a well-qualified teacher.
2. The teacher must be able to communicate the goal to be achieved by the trainee and the trainee can internally represent this goal during practice.
3. The teacher can describe a practice activity to attain the identified goal for performance and this activity allows the trainee to get immediate feedback on a given attempt.
4. The trainee is able to make repeated revised attempts that gradually approach the desired goal performance. (p. 4)

This differs from purposeful practice, which includes activities to improve performance without the benefit of an instructor or effective methods for practice. It also differs from naïve practice, which involves participating in activities that are directly aligned with the sport, game, or task without any instruction or direction and by simply responding to normal demands in one's own way (Ericsson & Harwell, 2019). Thus, deliberate practice is very distinct from other types of practice due to a focused engagement in domain-specific activities under the direction of a skilled instructor. The extent to which deliberate practice can be considered causal above and beyond naïve practice toward gaining expertise is difficult to state because both may be less than 100 percent mutually exclusive. In any case, the amount of practice is a significant contributor to expert performance with more practice leading to higher skill levels.

Although questions of deliberate practice remain, Macnamara and Maitra (2019) state that "expert performance is the result of prolonged practice, and that differences in levels of expertise are the results of differences in amounts of practice" (p. 2). Of course, expert levels of performance may not be a motivating factor for many people, either children or adults. Instead, they may be motivated to downhill ski so they can participate with friends and manage a single-diamond hill safely; a desire to compete and to be faster than everyone else may not be the single, driving factor. Regardless of motivation, how do we best and most effectively support acquisition of skill via practice? Do we practice the same skills over and over or do we attempt to support the variable nature of game play? Do we practice the skill as a whole or break it down to focus on specific problem areas? Is physical practice the only way we can learn and refine motor skills?

VARIABLE PRACTICE

Variable practice is practice that includes variations of the skill itself or the context of the skill in variable order. For example, there are multiple ways to throw a ball: sidearm (*A*), with a full windup (*B*), or with an underarm toss (*C*). If one were to execute each of those throws in a varied order, such as *BCACBAACBC*, that would be variable practice. The learner may never use the same throw twice in a row, but certainly the instructor will cue or create scenarios warranting the intermingling of the three throws during a practice session. By con-

trast, when one repeats the same skill in succession over and over during practice, this is considered **constant practice**.

In constant practice, the baseball instructor has the learner repeat many trials of the forceful overarm throw only. The constant practice schedule is more intuitive and the one many of us have experienced as early learners: a fixed amount of time or number of trials. This may seem reasonable because the learner can concentrate on one skill at a time and benefit from repetition and feedback.

Somewhat surprisingly, perhaps, variable practice tends to be superior to constant practice for learning a wide range of motor skills when a *novel* variation of the skill is required, such as open skills (Chua et al., 2019; James & Conatser, 2014; Yao & DeSola, 2009). Although not always explicitly stated, variable practice is advocated by each of the major models of skill acquisition described in chapter 5 albeit for different reasons. Variable practice develops schema and encourages new parameters of a generalized motor program so that people can respond to changing movement situations, according to the cognitive schema perspective of Schmidt (1975). Such practice provides the necessary variation of regulatory (e.g., opponent position, distance to target) and nonregulatory (e.g., crowd noise, fatigue) contexts in Gentile's stages model (1972, 2000). Finally, it gives learners the opportunity to explore and discover the perceptual motor landscape so that they can assemble functional motor patterns, according to dynamical systems and ecological theories (Davids et al., 2008).

Whereas variable practice is more effective for open skills, constant practice may be beneficial if the ultimate movement goal remains consistent across trials, such as in closed skills. For example, free throws in basketball always occur from the same distance with noninterfering opponents; hence, a novel response is not required. Breslin and colleagues (2012) demonstrated the benefit of constant practice over variable practice following 300 trials of a basketball free throw. Diving, gymnastics, throwing darts, playing cornhole, and so on, involve consistency across time and context rather than novel responses to changing environments. Also, constant practice may be superior to variable practice in acquiring force output patterns such as throwing for speed (King & Newell, 2013). See Ranganathan and Newell (2012) for a more complete discussion.

To theoretically situate the relevance of variability and skill learning, we now shift to the variability of practice hypothesis. The variability of practice hypothesis was first postulated by Schmidt (1975) in the context of generalized motor programs and schema development. When faced with a goal-oriented movement, the person retrieves a generalized motor program from long-term memory and then selects parameters that will dictate how the action will be executed (e.g., how forceful, how long). A generalized motor program is largely defined by invariant features—that is, characteristics of the movement that remain constant despite changes in parameters (see chapter 2). For example, an overarm throw for force usually has a stepping action, trunk rotation, arm action, wrist movement, and follow-through (see chapter 9, Object Control Skills in Childhood). Those are the invariant features of the throw and constitute the generalized motor program.

A throw has many variations depending on factors such as the object (e.g., ball or disc) and the intended distance of the throw. Variable practice involves variability in the parameters of the movement, not different movements. Different versions or variations of the throw might include parameters such as different required speeds, distances and trajectories, and player movements during a throw (e.g., throwing a fielded ball or throwing from a stationary position). The movement schema is an abstract or general memory representation of a set of rules that connect a person's actions to the parameters needed to produce the outcome (see chapter 2). Consider a softball player's decision, or desired outcome, to throw to a base for a force out or to throw to a teammate who needs to tag out a runner. This is achieved by using a generalized motor program of throwing, with the addition of *quickly changing the trajectory of the ball so that it may be caught in the mitt at chest height or caught low so that the defender can tag the runner out.* The variations of the throw (in italics) are the parameters that can change if the goal and context of the next play are different (e.g., the lead runner is the winning run or if the defense has a five-run lead and just wants outs to end an inning). Thus, a solution to a movement problem involves selecting the correct parameters from a generalized motor program.

With practice, the rules, or schema, are developed and used to determine the parameters required for different versions of a generalized motor program. Practice is variable because different parameters of the movement are included. Over time, the person learns relationships—for example, that different intensities and directions of forces generated by the hand produce successful throws for different distances and heights. Variable practice requires the learner to select new parameters for each movement trial; much less effort is required in constant practice because the same parameters are selected for many trials in a row. Strong schemas enable the person to select the appropriate parameters in novel contexts. For example, an outfielder needs to be able to select the appropriate amount of overall force to ensure his throw makes it to his intended target, which will vary based on how far the ball was hit to the outfield and the game situation.

Along with improved choice selection with motor skill performance, there is also an increased benefit of variable over constant practice when learning is assessed on tests of transfer and retention (Buszard et al., 2017; Pacheco & Newell, 2018). Consider the following scenario. You are teaching a lacrosse shot to your class. Group A tries a constant practice approach. Their task is to shoot a lacrosse ball to target on a wall in a gym that is 20 feet away. The target is stationary, and so there is a mark on the ground from where they shoot. They are to repeat this task 10 times and then move back 10 feet; repeat again and move back another 10 feet; then repeat and finish. Group B is the variable group. Group B has the same target on the wall with marks on the gym floor set at 10, 20, and 30 feet away from the target. At each floor spot, they have a basket of lacrosse balls. The instructions are to complete 30 throws without repeating any distance to the target two times in a row. In addition, they are told to vary whether they shoot the ball from a stationary position or after running a few steps. According to what we have learned in this chapter, so far, the constant group may perform better, initially, so at the end of that class period, they may report more targets hit than the variable group. However, during game play, the variable group seems to have an easier time shooting on goal when there is an active defense than the constant group. Furthermore, at the end of the unit, when the teacher retests the groups, the variable group scores higher than the constant group.

Thus, the benefits of variable practice may not appear in immediate performance but rather on later tests of transfer and retention. In other words, variable practice may appear to be adversely affecting performance during learning trials but will ultimately enhance learning (for a reminder of the differences between learning and performance, see chapter 1; to compare retention and transfer, see chapter 6). Variable practice may seem very sensible with open skills because they inherently include variability. After all, tennis players try to make it difficult for you to return the ball by hitting it with unexpected direction and force, and opponents are always trying to prevent you from receiving a pass from your lacrosse teammate. But even in closed skills, there are benefits from variable practice that might not seem so obvious at the outset. Closed skills with intertrial variability, such as golf, benefit from variable practice.

WHAT DO YOU THINK?

Exercise 19.1

Pick two activities. Describe how you would teach them using each type of practice. The overhand throw is provided as an example.

Activity	Type of practice	Practice session
Overhand throw	Constant	Throw 60 balls 20 yards.
	Variable	Throw 60 balls from either 20, 40, or 60 yards.
	Constant	
	Variable	
	Constant	
	Variable	

Golfers must perform under various wind conditions, on different fairway layouts, and under anxiety in competition, and they must make appropriate decisions, from the selection of clubs to how to putt given the layout of the green. Golfers may have a great deal of time to decide on a course of action, but shots must be parameterized to the physical and psychological playing conditions.

Many studies with children support the advantage of variable practice in motor skill learning (e.g., Gerson & Thomas, 1977; Kerr & Booth, 1978; Wulf, 1991; Zetou et al., 2014). However, other studies provided mixed or minimal support (e.g., Jarus & Goverover, 1999; Pease & Pupnow, 1983; Pigott & Shapiro, 1984; Wrisberg & Mead, 1981). The equivocal nature of these findings led Yan and colleagues (1998) to conduct a meta-analysis on the variable versus constant practice issue with children. The researchers located 39 effect sizes (ESs) in nine studies that included 272 boys and 336 girls ranging in age from 3 to 11 years. The overall ES between variable and constant practice regarding transfer to a new task was 0.28, a relatively small effect. That is, although variable practice was generally superior, the difference from constant practice was not great. The authors were also interested in the impact of age, type of task (rapid timing versus slow positioning), and type of movement (simple linear positioning versus complex or real sport movements such as throwing a beanbag). Age had a strong mediating influence on the advantage of variable practice over constant practice; there was a large ES (0.80) for young children aged 3 to 5 years but a relatively small ES for those between 6 and 11 years of age. The transfer benefits of variable practice over constant practice were greater for more ballistic tasks than for slow movements, as well as for more complex real-world movements than for simple movements. One can see that research findings can be quite complex and that generalizations and suggestions for practitioners might depend on age and the type of task or movement.

The original variability of practice hypothesis proposed that variability existed in movement parameters in a single gener-

---

TRY THIS

Who Is the Ringer?

Exercise 19.2

In this activity you will compare variable and constant practice for an underarm throw. Place a piece of tape on the wall of a gym. Measure distances of 4, 8, and 12 feet (1.2, 2.4, and 3.7 m) from the wall and mark each distance on the gym floor with tape. Create groups of two to four people. Half the group will practice the task using constant practice by underarm throwing a beanbag 30 times with the nondominant hand from 12 feet (3.7 m), tossing 30 beanbags in a row. The other half of the group will practice the task using variable practice by underarm throwing a beanbag 10 times from 4 feet (1.2 m), 10 times from 8 feet (2.4 m), and 10 times from 12 feet (3.7 m) without tossing from the same spot twice in a row. Count the number of times each person hits the target in 30 throws. This number is the performance score. Was there a difference between the constant and variable groups? Now have everyone throw 20 times to a small ring on the floor 6 feet (1.8 m) away (transfer task) and again count the number of hits. This number is the learning score. Was there a difference between the constant and variable groups? If not, what is your explanation? A month later, if you want a challenge, replicate the floor ring task and see who best retains their learning.

alized motor program. But what is known about organizing practices when variability appears to be different movements related to a sport or activity, such as passing, shooting, and cradling in lacrosse? Should a given practice include a mixture of the three skills, much like variable practice, or is it more effective to focus on only one of the skills for a considerable period before moving to the next skill? The area dealing with these nuances, known as contextual interference, addresses blocked, random, and serial practice.

CONTEXTUAL INTERFERENCE EFFECT

Contextual interference refers to the practicing of multiple skills in varied ways within any given session, or simply put, the amount of switching between tasks. Intuitively, it may seem logical that when novices are learning new skills, contextual interference would make performance more difficult. The **contextual interference effect** positively influences retention of learning and transfer from practice to game situations despite creating problems with performance during practice.

Variable practice can be designed with three different practice structures such as blocked, random, and serial practice. **Blocked practice** is rehearsal of one skill repeated over a fixed block of time before moving to the next skill. Blocked practice is like constant practice as described in the previous section because one skill is practiced repeatedly before switching to a new motor skill or variation of the same skill, as is often seen in repeated drills. **Random practice** is a practice sequence in which several skills are practiced in an unexpected order. An attempt is made to avoid rehearsal of the same skill twice in a row. In some ways random practice is like a competitive situation because movements, plays, and positions of opponents cannot be predicted in open skills. The organization of **serial practice** is like that of random practice in that various skills are intermingled during practice, but in a fixed format (e.g., layups, then rebounds, then chest pass and repeat). Serial practice is set up like repeated sequences or sets, such as practicing 10 passes, 10 free throws, and 10 layups, then repeating the sequence two more times. Table 19.1 shows how these forms of practice might appear across three 30-minute sessions of soccer.

The contextual interference effect is a paradox, because a random practice schedule can be detrimental during early skill acquisition but have a positive effect on learning and transfer for more skilled performances. Two main theories have been proposed to explain this paradox: the **elaboration and distinctive hypothesis** and the **forgetting and reconstruction hypothesis** (Lee, 2012; Magill, 2017; Schmidt & Wrisberg, 2008).

The elaboration and distinctive hypothesis was proposed by Shea and Morgan (1979). They suggested that random practice results in more cognitive strategies such as comparing and contrasting movements in working memory. As the learner shifts from one skill to the next, the distinct nature of each becomes clearer and more meaningful in long-term memory. This cognitive effort has a deleterious effect during acquisition but is advantageous later when learning is assessed. Of course, during blocked practice, people are not challenged to compare and contrast skills because they perform many repetitions of the same skill.

The second theoretical account, the forgetting and reconstruction hypothesis, was proposed by Lee and Magill (1985). They argued that the key explanation for the contextual interference effect is the action planning required for each skill. In random practice, the person must abandon the action plan used on the previous skill because a new one must be constructed. Thus, the action plan is forgotten initially but is renewed each time that skill is repeated later

Table 19.1 Three Lacrosse Classes With Three Skills and Three Practice Formats

Type of practice	Amount of contextual interference	Duration for each skill (in minutes)	Class 1	Class 2	Class 3
Constant	Zero	30	All passing	All shooting	All cradling
Blocked practice	Low	10	Passing	Passing	Passing
		10	Cradling	Cradling	Cradling
		10	Shooting	Shooting	Shooting
Serial practice	Moderate	5	Passing	Passing	Passing
		5	Cradling	Cradling	Cradling
		5	Shooting	Shooting	Shooting
		5	Passing	Passing	Passing
		5	Cradling	Cradling	Cradling
		5	Shooting	Shooting	Shooting
Random practice	High	Total of 30 min for all skills	Cradling Cradling Passing Shooting Passing And so on	Passing Shooting Cradling Shooting Cradling And so on	Shooting Shooting Passing Cradling Passing And so on

during practice. Random practice forces the learner to practice action planning, which is absent in blocked practice.

Both the elaboration and distinctive hypothesis and the forgetting and reconstruction hypothesis enjoy research support (Brady, 1998; Lee, 2012; Magill, 2017). Time will tell which one emerges as the more effective explanation, or whether some combination of the two is proposed.

The contextual interference effect is a relatively robust finding based on a great deal of empirical research (Lee, 2012) that included children (discussed later in this section), adults (e.g., Feghhi et al., 2011), and older adults (e.g., Lin et al., 2010). Practitioners should feel comfortable using random practice in most learning situations. Despite this general statement, though, some research findings have provided no, or limited, support for the contextual interference effect (e.g., Cheong et al., 2012; Ollis et al., 2005).

Unfortunately, clear and unequivocal guidelines that might tell us that a certain skill under a specific practice schedule will not yield the interference effect do not exist. More research is needed on this issue. But neither does the research suggest that blocked practice is generally more effective in motor skill acquisition than random practice (Ollis et al., 2005). When the contextual interference effect fails to enhance learning, the research usually shows a nonsignificant difference between blocked and random practice, not the superiority of blocked practice. A number of mediators have been proposed that cast doubt on the general benefit of contextual interference. These include age, skill level, type of skill, personality, motivation, and amount of interference (Ollis et al., 2004).

The contextual interference effect has been investigated with children. The superiority of random practice was shown on a handwriting task with five- to seven-year-olds (Ste-Marie et al., 2004). However, mixed results were found for the contextual interference effect for the forehand tennis groundstroke in two groups of 26 children aged 8 to 9 and 10 to 12 (Farrow & Maschette, 1997). The contextual inference

RESEARCH NOTES

Random Effects

Shea and Morgan (1979) conducted the first motor learning study that provided evidence of the contextual interference effect. The basic task was to move an arm and grasp a tennis ball and then knock over three of six small wooden barriers as quickly as possible and return the tennis ball to a final resting position. Participants had to learn three movement patterns (skills *A*, *B*, and *C*); patterns were illuminated by different-colored lights.

Two groups of university-aged students practiced the three-arm and hand movements under blocked or random conditions. The blocked group had 54 total practice trials: 18 consecutive trials for skill *A*, then 18 trials for skill *B*, and then 18 trials for skill *C*. The random group also had 54 trials to acquire the three skills but practiced them in random order, never performing a skill twice in a row over the 54 trials. As shown in figure 19.1, the blocked group produced quicker movements during the practice phase.

To assess learning, the researchers required the participants to perform a retention test, one 10 minutes after practice and one 10 days later. The retention tests were performed under both blocked and random formats. Figure 19.1 clearly demonstrates that the participants who had practiced under random conditions became much quicker at the movements than those who had practiced under blocked conditions. In fact, the random group maintained the speeds accomplished during acquisition, whereas the blocked group showed very poor performance during randomly ordered retention trials. In line with contextual interference predictions, blocked practice produced faster immediate performance, but random practice resulted in more learning.

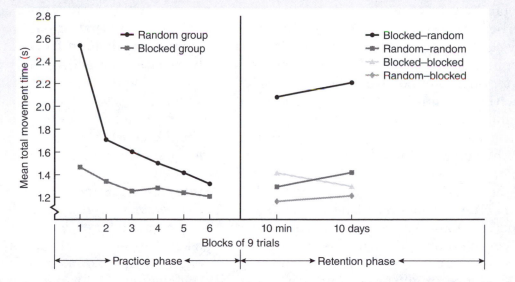

Figure 19.1   Performance on movement–speed tasks under random and blocked practice conditions. The relative amount that the groups learned is indicated by their retention performance at the right.

Reprinted by permission from J.B. Shea and R.L. Morgan, "Contextual Interference Effects on the Acquisition, Retention, and Transfer of a Motor Skill," *Journal of Experimental Psychology: Human Learning & Memory* 5, no. 2 (1979): 179-187.

effect was evident for the 10- to 12-year-olds in the retention phase on the preferred hand, and the random group was superior to the blocked group. However, the expected superiority of the blocked group during acquisition was not observed, and interference effects were not evident for the eight- and nine-year-olds. This mixed pattern of results with children is evident in other studies as well (Bortoli et al., 2001; Del Rey et al., 1983; Edwards et al., 1986; Pollock & Lee, 1997; Vera et al., 2008). In a meta-analysis of 61 studies comparing adults, youth, and children on motor learning effects of random practice, Brady (2004) found that the effect size for the youth and children was quite small. The author explains these findings by suggesting that young children may be overwhelmed with random practice because of their limited information-processing capabilities and the complexity of sport skills.

Newell and McDonald (1992) asserted that random practice would have more impact later in the process of learning, and Wulf and Schmidt (1994) suggested that random practice for novices may produce too much variability. In concert with these views, Herbert and colleagues (1996) found that low-skilled university students performed forehand and backhand tennis strokes better on a retention test following blocked practice. From a practical viewpoint, it might be wise to use some blocked practice during early stages of learning, regardless of age, before inserting some random practice. On the other hand, even young children might benefit from random practice when practicing skills with which they have some experience and knowledge (e.g., a talented soccer team of eight-year-olds).

Beyond age and skill, the amount of interference might be an important variable when we seek to understand the sometimes-equivocal nature of the contextual interference research (see previous Research Notes; Ollis et al., 2004). Perhaps contextual interference is more like a continuum than the two opposites of random practice (high interference) and blocked practice (low interference). Magill (2017) asserted that between the extremes falls moderate contextual interference, such as the serial practice, which can include a serial order of trials of all task variations or the serial repetition of short blocks of trials. Some repetition of a skill allows learners to adjust over a limited number of trials, but moving to another skill may invoke elaboration or action plan reconstruction to optimally benefit from some interference.

The benefits of contextual interference can be influenced by other factors. For example, the ability to self-regulate blocked and random practice has been found to benefit learning more than when blocked or random practice is assigned (Keetch & Lee, 2007). Other mediating variables might be motivation and attention (Lee & White, 1990). Because random practice necessitates more effort than blocked practice, tasks that are tedious or lacking in intrinsic interest might profit from contextual interference. A final potential mediator proposed by Brady (1998) is personality. He reviewed several studies whose results were consistent with the assertion that impulsive people might particularly benefit from random practice because such practice suppresses impulsivity, causing them to adopt a more reflective style.

One potential issue practitioners may encounter when using random practice is learners' disconnect between actual and perceived learning effects of contextual interference. Simon and Bjork (2001) found that learners who engaged in blocked practice predicted they would perform better on a keystroke-pattern task than learners who engaged in random practice even though their actual performance was worse on a retention test. The findings of this study suggest that learners may not be receptive or motivated to practice under a random practice schedule. Thus, hybrid approaches have been suggested as ways to combine blocked and random practice so that learners can

RESEARCH NOTES

Differential Effects of Age, Ability, and Complexity of Skill on Contextual Interference Effects

Ollis and colleagues (2004) explored the influence of professional expertise and task complexity on the potency of the contextual interference (CI) effect. In their study, the authors compared college students with professional firefighters and the task of knot tying regarding initial skill acquisition, retention, and transfer. Tasks included tying knots that were simple and those that were complex. Participants were randomly assigned to blocked (low CI), random-blocked (moderate CI), and random (high CI) groups. At the pretest, all firefighters were faster than the college students. At immediate posttest, all groups saw reductions in times, but the high CI group performed poorly in the beginning. Later on, however, the high CI group outperformed the low and moderate CI groups. At the retention test, all groups maintained gains indicating a lack of differential benefit from CI level. For the novices, high levels of contextual interference seemed most beneficial regardless of complexity. Moreover, higher levels of contextual interference best support transfer when transfer tasks appeared distant (e.g., tying simple versus tying complex knots blindfolded). Thus, complexity and experience affect the potency of contextual interference. These findings confirm that there is a need to understand baseline levels of performance before creating tasks that will optimize retention and transfer.

WHAT DO YOU THINK?

Exercise 19.3

1. Describe in your own words the two theories that attempt to explain the contextual interference effect.

2. Choose two sports and indicate how you would teach the skills associated with each sport using blocked, serial, and random practice.

SPORT 1: ASSOCIATED SKILLS:				
Practice type	**Time**	**Class 1**	**Class 2**	**Class 3**
Blocked				
Random				
Serial				

SPORT 2: ASSOCIATED SKILLS:				
Practice type	**Time**	**Class 1**	**Class 2**	**Class 3**
Blocked				
Random				
Serial				

experience immediate performance effects as well as long-term effects on learning (Lee & Carnahan, 2021).

PRACTICE SPECIFICITY

Promoting the advantages of variable and random practice might seem at odds with the concept of specificity of learning and transfer of learning (see chapter 6). Specificity of learning is the idea that practice experiences should reflect the movement components and environmental conditions of the target skill and target context. To state this differently, if we practice for the purpose of developing skills for game play or individual competition, our practice should resemble the game or competition as much as possible.

Specificity of practice may have two forms, sensory and motor specificity, and context specificity (Schmidt & Lee, 2005). The idea of sensory and motor specificity has emerged largely from the research of Proteau and colleagues (Proteau, 1987; Proteau et al., 1992; Soucy & Proteau, 2001). Primarily using aiming tasks such as placing a stylus on a target, they have manipulated the type and amount of feedback using techniques such as occluding vision of either the arm or the target. It is often assumed that over many practice trials, the need for sensory feedback diminishes or changes; for example, the learner depends less on visual feedback when kinesthetic feedback assumes more importance (Schmidt, 1975). However, Proteau's research challenges this assumption, because the findings show that performance deteriorates on a transfer task even following extensive practice if the transfer task includes more or less sensory feedback than in the practice conditions. Proteau (1992) stated, "Withdrawing or adding a significant source of information after a period of practice where it was respectively present or absent results in a deterioration of performance" (p. 96). Thus, if practice included restricted vision, provid-

ing more visual information on the transfer task will result in poorer, rather than better, performance. It is proposed that this effect of specificity of practice occurs because the learner develops a sensorimotor representation during practice that is disrupted if the real game (transfer task) adds or reduces sensory information. Performance is optimal when the practice conditions match the transfer conditions.

This line of thinking is supported in several studies that used powerlifting (Tremblay & Proteau, 1998), ball interception (Tremblay & Proteau, 2001), basketball free throws (Moradi et al., 2014), and balance beam walking (Robertson et al., 2002). Robertson and colleagues (2002) challenged some common practice rituals of teachers and coaches that do not match performance conditions. For example, it is fine to direct participants to visual cues on the beam, which should not differ in competition, but probably not to cues on the home gymnasium ceiling or floor, which are most certainly going to be different in competition. They also challenge the coaching practice of talking an athlete through a routine. This added auditory stimulation cannot occur during competition and therefore should be used cautiously during practice. Moreover, the authors recommend that therapists in rehabilitation settings emphasize function- and goal-directed activities rather than isolated muscle actions. Therapists should determine the sources of information required in the functional task and manipulate those in therapy.

Proteau's sensorimotor representation logic can be extended to a broader sense of context specificity. We often hear about the need to practice a task repeatedly as if to stamp it into the brain (Schmidt & Wrisberg, 2008). This type of thinking appears to coincide with the thousands of hours of practice that experts report (see chapter 17). Without question, slap shots in hockey, golfing tee shots, and new ways of getting out of bed after an accident are

Table 19.2   Skill Differences Between the Target Context and Blocked Practice

Target context	Blocked practice
Preceded by regular variable conditions	Not preceded by regular variable conditions
Requires the generation of a solution on each attempt	Requires the generation of a solution only on the first attempt
Allows only one chance for success	Allows many chances for success
Same movement not repeated on successive attempts	Same movement repeated on successive attempts
Corrections not allowed on next attempt	Corrections allowed on the next attempt

Reprinted by permission from R.A. Schmidt and C.A. Wrisberg, *Motor Learning and Performance: A Situation-Based Learning Approach*, 4th ed. (Champaign, IL: Human Kinetics, 2008), 264.

often practiced hundreds of times over only a few weeks. But more than one coach has noted that some players perform wonderfully in practice but cannot perform in the game or competition. One of the difficulties with constant and blocked practice is that the target skill may not be practiced in the target context. Dribbling a basketball while walking is simply not the same skill as dribbling in a game. In a similar vein, practicing skating while controlling the puck and passing to a teammate might be useful as a reminder of some passing or puck control techniques, but it ignores the reality that the timing of the pass is often dictated by the positioning of moving opponents and teammates. Athletes must be prepared to produce movements in various situations. The target context also refers to such things as elevated anxiety on the first hole of golf compared to the driving range because this is now competition, and the person wants to impress the other players in the foursome. Table 19.2 includes other features of a skill that might be different in the target context and blocked practice.

The idea of specificity of learning is to practice in a manner that brings learners as close as possible to the target skill and target context. Practitioners must consider the developmental level of the learners (i.e., age and skill level) and their degree of motivation (i.e., a team of elite 10-year-olds will be different from a fifth-grade class). There will certainly be times when teachers or therapists believe it is appropriate to use constant and blocked practice, but over time they should remember that such practice is unlikely to mimic the target skill and context. As Schmidt and Wrisberg (2008, p. 264) stated, "The main point is that many *repetitions* in practice are essential for highly skilled performance—but *repetitiveness* in practice is not effective."

PART AND WHOLE PRACTICE

Motor skills are often complex and difficult to learn, particularly for children, novices, and others who lack motivation or the structural constraints that match the skill. Instructors are faced with the decision of whether to teach a skill as a whole or break it into parts and teach the parts before combining them into the whole. Skills that overwhelm a learner, elicit some degree of fear, or even pose a real danger should certainly be broken into parts. The key assumption is that practicing one part of a skill will transfer to performing the whole skill (Lee et al., 2001). In fact, whether part practice transfers to performance of the whole skill is the ultimate test of its effectiveness. Concepts in this area of motor learning research very much depend on the nature of the task.

The literature on part and whole practice was brought forward by Naylor and Briggs (1963), who distinguished between task complexity and task organization (Magill & Anderson, 2013). **Task complexity** refers to the number of parts or components and the amount of attention required (information-processing demands). Serving a tennis ball, batting a baseball, and performing a dance routine are complex skills because they demand much attention and have many components. Low-complexity skills have few components and require little processing, such as underhand rolling or galloping. Of course, whether a task is complex also depends on the person's experience with that task.

Task organization deals with the relationships of the skill components. The layup in basketball is a skill with a high level of organization because the parts are interdependent in terms of time and space. Other examples are juggling, ski racing, and the golf drive. The time and space performance characteristics of one part depend on those of the part performed just prior to it. If part A is not performed well, part B cannot be performed well, and so on. Tasks with a low level of task organization are those in which the performance of each component is relatively independent. For example, a choreographed ballet dance has many components, but each task is independent of the one preceding it; someone who is a bit shaky

with the pirouette at one point in the dance can still perform the dance.

For skills that are low in complexity and high in organization, experts often recommend teaching the whole task because the high interdependency of the parts makes it difficult to practice parts outside the whole skill context. On the other hand, for skills that are high in complexity and low in organization, part practice can be effective because the interdependence of the parts is not critical and part practice can reduce the information-processing demands (Magill & Anderson, 2013; Naylor & Briggs, 1963). Teachers and coaches must therefore analyze tasks to judge their complexity and organization.

As noted, the person's experience with the task affects the level of complexity of the task. In the case of children, task complexity and organization are likely to be influenced by their physical and cognitive development. The benefits of part or whole practice might be influenced by age, but few studies of whole and part practice have included participants who differed

---

WHAT DO YOU THINK?

Exercise 19.4

Think of one task in each of the four quadrants shown. Tasks could be high in both complexity and organization, high in neither, high in complexity but low in organization, or low in complexity but high in organization.

	High organization	Low organization
High complexity		
Low complexity		

in development. An exception is Chan and colleagues (2015), who had first-, third-, and fifth-graders practice a three-beanbag juggling task. Whole practice involved 40 trials per day for six days, and part practice involved juggling with one ball for the first two days, two balls for the next two days, and three balls for the last two days. Based on the results from a retention test, the first- and third-graders benefited the most from part practice, and the fifth-graders retained more with whole practice. Juggling is a task of high complexity and organization, and authors reasoned that the fifth-graders (almost 11 years of age) could benefit from whole practice because of advanced neuro-maturation, information processing, and motor coordination. More developmental studies of this nature are warranted.

As you completed exercise 19.4, you might have realized that some skills are not easily categorized as high or low task complexity or organization. There may be some inter-mediate level of both organization and complexity, and thus the general guidelines for high organization–low complexity and low organization–high complexity may be difficult to follow. Did you identify any skills that were both low or both high on each factor? The skill classification of continuous, discrete, and serial skills may help here.

Continuous skills are usually high in organization because of the interdependence of the parts. Discrete skills may be low in complexity from the viewpoint of the number of parts, but some will still demand a great deal of attention or require perceptual skills such as for catching or batting. Most rapid discrete skills such as a bat swing and bimanual skills such as the toss and swing in a tennis serve might be the least likely candidates for part practice. They argued that such skills can be broken down into parts, but that the parts are quite arbitrary and practicing them in isolation contributes little to whole-task performance (the ultimate goal). For example, practicing the backswing of a golf shot by itself pro-

duces different dynamics than are produced in the whole swing because of the stop at the end of the backswing. Serial skills have levels of organization that depend on the skill but often are high in complexity because of the number of components.

Lee and colleagues (2001) also argued that despite the challenge of learning highly interdependent parts (high organization), the research literature does not generally demonstrate instances of negative transfer from part practice; rather, some benefits of part learning are usually described. In other words, if a task has high organiza-tion but would overwhelm and discourage a learner, some form of part practice might be necessary. The issue becomes which part practice technique to use. Four part practice techniques have been proposed: fractionation, segmentation, simplification, and attention cueing.

Fractionation

Fractionation is part practice that separates parts of an action that normally are exe-cuted simultaneously; for example, swim-ming instructors often have part practice drills for either the arms or legs for a given stroke. This seems to work because the arms and legs perform different movements, and instructors frequently move back and forth between the part and the whole. However, breaking a symmetrical movement like that of the arms of the breaststroke down into drills for each arm is likely counter-productive because the arms perform the same movement and the task is high in organization.

Lee and colleagues (2001) reviewed the fractionation studies and found that those with video games, tapping, tracking, and bimanual aiming tasks have usually shown part practice to be ineffective in promoting positive transfer to the whole task. This is likely because of the high degree of coor-dination and interdependence of the parts. For motor skills requiring symmetric (e.g., freestyle swimming stroke) and asymmetric (e.g., tennis serve) bimanual coordination, the evidence is mixed, with some support for both part and whole practice (Magill & Anderson, 2013). If skills with asymmetric bimanual coordination must be broken down, practicing with the limb that has the more difficult and complex task should probably come first. Rhythmical skills with bimanual coordination, such as the coordination used in music, are likely best learned with whole practice, but part practice has shown some effectiveness for pianists when rhythm and melody are separated (Lee et al., 2001).

Segmentation

Segmentation is part practice in which a task is segmented into parts along the dimension of time. For example, a gymnastic beam routine may be segmented into several different steps. In pure part practice, the different steps would be practiced separately; then all the parts would be gathered into the whole routine. Progressive part practice involves practicing the first part alone, then the second part alone, and then the first and second parts together. The whole task is achieved by progressively practicing larger versions of the whole task. Finally, in repetitive part practice, the first part is practiced alone and then the first and second parts are practiced together before the third part is added to the first and second. The three types of part practices are outlined in table 19.3, using the layup shot in basketball as the skill.

Part practice can be achieved by either forward or backward chaining. Forward chaining is the practice of the parts in their timed order: part 1, parts 1 and 2, and so on.

Learning the folk dance with forward chaining gradually assembles the whole dance. Backward chaining emphasizes practice of the last component and progressively adds on preceding components that are practiced in their typical order as the learner becomes proficient in each component. This might create motivation because the learner accomplishes the goal at the beginning of practice. For example, backward chaining of the basketball layup begins with the shot, then proceeds to the step–shot combination, the dribble–two-step–shot combination, and so on for several dribbles (Lee et al., 2001). Backward chaining has been demonstrated to be most effective when the end point of the chain requires accuracy, as in the layup. Forward chaining is more effective in tasks such as wrestling takedowns or dance sequences, in which each segment contributes equally to the task goal.

Progressive part practice takes advantage of both part and whole practice methods. Part practice reduces attention demands of the whole task so that the learner can concentrate on one aspect. Building toward the whole has the advantage of coordinating parts that may have some degree of interdependence.

Simplification

Simplification, a pedagogical principle that teachers have been using for decades, involves practicing an easier version of the task. Six ways in which skills can be simplified (Magill & Anderson, 2013) are as follows:

1. Reduce object difficulty (e.g., juggle

Table 19.3 Steps in the Types of Segmented Practice

Part	Repetitive part	Progressive part
1. Dribbling	1. Dribbling	1. Dribbling
2. Two-step combination	2. Dribbling, two-step combination	2. Two-step combination
3. Shot	3. Dribbling, two-step combination, shot	3. Dribbling, two-step combination
4. Dribbling, two-step combination, shot		4. Shot
		5. Dribbling, two-step combination, shot

WHAT DO YOU THINK?

Exercise 19.5

Choose a motor skill that is appropriate for segmentation. Next, break it down into a minimum of three components that can be practiced in isolation. Design a repetitive part forward chaining example with your motor skill. Then, design a progressive part backward chaining example using your motor skill.

1. Which type of segmented practice has the most steps?
2. Which type of segmented practice has the least number of steps?
3. Which practice design do you think is more appropriate for your skills? Explain.

with scarves, catch a larger ball, bat with a large plastic bat).

2. Reduce attention demands (e.g., provide physical assistance such as support in gymnastics).
3. Reduce speed.
4. Add auditory cues (e.g., clap to the rhythm of a skipping action).
5. Sequence skill progressions (e.g., hit baseballs from a tee, then a pitching machine, and later a pitcher; also use small-sided games in general).
6. Use simulators (e.g., rebounders in basketball) and virtual reality.

Although simplification is a common practice, research support of it is rather limited (Lee et al., 2001). If simplification creates a new task or changes the dynamics of the task dramatically, then part practice may not be effective. Mané and colleagues (1989; as cited by Lee et al., 2001) manipulated the speed of a video game. A slower speed transferred positively to the performance of the game at regular speed, but there was a limit. At some point, the reduced speed was ineffective, presumably because the game became quite a different one.

Attention Cueing

Attention cueing is not strictly a part practice method because the whole skill is performed. However, the performer directs attention to a specific part of the whole—for example, the backswing of the slap shot in hockey or the elbow on the recovery of the crawl stroke. Attention research supports the fact that selective focus is possible.

DISTRIBUTION OF PRACTICE

Is it better for learning to have fewer but longer practice sessions or more frequent but shorter practice sessions? Distribution of practice refers to the amount of practice within each period and the amount of rest between practice sessions to ensure optimal learning of motor skills (Magill & Anderson, 2013). This body of knowledge usually compares schedules of practice called massed and distributed. **Massed practice** involves longer practice sessions that involve many practice trials. This is contrasted to **distributed practice**, which has fewer practice trials in shorter practice sessions. Massed practice schedules have fewer practice sessions than distributed practice schedules. When the time between trials is a focus, massed practice has minimal or short rest periods, whereas distributed practice has longer rest intervals.

Early research (1930s to 1950s) on distributed practice investigated the length of the intertrial interval—that is, the rest time between trials (Magill & Anderson, 2013). Reviews of this literature point to the importance of the type of task when making this determination. Continuous skills are learned better with distributed schedules of practice than with massed schedules, whereas the reverse is true of discrete skills. Thus, swimming, dancing, and skiing would benefit from distributed practice, and hitting a golf ball or baseball would benefit from massed practice. Continuous tasks likely benefit from distributed practice because they can be physiologically fatiguing, whereas discrete tasks have naturally occurring breaks between trials.

Later research focused on examining the length of time between practice sessions, which has generally supported distributed practice. In a classic study, Baddeley and Longman (1978) found that postal workers who practiced a typing skill only once a day for one hour performed better than those who practice two times a day for one hour, one time a day for two hours, or two times a day for two hours. In medicine, there is a tradition of full-day training of surgical skills. Spruit and colleagues (2015) examined the effectiveness of this training by comparing the performance and retention of trainees who practiced for either three 75-minute sessions massed in a single day or three 75-minute sessions distributed over three weeks. The distributed practice was superior to massed practice in terms of skill acquisition as well as short- and long-term retention.

Little research has addressed the optimal number and length of practice sessions, but in general, researchers recommend more frequent and shorter sessions, as would occur in distributed practice (e.g., Kwon et al., 2015). More recently, Verhoeven and Newell (2018) proposed a new theoretical model that attempts to consolidate the many effects of practice distribution on performance to predict the optimal practice distribution. The model uses three assumptions (outlined next) to develop time scales that can be used to estimate between and within practice intervals.

1. The warm-up decrement (see chapter 6) is the result of a loss of set, which gets larger with an increase in the rest interval duration.

2. Fatigue, both physical and mental, has the strongest negative influence on performance in practice sessions and experimental designs with short rest intervals, but it can be alleviated by providing a rest break.

3. Learning a skill requires a rest interval that is long enough for the cellular and molecular mechanisms associated with memory formation to take place. However, if this rest interval is arbitrarily long, forgetting may occur. (p. 163)

Although distributed practice is advisable in many practice contexts, unfortunately, it is not always practical. Many educational, recreational, and rehabilitation situations have specified practice times, and practitioners have little flexibility in allotting practice time. For example, teachers know the number of days during the week that a given class will have physical education, and youth soccer teams have predetermined use of the practice fields. To complicate matters further, research has found that participants show a greater preference for massed practice (Son & Simon, 2012); thus, learner buy-in to a distributed practice schedule could be problematic to practitioners even when schedules allow for it.

MENTAL PRACTICE AND IMAGERY

It may surprise you to learn that just thinking about certain aspects of a skill can have performance and learning benefits (Lee et al., 2001; Schmidt & Wrisberg, 2008). **Mental practice** (or motor imagery) is cognitive rehearsal of a physical skill

---

TRY THIS

Kicking With the Nondominant Foot

Exercise 19.6

Let's compare massed and distributed practice for a kicking task using the nondominant leg and foot. The kick is a power kick of a soccer ball to a target 10 feet away. The target should include different circles that are concentric. The target can be displayed on a wall for ease if there are no actual soccer goals available. A direct hit in the center scores 5 points, one in the next circle scores 4 points, and so on. Establish a group of six. Three people kick under massed conditions, and three people kick under distributed conditions. The massed practice participants kick 40 times in succession. Record the scores from the 40 trials. The distributed group kicks in four sessions of 10 blocks with two minutes between blocks. Again, record the scores from the 40 trials. Compare the massed and distributed groups. Did you find differences that are consistent with the content in this Distribution of Practice section?

WHAT DO YOU THINK?

Exercise 19.7

You just learned about distributed and massed practice. Fill in the following table by indicating whether the skills can likely be taught more effectively under distributed or massed practice conditions based upon the type of motor skill.

Skill	Massed practice	Distributed practice
Dancing		
Long jump		
Chest pass		
Riding a bicycle		
Skipping rope		

---

without overt physical movements (Magill & Anderson, 2013). **Imagery** is a form of mental practice that involves a multisensory (visual, kinesthetic, etc.) representation of an experience. For example, a distance runner imaging a trail run might see trees along the race path, feel the breeze on her face, and hear her feet striking the ground. Research with children and adolescents suggests that imagery emerges around age 5 and improves with age, particularly between early adolescence and early adulthood (Gabbard, 2009). These forms of practice should be considered when physical practice is inconvenient or impractical, such as an injured athlete who wants to maintain motor skills for his sport.

Mental practice has a rather long history and usually involves rehearsing procedural or symbolic aspects of the skill. Rehearsing procedures could follow the series of movements in therapy or in a gymnastics or dance routine. Rehearsal might also be related to response selection procedures, such as the amount of force to use to pass a ball, or a decision-making strategy, such as *If my opponent backs away, I will keep the puck and drive to the net*. Recall the discussion of procedural knowledge in chapter 14. Symbolic aspects of skills refer to such things as remembering to follow through when throwing a ball.

Mental practice research usually compares mental practice conditions to a physical practice condition and a no-practice condition. Some studies have also incorporated experimental conditions combining physical and mental practice. Results typically demonstrate that mental practice is better for learning than no practice but not as effective as physical practice. The latter is hardly surprising given all that we have said about physical practice in this chapter. Yet, mental practice is recommended in combination with physical practice in recovery from stroke (Nilsen et al., 2010) and to improve surgical performance (Cocks et al., 2014) and music performance (Bernardi et al., 2013). Moreover, recent evidence suggests that mental practice can be as effective as physical practice in maintaining movement representation of a motor skill (de Paula Ferreira et al., 2021) and can aid in learning the relative timing of a motor skill (Apolinario-Souza et al., 2020).

Interestingly, some studies have shown that a combination of physical and mental practice is almost as effective as physical practice alone (e.g., Hird et al., 1991; Kolh et al., 1992) even though combined groups may only have half the physical practice of the physical practice groups. Magill and Anderson (2013) explained these findings from a cognitive problem-solving perspective. During mental practice, learners engage in cognitive practice strategies that normally are used during physical practice but can be developed during mental practice as well.

In a recent meta-analysis of 37 studies, Toth and colleagues (2020) examined the effects of mental practice on performance. They found both physical and mental practice had significantly positive effects on performance, and although physical practice resulted in higher performance gains than mental practice, they were not significantly different from one another. The authors also found that mental practice was beneficial to individuals of all skill levels as well as for those in both individual and team activities. The most effective mental practice programs were between 1 and 6 weeks, and the optimal session length was 20 minutes. Mental practice was equally effective across different settings but was better when it consisted of kinesthetic or mixed imagery.

Children have also been shown to benefit from mental practice. In a finger opposition task, mental practice was as effective as physical practice for immediate and long-term learning with 9- and 10-year-olds (Asa et al., 2014). Moreover, Takazono and Teixeira (2018) found that 9- to 10-year-old children who performed a combination of physical practice and imagery improved their performance on both elements of a novel task while the physical practice group only improved on one element.

Mental imagery is frequently used by athletes, dancers, exercisers, and rehabilitation patients. Divers might mentally view themselves rotating, twisting, and opening prior to the actual dive while patients recovering from a stroke might image themselves performing a rehabilitation exercise or daily activity. Paivio (1986) proposed a framework for classifying imagery content. In his framework, imagery content can either be cognitive or motivational at the specific or general level. This combination resulted in four categories: cognitive specific (skill rehearsal), such as performing a golf putt; cognitive general (strategy rehearsal), such as overcoming a full-court press in basketball; motivational specific (goal setting), such as winning a medal for first place; and motivational general (arousal and mastery), such as relaxing in a calm environment or succeeding at an event. Based on research (Salmon et al., 1994) and the development of the Sport Imagery Questionnaire (Hall et al., 1998), the motivational-general category was later divided into two separate categories of motivational general—arousal and motivational general—mastery.

Imagery has many characteristics. For example, images are often visual (seeing the movement) and kinesthetic (feeling the movement) but can include other sensory modalities, such as audition (sounds) and olfaction (smells). Imagery can be experienced in real time or slow motion and from a first-person (viewing images through your own eyes) to third-person (viewing images as a spectator) perspective. When using a third-person perspective, individuals can modify the viewing angle of the image as well as choose to image their own performance or the performance of someone else. Imagery also varies in the degree to which the individual is consciously aware of the imagery and its intended purpose. Imagery that is specifically planned and used to achieve a goal, such as regulating arousal before competition, is much more deliberative than imagery that was triggered by an internal or external source, such as a song reminding an individual about a specific event in their life.

Over two decades ago, Martin and colleagues (1999) proposed the applied model of imagery use to provide a theoretical understanding of imagery use in sport. More recently, Cumming and Williams (2013), updated the model based on newer research, which they called the revised model of deliberative imagery use. The model contains nine components that practitioners should consider when designing imagery interventions: where, when, who, why, what, how, meaning, imagery ability, and outcome. The *where* and *when* components focus on the location and situation in which the imagery is used. Research suggests that imagery is more beneficial when it matches the environment in which the skill is performed (Holmes & Collins, 2001), such as a stroke patient imaging a daily activity while at home. The *who* component refers to the individual, whose characteristics (e.g., gender, skill level, age) may also influence imagery effectiveness. For example, male exercisers are more likely to image their task-relevant information (technique) than female exercisers (Cumming, 2008).

The *why* component concerns the reason for the imagery while the *what* component refers to the imagery content. Although these components appear related, they are, in fact, distinct from one another. For example, a baseball player imaging the successful execution of his next pitch (*what*) could be doing so to improve his performance *or* increase his confidence. *How* refers to the characteristics of imagery discussed in the previous paragraph (e.g., sensory modality, or perspective) as well as duration and frequency. The *meaning* of the imagery to the individual should also be considered when planning the content of the imagery. For example, imaging 10 successful putts from a short distance to the hole may be considered unhelpful to an experienced golfer but may be viewed as very helpful to a novice.

The effectiveness of imagery can be influenced by one's *imagery ability*. Imagery ability concerns the vividness of one's images as well as how well they can control and maintain the images. Research suggests that individuals with higher imagery ability benefit more from imagery use than those with lower imagery ability (Robin et al., 2007). However, imagery ability can be improved with practice (Cumming & Williams, 2012). Within the model, imagery ability is thought to influence *what* is imaged and *how* in that individuals are more likely to image content and use imagery characteristics that are easy for them to produce. The *outcome* of the imagery can be categorized, generally,

WHAT DO YOU THINK?

Exercise 19.8

You just learned that mental practice has performance and learning benefits. How could you incorporate mental practice into instructional or therapeutic settings? When would be the most appropriate times to encourage the use of mental practice in each of these settings? Explain.

as affective, behavioral, or cognitive; however, domain-specific outcomes have been proposed within sport, dance, exercise, and rehabilitation. Although deliberate imagery such as enhanced performance is used with a specific outcome in mind, unintentional positive outcomes may also be achieved, such as increased confidence. However, it's important to understand that unintentional negative outcomes can also occur when imagery is not used correctly.

Magill and Anderson (2013) described three generally accepted hypotheses for why mental practice and imagery are effective. First, a psychoneuromuscular hypothesis links the mental practice of an action, such as bending the elbow, to electromyographic activity in the muscles responsible for the bending that may activate the neuromotor pathways involved in learning. Second, the brain activity hypothesis comes from brain scan results indicating that motor pathways activated during imagining an action are like those activated during actual performance (Jeannerod, 1999). The third explanation is the cognitive hypothesis, which asserts that mental practice aids the learner in creating a mental blueprint for the movement. This helps with the first stage of motor learning, which involves a high degree of cognitive activity for people who struggle with performance-related questions. Research suggests that mental practice is tied to planning rather than execution, which provides some support for the cognitive hypothesis (Bach et al., 2014).

SUMMARY

Physical practice is by far the most important factor in learning motor skills. And Benny, the boy in the chapter-opening scenario, now realizes that the goal of practice is to perform the skill outside the therapeutic practice venue, in the context of activities of daily living, recreation, or competition. To some extent, the amount of practice depends on the learner's goals and aspirations. The research evidence suggests that more practice is necessary when higher levels of performance are sought. Will Benny be satisfied when he can run to the store, or might he aspire to become a Paralympian?

How to organize and schedule practice sessions so that people can reach their goals was the focus of this chapter. We explored variable, constant, random, blocked, part, whole, mental, mass, and distributed practice and attempted to describe the best practice conditions. However, sometimes the research is incomplete, and the results are controversial or equivocal. Although we would like to have offered simple summary statements on exactly how therapists, teachers, and coaches should organize their practices, learning motor skills is simply too complex and is influenced by a host of factors beyond practice schedules. So, we highlighted the moderating factors available from the research, including age, level of skill, type of task (laboratory or real world), type of skill, motivation, attention, and personality.

> **ONLINE ACTIVITIES**

The student material found in HK*Propel* includes exercises, labs, and videos to enhance learning and encourage practical application of important concepts.

LEARNING AIDS

Supplemental Activities

1. Biographies of highly skilled athletes and musicians often speak to the issue of practice. Select a person you admire or would like to know more about and read their biography. What are the person's reflections about practice?

2. Locate an experienced therapist you know and ask for an interview about practice. Does this person distinguish between the many types of practice discussed in this chapter? Do they see instances of the contextual interference effect? Do they use mental imagery?

Glossary

blocked practice—A practice sequence in which one skill is repeated over a fixed block of time before moving to the next skill. This is usually contrasted to random practice, which involves different skills intermingled during a designated time period.

constant practice—A practice sequence in which one skill is repeated for a fixed amount of time or number of trials.

contextual interference—The memory and performance disruption that results from performing multiple skills or variations of a skill within the context of practice. This disruption has a negative effect when people are attempting to learn several tasks at the same time.

contextual interference effect—The learning benefit resulting from performing multiple skills using a high contextual interference practice schedule.

distributed practice—Practice that typically involves a short session with few practice trials and long rest intervals.

elaboration and distinctive hypothesis—The idea that random practice results in the use of cognitive strategies. When learners shift from one skill to another, the nature of each strategy becomes clearer and more meaningful in long-term memory. This cognitive effort has a deleterious effect during skill acquisition but is beneficial to skill learning.

forgetting and reconstruction hypothesis—The hypothesis that the key to understanding the contextual interference effect is to consider the action planning required for each skill. Random practice forces learners to practice action planning, because they must reconstruct a new action plan each time they learn a new skill.

imagery—A form of mental practice that involves a visual or kinesthetic representation of performance; the visualization or cognitive rehearsal of a movement.

massed practice—Long practice sessions with many practice trials.

mental practice—The cognitive rehearsal of a physical skill without overt physical movements.

random practice—A practice sequence in which several skills are mixed in a random order. Rehearsal of the same skill twice in a row is avoided.

serial practice—A practice sequence in which skills are performed in a mixed order but in a fixed format.

task complexity—The number of parts or components of a skill and the amount of attention required to complete the skill.

task organization—The relationships of the skill components.

variable practice—A practice sequence in which several variations of the same skill occur in a mixed order.

20

FEEDBACK

CHAPTER OBJECTIVES

After reading this chapter, you should be able to do the following:

- Explain why extrinsic feedback is an essential component of motor skill acquisition.
- Provide examples of types of extrinsic feedback.
- Identify the main functions of extrinsic feedback.
- Understand feedback schedules including when and how to use them.
- Describe factors that should be considered to provide feedback effectively.
- Explain how the timing of feedback following a performance attempt affects motor learning.

Are You Ready for Feedback?

Jesse's love of hockey began with her first puck at age 5. Throughout her childhood, she found herself playing not only hockey but also virtually any sport she could, including some in which she was the only girl on the team. In high school she excelled as an athlete and was highly sought after as a top college hockey recruit for Boston University. Feeling on top of the world, Jesse expected to begin her college career on the starting lineup. Instead, she found herself on the bench. Her coach told her she can score goals but needs to improve her defense. However, she soon found herself sitting even further down the bench. While on the bench, she started analyzing the game, noticing that when the puck is passed to one side, the defense shifted, and the corner was wide open. She thought, *When I get my opportunity, I'm going to go to that open spot.* She deeply yearned to play and started listening to her coach's feedback to focus on her defense. Jesse did just that. She started to focus on her defense and became a starter.

Although feedback is an important part of the learning process, accepting it and making the necessary changes is not always easy. You have likely experienced a situation, perhaps like Jesse's, in which you did not agree with the feedback you received or felt frustrated even hearing it. If so, you are probably not surprised to learn that when someone is not open to receiving feedback, it is not going to help. So, how can instructors, coaches, and therapists provide critical feedback in these situations? What are the most effective methods of providing feedback? Siedentop and Tannehill (2000) reported that the feedback delivered in athletic and clinical settings is often not optimal in terms of type, accuracy, and frequency. This chapter discusses the many variables that determine the appropriateness and effectiveness of feedback to people of varying ages and skill levels and based on skill difficulty. It also presents some common myths about feedback delivery.

Feedback is critical when learning new motor skills, especially complex ones. It is also necessary for highly skilled athletes such as Jesse, as well as injured people trying to reacquire motor skills, whether they are sport-specific skills (e.g., making sharp cuts on the ice rink following an anterior cruciate ligament tear) or relevant life skills (e.g., relearning to walk, write, or even brush one's teeth). Injured people often must either relearn a motor skill, modify a motor skill, or learn a new motor skill. Occupational and physical therapists must understand how to provide feedback in a way that maximizes patients' learning. When practitioners are providing feedback to facilitate motor learning, regardless of the situation (e.g., an unskilled person learning a new motor skill, or someone recovering from injury or illness), they must consider the type, frequency, and timing of their feedback.

FUNCTIONS OF FEEDBACK

The three main functions of extrinsic feedback are information, motivation, and reinforcement (see figure 20.1). Feedback that provides information helps learners understand how they are moving, what they are doing correctly or incorrectly, and how they can correct errors. This information can guide them to better performances. Feedback to correct performance errors addresses the performance outcome (knowledge of results), sensations produced by the movement (intrinsic feedback), the nature of the errors (descriptive feedback), and suggestions on how to correct errors (prescriptive feedback). For example, a pole-vaulter will receive information about his movement from multiple sources. He will see the outcome of the vault, hear the pole contact the vaulting box and hear it fall if it hits too hard, feel whether he pulled his body up and around the bar or hit the bar, and likely know the outcome before he is even near the bar. These are all types of intrinsic feedback. The pole-vaulter may also receive extrinsic feedback from a coach or a teammate who describes his form or provides corrective information.

Feedback also functions to motivate learners. When learners receive feedback on their movement performances, they can compare it with their performance goals. Those who are progressively improving should receive feedback that indicates they are moving closer and closer to their goals. Improved performance is very rewarding and provides an incentive to continue practicing to achieve further success. Conversely, learners who see little improvement or get worse often become frustrated with the task. Frustrated learners are likely to decrease their effort or even quit. To increase motivation, instructors can provide more feedback on correct aspects of

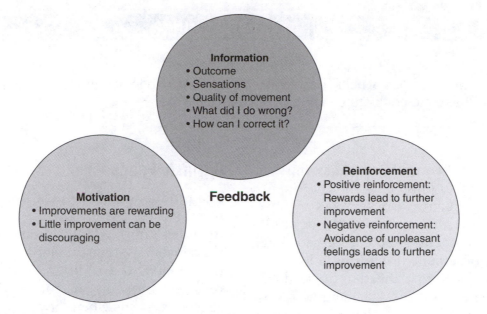

Figure 20.1 Extrinsic feedback has three main functions: guiding the learner to better performances, providing an incentive to motivate the learner, and reinforcing the movement.

the performance attempts than on errors to reduce some of the frustration learners may be experiencing.

The third function of feedback is **reinforcement**. Reinforcement occurs when the feedback following a performance attempt increases the probability of similar performance attempts in the future. Feedback can provide positive and negative reinforcement. **Positive reinforcement** following a performance attempt can be rewarding. This reward is intended to increase the likelihood that successful attempts will occur more consistently; however, it should be provided immediately following the attempt to be most beneficial. Positive reinforcement can be given verbally through compliments or praise, such as *Great job on the backswing!* or *You're getting there! You can do it!* This reinforcement can motivate learners to continue their efforts. These phrases should be used sparingly and only when deserved. If a learner is having very little success, the instructor should find at least some aspect of the movement pattern, however small, to praise. Nonverbal gestures can also provide positive reinforcement, such as a smile, a

thumbs-up, or a pat on the back.

For extrinsic feedback to be positively reinforcing, the learner must perceive it as a reward (Rose & Christina, 2006; Wulf & Lewthwaite, 2016). Consider a coach who increases the intensity or duration of practice because they believe the athlete can improve to the next level. If the coach does not explain the reason behind the change, the athlete may perceive the added workload as a punishment. Similarly, a coach may switch a player's position because of the player's well-rounded athleticism. However, the athlete may interpret the change as suggesting an inability to play the position well rather than an enhanced capability to play multiple positions.

Feedback that evokes unpleasant feelings that the learner will want to avoid at all costs is **negative reinforcement**. Negative reinforcement can be derived simply from embarrassment over a poor performance, such as a missed shot, a poor throw, or a missed catch. A hurdler with a knee injury may avoid hitting the hurdle with his trail leg at all costs to avoid the pain. An inexperienced driver learning how to drive a car

WHAT DO YOU THINK?

Exercise 20.1

Describe two examples of using negative reinforcement for one or more motor skills. Why do you think these methods are effective or not effective?

with a manual transmission may initially cause the car to jump or stall. The embarrassment this causes can serve as negative reinforcement, strengthening the desire to learn. A golf teaching aid can provide negative reinforcement to eliminate lunging. The aid is placed just ahead of the lead leg; during the swing, the learner must stay behind the pad through ball impact. Hitting the pad tells the learner that she has moved ahead of the ball (negative reinforcement).

Another common negative reinforcer is the beeping or dinging sound in a car that indicates that the seat belt is not fastened. Fastening the seat belt (correct movement) is reinforced to avoid hearing the annoying sound. To decrease the length of a batter's step, a coach can place a wooden barrier on the ground; contacting the barrier with the foot indicates that the step is too long. Shorter steps (correct movement) are because the batter wants to avoid contacting the barrier (negative reinforcer).

TYPES AND MODALITIES OF FEEDBACK

The two most general types of feedback are intrinsic feedback (i.e., derived from sensory systems) and extrinsic feedback (i.e., provided by external sources). Effective extrinsic feedback is an essential component of clinical, educational, and athletic programs. The only variable more important than extrinsic feedback in learning a motor skill is practice (Bilodeau, 1966; Robert et al., 2017). We will take a closer look at these two types of feedback but focus mostly on extrinsic feedback.

Intrinsic Feedback

The production of the task itself generates intrinsic feedback. **Intrinsic feedback** includes any feedback received through the sensory systems, including vision, proprioception, and audition. A hockey player receives information from each of these sensory systems when they take a slap shot. They feel the release of the shot and the force with which they made it (proprioceptive intrinsic feedback). They see the trajectory of the puck and whether it goes into the net, hits the bar, or gets blocked by the goalie (visual intrinsic feedback), and they hear the swoosh of the puck into the net (auditory intrinsic feedback). A skilled hockey player often knows whether they are going to make the shot long before the shot even approaches the net. Intrinsic feedback can be supplemented by coaches, instructors, peers, and equipment.

Extrinsic Feedback

Feedback that is supplemental to the intrinsic sources of feedback is termed **extrinsic feedback**. Any feedback provided by an instructor, trainer, therapist, coach, or even a friend is extrinsic feedback. A fitness trainer who tells their client that their reps are too fast or a fencing coach instructing their student to lunge more when striking is giving extrinsic feedback. Equipment (e.g., a stopwatch, a heart rate monitor, a video replay system) also provides a type of extrinsic feedback.

Providing appropriate feedback is one of the most important responsibilities of an instructor. Important considerations for extrinsic feedback are determining the most appropriate type, precision, and frequency of feedback, as well as when to schedule the presentation of feedback. Extrinsic feedback can result in quick learning and enhance retention while also increasing learner motivation. Learners who cannot detect their own errors may spend countless hours trying different techniques, which would not be necessary if they received a simple tip from an instructor who had observed their attempts.

Extrinsic feedback is pivotal in rehabilitation settings as well. Patients with perceptual or cognitive deficits may only be able to use limited intrinsic feedback (Flinn & Radomski, 2002; Harvey, 2019). They may

---

TRY THIS

Providing Verbal Knowledge of Results

Exercise 20.2

a. Form pairs. Each pair has three different-colored pens, markers, or pencils; a piece of paper; and a blindfold. One student is the participant, and the other is the experimenter, providing feedback.

b. On the piece of paper, the experimenter draws a basketball hoop and a stick figure of a person about to shoot the basketball.

c. The participant then puts on the blindfold and draws a line from the hands of the stick figure to the hoop using a typical basketball shot trajectory. The participant does this 10 times with no feedback and without looking at the picture, although the experimenter does place the pen at the starting point after each attempt. The participant remains blindfolded throughout the experiment.

d. For a second group of trials, the participant uses a different-colored writing implement and completes the same task 10 times, but during these trials, the experimenter provides KR (knowledge of results) after each attempt, such as *You missed the hoop.* The participant remains blindfolded throughout the experiment.

e. For a third group of trials, the participant uses a different-colored writing tool and completes the same task 10 times, but during these trials, the experimenter provides KP after each attempt. This is feedback on the quality of the movement, such as *You need more arc and need to continue the line farther.* The participant remains blindfolded throughout the experiment.

f. When you are finished, switch roles with your partner and complete the activity again.

g. Compare your results after receiving no feedback, after receiving KR, and after receiving KP (knowledge of performance).

Questions

1. How detailed was the feedback you and your partner provided for KR or KP?

2. Do you think the detail of feedback from your partner may have affected your results during the KR and KP trials?

3. What other factors do you think may have affected your results for each condition?

rely on extrinsic feedback to even understand how they are performing because they cannot accurately feel the movement or see the outcome.

Extrinsic feedback occurs in many forms. Most simply, it can be provided verbally or nonverbally. Nonverbal forms of extrinsic feedback include a buzzer that sounds following poor performances or a stopwatch that displays a race time. Extrinsic feedback can be provided either during the movement (**concurrent feedback**) or following the movement (**terminal feedback**). A one-mile (1.5 km) race time is terminal feedback. However, running splits, such as race times during set intervals such as a quarter mile or half mile, is an example of concurrent feedback because the runner receives pace information during the run. To optimize and accelerate motor learning in learners, athletes, or patients, practitioners should manipulate factors such as task complexity, feedback designs, and feedback modalities—such as visual modalities (videos, head-mounted displays), auditory modalities (speakers, headphones, timers, practitioners), and haptic modalities (robots, vibrotactile actuators), or a combination of them (Sigrist et al., 2013).

Verbal Feedback

Perhaps the most common type of feedback is verbal. We often think of a coach providing feedback in terms of what athletes did incorrectly such as putting the shot without a whipping motion; how they can perform better the next time, such as hitting down on the golf ball; or the outcome of the performance, such as indicating a distance on a long jump attempt. Verbal feedback provides **knowledge of results (KR)** or **knowledge of performance (KP)**. These give learners feedback regarding the outcome (KR) and the quality of their performances (KP).

Knowledge of results is terminal feedback that describes the outcome of the movement (e.g., a gymnastics score, the distance of a punt, the score on a sit and reach test, the speed of a pitch). Knowledge of performance provides specific feedback about the quality of the movement. It informs the learner about the components of the movement pattern that led to the outcome (e.g., the need to shift the weight more, use more force with the follow-through, or use more torso rotation when throwing). Most instructors and clinicians emphasize the outcome of the performance and fail to provide appropriate feedback regarding the movement itself (Fishman & Tobey, 1978). Outcome-based feedback is often inadequate in guiding the learner to perform the skill correctly (Newell & Walter, 1981; Sharma et al., 2016).

There are two types of knowledge of performance: descriptive feedback and prescriptive feedback. **Descriptive feed-**

WHAT DO YOU THINK?

Exercise 20.3

Label each of the following examples as either KR or KP.

1. You snapped your wrist too early.
2. You just missed the pin by two inches (five cm).
3. You stepped on the line when you shot the free throw.
4. You swam that 50 m two seconds faster than the last time.
5. Step with your sticker foot.
6. Keep your back straight on that lift.

back, as the name implies, describes the movement pattern. This type of feedback is useful for explaining what learners are doing incorrectly. One of the most common errors in golf is an exaggerated twist of the backswing. Novice golfers often incorrectly assume that a greater twist of the backswing will help them generate more force. Instructors can provide descriptive feedback by describing this exaggerated twist.

Prescriptive feedback provides suggestions to correct the error. An instructor could tell a novice golfer, "By exaggerating your twist, you will not be able to stay in the same swing plane, which will be very difficult for you to compensate for. You need to maintain perfect posture and swing fluidly. This will help you to maintain contact with the ball and avoid twisting too far on the backswing." The appropriate type of feedback depends on the skill level of the learner. Novice learners need more prescriptive feedback than skilled performers do, because they have not yet learned how to correct errors. Regardless of skill level, a combination of both descriptive and prescriptive feedback is most effective. When given both types of KP, learners begin to associate the causes of errors with the appropriate corrections.

Nonverbal Feedback

Although we often think of feedback as verbal, most people use many forms of nonverbal feedback. Nonverbal feedback includes visual feedback (e.g., pictures or videos) and auditory feedback such as a buzzer, a metronome, or a sound consequent to a movement. An example of a consequent sound is the sound of a racquetball hitting the wall. This sound can provide the player with information regarding the ball's speed and even trajectory. Consequent sounds can also provide information about the rhythm of a movement, such as double Dutch rope jumping, a skill in which the rhythm is crucial. Now we will shift away from auditory feedback to other sources such as equipment, biofeedback, and visual feedback.

Equipment   Feedback can be provided from a wide variety of equipment. An example is equipment for monitoring performance, such as radar guns to monitor the speed of a pitch. Nowadays, many people have activity-tracking apps or watches that monitor their physical activity levels, including number of steps, distance run, pace, splits, and even heart rate. Many devices have been developed to improve the golf swing, perhaps even more so than for any other motor

---

WHAT DO YOU THINK?

Exercise 20.4

Label each of the following examples of feedback statements as descriptive or prescriptive feedback.

1. You broke your wrists.
2. Keep your left arm straight.
3. Follow through to the right hip.
4. You need to stop sooner.
5. You swung too hard.
6. Follow through across the midline.

skill, such as helping to eliminate swaying and lunging and facilitating proper impact. Equipment is also critical for therapists to assist clients with walking, regaining balance, and increasing strength.

Biofeedback **Biofeedback** is extrinsic feedback that provides concurrent information related to physiological processes (Magill, 2007). Biofeedback has been well known since the 1950s (Schwarz et al., 2003) and is used to shape behavior during performance. One of the most used forms of biofeedback is the heart rate monitor. Heart rate monitors, readily available at department or sporting goods stores and integrated into popular activity trackers, continuously display the person's current heart rate. They help people adjust their intensity levels throughout a workout based on their heart rates. Blood pressure monitors and chronometers are other sources of biofeedback. Blood pressure may be continuously monitored for people with cardiovascular problems. Chronometers provide swimmers with real-time, nonverbal biofeedback without interfering with their performances (Pèrez et al., 2009). Providing feedback during water sports has been particularly difficult because of the pool environment. Chronometers have been found to be beneficial for improving swim times while also allowing the instructor to focus on other aspects of the performance or on other swimmers.

Biofeedback is also commonly used in rehabilitation settings. Feedback can be provided for muscular activation and joint angle excursions. By viewing electromyographic biofeedback, patients have increased voluntary activation in particular muscle groups (Brucker & Bulaeva, 1996) and relearned to walk following a stroke by changing their walking patterns (Intiso et al., 1994). Biofeedback devices can improve postural control and gait using audio-biofeedback, which reports the amount and direction of postural sway (Dozza et al., 2011). Unfortunately, these benefits are generally lost once the biofeedback is removed; thus, the use

of these devices should be limited so that learners do not become overreliant on them.

Visual Feedback Visual feedback, which can be very beneficial during the learning process, can take the form of visual displays of kinetic and kinematic feedback. Kinetic and kinematic feedback, types of knowledge of performance that provide information in addition to intrinsic feedback, have been shown to be more effective than knowledge of results (Newell & Carlton, 1987; Young & Schmidt, 1992).

Kinematic feedback provides information on the observable aspects of the movement (e.g., the space–time properties of a performance) and can be very beneficial during the learning process. The most used forms of kinematic feedback are pictures, illustrations, and video replays of limb position, velocity, or acceleration (see figure 20.2). For example, illustrating the aiming trajectory of the rifle barrel, an essential aspect of shooting performance (Konttinen et al., 1998), provides information on the movement of the barrel and supplements intrinsic feedback (Mononen et al., 2003). **Kinetic feedback** provides information on the underlying processes of the movement, such as force. Graphs illustrating force–time curves for a motor skill have been found to be useful for such actions as the jump out of starting blocks for runners and the trigger squeeze and release for rifle shooters. Learners can see whether they need more or less force and learn the appropriate timing in relation to the amount of force required.

For kinematic feedback to benefit the acquisition and retention of motor skills, it must supplement the feedback regarding goal achievement (KR) (Rucci & Tomporowski, 2010). The goal for most motor skills is to induce a change in the environment through a particular movement or set of movements, such as batting in baseball. Because separating the movement patterns in batting (the kinematics of the swing) from the outcome (where the ball was directed and landed, or KR) is easy,

Figure 20.2   A series of photographs of a golf swing that provide kinematic feedback. They illustrate the changing form and the correct alignment of the body relative to the club throughout the swing.

learners are likely to benefit from kinematic feedback. For other tasks, such as gymnastics, dance, and figure skating, the information on movement production and goal achievement would be the same (Newell et al., 1983). In this case, rather than *affecting* goal achievement, the movement pattern *is* the goal achievement. For these tasks, then, the kinematics of the movement and goal achievement cannot be separated.

The most effective kinematic patterns are generally known for most sporting activities, and kinematic feedback is very commonly provided to optimize learners' movement patterns. Feedback on some kinematic variables is more beneficial to learning than is feedback on others. Although the most appropriate feedback is on kinematic variables that are motor skill specific, feedback on spatial characteristics (positional information) tends to be more effective for learning than feedback on temporal aspects (Young & Schmidt, 1992). It is probably easier for learners to visualize where to place and move body parts and equipment, such as a racket, than to understand the timing of the movement, because this is more abstract and harder to conceptualize.

Video Feedback Learners may believe that they are performing a task correctly until they see for themselves via pictures or a video that they are not. Although video feedback can be quite useful, practitioners must consider several factors when using it, such as the time during which the video is presented, the skill level of the learner, and whether the video is supplemented with feedback from the instructor.

Video feedback is more useful when it is provided over an extended period. Because this type of feedback provides so much information, learners need time to fully benefit from it. The longer time also gives learners more opportunities to practice the motor skill. Research studies have shown that video feedback used for less than five weeks resulted in no improved performance (Rose & Christina, 2006).

Providing video feedback without cueing the learner to specific aspects of the movement is also ineffective, especially for novice learners, and it may be detrimental (Jarodzka et al., 2013; Rucci & Tomporowski, 2010). This is likely because video feedback provides too much information. Video feedback is not effective for learners who do not understand what they should be looking for in the video or how to interpret the information. Skilled performers, on the other hand,

know the aspects of the movement pattern they need to focus on and can benefit from viewing videos of their performances with little to no supplementation.

Minimally, novices should be given attention-directed cues (Newell & Walter, 1981) when they view videos. Because they have little experience with performing the movement pattern correctly, they may become overwhelmed with all the information available on the video. **Attention-directed cues** direct attention to the most important aspects of the movement pattern. For instance, a juggler may be instructed to focus on the height of the toss; a golfer, on the position of the club during the backswing; and a soccer player, on the plant foot position. The benefits of attention-directing cues are not limited to novice performers. Highly skilled athletes have also benefited from these cues when viewing videos (Menickelli et al., 2000).

Although attention-directed cues have been found to improve performance following video feedback, attention-focusing cues provide the greatest benefit (Kernodle & Carlton, 1992). **Attention-focusing cues** not only direct the learner's attention to specific aspects of the movement pattern, but they also include error correction suggestions. For instance, rather than simply

---

RESEARCH NOTES

Balance It Up!

To examine the influence of success-related feedback provided on learning and retention, Ong and Hodges (2018) had university students perform a balance task. There were two different experimental balance tasks. In task 1, participants used a stabilimeter and received different types of feedback with goals based upon time on task. Unfortunately, goal structures provided no differential effects for learning or retention in study 1. In sum, whether the task was too easy, too hard, or somewhere in between, there were no differences in learning. In task 2, some participants received positive or negative feedback, and others received no feedback at all. Interestingly, only the negative feedback group showed significantly higher motivation and arousal than other conditions. No condition affected balance outcomes. Thus, the authors question that perceptions of success actually affects outcomes.

directing the juggler's attention to the toss, the instructor could inform the learner that she needs to make tosses that peak between the shoulder and the head. The golf instructor could inform novice golfers that they need to avoid overswinging the club because they will lose control of it, preventing them from staying in the same plane of motion.

A soccer coach could inform novice players that the position of the plant foot is critical to dribbling. Correctly positioning the plant foot allows the player to control the speed and direction of the dribble. See table 20.1 for examples of attention-focusing and attention-directed cues.

Table 20.1 Attention-Focusing and Attention-Directed Cues (Suggested Corrections) for the Front Crawl Freestyle Swim Stroke

Attention-focusing cues	Attention-directed cues
1. Focus on the position of your arms.	1a. Keep your elbow up. 1b. Reach to the midline.
2. Focus on touching the water with your fingertips followed by extending your arm.	2. When you place your hands into the water, lead with your fingertips toward the midline and then to your hip.
3. Focus on creating little splash.	3. The leg motion should activate from the hips, keep your toes pointed, and flutter to reduce splash.

RESEARCH NOTES

Who Needs Verbal Cues Anyway?

Kernodle and Carlton (1992) illustrated the benefits of supplementing video feedback in a study of participants who threw sponge balls at a target with their eyes closed. Participants were separated into four groups. One group was provided only KR (the distance the ball was thrown, no video); one group was provided only KP (a video); one group viewed the video and received attention-directing cues such as focusing on the hips when throwing; and the final group viewed the video and received attention-focused cues such as *Rotate the hips from left to right during the throwing phase*. Although all groups started at approximately the same level, the greatest gains in performances were seen in the group that received the attention-focusing cues (video + correcting cues). Significant benefits were also found for the attention-directed cues (video + attention cues) over the KR-only and KP-only (video) groups. No significant differences were found between the KR-only and KP-only groups, which indicated that providing video feedback without attention-focusing or attention-directing cues provides no more benefit than simply providing KR. For example, *You threw the ball 35 feet*.

A more recent study (Rucci & Tomporowski, 2010) revealed similar results for learning the hang power clean over six training sessions. Participants were separated into three groups: visual feedback only, verbal feedback only, and verbal and video feedback. Dartfish video analyses revealed that the video-only group did not significantly improve, whereas the other two groups did.

These studies indicated that video feedback that is not supplemented with verbal cues is not effective for novices. Most learners need some form of verbal cues to improve their skills. Videos should be supplemented by an instructor who can direct learners' attention to the most important cues and describe how they can correct their errors to maximize learning.

Table 20.2   Video Feedback Learning Stages

Stage	Learner characteristics	Instructor's role
Shock	Learners are preoccupied with appearance.	• Allow learners to become familiar with viewing videos. • Hold off on further instruction until learners are ready.
Error detection	• Learners critically observe their performances. • They identify some performance errors.	• Distinguish relevant and irrelevant cues. • Provide attention-focusing cues.
Error correction	• Learners can now identify their errors. • They know the causes of their errors. • They focus on learning how to correct the identified errors.	Encourage problem solving.
Independence	• Learners detect and correct their errors. • They have little to no dependence on the instructor.	• Recognize a minimal or nonexistent supplemental role. • Provide encouragement.

WHAT DO YOU THINK?

Exercise 20.5

1. What are some advantages to using videos to enhance motor skill learning?
2. What are some disadvantages of using videos for motor skill learning?
3. Video feedback is most effective for learners at what level of skill?
4. When is using video feedback least effective?

Four stages have been described for learners who are introduced to video feedback: (a) shock, (b) error detection, (c) error correction, and (d) independence (see table 20.2; Darden, 1999). When learners are introduced to video feedback, they are often more focused on their visual appearance than on their movement patterns or performances. Because of this preoccupation with irrelevant factors (overall appearance rather than movement patterns), this stage has been termed the **shock stage**. Darden stated that until learners have adjusted to viewing themselves on video, further instruction is ineffective. During stage 2, the **error detection stage**, instructors should supplement the video feedback with attention-focusing cues. This is especially important for novice learners who may not know the task-relevant cues for the motor skill and may be focusing on irrelevant cues. These cues enable them to begin to critically analyze their performances and prepare them to detect

and correct their errors. Learners who can identify their errors and understand the causes of their errors have advanced to stage 3, the **error correction stage**. During this stage, learners are developing error correction strategies. With learners in this stage, the instructor's role is to focus on problem-solving skills. The **independence stage** is the final video feedback learning stage. Learners who reach this stage require minimal to no video supplementation by an instructor. Skilled performers know exactly what to look for when viewing the videos and can identify and correct their errors.

PROVIDING EFFECTIVE FEEDBACK

Instructors and clinicians often spend much time preparing the learning situation by properly setting up the environment, setting goals, and designing the practice sessions,

RESEARCH NOTES

Can Video Feedback Support Learning During a Pandemic?

Souissi and colleagues (2021) described how the COVID-19 pandemic shifted the educational landscape requiring the need for distance learning modalities for instruction. In this study the authors contrast (a) video feedback plus online pedagogy; (b) only video feedback; and (c) a control group among those learning to perform the snatch weightlifting technique. Thirty-five school-aged children participated in the study and were randomly assigned to one of the three aforementioned conditions. All students were pretested, received six sessions of training, were posttested immediately afterward, and then retention tested a week later.

During this distance learning time, all students were asked to watch a video demonstration of the snatch skill along with hearing cues for success. Students in the video feedback and pedagogical activity group (VF-PA) were able to watch their own video feedback in slow motion with options for replay and pause. In this condition, learners were provided with key images and cues of the snatch to help them better error detect. Afterward, students had to correct their errors during the next trial. The video feedback–only group (VF) were provided with pause and replay options but no pedagogical support. The control group did not receive any augmented feedback or pedagogical aids. All distance learning sessions were led by a physical education teacher through Zoom.

The results showed that the VF-PA group was better able to error detect than the VF and control groups. The VF group was significantly better than the control group regarding error detection. Unsurprisingly, novice movers struggle with error detection, and these struggles are reduced by augmented feedback. It is key for instructors to remember the importance of including attention or correcting cues (or both) with videos. These data might influence distance delivery methods in the future.

but many do not provide effective feedback. Important factors include the frequency, timing, and scheduling of feedback.

Corrective or Error-Based Feedback

Instructors must determine whether to provide feedback on the correct aspects of the movement pattern or instructional cues on the learner's errors. The effectiveness of error versus corrective feedback largely depends on the learner's skill level, motivation, and interest. For novices, feedback focused on errors can be very effective. This guides them to the correct movement patterns. Learners who are not very motivated toward or interested in the activity benefit more from feedback on the correct aspects of the movement pattern. This feedback encourages them to continue their efforts by confirming their progress.

Tzetzis and colleagues (2008) examined the effect of different corrective feedback methods on badminton performance for a low-difficulty and high-difficulty skill. Participants were separated into four groups: a control group and three practice groups referred to as group 1, group 2, and group 3. Group 1 received positive feedback and instructional cues on how to correct technique; group 2 received only instructional cues on how to correct technique; and group 3 received positive feedback, instructional cues on how to correct technique, and instructional cues on errors. The group with all three (group 3) improved the most in the high-difficulty skill, but groups 1 and 2 performed better in the low-difficulty skill. The authors concluded that the feedback that is most appropriate might depend on the level of difficulty of the motor skill. This finding is also supported by Souissi et al. (2021).

In general, it is optimal to provide feedback on *both* the errors and the correct components of the movement. The sandwich approach (see figure 20.3) is a recommended strategy for providing feedback on both errors and correct components (Fischman & Oxendine, 2001). In the sandwich, the bread is praise, and constructive criticism is the meat. Initially, instructors praise the learner's strengths to reinforce correct performance, as in *Good! You kept your eye on the ball, and you had good timing.* Improvements

are then suggested based on the learner's errors. For example, *Next time, spread your feet a little wider.* The instructor concludes with motivational information, encouraging the learner by discussing the benefits of correcting the error, such as *Spreading your feet wider will help your balance.*

Feedback Frequency

Traditionally, researchers believed that the more frequently feedback was provided following performance attempts, the greater the gains in learning would be (Thorndike, 1931). This line of thinking developed because performance tends to increase more and at a faster rate when extrinsic feedback is

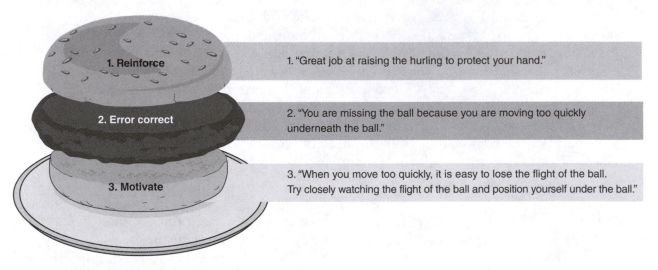

Figure 20.3 The sandwich approach to providing error feedback.

WHAT DO YOU THINK?

Exercise 20.6

1. Using the sandwich approach, change the following statement for the skill of fielding a ground ball: *I told you this would happen! How many times do I have to tell you to keep your head down? Why won't you listen?* Be sure to add something that the learner did correctly and discuss the benefits of keeping your head down.

2. Devise a feedback example using a motor skill of your choice using the sandwich approach.

3. Describe how each step of the sandwich benefits the learner.

given most or all the time. However, current research has indicated that too much feedback is detrimental to learning (Anderson et al., 2005). The **guidance hypothesis** asserts that novices benefit from high-frequency KR initially, even as much as feedback on every attempt; then, as they improve, the frequency of feedback should be gradually reduced. If extrinsic feedback is given frequently for too long, learners can become overly dependent on it, often relying more on the extrinsic feedback than on their own sensory sources of feedback. This promotes passive learning; that is, learners do not develop the critical problem-solving skills necessary for performing the motor skill without extrinsic feedback. On the other hand, learners who receive extrinsic feedback at a lower frequency become much more active in the process. They reflect and evaluate their movements. This active process helps them perform the motor skill without feedback. It should be noted that feedback frequency is task and skill dependent. How much to reduce the feedback is not a one-size-fits-all variable. More complex tasks require additional feedback, and reducing the frequency of feedback can degrade learning under certain practice conditions (Wu et al., 2011).

Feedback Precision

Adjusting feedback precision based on the skill level of the learner is also important. Feedback should be less precise for beginners. When learners are introduced to a task, they are simply trying to obtain a broad understanding of the movement pattern. More general instructions can be effective during this stage. As they progress from the cognitive stage to the associative stage, their focus shifts to refining the task. Currently, more precise feedback is more meaningful.

Feedback given only when performance is outside a particular range is referred to as **bandwidth feedback**. For example, a long snapper on an American football team may receive feedback only when the snap exceeds a range of correctness, such as above the chin or below the knees of the kicker; a volleyball player may receive feedback only when her toss is not directly in front of her dominant arm; and a long jumper may receive feedback on his takeoff only when his foot lands more than 3 inches (7.6 cm) behind the line. These players know that if they do not receive feedback, they have performed satisfactorily. With this method, the absence of feedback provides positive reinforcement and can be motivational.

Bandwidth feedback eliminates the provision of too much feedback because learners receive feedback only when they are outside a predefined range of correctness. Bandwidth feedback has been found to promote significantly more retention than both high- and low-frequency KR (Lai & Shea, 1999; Lee & Carnahan, 1990; Sherwood, 1988) as well as the learning of complex motor skills such as a gymnastics sequence (Sadowski et al., 2013). These benefits may result from the fact that the strategy inherently involves a fading schedule. Novice performers require more feedback than skilled performers do because they are performing outside of the satisfactory range much more often. With practice and increased consistency of movement, learners perform more and more in the satisfactory range, so they receive progressively less and less feedback. The benefit of bandwidth feedback can be further increased by providing positive feedback when the learner is within the bandwidth. In this case learners are receiving less quantitative, or error-based, feedback as they progress, while also receiving the motivational benefit of positive feedback with better performances (Agethan & Krause, 2016).

Choosing an appropriate bandwidth is an important consideration for instructors. Depending on the task, it may be better to have a larger bandwidth for beginners. As learners progress, the bandwidth can be slowly decreased. The goal is to provide the most feedback initially, but the task should not be so challenging that the learner does not achieve any success or see much progress. Tasks that are perceived as too challenging can cause learners to quickly lose motivation or interest in the activity.

Feedback Schedules

Although providing too much KR continuously can be detrimental, so can providing not enough KR during the initial stages of learning (see figure 20.4). Novices who receive very little KR do not receive the guidance they need to improve movement patterns. Beginners do not yet know what they are doing correctly or incorrectly and may spend significant amounts of time trying new strategies. Those who do not receive enough KR during these initial stages require significantly more time to improve and may lose motivation or interest during the process.

Although research has determined that the traditional concept of *more is better* is not valid for providing KR, no optimal reduced-frequency feedback schedule has been found to be most effective. This section describes several reduced-frequency feedback schedules. The appropriateness of each depends on the complexity and duration of the task and the intrinsic factors of the learner.

Faded Feedback

Winstein and Schmidt (1990) developed a feedback schedule in which the amount of feedback is based on the skill level of the learner; it is appropriately termed **faded feedback**. Beginners receive high-frequency feedback to guide their movements and reinforce the correct aspects of their movements. An effective amount of feedback for a beginner may be as high as 80 to 100 percent relative frequency of KR depending on the complexity and duration of the motor skill. The **relative frequency of KR** is the percentage of performance attempts in which KR is provided. To calculate the relative frequency of KR, the number of trials with which KR was used (i.e., the **absolute frequency of KR**) is divided by the total number of trials. This number is then multiplied by 100 percent. For example, if a gymnast receives feedback following four out of eight vaults, then the absolute frequency is four attempts and the relative frequency is 50 percent, because she received feedback 50 percent of the time. As learners improve, the relative frequency of KR should be progressively reduced. This feedback schedule should be tailored to the learner and should not be reduced until the learner has reached a certain level of proficiency. Children may require longer periods of practice than adults do, and their feedback should be reduced more gradually than that of adults (Sullivan et al., 2008).

Summary Feedback

Summary feedback is feedback following a set number of performance attempts in which the instructor summarizes each attempt. For example, a gymnast could

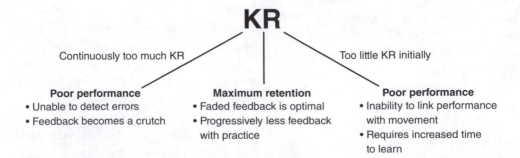

Figure 20.4 Negative outcomes can result from both continuously providing KR and not providing enough KR.

WHAT DO YOU THINK?

Exercise 20.7

1. Calculate the relative frequency of KR when the absolute frequency of KR is 10 trials and the total number of trials is 40.

2. Calculate the absolute frequency of KR for a relative frequency of 80 percent and a total number of trials of 60.

3. Calculate the total number of trials for an absolute frequency of five trials and a relative frequency of 50 percent.

complete an entire floor routine, after which the coach would provide feedback on each of the moves. Similarly, a learner could perform a set number of attempts for a discrete skill, such as shooting a foul shot or throwing a shot put, before receiving summary feedback. Videos are also a source of summary feedback. Learners can watch a video following the completion of a series of moves and preferably receive attention-directed feedback regarding their performance attempts. The number of performance attempts appropriate for a motor skill would depend on the complexity and duration of the task. Fewer trials should be summarized with longer or more complex motor skills.

Average Feedback

Average feedback is very similar to summary feedback in that both occur following a set number of performance attempts. However, rather than providing feedback on every attempt or movement, the practitioner discusses only the average performance error(s) or the essence of the performances with the learner. Summary and average feedback also differ with respect to the amount provided. Average feedback provides less high-focused feedback than summary feedback does. Summary feedback and average feedback have been found to be equally effective (Weeks & Sherwood, 1994), but average feedback may be more appealing to practitioners. Given the demands and

time constraints imposed on most instructors, clinicians, and coaches, it is unlikely that they can devote attention to many performance attempts for one learner and provide specific feedback on each attempt. Providing a description of the quality of the performances overall (average feedback) is more practical. Average feedback is also advantageous to learners because they are less likely to become overwhelmed with too much information.

Learner-Regulated Feedback

All the feedback schedules we have considered so far are designed and implemented by the practitioner. One feedback schedule, which has been the focus of many research studies, puts learners in control of feedback by allowing them to decide how often to receive extrinsic feedback and after which trials. This is called **learner-regulated feedback**. Shifting the control of the provision of feedback from the instructor to the learner resulted in more learning than in matched participants who received feedback at the instructor's discretion (Chiviacowsky et al., 2008). The only difference between the groups in this study was that one group decided *when* they would receive feedback. The possible benefits to learner-regulated feedback are (a) a more active role, providing learners with more opportunity to process the movement and the feedback cognitively (Wulf et al., 2001), and (b) increased motivation (Chiviacowsky

& Wulf, 2007). The frequency with which learners request feedback largely depends on their characteristics, including skill level and age, as well as characteristics of the task such as complexity and duration. As previously discussed, beginners require more feedback until they obtain a certain level of proficiency. More feedback is also required for more complex and longer tasks.

Extrinsic Feedback Timing

Another critical issue is the timing of extrinsic feedback (see figure 20.5). In other words, when is it most appropriate to provide extrinsic feedback? Many instructors and clinicians assume that feedback is most effective immediately following a performance attempt. Although one might expect immediate feedback to be most ben-

eficial because it allows learners to link the performance with the outcome or quality of the movement before their memory of the movement production fades, immediate feedback prevents learners from reflecting on the movement. Just as the provision of high-frequency KR (i.e., 80-100 percent relative KR) eliminates active processing, feedback provided too soon after a performance attempt promotes passive learning. The learner will become reliant on the feedback and will not develop the critical problem-solving skills necessary for performing the motor skill without the guidance of the extrinsic feedback.

The time between one performance attempt and the next is termed the **interresponse interval**. This period is broken down into two other temporal intervals—the feed-

---

RESEARCH NOTES

How Much Feedback Do I Need? Autonomy With Feedback

Chiviacowsky and Lessa (2017) investigated the effectiveness of autonomy supported feedback in adults, comparing the presence of choice with requests for feedback with their learning. Previously, it had been found that children who requested feedback (learner-regulated group) learned the task more effectively than did children who received feedback on the same schedule but did not control when they received it (Chiviacowsky & Wulf, 2006). However, research with adults is a bit scarcer. Adults were divided into choice versus no-choice groups regarding when they received feedback. The choice group showed enhanced learning in comparison to the no-choice group. The authors suggested these data and findings support previous autonomy-supported inquiries.

Providing autonomy with feedback might help support individual differences and needs (Laughlin et al., 2015) and promote higher order levels of thinking (Grand et al., 2015), by prompting one to think about error detection (Carter et al., 2014) and potentially satisfying different motivations (Sanli et al., 2013).

It is also important to consider the type of feedback that is appropriate for children. Typically, positive feedback is very effective; however, this may not be the case for all positive feedback. In a study of 10-year-olds performing kicking and throwing tasks, those who received generic feedback such as feedback reflecting inherent ability improved less than did those who were pushed to think differently and change ability conceptions (Chiviacowsky & Drews, 2014). These effects provided both short- and long-term benefits. Feedback that teaches children that they are in control of their performances was more likely to change their performances, which led to improvements.

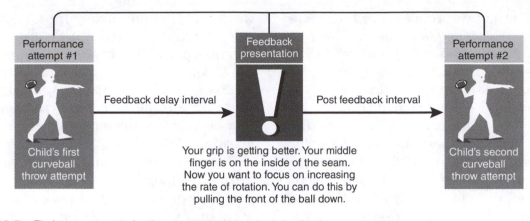

Figure 20.5   Timing components for the presentation of extrinsic feedback.
Based on Coker (2009).

back delay interval (the time between the first attempt and the provision of feedback) and the postfeedback delay interval (the time between the provision of feedback and the second attempt). The following sections describe these intervals further because their duration has important implications for learning.

Feedback Delay Interval

Researchers have examined the timing of feedback to determine the most effective time lapse between the completion of a performance and the provision of KR. The time between the completion of an attempt and the presentation of feedback is termed the **feedback delay interval**. The length of the feedback delay interval is a critical component in the presentation of extrinsic feedback. The learner needs adequate time to focus on proprioceptive, auditory, and visual feedback from the attempt (Magill, 2001). If the feedback delay interval is too long, then the learner will have forgotten much about the movement production. On the other hand, if the feedback delay interval is too short, the learner will not have time to engage in the cognitive operations needed to detect errors and create correction strategies (Salmoni et al., 1984; Swinnen et al., 1990).

The key question is *How long should instructors and clinicians wait before providing extrinsic feedback?* The feedback delay interval does not need to be lengthy. It simply needs to be long enough to allow learners to process and evaluate their own intrinsic feedback. Learners need to think about how the movement felt, how they performed, what errors they may have made, and how to correct them. Even just a few seconds can be long enough to do this. However, research has indicated that longer delays do not adversely affect learning (Bilodeau & Bilodeau, 1958). Although a longer feedback delay interval is less likely to negatively affect learning than immediate extrinsic feedback (a very small feedback delay interval), motor forgetting can occur during this time, which makes it more difficult for learners to link their performances to extrinsic feedback.

Consider an instructor who has chosen a feedback delay interval of five seconds. How does he know that the learners are reflecting during this time and not simply waiting for his feedback? The truth is that he does not know unless he asks. Prompting learners to self-reflect and evaluate their performances during this break leads to increased retention (Swinnen et al., 1990). To promote self-evaluation following a performance attempt, the instructor should ask learners directed questions. The questions could be general, such as *How do you think you did?* or *What do you think you did wrong [or right] during that attempt?* The instructor could then follow up by asking *How did you come to the conclusion that [a particular aspect of the movement] was correct [or incorrect]?* or *What about that movement was incorrect?* or *How could you correct that mistake?*

Self-evaluation is a learned strategy that takes time to develop. It may be more effective to ask specific questions, especially with beginners, because they will likely not know the causes of their errors or how to correct them. For example, an instructor could ask leading questions, such as *Do you think you followed through on the release of the ball?* or *Where did you make contact with the ball? Was it the correct location?* As learners develop better self-evaluation strategies and improve their performances, the questions can become more general. Eventually, they will be able to self-evaluate with little to no help from the instructor.

Postfeedback Delay Interval

The time between the presentation of extrinsic feedback and the subsequent performance attempt is called the **postfeedback delay interval**. In contrast to the feedback delay interval, learners are likely focusing more on evaluating the feedback just received than on their own intrinsic feedback (Magill, 2001). However, if this interval is too short, learning can be negatively affected (Gallagher & Thomas, 1980). Learners need sufficient time to process the information provided through extrinsic feedback and to plan the next attempt (Rose & Christina, 2006).

The appropriate length of the postfeedback delay interval depends on the age of the learner; children require longer intervals (Barclay & Newell, 1980). As previously mentioned, children have greater processing limitations than adults have. Increased postfeedback delay intervals give young learners more time to develop the error detection and correction mechanism necessary for learning motor skills.

Conversely, older adults are negatively affected by longer postfeedback delay intervals (Liu et al., 2013). However, delays of even three or six seconds longer in duration in the postfeedback delay interval degraded their performance. This is likely due to their reduced attention and working memory capabilities. Older adults may switch their attention from their intrinsic feedback to the KR in short intervals and rely too heavily on KR feedback (Yan & Dick, 2006).

To facilitate cognitive processing during the postfeedback delay interval, the instructor can ask learners how they are going to execute the next attempt, or more specifically, what they are going to do differently from the previous attempt. By encouraging learners to further process this information, the instructor can check how well they understand their performance errors and the effectiveness of the feedback.

Misconceptions About Feedback

Now that you've looked at various types and schedules of feedback, it's important that you also understand some misconceptions about feedback. Table 20.3 outlines three common misconceptions about feedback and provides best practices to address each.

Table 20.3 Misconceptions About and Best Practices for Extrinsic Feedback

Misconception	Best practice
More is better: The more feedback provided, the better the learning.	Fade the amount of feedback provided.
The faster, the better: Providing feedback immediately following the performance attempt is most effective.	Allow processing time after the performance attempt and after providing feedback.
Increased precision is better: Decreasing the bandwidth is more effective.	Fade the bandwidth (expect progressively better performances as skill level increases).

Note that for each best practice, the skill level of the learner, the difficulty of the motor skill, and the age of the learner should be considered.

SUMMARY

Feedback is one of the most important factors in skill acquisition, second only to practice. Feedback helps guide performers toward executing proper movement patterns, motivates learners, and reinforces successful performances. Feedback received via the sensory systems is intrinsic feedback, whereas feedback that has been given in addition to sensory sources is extrinsic feedback. The two main forms of extrinsic feedback are knowledge of results (performance outcome) and knowledge of performance (quality of the movement pattern). Knowledge of performance can be descriptive or prescriptive but providing both is most effective.

Novice learners require more extrinsic feedback than skilled learners do. Feedback during the initial stages of learning can decrease learning time by helping learners link successful performances with the movement patterns produced. As learners progress, the amount of feedback provided should decrease, which is known as faded feedback. Practitioners can accomplish this by progressively providing less relative KR or by providing bandwidth KR, because more skilled learners will perform within the bandwidth progressively more and more and therefore receive less feedback. Learner-regulated KR is also very effective, especially for adults. Because learners generally ask for KR only when they need the feedback, they do not receive too much and feel a greater sense of control over the learning situation.

The importance of appropriate extrinsic feedback cannot be overemphasized. Often, movement educators provide extrinsic feedback too frequently or too soon, without realizing the negative effects this has on both short- and long-term retention. Just like practice, feedback should be designed around the learner and the task.

> ## › ONLINE ACTIVITIES

The student material found in HK*Propel* includes exercises, labs, and videos to enhance learning and encourage practical application of important concepts.

LEARNING AIDS

Supplemental Activities

1. Many variables influence the effectiveness of extrinsic feedback, including the skill level and age of the learner and the difficulty of the task. Practitioners should consider the type of feedback that would be most appropriate, as well as the frequency at which to provide the feedback. Answer the following questions regarding these important considerations:

   a. What are the benefits of providing extrinsic feedback?

   b. When might extrinsic feedback not be needed?

   c. When might extrinsic feedback enhance skill acquisition?

   d. When can extrinsic feedback be counterproductive—that is, when can it degrade skill acquisition?

   e. Counter the misconceptions listed in table 20.3. Explain why each is a misconception.

2. If you were teaching someone a new motor skill, how would you incorporate feedback into your program? Provide a progression of feedback instruction from the initial instruction to skill refinement. You could design this feedback schedule for any motor skill, from teaching striking skills to a child to teaching an adult how to walk following an injury. Describe the motor skill you are teaching and the characteristics of the learner. Be sure to include a timeline for this progression.

Glossary

absolute frequency of KR—The number of trials in which KR was used.

attention-directed cues—Cues that direct attention to the most important aspects of the movement pattern.

attention-focusing cues—Cues that not only direct attention to specific aspects of the movement pattern but also include error-correcting suggestions.

average feedback—Feedback that includes only the average performance error(s), or the essence of the performances.

bandwidth feedback—Feedback given only when the performance is outside a particular range.

biofeedback—Extrinsic feedback that provides concurrent kinematic information related to physiological processes.

concurrent feedback—Feedback received during the movement.

descriptive feedback—Feedback that describes the nature of a performance error.

error correction stage—Stage 3 of the video learning stages, in which learners can identify their errors and, in some cases, understand the causes.

error detection stage—Stage 2 of the video learning stages, in which learners are comfortable viewing their performances. Attention-focused cues should be used to help them detect their errors during this stage.

extrinsic feedback—Feedback that comes from an external source in addition to sensory information.

faded feedback—Feedback based on the skill level of the learner; beginners receive high-frequency feedback initially and progressively less feedback with improvement.

feedback delay interval—The time between the completion of a performance attempt and the presentation of feedback.

guidance hypothesis—The hypothesis that the benefits of high-frequency KR can be deceiving because learners tend to perform better initially than they would if they had received lower frequency KR.

independence stage—The final stage of the video feedback learning stages, in which learners require minimal to no video supplementation by an instructor.

interresponse interval—The period between two performance attempts.

intrinsic feedback—Response-produced information that is received from sensory sources before, during, and after a movement.

kinematic feedback—Feedback on the observable aspects of the movement, such as the space–time properties of a performance.

kinetic feedback—Feedback on the underlying processes of the movement, such as force.

knowledge of performance (KP)—Feedback that provides information about the characteristics of the movement pattern produced.

knowledge of results (KR)—Terminal feedback that describes the outcome of the movement.

learner-regulated feedback—A feedback schedule that puts learners in control of feedback by allowing them to decide how often to receive extrinsic feedback and after which trials.

negative reinforcement—Feedback that elicits unpleasant feelings that the learner will want to avoid.

positive reinforcement—Feedback following a movement that promotes the recurrence of the same movement pattern.

postfeedback delay interval—The time between the presentation of extrinsic feedback and the subsequent performance attempt.

prescriptive feedback—Feedback that provides suggestions for correcting performance errors.

reinforcement—A benefit of feedback that occurs when the feedback increases the probability of similar performance attempts in the future.

relative frequency of KR—The percentage of performance attempts for which KR is provided.

shock stage—Stage 1 of the video learning stages, in which learners are often more focused on their visual appearance on video than on their movement patterns or performances.

summary feedback—Feedback provided on all attempts following a set number of performance attempts.

terminal feedback—Feedback provided following the movement.

21

PROGRAM DESIGN

After reading this chapter, you should be able to do the following:

- Compare different pedagogical styles.
- Develop ecological task analyses.
- Develop upward and downward extensions.
- Universally design tasks.
- Create a block plan.

In this textbook you have learned about many concepts related to motor learning and motor development. You have learned how to classify motor skills, which is particularly helpful for creating appropriate practice and feedback schedules. You have also learned how to measure learning and maximize performance and, most important, you have learned about long-term retention based on variables such as the complexity and duration of the motor skill and the developmental and skill levels of the learner by manipulating the task and the environment. You will now put all these concepts together to design your own program.

Assessment is the first place one should start when designing one's own program. Whether the program is for rehabilitation, physical education, or intervention, one must establish a baseline or present level of performance before any decisions on programming can commence. As we learned in chapter 11, there are many ways in which one can assess the gross motor development. However, how we evaluate our assessment results is up for debate.

GOLD STANDARDS VERSUS VARIABILITY

Instructors of physical skills sometimes teach with a template in mind (e.g., the movement pattern of a highly skilled athlete). After all, does it not make sense to imitate the best? A skiing instructor might encourage her students to emulate the style of the last Olympic champion, and the track coach might highlight the running pattern of Usain Bolt. Because the assumption is that everyone should strive for the gold standard, instructors' feedback is often directed at making everyone similar. However, motor learning theories challenge this gold standard thinking.

As discussed in chapter 2, most motor learning theorists agree that the single motor program idea does not provide a logi-cal or theoretical explanation for how novel movements are produced. These questions about storage and novel movements led to the notion of a generalized motor program (see chapter 2).

The generalized motor program is argued to contain the skeleton, or abstraction, of a movement pattern rather than a specific movement. For example, an overhead throwing action might be a motor program that contains feet placement, arm flexion, sequential trunk rotation, weight transfer, arm follow-through, and visual contact with a target. As previously described, the generalized motor program likely includes information about the sequence and relative timing and force of actions. Performers use that program when the task calls for an overhead throw, but it can be modified to meet specific environmental demands. Thus, in baseball, the second baseman throws the ball to first base with less arm flexion than the third baseman uses because the distance of the throw is shorter, and both know to hurry the throw when the runner is particularly quick. These situations require variations of the generalized motor program and produce different movement skills that can accomplish the task of getting the ball to the first baseman before the runner. Teachers and coaches need to include throwing variation in their practices to help learners develop generalized motor programs so that they can respond to a variety of movement situations.

Supporters of ecological and dynamic systems thinking also promote variation in movement patterns in practice but for different theoretical reasons than those of supporters of information processing. Variability is viewed very positively in dynamic systems thinking because each person is considered to have a unique signature, or style, in most motor patterns. As a result of varying intrinsic dynamics such as body size, strength, and experience, as well as the self-organizing nature of systems, people are expected to solve movement challenges in different ways. For example, basketball players have been shown to have quite distinct shooting patterns (Button et al., 2003). People with cerebral palsy will certainly walk or reach differently than individuals without disabilities, or even differently in comparison to other individuals who have cerebral palsy. Observation of ice hockey players skating quickly reveals unique patterns even to the naked eye. Practice experiences must recognize these differences by presenting opportunities for learners to build on their personal and current capabilities. An instructor may demonstrate one way to shoot a basketball or one way to ice skate but should anticipate that other patterns will naturally emerge. At other times, an instructor may watch a class and determine that a very direct comment about performance is necessary, perhaps because some learners are struggling. At other times a direct approach may be necessary to ensure safety in activities such as gymnastics, skiing, and diving. Although **guided discovery**, an approach to learning in which the teacher creates an environment and tasks to help learners find their own solutions, has many benefits, the skilled instructor knows when to be direct.

Variability in practice is also viewed positively by ecological and dynamic systems thinkers because it mirrors the actual situations in games and sport. Particularly in open sports, participants must frequently adapt their movements to their opponents' actions. Constant practice of the bounce pass in basketball without movement and opponents will not prepare players to lean to one side and pass around a moving opponent. More formally, if the attractor state for a bounce pass in basketball is too stable, the player will have difficulty with the phase shift necessary to solve the dynamics of the game. Similarly, physical and occupational therapists who may be concerned with improving walking must design practices on surfaces that vary in size and slope.

Davids and colleagues (2008) summarized these thoughts about variability when they wrote: "Practitioners' traditional emphasis on reducing errors during skill practice by encouraging consistency in motor patterns should be revised to acknowledge the valuable goal of variability in moment-to-moment control as well as long-term learning" (p. 151). According to Davids and colleagues, less time should be devoted to teacher-directed promotion of identical motor patterns, and more time should be devoted to problem solving, discovery learning, and self-regulation. As noted previously, this does not mean that a direct instructional approach is never appropriate. These authors proposed the term **nonlinear pedagogy** as the foundation of instruction based on dynamic systems—*nonlinear* because of findings that learning is often characterized by rather sudden changes in performance (e.g., to new and more sophisticated motor patterns) rather than by linear increments, as traditionally proposed by most other learning theorists.

Consistent with the principles of dynamic systems theory, nonlinear practitioners recognize that a learner's solution to a movement challenge is a unique coordination pattern resulting from the self-organization of numerous body systems. Variability among people is natural, and therapists, teachers, and coaches should design practices with this in mind. Also, by changing task, environment, and personal constraints, practitioners can nudge people to new levels of performance and can better replicate in practice the dynamics that exist in real games or life contexts. Of course, in some circumstances, a therapist or instructor will intervene with a particular person and suggest a change in movement pattern, but this is quite different from expecting everyone to perform skills in identical ways.

Davids and colleagues (2008) also proposed that teachers and coaches be called **hands-off practitioners** to reflect a new role consistent with dynamic systems theory. The hands-off practitioner is just as involved as the traditional practitioner, only in different ways. Davids and colleagues suggested that practitioners using traditional methods present drills to perfect a gold standard of performance for all, use practice skills outside the real context of performance, provide too much instruction and feedback, and overly manage the practice environment. The hands-off practitioner creates "a learning environment for the discovery of optimal solutions by manipulating constraints, interpreting movement variability, and nurturing learners in their search activities" (p. 100). Because there is no one movement solution for all learners, the hands-off teacher or therapist allows greater opportunity for learners to find appropriate personal motor patterns within practice. This prepares them to deal with changing dynamics in real performance situations, particularly in open sports and games. However, even in closed activities such as bowling and golf, movement patterns must change subtly to accommodate changes in the physical environment or in psychological functioning.

Problem solving, discovery learning, and self-regulation are embraced in dynamic systems thinking as well as in generalized motor programs theory and knowledge-based perspectives, although the theoretical explanations differ (Wall et al., 2007). Even thoughtful educational philosophers (e.g., Dewey) have acknowledged for many

WHAT DO YOU THINK?

Exercise 21.1

1. You just read about generalized motor programs. Choose two skills and complete the following table. (The overhand throw is provided as an example.)

2. Describe the role of the practitioner according to dynamic systems theory.

3. Considering your own beliefs about teaching and coaching is important. This chapter presents a role of teachers and coaches that you were likely not exposed to as a child. Will you adopt this role easily, or will you be tempted to take on a more traditional role? For example, will you provide opportunities for students to make choices based on their interests, or do you prefer to be in control? Explain and justify.

Skill	Sequence of actions	Task goal	Parameters
Overhand throw	Foot placement, arm flexion, sequential trunk rotation, weight transfer, arm follow-through, and visual contact with a target	Getting the ball to first base before the runner	Increased arm flexion to throw far; decreased arm flexion to throw a short distance

years that the most effective learning occurs through discovery and problem-based activities. So, how can the physical dimensions of the learning environment be manipulated to encourage problem solving, discovery learning, and self-regulation?

It might not need stating, but just in case—the learning environment for motor skills should be structured to promote fun. Children, adolescents, and adults list other reasons for participating in sport and physical activity (Gould et al., 1985; Weiss & Williams, 2004), but fun is often at the top of the list. Recall that intrinsic motivation is based on the pure joy of participating, and fun activities would seem to promote this. If you have seen a toddler making noise and repeating actions while playing with toys or an elementary school gymnasium during a class, you may realize the value of fun and the notion of intrinsic motivation.

Without understanding assessment, development of a present level of performance, and then different pedagogical strategies to coaching, teaching, and even rehabilitation, one cannot develop the content within their program. Now that you understand the present level of performance, we now shift to task analysis, the crux of content development.

ECOLOGICAL TASK ANALYSIS

Traditional task analysis is a method of analyzing movement performance by comparing learners' movement patterns to a correct model. This approach has several problems. The main one is that comparing learners with a model, or correct form, assumes that the structural constraints of the learner are like those of the model—in other words, that the learner can move like the model. Traditional task analysis is also problematic because everyone is placed on a continuum of performance ranging from incorrect to correct. The instructor observes the learner and corrects the movements that deviate from the correct form. This type of

correction assumes there is only one way to do something and rarely takes individual differences and environment into account. Finally, the traditional task analysis model does not account for the interaction between the task and the environment.

The **ecological task analysis**, on the other hand, accounts for learners' individual differences. This is accomplished by manipulating the environment and task on a progression of complexity, allowing learners to increase the complexity on one or more levels of a motor skill at a time. Davis and Burton (1991) identified four major steps for designing an ecological task analysis:

1. The instructor selects the task goal and structures the environmental constraints around it. An important component in the ecological task model is the involvement of the learner in this process.

2. The instructor provides learners with movement options rather than constraining their movements by instructing them to complete the movement pattern in a particular way (as in the traditional task analysis model). The instructor may even provide equipment options, such as different-sized balls. Learners may decide to make the task more or less challenging, depending on the size or bounciness of the ball. Learners who are presented with choices are likely to take more ownership of the learning process and remain motivated.

3. After learners have attempted the movement pattern, the instructor manipulates the environment, task, or both, to enhance performance.

4. The instructor then gives learners augmented feedback.

Creating an ecological task analysis for a motor skill involves three steps. The first is making a list of all the constraints associated with performing the motor skill. For playing basketball, important constraints are coordination, balance, agility, strength, and control. Once the individual constraints are established, the second step is to list the interactions between the task and the environment. In other words, how can the task of playing basketball be simplified? The equipment can be modified for smaller children, such as using a smaller or lighter ball, to account for constraints such as height and strength. The hoop could be lowered, and the court size could be decreased. A beginner would likely practice shooting balls while stationary to decrease the balance and coordination constraints. The third step is to develop a range from simple to complex for each task and environmental constraint.

Keep in mind that large changes in performance can result from small variations in a constraint. Task analyses are also helpful in therapeutic situations by providing patients with multiple options and progressions as they improve.

Task analysis can be an easy way for both instructors and learners to manipulate the task and the environment, and it helps in the creation of individualized programs even in group settings. For instance, one learner could be at the lowest level for catching in all six examples in table 21.1, whereas another may be using a medium-sized, heavy ball that is traveling at a slow speed (a relatively complex catching task). Learners who are

Table 21.1 Ecological Task Analysis for Catching

FACTORS						
	Size of object being caught	Distance for object being thrown	Weight of object being caught	Speed at which ball is coming	Predictability of trajectory of object being caught	Anticipation of ball coming and getting hands ready
Level of difficulty: simple	Large	Short	Light	Slow	Along the ground	Hands up when it gets close
Level of difficulty: moderate	Medium	Medium	Moderate	Moderate	Bounced along the ground	Hands up when it's on its way
Level of difficulty: complex	Small	Long	Heavy	Fast	In the air	Hands up before the ball is thrown

RESEARCH NOTES

SKIPping With Teachers

In 2017, Brian and colleagues implemented a gross motor skill intervention to preschoolers experiencing gross motor developmental delays. Teachers received continuous professional development to implement the program. The program featured task analyses, unit plans, assessments of program implementation (i.e., fidelity), and strong theoretical underpinning from motor development, physical education, and motor learning literature bases. After implementing their program, Brian and colleagues found that children did remediate their delays. Furthermore, the higher the teacher's fidelity of intervention (e.g., the more aligned they were with following task analyses and unit plans), the more students learned. Thus, task analyses, extensions, and planning works to support programmatic design and decisions in school settings.

given the opportunity to manipulate the task conditions often find the activity more interesting and rewarding.

Ecological task analysis is a method of outlining several possible task and environmental constraints at various levels of difficulty. Once an ecological task analysis is developed, it can become a tool for both the instructor (or therapist) and the learner (or client) to use to manipulate the complexity of the task and assess the level of the learner or client. Ecological task analysis allows for easy comparisons across individuals by comparing learners' levels for each factor rather than by evaluating product outcomes (e.g., distance or accuracy). Product outcomes are limiting given that some learners adopt unorthodox techniques to throw farther. For example, a learner who catches more balls than another learner (product outcome) may be using his chest in the catch (poor technique).

Now that we understand the way in which skills can be taught based upon present level of performance through task analysis, we now need to understand how to change the task to maximize learning based upon how the person performs the task. Sometimes even the best laid plans need to change. If a task is too easy, performers may get bored. If the task is too difficult, performers could learn incorrect movement patterns or quit. Creating a task analysis can provide options from which the instructor or therapist can shift from task to task and within the task. From a physical education perspective, shifting within a task to make it easier (downward) or harder (upward) is considered an extension task (Rink, 2014). However, to understand what makes an extension task developmentally appropriate, one needs to grasp the principles of motor development. Specifically, there are two concepts that really need to inform any task analysis including extensions. These concepts are developmental direction and the orderly manner through which we learn motor control.

As we learned in chapter 1, we learn to control our movements from head to toe (cephalocaudally) and from midline to extremities (proximodistally). In addition, we tend to learn our gross motor skills before our fine motor skills (generospecifically). Thus, it is easier for a young child to catch a ball tossed toward their chest and closer to their head than their waist. Understanding these concepts will help design tasks and support proper technique when teaching motor skills. Practitioners who are designing programs need to take these concepts into account when designing tasks and their task analyses that range from simple to more challenging.

In addition, we learn to control our movements in the following predictable way: **unilateral** (one appendage), bilaterally (two appendages at the same time), ipsilaterally (appendages on the same hemisphere—right arm and right leg), and contralaterally (appendages moving in opposition such as right leg and left arm). If children learn to

WHAT DO YOU THINK?

Exercise 21.2

1. Design an ecological task analysis for a sport-specific motor skill of your choice. Include at least five factors and vary them in difficulty from simple to complex using at least three levels.

2. Design an ecological task analysis for a balance skill. Include at least five factors and vary them in difficulty from simple to complex using at least three levels.

control movements in ways that are not necessarily best for power, mobility, or efficiency (e.g., **bilateral** throwing is not as powerful as contralateral movements), then we need to design tasks that push learners away from sequences that tend to emerge more organically. For example, young children tend to throw with an **ipsilateral** pattern. Oppositional movement (e.g., stepping with a foot opposite of the arm) tends to be a more advanced developmental milestone than movement within the same body hemisphere (e.g., right arm and right leg). Tasks should be designed to encourage a **contralateral** pattern, stepping with opposition (refer to exercise 21.3 for an example).

Having knowledge of extensions within tasks, task analyses, and assessment data is critical to creating programs that maximize learning for all students. However, when designing programs, practitioners must consider the needs of all students prior to program design. Rather than starting with a task designed for the average performer (student at an intermediate level), practitioners

should design tasks that meet all performers' needs ahead of time to support learning for all. Universal design for learning (UDL) is a framework created to help practitioners do just that—include students of all capabilities from the start. For an in-depth guide on implementing UDL in programs, please refer to *Universal Design for Learning in Physical Education* (Lieberman et al., 2020).

At the heart of UDL are three core concepts that best translate to motor learning and development. These core concepts include (a) featuring a product rather than a process orientation, (b) always providing multiple variations and options to all learners, and (c) designing tasks to reduce students being on display as much as possible.

Featuring a product orientation focuses on function and mobility rather than the process of movement. Product-oriented goals better support students with disabilities and varied presentations because product goals do not depend upon how one functions or moves but rather on one's ability to achieve one's goal of the movement.

WHAT DO YOU THINK?

Exercise 21.3

Skill	Task	Issue	Extension
Throwing	Throw a ball to a target five ft (1.5 m) away	The child is stepping ipsilaterally.	• *Upper extension:* Move the child farther away. Prompt to throw as hard as they can. Orient them sideways to start. • *Downward extension:* Place a sticker on their opposite foot and tell them to step with their sticker foot.
Catching	Catch a tennis ball with two hands gently tossed from 15 ft (4.6 m) away	The child is missing the ball and turning their head away.	• *Downward extension:* Change from a tennis ball to a beach ball. • *Downward extension:* Prompt the child to use their hands.
Lunging	In a rehabilitation setting, the patient does forward lunges to increase strength and flexibility	The patient is struggling to meet the appropriate depth with the leg (either not far down enough or too far).	*Downward extension:* Place a mirror in front of the patient. Provide rails or use your arms to assist them with the maneuver. Provide feedback regarding the depth.

Think of two other skills and create extensions.

RESEARCH NOTES

Universal Design for Learning

Kennedy and colleagues (2018) conducted a scoping review to document how UDL principles are being used by rehabilitation professionals in school settings. Specifically, they combed the occupational, physical, and speech-language therapy literature bases. Of the approximately 4,000 manuscripts found, 45 met their inclusion criteria. Overall, the authors deemed UDL a promising approach for rehabilitation in school settings. Here are their recommendations: (a) do a better job of describing your methods and operationalizing UDL, (b) use a team, (c) maximize visual supports where possible, (d) be sure to provide multiple avenues for student expression, (e) utilize variety with rehabilitation and curricular choices, and (f) do your best to keep students motivated in ways that are meaningful to them. The authors conclude that more empirical studies are needed to corroborate the use of UDL with achievement-based outcomes.

Being on display can be embarrassing. Thus, using a product orientation, providing all options, and setting personal goals for individual improvement (e.g., improving one's time rather than comparing against a peer) reduces students being on display and improves the likelihood for participant success, learning, and enjoyment with their choices. Table 21.2 shows examples of each of the UDL concepts.

Table 21.2   UDL Concepts

Skill	Example	Product	All options available?	On display?
Running	Correct—Running as many laps as you can in 4 min	Yes	Yes	No. All students focus on their own goals and stop the task at the same time.
Running	Incorrect—Run until you reach four laps	Yes	Yes	Yes. Students are on display. When the faster students finish, they will watch the slower participants until they finish the task.
Soccer dribbling	Correct—Each participant has their own ball, and they are working on foot dribbling to their own designated goal.	Yes. Score as many goals as possible within the allotted time.	Yes. Students can choose their distance and size or type of ball.	No. All students focus on their own goals and stop the task at the same time.
Soccer dribbling	Incorrect—Students are in line. One participant has a ball, dribbles down the soccer field, and shoots on goal.	No. Practice until you score two goals.	No. All participants use the regulation soccer ball, field, and goal.	Yes. More advanced performers will stare at those who are newer or less efficient with soccer.
Physical therapy session	Incorrect—The patient is in an open room with multiple patients. They are asked to walk to one end of the room and back. The patient is also asked to lie on their side while the therapist applies treatment.	No. The therapist was focused on the quality of movement.	No. There were no supports in place to aid with ambulation.	Yes. There are other patients in the same space.

WHAT DO YOU THINK?

Exercise 21.4

What are your experiences in physical education? Do the previous concepts of developmental direction, orderly progression, and increases of complexity of skill reflect your experiences? Now, create your own yearly plan and integrate all the concepts discussed. Remember to start from the least complex and end with the most complex skills.

Week	Concept	Task(s)	Goal(s)
1	Baseline assessment		Establish present level of performance
End of year	Postassessment		Participant and program evaluation

---

Now you create two tasks and include a correct and an incorrect example for each of the tasks and fill in the UDL orientations for each.

Not only do children follow the concept of developmental direction and learn to control in orderly ways, but certain motor skills are also easier to learn than others. Ease with learning goes in concert with increases in complexity. According to Monsma and colleagues (2020), balance increases in complexity in the following way: feet shoulder-width apart, feet together, feet partially in tandem, feet in tandem, and on one foot with eyes open. Locomotor skills increase in complexity in the following way: run, jump, gallop, hop, and skip. Object control skills increase in complexity from throw, kick, catch, strike, and then ball bounce. Understanding all these concepts helps us to create developmentally appropriate yearly block plans across numerous disciplines. For a complete description of block planning, please refer to Rink (2014).

SUMMARY

This final chapter provided a blueprint from which to create a program. Movement professionals must have a solid understanding of these concepts to prepare the environment and instruct learners, whether they are athletes, students, classes, patients, or clients, based on their individual constraints. The task and environment should be designed ahead of time to be the most effective practice sessions for individuals or groups. Tasks that are designed ahead of time can better utilize UDL and reduce placing practitioners, students, and clients on display. Finally, utilizing unit and block plans can help create developmentally appropriate environments, which feature task analyses that maximize desired learning and rehabilitation outcomes.

> **ONLINE ACTIVITIES**

The student material found in HK*Propel* includes exercises, labs, and videos to enhance learning and encourage practical application of important concepts.

LEARNING AIDS

Supplemental Activities

1. For this task, you will need several items to catch. Please choose from the following task structures (a) toss and catch by yourself, (b) toss and catch back and forth with a partner, (c) self-toss and catch a ball off a wall, (d) partner tosses a ball off the wall for you to catch. For partner catching, measure distances of 4, 8, and 12 feet (1.2, 2.4, and 3.7 m, respectively) and choose your distance. Equipment choices can include beanbags, tennis balls, beach balls, playground balls, scarves, and so on. Count the number of times you catch your object. Change task parameters at least two times. In which task parameter were you most successful? Which task do you think would best support novice performers? Experts? Were you on display? Which tasks would be most or least on display?

2. Locate a physical therapy center and ask if you can observe for a few sessions. Can you find any examples of UDL? If not, what would you do? Do you see any patients on display? How so or how not? What would you incorporate into your future practice or what would you do differently?

Glossary

bilateral—Movement with two arms.

contralateral—Oppositional movement with an arm and leg such as the right arm moving with the left leg.

ecological task analysis—A method of analyzing movement performance that accounts for individual differences by manipulating the environment and task on a progression of complexity, allowing learners to increase complexity on one or more levels of a skill at a time.

guided discovery—An approach to learning in which the teacher creates an environment and tasks to help learners find their own solutions.

hands-off practitioners—Based on dynamic systems theory, practitioners who incorporate problem solving, self-discovery, and self-regulation into the learning environment to encourage learners to discover appropriate personal motor patterns.

ipsilateral—Movement within the same hemisphere across two limbs such as the right arm and right leg.

nonlinear pedagogy—The foundation of instruction based on dynamic systems theory, in which practitioners promote problem solving, discovery learning, and self-regulation.

traditional task analysis—A method of analyzing movement performance by comparing the movement pattern to a correct model.

unilateral—Movement of one limb such as the right arm only.

REFERENCES

Chapter 1

Argyle, M., & Kendon, A. (1967). The experimental analysis of social performance. In *Advances in experimental social psychology, 3*, 55-98. Academic Press.

Barnett, L.M., Stodden, D.F., Hulteen, R.M., & Sacko, R. (2020). Motor competence assessment. In T. Brusseau, S. Fairclough, & D. Lubans (Eds.), *The Routledge handbook of youth physical activity*. Routledge.

Bernstein, N. (1967). *The co-ordination and regulation of movement.* Pergamon Press.

Calvo-Merino, B., Glaser, D.E., Grezes, J., Passingham, R.E., & Haggard, P. (2005). Action observation and acquired motor skills: An fMRI study with expert dancers. *Cerebral Cortex, 15*, 1243-1249.

Clark, J.E., & Metcalfe, J.S. (2002). The mountain of motor development: A metaphor. In J.E. Clark, & J. Humphrey (Eds.), *Motor development: Research and reviews* (pp. 163-190). Reston, VA: NASPE Publications.

Clark, J.E., & Whitall, J. (1989). What is motor development? The lessons of history. *Quest, 41,* 183-202.

Cohen, R.G., & Rosenbaum, D.A. (2004). Where objects are grasped reveals how grasps are planned: Generation and recall of motor plans. *Experimental Brain Research, 157,* 486-495.

Darwin, C. (1859). *On the origin of species by means of natural selection, or the preservation of favoured races in the struggle for life.* John Murray.

Darwin, C. (1871). *The descent of man, and selection in relation to sex.* John Murray.

Darwin, C. (1872). *The origin of species by means of natural selection, or the preservation of favoured races in the struggle for life* (6th ed.). John Murray.

di Pellegrino, G., Fadiga, L., Fogassi, L., Gallese, V., & Rizzolatti, G. (1992). Understanding motor events: A neurophysiological study. *Experimental Brain Research, 91,* 176-180. https://doi.org/10.1007/BF00230027

Dwyer, G.M., Baur, L.A., & Hardy, L.L. (2009). The challenge of understanding and assessing physical activity in preschool-age children: Thinking beyond the framework of intensity, duration and frequency of activity. *Journal of Science & Medicine in Sport, 12*(5): 534-536. https://doi.org/10.1016/j.jsams.2008.10.005

Elisa, F., Josee, L., Oreste, F., Claudia, A., Antonella, L., Sabrina, S., & Giovanni, L. (2002). Gross motor development and reach on sound as critical tools for the development of the blind child. *Brain & Development, 24,* 269-275. https://doi.org/10.1016/S0387-7604(02)00021-9

Fox, P.W., Hershberger, S.L., & Bouchard, T.J. (1996). Genetic and environmental contributions to the acquisition of a motor skill. *Nature, 384,* 356-358. https://doi.org/10.1038/384356a0

Gesell, A. (1928). *Infancy and human growth.* Macmillan.

Gesell, A. (1954). The ontogenesis of infant behavior. In L. Carmichael (Ed.), *Manual of child psychology* (2nd ed.). Wiley.

Gray, R. (2020). Changes in movement coordination associated with skill acquisition in baseball batting: Freezing/freeing degrees of freedom and functional variability. *Frontiers in Psychology, 11,* 1-17. https://doi.org/10.3389/fpsyg.2020.01295

Haibach, P., Lieberman, L., & Pritchett, J. (2011). Balance in adolescents with and without visual impairments. *Insight Journal, 4*(3), 112-123.

Halverson, L.E. (1970). *Research in motor development: Implications for program in early childhood education* [Paper presentation]. Midwest Association for Health, Physical Education and Recreation, Chicago, IL.

Hirsiger, S., Pickett, K., & Konczak, J. (2012). The integration of size and weight cues for perception and action: Evidence for a weight-size illusion. *Experimental Brain Research, 223,* 137-147.

Howard, R.W. (2014). Learning curves in highly skilled chess players: A test of the generality of the power law of practice. *Acta Psychologica, 151,* 16-23. https://doi.org/10.1016/j.actpsy.2014.05.013

Hulteen, R.M., Morgan, P.J., Barnett, L.M., Stodden, D.F., & Lubans, D.R. (2018). Development of foundational movement skills: A conceptual model for physical activity across the lifespan. *Sports Medicine, 48*(7), 1533-1540. https://doi.org/10.1007/s40279-018-0892-6

Kandel, S., & Perret, C. (2015). How do movements to produce letters become automatic during writing acquisition? Investigating the development of motor anticipation. *International Journal of Behavioral Development, 39*(2), 113-120.

Knapp, B. (1963). *Skill in sport.* Routledge & Kegan Paul.

Lashley, K.S. (1951). The problem of serial order in behavior. In L.A. Jeffress (Ed.), *Cerebral mechanisms in behavior* (pp. 112-131). Wiley.

Logan, G.D. (1988). Toward an instance theory of automatization. *Psychological Review, 95,* 492-527.

Malina, R. M. (2014). Top 10 research questions related to growth and maturation of relevance to physical activity, performance, and fitness. *Research Quarterly in Exercise & Sport 85*(2), 157-173. https://doi.org/10.1080/02701367.2014.897592

McGraw, M. (1935). *Growth: A study of Johnny and Jimmy.* Appleton-Century-Crofts.

McGraw, M.B. (1940). Signals of growth. *Child Study, 18,* 8-10.

McGraw, M.B. (1969). *The neuromuscular maturation of the human infant.* Hafner. (Original work published 1945)

Mendres-Smith, A.E., Borrero, J.C., Castillo, M.I., Davis, B.J., Becraft, J.L., & Hussey-Gardner, B. (2020). Tummy time without the tears: The impact of parent positioning and play. *Journal of Applied Behavior Analysis, 53*(4), 2090-2107. https://doi.org/10.1002/jaba.715

Mukamel, R., Ekstrom, A.D., Kaplan, J., Iacoboni, M., & Fried, I. (2010). Single-neuron responses in humans during execution and observation of actions. *Current Biology* 20, 750-756. https://doi.org/10.1016/j.cub.2010.02.045

Newell, K.M (1986). Constraint on the development of coordination. In M.G. Wade & H.TA. Whiting (Eds.), *Motor skill acquisition in children: Aspects of coordination and control.* (pp. 341-360). Martinis NIJHOS.

Newell, K.M. (2020). What are fundamental motor skills and what is fundamental about them? *Journal of Motor Learning & Development, 8,* 280-314. doi.org/10.1123/jmld.2020-0013

Newell, A., & Rosenbloom, P.S. (1981). Mechanisms of skill acquisition and the law of practice. In J.R. Anderson (Ed.), *Cognitive skills and their acquisition* (pp. 1-55). Hillsdale, N.J.: Erlbaum.

Rosenbaum, D.A. (2010). *Human motor control* (2nd ed.). Academic Press.

Sasaki, J.Y., & Kim, H.S. (2017). Nature, nurture, and their interplay: A review of cultural neuroscience. *Journal of Cross-Cultural Psychology, 48*(1), 4-22. https://doi.org/10.1177/0022022116680481

Schmidt, R.A., & Lee, T.D. (2014). *Motor learning and performance* (5th ed.). Human Kinetics.

Seefeldt V. (1980). Developmental motor patterns: Implications for elementary school physical education. In C. Nadeau, W. Holliwell, & G. Roberts (Eds.), *Psychology of motor behavior and sport* (pp. 314-323). Human Kinetics.

Shirley, M.M. (1931). *The first two years: A study of twenty-five babies: Vol. 1. Postural and locomotor development.* University of Minnesota Press.

Siedentop, D., & Tannehill, D. (2000). *Developing teaching skills in physical education.* Mayfield.

Snyder, K.M. & Logan, G.D. (2014). The problem of serial order in skilled typing. *Journal of Experimental Psychology: Human Perception & Performance, 40*(4), 1697-1717. https://doi.org/10.1037/a0037199

Sparrow, W.A. (1992). Measuring changes in coordination and control. In J.J. Summers (Ed.), *Approaches to the study of motor control and learning* (pp. 147-162). North-Holland.

Spirduso, W.W., Francis, K.L., & MacRae, P.G. (2005). *Physical dimensions of aging* (2nd ed.). Human Kinetics.

Stodden, D.F., Goodway, J.D., Langendorer, S.J., Roberton, M.A., Rudisill, M.E., Garcia, C., & Garcia, L.E. (2008). A developmental perspective on the role of motor skill competence in physical activity: An emergent relationship. *Quest, 60*(2), 290-306.

Thelen, E., Fisher, D.M., Ridley-Johnson, R., & Griffin, N.J. (1982). Effects of body build and arousal on newborn infant stepping. *Developmental Psychobiology, 15*(5), 447-453.

Turvey, M.T. (1990). Coordination. *American Psychologist, 45*(8), 938-953.

Van Dalen, D.B., & Bennett., B.L. (1971). *A world history of physical education: Cultural, philosophical, comparative* (2nd ed.). Prentice-Hall.

Viera, A.P.B., Carvalho, R.P., Barela, A.M.F., & Barela, J.A. (2019). Infants' age and walking experience shapes perception-action coupling when crossing obstacles. *Perceptual & Motor Skills, 162*(2), 185-201. https://doi.org/10.1177/0031512518820791

Wagner, M.O., Haibach, P.S., & Lieberman, L.J. (2013). Gross motor skill performance in children with and without visual impairments—Research to practice. *Research in Developmental Disabilities, 34*(10), 3246-3252.

Williams, L.R., & Gross, J.B. (1980). Heritability of motor skill. *Acta Geneticae Medicae Et Gemellologiae: Twin Research, 29*(2), 127-136. https://doi.org/10.1017/S0001566000008606

Chapter 2

Adolph, K.E., Eppler, M.A., & Gibson, E.J. (1993). Crawling versus walking infants' perception of affordances for locomotion over sloping surfaces. *Child Development, 64*(4), 1158-1174.

Bhalla, J.A., & Weiss, M.R. (2010). A cross-cultural perspective of parental influence on female adolescents' achievement beliefs and behaviors in sport and school domains, *Research Quarterly for Exercise and Sport, 81*(4), 494-505. https://doi.org/10.1080/02701367.2010.10599711

Clark, J.E., & Whitall, J. (1989). What is motor development? The lessons of history. *Quest, 41,* 183-202.

Ennis, C. (1992). Reconceptualizing learning as a dynamical system. *Journal of Curriculum and Supervision, 7*(2), 115-130.

Fitts, P.M. (1954). The information capacity of the human motor system in controlling the amplitude of movement. *Journal of Experimental Psychology, 47,* 381-391.

Fitts, P., & Posner, M.I. (1967). *Human performance.* Brooks/Cole.

Gibson, J.J. (1966). *The senses considered as perceptual systems.* Houghton Mifflin.

Gibson, J.J. (1977). The theory of affordances. *Hilldale, USA, 1*(2), 67-82.

Gibson, J.J. (1979). *The ecological approach to visual perception.* Houghton Mifflin.

Henry, F.M., & Rogers, D.E. (1960). Increased response latency for complicated movements and the "memory drum" theory of neuromotor reaction. *Research Quarterly, 31,* 448-458.

Keele, S.W. (1973). *Attention and human performance.* Goodyear.

Kugler, P.N., Kelso, J.A.S., & Turvey, M.T. (1982). On the control and coordination of naturally developing systems. In J.A.S. Kelso & J.E. Clark (Eds.), *The development of movement control and coordination* (pp. 5-78). Wiley.

Marteniuk, R.G. (1976). *Information processing in motor skills.* Holt, Rinehart & Winston.

Michaels, C.F., & Carello, C. (1981). *Direct perception.* Prentice Hall.

Newell, K.M. (1986). Constraints on the development of coordination. In M.G. Wade & H.T.A Whiting (Eds.), *Motor development in children: Aspects of coordination and control* (pp. 341-360). Martinus Nijhoff.

Polit, A., & Bizzi, E. (1978). Processes controlling arm movements in monkeys. *Science, 201* (4362), 1235-1237.

Rival, C., Olivier, I., & Ceyte, H. (2003). Effects of temporal and/or spatial instructions on the speed–accuracy trade-off of pointing movements in children. *Neuroscience Letters, 336,* 65-69.

Schmidt, R.A. (1975). *Motor skills.* Harper & Row.

Thelen, E., & Ulrich, B.D. (1991). Hidden skills: A dynamical systems analysis of treadmill stepping during the first year. *Monographs of the Society for Research in Child Development, 56,* (1, Serial No. 223).

Warren, W.H., Jr. (1984). Perceiving affordances: Visual guidance of stair climbing. *Journal of Experimental Psychology: Human Perception and Performance, 10,* 683-703.

Woodworth, R.S. (1899). The accuracy of voluntary movement. *Psychological Review, 3* (Suppl. 2), 1-114.

Chapter 3

Adams, R., & Dijkstra, S. (1966). Short-term memory for motor responses. *Journal of Experimental Psychology, 71,* 314-318.

Allen, P.A., Smith, A.F., Vires-Collins, H., & Sperry, S. (1998). The psychological refractory period: Evidence for age differences in attentional time-sharing. *Psychology and Aging, 13,* 218-229.

Atkinson, R.C., & Shiffrin, R.M. (1968). Human memory: A proposed system and its control processes. In K.W. Spence & J.T. Spence (Eds.), *The psychology of learning and motivation: Advances in research and theory* (Vol. 2, pp. 89-197). Academic Press.

Baddeley, A.D. (1986). *Working memory.* Oxford University Press.

Baddeley, A.D. (1995). Working memory. In M.S. Gazzaniga (Ed.), *The cognitive neurosciences* (pp. 755-764). MIT Press.

Cherry, E.C. (1953). Some experiments on the recognition of speech, with one and with two ears. *The Journal of the Acoustical Society of America, 25*(5), 975-979.

Cooper, A., Goodman, A., Page, A., Sherar, L.B., Esliger, D.W., van Sluijs, E., Andersen, L., Anderssen, S., . . . Ekelund, U. (2015). Objectively measured physical activity and sedentary time in youth: The international children's accelerometry database (ICAD). *The International Journal of Behavioral Nutrition and Physical Activity, 12*(1), 113.

Dunn, J.C. (2008). The dimensionality of the remember-know task: A state-trace analysis. *Psychological Review, 115,* 426-446.

Easterbrook, J.A. (1959). The effect of emotion on cue utilization and the organization of behavior. *Psychological Review, 66,* 183-201.

Freudheim, A.M., Wulf, G., Madureira, F., Pasetto, S.C., & Correa, U.C. (2010). An external focus of attention results in greater swimming speed. *International Journal of Sports Science and Coaching, 5,* 533-542.

Gallahue, D.L., Ozmun, J.C., & Goodway, J.D. (2012). *Understanding motor development: Infants, children, adolescents and adults* (7th ed.). McGraw-Hill.

Ghetti, S., & Lee, J. (2011). Children's episodic memory. Wiley Interdisciplinary Reviews: *Cognitive Science, 2,* 365-373.

Haywood, K.M., & Getchell, N. (2014). *Life span motor development* (6th ed.). Human Kinetics.

Helsen, W., & Pauwels, J.M. (1993). The relationship between expertise and visual information processing in sport. In J.L. Starkes & F. Allard (Eds.), *Cognitive issues in motor expertise* (pp. 109-134). Elsevier Science.

Hick, W.E. (1952). On the rate of gain of information. *Quarterly Journal of Experimental Psychology, 4,* 11-26.

Hitzeman, S.A., & Beckerman, S.A. (1993). What the literature says about sports vision. *Optometry Clinics, 3*(1), 145-169.

Ille, A., & Cadopi, M. (1999). Memory for movement sequences in gymnastics: Effects of age and skill level. *Journal of Motor Behavior, 31,* 290-300.

Kahneman, D. (1973). *Attention and effort.* Prentice Hall.

Koenig, L., Wimmer, M.C., & Hollins, T.J. (2015). Process dissociation of familiarity and recollection in children: Response deadline affects recollection but not familiarity. *Journal of Experimental Child Psychology, 131,* 120-134.

Kohmura, Y., Yoshigi, H., Sakuraba, K., Aoki, K., & Totsuka, R. (2008). Development and gender differences in dynamic and kinetic visual acuities in children from 8 to 17 years of age. *International Journal of Sport and Health Science, 6,* 128-134.

Landers, D.M., & Arent, S.M. (2010). Arousal-performance relationships. In J.M. Williams (Ed.), *Applied sport psychology: Personal growth to peak performance* (6th ed., pp. 221-226). McGraw-Hill.

Leavitt, J.L. (1979). Cognitive demands of skating and stick handling in ice hockey. *Canadian Journal of Applied Sport Science, 4,* 46-55.

Li, K., Su, W., Fu, H., & Pickett, K.A. (2015). Kinesthetic deficit in children with developmental coordination disorder. *Research in Developmental Disabilities, 38,* 125-133.

Magill, R., & Anderson, D. (2013). *Motor learning and control: Concepts and applications* (10th ed.). McGraw-Hill.

Marieb, E.N., Wilhelm, P.B., & Mallatt, J.B. (2017). *Human anatomy* (8th ed.). Pearson Education.

McNevin, N.H., Shea, C.H., & Wulf, G. (2003). Increasing the distance of an external focus of attention enhances learning. *Psychological Research, 67,* 22-29.

Miller, G.A. (1956). The magical number seven plus or minus two: Some limits on our capacity for processing information. *Psychological Review, 63,* 81-97.

Nideffer, R.M. (1976). Test of attentional and interpersonal style. *Journal of Personality and Social Psychology, 34,* 394-404.

Perreault, M.E., & French, K.E. (2015). External-focus feedback benefits free-throw learning in children. *Research Quarterly for Exercise and Sport, 86,* 422-427.

Schmidt, R.A., & Lee, T.D. (2011). *Motor control and learning: A behavioral emphasis* (5th ed.). Human Kinetics.

Schrauf, M., Wist, E.R., & Ehrenstein, W.H. (1999). Development of dynamic vision based on motion contrast. *Experimental Brain Research, 124,* 469-473.

Smith, M.C. (1967). Theories of the psychological refractory period. *Psychological Bulletin, 67,* 202-213.

Starkes, J.L., Deakin, J.M., Lindley, S., & Crisp, F. (1987). Motor versus verbal recall of ballet sequences by young expert dancers. *Journal of Sport Psychology, 9,* 222-230.

Tsushima, W.T., Siu, A.M., Ahn, H.J., Chang, B.L., & Murata, B.M. (2019). Incidence and risk of concussions in youth athletes: Comparisons of age, sex, concussion history, sport, and football position. *Archives of Clinical Neuropsychology, 34*(1), 60-69. https://doi.org/10.1093/arclin/acy019

Vance, J., Wulf, G., Töllner, T., McNevin, N., & Mercer, J. (2004). EMG activity as a function of the performer's focus of attention. *Journal of Motor Behavior, 36,* 450-459.

Vaughan, R.S., Hagyard, J.D., Brimmell, J., & Edwards, E.J. (2021). The effect of trait emotional intelligence on working memory across athletic expertise. *Journal of Sports Sciences, 39*(6), 629-637. https://doi.org/10.1080/02640414.2020.1840039

Visser, J., & Geuze, R.H. (2000). Kinaesthetic acuity in adolescent boys: A longitudinal study. *Developmental Medicine & Child Neurology, 42,* 93-96.

Weinberg, R.S., & Gould, D. (2015). *Foundations of sport and exercise psychology* (6th ed.). Human Kinetics.

Wickens, C.D. (1980). The structure of processing resources. In R. Nickerson (Ed.), *Attention and performance VII* (pp. 239-257). Erlbaum.

Wickens, C.D. (1992). *Engineering psychology and human performance* (2nd ed.). HarperCollins.

Wixted, J.T. (2007). Dual-process theory and signal-detection theory of recognition memory. *Psychological Review, 114*(1),152-76. https://doi: 10.1037/0033-295X.114.1.152

Wulf, G. (2013). Attentional focus and motor learning: A review of 15 years. *International Review of Sport and Exercise Psychology, 6,* 77-104.

Wulf, G., Dufek, J.S., Lozano, L., & Pettigrew, C. (2010). Increased jump height and reduced EMG activity with an external focus. *Human Movement Science, 29*(3), 440-448.

Wulf, G., Höß, M., & Prinz, W. (1998). Instructions for motor learning: Differential effects of internal versus external focus of attention. *Journal of Motor Behavior, 30,* 169-179.

Wulf, G., & Lewthwaite, R. (2010). Effortless motor learning? An external focus of attention enhances movement effectiveness and efficiency. In B. Bruya (Ed.), *Effortless attention: A new perspective in the cognitive science of attention and action* (pp. 75-101). The MIT Press.

Wulf, G., McNevin, N.H., & Shea, C.H. (2001). The automaticity of complex motor skill learning as a function of attentional focus. *The Quarterly Journal of Experimental Psychology, 54A,* 1143-1154.

Wulf, G., & Su, J. (2007). An external focus of attention enhances golf shot accuracy in beginners and experts. *Research Quarterly for Exercise and Sport, 78,* 384-389.

Wulf, G., Wächter, S., & Wortmann, S. (2003). Attentional focus in motor skill learning: Do females benefit from an external focus? *Women in Sport and Physical Activity Journal, 12,* 37-52.

Yonelinas, A.P. (2002). The nature of recollection and familiarity: A review of 30 years of research. *Journal of Memory and Language, 46,* 441-517

Yoo, H., Reichow, A., Erickson, G., & Citek, K. (2009). Static and dynamic visual acuities of athletes. *Journal of Vision, 9*(8), 411, 411a. https://doi.org/10.1167/9.8.411

Chapter 4

Adams, D.L. (1999). Develop better motor skill progressions with Gentile's taxonomy of tasks. *Journal of Physical Education, Recreation and Dance, 70*(8), 35.

Argyle, M., & Kendon, A. (1967). The experimental analysis of social performance. In L. Berkowitz (Ed.), *Advances in experimental social psychology.* Academic Press.

Brace, D.K. (1927). *Measuring motor ability.* A.S. Barnes.

Fitts, P., & Posner, M.I. (1967). *Human performance.* Brooks/Cole.

Fleishman, E.A. (1962). The description and prediction of perceptual motor skill learning. In R. Glasser (Ed.), *Training research and education* (pp. 137-175). University of Pittsburgh Press.

Fleishman, E.A. (1964). *The structure and measurement of physical fitness.* Prentice Hall.

Gallahue, D.L., Ozmun, J.C., & Goodway, J.D. (2012). *Understanding motor development* (7th ed.). McGraw-Hill.

Gentile, A.M. (2000). Skill acquisition: Action, movement and neuromotor processes. In J.H. Carr & R.B. Shepherd (Eds.), *Movement science: Foundations for physical therapy in rehabilitation* (2nd ed., pp. 111-187). Aspen.

Henry, F.M. (1968). Specificity vs. generality in learning motor skills. In R.C. Brown & G.S. Kenyon (Eds.), *Classical studies on physical activity* (pp. 331-340). Prentice Hall.

Honeybourne, J. (2006). *Acquiring skill in sport: An introduction.* Routledge.

Kenyon, L.K., & Blackinton, M.T. (2011) Applying motor-control theory to physical therapy practice: A case report. *Physiotherapy Canada, 63,* 345-354.

Knapp, B. (1963). *Skill in sport.* Routledge & Kegan Paul.

Talović, M., Hodžić, M., Bajramović, I., Jelešković, E., & Alić, H. (2009). Influence of the motor and functional abilities to the efficiency of football techniques elements performance. *Homo Sporticus, 11*(1), 41-44.

Chapter 5

Arutyunyan, G.A., Gurfinkel, V.S., & Mirskii, M.L. (1968). Study of taking aim at a target. *Biophysics, 13,* 536-538.

Arutyunyan, G.A., Gurfinkel, V.S., & Mirskii, M.L. (1969). The organization of movements in human execution of a task involving exactness of post. *Biophysics, 14,* 1162-1167.

Bernardi, N., Darainy, M., & Ostry, D.J. (2015). Somatosensory contributions to the initial stages of human motor learning. *The Journal of Neuroscience, 35*(42), 14316-14326.

Bernstein, N. (1967). *The co-ordination and regulation of movement.* Pergamon Press.

Birrer, D., Rothlin, P., & Morgan, G. (2012). Mindfulness to enhance athletic performance: Theoretical considerations and possible impact mechanisms. *Mindfulness, 3*(3), 235-246. https://doi.10.1007/s12671-012-0109-2

Carson, H.J, & Collins, D. (2011). Refining and regaining skills in fixation/diversification stage performers: The five-A model. *International Review of Sport and Exercise Psychology, 4*(2), 146-167.

Chow, J.Y., Davids, K., Button, C., & Koh, M. (2008). Coordination changes in a discrete multi-articular action as a function of practice. *Acta Psychologica, 127,* 163-176.

Diedrich, F.J., & Warren, W.H. (1995). Why change gait? Dynamics of the walk-run transition. *Journal of Experimental Psychology: Human Perception & Performance, 21,* 183-202.

Dutt-Mazumder, A., & Newell, K.M. (2018). Influence of skill level on acquisition of dynamic cyclical postural stability as a function of practice. *Scandinavian Journal of Medicine and Science in Sports, 28,* 1604-1614.

Fitts, P., & Posner, M.I. (1967). *Human performance.* Brooks/Cole.

Gentile, A.M. (1972). A working model of skill acquisition with application to teaching. *Quest, 17,* 3-23.

Gentile, A.M. (1987). Skill acquisition: Action, movement and neuromotor processes. In J.H. Carr, R.B. Shepherd, J. Gordon, A.M. Gentile, & J.M. Held (Eds.), *Movement science: Foundations for physical therapy in rehabilitation* (pp. 93-154). Rockville, MD: Aspen.

Gentile, A.M. (2000). Skill acquisition: Action, movement and neuromotor processes. In J.H. Carr & R.B. Shepherd (Eds.), *Movement science: Foundations for physical therapy in rehabilitation* (2nd ed., pp. 111-187). Aspen.

Kee, Y.H. (2019). Reflections on athletes' mindfulness skills development: Fitts and Posner's (1967) three stages of learning. *Journal of Sport Psychology in Action, 10*(4), 214-219.

Kelso, J.A.S. (1995). *Dynamic Patterns.* MIT Press.

Ko, Y.G., Challis, J.H., & Newell, K.M. (2003). Learning to coordinate redundant degrees of freedom in a dynamic balance task. *Human Movement Science, 22,* 47-66.

Konczak, J., Velden, H.V., & Jaeger, L. (2009). Learning to play the violin: Motor control by freezing, not freeing degrees of freedom. *Journal of Motor Behavior, 41,* 243-252.

Newell, K.M., Kugler, P.N., van Emmerik, R.E.A., & McDonald, P.V. (1989). Search strategies and the acquisition of coordination. In S.A. Wallace (Ed.), *Perspectives on the coordination of movement* (pp. 85-122). North-Holland.

Newell, K.M., & Liu, Y.T. (2021). Collective variables and task constraints in movement coordination, control and skill. *Journal of Motor Behavior, 53*(6), 770-796.

Newell, K.M., & Vaillancourt, D.E. (2001). Dimensional change in motor learning. *Human Movement Science, 20*(4-5), 695-715.

Newell, K.M., & van Emmerik, R.E.A. (1989). The acquisition of coordination: Preliminary analysis of learning to write. *Human Movement Science, 8,* 17-32.

Rose, D.J., & Christina, R.W. (2006). *A multilevel approach to the study of motor control and learning* (2nd ed.). Pearson Benjamin Cummings.

Seefeldt, V. (1980). Developmental motor patterns: Implications for elementary school physical education. In C. Nadeau, W. Holliwell, K. Newell, & G. Roberts (Eds.), *Psychology of motor behavior and sport* (pp. 314-323). Human Kinetics.

Shank, M.D., & Haywood, K.M. (1987). Eye movements while viewing a baseball pitch. *Perceptual and Motor Skills, 64,* 1191-1197.

Vereijken, B. (1991). *The dynamics of skill acquisition* [Unpublished doctoral dissertation], Free University.

Vereijken, B., van Emmerik, R.E.A., Whiting, H.T.A., & Newell, K.M. (1992). Free(z)ing degrees of freedom in skill acquisition. *Journal of Motor Behavior, 24*(1), 133-142.

Verrel, J., Pologe, S., Manselle, W., Lindenberger, U., & Woollacott, M. (2013). Coordination of degrees of freedom and stabilization of task variables in a complex motor skill: Expertise-related differences in cello bowing. *Experimental Brain Research, 224*(3), 323-334.

Zanone, P.G., & Kelso, J.A.S. (1994). The coordination dynamics of learning: Theoretical structure and experimental agenda. In S. Swinnen, H. Heuer, J. Massion, & P. Casaer (Eds.), *Interlimb coordination: Neural, dynamical, and cognitive constraints* (pp. 461-490). Academic Press.

Chapter 6

Almond, L. (1986). Primary and secondary rules. In R. Thorpe, D. Bunker, & L. Almond (Eds.), *Rethinking games teaching* (pp. 38-40). University of Technology, Loughborough.

Anderson, J.R. (1993). *Rules of mind*. Erlbaum.

Asher, J.J. (1964). Vision and audition in language learning. *Perceptual and Motor Skills, 19*, 255-300.

Bransford, J.D., Franks, J.J., Morris, C.D., & Stein, B.S. (1979). Some general constraints on learning and memory research. In L.S. Cermak & F.I.M. Craik (Eds.), *Levels of processing in human memory* (pp. 331-354). Erlbaum.

Cook, V.J. (1997). L2 users and English spelling. *Journal of Multilingual and Multicultural Development, 18*, 474-488.

Ebbinghaus, H. (1913). Memory: A contribution to experimental psychology (H.A. Ruger & C.E. Bussenius, Trans.).Bureau of Publications, Teachers College, Columbia University.

Figueredo, L. (2006). Using the known to chart the unknown: A review of first-language influence on the development of English-as-a-second-language spelling skill. *Reading and Writing, 19*, 873-905.

Fitts, P., & Posner, M.I. (1967). *Human performance*. Brooks/Cole.

Forrester, L.W., Wheaton, L.A., & Luft, A.R. (2008). Exercise-mediated locomotor recovery and lower-limb neuroplasticity after stroke. *Journal of Rehabilitation Research & Development, 45*(2), 205.

Haibach, P.S., Daniels, G.L., & Newell, K.M. (2004). Coordination changes in the early stages of learning to cascade juggle. *Human Movement Science, 23*, 185-206.

Hanseeuw, B.J., Seron, X., & Ivanoiu, A. (2012). Increased sensitivity to proactive and retroactive interference in amnestic mild cognitive impairment: New insights. *Brain and Cognition, 80*(1), 104-110.

Hopper, T., & Bell, R. (1999). Games classification system: Teaching strategic understanding and tactical awareness. *California Association for Health, Physical Education, Recreation and Dance, 66*(4), 14-19.

Howard, R.W. (2014). Learning curves in highly skilled chess players: A test of the generality of the power law of practice. *Acta Psychologica, 151*, 16-23.

Lee, T., & Carnahan, H. (2021). Motor learning: Reflections on the past 40 years of research. *Kinesiology Review, 10*, 274-282. https://doi.org/10.1123/kr.2021-0018

Loy, J. (1968). The nature of sport: A definitional effort. *Quest, 10*, 1-15.

Majed, L., Heugas, A.-M., Chamon, M., & Siegler, I.A. (2012). Learning an energy-demanding and biomechanically constrained motor skill, racewalking: Movement reorganization and contribution of metabolic efficiency and sensory information. *Human Movement Science, 31*, 1598-1614.

Morris, L. (2001). Going through a bad spell: What the spelling errors of young ESL learners reveal about their grammatical knowledge. *Canadian Modern Language Review, 58*, 273-286.

Mount, J. (1996). Effect of practice of a throwing skill in one body position on performance of the skill in an alternate position. *Perceptual and Motor Skills, 83*, 723-732.

Neumann, O. (1984). On controlled and automatic processes. In W. Prinz & A. Sanders (Eds.), *Cognition and motor processes* (pp. 225-295). Springer.

Newell, K.M., Liu, Y.T., & Mayer-Kress, G. (2006). Human learning: Power laws or multiple characteristic time scales? *Tutorials in Quantitative Methods for Psychology, 2*, 66-76.

Newell, K.M., & Rosenbloom, P.S. (1981). Mechanisms of skill acquisition and the law of practice. In J.R. Anderson (Ed.), *Cognitive skills and their acquisition* (pp. 1-55). Erlbaum.

Rink, J. (1998). Teaching concepts and content-specific pedagogy. In *Teaching physical education for learning* (pp. 281-292). McGraw-Hill.

Rose, D.J., & Christina, R.W. (2006). *A multilevel approach to the study of motor control and learning* (2nd ed.). Pearson Benjamin Cummings.

Siedentop, D. (2012). *Introduction to physical education fitness and sport* (8th ed.). New York: McGraw-Hill.

Snoddy, G.S. (1926). Learning and stability: A psychophysical analysis of a case of motor learning with clinical applications. *Journal of Applied Psychology, 10*, 1-36.

Sparrow, W.A., & Newell, K.M. (1998). Metabolic energy expenditure and the regulation of movement economy. *Psychonomic Bulletin & Review, 5*(2), 173-196. https://doi.org/10.3758/BF03212943

Thorndike, E.L. (1914). *Educational psychology*. Columbia University.

Thorpe, R., Bunker, D., & Almond, L. (1986). *Rethinking games teaching*. University of Technology, Loughborough.

Voss, D.E., Ionta, M.K., & Myers, B.J. (1985). *Proprioceptive neuromuscular facilitation* (3rd ed.). Harper & Row.

Verhoeven, F.M., & Newell, K.M. (2018). Unifying practice schedules in the timescales of motor learning and performance. *Human Movement Science, 59*, 153-169. https://doi.org/10.1016/j.humov.2018.04.004

Verneau, M., van der Kamp, J., Savelsbergh, G.J.P., & de Looze, M.P. (2015). Proactive and retroactive transfer of middle age adults in a sequential motor learning task. *Acta Psychologica*, 57-63. https://doi.org/10.1016/j.actpsy.2015.01.009

Werner, P., & Almond, L. (1990). Models of games education. *Journal of Physical Education, Recreation and Dance, 61*(4), 23-27.

Wulf, G., & Lewthwaite, R. (2016). Optimizing performance through intrinsic motivation and attention for learning: The OPTIMAL theory of motor learning. *Psychonomic Bulletin & Review, 23*(5), 1382-1414. https://doi.org/10.3758/s13423-015-0999-9

Chapter 7

Abernathy, B., Kippers, V., Mackinnon, L.T., Neal, R.J., & Hanrahan, S. (1996). *The biophysical foundations of human movement*. Macmillan Education Australia.

ACOG Committee. (2020). Physical activity and exercise during pregnancy and the postpartum period: ACOG

Committee opinion, number 804. *Obstetrics & Gynecology*, 135, e178-e188.

Addila, A.E., Azale, T., Gete, Y.K., & Yitayal, M. (2021). The effects of maternal alcohol consumption during pregnancy on adverse fetal outcomes among pregnant women attending antenatal care at public health facilities in Gondar town, Northwest Ethiopia: A prospective cohort study. *Substance Abuse Treatment, Prevention, and Policy, 16*(1). https://link.gale.com/apps/doc/A675222605/AONE?u=brockport&sid=bookmark-AONE&xid=c47382bc

Adolph, K.E., Bertenthal, B.I., Boker, S.M., Goldfield, E.C., & Gibson, E.J. (1997). Learning in the development of infant locomotion. *Monographs of the society for research in child development*, i-162.

Adolph, K.E. (2008). Learning to move. *Current Directions in Psychological Science, 17*, 213-218.

Adolph, K.E., & Berger, S.E. (2006). Motor development. In W. Damon & R.M. Lerner (Series Eds.) and D. Kuhn & R.S. Siegler (Vol. Eds.), *Handbook of child psychology: Vol. 2. Cognition, perception, and language* (6th ed., pp. 161-213). Wiley.

Adolph, K.E., & Hoch, J.E. (2018). Motor development: Embodied, embedded, enculturated, and enabling. *Annual Review of Psychology, 70*, 141-164. https://doi.org.10.1146/annurev-psych-010418102836

Aicardi, J., & Bax, M. (1992). Cerebral palsy. In J. Aicardi (Ed.), *Diseases of the nervous system in childhood* (2nd ed., pp. 210-239). Mac Keith Press.

American Academy of Pediatrics Task Force on Infant Positioning and SIDS. (1992). Positioning and SIDS. *Pediatrics, 89*, 1120-1126.

Angulo-Barroso, R., Burghardt, A.R., Lloyd, M., & Ulrich, D. (2007). Physical activity in infants with Down syndrome receiving a treadmill intervention. *Infant Behavior and Development, 31*(2), 255-269.

Benson, J.M. (1993). Season of birth and onset of locomotion: theoretical and methodological implications. *Infant Behavior and Development, 16*, 69-81.

Bremond-Gignac, D., Cussenot, O., Deplus, S., Peuchmar, M., Ferkadji, L., Emaleh, M., & Lassau, J.P. (1994). Computation of eyeball growth by magnetic resonance imaging (26.11. 93). *Surgical and Radiologic Anatomy,16*(1), 113-115.Campos, A.C., Rocha, N.A.C.F., & Savelsbergh, G.J.P. (2009). Reaching and grasping movements in infants at risk: A review. *Research in Developmental Disabilities, 30*, 819-826.

Campos, J.J., Witherington, D., Anderson, D.I., Frankel, C.I., Uchiyama, I., & Barbu-Roth, M.A. (2008). Rediscovering development in infancy. *Child Development, 79*(6), 1625-1632.

Carmichael, L. (1946). The onset and early development of behavior. In L. Carmichael (Ed.), *Manual of child psychology* (pp. 43-166). Wiley.

Carr, J. (1970). Mental and motor development in young Mongol children. *Journal of Mental Deficiency Research, 14*, 205-220.

Chinello, A., DiGangi, V., & Valenza, E. (2018). Persistent primary reflexes affect motor acts: Potential implications for autism spectrum disorder. *Research in Developmental Disabilities*, 287-295. https://doi.org/10/1016/j.ridd.2016.07.010

Cintas, H.L. (1995). Cross-cultural similarities and differences in development and the impact of parental expectations on motor behavior. *Pediatric Physical Therapy, 7*, 103-111.

Courage, M.L., & Adams, R.J. (1990). Visual acuity assessment from birth to three years using the acuity card procedures: Cross-sectional and longitudinal samples. *Optometry and Vision Science, 67*, 713-718.

Di Mascio, D., Khalil, A., Saccone, G., Rizzo, G., Buca, D., Liberati, M., Vecchiet, J., Nappi, L., Scambia, G., Berghella, V., & D'Antonio, F. (2020). Outcome of coronavirus spectrum infections (SARS, MERS, COVID-19) during pregnancy: A systematic review and meta-analysis. *American Journal of Obstetrics & Gynecology MFM 2*, 100107. https://doi:10.1016/j.ajogmf.2020.100107

Drover, J.R., Felius, J., Cheng, C.S., Morale, S.E., Wyatt, L., & Birch, E.E. (2018). Normative pediatric visual acuity using single surrounded HOTV optotypes on the electronic visual acuity tester following the Amblyopia Treatment Study protocol. *Journal of the American Association for Pediatric Ophthalmology and Strabismus, 12*(2), 145-149. https://doi.org/10.1016/j.jaapos.2007.08.014

Dusing, S.C., & Harbourne, T.H. (2010). Variability in postural control during infancy: Implications for development, assessment, and intervention. *Physical Therapy, 90*(12), 1838-1849.

Eimas, P.D. (1975). Auditory and phonetic coding of the cues for speech: Discrimination of the [r-l] distinction by young infants. *Perception & Psychophysics, 18*, 341-347.

Evans, P.M., & Alberman, E. (1985). Recording motor deficits of children with cerebral palsy. *Developmental Medicine and Child Neurology, 27*, 401-406.

Frantz, R.L. (1963). Pattern vision in newborn infants. *Science, 140*(3564), 296-297.

Gabbard, C. (2021). *Lifelong motor development*. Lippincott Williams & Wilkins.

Gesell, A. (1946). The ontogenesis of infant behavior. In L. Charmichael (Ed.), *Manual of child psychology* (pp. 295-331). Wiley.

Gesell, A., & Ames, L.B. (1940). The ontogenetic organization of prone behavior in human infancy. *Journal of Genetic Psychology, 56*, 247-263.

Gibson, E.J., & Pick, A.P. (2000). An ecological approach to perceptual development. In E.J. Gibson & A.P. Pick (Eds.), *An ecological approach to perceptual learning and development* (pp. 14-25). Oxford University Press.

Hadders-Algra, M. (2000). The neuronal group selection theory: A framework to explain variation in normal motor development. *Developmental Medicine and Child Neurology, 42*, 566-572.

Hadders-Algra, M. (2018). Early human motor development: From variation to the ability to vary and adapt. *Neuroscience & Biobehavioral Review, 90*, 411-427. https://doi.org/10.1016/j.neubiorev.2018.05.009

Handryastuti, S., Fadiana, G., Ismael, S., Sastroasmoro, S., Aminullah, A., Idris, F.H., Saptogino, A., & Hapsara, S. (2018). Early detection of cerebral palsy in high-risk infants: Diagnostic value of primitive and developmental reflexes as well as ultrasound. *Paediatrica Indoneisana, 58*(1), 5-12. http://dx.doi.org/10.14238/pi58.1.2018.5-12

Harlow, H.F. (1949). The formation of learning sets. *Psychological Review, 56*, 51-65.

Henderson, S.E. (1985). Motor skill development. In D. Lane & B. Stratford (Eds.), *Current approaches to Down syndrome* (pp. 397-405). Holt, Rinehart & Winston.

Henderson, S.E. (1986). Some aspects of the motor development of motor control in Down's syndrome. In H.T.A. Whiting & M.G. Wade (Eds.), *Themes in motor development* (pp. 69-92). Martinus Nijhoff.

Herring, J.A. (2020). The orthopaedic examination: A comprehensive overview. In *Tachdijian's pediatric orthopaedics*. pp. 25-61. *E-Book*. Elsevier Health Sciences.

Hogg, J., & Moss, S.C. (1983). Prehensile development in Down's syndrome and non-handicapped preschool children. *British Journal of Developmental Psychology, 1*(2), 189-204.

Hox, J.J., Moerbeek, M., & Van de Schoot, R. (2010). Multilevel analysis: Techniques and applications. Routledge.

Jenkins, K.J., Correa, A., Feinstein, J.A., Botto, L., Britt, A.E., Daniels, S.R., . . . & Webb, C.L. (2007). Noninherited risk factors and congenital cardiovascular defects: current knowledge: a scientific statement from the American Heart Association Council on Cardiovascular Disease in the Young: endorsed by the American Academy of Pediatrics. *Circulation, 115*(23), 2995-3014.

Kaiser, L.L., & Campbell, C.G. (2014). Practice paper of the Academy of Nutrition and Dietetics abstract: Nutrition and lifestyle for a healthy pregnancy outcome. *Journal of the Academy of Nutrition and Dietetics, 114*(9), 1447.

Karasik, L.B., Tamis-LeMonda, C.S., Adolph, K.E., & Bornstein, M.H. (2015). Places and postures: A cultural comparison of sitting in 5-month-olds. *Journal of Cross-Cultural Psychology, 46*, 1023-1038.

Karch, D., Kang, K.-S., Wochner, K., Philippi, H., Hadders-Algra, M., Pietz, J., & Dickhaus, H. (2012). Kinematic assessment of stereotypy in spontaneous movements in infants. *Gait & Posture, 36*, 307-311.

Kisilevsky, B.S., Hains, S.M., Lee, K., Xie, X., Huang, H., Ye, H.H., Zhang, K., & Wang, Z. (2003). Effects of experience on fetal voice recognition. *Psychology Science, 14*, 220-224.

Koshy, G., Delpisheh, A., & Brabin, B.J. (2010). Dose response association of pregnancy cigarette smoking exposure, childhood stature, overweight and obesity. *European Journal of Public Health, 173*, 286-291.

Kuhl, P.K. (2010). Brain mechanisms in early language acquisition. *Neuron, 67,* 713-727. http://dx.doi.org/10.1016/j.neuron.2010.08.038

Kuhl, P.K., Williams, K.A., Lacerda, F., Stevens, K.N., & Lindblom, B. (1992). Language experience alters phonetic perception in infants by 6 months of age. *Science, 255,* 606-608.

Lee, R., Serene, T., & Tan, K.H. (2020). Guidelines on physical activity and exercise in pregnancy. *Perinatal Society of Singapore, Singapore,* 9-16.

Lenke, M.C. (2003). Motor outcomes in premature infants. *Newborn and Infant Nursing Reviews, 3,* 104-109.

Lloyd, M., Burghardt, A., Ulrich, D.A., & Angulo-Barroso, R. (2010). Physical activity and walking onset in infants with Down syndrome. *Adapted Physical Activity Quarterly, 27,* 1-16.

Lydic, J.S., & Steele, C. (1979). Assessment of the quality of sitting and gait patterns in children with Down's syndrome. *Physical Therapy, 12*(59), 1489-1494.

Lynch, T.A., & Abel, D.E. (2015). Teratogens and congenital heart disease. *Journal of Diagnostic Medical Sonography, 31*(5), 301-305.

Maitre, N.L., Slaughter, J.C., & Aschner, J.L. (2013). Early prediction of cerebral palsy after neonatal intensive care using motor development trajectories in infancy. *Early Human Development, 89*(10), 781-786.

McGraw, M.B. (1943). *The neuromuscular maturation of the human infant*. Columbia University Press.

Mercer, J. (1998). *Infant development: A multidisciplinary introduction*. Brooks/Cole.

Moon, C., Lagercrantz, H., & Kuhl, P.K. (2013). Language experienced in utero affects vowel perception after birth: A two-country study. *Acta Paediatrica, 102,* 156-160. http://dx.doi.org/10.1111/apa.12098

Moore, M.L. (2003). Preterm labor and birth: What have we learned in the past two decades? *Journal of Obstetric, Gynecologic, and Neonatal Nursing, 32,* 638-649.

Monson, R.M., Deitz, J., & Kartin, D. (2003). The relationship between awake positioning and motor performance among infants who slept supine. *Pediatric Physical Therapy, 15*(4), 196-203.

Mottola, M.F., Davenport, M.H., Ruchat, S.M., Davies, G.A., Poitras, V.J., Gray, C.E., . . . & Zehr, L. (2018). 2019 Canadian guideline for physical activity throughout pregnancy. *British journal of sports medicine, 52*(21), 1339-1346.

Nascimento, S.L., Surita, F.G., Godoy, A.C., Kasawara, K.T., & Morais, S.S. (2015). Physical activity patterns and factors related to exercise during pregnancy: A cross sectional study. *PLoS One, 10,* e0128953.

Newell, K.M. (1986). Constraints on the development of coordination. In M.G. Wade & H.T.A. Whiting (Eds.), *Motor development in children: Aspects of coordination and control* (pp. 341-361). Nijhoff.

Newell, K.M., Liu, Y.-T., & Mayer-Kress, G. (2003). A dynamical systems interpretation of epigenetic landscapes for infant motor development. *Infant Behavior & Development*, 26, 449-472.

Newell, K.M., McDonald, P.V., & Baillargeon, R. (1993). Body scale and infant grip configurations. *Developmental Psychobiology*, 26(4), 195-205.

Piek, J.P. (2006). *Infant motor development*. Human Kinetics.

Pollock, A.S., Durward, B.R., Rowe P.J., & Paul, J.P. (2000). What is balance? *Clinical Rehabilitation*, 14(4), 402-406.

Robinson, J.S., Moore, V.M., Owens, J.A., & McMillen, I.C. (2000). Origins of fetal growth restriction. *European Journal of Obstetrics & Gynecology and Reproductive Biology*, 92(1), 13-19.

Rosenbaum, P., Paneth, N., Leviton, A., Goldstein, M., Bax, M., Damiano, D., Dan, B., & Jacobsson B. (2007). A report: The definition and classification of cerebral palsy—April 2006. *Developmental Medicine & Child Neurology Supplement*, 109, 8-14.

Rothwell, P.M., Howard, S.C., Dolan, E., O'Brien, E., Dobson, J.E., Dahlöf, B., Sever, P.S., & Poulter, N.R. (2010). *Lancet*, 375(9718), 895-905.

Rudin, L.R., Dunn, L., Lyons, K., Livingston, J., Waring, M.E., & Pescatello, L.S. (2021). Professional exercise recommendations for healthy women who are pregnant: A systematic review. *Women's Health Reports*, 2(1), 400-412.

Salls, J.S., Silverman, L.N., & Gatty, C.M. (2002). The relationship of infant sleep and play positioning to motor milestone achievement. *American Journal of Occupational Therapy*, 56(5), 577-580.

Shirley, M.M. (1931). *The first two years: A study of twenty-five babies: Vol 1. Locomotor development*. The University of Minnesota Press.

Spencer, J.T., Clearfield, M., Corbetta, D., Ulrich, B., Buchanan, P., & Schoner, G. (2006). Moving towards a grand theory of development: In memory of Esther Thelen. *Child Development*, 77(6), 1521-1538.

Sporns, O., & Edelman, G. (1993). Solving Bernstein's problem: A proposal for the development of coordinated movement by selection. *Child Development*, 64, 960-981.

Thelen, E. (1985). Developmental origins of motor coordination: Leg movements in human infants. *Developmental Psychobiology*, 18 (1), 1-22.

Thelen, E. (1992). Development as a dynamic system. *Current Directions in Psychological Science*, 1, 189-193.

Thelen, E. (1995). Motor development: A new synthesis. *American Psychologist*, 50(2), 79-95.

Thelen, E., Corbetta, D., & Spencer, J.P. (1996). The development of reaching during the first year: The role of movement speed. *Journal of Experimental Psychology: Human Perception and Performance*, 22, 1059-1076.

Thelen, E., Ulrich, B.D., & Wolff, P.H. (1991). Hidden skills: A dynamic systems analysis of treadmill stepping during the first year. *Monographs of the society for research in child development*, i-103.

Timiras, P.S. (1972). *Developmental physiology and aging*. Macmillan.

Tracy, E.E. (2013). Alcohol: An unfortunate teratogen; Fetal alcohol syndrome is entirely preventable: We need to remind ourselves and our patients of this fact. *OBG Management*, 25(1), 36-45.

Trettien, A.W. (1900). Creeping and walking. *American Journal of Psychology*, 12, 1-57.

Ulrich, B.D., & Ulrich, D.A. (1993). Dynamic systems approach to understanding motor delay in infants with Down syndrome. In *Advances in psychology* (Vol. 97, pp. 445-459). North-Holland.

Ulrich, B.D., Ulrich, D.A. & Collier, D.H. (1992). Alternating stepping patterns: Hidden abilities of 11-month-old infants with Down syndrome. *Developmental Medicine and Child Neurology*, 34, 233-239.

Ulrich, B.D., Ulrich, D.A., Collier, D., & Cole, E. (1993). Developmental shifts in the ability of infants with Down syndrome to produce treadmill steps. *Physical Therapy*, 7(1), 14-23.

Von Hofsten, C. (1984). Developmental changes in the organization of pre-reaching movements. *Developmental Psychobiology*, 20, 378-388.

Vouloumanos, A., & Werker, J.F. (2004). Turned to the signal: The privileged status of speech for young infants. *Developmental Status*, 7, 270-276.

Wastnedge, E.A.N., Reynolds, R.M., van Boeckel, S.R., Stock, S.J., Denison, F.C., Maybin, J.A., & Critchley, H.O.D. (2021). Pregnancy & COVID-19. *Physiological Reviews*, 101(1), 303-318.

Werker, J.J., & Hensch, T.K. (2015). Critical periods in speech perception: New directions. *Annual Review of Psychology*, 66, 173-196. http://dx.doi.org/10.1146/annurev-psych-010814-015104

Wong, H.B., Machin, D., Tan, S.B., Wong, T.Y., & Saw, S.M. (2010). Ocular component growth curves among Singaporean children with different refractive error status. *Investigative Ophthalmology & Visual Science*, 51(3), 1341-1347.

Zelazo, P.R., Zelazo, N.A., & Kolb, S. (1972). "Walking" in the newborn. *Science*, 176, 314-315.

Chapter 8

Adolph, K.E. (2008). The growing body in action: What infant locomotion tells us about perceptually guided action. In R. Klatzky, M. Behrmann, & B. MacWhinney (Eds.), *Embodiment, ego-space, and action: Carnegie Mellon Symposium* (pp. 275-321). Erlbaum.

Barnett, L.M., Stodden, D.F., Hulteen, R.M., & Sacko, R.S. (2020). Motor proficiency assessment. In T.A. Brusseau (Ed.), *The Routledge handbook of pediatric physical activity*, (pp. 384-408). Routledge.

Bayley, N. (1935). The development of motor abilities during the first three years. *Monographs of the Society for Research in Child Development*, 1, 1.

Brian, A., Getchell, N., True, L., De Meester, A., & Stodden, D.F. (2020). Reconceptualizing and operationalizing Seefeldt's proficiency barrier: Applications and future directions. *Sports Medicine*, 50(11), 1889-1900.

Brian, A., Pennelli, A., Taunton, S., Starrett, A., Howard-Shaughnessy, C., Goodway, J.D., Wadsworth, D., Rudisill, M., & Stodden, D. (2019). Motor competence levels and developmental delay in early childhood: A multicenter crosssectional study conducted in the USA. *Sports Medicine, 49*, 1609-1618.

Clark, J.E., & Metcalf, J.M. (2002). The mountain of motor development: A metaphor. In J.E. Clark & J.H. Humphrey (Eds.), *Motor development: Research and reviews* (Vol. 2, pp. 163-190). National Association for Sport and Physical Education.

Clark, J.E., Phillips, S.J., & Peterson, R. (1989). Developmental stability in jumping. *Developmental Psychology, 25*, 929-935.

Cole, W.G., Chan, G., Vereijken, B., & Adolph, K.E. (2013). Perceiving affordances for different motor skills. *Experimental Brain Research, 225*(3), 309-319.

De Meester, A., Stodden, D., Goodway, J., True, L., Brian, A., Ferkel, R., & Haerens, L. (2018). Identifying a motor proficiency barrier for meeting physical activity guidelines in children. *Journal of Science and Medicine in Sport, 21*(1), 58-62.

DeOreo, K., & Keogh, J. (1980). Performance of fundamental motor tasks. In C.B. Corbin (Ed.), *A textbook of motor development* (2nd ed., pp. 76-91). Brown.

Gabbard, C. (2012). *Lifelong motor development* (6th ed.). Benjamin Cummings.

Goodway, J.D. (2015, March 24). *Friday colloquia Jackie Goodway* [Video file]. Youtube. www.youtube.com/watch?v=0iQLj-aRUtk&t=1832s

Goodway, J.D., & Branta, C.F. (2003). Influence of a motor skill intervention on fundamental motor skill development of disadvantaged preschool children. *Research Quarterly for Exercise and Sport, 74*, 36-47.

Goodway, J., Ozmun, J., & Gallahue, D. (2019). *Understanding motor development: Infants, children, adolescents, adults* (8th ed.). McGraw-Hill.

Gutteridge, M.V. (1939). A study of motor achievements of young children. *Archives of Psychology, 244*, 1-178.

Halverson, L.E., & Williams, K. (1985). Developmental sequences for hopping over distance: A prelongitudinal screening. *Research Quarterly for Exercise and Sport, 56*, 37-44.

Haubenstricker, J.L., Seefeldt, V.D., & Branta, C.F. (1983, April). *Preliminary validation of a developmental sequence for the standing long jump* [Paper presentation]. Meeting of the American Alliance for Health, Physical Education, Recreation and Dance, Houston, TX.

Haywood, K., & Getchell, N. (2020). *Lifespan motor development* (7th ed.). Human Kinetics.

Kretch, K.S., & Adolph, K.E. (2015). Active vision in passive locomotion: Real-world free viewing in infants and adults. *Developmental Science, 18*, 736-750.

Logan, S.W., Ross, S.M., Chee, K., Stodden, D.F., & Robinson, L.E. (2018). Fundamental motor skills: A systematic review of terminology. *Journal of Sport Sciences, 36*(7), 781-796.

Lopes, V.P., Lopes, L., Santos, R., Stodden, D.F., & Rodrigues, L.P. (2017). Testing the motor proficiency barrier hypothesis for physical activity and weight status. *Journal of Sport and Exercise Psychology, 39*(S), S24-S24.

McCaskill, C.L., & Wellman, B.L. (1938). A study of common motor achievements at the pre-school ages. *Child Development, 9*, 141.

Newell, K.M. (1986). Constraints on the development of coordination. In M.G. Wade & H.T.A Whiting (Eds.), *Motor development in children: Aspects of coordination and control* (pp. 341-360). Martinus Nijhoff.

Newell, K.M. (2020). What are fundamental motor skills and what is so fundamental about them? *Journal of Motor Learning and Development, 8*, 280-314.

Owen, N., Healy, G.N., Matthews, C.E., & Dunstan, D.W. (2010). Too much sitting: The population health science of sedentary behavior. *Exercise Sport Science Review, 38*(3), 105-113.

Payne, G.V., & Isaacs, L.D. (2016). *Human life motor development: A lifespan approach* (9th ed.). McGraw-Hill.

Roberton, M.A. (1977). Stability of stage categorizations across trials: Implications for the "stage theory" of overarm throw development. *Journal of Human Movement Studies, 3*, 49-59.

Roberton, M.A., & Halverson, L.E. (1984). *Developing children: Their changing movement*. Lea & Febiger.

Roberton, M.A., & Konczak, J. (2001). Predicting children's overarm throw ball velocities from their developmental levels in throwing. *Research Quarterly for Exercise and Sport, 72*, 91-103.

Robinson, L.E., Stodden, D.F., Barnett, L.M., Lopes, V.P., Logan, S.W., Rodrigues, L.P., & D'Hondt, E. (2015). Motor competence and its effect on positive developmental trajectories of health. *Sports Medicine, 45*, 1273-1284.

Savelsbergh, G., Davids, K., van der Kamp, J., & Bennett, J. (2003). *Development of movement co-ordination in children: Applications in the field of ergonomics, health sciences and sport*. Routledge.

Seefeldt, V. (1980). Developmental motor patterns: Implications for elementary school physical education. In C. Nadeau, W. Holliwell & G. Roberts (Eds.), *Psychology of motor behavior and sport* (pp. 314-323). Human Kinetics.

Shirley, M.M. (1931). *The first two years: A study of twenty five babies: Vol. 1. Postural and locomotor development*. University of Minnesota Press.

Soska, K.C., Adolph, K.E., & Johnson, S.P. (2010). Systems in development: Motor skill acquisition facilitates three-dimensional object completion. *Developmental Psychology, 46*, 129-138.

Spencer, J.P., Perone, S., & Buss, A.T. (2011). Twenty years and going strong: A dynamic systems revolution in motor and cognitive development. *Child Development Perspectives, 5*(4), 260-266.

Stodden, D.F., Goodway, J.D., Langendorfer, S., Roberton, M.A., Rudisill, M.E., Garcia C., & Garcia, L.E. (2008). A developmental perspective on the role of physical competence in physical activity: An emergent relationship. *Quest, 60*, 290-306.

Sutherland, D. (1997). The development of mature gait. *Gait & Posture, 6*(2), 163-170.

Tamplain, P., Webster, E.K., Brian, A., & Valentini, N.C. (2019). Assessment of motor development in childhood: Contemporary issues, considerations, and future directions. *Journal of Motor Learning and Development, 8*, 391-409.

Thelen, E. (1985). Developmental origins of motor coordination: Leg movements in human infants. *Developmental Psychobiology, 18*, 1-22.

Thelen, E., & Ulrich, B.D. (1991). Hidden skills: A dynamic systems analysis of treadmill stepping during the first year. *Monographs of the Society for Research in Child Development, 56*(1, Serial No. 223).

Ulrich, B. (2010). Opportunities for early intervention based on theory, basic neuroscience, and clinical science. *Physical Therapy Journal, 90*, 1868-1880.

Whitall, J. (2003). Development of locomotor coordination and control in children. In G. Savelsbergh, K. Davids, J. Van der Kamp, & S. Bennett (Ed.), *Development of movement co-ordination in children: Applications in the field of ergonomics, health sciences and sport* (pp. 251-270). Routledge.

Wickstrom, R.L. (1983). *Fundamental motor patterns* (3rd ed.). Lea & Febiger.

Wild, M. (1938). The behavior pattern of throwing and some observations concerning its course of development in children. *Research Quarterly, 9*(3), 20.

Yoshida, H., & Smith, L.B. (2008). What's in view for toddlers? Using a head camera to study visual experience. *Infancy, 13*(3), 229-248.

Chapter 9

Atwater, A.E. (1979). Biomechanics of overarm throwing movements and of throwing injuries. *Exercise and Sport Sciences Reviews, 7*, 43-85.

Barnett, L.M., van Beurden, E., Morgan, P.J., Brooks, L.O., & Beard, J.R. (2009). Childhood motor skill proficiency as a predictor of adolescent physical activity. *The Journal of Adolescent Health, 44*(3), 252-259. https://doi.org/10.1016/j.jadohealth.2008.07.004

Barnett, L.M., van Beurden, E., Morgan, P.J., Brooks, L.O., & Beard, J.R. (2010). Gender differences in motor skill proficiency from childhood to adolescence: A longitudinal study. *Research Quarterly for Exercise and Sport, 81*(2), 162-170. https://doi.org/10.1080/02701367.2010.10599663

Bolger, L.E., Bolger, L.A., O'Neill, C., Coughlan, E., O'Brien, W., Lacey, S., Burns, C., & Bardid, F. (2021). Global levels of fundamental motor skills in children: A systematic review. *Journal of Sports Sciences, 39*(7), 717-753. https://doi.org/10.1080/02640414.2020.1841405

Clark, J.E., & Metcalf, J.M. (2002). The mountain of motor development: A metaphor. In J.E. Clark & J.H. Humphrey (Eds.), *Motor development: Research and reviews* (Vol. 2, pp. 163-190). National Association for Sport and Physical Education.

Clarke, P. (2003). *Where the ancestors walked: Australia as an Aboriginal landscape.* Allen & Unwin.

Eckert, H. (1987). *Motor development.* Benchmark Press.

Field, S.C., Esposito Bosma, C.B., & Temple, V.A. (2020). Comparability of the Test of Gross Motor Development–Second Edition and the Test of Gross Motor Development–Third Edition. *Journal of Motor Learning & Development, 8*(1), 107-125. https://doi.org/10.1123/jmld.2018-0058

Gabbard, C. (2021). *Lifelong motor development* (8th ed.). Wolters Kluwer.

Goodway, J., Ozmun, J., & Gallahue, D. (2020). *Understanding motor development: Infants, children, adolescents, adults* (8th ed.). Jones & Bartlett Learning.

Halverson, L.E., Roberton, M.A., & Landendorfer, S. (1982). Development of the overarm throw: Movement and ball velocity changes by seventh grade. *Research Quarterly for Exercise and Sport, 53*, 198-205.

Haubenstricker, J.L., Seefeldt, V.D., & Branta, C.F. (1983). *Preliminary validation of a developmental sequence for the standing long jump.* [Paper presentation]. Meeting of the American Alliance for Health, Physical Education, Recreation and Dance, Houston, TX.

Haywood, K., & Getchell, N. (2019). *Lifespan motor development* (7th ed.). Human Kinetics.

Owen, N., Healy, G.N., Matthews, C.E., & Dunstan, D.W. (2010). Too much sitting: The population health science of sedentary behavior. *Exercise Sport Science Review, 38*(3), 105-113.

Payne, G.V., & Isaacs, L.D. (2020). *Human motor development: A lifespan approach* (10th ed.). Routledge.

Petranek, L.J., & Barton, G.V. (2011). The overarm-throwing pattern among U-14 ASA female softball players: a comparative study of gender, culture, and experience. *Research Quarterly for Exercise and Sport, 82*(2), 220-228.

Roberton, M.A., & Konczak, J. (2001). Predicting children's overarm throw ball velocities from their developmental levels in throwing. *Research Quarterly for Exercise and Sport, 72*, 91-103.

Runion, B., Roberton, M.A., & Langendorfer, S.J. (2003). Forceful overarm throwing: A comparison of two cohorts measured 20 years apart. *Research Quarterly for Exercise and Sport, 74*, 334-330.

Savelsbergh, G., Davids, K., van der Kamp, J., & Bennett, J. (2003). *Development of movement co-ordination in children: Applications in the field of ergonomics, health sciences and sport.* Routledge.

Seefeldt, V., & Haubenstricker, J. (1975). *Developmental sequence of kicking* (Rev. ed.) [Unpublished research], Michigan State University, East Lansing.

Sheehan, D.P., Lienhard, K., & Ammar, D. (2020). Reducing the object control skills gender gap in elementary school boys and girls. *Advances in Physical Education, 10*(2), 155-168. https://doi.org/10.4236/ape.2020.102014

Taunton Miedema, S., Mulvey, K.L., & Brian, A. (2021). "You throw like a girl!" Young children's gender stereotypes about object control skills. *Research Quarterly for Exercise and Sport.* https://doi.org/10.1080/02701367.2021.1976374

Thomas, J.R., Alderson J., Thomas K., Campbell A., & Elliott, B. (2010). Developmental gender differences for overhand throwing in Aboriginal Australian children. *Research Quarterly for Exercise and Sport, 81*(4), 432-441.

Thomas, J.R., & French, K.E. (1985). Gender differences across age in motor performance: A meta-analysis. *Psychological Bulletin, 98*, 260-282.

Thomas, J.R., & Marzke, M.W. (1992). The development of gender differences in throwing: Is human evolution a factor. *Enhancing human performance in sport: New concepts and developments*, 60-76.

Ulrich, B. (2010). Opportunities for early intervention based on theory, basic neuroscience, and clinical science. *Physical Therapy Journal, 90*, 1868-1880.

Ulrich, D.A. (2000). *Test of gross motor development* (2nd ed.). Austin, TX: Pro-Ed.

Ulrich, D.A. (2019). *Test of gross motor development* (3rd ed.). Austin, TX: Pro-Ed.

Wickstrom, R.L. (1983). *Fundamental motor patterns* (3rd ed.). Lea & Febiger.

Wild, M. (1938). The behavior pattern of throwing and some observations concerning its course of development in children. *Research Quarterly, 9*(3), 20.

Chapter 10

Adrian, M.J., & Cooper, J.M. (1995). *Biomechanics of human movement* (2nd ed.). Benchmark Press.

Allen, S.V., & Hopkins, W.G. (2015). Age of peak competitive performance of elite athletes: A systematic review. *Sports Medicine, 45*, 1431–1441. https://doi.org/10.1007/s40279-015-0354-3

AGS Panel on Persistent Pain in Older Persons. (2002). The management of persistent pain in older persons. *Journal of the American Geriatric Society, 50*(Suppl. 6), S205-S224.

Ajzen, I. (1985). From intentions to actions: A theory of planned behaviour. In J. Kuhl & J. Beckman (Eds.), *Action control: From cognition to behavior* (pp. 11-39). Springer.

Ajzen, I. (1991). The theory of planned behavior. *Organizational Behavior and Human Decision Processes, 50*(2), 179-211.

Baert, V, Gorus, E., Mets, T., Geerts, C., & Bautmans, I. (2011). Motivators and barriers for physical activity in the oldest old: A systematic review. *Ageing Research Review, 10*, 464-474.

Belsky, J.K. (1984). *The psychology of aging.* Brooks/Cole.

Berger, B.G., & Hecht, L.M. (1989). Exercise, aging, and psychological well-being: The mind-body question. In A.C. Ostrow (Ed.), *Aging and motor behavior.* Benchmark Press.

Berger, B.G., & McInman, A. (1993). Exercise and the quality of life. In R.N. Singer, M. Murphy, & L.K. Tennant (Eds.), *Handbook of research on sport psychology.* Macmillan.

Bernard, T., Sultana, F., Lepers, R., Hauss-Wirth, C., & Brisswalter, J. (2009). Age-related decline in Olympic triathlon performance: Effect of locomotion mode. *Experimental Aging Research, 36*(1), 64-78.

Beurskens, R., & Bock, O. (2012). Age-related deficits of dual-task walking: A review. *Neural Plasticity*, 131608. https://doi.org.10.1155/2012/131608

Blackwell, D.L., & Clarke, T.C. (2018). State Variation in Meeting the 2008 Federal Guidelines for Both Aerobic and Muscle-strengthening Activities Through Leisure-time Physical Activity Among Adults Aged 18-64: United States, 2010-2015. *National Health Statistics Reports*, 112, 1-22.

Bradbury, J.C. (2009). Peak athletic performance and ageing: Evidence from baseball. *Journal of Sports Sciences, 27*(6), 599-610. https://doi.org.10.1080/02640410802691348

Braver, E.R., & Trempel, R.E. (2003). Are older drivers at higher risk of involvement in crashes resulting in deaths or nonfatal injuries among their passengers or other road users? *American Journal of Epidemiology, 157*, S50.

Burns, R.A., Browning, C., & Kendig, H.L. (2017). Living well with chronic disease for those older adults living in the community. *International Psychogeriatrics, 29*(5), 835843. https://doi.org/10.1017/S1041610216002398

Butler, R.J., Crowell, H.P., & Davis, I.M. (2003). Lower extremity stiffness: Implications for performance and injury. *Clinical Biomechanics, 18*, 511-517.

Castro, C., Martínez, C., & Tornay, F.J. (2005). Vehicle distance estimations in nighttime driving: A real-setting study. *Transportation Research Report Part F: Traffic Psychology and Behavior, 8*(1), 31-45.

Centers for Disease Control and Prevention. (2015). *Leading indicators for chronic diseases and risk factors.* chronicdata.cdc.gov

Cole, K.J., Rotella, D.L., & Harper, J.G. (1999). Mechanisms for age-related changes of fingertip forces during precision gripping and lifting in adults. *Journal of Neuroscience, 19*, 3228-3247.

Comfort, A. (1979). *Aging, the biology of senescence* (2nd ed.). Holt, Rinehart, Winston.

Crews, D.J., Lochbaum, M.R., & Karoly, P. (2000). Self-regulation: Concepts, methods and strategies in sport and exercise. In R.N. Singer, H.A. Hausenblas, & C.M. Janelle (Eds.), *Handbook of sport psychology* (2nd ed., pp. 566-581). Wiley.

Deford, F. (1980, July 14). A match goes down in history. *Sports Illustrated.*

DeSimone, B. (2006, September 11). *Act II of Navratilova's career ends with a win.* www.espn.com/sports/tennis/usopen06/news/story?id=2578105

Dickerson, A.E., Molnar, L.J., Bédard, M., Eby, D.W., Berg-Weger, M., Choi, M., Grigg, J., Horowitz, A., Meuser,

T., Myers, A., O'Connor, M., & Silverstein, N.M. (2019). Transportation and aging: An updated research agenda to advance safe mobility among older adults transitioning from driving to non-driving. *The Gerontologist, 59*(2), 215-221. https://doi.org/10.1093/geront/gnx120

Diermayr, G., McIsaac, T.L., & Gordon, A.M. (2011). Finger force coordination underlying object manipulation in the elderly—a mini-review. *Gerontology, 57*, 217-227. https://doi.org10.1159/000295921.

DiPietro, L., Williamson, D.F., Caspersen, C.J., & Eaker, E. (1993). The descriptive epidemiology of selected physical activities and body weight among adults trying to lose weight: The Behavioral Risk Factor Surveillance System Survey, 1989. *International Journal of Obesity, 17*, 69-76.

Donato, A.J., Tench, K., Glueck, D.H., Seals, D.R., Eskurza, I., & Tanaka, H. (2003). Declines in physiological functional capacity with age: A longitudinal study in peak swimming performance. *Journal of Applied Physiology, 94*(2), 764-769.

Donorfio, L.K.M., Mohyde, M., Coughlin, J., & D'Ambrosio, L. (2008). A qualitative exploration of self-regulation behaviors among older drivers. *Journal of Aging and Social Policy, 20*(3), 323-339.

Elble, R.J. (1997). Changes in gait with normal aging. In J.C. Masdeu, L. Sudarsky, & L. Wolfson (Eds.), *Gait disorders of aging: Falls and therapeutic strategies* (pp. 93-106). Lippincott-Raven.

Errata. (2016). *MMWR Morbidity and Mortality Weekly Report, 65*(36), 1152. http://dx.doi.org/10.15585/mmwr.mm6541a7

Flanagan, E.P., & Harrison, A.J. (2007). Muscle dynamics differences between legs in healthy adults. *Journal of Strength and Conditioning Research, 21*, 67-72.

Foley, D.J., Heimovitz, H.K., Guralnik, J.M., & Brock, D.B. (2002). Driving life expectancy of persons aged 70 years and older in the United States. *American Journal of Public Health, 92*, 1284-1289.

Fried, L.P., Storer, D.J., King, D.E., & Lodder, F. (1991). Diagnosis of illness presentations in the elderly. *Journal of the American Geriatric Society, 39*, 117-123.

Gabbard, C.P. (2012). *Lifelong motor development* (6th ed.). Pearson.

Goethals, L., Barth, N., Guyot, J., Hupin, D., Celarier, T., & Bongue, B. (2020). Impact of Home Quarantine on Physical Activity Among Older Adults Living at Home During the COVID-19 Pandemic: Qualitative interview study. *JMIR Aging, 3*(1), e19007. https://doi.org.10.2196/19007

Gray, P.M., Murphy, M.H., Gallagher, A.M., & Simpson, E.E.A. (2016). Motives and barriers to physical activity among older adults of different socioeconomic status. *Journal of Aging and Physical Activity, 24*, 419-429.

Hackney, A.C. (2021). Endocrine system changes. In D.R. Bouchard (Ed.), *Exercise & physical activity for older adults*. Human Kinetics.

Haguenauer, M., Legreneur, P., & Monteil, K.M. (2005). Vertical jumping reorganization with aging: A kinematic comparison between young and elderly men. *Journal of Applied Biomechanics, 21*(3), 236-246. https://doi.org/10.1123/jab.21.3.236

Halverson, L.E., Roberton, M.A., & Landendorfer, S. (1982). Development of the overarm throw: Movement and ball velocity changes by seventh grade. *Research Quarterly for Exercise and Sport, 53*, 198-205.

Harvey, J.A., Chastin, S.F.M., & Skelton, D.A. (2015). How sedentary are older people? A systematic review of the amount of sedentary behavior. *Journal of Aging and Physical Activity, 23*(3), 471-487. https://doi.org/10.1123/japa.2014-0164

Hausenblas, H.A., Carron, A.V., & Mack, D.E. (1997). Application of the theories of reasoned action and planned behavior to exercise behavior: A meta-analysis. *Journal of Sport and Exercise Psychology, 19*, 36-51.

Hertel, J., Friedrich, N., Wittfeld, K., Pietzner, M., Budde, K., Van der Auwera, S., Lohmann, T., Teumer, A., Vo Izke, H., Nauck, M., & Jorgen Grabe, H. (2016). Measuring biological age via metabonomics: The metabolic age score. *The Journal of Proteome Research, 15*, 400-410.

Hill, A.V. (1925). The physiological basis of athletic records. *Lancet, 209*(2), 483-486.

Horníková, H., Doležajová, L., & Zemková, E. (2018). Playing table tennis contributes to better agility performance in middle-aged and older subjects. *Acta Gymnica, 48*(1), 15-20. https://doi.org.10.5507/ag.2018.004

Jagacinski, R.J., Greenberg, N., & Liao, M.J. (1997). Tempo, rhythm, and aging in golf. *Journal of Motor Behavior, 29*(2), 159-173.

Jia, L., Zhang, W., & Chen, X. (2017). Common methods of biological age estimation. *Clinical Interventions in Aging, 12*, 759-772. https://doi.org.10.2147/CIA.S134921

Johnson, E.E. (2003). Transportation mobility and older drivers. *Journal of Gerontological Nursing, 29*(4), 34-41.

Kalman, Y.M., Kavé, G., & Umanski, D. (2015). Writing in a digital world: Self-correction while typing in younger and older adults. *International Journal of Environment Research & Public Health, 12*, 12723-12734.

Kenney, W.L., Wilmore, J., & Costill, D. (2015). *Physiology of sport & exercise* (6th ed.). Human Kinetics.

Kirschenbaum, D.S. (1984). Self-regulation and sport psychology: Nurturing and emerging symbiosis. *Journal of Sport Psychology, 6*, 159-183.

Kirschenbaum, D.S. (1987). Self-regulation of sport performance. *Medicine & Science in Sports & Exercise, 19*, S106-S113.

Klinger, A., Masataka, T., Adrian, M., & Smith, E. (1980). *Temporal and spatial characteristics of movement patterns of women over 60*. Paper presented at the National Conference of the American Alliance for Health, Physical Education, Recreation and Dance, Detroit.

Knechtle, B., Rüst, C.A., Rosemann, T., & Lepers, R. (2012). Age-related changes in 100-km ultra-marathon running performance. *AGE, 34*, 1033-1045.

Kocaman, S.A., Cetin, M., Durakoglugil, M.E., Erdogan, T., Canga, A., & Cicek, Y. (2012). The degree of premature hair graying as an independent risk marker for coronary artery disease: A predictor of biological age rather than chronological age. *The Anatolian Journal of Cardiology, 12*(6), 457.

Kosma, M. (2012). An expanded framework to determine physical activity and falls risks among diverse older adults. *Research on Aging, 36*(1), 95-114.

Lees, F.D., Clark, P.G., Nigg, C.R., & Newman, P. (2005). Barriers to exercise behavior among older adults: A focus-group study. *Journal of Aging and Physical Activity, 13*(1), 23-33.

Lindgren De Groot, G.C., & Fagerström, L. (2011). Older adults motivating factors and barriers to exercise to prevent falls. *Scandinavian Journal of Occupational Therapy, 18*, 153-160.

Lorson, K.M., Stodden, D.F., Langendorfer, S.J., & Goodway, J.D. (2013). Age and gender differences in adolescent and adult overarm throwing. *Research Quarterly for Exercise and Sport, 84*, 239-244.

Macera, C.A., Cavanaugh, A., & Bellettiere, J. (2015). State of the art review: Physical activity and older adults. *American Journal of Lifestyle Medicine, 11*(1), 42-57.

Marshall, S.C. (2008). The role of reduced fitness to drive due to medical impairments in explaining crashes involving older drivers. *Traffic Injury Prevention, 9*, 291-298.

Martinez-Valdes, E., & De Nunzio, A.M. (2021). Motor control. In D.R. Bouchard (Ed.), *Exercise & physical activity for older adults* (pp. 151-172). Human Kinetics.

Massey, M.V., Meyer, B.B. & Naylor, A.H. (2015). Self-regulation strategies in mixed martial arts. *Journal of Sport Behavior, 38*(2), 192-211.

Meltzer, D.E. (1994). Age dependence of Olympic weightlifting ability. *Medicine & Science in Sports & Exercise, 26*(8), 1053-1067.

Meng, A., & Siren, A.K. (2012). Cognitive problems, self-rated changes in driving skills, driving-related discomfort and self-regulation of driving in old drivers. *Accident Analysis & Prevention, 49*, 322-329.

Motalebi, S.A., Iranagh, J.A., Abdollahi, A., & Lim, W.K. (2014). Applying of theory of planned behavior to promote physical activity and exercise. *Journal of Physical Education and Sport, 14*(4), 562-568.

Murray, M.P., Kory, R.C., & Sepic, B.C. (1970). Walking patterns of normal women. *Archives of Physical Medicine and Rehabilitation, 51*, 637-650.

National Centers for Health Statistics. (2020). https://www.cdc.gov/nchs/about/fact_sheets.htm

National Highway Traffic Safety Administration. (2017). 2016 fatal motor vehicle crashes: Overview. National Center for Statistics and Analysis, Research and Development. National Highway Traffic Safety Administration.

Nelson, C.J. (1981). *Locomotor patterns of women over 57.* [Unpublished master's thesis]. Washington State University, Pullman.

Payne, G.V., & Isaacs, L.D. (2016). *Human life motor development: A lifespan approach* (9th ed.). McGraw-Hill.

Ranganathan, V.K., Siemionow, V., Sahgal, V., Liu, J.Z., & Yue, G.H. (2001). Skilled finger movement exercise improves hand function. *Journal of Gerontology A: Biological Science and Medical Science, 56*, M518-M522.

Reider, B. (2008). Live long and prosper. *American Journal of Sports Medicine, 36*(3), 441-442.

Rhodes, R.E., Martin, A.D., Taunton, J.E., Rhodes, E.C., Donnelly, M., & Elliot, J. (1999). Factors associated with exercise adherence among older adults: An individual perspective. *Sports Medicine, 28*(6), 397-411.

Roberton, M.A., & Halverson, L.E. (1984). *Developing children: Their changing movement.* Lea & Febiger.

Roberton, M.A., & Konczak, J. (2001). Predicting children's overarm throw ball velocities from their developmental levels in throwing. *Research Quarterly for Exercise and Sport, 72*, 91-103.

Rosenblum, S., & Werner, P. (2005). Assessing the handwriting process in healthy elderly persons using a computerized system. *Aging Clinical and Experimental Research, 18*(5), 433-439.

Saftari, L.N., & Kwon, O.S. (2018). Ageing vision and falls: A review. *Journal of Physiological Anthropology, 37*, 11. https://doi.org.10.1186/s40101-018-0170-1

Schulz, R., & Curnow, C. (1988). Peak performance and age among superathletes: Track and field, swimming, baseball, tennis, and golf. *Journal of Gerontology, 43*(5), 113-120.

Shephard, R.J. (2008). *Aging, physical activity, and health.* Human Kinetics.

Spirduso, W.W., Francis, K.L., & MacRae, P.G. (2005). *Physical dimensions of aging* (2nd ed.). Human Kinetics.

Steffen, T.M., Hacker, T.A., & Mollinger, L. (2002). Age and gender-related test performance in community-dwelling elderly people: Six-minute walk test, Berg balance scale, timed up & go test, and gait speeds. *Physical Therapy, 82*(2), 128-137.

Stephens, T., & Craig, C.L. (1990). *The well-being of Canadians: Highlights of the 1988 Campbell's Soup survey.* Canadian Fitness and Lifestyle Research Institute.

Thapa, P., Gideon, P., Fought, R., Kormicki, M., & Ray, W. (1994). Comparison of clinical and biomechanical measures of balance and mobility in elderly nursing home residents. *Journal of the American Geriatrics Society, 42*, 493-500.

Tseng, M.H., & Cermak, S.A. (1993). The influence of ergonomic factors and perceptual-motor abilities on handwriting performance. *American Journal of Occupational Therapy, 47*, 919-926.

Tufano, J.T. (2019). Assisted jumping: A possible method of incorporating high-velocity exercise in older populations. *Medical Hypotheses, 126*, 131-134. https://doi.org/10.1016/j.mehy.2019.03.028

U.S. Department of Health and Human Services. (2018). *Physical Activity Guidelines for Americans, 2nd edition.* U.S. Department of Health and Human Services. https://health.gov/sites/default/files/2019-09/Physical_Activity_Guidelines_2nd_edition.pdf#page=56

U.S. Department of Health and Human Services, Administration for Community Living. (2015). Administration on Aging.

Valois, P., Shephard, R.J., & Godin, G. (1986). Relationship of habit and perceived physical ability to exercise behavior. *Perceptual and Motor Skills, 62,* 811-817.

Wang, L. (2008). The kinetics and stiffness characteristics of the lower extremity in older adults during vertical jumping. *Journal of Sports Science and Medicine, 7,* 379-386.

Waschall, S.B., & Kernis, M.H. (1996). Level and stability of self-esteem as predictors of children's intrinsic motivation and reactions to anger. *Personality and Social Psychology Bulletin, 22,* 4-13.

Weiss, G., & Gould, D. (2015). *Foundations of Sport and Exercise Psychology* (6th ed.). Human Kinetics.

White, K.M., Terry, D.J., Troup, C., Rempel, L.A., Norman, P., Mummery, K., Riley, M., Posner, N., & Kenardy, J. (2012). An extended theory of planned behavior intervention for older adults with type 2 diabetes and cardiovascular disease. *Journal of Aging and Physical Activity, 20*(3), 281-299.

Williams, J.M., & Leffingwell, T.R. (1996). Cognitive strategies in sport and exercise psychology. In J.L. Van Raalte & B.W. Brewer (Eds.), *Exploring sport and exercise psychology* (pp. 51-73). American Psychological Association.

Williams, K., Haywood, K., & VanSant, A. (1990). Characteristics of older adult throwers. In J.E. Clark & J. Humphrey (Eds.), *Advances in motor development research* (Vol. 3, pp. 29-44). AMS Press.

Williams, K., Haywood, K., & VanSant, A. (1991). Throwing patterns of older adults: A follow-up investigation. *International Journal of Aging and Human Development, 33*(4), 279-294.

Williams, K., Haywood, K., & VanSant, A. (1998). Changes in throwing by older adults: A longitudinal investigation. *Research Quarterly for Exercise and Sport, 66*(1), 1-10.

Willmott, M. (1986). The effect of vinyl floor surface and carpeted floor surface upon walking in elderly hospital inpatients. *Age and Ageing, 15,* 119-120.

Wright, V.J., & Perricelli, B.C. (2008). Age-related rates of decline in performance among elite senior athletes. *American Journal of Sports Medicine, 36*(3), 443-450.

Yardley, L., Donovan-Hall, M., Francis, K., & Todd, C. (2007). Attitudes and beliefs that predict older people's intention to undertake strength and balance training. *Journals of Gerontology B Psychological Sciences & Social Sciences, 62*(2), P119-P125.

Zinsser, N., Bunker, L.K., & Williams, J.M. (2001). Cognitive techniques for building confidence and enhancing performance. In J.M. Williams (Ed.), *Applied sport psychology: Personal growth to peak performance* (4th ed., pp. 284-311). Mayfield.

Chapter 11

Barnett, L.M., Stodden, D., Cohen, K.E., Smith, J.J., Lubans, D.R., Lenoir, M., . . . & Morgan, P.J. (2016). Fundamental movement skills: An important focus. *Journal of Teaching in Physical Education, 35*(3), 219-225.

Brian, A., Pennell, A., Taunton, S., Starrett, A., Howard-Shaughnessy, C., Goodway, J. D., Wadsworth, D., Rudisil, M., & Stodden, D. (2019). Motor competence levels and developmental delay in early childhood: A multicenter cross-sectional study conducted in the USA. *Sports Medicine, 49*(10), 1609-1618.

Bruininks, R.H., & Bruininks, B.D. (2005). *Test of motor proficiency* (2nd ed.). AGS Publishing.

Clark, J.E. (2007). On the problem of motor skill development. *Journal of Physical Education, Recreation & Dance, 78*(5), 39-44.

Clark, J.E., & Whitall, J. (1989). What is motor development? The lessons of history. *Quest, 41*(3), 183-202.

Folio, R. & Fewell, R. (2000). *Peabody developmental motor scales. Examiners manual.* Pro-ED. Inc.

Getchell, N., Schott, N., & Brian, A. (2019). Motor development research: Designs, analyses, and future directions. *Journal of Motor Learning and Development, 8*(2), 410-437.

Henderson, S., Sugden, D., & Barnett, A. (2007). *Movement assessment battery for children* (2nd ed.). Harcourt Assessment.

Kiphard, E.J., & Shilling, F. (1974). *Körperkoordinationtest für Kinder.* Beltz.

Logan, S.W., Barnett, L.M., Goodway, J.D., & Stodden, D.F. (2017). Comparison of performance on process-and product-oriented assessments of fundamental motor skills across childhood. *Journal of Sports Sciences, 35*(7), 634-641.

Palmer, K.K., & Brian, A. (2016). Test of Gross Motor Development-2 scores differ between expert and novice coders. *Journal of Motor Learning and Development, 4*(2), 142-151.

Rink, J. (2014). *Teaching physical education for learning.* McGraw-Hill Higher Education.

Tamplain, P., Webster, E.K., Brian, A., & Valentini, N.C. (2019). Assessment of motor development in childhood: Contemporary issues, considerations, and future directions. *Journal of Motor Learning and Development, 8*(2), 391-409.

True, L., Brian, A., Goodway, J., & Stodden, D. (2017). Relationships between product-and process-oriented measures of motor competence and perceived competence. *Journal of Motor Learning and Development, 5*(2), 319-335.

Ulrich, D. (2019). *Test of Gross Motor Development* (3rd ed.). Pro-ed.

Chapter 12

Ashtari M., & Cyckowski L. (2012). Brain development during adolescence. In V. Preedy (Ed.), *Handbook of growth and growth monitoring in health and disease* (pp. 1213-1229). Springer. https://doi-org.brockport.idm.oclc.org/10.1007/978-1-4419-1795-9_72

Baker, J., & Davids, K. (2007). Introduction. *International Journal of Sport Psychology, 38,* 1-3.

Bataweel, E.A., & Ibrahim, A.I. (2020). Balance and musculoskeletal flexibility in children with obesity: A cross-sectional study. *Annals of Saudi Medicine, 40*(2), 120-115. https://doi.org.10.5144/0256-4947

Bogin, B. (1998, February). The tall and the short of it. *Discover,* 40-44.

Bouchard, C., An, P., Rice, T., Skinner, J.S., Wilmore, J.H., Gagnon, J., Perusse, L., Leon, A.S., & Rao, D.C. (1999). Familial aggregation of $\dot{V}O_2$ max response to exercise training: Results from the HERITAGE family study. *Journal of Applied Physiology, 87*, 1003-1008.

Bushnell, I. (2001). Mother's face recognition in newborn infants: Learning and memory. *Infant Child Development, 10*, 67-74. https://doi.org/10.1002/icd.248

Clarke, H.H. (1975). Joint and body range of movement. *Physical Fitness Research Digest, 5*, 16-18.

Clark, J.E. (2007). On the problem of motor skill development. *Journal of Physical Education, Recreation and Dance, 78*(5), 39-44.

Cooper, D.M., Nemet, D., & Galassetti, P. (2004). Exercise, stress, and inflammation in the growing child: From the bench to the playground. *Current Opinions in Pediatrics, 16*, 286-292.

Davids, K., & Baker, J. (2007). Genes, environment and sport performance: Why the nature-nurture dualism is no longer relevant. *Sports Medicine, 37*, 961-980.

Dias Quiterio, A.L., Carnero, E.A., Baptista, F.M., & Sardinha, L.B. (2011). Skeletal mass in adolescent male athletes and nonathletes: relationships with high-impact sports. *Journal of Strength Conditioning Research*, (12), 3439-47. https://doi: 10.1519/JSC.0b013e318216003b

Ericsson, K.A. (2003). Development of elite performance and deliberate practice: An update from the perspective of the expert performance approach. In J.L. Starkes & K.A. Ericsson (Eds.), *Expert performance in sports* (pp. 49-83). Human Kinetics.

Ericsson, K.A. (2007). Deliberate practice and the modifiability of body and mind: Toward a science of the structure and acquisition of expert and elite performance. *International Journal of Sport Psychology, 38*, 109-123.

Ericsson, K.A. (2013). Training history, deliberate practice and elite sports performance: An analysis in response to Tucker and Collins review—what makes champions? *British Journal of Sports Medicine, 47*, 533-535.

Ericsson, K.A. (2016). Summing up hours of any type of practice versus identifying optimal practice activities: Commentary on Macnamara, Moreau, & Hambrick. *Perspectives on Psychological Science, 11*, 351-354.

Fox, P.W., Hershberger, S.L., & Bouchard, T.J. (1996). Genetic and environmental contributions to the acquisition of motor skill. *Nature, 384*, 356-358.

Gabbard, C.P. (2012). *Lifelong motor development* (6th ed.). Benjamin Cummings.

Galassetti P., & Pablico, P.C. (2012). Growth hormone response to exercise: Implications for body growth. In V. Preedy (Ed.), *Handbook of growth and growth monitoring in health and disease* (pp. 2473-2490). Springer. https://doi-org.brockport.idm.oclc.org/10.1007/978-1-4419-1795-9_147

Garcia-Pinillos, F., Ruiz-Ariza, A., Moreno del Castillo, R., & Latorre-Roman, P.A. (2015). Impact of limited hamstring flexibility on vertical jump, kicking speed, spring and agility in young football players. *Journal of Sports Sciences, 33*(12), 1293-1297.

Geladas, N., Koskolou, M., & Klissouras, V. (2007). Nature or nurture: Not an either-or question. *International Journal of Sport Psychology, 38*, 124-134.

Georgiades, E., Klissouras, V., Baulch, J., Wang, G. & Pitsiladis, Y. (2017). Why nature prevails over nurture in the making of an elite athlete. *BMC Genomics, 18*(8), 835. https://doi.org.10.1186/s12864-017-4190-8

Gollnick, P.D., Timson, B.F., Moore, R.L., & Riedy, M. (1981). Muscle enlargement and number of fibers in skeletal muscles of rats. *Journal of Applied Physiology, 50*, 936-943.

Hannon, E.E., Schachner, A., Nave-Blodgett, J.E. (2017). Babies know bad dancing when they see it: Older but not younger infants discriminate between synchronous and asynchronous audiovisual musical displays. *Journal of Experimental Child Psychology, 159*, 159-174. https://doi.org/10.1016/j.jecp.2017.01.006

Haubenstricker, J., Wisner, D., Seefeldt, V., & Branta, C. (1997). Gender differences and mixed longitudinal norms on selected motor skills for children and youth. *Journal of Sport and Exercise Psychology: NASPSPA Abstracts, 19*(6), S63.

Howe, M.J.A., Davidson, J.W., & Sloboda, J.A. (1998). Innate talents: Reality or myth? *Behavioral and Brain Sciences, 21*, 399-442.

Joyner, M.J. (1993). Physiological limiting factors and distance running: Influence of gender and age on record performances. *Exercise and Sport Science Reviews, 21*, 103-133.

Kail, R.V., & Cavanaugh, J.C. (2016). *Human development: A lifespan view* (7th ed.). Nelson.

Kellman, P.J., & Arterberry, M.E. (1998). *The cradle of knowledge: Development of perception in infancy*. MIT Press.

Keogh, J., & Sugden, D. (1985). *Movement skill development*. Macmillan.

Klissouras, V., Geladas, N., & Koskolou, M. (2007). Nature prevails over nurture. *International Journal of Sport Psychology, 38*, 35-67.

Krogman, W.M. (1972). *Child growth*. University of Michigan Press.

Macnamara, B.N., Moreau, D., & Hambrick, D.Z. (2016). The relationship between deliberate practice and performance in sports: A meta-analysis. *Perspectives on Psychological Science, 11*, 333-350.

Malina, R.M. (1978). Growth of muscle tissue and muscle mass. In F. Faulkner & J.M. Tanner (Eds.), *Human growth: A comprehensive treatise* (pp. 273-294). Plenum Press.

Malina, R.M., & Bouchard, C. (1991). *Growth, maturation, and physical activity*. Human Kinetics.

Malina, R.M., Bouchard, C., & Bar-Or, O. (2004). *Growth, maturation, and physical activity* (2nd ed.). Human Kinetics.

Malina, R.M. Bouchard, C., & Beunen, G. (1988). Human growth: Selected aspects of current research on well-nourished children. *Annual Review of Anthropology, 17*, 187-219.

Marisi, D.Q. (1977). Genetic and extragenetic variance in motor performance. *Acta Genetica Medica, 26*, 3-4.

Marshall, J.D., & Bouffard, M. (1994). Obesity and movement competency in children. *Adapted Physical Activity Quarterly, 11*, 297-305.

Marshall, J.D., & Bouffard, M. (1997). The effects of quality daily physical education on movement competency in obese versus nonobese children. *Adapted Physical Activity Quarterly, 14*, 222-237.

Maruta, J., Spielman, L.A., Rajashekar, U., & Ghajar, J. (2017). Visual tracking in development and aging. *Frontiers in Neurology, 8*, 640.

McGraw, M. (1935). *Growth: A study of Johnny and Jimmy.* Appleton-Century-Crofts.

Morris, G.S. (1980). *Elementary physical education: Toward inclusion.* Brighton.

Neuman, A.C., & Hochberg, I. (1983). Children's perception of speech in reverberation. *Journal of the Acoustical Society of America, 73*, 2145-2149.

Newell, K.M. (1984). Physical constraints to development of motor skills. In J.R. Thomas (Ed.), *Motor development during childhood and adolescence* (pp. 105-120). Burgess.

Ong, K.K., Elks, C.E., Li, S., Zhao, J.H., Luan, J., Andersen, L.B., Bingham, S.A., Brage, S., Smith, G.D., Ekelund, U., Gillson, C.J., Glaser, B., Golding, J., Hardy, R., Khaw, K.T., Kuh, D., Luben, R., Marcus, M., McGeehin, M.A., . . .Wareham, N.J. (2009). Genetic variation in LIN28B is associated with the timing of puberty. *Nature Genetics, 41*, 729-733.

Payne, G.V., & Isaacs, L.D. (2008). *Human life motor development: A lifespan approach* (7th ed.). McGraw-Hill.

Piek, J.P. (2006). *Infant motor development.* Human Kinetics.

Poole, C., Miller, S.A., & Booth Church, E. (2006). Ages & stages: All about body awareness. *Early Childhood Today.* www.scholastic.com/teachers/articles/teaching-content/ages-stages-all-about-body-awareness

Preedy, V.R. (2012). *Handbook of growth and growth monitoring in health and disease.* Springer.

Sermaxhaj, S., Arifi, F., Havolli, J., Luta, F., & Isufi, I. (2021). The effect of physical exercise according to a programme for the development of flexibility in the motor abilities of young football players. *SportMont*, https://doi.org.10.26773/smj.210209

Shulman, C. (2016). Nature-nurture controversy and its implications for infant and early childhood mental health. In *Research and practice in infant and childhood mental health* (Vol. 13, pp. 67-79). Springer.

Thelen, E., & Smith, L.B. (1994). *A dynamic processes approach to development of cognition and action.* MIT Press/Bradford.

Thodberg, H.H., Juul, A., Lomholt, J., Martin, D.D., Jenni, O.G., Caflisch, J., Ranke, M.B., & Kreiborg, S. (2012). Adult height prediction models. In V. Preedy (Ed.), *Handbook of growth and growth monitoring in health and disease* (pp. 27-57). Springer. https://doi-org.brockport.idm.oclc.org/10.1007/978-1-4419-1795-9_3

Tucker, R., & Collins, M. (2012). What makes champions? A review of the relative contribution of genes and training to sporting success. *British Journal of Sports Medicine, 46*, 555-561.

Turner, C.H., & Robling, A.G. (2003). Designing exercise regimens to increase bone strength. *Exercise and Sport Sciences Reviews, 31*, 45-50.

Ulrich, D.A., Ulrich, B.D., Angulo-Kinzler, R.M., & Yun, J. (2001). Treadmill training of infants with Down syndrome: Evidence-based developmental outcomes. *Pediatrics, 108*, 84-91.

van den Berg, M.E., Rijnbeek, P.R., Niemeijer, M.N., Hofman, A., van Herpen, G., Bots, M.L., Hillege, H., Swenne, C.A., Eijgelsheim, M., Stricker, B.H. & Kors, J.A. (2018). Normal values of corrected heart-rate variability in 10-second electrocardiograms for all ages. *Frontiers in Physiology, 9*, 424. https://doi.10.3389/fphys.2018.00424

Wattam-Bell, J. (1996). Visual motion processing in one month old infants: Habituation experiments. *Vision Research, 36*, 1679-1685.

Williams, H.G. (1983). *Perceptual and motor development.* Prentice Hall.

Chapter 13

Akima, H. I R. O. S. H. I., Kano, Y. U. T. A. K. A., Enomoto, Y. O. S. H. I. T. A. K. A., Ishizu, M. A. S. A. O., Okada, M. O. R. I. H. I. K. O., Oishi, Y. O. S. H. I. E., . . . & Kuno, S. (2001). Muscle function in 164 men and women aged 20--84 yr. *Medicine and science in sports and exercise, 33*(2), 220-226.

Baptista de Oliveira Medeiros, H., Sardinha Mendes Soares de Araújo, D., & Gil Soares de Araújo, C. (2013). Age-related mobility loss is joint-specific: An analysis from 6,000 Flexitest results. *Age, 35*(6), 2399-2407. https://doi:10.1007/s11357-013-9525-z

Barbour, K.E., Helmick, C.G., Boring, M., & Brady, T.J. (2017). Vital signs: prevalence of doctor-diagnosed arthritis and arthritis-attributable activity limitation—United States, 2013–2015. *Morbidity and Mortality Weekly Report, 66*(9), 246.Barzilai, N., & Gabriely, I. (2010). Genetic studies reveal the role of the endocrine and metabolic systems in aging. *The Journal of Clinical Endocrinology & Metabolism, 95*(10), 18-29.

Bassey, E.J., Fiatarone, M.A., O'Neill, E.F., Kelly, M., Evans, W.J., & Lipsitz, L.A. (1992). Leg extensor power and functional performance in very old men and women. *Clinical Science, 82*, 321-327.

Bemben, D.A., & Bemben, M.G. (2011). Dose-response effect of 40 weeks of resistance training on bone mineral density in older adults. *Osteoporosis International, 22*, 179-186. https://doi:10.1007/s00198-010-1182-9

Blair, S.N. (2009). Physical inactivity: The biggest public health problem of the 21st century. *British Journal of Sports Medicine, 43*, 1-2.

Boisvert-Vigneault, K., & Dionne, I.J. (2021). Body composition & age-related changes. In D.R. Bouchard (Ed.), *Exercise & physical activity for older adults* (pp. 43-56). Human Kinetics.

Bradley, E.G. (2007). Nursing management: Hypertension. In S.L. Lewis, M.M. Heitkemper, S.R. Dirksen, P.G. O'Brien, & L. Bucher (Eds.), *Medical-surgical nursing* (7th ed., pp. 761-783). Mosby Elsevier.

Clark, B.C., & Manini, T.M. (2008). Sarcopenia =/= dynapenia. *The Journals of Gerontology: Series A, 63*(8), 829-834.

Coker, C.A. (2013). *Motor learning and control for practitioners* (3rd ed.). Holcomb Hathaway.

Corso, J.F. (1987). Sensory-perceptual processes and aging. *Annual Review of Gerontology and Geriatrics, 7,* 29-55.

Cunningham, D.A., Paterson, D.H., Koval, J.J., & St Croix, C.M. (1997). A model of oxygen transport capacity changes for independently living older men and women. *Canadian Journal of Applied Physiology, 22*(5), 439-453.

Delmonico, M.J., Harris, T.B., Visser, M., Park, S.W., Conroy, M.B., Velasquez-Mieryer, P., Boudreau, M., Manini, T.M., Nevitt, M., & Newman, A.B. (2009). Longitudinal study of muscle strength, quality, and adipose tissues infiltration. *American Journal of Clinical Nutrition, 90*(6), 1579-1585. https://doi.org1.3945/ajcn.2009.28047

Dempsey, J.A., & Seals, D.R. (1995). Aging, exercise and cardiopulmonary function. In D.R. Lamb, C.V. Gisolfi, & E. Nadel (Eds.), *Perspectives in exercise science and sports medicine: Vol. 8. Exercise in older adults* (pp. 237-297). Benchmark Press.

DeStefano, F., Coulehan, J., & Wiant, M. (1979). Blood pressure survey on the Navajo Indian reservation. *American Journal of Epidemiology, 109*(3), 335-345.

dos Santos, L., Cyrino, E.S, Antunes, M., Santos, D.A., & Sardinha, L.B. (2017). Sarcopenia and physical independence in older adults: The independent and synergic role of muscle mass and muscle function. *Journal of Cachexia, Sarcopenia and Muscle, 8*(2), 245-250. https://doi.org10.1002/jcsm.1260

Eskurza, I., Donato, A.J., Moreau, K.L., Seals, D.R., & Tanaka, H. (2002). Changes in maximal aerobic capacity with age in endurance-trained women: 7 year follow-up. *Journal of Applied Physiology, 92,* 2303-2308.

Evans, S.L., Davy, P., Stevenson, E.T., & Seals, D.R. (1995). Physiological determinants of 10-km performance in highly trained female runners of different ages. *Journal of Applied Physiology, 78,* 1931-1941.

Fagard, R., Thijs, L., & Amery, A. (1993). Age and the hemodynamic response to posture and to exercise. *American Journal of Geriatric Cardiology, 2*(2), 23-30.

Faulkner, J.A., & Brooks, S.V. (1995). Muscle fatigue in old animals. Unique aspects of fatigue in elderly humans. *Advancements in Experimental Medicine and Biology, 384,* 471-480.

Faulkner, J.A., Larkin, L.M., Claflin, D.R., & Brooks, S.V. (2007). Age-related changes in the structure and function of skeletal muscles. *Clinical and Experimental Pharmacology and Physiology, 34,* 1091-1096.

Fazzi, E., Lanners, J., Ferrari-Ginevra, O., Achille, C., Luparia, A., Signorini, S., & Lanzi, G. (2002). Gross motor development and reach on sound as critical tools for the development of the blind child. *Brain and Development, 24,* 269-275.

Ferlinc, A., Fabiani, E., Velnar, T., & Gradisnik, L. (2019). The importance and role of proprioception in the elderly: A short review. *Materia Socio-Medica, 31*(3), 219-221. https://doi.org/10.5455/msm.2019.31.219-221

Foroughi, C., Monfort, S.S., Paczynski, M., McKnight, P.E., & Greenwood, P.M. (2016). Placebo effects in cognitive training. *Proceedings of the National Academy of Sciences of the United States of America, 113*(27), 7470-7474. https://doi.org10.1073/pnas.1601243113

Gabbard, C.P. (2012). *Lifelong motor development* (6th ed.). Benjamin Cummings.

Gant, J.C., Kadish, I., Chen, K-C., Thibault, O., Blalock, E.M., Porter, N., & Landfield, P.W. (2018). Aging-related calcium dysregulation in rat entorhinal neurons homologous with the human entorhinal neurons in which Alzheimer's disease neurofibrillary tangles first appear. *Journal of Alzheimer's Disease, 66*(4), 1371-1378.

Garzia, R., & Trick, L. (1992). Vision in the 90's: The aging eye. *Journal of Optometric Vision Development, 23*(1), 4-41.

Goodpaster, B.H., Park, S.W., Harris, T.B., Kritchevsky, S.B., Nevitt, M., Schwartz, A.V., . . . & Newman, A.B. (2006). The loss of skeletal muscle strength, mass, and quality in older adults: The health, aging and body composition study. *The Journals of Gerontology Series A: Biological Sciences and Medical Sciences, 61*(10), 1059-1064.Hackney, A.C. (2021). Endocrine system changes. In D.R. Bouchard (Ed.), *Exercise & physical activity for older adults* (pp.111-126). Human Kinetics.

Hagberg, J.M. (1988). Effect of exercise and training on older men and women with essential hypertension. In W.W. Spirduso & H.M. Eckert (Eds.), *The academy papers: Physical activity and aging* (pp. 187-191). Human Kinetics.

Harridge, S.D.R., & Lazarus, N.R. (2017). Physical activity, aging and physiological function. *Journal of Physiology, 32*(2), 152-161.

Hashizume, K., Suzuki, S., Takeda, T., Shigematsu, S., Ichikawa, K., & Koizumi, Y. (2006). Endocrinological aspects of aging: Adaptation to and acceleration of aging by the endocrine system. *Geriatrics & Gerontology International, 6,* 1-6.

Hayes, L.D., Grace, F.M., Sculthorpe, N., Herbert, P., Ratcliffe, J.W., Kilduff, L.P. & Baker, J.S. (2013). The effects of a formal exercise training programme on salivary hormone concentrations and body composition in previously sedentary aging men. *Springerplus 2,* 18.

Hernandez, J. (2008). Prehypertension: Why should we worry? *Advance for Nurse Practitioners, 16*(1), 65-73.

Heuninckx, S., Wenderoth, N., & Swinnen, S. (2008). Systems neuroplasticity in the aging brain: Recruiting additional neural resources for successful motor performance in elderly persons. *Journal of Neuroscience, 28,* 91-99. https://doi.org.10.1523/JNEUROSCI.3300-07.2008

Hunter, D.J., & Sambrook, P.N. (2000). Bone loss: Epidemiology of one loss. *Arthritis Research, 2*(6), 441-445. https://doi.org.10.1186/ar125

Hyde, T.E., & Gengenbach, M.S. (2007). *Conservative management of sports injuries* (2nd ed., p. 845). Jones & Bartlett.

Jackson, A.S., Janssen, I., Sui, X., Church, T.S., & Blair, S.N. (2012). Longitudinal changes in body composition associated with healthy ageing: Men, aged 20-96 years. *The British Journal of Nutrition, 107*(7), 1085-1091. https://doi.org.10.1017/S0007114511003886

Kanis, J.A., Johnell, O., Oden, A., Sernbo, I., Redlund-Johnell, I., Dawson, A., . . . & Jonsson, B. (2000). Long-term risk of osteoporotic fracture in Malmö. *Osteoporosis international, 11*(8), 669-674.Kannel, W., Sorlie, P., & Gordon, T. (1980). Labile hypertension: A faulty concept? The Framingham Study. *Circulation, 61*(6), 1183-1187.

Kasch, F.W., Wallace, J.P., Van Camp, S.P., & Verity, L. (1988). A longitudinal study of cardiovascular stability in active men aged 45-65 years. *Physician and Sportsmedicine, 16*(1), 117-126.

Kenshalo, D.R. (1977). Age changes in touch, vibration, temperature, kinesthesis, and pain sensitivity. In J.E. Birren & K.W. Schaie (Eds.), *Handbook of the psychology of aging* (pp. 562-579). Van Nostrand Reinhold.

Lazarus, N.R., & Harridge, S.D.R. (2010). Exercise, physiological function, and the selection of participants for aging research. *Journals of Gerontology, Series A: Biological Sciences and Medical Sciences, 65A,* 854-857.

Lazarus, N.R., Lord, J.M., & Harridge, S.D. (2019). The relationships and interactions between age, exercise and physiological function. *The Journal of physiology, 597*(5), 1299-1309.

Lee, T. (2010). Intrepid exploring: Looking past fears of short-term memory loss in aging to deploy the brain's long-term memories and-wisdom. *Journal of Aging, Humanities, and the Arts, 4,* 18-29. https://doi.org.10.1080/19325610903551541

Lexell, J. (1995). Human aging, muscle mass, and fiber type composition. *Journals of Gerontology: Biological Sciences and Medical Sciences, 50*(special issue), 11-16.

Linton, A.D. (2007). Age-related changes in the special senses. In A.D. Linton & H.W. Lach (Eds.), *Matteson & McConnell's gerontological nursing* (3rd ed., pp. 600-627). Saunders Elsevier.

Martinez-Valdes, E., & De Nunzio, A.M. (2021). Motor control. In D.R. Bouchard (Ed.), *Exercise & physical activity for older adults* (pp. 151-172). Human Kinetics.

McArdle, W., Katch, F., & Katch, V. (2001). *Exercise physiology: Energy, nutrition, and human performance* (5th ed.). Lippincott Williams & Wilkins.

Millodot, M. (1977). The influence of age on the sensitivity of the cornea. *Investigative Ophthalmology & Visual Science, 16*(3), 240-242.

Morgan, D.W., & Craig, M. (1992). Physiological aspects of running economy. *Medicine & Science in Sports & Exercise, 24,* 456-461.

Nam, H.S., Kweon, S.S., Choi, J.S., Zmuda, J.M., Leung, P.C., Lui, L.Y., . . . & Cauley, J.A. (2013). Racial/ethnic differences in bone mineral density among older women. *Journal of Bone and Mineral Metabolism, 31*(2), 190-198.

National Center for Health Statistics. (2021). Health, United States (2019). Table 22. www.cdc.gov/nchs/hus/contents2019.htm

Niinimaa, V., & Shephard, R.J. (1978). Training and exercise conductance in the elderly. II. The cardiovascular system. *Journal of Gerontology, 35,* 672-682.

Nillsson, B.E., & Westlin, N.E. (1971). Bone density in athletes. *Clinical Orthopaedics, 77,* 179-182.

Nouchi, R., Taki, Y., Takeuchi, H., Hashizume, H., Akitsuki, Y., Shigemune, Y., Sekigushi, A., Kotozaki, Y., Tsukiura, T., Yomogida, Y., & Kawashima, R. (2012). Brain training game improves executive functions and processing speed in the elderly: A randomized controlled trial. *PLOS One, 7*(1), e29676. https://doi.org.10.1371/journal.pone.0029676

Owsley, C., & Ball, K. (1993). Assessing visual function in the older driver. *Clinics in Geriatric Medicine, 9*(2), 389-401.

Paterson, D.H., Cunningham, D.A., & Babcock, M.A. (1989). Oxygen kinetics in the elderly. In G.D. Swanson, F.S. Grodins, & R.L. Hughson (Eds.), *Respiratory control: A modelling perspective* (pp. 171-178). Plenum Press.

Paterson, D.H., & Warburton, D.E. (2010). Physical activity and functional limitations in older adults: A systematic review related to Canada's Physical Activity Guidelines. *International Journal of Behavioral Nutrition and Physical Activity, 7,* 38. https://doi.org.10.1186/1479-5868-7-38

Pimentel, A.E., Gentile, C.L., Tanaka, H., Seals, D.R., & Gates, P.E. (2003). Greater rate of decline in maximal aerobic capacity with age in endurance-trained than in sedentary men. *Journal of Applied Physiology, 94*(6), 2406-2413.

Pogliaghi, S., & Murias, J.M. (2021). Cardiovascular changes. In D.R. Bouchard (Ed.), *Exercise & physical activity for older adults* (pp. 79-96). Human Kinetics.

Ratey, J.J. (2001). *A user's guide to the brain: Perception, attention, and the four theaters of the brain.* Vintage Books.

Raz, N., Lindenberger, U., Rodrigue, K.M., Kennedy, K.M. Head, D., Williamson, A., Dahle, C., Gerstorf, D., & Acker, J.D. (2005). Regional brain changes in aging healthy adults: General trends, individual differences and modifiers. *Cerebral Cortex, 15,* 1676-1689. https://doi.org.10.1093/cercor/bhi044

Reeve, J., Walton, J., Russell, L.J., Lunt, M., Wolman, R., Abraham, R.A., . . . & Mitchell, A. (1999). Determinants of the first decade of bone loss after menopause at spine, hip and radius. *QJM, 92*(5), 261-273.Riebe, D., Ehrman, J.K., Liguori, G., & Magal, M. (Eds.). (2018). *ACSMs guidelines for exercise testing and prescription* (10th ed.). Wolters Kluwer Health.

Rowell, L.B. (1993). *Human cardiovascular control.* Oxford University Press. https://doi.org/10.1002/clc.4960170212

Sachs, C., Hamberger, B., & Kaijser, L. (1985). Cardiovascular responses and plasma catecholamines in old age. *Clinical Physiology, 5,* 239-249.

Salat, D.H., Buckner, R.L., Snyder, A.Z., Greve, D.N., Desikan, R.S.R., Busa, E., . . . & Fischl, B. (2004). Thinning of the cerebral cortex in aging. *Cerebral Cortex, 14,* 721-730. https://doi.org.10.1093/cercor/bhh032

Saxon, S.V., Etten, M.J., & Perkins, E.A. (2010). *Physical change & aging: A guide for the helping professions* (5th ed.). Springer.

Schieber, F. (1992). Aging and the senses. In J.E. Birren, R.B. Sloane, & G.D. Cohen (Eds.), *Handbook of mental health and aging* (2nd ed., pp. 252-306). Academic Press.

Schultheis, L. (1991). The mechanical control system of bone in weightless spaceflight and in aging. *Experimental Gerontology, 26,* 203-214.

Schwartz, R. (1990). Body fat distribution in healthy young and older men. *Journal of Gerontology, 46*(6), 181-185.

Shank, M.D., & Haywood, K.M. (1987). Eye movements while viewing a baseball pitch. *Perceptual and Motor Skills, 64,* 1191-1197.

Shephard, R.J. (1991). Fitness and aging. In C. Blais (Ed.), *Aging into the twenty-first century* (pp. 22-35). Captus University.

Shephard, R.J. (1993). *Health and aerobic fitness.* Human Kinetics.

Shephard, R.J. (1997). *Aging, physical activity, and health.* Human Kinetics.

Shephard, R.J. (1998). Aging and exercise. In T.D. Fahey (Ed.), *Encyclopedia of sports medicine and science.* Internet Society for Sport Science. http://sportsci.org.

Shephard, R.J. (2008). Aging, physical activity and health. *International Encyclopedia of Public Health* (pp. 61-69). https://doi.org.10.1016/B978-012373960-5.00627-4

Snijders, T., Verdijk, L.B., van Loon, L.J. (2009). The impact of sarcopenia and exercise training on skeletal muscle satellite cells. *Ageing Research Reviews, 8,* 328-338.

Snowdon, D.A. (2003). Healthy aging and dementia: Findings from the nun study. *Annals of Internal Medicine, 139*(5), 450-454.

Sowers, M.F., Beebe, J.L., McConnell, D., Randolph, J., & Jannausch, M. (2001). Testosterone concentrations in women aged 25-50 years: Associations with lifestyle, body composition, and ovarian status. *American Journal of Epidemiology, 153,* 256-264.

Spirduso, W.W., Francis, K.L., & MacRae, P.G. (2005). *Physical dimensions of aging* (2nd ed.). Human Kinetics.

Svänborg, A., Eden, S., & Mellstrom, D. (1991). Metabolic changes in aging as predictors of disease: The Swedish experience. In D.K. Ingram, G.T. Baker, & N.W. Shock (Eds.), *The potential for nutritional modulation of aging* (pp. 81-90). Food & Nutrition Press.

Tanaka, H., Monahan, K.D., & Seals, D.R. (2001). Age-predicted maximal heart rate revisited. *Journal of the American College of Cardiology, 37*(1), 153-156. https://doi.org.S0735-1097(00)01054-8

Tanaka, H., & Seals, D.R. (2003). Dynamic exercise performance in masters athletes: Insight into the effects of primary human aging on physiological functional capacity. *Journal of Applied Physiology, 95,* 2152-2162.

Tate, C., Hyek, M., & Taffet, G. (1994). Mechanisms for the response of cardiac muscle to physical activity in old age. *Medicine & Science in Sports & Exercise, 26*(5), 561-567.

Van Norman, K. (1995). *Exercise programming for older adults.* Human Kinetics.

Weale, R. (1963). New light on old eyes. *Nature, 198,* 944-946.

Wilson, T.M., & Tanaka, H. (2000). Meta-analysis of the age-associated decline in maximal aerobic capacity in men: Relation to training status. *American Journal of Physiology-Heart and Circulatory Physiology, 278*(3), 829-834.

Zerzawy, R. (1987). Hämodynamische Reaktionen unter verschiedenen Belastungsformen [Hemodynamic reactions to different types of work]. In R. Rost & F. Webering (Eds.), *Kardiology im Sport [Cardiology in sport].* German Sports Medicine Federation.

Chapter 14

Abernethy, B. (1991). Visual search strategies and decision-making in sport. *International Journal of Sport Psychology, 22,* 189-210.

Atkinson, J., & Braddick, O. (2012). Visual attention in the first years: Typical development and developmental disorders. *Developmental Medicine and Child Neurology 54,* 589-595.

Bert, H., Petrie, T.A., MacIntire, M.M., & Jones, G. (2010). The influences of skill level, anxiety, and psychological skills use on amateur golfers' performances. *Journal of Applied Sport Psychology, 22*(2), 123-133.

Bherer, L., Kramer, A.F., & Peterson, M.S. (2008). Transfer effects in task-set cost and dual-task cost after dual-task training in older and younger adults: Further evidence for cognitive plasticity in attentional control in late adulthood. *Experimental Aging Research, 34,* 188-219.

Bjorklund, D.F., & Douglas, R.N. (1997). The development of memory strategies. In N. Cowan (Ed.), *The development of memory in childhood* (pp. 201-246). The Psychology Press.

Brown, A.L. (1975). The development of memory: Knowing, knowing about knowing, and knowing how to know. In H.W. Reese (Ed.), *Advances in child development and behavior* (Vol. 10, pp. 103-152). Academic Press.

Brown, A.L. (1978). Knowing when, where, and how to remember: A problem of metacognition. In R. Glaser (Ed.), *Advances in instructional psychology* (pp. 77-165). Erlbaum.

Chase, W.G., & Simon, H.A. (1973). Perception in chess. *Cognitive Psychology, 4,* 55-81.

Chi, M.T.H. (1978). Knowledge structures and memory development. In R.S. Siegler (Ed.), *Children's thinking: What develops?* (pp. 73-105). Erlbaum.

Craik, F.I.M. (1986). A functional account of age differences in memory. In F. Flix & H. Hagendorf (Eds.), *Human memory and cognitive capabilities, mechanisms, and performance* (pp. 409-422). Elsevier, North-Holland.

Crain, W.C. (1985). *Theories of development: Concepts and applications* (2nd ed.). Prentice Hall.

Cuevas, K., & Bell, M.A. (2014). Infant attention and early childhood executive function. *Child Development, 85,* 397-404.

Easterbrook, J.A. (1959). The effect of emotion on cue utilization and the organization of behavior. *Psychological Review, 66,* 183-201.

Eimer, M., Nattkemper, D., Schröger, E., & Prinz, W. (1996). Involuntary attention. In O. Neumann & A.F. Sanders (Eds.), *Handbook of perception and action: Vol. 3. Attention* (pp. 155-184). Academic Press.

Ericsson, K.A. (2003). Development of elite performance and deliberate practice: An update from the perspective of the expert performance approach. In J.L. Starkes & K.A. Ericsson (Eds.), *Expert performance in sports* (pp. 49-83). Human Kinetics.

Fantz, R.L. (1963). Patterned vision in newborn infants. *Science, 140,* 296-297.

Fantz, R.L. (1964). Visual experience in infants: Decreased attention to familiar patterns relative to novel ones. *Science, 146,* 668-670.

Fitts, P., & Posner, M.I. (1967). *Human performance.* Brooks/Cole.

Flavell, J.H. (1979). Metacognition and cognitive monitoring: A new area of cognitive-developmental inquiry. *American Psychologist, 34,* 906-911.

Flavell, J.H., Beach, D.H., & Chinsky, J.M. (1966). Spontaneous verbal rehearsal in a memory task as a function of age. *Child Development, 37,* 283-299.

Flavell, J.H., Friedrichs, A.G., & Hoyt, J.D. (1970). Developmental changes in memorization processes. *Cognitive Psychology, 1,* 324-340.

French, K.E., Spurgeon, J.H., & Nevett, M.E. (1995). Expert-novice differences in cognitive and skill execution components of youth baseball performance. *Research Quarterly for Exercise and Sport, 66,* 194-201.

French, K.E., & Thomas, J.R. (1987). The relation of knowledge to children's basketball performance. *Journal of Sport Psychology, 9,* 15-32.

Gallagher, J.D., & Thomas, J.R. (1984). Rehearsal strategy effects on developmental differences for recall of a movement series. *Research Quarterly for Exercise and Sport, 55,* 123-128.

Ginsburg, H., & Opper, S. (1969). *Piaget's theory of intellectual development: An introduction.* Prentice Hall.

Hastie, P.A., Calderon, A., Rolim, R.J., & Guarino, A.J. (2013). The development of skill and knowledge during a sport education season of track and field. *Research Quarterly for Exercise and Sport, 84,* 336-344.

Hess, T.M., Follett, K.J., & McGee, K.A. (1998). Aging and impression formation: The impact of processing skills and goals. *Journals of Gerontology: Psychological Sciences and Social Sciences, 53B,* 175-187.

Hick, W.E. (1952). On the rate of gain of information. *Quarterly Journal of Experimental Psychology, 4,* 11-26.

Hoover, J.H., & Wade, M. (1985). Motor learning theory and mentally retarded individuals: A historical review. *Adapted Physical Activity Quarterly, 2,* 228-252.

Keogh, J., & Sugden, D. (1985). *Movement skill development.* Macmillan.

Kourtessis, T., & Reid, G. (1997). Knowledge and skill of ball catching in children with cerebral palsy and other physical disabilities. *Adapted Physical Activity Quarterly, 14,* 24-42.

Lefebvre, C., & Reid, G. (1998). Prediction in ball catching by children with and without a developmental coordination disorder. *Adapted Physical Activity Quarterly, 15,* 299-315.

Liu, T., & Jensen. J.L. (2011). Effects of strategy use on children's motor performance in a continuous timing task. *Research Quarterly for Exercise and Sport, 82,* 198-209.

Luo, L., & Craik, F.I.M. (2008). Aging and memory: A cognitive approach. *La Revue Canadienne de Psychiatrie, 53*(6), 346-353.

Lustig, C., & Meck, W.H. (2001). Paying attention to time as one gets older. *Psychological Science, 12*(6), 478-484.

Määttä, S., Pääkkönnen, A., Saavalainen, P., & Partanen, J. (2005). Selective attention event-related potential effects from auditory novel stimuli in children and adults. *Clinical Neurophysiology, 116,* 129-141.

Magill, R.A. (2007). *Motor learning and control: Concepts and applications* (8th ed.). McGraw-Hill.

Molander, B., & Bäckman, L. (1989). Age differences in heart rate patterns during concentration in a precision sport: Implications for attentional functioning. *Journal of Gerontology: Psychological Sciences, 44,* 80-87.

Molander, B., & Bäckman, L. (1994). Attention and performance in miniature golf across the life span. *Journal of Gerontology: Psychological Sciences, 49*(2), 35-41.

Mowla, A., Ashkani, H., Ghanizadeh, A., Dehbozorgi, G.R., Sabayan, B., & Chohedri, A.H. (2007). Do memory complaints represent impaired memory performance in patients with major depressive disorder? *Depression & Anxiety, 25*(10), 92-96.

Nyberg, L., Lövdén, M., Riklund, K., Lindenberger, U., & Bäckman, L. (2012). Memory aging and brain maintenance. *Trends in Cognitive Sciences, 16*(5), 292-305.

Ornstein, P.A., & Naus, M.J. (1978). Rehearsal processes in children's memory. In P.A. Ornstein (Ed.), *Memory development in children.* Erlbaum.

Payne, G.V., & Isaacs, L.D. (2008). *Human life motor development: A lifespan approach* (7th ed.). McGraw-Hill.

Piaget, J. (1976). *The child and reality* (A. Rosin, Trans.) Grossman.

Reid, G. (1980b). Overt and covert rehearsal in short-term motor memory of mentally retarded and nonretarded persons. *American Journal of Mental Deficiency, 85,* 69-77.

Reid, G. (1980a). The effects of memory strategy instruction in short term motor memory of the mentally retarded. *Journal of Motor Behavior, 112,* 221-227.

Reynolds, G.D., Courage, M.L., & Richards, J.E. (2013). The development of attention. In D. Reisberg (Ed.), *Oxford handbook of cognitive psychology* (pp. 1000-1013). Oxford University Press.

Ross, A.O. (1978). *Psychological aspects of learning disabilities and reading disorders.* New York: McGraw-Hill.

Schneider, W., & Ornstein, P.A. (2015). The development of children's memory. *Child Development Perspectives, 9,* 190-195.

Shaffer, D. (1999). *Developmental psychology: Childhood and adolescence* (5th ed.). Brookes/Cole.

Stanley, J., & Krakauer, J.W. (2013). Motor skill depends on knowledge of facts. *Frontiers in Human Neuroscience, 7,* 503.

Starkes, J.L., & Allard, F. (1991). Motor-skill experts in sports, dance, and other domains. In K.A. Ericsson & J. Smith (Eds.), *Towards a general theory of expertise: Prospects and limits* (pp. 126-152). Cambridge University Press.

Starkes, J.L., Deakin, J.M., Lindley, S., & Crisp, F. (1987). Motor versus verbal recall of ballet sequences by young expert dancers. *Journal of Sport Psychology, 9,* 222-230.

Starkes, J.L., & Ericsson, K.A. (Eds.). (2003). *Expert performance in sports.* Human Kinetics.

Ste-Marie, D. M. (1999). Expert–novice differences in gymnastic judging: An information-processing perspective. *Applied Cognitive Psychology, 13*(3), 269–281. https://doi.org/10.1002/(SICI)1099-0720(199906)13:3<269::AID-ACP567>3.0.CO;2-Y

Sugden, D.A. (1978). Visual motor short term memory in educationally subnormal boys. *British Journal of Educational Psychology, 48,* 330-339.

Thomas, J.R., Thomas, K.T., & Gallagher, J.D. (1993). Developmental considerations in skill acquisition. In R.N. Singer, M. Murphey, & L.K. Tennant (Eds.), *Handbook of research on sport psychology* (pp. 73-105). Macmillan.

Toner, J. (2014). Knowledge of facts mediate 'continuous improvement' in elite sport: A comment on Stanley and Krakauer [2013]. *Frontiers in Human Neuroscience, 10,* 142.

Tulving, E. (1985). How many memory systems are there? *American Psychologist, 40,* 385-398.

Tulving, E. (2002). Episodic memory: From mind to brain. *Annual Review of Psychology, 53,* 1-25.

Van Gerven, P.W.M., & Guerreiro, M.J.S. (2016). Selective attention and sensory modality in aging: Curses and blessings. *Frontiers in Human Neuroscience, 10,* 1-7.

Verhaeghen, P., Steitz, W. D., Sliwinski, M.J., & Cerella, J. (2003). Aging and dual-task performance: A meta-analysis. *Psychology and Aging, 18,* 443-460.

Vestergren, P., & Nilsson, L.G. (2011). Perceived causes of everyday memory problems in a population-based sample aged 39-99. *Applied Cognitive Psychology, 25,* 641-646.

Wall, A.E., McClements, J., Bouffard, M., Findlay, H., & Taylor, J. (1985). A knowledge-based approach to motor development: Implications for the physically awkward. *Adapted Physical Activity Quarterly, 2,* 21-42.

Wall, A.E., Reid, G., & Harvey, W.J. (2007). Interface of the KB and ETA approaches. In W.E. Davis & G.D. Broadhead (Eds.), *Ecological task analysis and movement* (pp. 259-277). Human Kinetics.

Weiss, M.R. (1983). Modeling and motor performance: A developmental perspective. *Research Quarterly for Exercise and Sport, 54,* 190-197.

Wetzel, N. (2014). Development of control of attention from different perspectives. *Frontiers in Psychology, 5,* 1000.

Wickens, C.D., & Benel, D.C.R. (1982). The development of time-sharing skills. In J.A.S. Kelso & J.E. Clark (Eds.), *The development of movement control and coordination* (pp. 253-272). Wiley.

Williams, A.M., & Davids, K. (1998). Visual search strategy, selective attention, and expertise in soccer. *Research Quarterly for Exercise and Sport, 69,* 127-135.

Winther, K.T., & Thomas, J.R. (1981). Developmental differences in children's labeling of movement. *Journal of Motor Behavior, 13,* 77-90.

Zelinski, E.M., & Kennison, R.F. (2001). The Long Beach Longitudinal Study: Evaluation of longitudinal effects of aging on memory and cognition. *Home Health Care Services Quarterly, 19*(3), 45-55.

Chapter 15

Aiken, C.H., Fairbrother, J.T., & Post, P.G. (2012). The effects of self-controlled video feedback on the learning of the basketball set shot. *Frontiers in Psychology, 3,* 338.

Andrieux, M., Boutin, A., & Thon, B. (2016). Self-control of task difficulty during early practice promotes motor skill learning. *Journal of Motor Behavior, 48,* 57-65.

Babic, M.J., Morgan, P.J., Plotnikoff, R.C., Lonsdale, C., White, R.L., & Lubans, D.R. (2014). Physical activity and physical self-concept in youth: Systematic review and meta-analysis. *Sports Medicine, 44,* 1589-1601.

Bailey, R., Cope E.J., & Pearce, G. (2013). Why do children take part and remain involved in sport? A literature review and discussion of implications for sport coaches. *International Journal of Coaching Science, 7,* 56-75.

Bai, Y., Chen, S., Vazou, S., Welk, G.J., & Schaben, J. (2015). Mediated effects of perceived competence on youth physical activity and sedentary behavior. *Research Quarterly for Exercise and Sport, 86,* 406-413.

Balish, S.M., McLaren, C., Rainham, D., & Blanchard, C. (2014). Correlates of youth sport attrition: A review and future directions. *Psychology of Sport and Exercise, 15,* 429-439.

Bandura, A. (1997). *Self-efficacy: The exercise of control.* Freeman.

Barnett, L.M., Ridgers, N.D., & Salmon, J. (2015). Associations between young children's perceived and actual ball skill competence and physical activity. *Journal of Science and Medicine in Sport, 18,* 167-171.

Bauman, A.E., Reis, R.S., Sallis, J.F., Wells, J.C., Loos, R.J.F., & Martin, B.W. (2012). Correlates of physical activity: Why are some people active and others not? *Lancet, 380,* 258-271.

Cairney, J., Kwan, M.Y.W., Velduizen, S., Hay, J., Bray, S.R., & Faught, B.F. (2012). Gender, perceived competence and the enjoyment of physical education in children: A longitudinal examination. *International Journal of Behavioral Nutrition and Physical Activity, 9,* 26.

Caprara, G.V., Pastorelli, C., & Weiner, B. (1997). Linkages between causal ascriptions, emotion, and behavior. *International Journal of Behavioral Development, 20,* 153-162.

Ceria-Ulep, C.D., Serafica, R.C., & Tse, A. (2011). Filipino older adults' beliefs about exercise activity. *Nursing Forum, 46*(4), 240-250.

Chase, M.A. (2001). Children's self-efficacy, motivational intentions, and attributions in physical education and sport. *Research Quarterly for Exercise and Sport, 72,* 47-54.

Chiviacowsky, S., & Wulf, G. (2005). Self-controlled feedback is effective if it is based on the learner's performance. *Research Quarterly for Exercise and Sport, 76,* 42-48.

Chiviacowsky, S., Wulf, G., de Medeiros, F.L., Kaefer, A., & Tani, G. (2008). Learning benefits of self-controlled knowledge of results in 10-year-old children. *Research Quarterly for Exercise and Sport, 79,* 405-410.

Cleary, T.J., & Zimmerman, B.J. (2001). Self-regulation differences during athletic practice by experts, non-experts and novices. *Journal of Applied Sport Psychology, 13,* 185-206.

Côté, J., Baker, J., & Abernethy, B. (2003). From play to practice: A developmental framework for acquisition of expertise in team sports. In J.L. Starkes & K.A. Ericsson (Eds.), *Expert performance in sports* (pp. 89-113). Human Kinetics.

Crain, W.C. (1985). *Theories of development: Concepts and applications* (2nd ed.). Prentice Hall.

Crocker, P.R.E., Hoar, S.D., McDonough, M.H., Kowaski, K.C., & Niefer, C.B. (2004). Emotional experiences in youth sport. In M.R. Weiss (Ed.), *Developmental sport and exercise psychology: A lifespan perspective* (pp. 197-221). Fitness Information Technology.

Dacey, M., Baltzell, A., & Zalchkowsky, L. (2008). Older adults' intrinsic and extrinsic motivation toward physical activity. *American Journal of Health Behavior, 32*(5), 570-582.

Deci, E.L., & Flaste, R. (1995). *Why we do what we do: The dynamics of personal autonomy.* Putnam.

Deci, E.L., & Ryan, R.M. (1985). *Intrinsic motivation and self-determination in human behavior.* Plenum Press.

De Meester, A., Maes, J., Stodden, D., Cardon, G., Goodway, J., Lenoir, M., & Haerens, L., (2016). Identifying profiles of actual and perceived motor competence among adolescents: Associations with motivation, physical activity, and sports participation. *Journal of Sports Sciences, 34*(21), 2027-2037. https://doi.org/10.1080/02640414.2016.1149608

Dishman, R.K. (1994). *Advances in exercise adherence.* Human Kinetics.

Erikson, E.H. (1963). *Childhood and society* (2nd ed.). Norton.

Feltz, D.L., Short, S.E., & Sullivan, P.J. (2008). *Self-efficacy in sport.* Human Kinetics.

Garner, P.W., & Waajid, B. (2012). Emotional knowledge and self-regulation as predictors of preschools' cognitive ability, classroom behavior, and social competence. *Journal of Psychoeducational Assessment, 30,* 330-343.

Harter, S. (1978). Effectance motivation reconsidered: Toward a developmental model. *Human Development, 21,* 34-64.

Harter, S. (1999). *The construction of self: A developmental perspective.* Guilford.

Haywood, K.M., & Getchell, N. (2014). *Life span motor development* (6th ed.). Human Kinetics.

Horn, T.S. (1987). The influence of teacher-coach behavior on the psychological development of children. In D. Gould & M.R. Weiss (Eds.), *Advances in pediatric sport science: Vol. 2. Behavioral issues* (pp. 121-142). Human Kinetics.

Jokic, C.S., Polatajko, H., & Whitebread, D. (2013). Self-regulation as a mediator in motor learning: The effect of the cognitive orientation to occupational performance approach on children with DCD. *Adapted Physical Activity Quarterly, 29,* 103-126.

Janelle, C.M., Barba, D.A., Frehlich, S.G., Tennant, L.K., & Cauraugh, J.H. (1997). Maximizing performance feedback effectiveness through videotape replay and a self-controlled learning environment. *Research Quarterly for Exercise and Sport, 68*(4), 269-279.

Keetch, K.M., & Lee, T.D. (2007). The effect of self-regulated and experimenter-imposed practice schedules on motor learning for tasks of varying difficulty. *Research Quarterly for Exercise and Sport, 78,* 476-486.

Kitsantas, A., & Zimmerman, B.J. (1998). Self-regulation of motoric learning: A strategic cycle view. *Journal of Applied Sport Psychology, 10,* 220-239.

Kolovelonis, A., Goudas, M., Hassandra, M., & Dermitzaki, I. (2012). Self-regulated learning in physical education: Examining the effects of emulative and self-control practice. *Psychology of Sport and Exercise, 13,* 383-389.

LeGear, M., Greyling, L., Sloan, E., Bell, R.I., Williams, B.-L., Naylor, P-J., & Temple, V. (2012). A window of opportunity? Motor skills and perceptions of competence of children in kindergarten. *International Journal of Behavioral Nutrition and Physical Activity, 9,* 29.

Leversen, I., Danielsen, A.G., Wold, B., & Samdal, O. (2012). What they want and what they get: Self-reported motives, perceived competence, and relatedness in adolescent leisure activities. *Child Development Research,* article 684157. https://doi.org/ 10.1155/2012/684157

Lewthwaite, R., Chiviacowsky, S., Drews, R., & Wulf, G. (2015). Choose to move: The motivational impact of autonomy support on motor learning. *Psychonomic Bulletin & Review, 22,* 1383-1388.

Litt, M., Kleppinger, A., & Judge, J. (2002). Initiation and maintenance of exercise behavior in older women: Predictors from social learning model. *Journal of Behavioral Medicine, 25*(1), 83-97.

Lloyd, M., Reid, G., & Bouffard, M. (2006). Self-regulation of sport-specific and educational problem solving tasks by boys with and without DCD. *Adapted Physical Activity Quarterly, 23*, 370-389.

Lubans, D.R., Plotnikiff, R.C., & Lubans, N.J. (2012). Review: A systematic review of the impact of physical activity programmes on social and emotional well-being in at-risk youth. *Child and Adolescent Mental Health, 17*, 2-13.

Maatta, S., Ray, C., & Roos, E. (2014). Associations of parental influence and 10-11-year-old children's physical activity: Are they mediated by children's perceived competence and attraction to physical activity? *Scandinavian Journal of Public Health, 42*, 45-51.

McAuley, E. (1992). The role of efficacy cognitions in the prediction of exercise behaviour in middle aged adults. *Journal of Behavioral Medicine, 15*, 65-88.

Nasuti, G., & Rhodes, R.E. (2013). Affective judgement and physical activity in youth: Review and meta-analysis. *Annals of Behavioral Medicine, 45*, 357-376.

Petlichkoff, L.M. (2004). Self-regulation skills for children and adolescents. In M.R. Weiss (Ed.), *Developmental sport and exercise psychology: A lifespan perspective* (pp. 269-288). Fitness Information Technology.

Post, P.G., Fairbrother, J.T., & Barros, J.A.C. (2011). Self-controlled amount of practice benefits learning a motor skill. *Research Quarterly for Exercise and Sport, 82*(3), 474-481. https://doi.org/ 10.1080/02701367.2011.10599780

Post, P.G., Fairbrother, J.T., Barros, J.A.C., & Kulpa, J.D. (2014). Self-controlled practice with a fixed time period facilitates the learning of a basketball set shot. *Journal of Motor Learning and Development, 3*, 9-15.

Robinson, L.E., Stodden, D.F., Barnett, L.M., Lopes, V.T., Logan, S.W., Rodrigues, L.P., & D'Hondt, E. (2015). Motor competence and its effect on positive developmental trajectories of health. *Sports Medicine, 45*, 1273-1284.

Rodgers, W.M., Markland, D., Selzler, A.-M., Murray, T., & Wilson, P.M. (2014). Distinguishing perceived competence and self-efficacy: An example from exercise. *Research Quarterly for Exercise and Sport, 85*, 527-539.

Ryan, R.M., & Deci, E.L. (2000). Self-determination theory and the facilitation of intrinsic motivation, social development, and well-being. *American Psychologist, 55*, 68-78.

Sanli, E.A., Patterson, J.T., Bray, S.R., & Lee, T.D. (2013). Understanding self-controlled motor learning through the self-determination theory. *Frontiers in Psychology, 3*, 611.

Seabra, A.C., Seabra, A.F., Mendonca, D.M., Brustad, R., Maia, J.A., Fonseca, A.M., & Malina, R.M. (2012). Psychosocial correlates of physical activity in school children aged 8-10 years. *European Journal of Public Health, 23*(5), 794-798. https://doi.org/ 10.1093/eurpub/cks149

Seligman, M. (1975). *Helplessness: On depression, development, and death*. Freeman.

Shaffer, D. (1999). *Developmental psychology: Childhood and adolescence* (5th ed.). Brooks/Cole.

Singer, R.N. (2002). Preperformance state, routines, and automaticity: What does it take to realize expertise in self-paced events? *Journal of Sport and Exercise Psychology, 24*, 359-375.

Stephens, T., & Craig, C.L. (1990). *The well-being of Canadians: Highlights of the 1988 Campbell's Soup Survey*. Canadian Fitness and Lifestyle Research Institute.

Stodden, D.F., Goodway, J.D., Langendorfer, S.J., Roberton, M.A., Rudisill, M.E., Garcia, C., & Garcia, L.E. (2008). A developmental perspective on the role of motor skill competence in physical activity: An emergent relationship. *Quest, 60*, 290-306.

Sun, H., & Chen, A. (2010). A pedagogical understanding of the self-determination theory in physical education. *Quest, 62*, 364-384.

Tamminen, K.A., & Crocker, P.R.E. (2013). 'I control my own emotions for the sake of the team': Emotional self-regulation and interpersonal emotion regulation among female high-performance curlers. *Psychology of Sport and Exercise, 14*, 737-747.

Teixeira, P.J., Carraca, E.L., Markland, D., Silva, M.N., & Ryan, R.M. (2012). Exercise, physical activity, and self-determination theory: A systematic review. *International Journal of Behavioral Nutrition and Physical Activity, 9*, 78.

Vallerand, R.J. (1997). Toward a hierarchical model of intrinsic and extrinsic motivation. In M.P. Zanna (Ed.), *Advances in experimental social psychology* (Vol. 2 pp. 271-360). Academic Press.

Vallerand, R.J. (2007). Intrinsic and extrinsic motivation in sport and physical activity: A review and a look at the future. In G. Tenenbaum & E. Eklund (Eds.), *Handbook of sport psychology* (3rd ed., pp. 49-83). Wiley.

Van den Berghe, L., Vansteenkiste, M., Cardon, G., Kirk, D., & Haerens, L. (2014). Research on self-determination in physical education: Key findings and proposals for future research. *Physical Education and Sport Pedagogy, 19*, 97-121.

Weiner, B. (1985). An attribution theory of achievement motivation and emotion. *Psychological Review, 92*, 548-573.

Weiss, M.R., McCullagh, P., Smith, A.L., & Berlant, A.R. (1998). Observational learning and the fearful child: Influence of peer models on swimming skill performance and psychological responses. *Research Quarterly for Exercise and Sport, 69*, 380-394.

Weiss, M.R., & Williams, L. (2004). The why of youth sport involvement: A developmental perspective on motivational processes. In M.R. Weiss (Ed.), *Developmental sport and exercise psychology: A lifespan perspective* (pp. 223-268). Fitness Information Technology.

Wulf, G., & Toole, T. (1999). Physical assistance devices in complex motor skill learning: Benefits of a self-controlled practice schedule. *Research Quarterly for Exercise and Sport, 70*, 265-272.

Wu, W.F.W., & Magill, R.A. (2011). Allowing learners to choose: Self-controlled practice schedules for learning multiple movement patterns. *Research Quarterly for Exercise and Sport, 82*, 449-457.

Zimmerman, B.J. (2000). Attaining self-regulation: A social cognitive perspective. In M. Boekaerts, P.R. Pintrich, & M. Zeidner (Eds.), *Handbook of self-regulation* (pp. 13-39). Academic Press.

Zimmerman, B.J., & Kitsantas, A. (1997). Developmental phases in self-regulation: Shifting from process goals to outcome goals. *Journal of Educational Psychology, 89,* 29-36.

Zimmerman, B.J., & Kitsantas, A. (1999). Acquiring writing revision skill: Shifting from process to outcome self-regulatory goals. *Journal of Educational Psychology, 91,* 241-250.

Chapter 16

Abdul Razak, M.T., Omar Fauzee, M.S., & Abd Latif, R. (2010). The perspective of Arabic Muslim women toward sport participation. *Journal of Asia Pacific Studies, 1*(2), 264-377.

Beilock, S.L., Jellison, W.A., Rydell, R J., McConnell, A.R., & Carr, T.H. (2006). On the causal mechanisms of stereotype threat: Can skills that don't rely heavily on working memory still be threatened? *Personality and Social Psychology Bulletin, 32*(8), 1059-1071. http://dx.doi.org/10.1177/0146167206288489

Bem, S.L. (1981). Gender schema theory: A cognitive account of sex typing. *Psychological Review, 88*(4), 354-364.

Bickmore, T.W., Caruso, L., Clough-Gorr, K., & Heeren, T. (2005). "It's just like you talk to a friend" relational agents for older adults. *Interacting with Computers, 17,* 711-735. https://doi.org/10.1016/j.intcom.2005.09.002

Billings, A.C., & Eastman, S.T. (2002). Selective representation of gender, ethnicity, and nationality in American television coverage of the 2000 summer Olympics. *International Review for the Sociology of Sport, 37*(3), 351-370. http://irs.sagepub.com/cgi/content/abstract/37/3-4/351

Bopp, T., & Sagas, M. (2014). Racial tasking and the college quarterback: Redefining the stacking phenomenon. *Journal of Sport Management, 28*(2), 136-142. http://dx.doi.org/10.1123/jsm.2012-0296

Centers for Disease Control and Prevention. (2021, March 31). *Adult obesity prevalence maps.* www.cdc.gov/obesity/data/prevalence-maps.html

Chalabaev, A., Stone, J., Sarrazin, P., & Croizet, J.-C. (2008). Investigating physiological and self-reported mediators of stereotype lift effects on a motor task. *Basic and Applied Social Psychology, 30*(1), 18-26. http://dx.doi.org/10.1080/01973530701665256

Chen, D.W. (2022, May 24). *Transgender athletes face bans from girls' sports in 10 U.S. states.* The New York Times. https://www.nytimes.com/article/transgender-athlete-ban.html

Cherney, I.D. (2018). Characteristics of masculine and feminine toys and gender-differentiated play. In E. Weisgram & L. Dinella (Eds.), *Gender typing of children's toys: How early play experiences impact development* (pp. 73-93). American Psychological Association.

Chogahara, M., O'Brien Cousins, S., & Wankel, L.M. (1998). Social influences on physical activity in older adults: A review. *Journal of Aging and Physical Activity, 6*(1), 1-17. https://doi.org/10.1123/japa.6.1.1

Coleman, C.A., & Scott, J. (2018). Sports are not colorblind: The role of race and segregation in NFL positions. *Journal of Emerging Investigators.* www.emerginginvestigators.org/articles/sports-are-not-colorblind-the-role-of-race-and-segregation-in-nfl-positions/pdf

Convention on the Rights of Persons with Disabilities (2006, December 13). A/RES/61/106. United Nations, New York, NY.

Cros, B. (2013). Managing racial diversity: Positional segregation in South African rugby union in the post-apartheid era. *Cadernos de Estudos Africanos, 26,* 153-176. https://doi.org/10.4000/cea.1154

Darlow, S.D., & Xu, X. (2011). The influence of close others' exercise habits and perceived social support on exercise. *Psychology of Sport and Exercise, 12*(5), 575-578. https://doi.org/10.1016/J.PSYCHSPORT.2011.04.004

Eccles (Parsons), J., Adler, T.F., Futterman, R., Goff, S.B., Kaczala, C.M., Meece, J.L., & Midgley, C. (1983). Expectations, values and academic behaviors. In J.T. Spence (Ed.), *Achievement and achievement motivation* (pp. 75-146). W.H. Freeman.

Edwards, H. (1973). *Sociology of sport.* Dorsey.

Eime, R.M., Charity, M.J., Harvey, J.T., & Payne, W.R. (2015). Participation in sport and physical activity: Associations with socio-economic status and geographical remoteness. *BMC Public Health, 15,* Article 434. https://doi.org/10.1186/s12889-015-1796-0

Eitzen, D.S., & Furst, D. (1989). Racial bias in women's collegiate volleyball. *Journal of Sport and Social Issues, 13*(1), 46-51.

Equality Act, H.R. 5, 117th Congress. (2021). www.congress.gov/bill/117th-congress/house-bill/5

Federico, B., Falese, L., Marandola, D., & Capelli, G. (2013). Socioeconomic differences in sport and physical activity among Italian adults. *Journal of Sports Sciences, 31*(4), 451-458. https://doi.org/10.1080/02640414.2012.736630

Gabbard, C.P. (2012). *Lifelong motor development* (6th ed.). Benjamin Cummings.

Gallahue, D.L., Ozmun, J.C., & Goodway, J.D. (2012). *Understanding motor development: Infants, children, adolescents, adults* (7th ed.). McGraw-Hill.

Garcia, C. (2011). Gender expression and homophobia. *Journal of Physical Education, Recreation & Dance, 82*(8), 47-49. https://doi.org/10.1080/07303084.2011.10598678

Gardner, P.J. (2011). Natural neighborhood networks—Important social networks in the lives of older adults aging in place. *Journal of Aging Studies, 25*(3), 263-271. https://doi.org/10.1016/j.jaging.2011.03.007

Gender Neutral Retail Departments, Cal. Assemb. B. 1084 (2021), Chapter 750 (Cal. Stat. 2021). https://leginfo.legislature.ca.gov/faces/billNavClient.xhtml?bill_id=202120220AB1084

Gordon-Larsen, P., Nelson, M.C., Page, P., & Popkin, B.M. (2006). Inequality in the built environment underlies key health disparities in physical activity and obesity. *Pediatrics, 117*(2), 417-424. https://doi.org/10.1542/peds.2005-0058

Hallinan, C.J. (1991). Aborigines and positional segregation in Australian rugby league. *International Review for Sociology of Sport, 26*(2), 69-79.

Harms, L., & Kansen, M. (2018). *Cycling facts*. Netherlands Institute for Transport Policy Analysis. https://government.nl/binaries/government/documenten/reports/2018/04/01/cycling-facts-2018/Cycling+facts+2018.pdf

Hermann, J.M., & Vollmeyer, R. (2016). "Girls should cook, rather than kick!"—Female soccer players under stereotype treat. *Psychology of Sport and Exercise, 26*, 94-101. https://doi.org/10.1016/j.psychsport.2016.06.010

Hively, K., & El-Alayli, A. (2014). 'You throw like a girl': The effect of stereotype threat on women's athletic performance and gender stereotypes. *Psychology of Sport and Exercise, 15*(1), 48-55. https://doi.org/10. 1016/j.psychsport.2013.09.001

Hulteen, R.M., Smith, J.J., Morgan, P.J., Barnett, L.M., Hallal, P.C., Colyvas, K., & Lubans, D.R. (2017). Global participation in sport and leisure-time physical activities: A systematic review and meta-analysis. *Preventive Medicine, 95*, 14-25. https://doi.org/10.1016/j.ypmed.2016.11.027

Individuals With Disabilities Education Act, 20 U.S.C. § 1400 (2004).

Jones, B.A., Arcelus, J., Bouman, W.P., & Haycraft, E. (2017). Sport and transgender people: A systematic review of the literature relating to sport participation and competitive sport policies. *Sports Medicine, 47*, 701-716. https://doi.org/10.1007/s40279-016-0621-y

Kaestner, R., & Xu, X. (2006). Effects of Title IX and sports participation on girls' physical activity and weight. *Advances in Health Economics and Health Services Research, 17*, 79-114.

Kaestner, R., & Xu, X. (2010). Title IX, girls' sports participation, and adult female physical activity and weight. *Evaluation Review, 34*(1), 52-78. https://doi.org/10.1177/0193841X09353539

Kamphuis, C.B., van Lenthe, F.J., Giskes, K., Brug, J., & Mackenbach, J.P. (2007). Perceived environmental determinants of physical activity and fruit and vegetable consumption among high and low socioeconomic groups in the Netherlands. *Health & Place, 13*(2), 493-503. https://doi.org/10.1016/j.healthplace.2006.05.008

Kobach, M.J., & Potter, R.F. (2013). The role of mediated sports programming on implicit racial stereotypes. *Sport in Society, 16*(10), 1414-1428. https://doi.org/10.1080/17430437.2013.821254

Krishnakumar, P. (2021, April 15). *This record-breaking year for anti-transgender legislation would affect minors the most*. CNN. www.cnn.com/2021/04/15/politics/anti-transgender-legislation-2021/index.html

Lapchick, R. (2020). *2020 Racial and gender report card*. Institute for Diversity and Ethics in Sport. www.tidesport.org/complete-sport

Limstrand, T. (2008). Environmental characteristics relevant to young people's use of sports facilities: A review. *Scandinavian Journal of Medicine and Science in Sports, 18*, 275-287. https://doi.org/10.1111/j.1600-0838.2007.00742.x

Loy, J., & McElvogue, J. (1970). Racial segregation in American sport. *International Review of Sport Sociology, 5*(1), 5-23. https://doi.org/10.1177/101269027000500101

Malcolm, D. (1997). Stacking in cricket: A figurational sociological reappraisal of centrality. *Sociology of Sport Journal, 14*, 263-282.

Margolis, B., & Piliavin, J.A. (1999). "Stacking" in major league baseball: A multivariate analysis. *Sociology of Sport Journal, 16*, 16-34.

Metheny, E. (1965). *Connotations of movement in sport and dance*. Wm. C. Brown.

Miedema, S.T., Mulvey, K.L., & Brian, A. (2021). "You throw like a girl!": Young children's gender stereotypes about object control skills. *Research Quarterly for Exercise and Sport*. https://doi.org/10.1080/02701367.2021.1976374

Mihalik, B.J., O'Leary, J.T., Mcguire, F.A., & Dottavio, F.D. (1989). Sports involvement across the life span: Expansion and contraction of sports activities. *Research Quarterly for Exercise and Sport, 60*(4), 396-398. https://doi.org/10.1080/02701367.1989.10607470

National Federation of State High School Associations. (2019). *2018-19 high school athletics participation survey*. www.nfhs.org/sports-resource-content/high-school-participation-survey-archive/

Pan, S.Y., Cameron, C., DesMeules, M., Morrison, H., Craig, C.L., & Jiang, X. (2009). Individual, social, environmental, and physical environmental correlates with physical activity among Canadians: A cross-sectional study. *BMC Public Health, 9*, 21. https://doi.org/10.1186/1471-2458-9-21

Plaza, M., Boiche, J., Brunel, L., & Ruchaud, F. (2017). Sport = male . . . but not all sports: Investigating the gender stereotypes of sport activities at the explicit and implicit levels. *Sex Roles, 76*, 202-217. https://doi.org/ 10.1007/s11199-016-0650-x

Rackow, P., Scholz, U., & Hornung, R. (2014). Effects of a new sports companion on received social support and physical exercise: An intervention study. *Applied Psychology: Health and Well-Being, 6*(3), 300-317.

Rackow, P., Scholz, U., & Hornung, R. (2014). Effects of a new sports companion on received social support and physical exercise: An intervention study. *Applied Psychology: Health and Well-Being, 6*(3), 300-317. https://doi.org/10.1111/aphw.12029

Reimers, A.K., Wagner, M., Alvanides, S., Steinmayr, A., Reiner, M., Schmidt, S., & Woll, A. (2014). Proximity to sports facilities and sports participation for adolescents in Germany. *PLoS ONE, 9*(3), e93059. https://doi.org/10.1371/journal.pone.0093059

Riemer, B.A., & Visio, M.E. (2003). Gender typing of sports: An investigation of Metheny's classification. *Research Quarterly for Exercise and Sport, 74*(2), 193-204. https://doi.org/10.1080/02701367.2003.10609081

Rook, K.S. (2000). The evolution of social relationships in later adulthood. In S.H. Qualls & N. Abeles (Eds.), *Psychology and the aging revolution: How we adapt to longer life* (pp. 173-191). American Psychological Association.

Rose, A.J., & Smith, R.L. (2018). Gender and peer relationships. In W.M. Bukowski, B. Laursen, & K.H. Rubin (Eds.), *Handbook of peer interactions, relationships, and groups* (pp. 571-589). Guilford Press.

Ruble, D.N., & Martin, C.L. (1998). Gender development. In N. Eisenberg (Ed.), *Handbook of child psychology: Vol. 3. Social, emotional, and personality development* (5th ed., pp. 933-1016). John Wiley & Sons.

Schaie, K.W., & Willis, S.L. (1991). *Adult development and aging* (3rd ed.). HarperCollins.

Shields, N., Synnot, A.J., & Barr, M. (2012). Perceived barriers and facilitator to physical activity for children with disability: A systematic review. *British Journal of Sports Medicine, 46*, 989-997. https://doi.org/10.1136/bjsports-2012-090236

Siler, K. (2019). Pipeline on the gridiron: Player backgrounds, opportunity structures and racial stratification in American college football. *Sociology of Sport Journal, 36*, 57-76. https://doi.org/10.1123/ssj.2017-0125

Steele, C.M., & Aronson, J. (1995). Stereotype threat and the intellectual test performance of African Americans. *Journal of Personality and Social Psychology, 69*(5), 797–811. https://doi.org/10.1037/0022-3514.69.5.797

Stephens, T., & Craig, C.L. (1990). *The well-being of Canadians: Highlights of the 1988 Campbell's Soup Survey.* Canadian Fitness and Lifestyle Research Institute.

Stone, J. (2002). Battling doubt by avoiding practice: The effects of stereotype threat on self-handicapping in White athletes. *Personality and Social Psychology Bulletin, 28*(12), 1667-1678. https://doi.org/10.1177/014616702237648

Stone, J., Lynch, C.I., Sjomeling, M., & Darley, J.M. (1999). Stereotype treat effects on Black and White athletic performance. *Journal of Personality and Social Psychology, 77*(6), 1213-1227.

Tanimoto, C., & Miwa, K. (2021). Factors influencing acceptance of transgender athletes. *Sport Management Review, 24*(3), 452-474. https://doi.org/10.1080/14413523.2021.1880771

Thomas, J.R., & French, K.E. (1985). Gender differences across age in motor performance. A meta-analysis. *Psychological Bulletin, 98*(2), 260-282. https://doi.org/10.1037//0033-2909.98.2.260

Todd, B.K., Fischer, R.A., Di Costa, S., Roestorf, A., Harbour, K., Hardiman, P., & Barry, J.A. (2018). Sex differences in children's toy preferences: A systematic review, meta-regression, and meta-analysis. *Infant and Child Development, 27*(2), e2064. https://doi.org/10.1002/icd.2064

U.S. Department of Transportation. (2020). *Transportation statistics annual report.* https://doi.org/10.21949/1520449

Wiggins, D.K. (1997). *Glory bound: Black athletes in a White America.* Syracuse University Press.

Wolbring, G. (2012). Expanding ableism: Taking down the ghettoization of impact of disability studies scholars. *Societies, 2*, 75-83. https://doi.org/10.3390/soc2030075

World Atlas. (2021). *The most popular sports in the world.* www.worldatlas.com/articles/what-are-the-most-popular-sports-in-the-world.html

Yanus, A.B., & O'Connor, K. (2016). To comply or not to comply: Evaluating compliance with Title IX of the Educational Amendments of 1972. *Journal of Women, Politics & Policy, 37*(3), 341-358. https://doi.org/10.1080/1554477X.2016.1188601

Chapter 17

Balyi, I., Way, R., & Higgs, C. (2013). *Long-term athlete development.* Human Kinetics.

Barnett, L.M., Ridgers, N.D., & Salmon, J. (2015). Associations between young children's perceived and actual ball skill competence and physical activity. *Journal of Science and Medicine in Sport, 18*, 167-171. https://doi.org/10.1016/j.jsams.2014.03.001

Bergeron, M.F., Mountjoy, M., Armstrong, N., Chia, M., Côté, J., Emery, C.A., . . . & Engebretsen, L. (2015). International Olympic Committee consensus statement on youth athletic development. *British Journal of Sports Medicine, 49*(13), 843-851. http://dx.doi.org/10.1136/bjsports-2015-094962

Bloom, B.S. (Ed.). (1985). *Developing talent in young people.* Ballantine.

Clark, J.E. (2007). On the problem of motor skill development. *Journal of Physical Education, Recreation and Dance, 78*(5), 39-44. https://doi.org/10.1080/07303084.2007.10598023

Clark, J.E., & Metcalf, J.M. (2002). The mountain of motor development: A metaphor. In J.E. Clark & J.H. Humphrey (Eds.), *Motor development: Research and reviews* (Vol. 2, pp. 163-190). National Association for Sport and Physical Education.

Côté, J. (1999). The influence of the family in the development of talent in sport. *Sport Psychologist, 13*, 395-417. https://doi.org/ 10.1123/tsp.13.4.395

Côté, J., Baker, J., & Abernethy, B. (2003). From play to practice: A developmental framework for acquisition of expertise in team sports. In J.L. Starkes & K.A. Ericsson (Eds.), *Expert performance in sports* (pp. 89-113). Human Kinetics.

Coté, J., Baker, J., & Abernethy, B. (2007). Practice and play in the development of sport expertise. In R. Eklund & G. Tenenbaum (Eds.), *Handbook of sport psychology* (3rd ed. pp. 184-202). Wiley.

Coté, J., Lidor, R., & Hackfort, D. (2009). ISSP position stand: To sample or to specialize? Seven postulates about youth sport activities that lead to continued participation and elite performance. *International Journal of Sport and Exercise Physiology, 9*, 7-17. https://doi.org/10.1080/161219 7X.2009.9671889

De Meester, A., Stodden, D., Goodway, J., True, L., Brian, A., Ferkel, R., & Haerens, L. (2018). Identifying a motor proficiency barrier for meeting physical activity guidelines in children. *Journal of science and medicine in sport, 21*(1), 58-62. https://doi.org/10.1016/j.jsams.2017.05.007

Drost, D.K., Brown, K., Wirth, C.K., & Greska, E.K. (2015). Teaching elementary-age youth catching skills using theoretically based motor-development strategies. *Journal of Physical Education, Recreation, and Dance, 86*(1), 30-35. https://doi.org/10.1080/07303084.2014.978420

Gallahue, D.L., Ozmun, J.C., & Goodway, J.D. (2012). *Understanding motor development: Infants, children, adolescents and adults* (7th ed.). McGraw-Hill.

Goncalves, C.E.B., Rama, L.M.L., & Figueiredo, A.B. (2012). Talent identification and specialization in sport: An overview of some unanswered questions. *International Journal of Sports Physiology and Performance, 7*, 390-393. https://doi.org/10.1123/ijspp.7.4.390

Goodway, J.D., Ozmun, J.C., & Gallahue, D.L. (2012). Motor development in young children. In O. Saracho & B. Spodek (Eds.), *Handbook of research on the education of young children*. Routledge.

Goodway, J.D., & Robinson, L.E. (2015). Developmental trajectories in early sport specialization: A case for early sampling from a physical growth and motor development perspective. *Kinesiology Reviews, 4*(3), 267-278. https://doi.org/10.1123/kr.2015-0028

Gulbin, J.P., Croser, M.J., Morley, E.J., & Weissensteiner, J.R. (2013). An integrated framework for the optimization of sport and athlete development: A practitioner approach. *Journal of Sport Sciences, 31*(12), 1319-1331. http://dx.doi.org/10.1080/02640414.2013.781661

Harter, S. (1999). *The construction of self: A developmental perspective*. Guilford.

Holfelder, B., & Schott, N. (2014). Relationship of fundamental movement skills and physical activity in children and adolescents: A systematic review. *Psychology of Sport and Exercise, 15* 382-391. https://doi.org/10.1016/j.psychsport.2014.03.005

Janelle, C.M., & Hillman, C.H. (2003). Expert performance in sport: Current perspectives and critical issues. In J.L. Starkes & K.A. Ericsson (Eds.), *Expert performance in sports* (pp. 19-47). Human Kinetics.

Johnston, K., Wattie, N., Schorer, J., & Baker, J. (2018). Talent identification in sport: A systematic review. *Sports Medicine, 48*, 97-109. https://doi.org/10.1007/s40279-017-0803-2

Lloyd, M., Saunders, T.J., Bremer, E., & Tremblay, M.S. (2014). Long-term importance of fundamental motor skills: A 20-year follow-up study. *Adapted Physical Activity Quarterly, 31*, 67-78. https://doi.org/10.1123/apaq:2013-0048

Lubans, D.R., Morgan, P.J., Cliff, D.P., Barnett, L.M., & Okely, A.D. (2010). Fundamental movement skills in children and adolescents: Review of associated health benefits. *Sports Medicine, 40*, 1019-1035. https://doi.org/10.2165/11536850-000000000-00000

Newell, K. (1984). Physical constraints to development of motor skills. In J. Thomas (Ed.), *Motor development during preschool and elementary years* (pp. 105-120). Burgess.

Newell, K. (1986). Constraints on the development of coordination. In M.G. Wade & H.T. Whiting (Eds.), *Motor development in children: Aspects of coordination and control* (pp. 341-360). Nijhoff.

Newell, K.M. (2020). What are fundamental motor skills and what is fundamental about them? *Journal of Motor Learning and Development, 8*, 280-314. https://doi.org/10.1123/jmld.2020-0013

Patatas, J.M., De Bosscher, V., Derom, I., & Winckler, C. (2020). Stakeholders' perceptions of athletic career pathways in Paralympic sport: From participation to excellence. *Sport in Society*. https://doi.org/10.1080/17430437.2020.1789104

Robinson, L.E. (2010). The relationship between perceived physical competence and fundamental motor skills in preschool children. *Child: Care, Health, and Development, 37*, 589-596. https://doi.org/ 10.1111/j.1365-2214.2010.01187.x

Robinson, L.E., Stodden, D.F., Barnett, L.M., Lopes, V.P., Logan, S.W., Rodrigues, L.P., & D'Hondt, E. (2015). Motor competence and its effect on positive developmental trajectories of health. *Sports Medicine, 45*(9), 1273–1284. https://doi.org/10.1007/s40279-015-0351-6

Seefeldt, V. (1980). Developmental motor patterns: Implications for elementary school physical education. In C. Nadeau, W. Holliwell, K. Newell, & G. Roberts (Eds.), *Psychology of motor behavior and sport* (pp. 314-323). Human Kinetics.

Stodden, D.F., Gao, Z., Goodway, J.D., & Langendorfer, S.J. (2014). Dynamic relationships between motor skill competence and health-related fitness in youth. *Pediatric Exercise Science, 26*, 231-241. https://doi.org/ 10.1123/pes.2013-0027

Stodden, D.F., & Goodway, J.D (2007). The dynamic association between motor skill development and physical activity. *Journal of Physical Education, Recreation and Dance, 78*, 33-49. https://doi.org/10.1080/07303084.2007.10598077

Stodden, D.F., Goodway, J.D., Langendorfer, S.J., Roberton, M.A., Rudisill, M.E., Garcia, C., & Garcia, L.E. (2008). A developmental perspective on the role of motor skill competence in physical activity: An emergent relationship. *Quest, 60*, 290-306. https://doi.org/10.1080/00336297.2008.10483582

Stodden, D., Ture, L.K., Langendorfer, S.J., & Gao, Z. (2013). Associations among selected motor skills and health-related fitness: Indirect evidence for Seefeldt's proficiency barrier in young adults. *Research Quarterly for Exercise and Sport, 84*, 397-403. https://doi.org/10.1080/02701367.2013.814910

Wall, A.E., Reid, G., & Harvey, W.J. (2007). Interface of the KB and ETA approaches. In W.E. Davis & G.D. Broadhead (Eds.), *Ecological task analysis and movement* (pp. 259-277). Human Kinetics.

Weiss, M.R., & Williams, L. (2004). The why of youth sport involvement: A developmental perspective on motivational processes. In M. R. Weiss (Ed.), *Developmental sport and exercise psychology: A lifespan perspective* (pp. 223–268). Fitness Information Technology.

Chapter 18

Adams, J.A. (1971). A closed-loop theory of motor learning. *Journal of Motor Behavior, 3,* 111-150.

Alanko, T., Karhula, M., Kröger, T., Piirainen, A., & Nikander, R. (2019). Rehabilitees perspective on goal setting in rehabilitation–a phenomenological approach. *Disability and Rehabilitation, 41*(19), 2280-2288.

Andrieux, M., & Proteau, L. (2013). Observation learning of a motor task: Who and when? *Experimental Brain Research, 229,* 125-137.

Andrieux, M., & Proteau, L. (2014). Mixed observation favors motor learning through better estimation of the model's performance. *Experimental Brain Research, 232,* 3121-3132.

Ashford, K., Bennett, S.J., & Davids, K. (2006). Observational modeling effects for movement dynamics and movement outcome measures across differing task constraints: A meta-analysis. *Journal of Motor Behavior, 38,* 185-205.

Ashford, K., Davids, K., & Bennett, S.J. (2007). Developmental effects influencing observational modeling: A meta-analysis. *Journal of Sports Sciences, 25,* 547-558.

Avila, L.T.G., Chiviacowsky, S., & Wulf, G. (2012). Positive social-comparative feedback enhances motor learning in children. *Psychology of Sport and Exercise, 13,* 849-853.

Bandura, A. (1986). *Social foundations of thought and action: A social cognitive theory.* Prentice Hall.

Bandura, A. (1997). *Self-efficacy: The exercise of control.* Freeman.

Bayón, C., Martín-Lorenzo, T., Moral-Saiz, B., Ramírez, Ó., Pérez-Somarriba, Á., Lerma-Lara, S., . . . & Rocon, E. (2018). A robot-based gait training therapy for pediatric population with cerebral palsy: goal setting, proposal and preliminary clinical implementation. *Journal of neuroengineering and rehabilitation, 15*(1), 1-15.

Blandin, Y., & Proteau, L. (2000). On the cognitive basis of observational learning: Development of mechanisms for the detection and correction of errors. *Quarterly Journal of Experimental Psychology, 53A,* 846-867.

Bouffard, M., & Dunn, J.G.H. (1993). Children's self-regulated learning of movement sequences. *Research Quarterly for Exercise and Sport, 64,* 393-403.

Boyce, B.A. (1992). Effects of assigned versus participant set goals on skill acquisition and retention of a selected shooting task. *Journal of Teaching Physical Education, 11,* 220-234.

Breslin, G., Hodges, N.J., & Williams, A.M. (2009). Effect of information load and time on observational learning. *Research Quarterly for Exercise and Sport, 80,* 480-490.

Cadopi, M., Chatillon, J.F., & Baldy, R. (1995). Representation and performance: Reproduction of form and quality of movement in dance by eight- and 11-year-old novices. *British Journal of Psychology, 86,* 217-225.

Carroll, W.R., & Bandura, A. (1990). Representational guidance of action production in observational learning: A causal analysis. *Journal of Motor Behavior, 22,* 85-97.

Chiviacowsky, S., Wulf, G., & Avila, L.T.G. (2012). An external focus of attention enhances motor learning in children with intellectual disabilities. *Journal of Intellectual Disability Research, 57,* 627-634.

Darden, G.F. (1997). Demonstrating motor skills: Rethinking that expert demonstration. *Journal of Physical Education, Recreation and Dance, 68*(6), 31-35.

Domuracki, K., Wong, A., Olivieri, L., & Grierson, L.E.M. (2015). The impacts of observing flawed and flawless demonstrations on clinical skill learning. *Medical Education, 49,* 186-192.

Fagundes, J., Chen, D.D., & Laguna, P. (2013). Self-control and frequency of model presentation: Effects on learning a ballet passé relevé. *Human Movement Science, 32*(4), 847-856.

Farrow, D., & Abernethy, B. (2002). Can anticipatory skills be learned through implicit video-based perceptual training? *Journal of Sports Sciences, 20,* 471-485.

Ferrari, S.F., Borges, P.H., Teixeira, D., & Marques, P.G. (2018). Impact of verbal instruction and demonstration methods on self-efficacy and motor learning in inexperienced handball players. *Journal of Physical Education and Sport, 18*(2), 816-820.

Fitts, P., & Posner, M.I. (1967). *Human performance.* Brooks/Cole.

Gentile, A.M. (1972). A working model of skill acquisition with application to teaching. *Quest, 17,* 3-23.

Gentile, A.M. (1998). Implicit and explicit processes during acquisition of functional skills. *Scandinavian Journal of Occupational Therapy, 5,* 7-16.

Gould, D. (2006). Goal setting for peak performance. In J.M. Williams (Ed.), *Applied sport psychology: Personal growth to peak performance* (pp. 240-259). McGraw-Hill.

Gould, D., & Chung, Y. (2004). Self-regulation skills in young, middle, and older adulthood. In M. Weiss (Ed.), *Developmental sport and exercise psychology: A lifespan perspective* (pp. 383-402). Fitness Information Technology.

Gould, D., Nalepa, J., & Mignano, M. (2020). Coaching Generation Z athletes. *Journal of Applied Sport Psychology, 32*(1), 104-120.

Goulet, C., Bard, C., & Fleury, M. (1989). Expertise differences in preparing to return a tennis serve: A visual information processing approach. *Journal of Sport and Exercise Psychology, 11,* 382-398.

Gredin, V., & Williams M. (2016). The relative effectiveness of various instructional approaches during the performance and learning of motor skills. *Journal of Motor Behavior, 48,* 86-97.

Green, T.D., & Flowers, J.H. (1991). Implicit versus explicit learning processes in probabilistic, continuous fine-motor catching task. *Journal of Motor Behavior, 23,* 293-300.

Hodges, N., & Franks, I.M. (2002). Modelling coaching practice: The role and demonstration. *Journal of Sports Sciences, 20*, 793-811.

Huff, M., & Schwan, S. (2012). The verbal facilitation effect in learning to tie nautical knots. *Learning and Instruction, 22*, 376-385.

Kitsantas, A., & Zimmerman, B.J. (1998). Self-regulation of motoric learning: A strategic cycle view. *Journal of Applied Sport Psychology, 10*, 220-239.

Kolovelonis, A., Goudas, M., & Dermitzaki, I. (2011). The effect of different goals and self-recording on self-regulation of learning a motor skill in a physical education setting. *Learning and Instruction, 21*, 355-364.

Kolovelonis, A., Goudas, M., & Dermitzaki, I. (2012). The effects of self-talk and goal setting on self-regulation of learning and new motor skill in physical education. *International Journal of Sport and Exercise Psychology, 10*, 221-235.

Kyllo, L.B., & Landers, D.M. (1995). Goal setting in sport and exercise: A research synthesis to resolve the controversy. *Journal of Sport and Exercise Psychology, 17*, 117-137.

Lago-Rodriguez, A., Cheeran, B., Koch, G., Hortobagyi, T., & Fernandez-del-Olmo, M. (2014). The role of mirror neurons in observation motor learning: An integrative review. *European Journal of Human Movement, 32*, 82-103.

Lee, T.D., Chamberlin, C.J., & Hodges, N. (2001). Practice. In R.N. Singer, H.A. Hausenblas, & C.M. Janelle (Eds.), *Handbook of sport psychology* (2nd ed., pp. 115-143). Wiley.

Lee, T.D., & White, M.A. (1990). Influence of an unskilled model's practice schedule on observational learning. *Human Movement Science, 9*, 349-367.

Lefebvre, C., & Reid, G. (1998). Prediction in ball catching by children with and without a developmental coordination disorder. *Adapted Physical Activity Quarterly, 15*, 299-318.

Locke, E.A., & Latham, G.P. (1985). The application of goal setting to sports. *Sport Psychology Today, 7*, 205-222.

Magill, R., & Anderson, D. (2021). *Motor learning and control: Concepts and applications.* (12th ed.). New York, NY: McGraw-Hill.

Martens, R., Burwitz, L., & Zuckerman, J. (1976). Modeling effects on motor performance. *Research Quarterly, 47*, 277-291.

McCullagh, P., & Weiss, M.R. (2001). Modeling: Considerations for motor skill performance and psychological responses. In R.N. Singer, H.A. Hausenblas, & C.M. Janelle (Eds.), *Handbook of sport psychology* (2nd ed., pp. 205-238). Wiley.

Meaney, K.S. (1994). Developmental modeling effects on the acquisition, retention, and transfer of a novel motor task. *Research Quarterly for Exercise and Sport, 65*, 31-39.

Newell, K.M. (1981). Skill learning. In D. Holding (Ed.), *Human skills* (pp. 203-226). Wiley.

Purdy, L. (2017). *Sports coaching: The basics.* Routledge.

Ringenbach, S.D.R., & Lantero, D.A. (2005). Bimanual coordination preferences in adults with Down syndrome. *Adapted Physical Activity Quarterly, 22*, 83-98.

Rink, J. (2014). *Teaching physical education for learning* (7th ed.). New York, NY: McGraw-Hill.

Saemi, E., Porter, J., Wulf, G., Ghotbi-Varzaneh, A., & Bakhtari, S. (2013). Adopting an external focus of attention facilitates motor learning in children with attention deficit hyperactivity disorder. *Kinesiology, 45*, 179-185.

Sanchez, D.J., & Reber, P.J. (2013). Explicit pre-training does not improve implicit perceptual–motor sequence learning. *Cognition, 126*, 341-351.

Schmidt, R.A. (1975). The schema theory of discrete motor skill learning. *Psychological Review, 82*, 225-260.

Schmidt, R.A., & Lee, T.D. (2005). *Motor control and learning: A behavioral emphasis* (4th ed.). Human Kinetics.

Scully, D.M., & Newell, K.M. (1985). Observational learning and the acquisition of motor skills: Towards a visual perception perspective. *Journal of Human Movement Studies, 11*, 169-186.

Siedentop, D., & Tannehill, D. (2000). *Developing teaching skills in physical education* (4th ed.). Mountain View, CA: Mayfield.

Ste-Marie, D. M., Lelievre, N., & St. Germain, L. (2020). Revisiting the applied model for the use of observation: A review of articles spanning 2011–2018. *Research Quarterly for Exercise and Sport, 91*(4), 594-617.

Ste-Marie, D.M., Law, B., Rymal, A.M., Jenny, O., Hall, C., & McCullagh, P. (2012). Observation interventions for motor learning and performance: An applied model for the use of observations. *International Review of Sport and Exercise Psychology, 5*, 145-176.

Ste-Marie, D.M., Vertes, K., Rymal, A.M., & Martini, R. (2011). Feedforward self-modeling enhances skill acquisition in children learning trampoline skills. *Frontiers in Psychology, 2*, 155.

Weeks, D.L. (1992). A comparison of modeling modalities in the observational learning of an externally paced skill. *Research Quarterly for Exercise and Sport, 63*, 373-380.

Weeks, D.L., & Anderson, L.P. (2000). The interaction of observational learning with overt practice: Effects on motor learning. *Acta Psychologica, 104*, 259-271.

Weinberg, R.S., & Gould, D. (2011). *Foundations of sport and exercise psychology* (5th ed.). Human Kinetics.

Weiss, M.R. (1983). Modeling and motor performance: A developmental perspective. *Research Quarterly for Exercise and Sport, 54*, 190-197.

Weiss, M.R., Ebbeck, V., & Wiese-Bjornstal, D.M. (1993). Developmental and psychological factors related to children's observational learning of physical skills. *Pediatric Exercise Science, 5*, 301-317.

Weiss, M.R., McCullagh, P., Smith, A.L., & Berlant, A.R. (1998). Observational learning and the fearful child: Influence of peer models on swimming skill performance and psychological responses. *Research Quarterly for Exercise and Sport, 69*, 380-394.

West, A.L., Edner, N.C., & Hastings, E.C. (2013). Linking goals and aging. In E.A. Locke & G.P. Latham (Eds.), *New developments in goal setting and performance* (pp. 439-459). Routledge.

Wiese-Bjornstal, D.M., & Weiss, M.R. (1992). Modeling effects on children's form kinematics, performance outcome, and cognitive recognition of a sport skill: An integrated perspective. *Research Quarterly for Exercise and Sport, 63*, 67-75.

Williams, A.M., & Davids, K. (1998). Visual search strategy, selective attention, and expertise in soccer. *Research Quarterly for Exercise and Sport, 69*, 127-135.

Williams, A.M., & Hodges, N.J. (2005). Practice, instruction and skill acquisition in soccer: Challenging tradition. *Journal of Sports Sciences, 23*, 637-650.

Williams, A.M., Ward, P., Smeeton, N.J., & Allen, D. (2004). Developing anticipation skills in tennis using on-court instruction: Perception versus perception and action. *Journal of Applied Sport Psychology, 16*, 350-360.

Williams, J.G. (1989). Visual demonstrations and movement production: Effects of timing variations in a model's action. *Perceptual and Motor Skills, 68*, 891-896.

Wrisberg, C.A., & Pein, R.L. (2002). Note of learners' control of the frequency of model presentation during skill acquisition. *Perceptual and Motor Skills, 94*, 792-794.

Wulf, G. (2013). Attention focus and motor learning: A review of 15 years. *International Review of Sport and Exercise Psychology, 6*, 77-104.

Wulf, G., Chiviacowsky, S., Schiller, E., & Avila, L.T.G. (2010). Frequent external-focus feedback enhances motor learning. *Frontiers in Psychology, 1*, 190.

Wulf, G., Raupach, M., & Pfeiffer, F. (2005). Self-controlled observational practice enhances learning. *Research Quarterly for Exercise and Sport, 76*, 107-111.

Wulf, G., & Weigelt, C. (1997). Instructions about physical principles in learning a complex skill: To tell or not to tell . . . *Research Quarterly for Exercise and Sport, 68*, 362-367.

Zimmerman, B.J. (2000). Attaining self-regulation: A social cognitive perspective. In M. Boekaerts, P.R. Pintrich, & M. Zeidner (Eds.), *Handbook of self-regulation* (pp. 13-39). Academic Press.

Zimmerman, B.J., & Kitsantas, A. (1996). Self-regulated learning of a motoric skill: The role of goal setting and self-monitoring. *Journal of Applied Sport Psychology, 8*, 60-75.

Zimmerman, B.J., & Kitsantas, A. (1997). Developmental phases in self-regulation: Shifting from process goals to outcome goals. *Journal of Educational Psychology, 89*, 29-36.

Chapter 19

Apolinario-Souza, T., de Paula Ferreira, B., de Oliveira, J.R.V., de Holanda Marinho Nogueira, N.G., Pinto, J.A.R., & Lage, G.M. (2020). Mental practice is associated with learning the relative timing dimension of a task. *Journal of Motor Behavior, 53*(6), 727-736. https://doi-org.brockport.idm.oclc.org/10.1080/00222895.2020.1852156

Asa, S.K.de P., Melo, M.C.S., & Piemonte, M.E.P. (2014). Effects of mental and physical practice on a finger opposition task among children. *Research Quarterly for Exercise and Sport, 85*, 308-315.

Bach, P., Allami, B.K., Tucker, M., & Ellis, R. (2014). Planning-related motor processes underlie mental practice and imitation learning. *Journal of Experimental Psychology: General, 143*, 1277-1294.

Baddeley, A.D., & Longman, D.J.A. (1978). The influence of length and frequency of training session on the rate of learning to type. *Ergonomics, 21*(8), 627-635. http://dx.doi.org/10.1080/00140137808931764

Bernardi, N.F., De Buglio, M., Trimarchi, P.D., Chielli, A., & Bricolo, E. (2013). Mental practice promotes motor anticipation: Evidence from skilled music performance. *Frontiers in Human Neuroscience, 7*, 451.

Bortoli, L., Spagolla, G., & Robazza, C. (2001). Variability effects on retention of a motor skill in elementary school children. *Perceptual and Motor Skills, 93*, 51-63.

Brady, F. (1998). A theoretical and empirical review of the contextual interference effect and the learning of motor skills. *Quest, 50*, 266-293.

Brady, F. (2004). Contextual interference: A meta-analytic study. *Perceptual and Motor Skills, 99*, 116-126.

Breslin, G., Hodges, N.J., Steenson, A., & Williams, A.M. (2012). Constant or variable practice: Recreating the especial skill effect. *Acta Psychologica, 140*, 154-157.

Buszard, T., Reid, M., Krause, L., Kovalchik, S., & Farrow, D. (2017). Quantifying contextual interference and its effect on skill transfer in skilled youth tennis players. *Frontiers in Psychology, 8*, 1931.

Chan, J.S.Y., Luo, Y., Yan, J.H., Cai, L., & Peng, K. (2015). Children's age modulates the effect of part and whole practice in motor learning. *Human Movement Science, 42*, 261-272.

Cheong, J.P.G., Lay, B., Grove, J.L., Medic, N., & Razman, R. (2012). Practicing field hockey skills along the contextual interference continuum: A comparison of five practice schedules. *Journal of Sports Science and Medicine, 11*, 304-311.

Chua, L.K., Dimapilis, M.K., Iwatsuki, T., Abdollahipour, R., Lewthwaite, R., & Wulf, G. (2019). Practice variability promotes an external focus of attention and enhances motor skill learning. *Human Movement Science, 64*, 307-319.

Cocks, M., Moulton, C.-A., Luu, S., & Cil, T. (2014). What surgeons can learn from athletes: Mental practice in sports and surgery. *Journal of Surgical Education, 7*, 262-269.

Cumming, J. (2008). Investigating the relationship between exercise imagery, leisure time exercise behaviour, and exercise self-efficacy. *Journal of Applied Sport Psychology, 20*, 184-198.

Cumming, J., & Williams, S.E. (2012). *The role of imagery in performance.* In S. Murphy (Ed), Handbook of sport and performance psychology (pp. 213-232). Oxford University Press.

Cumming, J., & Williams, S. E. (2013). Introducing the revised applied model of deliberate imagery use for sport, dance, exercise, and rehabilitation. *Movement & Sport Sciences, 82*, 69-81. https://doi.org/10.1051/sm/2013098

Davids, K., Button, C., & Bennett, S. (2008). *Dynamics of skill acquisition: A constraints-led approach.* Human Kinetics.

Deakin, J.M., & Cobley, S. (2003). A search for deliberate practice: An examination of the practice environments in figure skating and volleyball. In J.L. Starkes & K.A. Ericsson (Eds.), *Expert performance in sports* (pp. 115-135). Human Kinetics.

Del Rey, P., Whitehurst, M., & Wood, J. (1983). Effects of experience and contextual interference on learning and transfer. *Perceptual and Motor Skills, 56,* 581-582.

de Paula Ferreira, B., de Holanda Marinho Nogueira, N., Lage, G.M., de Oliveira, J.R.V., & Apolinario-Souza, T. (2021). The role of mental practice in decreasing forgetting after practicing a gymnastics motor skill. *Science of Gymnastics Journal, 13*(1), 119-126.

Edwards, J.M., Elliott, D., & Lee, T.D. (1986). Contextual interference effects during skill acquisition and transfer in Down's syndrome adolescents. *Adapted Physical Activity Quarterly, 3*(3), 250-258. https://doi.org/10.1123/apaq.3.3.250

Ericsson, K.A., & Harwell, K.W. (2019). Deliberate practice and proposed limits on the effects of practice on the acquisition of expert performance: Why the original definition matters and recommendations for future research. *Frontiers in Psychology, 10,* 2396.

Farrow, D., & Maschette, W. (1997). The effects of contextual interference on children learning forehand tennis groundstrokes. *Journal of Human Movement Studies 33,* 47-67.

Feghhi, I., Abdoli, B., & Valizadeh, R. (2011). Compare contextual interference effect and practice specificity in learning basketball free throw. *Procedia-Social and Behavioral Sciences, 15,* 2176-2180.

Gabbard, C. (2009). Studying action representation in children via motor imagery. *Brain and Cognition, 71,* 234-239.

Gentile, A.M. (1972). A working model of skill acquisition with application to teaching. *Quest, 17,* 3-23.

Gentile, A.M. (2000). Skill acquisition: Action, movement and neuromotor processes. In J.H. Carr & R.B. Shepherd (Eds.), *Movement science: Foundations for physical therapy in rehabilitation* (2nd ed., pp. 111-187). Aspen.

Gerson, R.F., & Thomas, J.R. (1977). Schema theory and practice variability within a neo-Piagetian framework. *Journal of Motor Behavior, 2,* 127-134.

Hall, C.R., Mack, D.E., Paivio, A., & Hausenblas, H.A. (1998). Imagery use by athletes: Development of the Sport Imagery Questionnaires. *International Journal of Sport Psychology, 29,* 73-89.

Herbert, E.P., Landin, D., & Solmon, M.A. (1996). Practice schedule effects on the performance and learning of low- and high-skilled students: An applied study. *Research Quarterly for Exercise and Sport, 67,* 52-58.

Hird, J.S., Landers, D.M., Thomas, J.R., & Horan, J.J. (1991). Physical practice is superior to mental practice in enhancing cognitive and motor task performance. *Journal of Sport and Exercise Psychology, 13,* 281-293.

Holmes, P.S., & Collins, D.J. (2001). The PETTLEP approach to motor imagery: A functional equivalence model for sport psychologists. *Journal of Applied Sport Psychology, 13,* 60-83.

James, E.G., & Conatser, P. (2014). Effects of practice variability on unimanual arm rotation. *Journal of Motor Behavior, 46,* 203-210.

Jarus, T., & Goverover, Y. (1999). Effects of contextual interference and age on acquisition, retention, and transfer of motor skill. *Perceptual and Motor Skills, 88,* 437-447.

Jeannerod, M. (1999). To act or not to act: Perspectives on the representation of actions. *Quarterly Journal of Experimental Psychology, 52A*(1), 1-29.

Keetch, K.M., & Lee, T.D. (2007). The effect of self-regulated and experimenter-imposed practice schedules on motor learning for tasks of varying difficulty. *Research Quarterly for Exercise and Sport, 78,* 476-486.

Kerr, R., & Booth, B. (1978). Specific and varied practice of motor skill. *Perceptual and Motor Skills, 46,* 395-401.

King, A.C., & Newell, K.M. (2013). The learning of isometric force time scales is differently influenced by constant and variable practice. *Experimental Brain Research, 227,* 149.

Kolh, R.M., Ellis, S.D., & Roenker, D.L. (1992). Alternating actual and imagery practice: Preliminary theoretical considerations. *Research Quarterly for Exercise and Sport, 63,* 162-170.

Kwon, Y.H., Kwon, J.W., & Lee, M.H. (2015). Effectiveness of motor sequential learning according to practice sessions in healthy adults: Distributed practice versus massed practice. *Journal of Physical Therapy Science, 27,* 769-772.

Lee, T.D. (2012). Contextual interference: Generalizability and limitations. In N. Hodges & M.A. Williams (Eds.), *Skill acquisition in sport: Research, theory and practice* (pp. 79-93). Routledge.

Lee, T.D., & Carnahan, H. (2021). Motor learning: Reflections on the past 40 years of research. *Kinesiology Review, 10,* 274-282. https://doi.org/10.1123/kr.2021-0018

Lee, T.D., Chamberlin, C.J., & Hodges, N. (2001). Practice. In R.N. Singer, H.A. Hausenblas, & C.M. Janelle (Eds.), *Handbook of sport psychology* (2nd ed., pp. 115-143). Wiley.

Lee, T.D., & Magill, R.A. (1985). Can forgetting facilitate skill acquisition? In D. Goodman, R.B. Wilberg, & I.M. Franks (Eds.), *Differing perspectives on memory, learning and control* (pp. 3-22). North-Holland.

Lee, T.D., & White, M.A. (1990). Influence of an unskilled model's practice schedule on observational learning. *Human Movement Science, 9,* 349-367.

Lin, C.-H.J., Wu, A.D., Udompholkul, P., & Knowlton, B.J. (2010). Contextual interference effects in sequence learning for young and older adults. *Psychology and Aging, 25,* 929-939.

Macnamara, B.N., & Maitra, M. (2019). The role of deliberate practice in expert performance: Revisiting Ericsson, Krampe & Tesch-Römer (1993). *Royal Society Open Science, 6*(8), 190327.

Magill, R.A. (2017). *Motor learning and control: Concepts and applications* (11th ed.). McGraw-Hill.

Magill, R.A., & Anderson, D. (2013). *Motor learning and control: Concepts and applications* (10th ed.). McGraw-Hill.

Mané, A.M., Adams, J.A., & Donchin, E. (1989). Adaptive and part-whole training in the acquisition of a complex perceptual-motor skill. *Acta Psychologica, 71*(1-3), 179-196. https://doi.org/10.1016/0001-6918(89)90008-5

Martin, K.A., Moritz, S.A., & Hall, C.R. (1999). Imagery use in sport: A literature review and applied model. *Sport Psychologist, 13*, 245-268.

Moradi, J., Movahedi, A., & Salehi, H. (2014). Specificity of learning a sport skill to the visual condition of acquisition. *Journal of Motor Behavior, 46*, 17-23.

Naylor, J.C., & Briggs, G.E. (1963). Effects of task complexity and task organization on the relative efficiency of part and whole training methods. *Journal of Experimental Psychology, 65*, 217-224.

Newell, K.M., & McDonald, P.V. (1992). Searching for solutions to the coordination function: Learning as exploratory behavior. *Advances in Psychology, 87*, 517-532.

Nilsen, D.M., Gillen, G., & Gordon, A.M. (2010). Use of mental practice to improve upper-limb recovery after stroke: A systematic review. *The American Journal of Occupational Therapy, 64*, 695-708.

Ollis, S., Button, C., & Fairweather, M. (2005). The influence of professional expertise and task complexity upon the potency of the contextual interference effect. *Acta Psychologica, 118*(3), 229-244.

Pacheco, M.M., & Newell, K.M. (2018). Learning a specific, individual and generalizable coordination function: Evaluating the variability of practice hypothesis in motor learning. *Experimental Brain Research, 236*(12), 3307-3318.

Paivio, A. (1986). *Mental representations: A dual coding approach.* Oxford University Press.

Pease, D.G., & Pupnow, A.A. (1983). Effects of varying force production in practice schedules of children learning a discrete motor task. *Perceptual and Motor Skills, 57*, 275-282.

Pigott, R.E., & Shapiro, D.C. (1984). Motor schema: The structure of the variability session. *Research Quarterly for Exercise and Sport, 55*, 41-45.

Pollock, B.J., & Lee, T.D. (1997). Dissociated contextual interference effects in children and adults. *Perceptual and Motor Skills, 84*, 851-858.

Proteau, L. (1992). On the specificity of learning and the role of visual information for movement control. In L. Proteau & D. Elliott (Eds.), *Vision and motor control* (pp. 67-103). North Holland.

Proteau, L., Marteniuk, R.G., Girourd, Y., & Dugas, C. (1987). On the type of information used to control and learn an aiming movement after moderate and extensive training. *Human Movement Science, 6*, 181-199.

Ranganathan, R., & Newell, K.M. (2012). Changing up the routine: Intervention-induced variability in motor learning. *Exercise and Sport Sciences Reviews, 41*, 64-70.

Robertson, S.D., Tremblay, L., Anson, J.G., & Elliott, D. (2002). Learning to cross a balance beam: Implications for teachers, coaches and therapists. In K. Davids, G. Savelsbergh, S. Bennett, & J. van der Kamps (Eds.), *Dynamic interception actions in sport: Current research and practical applications* (pp. 109-125). Taylor and Francis.

Robin, N., Dominique, L., Toussaint, L., Blandin, Y., Guillot, A., & Le Her, M. (2007). Effects of motor imagery training on service return accuracy in tennis: The role of imagery ability. *International Journal of Sport and Exercise Psychology, 2*, 175-186.

Salmon, J., Hall, C., & Haslam, I.R. (1994). The use of imagery by soccer players. *Journal of Applied Sport Psychology, 6*, 116-133.

Schmidt, R.A. (1975). A schema theory of discrete motor skill learning. *Psychological Review, 82*(4), 225–260. https://doi.org/10.1037/h0076770

Schmidt, R.A., & Lee, T.D. (2005). *Motor control and learning: A behavioral emphasis* (4th ed.). Human Kinetics.

Schmidt, R.A., & Wrisberg, C.A. (2008). *Motor learning and performance: A situation-based learning approach* (4th ed.). Human Kinetics.

Shea, J.B., & Morgan, R.L. (1979). Contextual interference effects on the acquisition, retention, and transfer of a motor skill. *Journal of Experimental Psychology: Human Learning and Memory, 5*, 179-187.

Simon, D.A., & Bjork, R.A. (2001). Metacognition in motor learning. *Journal of Experimental Psychology: Learning, Memory, and Cognition, 27*(4), 907-912. https://doi.org/10.1037/0278-7393.27.4.907

Son, L.K., & Simon, D.A. (2012). Distributed learning: Data, metacognition, and educational implications. *Educational Psychology Review, 24*(3), 379-399. http://dx.doi.org/10.1007/s10648-012-9206-y

Soucy, M.-C., & Proteau, L. (2001). Development of multiple movement representations with practice: Specificity versus flexibility. *Journal of Motor Behavior, 33*, 243-254.

Spruit, E.N., Band, G.P.H., & Hamming, J.F. (2015). Increasing efficiency of surgical training: Effects of spacing practice on skill acquisition and retention in laparoscopy training. *Surgical Endoscopy, 29*, 2235-2243.

Ste-Marie, D.M., Clark, S.E., Findlay, L.C., & Latimer, A.E. (2004). High levels of contextual interference influence handwriting skill writing acquisition. *Journal of Motor Behavior, 36*, 115-126.

Takazono, P.S., & Teixeira, L.A. (2018). Effect of association of imagery and physical practice on children's motor learning. *Brazilian Journal of Kinanthropometry & Human Performance, 20*(5), 363-372.

Toth, A.J., McNeill, E., Hayes, K., Moran, A.P., & Campbell, M. (2020). Does mental practice still enhance performance? A 24 year follow-up and meta-analytic replication extension. *Psychology of Sport & Exercise, 48*. https://doi.org/10.1016/j.psychsport.2020.101672

Tremblay, L., & Proteau, L. (1998). Specificity of practice: The case of powerlifting. *Research Quarterly for Exercise and Sport, 69*, 284-289.

Tremblay, L., & Proteau, L. (2001). Specificity of practice in a ball interception task. *Canadian Journal of Experimental Psychology, 55*, 207-218.

Vera, J.G., Alvarez, J.C., & Medina, M.M. (2008). Effects of different practice conditions on acquisition, retention, and transfer of soccer skills by 9-year-old school children. *Perceptual and Motor Skills, 106*, 447-460.

Wrisberg, C.A., & Mead, B.J. (1981). Anticipation of coincidence in children: A test of schema theory. *Perceptual and Motor Skills, 52*, 599-606.

Wulf, G. (1991). The effect of type of practice on motor learning in children. *Applied Cognitive Psychology, 5*, 123-134.

Wulf, G., & Schimdt, R.A. (1994). Feedback-induced variability and the learning of generalized motor programs. *Journal of Motor Behavior, 26*, 348-361.

Yan, J.H., Thomas, J.R., & Thomas, K.T. (1998). Children's age moderates the effect of practice variability: A quantitative review. *Research Quarterly for Exercise and Sport, 69*, 210-215.

Yao, W.X., & DeSola, W. (2009). Variable practice versus constant practice in the acquisition of wheelchair propulsive speeds. *Perceptual and Motor Skills, 109*, 133-139.

Zetou, E., Papadakis, L., Vernadakis, N., Derri, V., Bebetsos, E., & Filippou, F. (2014). The effect of variable and stable practice on performance and learning the header skill of young athletes in soccer. *Procedia-Social and Behavioral Sciences, 152*, 824-829.

Chapter 20

Agethan, M., & Krause, D. (2016). Effects of bandwidth feedback on the automatization of an arm movement sequence. *Human Movement Science, 45*, 71-83.

Anderson, D.L., Magill, R.A., Sekiya, H., & Ryan, G. (2005). Support for an explanation of the guidance effect in motor skill learning. *Journal of Motor Behavior, 37*(3), 231-238.

Barclay, C.R., & Newell, K.M. (1980). Children's processing of information in motor skill acquisition. *Journal of Experimental Child Psychology, 30*, 98-108.

Bilodeau, E.A., & Bilodeau, I.M. (1958). Variable frequency of knowledge of results and the learning of a simple skill. *Journal of Experimental Psychology, 55*, 379-383.

Bilodeau, I.M. (1966). Information feedback. In E.A. Bilodeau (Ed.), *Acquisition of skill* (pp. 225-296). Academic Press.

Brucker, B.S., & Bulaeva, N.V. (1996). Biofeedback effect on electromyographic responses in patients with spinal cord injury. *Archives of Physical Medicine and Rehabilitation, 77*, 133-137.

Carter, M.J., Carlsen, A.N., & Ste-Marie, D.M. (2014). Self-controlled feedback is effective if it is based on the learner's performance: A replication and extension of Chiviacowsky and Wulf (2005). *Frontiers in Psychology, 5*, Article 1325, 1-10.

Chiviacowsky, S., & Drews, R. (2014). Effects of generic versus non-generic feedback on motor learning in children. *PLOS One, 9*(2), e88989.

Chiviacowsky, S., & Lessa, H.T. (2017). Choices over feedback enhance motor learning in older adults. *Journal of Motor Learning and Development, 5*(2), 304-318.

Chiviacowsky, S., & Wulf, G. (2006). Self-controlled feedback: Does it enhance learning because performers get feedback when they need it? *Research Quarterly for Exercise and Sport, 73*, 408-415.

Chiviacowsky, S., & Wulf, G. (2007). Feedback after good trials enhances learning. *Research Quarterly for Exercise and Sport, 78*, 40-47.

Chiviacowsky, S., Wulf, G., Laroque de Medeiros, F., Kaefer, A., & Wally, R. (2008). Self-controlled feedback in 10-year-old children: Higher feedback frequencies enhance learning. *Research Quarterly for Exercise and Sport, 79*(1), 122-127.

Coker, C.A. (2009). *Motor learning and control for practitioners* (2nd ed.). Holcomb Hathaway.

Darden, G.F. (1999). Videotape feedback for student learning and performance: A learning stages approach. *Journal of Physical Education, Recreation and Dance, 70*(9), 40-45, 62.

Dozza, M., Chiari, L., Peterka, R.J., Wall, C., &. Horak, F.B. (2011). What is the most effective type of audio-biofeedback for postural motor learning? *Gait & Posture, 34*(3), 313-319.

Fischman, M.F., & Oxendine, J.B. (2001). Motor skill learning for effective coaching and performance. In J.M. Williams (Ed.), *Applied sport psychology: Personal growth to peak performance* (pp. 13-28). Mayfield.

Fishman, S., & Tobey, C. (1978). Augmented feedback. In W.G. Anderson & G.T. Barrette (Eds.), What's going on in gym: Descriptive studies of physical education classes [Monograph]. *Motor Skills: Theory Into Practice, 1*, 51-62.

Flinn, N.A., & Radomski, M.V. (2002). Learning. In C.A. Trombly & M.V. Radomski (Eds.), *Occupational therapy for physical dysfunction* (5th ed., pp. 283-297). Lippincott Williams & Wilkins.

Gallagher, J.D., & Thomas, J.R. (1980). Effects of varying post-KR intervals upon children's motor performance. *Journal of Motor Behavior, 12*, 41-46.

Grand, K.F., Bruzi, A.T., Dyke, F.B., Godwin, M.M., Leiker, A.M., Thompson, A.G., . . . Miller, M.W. (2015). Why self-controlled feedback enhances motor learning: Answers from electroencephalography and indices of motivation. *Human Movement Science, 43*, 23-32.

Harvey, P.D. (2019). Domains of cognition and their assessment. *Dialogues in clinical neuroscience, 21*(3), 227.

Intiso, D., Santilli, V., Grasso, M.G., Rossi, R., & Caruso, I. (1994). Rehabilitation of walking with electromyographic biofeedback in drop-foot after stroke. *Stroke, 25*, 1189-1192.

Jarodzka, H., Van Gog, T., Dorr, M., Scheiter, K., & Gerjets, P. (2013). Learning to see: Guiding students' attention via a model's eye movements fosters learning. *Learning and Instruction, 25*, 62-70.

Kernodle, M.W., & Carlton, L.G. (1992). Information feedback and the learning of multiple-degree-of-freedom activities. *Journal of Motor Behavior, 24*(2), 187-196.

Konttinen, N., Lyytinen, H., & Viitasalo, J. (1998). Rifle-balancing in precision shooting: Behavioral aspects and psychophysiological implication. *Scandinavian Journal of Medicine and Science in Sports, 8*, 78-83.

Lai, Q., & Shea, C.H. (1999). Bandwidth knowledge of results enhances generalized motor program learning. *Research Quarterly for Exercise and Sport, 70*, 79-83.

Laughlin, D.D., Fairbrother, J.T., Wrisberg, C.A., Alami, A., Fisher, L.A., & Huck, S.W. (2015). Self-control behaviors during the learning of a cascade juggling task. *Human Movement Science, 41*, 9-19.

Lee, T.D., & Carnahan, H. (1990). Bandwidth knowledge of results and motor learning. *Quarterly Journal of Experimental Psychology, 42*, 777-789.

Liu, Y., Cao, C., & Yan, J.H. (2013). Functional aging impairs the role of feedback in motor learning. *Geriatrics Gerontology International, 13*, 849-859.

Magill, R.A. (2001). Augmented feedback in motor skill acquisition. In R.N. Singer, H.A. Hausenbas, & C.M. Janelle (Eds.), *Handbook of sport psychology* (pp. 88-114). John Wiley and Sons.

Magill, R.A. (2007). *Motor learning and control: Concepts and applications* (8th ed.). McGraw-Hill.

Menickelli, J., Landin, D., Grisham, W., & Hebert, E. (2000). The effects of videotape feedback with augmented cues on the performances and thought processes of skilled gymnasts. *Journal of Sport Pedagogy, 6*, 56-72.

Mononen, K., Viitasalo, J.T., Konttinen, N., & Era, P. (2003). The effects of augmented kinematic feedback on motor skill learning in rifle shooting. *Journal of Sports Sciences, 21*, 867-876.

Newell, K.M., & Carlton, M.J. (1987). Augmented information feedback and the acquisition of isometric tasks. *Journal of Motor Behavior, 19*, 4-12.

Newell, K.M., Quinn, J.T., Jr., Sparrow, W.A., & Walter, C.B. (1983). Kinematic information feedback for learning a simple rapid response. *Human Movement Science, 2*, 255-270.

Newell, K.M., & Walter, C.B. (1981). Kinematic and kinetic parameters as information feedback in motor skill acquisition. *Journal of Human Movement Studies, 7*, 235-254.

Ong, N.T., & Hodges, N.J. (2018). Balancing our perceptions of the efficacy of success-based feedback manipulations on motor learning. *Journal of motor behavior, 50*(6), 614-630.

Pèrez, P., Liana, S., Brizuela, G., & Encarnación, A. (2009). Effects of three feedback conditions on aerobic swim speeds. *Journal of Sports Science and Medicine, 8*, 30-36.

Robert, M.T., Sambasivan, K., & Levin, M.F. (2017). Extrinsic feedback and upper limb motor skill learning in typically-developing children and children with cerebral palsy. *Restorative Neurology and Neuroscience, 35*(2), 171-184.

Rose, D.J., & Christina, R.W. (2006). *A multilevel approach to the study of motor control and learning* (2nd ed.). Pearson Benjamin Cummings.

Rucci, J.A., & Tomporowski, P.D. (2010). Three types of kinematic feedback and the execution of the hang power clean. *Journal of Strength and Conditioning Research, 24*(3), 771-778.

Sadowski, J., Mastalerz, A., & Niznikowski, T. (2013). Benefits of bandwidth feedback in learning a complex gymnastic skill. *Journal of Human Kinetics, 37*, 83-93.

Salmoni, A.W., Schmidt, R.A., & Walter, C.B. (1984). Knowledge of results and motor learning: A review and critical appraisal. *Psychological Bulletin, 95*, 355-386.

Sanli, E., Patterson, J., Bray, S., & Lee, T.D. (2013). Understanding self-controlled motor learning protocols through the self-determination theory. *Frontiers in Movement Science and Sport Psychology, 3*, 1-17.

Schwarz, M., Olson, P.R., & Andrasik, F. (2003). A historical perspective on the field of biofeedback and applied psychophysiology. *Biofeedback: A practitioner's guide* (3rd ed., pp. 3-19). Guilford.

Sharma, D.A., Chevidikuunan, M.F., Khan, F.R., & Gaowgzeh, R.A. (2016). Effectiveness of knowledge of result and knowledge of performance in the learning of a skilled motor activity by healthy young adults. *Journal of Physical Therapy Science, 28*(5), 1482-1486.

Sherwood, D.E. (1988). Effect of bandwidth knowledge of results on movement consistency. *Perceptual and Motor Skills, 66*, 535-542.

Siedentop, D., & Tannehill, D. (2000). *Developing teaching skills in physical education.* Mayfield.

Sigrist, R., Rauter, G., Riener, R., & Wolf, P. (2013). Augmented visual, auditory, haptic, and multimodal feedback in motor learning: A review. *Psychonomic Bulletin & Review, 20*, 21-53.

Souissi, M.A., Ammar, A., Trabelsi, O., Glenn, J.M., Boukhris, O., Trabelsi, K., & Souissi, N. (2021). Distance motor learning during the COVID-19 induced confinement: Video feedback with a pedagogical activity improves the snatch technique in young athletes. *International Journal of Environmental Research and Public Health, 18*(6), 3069.

Sullivan, K.J., Kantak, S.S., & Burtner, P.A. (2008). Motor learning in children: Feedback effects on skill acquisition. *Physical Therapy, 88*(6), 720-732.

Swinnen, P.S., Schmidt, R.A., Nicholson, D.E., & Shapiro, D.C. (1990). Information feedback for skill acquisition: Instantaneous knowledge of results degrades learning. *Journal of Experimental Psychology: Learning, Memory and Cognition, 16*, 706-716.

Thorndike, E.L. (1931). *Human Learning.* Century.

Tzetzis, G., Votsis, E., & Kourtessis, T. (2008). The effect of different corrective feedback methods on the outcome and self-confidence of young athletes. *Journal of Sports Science & Medicine, 7*(3), 371-378.

Weeks, D.L., & Sherwood, D.E. (1994). A comparison of knowledge of results scheduling methods for promoting motor skill acquisition and retention. *Research Quarterly for Exercise and Sport, 65*(2), 136-142.

Winstein, C.J., & Schmidt, R.A. (1990). Reduced frequency of knowledge of results enhances motor skill learning. *Journal of Experimental Psychology: Learning, Memory, and Cognition, 16*, 677-691.

Wu, W.F.W., Young, D.E., Schandler, S.L., Meir, G., Judy, R.L.M., Perez, J., & Cohen, M.J. (2011). Contextual interference and augmented feedback: Is there an additive effect for motor learning? *Human Movement Science, 30*(6), 1092-1101.

Wulf, G., Clauss, A., Shea, C.H., & Whitacre, C. (2001). Benefits of self-control in dyad practice. *Research Quarterly for Exercise and Sport, 72*, 299-303.

Wulf, G., & Lewthwaite, R. (2016). Optimizing performance through intrinsic motivation and attention for learning: The OPTIMAL theory of motor learning. *Psychonomic Bulletin & Review, 23*(5), 1382-1414.

Yan, J.H. & Dick, M.B. (2006). Practice effects on motor control in healthy seniors and patients with mild cognitive impairment or mild Alzheimer's disease. *Neuropsychology, Development, Cognition Section B Aging, Neuropsychology & Cognition, 13*, 385-410.

Young, D.E., & Schmidt, R.A. (1992). Augmented kinematic feedback for motor learning. *Journal of Motor Behavior, 24*, 261-273.

Chapter 21

Brian, A., Goodway, J.D., Logan, J.A., & Sutherland, S. (2017). SKIPing with Head Start teachers: Influence of T-SKIP on object-control skills. *Research Quarterly for Exercise and Sport, 88*(4), 479-491.

Button, C., MacLeod, M., Sanders, R., & Coleman, S. (2003). Examining movement variability in the basketball free-throw action at different levels. *Research Quarterly for Exercise and Sport, 74*(3), 257-269.

Davids, K., Button, C., & Bennett, S. (2008). *Dynamics of skill acquisition: A constraints-led approach*. Human Kinetics.

Davis, W.E., & Burton, A.W. (1991). Ecological task analysis: Translating movement behavior theory into practice. *Adapted Physical Activity Quarterly, 8*, 154-177.

Gould, D., Feltz, D., & Weiss, M.R. (1985). Motives for competing in competitive youth swimming. *International Journal of Sport Psychology, 16*, 126-140.

Kennedy, J., Missiuna, C., Pollock, N., Wu, S., Yost, J., & Campbell, W. (2018). A scoping review to explore how universal design for learning is described and implemented by rehabilitation health professionals in school settings. *Child: Care, Health and Development, 44*(5), 670-688.

Lieberman, L.J., Grenier, M., Brian, A., & Arndt, K. (2020). *Universal Design for Learning in Physical Education*. Human Kinetics.

Monsma, E.V., Taunton Miedema, S., Brian, A., & Williams, H.G. (2020). Assessment of gross motor development in preschool children. In Alfonso, Bracken, & Nagle (Eds) *Psychoeducational assessment of preschool children* (5th ed., pp. 283-319). Routledge.

Rink, J. (2014). *Teaching physical education for learning*. McGraw Hill Higher Education.

Wall, A.E., Reid, G., & Harvey, W.J. (2007). Interface of the KB and ETA approaches. In W.E. Davis & G.D. Broadhead (Eds.), *Ecological task analysis and movement* (pp. 259-277). Human Kinetics.

Weiss, M.R., & Williams, L. (2004). The why of youth sport involvement: A developmental perspective on motivational processes. In M.R. Weiss (Ed.), *Developmental sport and exercise psychology: A lifespan perspective* (pp. 223-268). Fitness Information Technology.

INDEX

Note: The italicized f and t following page numbers refer to figures and tables, respectively.

ABOUT THE AUTHORS

Pamela S. Beach, PhD, is a professor of motor behavior at State University of New York at Brockport (SUNY Brockport), where she serves as the associate director of the honors college. She is the cofounder and codirector of

Courtesy of SUNY Brockport.

the Institute of Movement Studies for Individuals with Visual Impairments (IMSVI). Dr. Beach regularly publishes and presents nationally and internationally. Her research focuses on motor competence and balance in individuals with and without sensory impairments. Dr. Beach is the author of over 65 peer-reviewed publications and has presented at over 125 national and international conferences. She has also organized the International Symposium on Physical Activity and Individuals with Visual Impairments or Deafblindness. She has authored two previous editions of the textbook *Motor Learning and Development*, published by Human Kinetics, which has been widely adopted in university courses. Dr. Beach serves as the vice president of the National Consortium for Physical Education for Individuals with Disabilities (NCPEID) and has served as chair of the National Association for Sport and Physical Education (NASPE) Motor Development and Learning Academy and as a board member of the American Kinesiology Association (AKA). She has earned the Chancellor's Award for Excellence in Teaching and the Roland Fontaine Award for Student Engagement from SUNY Brockport as well as the Corinne Kirchner Research Award from the American Federation for the Blind. She resides in western New York with her husband, three children, and two dogs.

Melanie E. Perreault, PhD, is an associate professor of motor behavior and the coordinator of the kinesiology program in the department of kinesiology, sport studies, and physical education at State University of New

Courtesy of SUNY Brockport.

York at Brockport (SUNY Brockport). She is also the communications director for the Institute of Movement Studies for Individuals with Visual Impairments (IMSVI). Dr. Perreault teaches undergraduate courses on motor development and motor learning and graduate courses on research. She received SUNY Brockport's Honors Mentor Award and Faculty-Student Engagement Award in 2022 for her work with undergraduate student research.

Dr. Perreault's main area of research focuses on motor development in children with sensory impairments. She has published over 25 peer-reviewed articles and contributed to four books, including *Lesson Planning for High School Physical Education* and *Motor Learning and Development, Second Edition,* published by Human Kinetics. Dr. Perreault and her research team received the Corinne Kirchner Research Award from the American Federation for the Blind in 2020 and the Re-cognition Award from the CHARGE Syndrome Foundation in 2021 for their contributions to the field. She currently serves on the board of the American Kinesiology Association (AKA) and as a member-at-large for the International Motor Development Research Consortium.

Ali S. Brian, PhD, CAPE, is an associate professor in the department of physical education at the University of South Carolina, where she serves as the founder and director of the Physical and Developmental Disabilities

Research Lab as well as the founder and coordinator of the new adapted physical education master's degree program. Dr. Brian has served as the chair of the Research Council for SHAPE America and as the vice president elect for the National Consortium for Physical Education for Individuals with Disabilities (NCPEID). She is also an associate editor for *Research Quarterly for Exercise and Sport* and serves on the editorial boards for *Research Quarterly for Exercise and Sport* and *Physical Education and Sports Pedagogy*. Dr. Brian was given the G. Lawrence Rarick Research Award by the NCPEID in 2021 as well as the Corinne Kirchner Research Award by the American Federation for the Blind in 2020.

Dr. Brian is the author of over 50 peer-reviewed publications and has presented at over 150 national and international conferences. Her research focuses on establishing underlying mechanisms (e.g., gross motor, psychological, and social-cognitive development) that drive positive developmental trajectories for the health of children and youth with and without disabilities.

Douglas H. Collier, PhD, is an associate professor in the department of kinesiology, sport studies, and physical education at State University of New York at Brockport (SUNY Brockport). Collier was a delegate to the Jasper

Courtesy of SUNY Brockport.

Talks (1985), a significant policy workshop that became the catalyst to Collier's career-long interest in motor development. For the past three decades, his research agenda has examined various facets of motor development that pertain to the education of typically developing children and those with identifiable disabilities. He is also interested in positive and proactive solutions to challenging behavior in school-age learners. Collier has presented his research at multiple national and international conferences concerned with the study of motor development and pedagogy.

Over the course of his 24-year career in higher education, Collier has served in multiple leadership positions at local, state, and national levels. He is a member of the North American Federation of Adapted Physical Activity (NAFAPA), the Society of Health and Physical Educators (SHAPE America), and the North American Society for the Psychology of Sport and Physical Activity (NASPSPA).

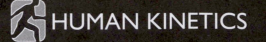

HUMAN KINETICS

Books

Ebooks

Continuing Education

Journals ...and more!

US.HumanKinetics.com
Canada.HumanKinetics.com